MICHIGAN GENEALOGY

Sources & Resources

Michigan Counties

1. Gogebic
2. Ontonagon
3. Houghton
4. Keweenaw
5. Baraga
6. Iron
7. Marquette
8. Dickinson
9. Menominee
10. Alger
11. Delta
12. Schoolcraft
13. Luce
14. Mackinac
15. Chippewa
16. Emmet
17. Charlevoix
18. Cheboygan
19. Presque Isle
20. Leelanau
21. Antrim
22. Otsego
23. Montmorency
24. Alpena
25. Benzie
26. Grand Traverse
27. Kalkaska
28. Crawford
29. Oscoda
30. Alcona
31. Manistee
32. Wexford
33. Missaukee
34. Roscommon
35. Ogemaw
36. Iosco
37. Mason
38. Lake
39. Osceola
40. Clare
41. Gladwin
42. Arenac
43. Oceana
44. Newaygo
45. Mecosta
46. Isabella
47. Midland
48. Bay
49. Muskegon
50. Ottawa
51. Kent
52. Montcalm
53. Gratiot
54. Saginaw
55. Tuscola
56. Huron
57. Sanilac
58. Ionia
59. Clinton
60. Shiawassee
61. Genesee
62. Lapeer
63. St. Clair
64. Allegan
65. Barry
66. Eaton
67. Ingham
68. Livingston
69. Oakland
70. Macomb
71. Van Buren
72. Kalamazoo
73. Calhoun
74. Jackson
75. Washtenaw
76. Wayne
77. Berrien
78. Cass
79. St. Joseph
80. Branch
81. Hillsdale
82. Lenawee
83. Monroe

See page 230 for an alphabetical listing of counties.

*** Isle Royale and the other islands on this map are among the more than 300 Michigan islands that dot the waters of the Great Lakes.**

MICHIGAN GENEALOGY

Sources & Resources

By Carol McGinnis

SECOND EDITION

Genealogical Publishing Co., Inc.
1001 N. Calvert St., Baltimore, MD 21202

Library of Congress Catalogue Card Number 2004115376
International Standard Book Number 0-8063-1755-8
Made in the United States of America

In memory of my mom,

Elaine Marie (Hall) McGinnis (1930-1994),
and our French Canadian, English, Irish,
and Swedish ancestors
who came to Michigan
to start a new life

Contents

Introduction

More than 20 years ago I made my first trip to a county courthouse.

Two of my friends had been inspired by the 1977 television miniseries "Roots" and were researching their own family lines. They talked about grandparents from Germany and Poland and other ancestors moving from New York to Michigan. I was fascinated by these stories, and I began to wonder about my own family roots – but not for the first time.

I had wondered about my family history as a child of 10 or so, but at that age I had no idea how to climb my family tree. Now, as an adult, I had friends to ask for advice. I already knew that my mother and my maternal grandparents all had been born in Ludington, Michigan, so my friends suggested that I search records in the Mason County Courthouse.

One warm July day I made the two-hour trek to Ludington, where I found my mother's birth record. And her parents' birth records. And my grandparents' marriage record. And my great-grandparents' death records. I also found birth, death, and marriage records on other assorted relatives, some of whom I hadn't known about.

On my drive back home, I was already planning my next research step – a trip to Saginaw County to ferret out information on a great-grandfather – and I decided on a way to organize my research by using color-coding. I was hooked.

Several years later, I visited the late Ray Gooldy's Ye Olde Genealogie Shoppe in Indianapolis, Indiana. When he discovered that I had a degree in journalism and had worked for several years as a reporter, he suggested that I use my writing skills to write genealogy guides. I had never considered merging my passion for writing with my passion for family history, and I was intrigued by the suggestion. The eventual result was the 1987 edition of *Michigan Genealogy* and later books about *West Virginia Genealogy* and *Virginia Genealogy.* (My dad has southern roots.)

Now it's the new millennium, and it's time for a revised and expanded edition of this book – not just to update the names and addresses of societies, the hours of libraries, or to talk about new print publications – but also to review the massive amounts of information about Michigan genealogy that's now available on the Internet. In fact, one new chapter is devoted to using the Internet for Michigan family history research, but Web addresses also are sprinkled liberally throughout other sections of the book. (Researchers should note that Web and e-mail addresses are placed within brackets to separate them from the period at the end of a sentence or other punctuation.)

Other new chapters explore the reasons why people settled in Michigan, who these people were, vital record laws in Michigan, and non-traditional sources for research, such as records of prisons and poorhouses. Several sections in other chapters, including those dealing with military, court, and land records, have been expanded. Like my earlier edition, much – but not all – of the information in the chapters about societies, libraries, and county records was gathered through written surveys.

Getting Started

What should you do if you are new to genealogy? It's simple. Start with what you know. Yourself. And then move backward in time to your parents. Grandparents. Great-grandparents.

Start by writing down everything you know, or think you know, about yourself and your family. At this stage, write down everything that you've heard. Finding the documentation to prove this information comes later.

After you've written down all that you know about your family, attempt to verify your memories of family dates and places by searching for sources in your home. These sources include:

- Birth, marriage, and death certificates
- Obituaries
- Newspaper clippings
- Photographs
- Old letters
- Diaries
- Wills

Ask your parents, grandparents, or great-grandparents if they know the locations of such items. Your goal should be to verify as many of your memories as possible. Ask if anyone else in your family has done genealogy research, and if so, plan to contact them to share information. These first steps are important to take, regardless of whether your ancestors are from Michigan or another area.

Once you've inventoried what you already know about your family, it's time to organize your information. You can do this with a number of standard forms used by genealogists, such as pedigree charts and family group sheets. It's also important to document or footnote your sources so that later you'll know where you discovered a particular fact. You can do this organization with pencil and paper, but now might be the time for you to consider whether you would like to use a computer and genealogy software to help you get organized.

After you've written down your memories, checked your home for family history sources, and organized the information you've found, what comes next?

Analyze the information you have. Think about what you'd like to learn next. It's best to narrow your focus to one family – or better yet – one individual. What do you know about this person? What would you like to learn? And how will you find this information? Be specific in your planning.

If great-grandpa's obituary, for example, says he died in Saginaw, Michigan, where he lived his entire life, do you want to try finding his death record? Or his tombstone? Or his marriage record? Do you want to locate him in census records? City directories?

Each time you learn more about your family, organize and analyze your information and think about the next steps to take to learn more.

If you haven't already, take some time to read a few basic genealogy guides to become familiar with family history records and research techniques. Many excellent how-to guides have been written, and one or more should be available at your local library or bookstore. Online "how-to" guides include RootsWeb.com's Guide to Tracing Family Trees <rwguide.rootsweb.com> and FamilySearch.org's Research Guidance <www.familysearch.org/Eng/Search/RG/frameset_rg.asp>.

If the focus of your family history research is Michigan, then you've come to the right place. *Michigan Genealogy* describes the sources and resources that are available to assist researchers in finding their Michigan ancestors – whether the ancestors moved to the area in the 17th century, the early 20th century, or anytime in between. In most cases, I describe why these records exist, where they are located now, and what information they may contain.

Michigan Genealogy starts by giving a brief overview of Michigan's history (Chapter 1), followed by an in-depth look at why settlers came to the state (Chapter 2). After these foundation chapters about Michigan's history, the rest of the book deals with genealogy sources and resources.

- Chapter 3 focuses on the territorial and state laws that governed the recording of vital records (births, deaths, marriages, and divorces) in Michigan. It also discusses the locations of these records.
- Chapter 4 talks about alternative sources for finding vital record information, such as church records, newspaper articles, county histories, and military records. These records, of course, may contain additional information about ancestors.
- Chapter 5 deals with census records – the backbone of family history research – and their substitutes, such as city directories. These are the sources where researchers are apt to find their ancestors in family units.
- Chapter 6 spotlights court and land records.
- Chapter 7 explores non-traditional sources, such as prison records.
- Chapter 8 highlights some of the many immigrant groups to settle in Michigan
- Chapter 9 reviews Internet sources.
- Chapter 10 profiles Michigan's 83 counties. Some of the information in this chapter comes from written surveys returned by 72 of Michigan's 83 county clerks.
- Chapter 11 describes genealogical or historical collections, both large and small, in libraries and archives throughout the state. Much of the information in this chapter is based on the surveys returned (120 out of 201) by librarians and archivists.

- Chapter 12 lists genealogical and historical societies in Michigan. Like the previous two chapters, much of the information in this chapter comes from the survey responses (143 out of 278) from society members.

I've made every attempt to present the most complete and current information about Michigan genealogy. I've spent years reading books and articles, visiting libraries, attending workshops and conferences, researching my own family lines, and surveying county clerks, libraries, and genealogical or historical societies. Still, Web site addresses change, sources conflict, and dates get transposed, so I take full responsibility for any mistakes that may be found within.

Special thanks go to all of those wonderful county clerks, librarians, archivists, or genealogical and historical society members who took time out from their busy routines to answer my surveys. During my many library visits, I've especially appreciated the helpful staffs at the Library of Michigan and the State Archives of Michigan. Finally, I'd like to thank Michael Tepper and Eileen Perkins at Genealogical Publishing Company. They patiently waited for the completion of this book and always have been appreciative and supportive of my work.

So now, settle back and prepare to learn more about Michigan's family history sources and resources. You may want to read this book from cover to cover, digest it a bit at a time, or focus on a section that's pertinent to your current research. In any event, enjoy. My wish is that it may help you in some small way to find branches of your family tree.

If you have questions or comments, please feel free to contact me through my Web site <michigan.genealogystuff.com> where updated Web addresses and other information will be posted from time to time.

– *Carol McGinnis*

1
"...the earthly paradise"

Detroit's founder Antoine de Lamothe Cadillac once called Michigan "the earthly paradise of North America."[1]

The French explorer and military officer referred specifically to the Detroit River and its access to the Great Lakes, the largest body of fresh water in the world. He easily could have referred to Michigan's thousands of interior lakes, rivers, and streams or to Michigan's fertile agricultural soil.

He could have mentioned the vast forests that sheltered the fur-bearing animals so prized by Europeans at that time, the same forests that later drew thousands to the state for the lumber industry. Or had he known about them, he could have mentioned the rich mineral deposits that drew thousands more to the state.

Whether Cadillac was right that Michigan was "an earthly paradise," it is clear that its rich natural resources helped attract its settlers.

Early Exploration

Michigan didn't become a state until 26 January 1837, but the French explored parts of it in the early 17th century. Etienne Brulé, for example, is believed to have reached "the vicinity of Sault Ste. Marie in the winter of 1618-19."[2] That's about two years before the Pilgrims founded the Plymouth Colony in December 1620 and about a decade after settlers established Jamestown in what would later become the state of Virginia.

In 1621 or 1622, Brulé and a companion are believed to have traveled up the Saint Mary's River into Lake Superior. Jean Nicolet, another Frenchman, traveled along the southern shore of the Upper Peninsula into Lake Michigan in 1634. "As early as 1641 [Jesuit priests] Isaac Jogues and Charles Raymbault held Catholic services at Sault Ste. Marie."[3] Michigan's first permanent settlement was a Catholic mission founded in 1668 at Sault Ste. Marie by Jesuit priest Jacques Marquette. He established a second mission at Saint Ignace in 1671, the same year that Simon Francois, Sieur de Saint Lusson, claimed for France "the Great Lakes and all lands 'bounded on the one side by the Northern and Western seas and the other side by the South Sea including all its length and breadth.'"[4] This claim took in all of present-day Michigan.

Fort de Buade also was established at Saint Ignace in 1671 or shortly thereafter. Later known as Fort Michilimackinac, it was the first military outpost in the state. Other early settlements established by the French included Fort Miami in 1679, near present-day Saint Joseph; Fort Saint Joseph in 1686, on the site of present-day Port Huron; another Fort Saint Joseph in 1691, this one south of today's city of Niles; and Fort Pontchartrain in 1701, which later became Detroit, Michigan's largest city.

At the time of these first settlements and explorations by the French, an estimated 15,000 Native Americans lived throughout the state and included the Chippewa (Ojibwa), Huron (Wyandot), Menominee, Miami, Potawatomi, and Ottawa (Odawa) nations. The Native people contributed much to the settlement of Michigan by serving as guides; teaching the European settlers how to raise corn, make maple sugar, and build birch bark canoes; and trapping animals for the fur trade. Many place names in Michigan come from Native words. In fact, Michigan is "derived from the Algonquin word Michigamea, and means literally 'a great lake.'"[5]

Other Michigan place names of Native origin include "Kalkaska, Osceola, Washtenaw, Shiawassee, Cheboygan, Mackinac, Saginaw, and Newaygo."[6]

Michigan remained French territory until 1763, when Great Britain won the French and Indian War. Great Britain lost possession of Michigan at the close of the Revolutionary War in 1783, but the British did not surrender Detroit or Fort Mackinac to the United States until 1796.

Seven years before, in 1787, the U.S. Congress had made Michigan a part of the Northwest Territory, and in 1800 the western portion of Michigan became part of the Indiana Territory. (The rest of Michigan became part of the Indiana Territory in 1803.) The Territory of Michigan, created by Congress in 1805, included all of the Lower Peninsula and the eastern Upper Peninsula.

Then after Illinois became a state in 1818, Michigan Territory expanded to include the area that is now present-day Wisconsin and part of present-day Minnesota (east of the Mississippi River). Michigan Territory was extended to the Missouri River in 1834 and included "all of [the] present states of Michigan, Wisconsin, Minnesota, Iowa, and part of North and South Dakota."[7] In 1836, Wisconsin Territory was created and Michigan lost the land in present-day Wisconsin, Minnesota, and Iowa. When Michigan became a state in 1837, the U.S. Congress gave Michigan the western three-quarters of the Upper Peninsula as a compromise to solve a boundary dispute with Ohio.

Even though present-day Michigan was included in the territory surrendered to the United States by Great Britain in 1783, federal law recognized the land of Michigan as belonging to the Native people of Michigan. "It remained the property of those tribes until it was ceded to the United States by treaty."[8] Between 1795 and 1842 the federal government acquired the land of Michigan through 11 treaties.

Settlers Arrive in Number

Despite the early settlements and exploration of Michigan by Europeans, the state remained largely unsettled until after the completion of the Erie Canal in 1825. The Canal connected the Hudson River in eastern New York with Lake Erie near Buffalo, New York, joining the Great Lakes system with the Atlantic ocean. This provided an easier way of transporting passengers and goods between the Eastern seaboard and Michigan. Although many New Yorkers and New Englanders had been migrating to Michigan before the canal's completion, after the canal was finished "a flood of Yankees hit Michigan from Monroe County in the east all the way to Berrien County on Lake Michigan's shores."[9]

Federal census records tell the story. In 1800, there were only 3,100 people enumerated in Michigan. (This number does not include Native Americans, who were not numbered in early censuses.) In 1820 the population had grown only to 8,900, but by 1830 it jumped to 29,000, and by 1840 it hit 210,000. Michigan had grown faster than any other state or territory during this decade.[10]

By 1860 there were three-quarters of a million people in the state.[11] Between 1870 and 1900 Michigan's population more than doubled from 1.2 million to 2.4 million.[12] "Except during the two decades from 1890 to 1910, Michigan's population grew more rapidly than that of the nation as a whole ... before 1890 the growth rate during each decade was often greatly in excess of 25 percent."[13]

Other factors influencing the settlement of Michigan was the availability of cheap land, the construction of roads from Detroit to the interior of the state, copper and iron mining that got underway in the Upper Peninsula in the mid-1840s, and the lumber industry that was booming by the late 19th century.

On the **Web**

Michigan's History, Arts, and Libraries site (HAL)
<www.michigan.gov/hal>
Part of the State of Michigan's Web site, with links to the State Archives of Michigan, Library of Michigan, Michigan Historical Museum System, and the Office of the State Archaeologist.

Michigan History Online
<www.michiganhistorymagazine.com/>
Michigan History magazine's Web site

Roots-l Michigan: History
<www.rootsweb.com/roots-l/USA/mi/history.html>
Michigan history links on Rootsweb.com

Michigan Historical Markers
<www.michmarkers.com/>
Designated historic sites in Michigan

Detroit News' Rearview Mirror
<info.detnews.com/history/>
Historical information from the archives of the *Detroit News*

In the 20th century, manufacturing – especially the auto industry – attracted many people. Henry Ford's announcement in 1914 of a minimum wage of $5 per eight-hour work day prompted workers from southern and eastern Europe "as well as blacks and whites from our southern states" to move to Detroit, creating "the largest industrial complex in the world."[14] By 1990 more than nine million people lived in Michigan, making it the eighth-largest state.[15]

A thorough history of Michigan is beyond the scope of this work, but some key dates and events are listed below. There are many excellent books devoted to Michigan's history, including Dunbar and May's *Michigan: A History of the Wolverine State* (1995). Researchers can consult the online card catalog of the Library of Michigan, available through the State of Michigan's History, Arts, and Libraries Web site <www.michigan.gov/hal>, or their favorite library for more suggestions.

Historical Highlights

1618-19 Etienne Brulé is the first European to explore Michigan. An estimated 15,000 Native people live throughout the state.[16]

1668 Father Jacques Marquette founds the first permanent settlement at Sault Ste. Marie.

1671 The French establish Fort de Buade at Saint Ignace; it is the first military outpost in the state. It is later known as Fort Michilimackinac and is the first of three forts in the Straits area to bear this name.

1679 The French build Fort Miami near present-day Saint Joseph, the first European settlement in the Lower Peninsula.

1686 The French built Fort Saint Joseph at Port Huron.

1691 The French built another Fort Saint Joseph on the Saint Joseph River, near the present-day site of Niles.

1701 In June, French army officer Antoine de LaMothe Cadillac and 100 soldiers and workmen establish Fort Pontchartrain de Détroit, at the present-day site of Detroit, in an effort to control trade through the Great Lakes. In September, the wives of Cadillac and his second-in-command arrive. Mesdames Marie-Therese Cadillac and Anne Picote de Tonty are the first European women to settle in Michigan.

Cadillac's party founds Ste. Anne's Church, the first Roman Catholic Church in the state.

1702 Therese de Tonty, the first child of European descent, is born in Detroit.

1710 Michigan's first census is taken at Detroit.

The first recorded marriage in Michigan takes place between European settlers Jean Baptiste Turpin and Margaret Fafard.

1756 France and England begin the Seven Years' War (also known as the French and Indian War). No battles are fought on Michigan soil.

1759 The French surrender to the English at Montreal. French influence begins to decline in Michigan.

1760 British forces occupy Detroit; there are about 2,000 inhabitants scattered on both sides of the Detroit River.

1761 British forces occupy Fort Michilimackinac.

1763 Chief Pontiac and his warriors attack Fort Pontchartrain; they lay siege for 152 days, the longest blockade ever made by Native people against European settlers. Meanwhile, Potawatomi warriors take Fort Saint Joseph, and the Chippewas capture the Fort at Michilimackinac.

1775 The American Revolution begins. The British control Michigan and use it as a base for raids elsewhere and to hold American prisoners. By 1780, there are 500 prisoners.

1779 The Detroit area population is 3,000.

1779-81 A fort is constructed on Mackinac Island.

1781 Spanish forces, helping the Americans against the British, capture an empty Fort Saint Joseph at Niles and raise the Spanish flag. Spanish rule is short-lived. The soldiers leave the next day, and the fort reverts to the British.

1783 The Treaty of Paris is signed, ending the Revolutionary War. However, the British continue to control Michigan for 13 more years, staying to protect their interest in the fur trade.

1787 Michigan becomes part of the Northwest Territory.

1795 The first major Indian land treaty involving Michigan is signed. The Treaty of Greenville (Ohio) grants land on the Detroit River, the Straits of Mackinc, and Mackinac Island to the United States.

1796 The British withdraw from Michigan.

1800 The western portion of Michigan becomes part of the Territory of Indiana.

1802 Detroit is incorporated as a town.

1803 All of Michigan becomes part of the Territory of Indiana.

1804 The United States establishes a land office at Detroit.

1805 Michigan Territory is created, with Detroit as the seat of government.

Fire destroys Detroit.

1807 The Treaty of Detroit cedes a large portion of southeastern Michigan to the United States.

1809 Michigan's first newspaper, the *Michigan Essay and Impartial Observer,* is printed in Detroit. It is also the first Catholic newspaper printed in English in the United States.

1810 Michigan Territory's population is 4,762.

1812 During the War of 1812, General Hull of the Northwestern Army invades Canada from Detroit. He retreats when he learns the British have captured Fort Mackinac. Later, Hull surrenders Detroit without a fight.

1813 American forces reenter Detroit.

1814 The War of 1812 ends.

1815 Americans return to Mackinac Island, but the British build a fort on Drummond Island and stay there until 1828.

1815 Wayne County, Michigan's first county, is created.

1818 Public land sales begin at Detroit, with land prices ranging from $2 to $40 per acre.

The first Protestant church building in Michigan is dedicated near Rouge River.

Walk-in-the-Water, the first steamboat on the upper Great Lakes, improves transportation between Detroit and Buffalo.

Regular ferry service between Detroit and Windsor, Ontario, begins.

1819 The Treaty of Saginaw with the Chippewa Indians cedes about 6 million acres of land around the Saginaw Bay to the United States.

1821 The Treaty of Chicago cedes the entire northwest third of the Lower Peninsula.

1823 The second land office opens at Monroe.

1825 The Eric Canal opens in New York, promoting the settlement of Michigan.

1828 The Historical Society of Michigan is organized but lasts briefly.

1830 The fur trade reaches its peak.

A daily boat line begins running between Detroit and Buffalo.

1831 The U.S. government opens the third land office in Michigan at White Pigeon.

1832 A seven-week cholera epidemic devastates Detroit.

1834 A second cholera epidemic at Detroit wipes out from 7 to 10 percent of the population.

1835 Michigan calls out the militia for the "Toledo War," a struggle focusing on the ownership of a 468-square-mile strip of land bordering Ohio.

1836 The Treaty of Washington cedes the entire eastern half of the Upper Peninsula to the United States.

1836 The Erie and Kalamazoo, first railroad built west of New York, opens. It runs from Adrian to Toledo, using horse-drawn trains. The next year it starts steam operations.

A Quaker preacher brings slaves into Cass County via the Underground Railroad, starting the movement of fugitive and freed slaves into the state.

1837 Michigan becomes the 26th state.

Michigan's first city directory is published at Detroit.

1840s Commercial lumbering begins.

1841 The University of Michigan opens at Ann Arbor; by1867, it is the largest university in the nation, with an enrollment of 1,255.

1842 The La Pointe Treaty cedes to the U.S. government all the Chippewa lands in the western Upper Peninsula.

Copper mining begins in the Upper Peninsula.

1845 Iron ore mining begins in the Upper Peninsula near Negaunee.

1846 Michigan abolishes capital punishment.

1847 Lansing becomes the new capital of the state.

Michigan becomes the nation's leader in copper production, a rank it holds for the next 40 years.

1850 Detroit residents found Temple Beth El, Michigan's first Jewish congregation.

1851 Michigan Central College (now Hillsdale College) graduates its first female student; it is the second college in the United States to admit women.

1853 Michigan State Normal School (later Eastern Michigan University) opens as the state's first teachers' college; it is the first state teachers' college west of New York.

1855 The Soo Ship Canal and Locks, a one-mile-long canal and two 350-foot locks at Sault Ste. Marie, are completed. This provides a stimulus for the state's mining industry.

1855 Michigan Agricultural College (now Michigan State University) is established. In 1862, it receives a grant of 240,000 acres from the U.S. government for the use or support of the college, making it the nation's oldest "land grant" college. It is also the first agricultural college in the nation.

1857 The first railroad in the Upper Peninsula begins operation, linking Marquette and Ishpeming.

1860 Salt mining begins in the Saginaw River Valley.

1865 By the end of the Civil War, more than 90,000 Michigan men have served in the military.

1867 Michigan requires statewide registration of vital records.

1868 Michigan becomes the nation's leader in iron production; it continues to do so until 1900.

1869 Michigan becomes the nation's leader in lumber production; it continues to lead the nation for 30 years.

1871 Forest fires rage across the state, destroying towns and thousands of acres of forest. Damage is in the millions of dollars.

1873 The *Detroit News* begins publication.

1874 The Historical Society of Michigan is reorganized as the Michigan Pioneer and Historical Society.

1876 An Ontonagon mine operator builds the first telephone system in Michigan.

1881 Railroad ferry service connects the Upper and Lower Peninsulas, making the Upper Peninsula easily reached for the first time.

Forest fires again scorch the state.

1885 The Michigan Soldiers' Home is established in Grand Rapids.

1888 Michigan's lumber boom peaks with the production of more than 4 billion board feet.

1891 The Grand Truck Railroad Tunnel under the Saint Clair River joins Port Huron, Michigan, and Sarnia, Ontario; it is the first underwater railroad tunnel that links two foreign countries.

Dickinson County, Michigan's last county, is created.

1892 The first railroad car ferry begins operating on the Great Lakes between Frankfort, Michigan, and Kewaunee, Wisconsin.

1897 Ransom E. Olds organizes the Olds Motor Vehicle Company, and the first Oldsmobile is produced.

1898 Michigan sends five regiments and the state's naval reserves to the Spanish-American War.

1899 Olds Motor Works forms as a result of a merger between Olds Motor Vehicle Company and Olds Gasoline Engine Works of Lansing; the first automobile factory in the United States is built by Olds in Detroit.

1901 Michigan leads the nation in gypsum production; it continues to do so until 1917.

1902 Henry M. Leland organizes the Cadillac Motor Car Company.

1903 Henry Ford incorporates the Ford Motor Company in Detroit.

1904 Buick Motor Company begins auto manufacturing in Flint.

1908 General Motors Company organizes, and Ford introduces the most famous of the early cars, the Model T. Fisher Body Corporation is founded.

1909 Woodward Avenue (between Six and Seven Mile Roads) in Detroit is the site of the world's first mile of poured concrete road.

1912 A limestone quarry opens at Rogers City; it becomes the world's largest.

Michigan is first in the nation in automobile production.

1914 Henry Ford announces a $5 minimum wage for an eight-hour workday.

Michigan produces 75 percent of all the cars in the United States.

1916 World War I rages in Europe; many Michigan men join Canadian units leaving for France.

Annual copper production peaks at nearly 270 million pounds of refined copper; iron ore production from the Upper Peninsula's Marquette Range is 5.5 million tons.

1918 By the end of World War I, about 175,000 Michigan men have served in the military; about 5,000 die and about 15,000 are wounded.

1919 The influenza pandemic kills 3,814 in Detroit.

1923 The first seasonal automobile ferry connects the Upper and Lower Peninsulas.

1925 Chrysler Motor Corporation organizes.

1929 Some large copper mines on the Keweenaw Peninsula close.

The Ambassador Bridge opens between Detroit and Windsor, Ontario.

1930 Michigan's population is almost 5 million, an increase of more than 1 million since 1920. Almost 70 percent of the population lives in cities, almost an exact reversal of the trend 50 years earlier.

1930 A vehicle tunnel opens between Detroit and Windsor, Ontario.

1933 Forty-six percent of Michigan's nonagricultural workforce is unemployed.

1935 United Automobile Workers organize in Detroit.

1938 International Blue Water Bridge connects Port Huron, Michigan, and Sarnia, Ontario.

1941 Michigan's auto plants are converted to the production of war materials; the state leads all other states in the production of war materials and becomes known as the "Arsenal of Democracy."

1945 By the end of World War II, 673,000 Michigan men and women have served in the military in this conflict.

1951 The State Office Building in Lansing is destroyed by fire.

1953 By the end of the Korean War, about 250,000 Michigan men and women have served in the military in this conflict.

1957 The Mackinac Bridge is completed; Michigan's two peninsulas are united by the five-mile-long structure, one of the world's longest suspension bridges.

1962 The International Bridge at Sault Ste. Marie opens; it connects the Upper Peninsula with Canada.

1966 The last operating mine on the Gogebic Iron Range closes.

1973 By the end of the Vietnam War, more than 400,000 Michigan men and women have served in the military in this conflict.

1987 Michigan celebrates its Sesquicentennial, the 150th anniversary of statehood.

1989 The state dedicates the Michigan Library and Historical Center in Lansing.

2001 Detroit celebrates its 300th anniversary.

2
The Settlement of Michigan

The fur trade dominated much of Michigan's early history and settlement. The profitable trade was important to both the French and English, contributed to changes in the lifestyle of Michigan's Native people, and attracted Michigan's first European settlers and explorers.

After the fur trade peaked in 1830, new factors in the settlement of Michigan came into play: the opening of the Eric canal in 1825, which improved transportation to and from the Eastern seaboard; other improvements in transportation; and the availability of cheap land for agriculture.

In the 1840s, the industries of lumbering, copper mining, and iron ore mining emerged. For the next few decades these industries brought thousands of settlers to Michigan. In the late 19th and early 20th centuries manufacturing, particularly the auto industry, brought hundreds of thousands more to the state.

Factors Influencing Settlement

The French and the Fur Trade: By the 16th century there was a shortage of fur-bearing animals in Europe and Russia, yet the demand for their pelts continued.

> Furs at that time were worn by the French aristocrats and the members of the wealthy middle class, which aped the styles and manners of the lords and their ladies. Since France became the fashion center of Europe under Louis XIV, the wearing of furs spread to other European countries. The limited supply of furs that could easily be obtained in Europe soon made the control of the vast fur resources of North America essential in meeting this growing demand for furs.[1]

As the French explored the Great Lakes area, they became aware of the region's potential as a source of furs. They took steps to secure their claim on the area by establishing a string of outposts to control fur trade routes. These outposts included Michilimackinac (Saint Ignace) and Sault Ste. Marie in Michigan's Upper Peninsula and Fort Saint Joseph (near the present-day city of Niles) and Detroit in the Lower Peninsula. Detroit, the first permanent settlement in Lower Michigan, was established in 1701 in part "to control access to the upper lakes."[2] Michigan became important not only as a source of furs but also as "a collecting point for shipment to the East."[3]

France controlled the fur trade in the Great Lakes region until 1760 when it turned possession of New France, which included present-day Michigan, over to Great Britain at the end of the French and Indian War. The French soldiers and government officials left Michigan, but the French civilians stayed. Detroit was the largest settlement at that time with about 2,000 inhabitants scattered along both sides of the Detroit River.[4]

Michigan Under the British: Michigan was under British control from 1760 to 1796, but during that time Michigan remained largely unsettled by Europeans. British policies angered native people and led to "a great Indian uprising ... in 1763 which finally centered around Detroit."[5] Pontiac, an Ottawa chief, and his warriors lay siege to Detroit for 152 days, the longest blockade ever made by Native Americans against European settlers. Meanwhile, Potawatomi warriors took Fort Saint Joseph, and Chippewa warriors captured the Fort at Michilimackinac. The Native Americans and British finally signed a peace treaty in 1766.

Partially in response to this uprising, the British Proclamation of 1763 reserved all the land west of the Alleghenies for Native Americans. "Thus, Michigan and the entire Great Lakes area remained Indian country, with the British asserting their authority only at a few isolated posts. In the interests of economy, garrisons were maintained after 1771 only at Detroit and Michilimackinac."[6]

The Revolutionary War began in 1775. No battles took place on Michigan soil, but the British held Michigan and used it as a base for raids into Kentucky by British soldiers and their Native American allies. Loyalists, who had fled from homes in western Pennsylvania, led some of these raids.[7] At the close of the Revolutionary War in 1783, Great Britain lost possession of Michigan, but the British refused to leave the forts at Detroit and Mackinac Island until 1796. One reason they stayed was to protect their interest in the fur trade.

By the end of the British era in Michigan, "Detroit and Mackinac were the major centers in the area, with a few white settlers on the Kalamazoo, Saint Joseph, and Grand rivers in the western part, and a few more along the River Raisin and near the present city of Monroe."[8] Detroit had about 500 residents, most of them of French ancestry.

War of 1812: Shortly after the end of the Revolutionary War, America came into conflict again with Great Britain. There were many causes of this war, including the charge by Americans that the Native Americans "received guns, ammunition, and murderous encouragement from British agents at Malden, a Canadian fort located at the head of Lake Erie 20 miles across the straits of Detroit."[9] Unlike earlier wars, several engagements took place in Michigan, including the battle of the River Raisin, "the bloodiest battle ever fought on Michigan soil."[10] Nearly 1,000 men were captured or killed. (Most of the men killed, however, were from Kentucky – not Michigan.) The War of 1812 ended in December 1814, and the Americans moved back onto Mackinac Island in 1815. (American forces had retaken Detroit in 1813). Michigan was now firmly under

American control. Its population was about 4,000; most were French Canadians who lived along the Detroit River. Few new settlers moved into the area for several years after the war.[11]

Geography: Michigan, surrounded by four of the five Great Lakes, is the only state in the United States consisting of two peninsulas. The Upper Peninsula contains more than 16,000 square miles and is "larger than that of the combined states of Massachusetts, Connecticut, and Delaware."[12] At its nearest point, the Upper Peninsula is separated from the Lower Peninsula by a few miles of water at the Straits of Mackinac; the Straits link Lakes Michigan and Huron. The two peninsulas were not connected by bridge until 1957, when the Mackinac Bridge was completed. Prior to that, the two peninsulas were connected by railroad ferry service in 1881 and automobile ferry service in 1923.

The Upper Peninsula is bordered on the north by Lake Superior, on the west by Wisconsin and Minnesota, and on the south by Lakes Michigan and Huron. The Lower Peninsula, consisting of more than 40,000 square miles, is bordered on the west by Lake Michigan, on the east by Lakes Huron and Erie, and on the south by Indiana and Ohio. Ontario, Canada, once known as Upper Canada, is north and east of Michigan; it is easily accessible across the rivers at Detroit and Port Huron in the Lower Peninsula and Sault Ste. Marie in the Upper Peninsula. The Detroit River, for example, has a gentle current and near Detroit is about a half-mile wide. In the 19th century "small boats regularly crossed to Canada; in the winter wagons could cross on the ice."[13]

Together, both peninsulas have more than 10,000 interior lakes and more than 36,000 miles of rivers and streams.[14]

At the time of European contact, coniferous (evergreen) and deciduous forests covered almost all of the state.[15] Exceptions included at least 60 large prairies – ranging in size from 30 to a few thousand acres – in southwestern Lower Michigan.[16] This grassy land type was "desired most by immigrants from New York and the upland South" since they didn't have to clear the land first for agriculture.[17] Rich mineral deposits were located throughout Michigan, particularly in the western Upper Peninsula, and the best soil for agriculture was located in southern Lower Michigan.

Islands: More than 300 islands, 32 of them greater than one-mile-square in size, are located in the Great Lakes within Michigan's present-day boundaries.[18] Many of these islands played a role in Michigan's history. Perhaps the most well known is Mackinac Island, located in the Straits of Mackinac just four miles east of Saint Ignace. The island was a significant crossroads in the fur trade; the French and later the British built forts there. Today, it is a popular summer tourist attraction with a state park, a museum, and the famous Grand Hotel. No automobiles are allowed on the island, and it is accessible only by a ferry service from Saint Ignace or Mackinaw City. Beaver Island, the largest island in Lake Michigan, became home to a community of Mormons in 1847, and Isle Royale in Lake Superior had a seasonal colony of Norwegian and Swedish fishermen. Drummond Island in

Lake Huron had a British fort and later several lumber camps, and North and South Manitou Islands in Lake Michigan had "wooding stations" to sell hardwood to fuel the boilers of passing steamships. Today, the Manitou Islands are part of the Sleeping Bear Dunes National Lakeshore. Settlers lived on these and other islands at various times in Michigan's history.

Misunderstandings: Early explorations of Michigan were done primarily by water, so there wasn't much accurate knowledge of the state's interior. One misperception was that there was "a physical barrier in the form of a high ridge, occasionally portrayed [on maps] as a mountain range" extending from north to south through the center of the Lower Peninsula.[19] Another misperception was that the interior was endlessly swampy. General Duncan McArthur, who was stationed at Detroit in 1814, wrote in a private letter that Michigan was "not worth defending, and merely a den for Indians and traitors."[20] Edward Tiffin, surveyor general of the United States, sent a surveying team into Michigan in 1815 to see if it was suitable to use for bounty land for veterans of the War of 1812. The surveyors examined land in Jackson County where drainage had always been a problem and sent an unfavorable report to Tiffin, who then told President Madison in 1816 "that Michigan apparently consisted of swamps, lakes, and poor, sandy soil not worth the cost of surveying" and that "not more than one acre in a hundred, or perhaps in a thousand, could be cultivated."[21]

There also were rumors that Michigan's climate was unhealthy because hundreds of soldiers at Detroit had died in 1813, most commonly from malaria. Typhoid fever also was a problem.

> In the East the warning about unhealthful conditions in Michigan was put into rhyme: 'Don't go to Michigan, that land of ills; The word means ague, fever, and chills.'[22]

Territorial Governor Lewis Cass sought to undo Michigan's poor image. In 1820, Cass and a team of soldiers, geographers, geologists, and others traveled by canoe north from Detroit to Mackinac Island and Sault Ste. Marie, west to the Mississippi River, and then south. Cass ended his trek, traveling by horseback from Fort Dearborn (Chicago) across Michigan to Detroit. Cass widely published his favorable report on the journey.

Transportation: Until the mid-1800s, most people in Michigan traveled on the lakes and the rivers, but "these routes were closed due to ice for about one-third of the year."[23] Early roads in Michigan were built by the military and tended to follow Indian trails. They included a road south from Detroit to Monroe, built during the War of 1812 and improved in 1818, and a road north from Detroit, which had gone only as far as present-day Pontiac by 1822. "Systematic road construction did not begin until the late 1820s, when immigrants began to move across the peninsula in substantial numbers," and "by the 1830s, Michigan had begun constructing an internal road network connecting interior points to central locations along major immigration routes."[24] Road networks in southern Lower Michigan expanded between 1835 and 1840.[25]

The first road westward through Michigan became known as the Chicago Road because it connected Detroit with Chicago (Fort Dearborn). "It followed the path of the Old Sauk Trail and is the approximate route of the present U.S. 12."[26] By the late 1820s, the eastern portion of the road was in use, and "by 1835 two stagecoaches a week operated between Detroit and Fort Dearborn."[27] After 1825, this road became a virtual extension of the Erie Canal, filtering settlers throughout southern Lower Michigan. Territorial Road, the second road westward, connected Ypsilanti with Saint Joseph by 1834. It generally followed the route of today's I-94. Grand River Road, the third road westward, generally followed the route of today's I-96. Trails branched off along these main routes.

Plank roads: Because Michigan's early dirt roads were often muddy and hard to use, plank roads became popular in the early 19th century. "Long boards were laid parallel to the road. Then thick, wide wooden planks were placed across the boards."[28] Sometimes the planks were covered with dirt and gravel. Often private companies built the roads and charged travelers a toll to use them.

Stagecoaches: By the time Michigan became a state, stagecoaches traveled over most of Michigan's main roads. They continued to do so until replaced by railroads. "Stagecoaches over short distances between neighboring communities and as feeders to the railroads continued to function into the early years of the 20th century."[29]

Erie Canal: Travel to Michigan from the east and the south was difficult in the 18th and early 19th centuries. "Until 1825, the only practical way to reach Detroit from New York City was a month's journey up the Hudson River to Albany, across upper New York by coach or wagon to Buffalo, and then by ship along the southern shore of Lake Erie."[30] Only 40 small sailing ships were available to travel between Michigan and Buffalo, New York, carrying furs, lumber, and other goods to Buffalo and returning to Michigan with supplies and passengers.[31] In addition, travel on Lake Erie "was regarded as more dangerous than on the Atlantic."[32] From the south, the 30-mile-wide Black Swamp in northwestern Ohio was virtually impassable during rainy seasons and blocked access to Michigan "from the Sandusky River on the east to the Indiana line on the west."[33]

In 1825, the State of New York completed construction of the Erie Canal, which "ran from the Hudson River in eastern New York State to Buffalo in the western part."[34] Now it was easier and faster to travel to Michigan; taking only two weeks to reach Michigan rather than a month. Many settlers from the east took advantage of this "first inexpensive and dependable transportation" between the Northeast and the Great Lakes.[35] "After 1833 this new stream of immigrants into Michigan became a flood when a packet line of lake steamers increased the transportation service available between Buffalo, the western terminal of the Erie Canal, and Detroit."[36]

In addition to promoting the settlement of Michigan, the Erie Canal increased the profitability of farming in Michigan. "Suddenly, it was faster and cheaper to ship goods of all kinds to New York City from Detroit than from most towns in

New York State."[37] Michigan farmers began shipping east such crops as wheat, corn, and fruit.

Steamers: Shipping of goods and passengers on the Great Lakes has been an important method of transportation since Michigan's early days. The first passenger steamboat on the Great Lakes was *Walk-in-the-Water,* which was launched from Buffalo, New York, in 1818; it did much to improve transportation between Detroit and Buffalo. Later, steamships carried passengers on the Great Lakes from one Michigan city to another or from Michigan to cities in other states, including Chicago or Cleveland. During the late 19th century, Muskegon was the second largest port on Lake Michigan next to Chicago, and Saginaw was "the most active port on Lake Huron."[38] Steamers served smaller communities, including Tawas, Au Sable, Au Gres, and Port Austin. Most immigrants who came to Michigan by way of the Great Lakes landed at Detroit, though some landed at Monroe, Saint Joseph or smaller ports on Lake Huron or Lake Michigan.[39] The expansion of water traffic in the early 19th century "opened the entire shoreline of the Lower Peninsula of Michigan to settlement."[40]

Railroads: Railroads came to Michigan in 1836, with the opening of the Erie and Kalamazoo. They dominated the state's inland transportation system between 1837 and the early 20th century, when 30 railroad companies operated 8,000 miles of railroad lines throughout the state.[41] The first railroad built west of New York, the Erie and Kalamazoo ran from Adrian to Toledo and used horse-drawn trains. In 1837, it started steam operations. By 1845, railroads had expanded into the interior of Michigan, but their routes were incomplete.[42] The first railroad in the Upper Peninsula began operation in 1857 and linked Marquette and Ishpeming. However, most of Michigan's railroad system developed after the Civil War. "Almost 2,000 miles were added between 1869 and 1873. The 559 miles built in 1871 were the most that were ever completed in Michigan during any single year."[43] By 1910, a total of 9,100 miles of railroad were in operation in Michigan, the most ever in Michigan's history.[44]

Railroads were an important factor in settlement, the most obvious reason being their speed. "Before the railroad came, it took a horse-drawn wagon anywhere from a day to a day and a half to go from Ann Arbor to Detroit. When the Michigan Central Railroad began operating in 1839, the train covered the same 38 miles in only two and a half hours."[45] This faster transportation improved a community's potential as a trading center, so many communities grew up along railroads to have access to them. In Calhoun County, for example, the population was about 10,000 when the first railroad was built in 1844. By 1870, the county was a railroad center with a population of 36,000. Similarly, Berrien County more than doubled its population between 1840 and 1850, the decade that the railroad first came to that county.[46] "The Pere Marquette and Grand Rapids and Indiana Railroads are probably responsible for the founding of more northern Michigan towns than any occurrence in its history."[47] Some of these towns, however, became "ghost towns" as railroad lines were abandoned and highways developed.

(See Chapter 6 for more on ghost towns.) Railroad expansion, and the existing water transportation on Michigan's many lakes and rivers, also aided in the development of the lumber and mining industries, both of which brought many settlers to Michigan.

In addition, railroad contractors often brought in their own laborers, many of them new immigrants. "Germans, Czechs, Irish, Italians, and natives from all parts of Europe disembarked at Port Huron, Port Austin, or Bay City and were taken to some newly established village along the line. After the railroads were completed the majority of these immigrants took up land and remained in the area."[48] A majority of the labor force building Michigan's railroads was Irish.[49]

Car Ferries: The Great Lakes and some of its connecting rivers interrupted railroad traffic. Railroad companies used car ferries to transport railroad cars across the Detroit and Saint Clair rivers. "Passengers could remain in railroad coaches while crossing the river, and freight could be transferred without the labor and expense of handling on both sides of the river."[50] Car ferries also were used across the Straits of Mackinac. Car ferry service across Lake Michigan was started in 1892 between the Betsie River in western Michigan and Kewaunee, Wisconsin. This was the first car ferry in the world to cross such a large expanse of water. Other car ferries soon operated from Menominee, Manistique, Ludington, and Grand Haven to ports in Wisconsin. Still later car ferries transported automobiles across the water.

Sault Sainte Marie Canal and Locks: Because Lake Superior is 19 feet higher than Lake Huron, Saint Marys River – which connects the two Great Lakes at Sault Ste. Marie – had rough rapids. The rapids were so difficult boats could not navigate the river; goods shipped by boats had to be unloaded at one lake, transported by wagon along the shoreline, and then reloaded on boats waiting in the other lake. In 1855, the Sault Sainte Marie (Soo) Canal and Locks were completed. The locks were used to raise and lower the water level so that boats could move from one lake to the other. This transportation improvement increased access to the region for goods and immigrants and was a tremendous boost to the mining industry. "Copper and iron could now be shipped easily to Chicago, Cleveland, Milwaukee, Detroit and other ports on the Great Lakes."[51]

Land and Agriculture: Starting in the early 19th century, the quantity, quality, and low cost of land in Michigan attracted settlers from the East who were finding it increasingly difficult to earn a living on their limited land resources. Farming in the East had become unprofitable due to "higher operating costs, increased land values, competition from western agriculture, and often declining output from worn-out lands."[52] Cheap and abundant land in Michigan also attracted settlers from European countries, including Great Britain, Germany, and the Netherlands. Between 1830 and 1837 Michigan became the most popular destination for pioneers moving west; this interest in the area became known as "Michigan Fever."[53]

The sale of public lands in Michigan increased more than threefold, from almost 150,000 acres in 1830 to nearly 500,000 acres in 1834.[54] In 1835 alone, however, two million acres were sold, an amount equal to the total amount of Michigan public lands sold to date.[55] Michigan Fever reached a peak in 1836 when four million acres of land were sold – almost 20 percent of the public domain land sold in the United States that year – and as many as 2,000 people arrived in a single day at the port of Detroit.[56] The sale of land, for example, at the Kalamazoo Land Office reached such a pace in the spring of 1836 that the land office had to be closed for 18 days to bring the office's records up to date.[57]

Between 1815 and 1860 settlers moving into southern Lower Michigan created "an export-oriented agricultural economy that formed the basis of the state's economy."[58] Settlers often followed in the wake of the lumbering industry, farming cut over lands. Agriculture was the predominant industry in the southern Lower Peninsula from the mid- to late 19th century, and Michigan became one of the leading agricultural states in the nation. (Farming in the Upper Peninsula got underway in the mid-19th century, mostly to provide food for settlers working in the lumber and mining industries.) Main cash crops were wheat, corn, and other grains. Northern Michigan became famous for potatoes, the Saginaw Valley and Thumb area (after 1890) for sugar beets and beans, and the narrow strip of land along Lake Michigan's shoreline for fruit, including strawberries, apples, peaches, and cherries.[59] The state also produced a number of specialty crops, such as peppermint oil. "By 1846, about 25 percent of the total American output of peppermint oil originated in Michigan, although its restricted market limited production to a small portion of Saint Joseph County."[60]

Recruitment Efforts: Between 1845 and 1885, the State of Michigan attempted to persuade immigrants to come to Michigan through the use of emigration agents who recruited settlers, many of them German. "Michigan was the first state to sponsor an official emigrant agency," setting one up seven years before any other state followed its example.[61] The first agent, John Almy of Grand Rapids, "was a public relations man who was already in New York City representing several Kent and Ottawa County landowners" when he was appointed to the post.[62] Almy wrote *State of Michigan – 1845 – To Emigrants,* a six-page booklet in both English and German, and distributed around 5,000 copies of it to immigrants arriving in New York, emigration societies, and others. Almy served as emigration agent only two months, and there is no record of the number of immigrants who may have been influenced to come to Michigan through his efforts.

Michigan's emigrant agency was not staffed again until 1849, when Edward H. Thomson of Flint took over as state emigration agent. He befriended shipping company executives and New York emigration officials and wrote and distributed a 47-page booklet, *The Emigrant's Guide to the State of Michigan,* which directed potential settlers to the Saginaw Valley and Thumb area and to parts of western and southwestern Michigan. He also produced editions in German and

Dutch for distribution in New York and "made arrangements with the Norwegian and Dutch consuls, and with several German consuls for the translation of his pamphlet and its distribution throughout their countries."[63] He also arranged for health officers in New York City to distribute the pamphlet to immigrants in quarantine. By 1850, Thomson claimed that he had sent around 2,800 immigrants to Michigan.[64] However, Thomson was not reappointed to his post, and it wasn't until 1859 that Michigan again had emigration agents, one working out of New York City and one working out of Detroit. Their work also was short lived, even though more than 1,500 German immigrants reportedly came to Michigan through their efforts.

In 1869, Michigan again appointed a state emigration agent. Max H. Allardt of East Saginaw was the first and only agent to be sent to Germany. From offices in Hamburg, he convinced nearly 3,000 Germans to settle in Michigan, many of them in the Saginaw Valley, an area with which he was familiar. In 1874 Allardt was recalled to Michigan. The state again named an emigration agent in 1881, and he worked in Detroit until 1885. The state abolished its immigration office in 1885 and only made "half-hearted attempts to induce immigration" after that date.[65]

In addition to the state's official attempts to promote settlement, various businesses and industries often recruited workers from Europe and other parts of the world. This became more common in the mid-19th century when the Civil War caused severe labor shortages. In fact, the U.S. Congress passed an act in 1864 "permitting the importation of contract labor, exempt from liability to military service."[66] Michigan mine companies – some through the Mining Emigrant Aid Association – recruited miners from Canada; Cornwall, England; Finland; Norway; Sweden; and other European countries. Many of the immigrant miners started off as contract laborers; a mining company paid the costs of the immigrant's transportation to Michigan and in return the immigrant agreed to work for the company until he repaid the transportation costs. "Between 1872 and 1884 lumbermen hired agents or worked with state immigration authorities to lure potential mill workers to the northern Michigan mill towns."[67] Manufacturers, such as Kalamazoo's Dewing and Sons Company, recruited other immigrants. Dewing and Sons Company, producers of sashes, doors, blinds, and lumber, advertised aggressively in the Netherlands.[68] In the 20th century, agents from automobile factories recruited employees from Michigan's Copper Country, prompting migration from the Upper Peninsula to southern Lower Michigan. "Two General Motors companies, Buick and Chevrolet, were among those heavily involved in the recruitment of blacks to Flint."[69]

Railroad companies also recruited settlers. Government subsidies in the form of more than 5.5 million acres of land grants were used to encourage railroads to construct their lines into the sparsely settled areas of Michigan's northern Lower Peninsula and the Upper Peninsula. The railroad companies sold some of this land to settlers, often in hopes that the settlers would use the railroads to transport their crops to market. Unlike public land sales, the railroads often sold land on credit and were willing to sell smaller lots. Railroads advertised to recruit people to purchase their land. For example, William L. Webber, head of the Pere Marquette's land division for 20 years, distributed pamphlets and planted hundreds of newspapers articles "throughout Ohio, upstate New York, New England, and in a half dozen leading agricultural periodicals" about the company's inexpensive lands.[70]

The Continental Improvement Company was a unique example of the involvement of railroad companies in recruiting settlers. It was formed by four Michigan railroads specifically to encourage Swedes and Norwegians to come to Michigan. "This company sent Reverend Josiah P. Tustin of Grand Rapids to Sweden in 1870 on his first 'recruiting mission.'"[71] Reverend Tustin offered potential settlers a number of perks, including free transportation from New York to Michigan, free shelter upon arrival until settlers could build their own homes, wages as railroad laborers ranging from $1.75 to $2 per day, and the opportunity to purchase land for $5 per acre. It's estimated that 1,000 Swedes came to New Bleking (later renamed Tustin) in Osceola County by 1871 due to Reverend Tustin's efforts.

Perhaps the most effective recruitment came from the personal letters sent from Michigan settlers to family and friends they left behind, either in Europe or in the eastern United States. Germans, Scandinavians, and others often wrote glowing testimonials about the quality and quantity of Michigan's land or the opportunities for jobs. "It would be difficult to over estimate the influence of these letters in the home districts in the Scandinavian countries. A letter received by one family might be passed around an entire district, and Michigan would thus become a definite destination in the minds of many prospective emigrants."[72] Some of these letters were reprinted in newspapers, making them available to a wider audience.

Events Outside of Michigan: Though many settlers came to Michigan for economic opportunity – cheap land or jobs in mining, lumbering, or manufacturing – others came "to practice dissenting religions, avoid political persecution, and escape slavery and racial discrimination."[73] German Lutherans, Dutch Calvinists, and Strangite Mormons were among those religious groups that came to Michigan to practice their beliefs. Political upheavals in Germany and other European countries and the 1845 potato famine in Ireland, Scotland, and other areas of Europe prompted others to find a new life in Michigan. Even political conditions in Canada brought new settlers to the state. "Although Michigan bordered Upper Canada, migration between the two regions had not been extensive before the Rebellion of 1837, a movement by radical elements opposed to a Canadian government they felt ignored their interests and discouraged economic development."[74] Many Canadian refugees settled in southwestern Michigan. African Americans, both slave and free, came to Michigan to escape slavery or racial discrimination in the south. Many fugitive slaves had followed the route of the Underground Railroad, a secret network that aided slaves in reaching freedom. "Quaker settlements in southern Michigan became integral components of the Underground Railroad as well as places for resettling former slaves."[75]

Lumbering: When European settlers first came to Michigan, most of the state was covered in forests so dense "some said a squirrel could travel on tree branches for hundreds of miles without ever touching the ground."[76] The state was rich in both white pine and hardwood, including yellow birch, sugar maple, hemlock, elm, basswood, and beech. In addition, Michigan's location on the Great Lakes and its numerous interior streams and rivers "gave it an unrivaled water transport network" for the development of a lumber industry.[77] Logs could be floated down rivers and streams to sawmills. Once cut into boards, the lumber could be shipped on the Great Lakes to Chicago or points east.

At first, settlers cut trees down for their own use: to build houses and barns, to clear land for crops, and to burn for cooking and heating. By the 1840s, however, settlers started cutting trees to sell, and commercial lumbering was well established in Michigan's Lower Peninsula by the 1850s. Large-scale commercial lumbering moved into the Upper Peninsula in the 1880s, prompted in part by the mining industry's need for wood to shore up mines.

Prior to 1850, most commercial lumbering had been done in the East, with the states of New York and Maine among the nation's leading lumber producers. When lumbermen in the East, particularly those in Maine, heard about Michigan's immense forests of white pine – the wood most used in construction in the 19th century – they moved their tools, techniques, and personnel to Michigan to develop the lumber industry. Lumber camps first moved into the Saginaw Valley, then "northward to the AuSable, westward to the Grand River Valley, and then northward along the west coast of the Lower Peninsula."[78]

By 1860, Michigan was the third leading lumber-producing state. Shortly after the Civil War, Michigan became the leading lumber-producing state, a rank it was to hold until the end of the 19th century. Throughout that time, lumbering was the prominent industry in the state's northern Lower Peninsula. "During the peak years of the lumber activity (around 1880), Michigan produced about a fourth of the nation's lumber, with its production nearly equaling that of the next three states combined."[79] The amount of wood harvested from Michigan forests during the last half of the 19th century equaled an amount that could have floored "the entire state of Michigan with one-inch boards and have enough left over to plank a road 60-feet wide from Detroit to San Francisco."[80] In the early 20th century, Michigan was "the leading hardwood producer in North America," most of this coming from the state's Upper Peninsula.[81]

Commercial lumbering brought thousands of settlers to Michigan's northern Lower Peninsula – where the best of Michigan's white pine grew – and later to the Upper Peninsula. Prior to the lumbering era, hardly anyone lived in the northern Lower Peninsula. The Saginaw Valley was the first region in the state where large-scale commercial lumbering developed, due in part to its network of rivers that could be used to float logs to sawmills. It was the state's leading lumbering area from 1840 to 1860. "On the western side of the Lower Peninsula the first sawmills were built at Grand Rapids in 1832 and in Muskegon in 1837," and by 1860 there were sawmills at the mouths of many rivers flowing into Lake Michigan.[82] In the Upper Peninsula, lumbering centers included Escanaba and Menominee. "By 1860, lumbering was second only to agriculture as the state's principal means of livelihood, and the industry created new towns, new railroads, new jobs, and new profits."[83]

From the 1860s to the turn of the 20th century lumbermen infiltrated and settled the interiors of the northern Lower Peninsula and the Upper Peninsula, establishing such communities as Cadillac, Roscommon, and Grayling. In the 1870s, there may have been more than 20,000 men in the lumber camps of Lower Michigan, and more than twice that number just 10 years later.[84] Lumber settlements often sprang up in a matter of days, and many lumbermen moved their families near lumber camps and established churches, schools, and stores. Later, many of these settlements became "ghost towns" when the lumber industry moved out of the area. (See Chapter 6 for more on ghost towns.) Other lumber camps were intended to be temporary; however, some of the towns that grew up near lumber camps lasted long after the trees had been cut down. Clare in Clare County, for example, was one of the busiest lumber communities in the northern Lower Peninsula. It grew from a population of less than 500 in 1871 to more than 7,500 in 1891. "At one point in the late 1870s, 150 logging camps were operating within 10 miles of Clare."[85] Today, Clare has a population of more than 3,000.

Most mill towns were located at the mouths of large rivers, and they included Alpena, Bay City, Cheboygan, Escanaba, Grand Haven, Ludington, Manistee, Manistique, Menominee, Muskegon, Oscoda, Pentwater, Petoskey, Port Huron, Saginaw, Traverse City, and Whitehall. "The greatest centers of mill activity, however, were the Saginaw and Bay City area, Muskegon, Manistee, and Menominee."[86]

In addition to experienced lumbermen from Maine, Vermont, New York, New England, and Pennsylvania, many immigrants worked in lumber camps, including French Canadians, Scots, Irishmen, Finns, Swedes, and Norwegians. In the early days of the lumber industry, some workers were local men draw from nearby settlements or young men from farms in southern Michigan who often spent one or more winters working in the northern Michigan camps, but most lumber workers were from the eastern United States. European immigrants, including Germans, Irishmen, and Scandinavians, started coming to Michigan in the 1840s and 1850s to work in the lumber industry. The largest number of immigrants was from Canada and included French Canadians and Scots.[87] Some French Canadian lumberjacks were seasonal residents of Michigan, and they returned to Canada after the spring log drives.[88] Some Europeans were recruited to the lumbering industry. "A Swede named Louis Sands brought Swedes, called 'Sandies,' into Michigan by the boatloads and trainloads."[89] By 1885, about 60 percent of the state's work force in the lumber industry "consisted of foreign-born."[90] "After World War I, some lumber companies encouraged migrant laborers from the mid-south to settle in the Upper Peninsula."[91] This included men from Kentucky and Tennessee.

Most early lumberjacks, also known as shanty boys, were single men between 20 and 30 years old.[92] Many also worked in sawmills in the summers. Other lumber workers included river drivers or "river hogs," who guided logs down streams to sawmills where sawmill workers converted logs into raw lumber. Though lumbering was a predominantly male industry, some women and children did lighter work around sawmills. Some women also worked in the kitchens of lumber camps.

The lumber industry brought much wealth and development to the state, but by the 1870s much of Michigan's forests had been cut, leaving stumps and branches to dry out on the forest floors. As a result, forest fires were frequent, and serious

On the **Web**

Michigan Historical Museum online exhibits trace the settlement of Michigan. They include:

The First People
<http://www.sos.state.mi.us/history/firstpeople/index.html>

Settling a State
<www.sos.state.mi.us/history/museum/explore/museums/hismus/prehist/settling/index.html>

Farming in Michigan
<www.sos.state.mi.us/history/museum/explore/museums/hismus/1900-75/erlyagri/index.html>

Lumbering in Michigan
<www.sos.state.mi.us/history/museum/explore/museums/hismus/prehist/lumber/index.html>

Mining in Michigan
<www.sos.state.mi.us/history/museum/explore/museums/hismus/prehist/mining/index.html>

Factories in Michigan
<www.sos.state.mi.us/history/museum/explore/museums/hismus/1900-75/erlyauto/index.html>

1930s Great Depression
<www.sos.state.mi.us/history/museum/explore/museums/hismus/1900-75/depressn/index.html>

The Arsenal of Democracy
<www.sos.state.mi.us/history/museum/explore/museums/hismus/1900-75/arsenal/index.html>

fires raged in the state in 1871 and 1881. (For more on these fires, see Chapter 7.) "Between the mammoth logging operations and the vast forest fires, 92 percent of the state's available forest was decimated by 1929."[93] Many of the workers in the lumber industry left Michigan to work in lumbering in Wisconsin or Minnesota or points farther west, became farmers in Michigan, or moved to cities for jobs in manufacturing.

Mining: Michigan also was rich in mineral resources, including coal, gold, gypsum, limestone, natural gas, oil, salt, sandstone, and silver. By the 1880s, for example, "Michigan was the leading source of salt in the country," supplying more than half of the nation's total.[94] But it was the rich deposits of copper and iron ore that stimulated settlement in Michigan's Upper Peninsula, and mining was the predominant industry in the Upper Peninsula from the mid- to late-19th century.

Copper Mining: Although copper was first mined in Michigan in 1771, it wasn't until the 1840s that copper mining became a serious venture. Prior to that time, the United States had imported much of its copper from England and other countries, but in the 1840s those sources were in decline. At the same time, the nation's need for copper was increasing; copper was used to sheath the hulls of wooden ships, to roof buildings, and to make copper pots, pans, coins, and plumbing pipes. Copper was combined with zinc to make brass or with tin to make bronze; both brass and bronze were used to make a variety of items, including machinery, weapons, and hardware.[95]

In his report to the Michigan legislature in 1841, state geologist Douglas Houghton talked about extensive copper deposits along the Lake Superior shore. His message inspired a rush of prospectors to the Keweenaw Peninsula (today's Houghton, Keweenaw, and Ontonagon counties), most of them arriving between 1843 and 1846. It was one of the nation's first mineral rushes, coming before the more famous California gold rush.

> Boom towns quickly sprang up at Copper Harbor, Eagle Harbor, Ontonagon, and a dozen lesser ports where the scurrying little schooners dropped anxious cargoes of prospectors. Loose ladies and saloonkeepers appeared as if by magic to set up shop on Superior's south shore line. Top-hatted, lace-frilled gamblers departed their Mississippi side-wheelers and leapt over hundreds of wilderness miles to deal cards under canvas in the new El Dorado. Yankee storekeepers dressed in homespun landed with pioneers garbed in buckskin. Soft-palmed clerks, whose heaviest work had been lifting ledgers and pushing quill pens, came ashore with picks slung over rounded shoulders. Tidewater easterners arrived in fishermen's outfits and made smug jokes about coasting fresh-water Superior in search of copper. Others were ex-lawyers, ex-preachers, ex-husbands, ex-everything you can think of except expert miners.[96]

By 1847, the initial boom frenzy had abated; fewer prospectors and greater numbers of professional miners and mining investors came to the area. Between 1845 and 1865, 300 mining companies organized, many short-lived and unprofitable. But the first successful mine – the Cliff Mine located near Eagle River in Keweenaw County – produced more than one million pounds of copper as early as 1849.[97] Other profitable ventures included the Minesota Mine, opened in 1847 and located near Rockland in Ontonagon County, and the Quincy Mine, opened in 1848 and located on Portage Lake in Houghton County. Deposits for what would later become the most productive mine in Michigan and the largest in the United States – the Calumet and Hecla – were discovered in 1859 between Copper Harbor and Hancock in Houghton County.

By 1860, three major copper producing areas had been located, all on the Keweenaw Peninsula. The Peninsula, which became known as the "Copper Country," contained the world's largest deposit of native copper. "Here, almost pure copper existed naturally in its metallic state, unalloyed with other elements."[98] For 40 years, from 1847 to 1887, Michigan produced more copper than any other state, filling as much as 80 to 90 percent of the nation's need for copper. Copper production peaked in 1916, with nearly 270 million pounds produced.[99]

Thousands of Americans and Europeans moved to the Keweenaw Peninsula for the employment opportunities in mining, increasing the population in the area from less than 1,000 in 1850 to more than 20,000 in 1870.[100] Houghton County alone grew from 9,000 in 1865 to 66,000 in 1900.[101] The earliest miners to come to the Copper Country were most often single men. Many had worked in silver, lead, or copper mines in Maine, Vermont, or other eastern states; some came from the Canadian fur trade; and others from Europe, primarily the British Isles and Germany.[102] Many of the early Cornish in the Upper Peninsula came from Wisconsin or other parts of the United States or Canada where they had been using their skills as miners. By 1846, however, the mine companies were going to Cornwall, England, to recruit experienced copper and tin miners.[103] Mine companies also sent agents to other European countries, such as Norway and Sweden, to recruit miners. Other Europeans moved to the area on their own as they searched for the chance to make better lives for themselves.

Soon, communities grew up near mines, families arrived, and in addition to the thousands working in mining jobs, thousands more "earned their living as merchants, farmers, clerks, manufacturers, or in the professions."[104] Cities that were built or grew because of the copper industry include Calumet (first called Red Jacket), Copper Harbor, Hancock, Houghton, Lake Linden, and Ontonagon. Many nationalities were represented in the Copper Country, the largest groups including Finns, Norwegians, and Swedes. But there also were many Cornish, Italians, Poles, African Americans, Germans, Irish, French Canadians, Native Americans, and more. "The proportion of foreign-born in the Copper Country and in the three iron ranges at the end of the [19th] century was as high or higher than any other comparable area in the state."[105]

Though copper mining continued well into the 20th century, it came upon hard times due to the nine-month copper strike of 1913-14, the post-World War I depression of 1921-22, and the Great Depression of the 1930s. Higher wages in automobile factories prompted thousands of Copper Country residents to move to Detroit, Milwaukee, or Chicago; many more moved to other mining fields, such as those at Butte, Montana. "Today, no copper is mined in Michigan, the last mine having closed in 1995."[106]

Iron Ore Mining: At the same time that copper mining was getting underway in the Keweenaw Peninsula, iron mining also was under development in other areas of the western Upper Peninsula. Iron ore was discovered near the present city of Negaunee in 1844, and iron mining began in 1845 with the formation of the Jackson Mining Company. "Before the Civil War, the major iron-producing region was the Marquette Range, but the postwar discovery of iron in the Menominee and Gogebic ranges greatly expanded Michigan's production capacity."[107] The Marquette Range, all of which is within Michigan, and the Menominee and Gogebic ranges, which are located in Michigan and Wisconsin, are three of the six principal iron ranges in the United States. By 1868, Michigan became the nation's leader in iron production, and it continued to do so until 1900. "The mines on the Menominee closed in the 1890s; the last mine on the Gogebic closed in 1966. Today, mining continues on the Marquette Range, where about 25 percent of the nation's iron ore is produced."[108]

The towns of Crystal Falls, Escanaba, Negaunee, Iron Mountain, Ironwood, Ishpeming, and Marquette developed with the iron mining industry. Iron mining, like copper mining, also attracted thousands of American and European settlers. "So many immigrants flocked to the region that the mining counties had the largest foreign population in the Upper Peninsula in the late 1800s: 12,000 in Houghton County, 10,000 in Marquette County, and 8,000 in Gogebic County."[109] Nationalities included the Irish, Welsh, Cornish, Italian, Swedish, Danish, Norwegian, Finnish, and French Canadian.

Manufacturing: Though Michigan may be best known for the manufacture of automobiles, manufacturing in Michigan dates back to the early 19th century – long before the invention of cars. Michigan's natural resources, transportation network, and location on the Great Lakes all contributed to the rise of manufacturing. "Much of the early manufacturing that developed in Michigan was in response to the need for farm machinery."[110] For example, George Gale and his son produced plows in southern Michigan's Hillsdale in the 1840s and later moved their operations to Albion, "where the Gale Manufacturing Company made that city famous for its plows and cultivators."[111] During the Civil War, farmers increasingly turned to labor-saving devices to help deal with the labor shortages caused by men leaving the state to become soldiers. Corn planters, threshing machines, forks, and hoes were among the other farming equipment produced in the state.

The state's rich resources of minerals and lumber also stimulated manufacturing. Grand Rapids, for example, became a center for the furniture industry, and many other cities in Michigan – including Detroit, Grand Ledge, Holland, Monroe, Muskegon, and Sturgis – had furniture firms.[112] In addition to furniture, the abundance of lumber in Michigan led to the development of other wood-related manufacturing, including "sashes, doors, window blinds, handles, even toothpicks and matches."[113] The shipbuilding, wagon and carriage, and paper industries all flourished in Michigan because of the availability of wood. Michigan's copper and iron deposits provided industries in Detroit with the raw materials to produce other goods, such as steel, railroad cars, ships, and stoves. As early as 1864 Bessemer steel was manufactured at Wyandotte. By 1890 Detroit was the nation's largest producer of railroad cars and ships and the world's largest producer of cast-iron stoves.[114] In other parts of the state, abundant salt deposits helped the development of the chemical industry, while limestone deposits helped the development of the cement industry. In addition to the raw materials, manufacturing benefited from the fortunes made in mining and lumbering; entrepreneurs of these industries reinvested their profits in manufacturing.

Early manufacturing consisted of "small and competitive local manufacturing establishments."[115] In time, companies began to replace individual owners, and large manufacturing facilities in larger cities began to dominate each industry. "By 1900 Detroit, Grand Rapids, Saginaw, Kalamazoo, Jackson, Battle Creek, Bay City, Muskegon, Port Huron, and Lansing contained the majority of the state's larger industries."[116] Detroit became the center of manufacturing activity in Michigan because of its size, location, labor pool, transportation facilities, and investment capital. By 1880, the city had more than 900 factories.[117] In addition to heating and cooking stoves, ships, and rail cars, Detroit manufacturing firms produced iron, steel, cigars, boots and shoes, soap and candles, beer, printed materials, paints, pharmaceuticals, and machinery.[118] By the start of the 20th century, it was well positioned to become the center of the automobile industry.

Auto Industry: Automobile production dominated the history and economy of Michigan for much of the 20th century. Experiments in auto production started in the 1890s, with Charles B. King, Henry Ford, and others building gasoline-powered vehicles.

> Between 1900 and 1910 at least 57 small firms made some kind of auto in Michigan. Many plants were nothing more than large garages. And the cars were mostly experimental. ... Cars were built in Adrian, Alpena, Chelsea, Constantine, Dundee, Gaylord, Grand Rapids, Hillsdale, Jackson, Jonesville, Kalamazoo, Marysville, Muskegon and Saginaw. ... The cars had many names – Roamer, Marquette, Earl, Hackett, Lion, Saxxon, Flanders, Brush, Hollier.[119]

Ransom E. Olds of Lansing, however, was the first person to successfully manufacture cars in Michigan in significant numbers; he organized the Olds

Motor Vehicle Company in 1897 and produced the first Oldsmobile. This was followed by his creation of the Olds Motor Works in 1899 and the location of the first automobile factory in the United States in Detroit. Soon other car companies began, including the Cadillac Automobile Company in 1902, Buick Motor Company and Ford Motor Company in 1903, and the General Motors Corporation in 1908.

The Ford Motor Company introduced in 1908 one of the most famous of the early cars, the Model T. Ford executives experimented with a moving assembly line to reduce production time and cost for the popular automobile and were successful by 1914. In that year a quarter of a million Model T Fords were produced at a retail price of $490 per car. That was nearly half the per-car retail price charged before the introduction of the assembly line.[120] The new affordable car became a vital part of the national economy and culture of the 1920s.

Also noteworthy in 1914 was the Ford Motor Company's January 5 announcement of a minimum wage of $5 for an eight-hour workday, about twice as much as the maximum pay for most workers in America. (However, single men, women, and African Americans were not eligible for the wage.[121]) Henry Ford also announced that the factory, which had been working two nine-hour shifts, would start working three eight-hour shifts. This would increase the number of jobs by 4,000 or 5,000. The announcement was front-page news in newspapers around the world. "At 7:30 the next morning, 10,000 men [seeking work] mobbed the Ford employment office."[122]

By 1912, Michigan was first in the nation in automobile production, and by the end of 1914, auto production accounted for 37 percent of Michigan's manufacturing output. Just two years later, Detroit produced more than half of the world's cars and trucks. Detroit had become "the automotive production capital of the world, the undisputed Motor City."[123]

Great Depression: Occurring between World War I and World War II, the Great Depression of the 1930s was the worst economic downturn in the nation's history. Michigan, particularly Detroit, was hard hit because the sales of automobiles plummeted. "Auto production fell from more than five million units in 1929 to only 1.3 million in 1932. Employment in the mines declined from 9,000 in 1929 to 2,700 in 1933."[124] Unemployment of the state's nonagricultural workers reached 20 percent in 1930 and grew to 29 percent in just a year. By 1932, about 50 percent of wage earners in Detroit were out of work; statewide unemployment of nonagricultural workers reached 43 percent in 1932 and 46 percent in 1933.[125] Between 1930 and 1935, Michigan lost about 28 percent of its population. The worst years of the Depression were over by 1935, but many families did not have a steady income until much later. Michigan did not become a popular destination again for job seekers until the manufacturing industry was revitalized by wartime production in the 1940s.

War Production: During World War I, and again during World War II, factories and shipyards were used to produce military supplies, such as steel ships, tanks, armored trucks, and airplane engines. Production during World War I wasn't as impressive as it was during World War II, when Michigan became known as the "Arsenal of Democracy," but it did highlight the importance of manufacturing in Michigan and opened up job opportunities for women and African Americans.

During World War II, the auto industry suspended civilian automobile production to use its full resources for war production. By war's end, the auto industry nationwide had produced nearly $50 billion worth of war materials, including aircraft and aircraft parts, military vehicles and parts, tanks, guns, artillery, and ammunition. Michigan led all other states in the production of military equipment during World War II, producing about 25 percent of all Allied war materials.[126]

The "best known of Michigan's war production achievements" was Ford Motor Company's Willow Run bomber plant, located just east of Ypsilanti in Washtenaw County.[127] The $100 million facility was the largest assembly plant ever built. It employed up to 43,000 men and women, and by war's end had produced more than 8,500 Liberator bombers.[128] Manufacturing plants throughout Michigan participated in war production, but the concentration was in southeastern Michigan, near Detroit.

Employment Opportunities: In the last half of the 19th century, manufacturing grew from an industry with less than 10,000 workers in 1850 to more than 160,000 workers in 1900. That was about 25 percent of the state's working population.[129] The auto industry created hundreds of thousands of additional jobs in the early 20th century. "Immigrants from southern and eastern Europe, Mexico, and the Middle East flocked to the opportunities the expanding automobile and other new industries offered, as did residents of Michigan's rural communities who saw more potential for improving their lives in the factories than on their worn out farms."[130] When European immigration was halted during World War I, thousands of people from the American South – many of them African Americans – came to Michigan for industrial jobs. Again, during World War II, industrial jobs brought more than 200,000 individuals to Michigan, many of them from the American South. Manufacturing ultimately drew more than half of the population of Michigan to cities for jobs in industry or services.

Settlement Patterns

Though Michigan's Upper Peninsula was the first to be explored, large-scale settlement of Michigan began in the state's southeastern Lower Peninsula, with the founding of Detroit in 1701. More than 100 years later "the territory's settlements were confined to a ring of towns circling Detroit – Mount Clemens, Pontiac, and Rochester in the Clinton River Valley, Ann Arbor and Ypsilanti on the Huron River, and Monroe, Tecumseh, and Adrian along the Raison River."[131] After the 1825 opening of the Erie Canal made it easier to travel to Michigan, settlers from the East poured into Detroit and fanned west along the Chicago, Territorial, and Grand River roads, settling the southern and southwestern portions of the Lower Peninsula. "By 1837, 25,000 people lived along the

Chicago Road and almost as many more in the Kalamazoo River Valley."[132] Other settlers moved north of Detroit into the Saginaw Valley or north and west to Ionia, Grand Rapids, and Grand Haven. Still, by 1840 about 99 percent of Michigan's non-Native American population lived south of an imaginary line from Saginaw Bay in the east and Muskegon in the west.[133] And the settled area "was essentially a collection of small scattered communities, scattered farms, and scattered wilderness outposts."[134] Ninety-six percent of the state's population lived in rural areas. Detroit and Monroe were the only two incorporated communities, and Detroit was the largest city, with a population of 9,102.[135]

During the mid- to late-19th century, the lumber industry brought setters to the northern Lower Peninsula and the Upper Peninsula east of Marquette and Dickinson counties. Many of these settlers lived near the mouths of rivers where sawmills turned logs into lumber. "This region's share of the state's population increased steadily, reaching 11.4 percent by 1880, 16.9 percent by 1890, and peaking at 18.3 percent in 1900."[136] The mining industry brought settlers to the western Upper Peninsula in the mid- to late-19th century, but by 1910 that region only had 7.7 percent of the state's population.[137] Later, as the mining and lumbering industries waned, settlers left the northern portion of the state, moving to Detroit or other communities in southern Lower Michigan or leaving the state entirely for opportunities elsewhere.

Rural to Urban: In 1860, about 85 percent of Michigan residents depended upon agriculture for their livelihood.[138] As late as 1890, Michigan still had major undeveloped areas and could still be said to be in "the frontier stage of development."[139] About 65 percent of the state's residents lived in towns or cities with a population of 2,500 or less.[140] In 1910, more than half of Michigan's population still lived in rural areas.[141] But the population of Michigan's cities had begun to grow four times as quickly as the population in the state's rural areas during the last three decades of the 19th century. Detroit, for example, had grown from 80,000 residents in 1870 to 286,000 in 1900.[142] With the development and growth of the auto industry in the early 20th century, "the pendulum swung quickly from rural to urban."[143] By 1920, about 60 percent of Michigan residents lived in urban areas, and "by 1930 fewer than one in three lived in rural areas."[144] By 1960, about a quarter of Michigan's population lived in rural areas, but "even fewer actually supported themselves through farming."[145]

Chain Migration: Some settlers (usually men) came to Michigan alone in search of work, often leaving families behind. Once established, however, they usually sent for their families to join them. Other settlers came with their immediate family or as part of a group. Sometimes these groups were formally organized with an agreement or a charter, while others were loose-knit groups of families, friends, and neighbors from common areas. "Often the desire to remain among former neighbors prompted people from one locale to all settle in the same vicinity on the frontier."[146] In Saint Joseph County, for example, as many as 150 families from Chatauqua County, New York, started settling there in 1830. Over the course of six years in the 1850s, about 50 families from Ohio settled near Elsie in Clinton County.[147] This process of chain migration, where earlier settlers provided support and encouragement to more recent arrivals from the same geographic area or from the same ethnic group, occurred often in Michigan.

Covenanted Communities: Covenanted communities were those organized around an agreement or a common set of rules and expectations. "Three general types of covenanted communities appeared in antebellum Michigan: communities based on common economic interests and ideals, and often a common faith; those settled by foreign colonists bound by religion, ethnicity, language, and a formal organization; and experimental communities organized around communitarian principles."[148] Settlements of common interest included Vermontville and Olivet in Eaton County, Benzonia Colony in Benzie County, the Rochester Colony in Clinton County, and the settlement of the Kalamazoo Emigration Society near Gull Prairie in Kalamazoo County. Covenanted communities settled by Europeans included Westphalia in Clinton County; Frankenhilf, Frankenlust, Frankenmuth, and Frankentrost in Saginaw County; and Graafschap, Groningen, Holland, Noordeloos, Overisel, and Zeeland in Allegan and Ottawa counties. Experimental or communitarian communities included Alphadelphia in Kalamazoo County, James Jesse Strang's Mormon settlement on Beaver Island, the Israelite House of David in Berrien County, and Ora et Labora and Palestine in Huron County.

Alphadelphia: In 1844, Michigan Universalists founded Alphadelphia, a short-lived experimental community in Kalamazoo County, near Galesburg. Members gave up personal and real property in exchange for stock in the organization. They received housing, supplies, and wages for their work and were to receive a return on their investment. At its peak, there were no more than 300 members.[149] Within four years of its founding, the experiment collapsed due to internal strife. For more information on Alphadelphia, see Thomas' article, "The Alphadelphia Experiment," published in the Fall 1971 issue of *Michigan History.* In addition, information on Alphadelphia also is available at the Galesburg Memorial Library (see pages 318-319).

Benzonia Colony: In 1858, the Reverend Charles E. Bailey, a Congregationalist minister, and a group of his followers came to Benzie County to establish Benzonia Colony, which was to be based upon earlier settlements in Oberlin, Ohio, and Olivet, Michigan. They established the Institution of Higher Learning near Benzonia, later named Grand Traverse College (1863), Benzonia College (1891), and Benzonia Academy (1900). The college closed in 1918.[150]

Dutch Communities in Western Michigan: In the 1840s, members of Holland's Seceder movement began settling in Allegan and Ottawa counties. Their communities included Graafschap, Groningen, Holland, Noordeloos, Overisel, and Zealand. (See Chapter 8 for more.)

Israelite House of David: This religious commune was founded in Benton Harbor during the spring of 1903. The Israelite House of David split into two separate communes in 1930, with one keeping the original name and the other calling itself The City of David. At its peak in the 1920s, the House of David had about 1,000 members, and members came from "all parts of the United States, Canada, Australia and several European countries."[151] By 1990, membership in the two factions had dwindled to 39.[152] Information about House of David members taken from the 1920 federal census can be found online <www.usgennet.org/usa/mi/county/berrien/HOD1920.html>. Mary's City of David <www.maryscityofdavid.org/> has a large collection of materials about the reorganized House of David <www.israelitehouseofdavid.org/>.

Kalamazoo Emigration Society: Many organized settlements "involved relocations of entire congregations, led by their clergymen" or groups of families.[153] The Kalamazoo Emigration Society, which settled near Gull Prairie in Kalamazoo County in 1832, was a different sort of covenanted community. The charter "set no conditions for membership but promoted the Michigan venture as both an evangelical mission and a good business proposition."[154] Society members included families from Connecticut, Massachusetts, and Vermont. For more information on the venture, see Gray's *The Yankee West: Community Life on the Michigan Frontier* (1996).

Lutheran Communities in Saginaw County: In the 1840s, the Saginaw Valley became the focus of the second German missionary center in Michigan. Germans founded Frankenhilf, Frankenlust, Frankenmuth, and Frankentrost. (See Chapter 8 for more.)

Mormon Colony on Beaver Island: At the death of Mormon founder Joseph Smith, most Mormons accepted the leadership of Brigham Young. Some, however, followed the leadership of James Jesse Strang and moved with him in the late 1840s to a settlement on Beaver Island in northern Lake Michigan. There were four Mormon families on Beaver Island in 1847, 12 families by 1848, and 50 families by the summer of 1850, when Strang crowned himself "King" and "assumed dictatorial power in formulating rules governing moral and religious practices."[155] The Mormons' growing political and economic strength "gave it control of local government, and Strang was a state legislator from 1853 to 1856."[156] This caused tension with the local non-Mormons, many of them Irish fishermen. An 1853 conflict between the two groups became known as the Battle of Pine River and resulted in the fishermen fleeing the Pine River area, now Charlevoix in Charlevoix County. The Mormons established a mainland community at Pine River, and by 1855, there were more than 2,500 Mormons in the county. Enemies assassinated Strang in 1856, and non-Mormons attacked the settlement at Beaver Island, forcing the Mormons to flee. By 1936, only 15 Strangite Mormons were reported to be in Michigan.[157] Young's *Strangite Mormons: A Finding Aid* (1996) is an alphabetical list of several hundred followers of Strang, many of them from Beaver Island. It includes genealogical notes and references for further study about most of the individuals. For more information on Strang's colony, see Quaife's *The Kingdom of Saint James* (1930).

Olivet: "The Congregational community at Oberlin, Ohio, founded a Christian community and college at Olivet under their missionary leader, the Reverend John Jay Shipherd."[158] Shipherd and his 39 followers founded the community in 1843 in southern Eaton County; they opened Olivet Institute (later Olivet College) in 1844. The community was not established through a formal agreement, but its founders "shared a common origin and purpose."[159]

Ora et Labora: Sponsored by the German Methodist Church, the short-lived Ora et Labora (Latin for "Pray and Work") was established in 1857 on the shores of Wild Fowl Bay, near Bay Port in Huron County. Two hundred eighty-eight individuals signed the community's "initial articles of agreement" that reflected Methodist beliefs but also "intended to preserve German customs and language."[160] Members worked on communal projects and were paid for their labor from the community's store. By 1861, however, male workers were pulled away by the Civil War; the community's isolation and the members' lack of farming experience also contributed to the experiment's failure. "Only 14 families remained when the colony disbanded in 1867."[161]

Palestine: In 1891, 16 Russian Jewish peddlers from Bay City – all recent immigrants – purchased 640 acres near Bad Axe in Huron County. They had hoped to earn a living on a Jewish agricultural settlement they named Palestine. However, the immigrants lacked agricultural experience and expertise, and the colony failed after about a decade. By 1895 the colony had grown to 800 acres and 70 people, but five years later there were only eight families on the land "and in time these soon departed."[162]

Rochester Colony: Twenty-six families from Rochester, New York, established the nonsectarian Rochester Colony in 1836. (This is not to be confused with Oakland County's Rochester, first settled in 1817, and also named for Rochester, New York.) The organization acquired more than 4,000 acres in northeastern Clinton County. It did not have as rigid an organizational structure as some covenanted communities, and as a result it didn't grow to become more than a rural community. In 1837, it was platted as Mapleton and its name was changed to Duplain in 1841. "Today little remains of Duplain, but descendants of the Rochester pioneers still live on land their ancestors settled and farmed."[163]

Vermontville: Under the direction of Congregational minister Sylvester Cochrane, a group of men from Bennington, Benson, Orwell, Poultney, and other Vermont communities signed a contract to establish Eaton County's Vermontville in 1836. "Although the contract obliged the signers to adhere to certain moral principles, such as observing the Sabbath and refraining from the consumption of alcohol, it did not establish a particular religion or otherwise attempt to regulate their behavior."[164] As part of the agreement, each settler was to receive 160 acres of land. Building a school and a church also were among the provisions of the master plan. Later, a doctor arrived and a store opened. Soon the community became a regional trade center. Barber's *The Vermontville Colony* (1897) is a complete history of the undertaking and includes biographical sketches of the community's founding settlers. The book is available online through American Memory's Pioneering the Upper Midwest: Books from Michigan, Minnesota, and Wisconsin, ca. 1820 to 1910 <memory.loc.gov/ammem/umhtml/umhome.html>.

Westphalia: "Catholic Germans emigrating from the Prussian provinces of Westfalia and the Rhineland established the earliest foreign covenanted community in Michigan."[165] Named Westphalia, settlement began in 1836 when Catholic priest Anton Kopp purchased 560 acres in western Clinton County.[166] This became the center for a successful self-sustaining agricultural community. Membership in the church admitted settlers to the community's covenant.[167]

Phased Migration: Some settlers came to Michigan directly from the East, Canada, or Europe, while others lived for a time elsewhere before making Michigan their home. However, many – or perhaps most – New England families that came to Michigan lived elsewhere first. They moved west in "phases" or "stages," "settling first in western New York or northern Pennsylvania, or perhaps in Upper (Quebec) Canada, followed sometimes by a stop in the Western Reserve [in Northeastern Ohio] or Lower (Ontario) Canada, before finally arriving in Michigan."[168] Other settlers from New England or western New York spent a few years in Indiana before moving on to Michigan.[169] French Canadians, who migrated to Michigan for the lumber or mining industries, frequently lived in New York, Maine, Vermont, New Hampshire, Massachusetts, or Rhode Island before moving to Michigan. Many of them also returned to Canada for short periods of time, moving back and forth to Michigan.[170]

Once immigrants arrived in Michigan, "mobility was a fact of life" for settlers; many moved several times within the state before settling down for good.[171] Others stayed in Michigan only a few years before moving farther west, some to follow opportunities in lumbering or mining and others to buy land for farming. Many Norwegians, for example, worked in lumbering or mining in Michigan to save money for a land purchase. They later moved to Wisconsin, Minnesota, or farther west.

Some immigrants came to Michigan, moved elsewhere for some time, and then returned to Michigan. William Bray, for example, moved from Cornwall, England, at age 12 and settled in Vermont. He later went to the Carolinas. "He moved back and forth between South Carolina, Michigan, Illinois, Missouri, Duluth, Ontonagon – wherever prospects beckoned – until he settled at Iron Mountain."[172] Another Cornish miner moved from California to Michigan, later took up gold mining in the Dakotas and Colorado, and then returned to Michigan.[173] Other immigrant groups also moved back and forth to Michigan.

Those who left Michigan for good tended to move into surrounding states or farther west. By 1850, for example, Ohio had 2,238 Michigan-born residents. This was the most Michigan-born residents located outside of Michigan. Other states with high numbers of Michigan-born residents included Illinois with 2,158, New York with 1,921, Wisconsin with 1,900, and Indiana with 1,817.[174] By 1880

Michigan residents had started to move farther west into Minnesota, Iowa, Nebraska, Missouri, Kansas, and California. "In 1910 most of Michigan's natives moved into the states surrounding it, and also to the three Pacific Coast states, with secondary movements toward the Great Plains and the East Coast."[175]

Records that Give Clues About Immigration or Migration

Clues about where Michigan settlers came from or where they moved to can often be found in such sources as court, land, or church records; censuses; obituaries and other newspaper articles; and county histories or other biographical sketches. These records are explored in later chapters. Other records that may have clues about migration or immigration are passenger lists, passenger agent records, border crossings, naturalization records, or the Michigan Migration Project.

Passenger Lists: European setters en route to Michigan usually landed at New York City or other East Coast ports and then made their way inland to Michigan. Others traveled to Canada first and then crossed the border into Michigan. Colletta's *They Came in Ships: A Guide to Finding Your Immigrant Ancestor's Arrival Record* (2002) is an excellent introduction to researching ship passenger lists. More information about ship passenger lists can be found online through the National Archives Web site <www.archives.gov/research_room/genealogy/immigrant_arrivals/passenger_records.html>. Passenger lists for several ships used by some of the first settlers to west Michigan also can be found online <www.macatawa.org/~devries/Shipindex.htm>.

Passenger Agent Records: More than 6,000 passengers, most immigrants from Great Britain and Europe, are mentioned in the account ledger of Detroit passenger agent Richard Robert Elliott. Duncan's *Passage to America 1851-1869: The Records of Richard Elliott, Passenger Agent, Detroit, Michigan* (1999) transcribes and indexes the ledger and includes the names of the passengers, names of the individuals paying passage, ports of departure, and destinations. The ledger also lists "those who obtained passage from Detroit outward bound to European ports."[176] The original ledger is located in the Burton Historical Collection of the Detroit Public Library. The Burton Historical Collection also has 11 bound volumes of letters written to Elliott from those submitting money for passage; many letters "contain references to family relationships and exact addresses."[177]

Border Crossings: Through much of Michigan's history, records of border crossings between Canada and Michigan were not kept. However, there are some exceptions.

Saint Albans Lists: From the mid- to late-19th century, greater and greater numbers of European immigrants crossed into the United States by way of Canada, sometimes because ship passenger fares to Canada were less costly than those to the United States and sometimes to bypass U.S. immigration inspectors. The United States responded by asking Canada to assist them in requesting documentation from U.S.-bound immigrants. "Under a U.S.-Canadian agreement signed in 1894, immigrants destined to the United States were inspected and recorded by U.S. immigrant inspectors at Canadian ports of entry."[178] The resulting Saint Albans Lists include information on immigrants who crossed from Canada into the United States between 1895 and 1954. Though Saint Albans is located in Vermont, the Saint Albans records list crossings from all along the U.S.-Canadian border, including Michigan. The records include ship, train, and airplane passengers. The records have been arranged by Soundex, and the Soundex cards indicate the immigrant's admission date and port of entry. The manifest lists include other details, such as the names of those accompanying the passenger; the passenger's birthplace, age, gender, marital status, last permanent residence, occupation, language, race, and nationality; the name and address of the nearest relative or friend in the passenger's country of origin; whether the passenger had been in the United States before (when and where); destination, name, and address of friend or relative the passenger planned to join in the United States; purpose of coming to the United States and time remaining in country; seaport, date of landing, and name of steamship; and personal description (height, complexion, eye and hair color, and distinguishing marks). The passenger manifests and soundexes are available on microfilm from the National Archives, Family History Centers, and several libraries, including the Library of Michigan. In addition, the Michigan Family History Network has placed some of these lists online <www.mifamilyhistory.org/glpassengers/default.asp>. Additional information about Saint Albans lists can be found on the National Archives Web site <www.archives.gov/publications/prologue/fall_2000_us_canada_immigration_records_1.html>.

Port of Detroit: Microfilmed records for the Port of Detroit include "the original card manifests, arranged alphabetically, for persons entering the United States through Detroit, and some other Michigan ports from 1906 to 1954."[179] This 117-roll set of microfilm is available through the National Archives, Family History Centers, and the Library of Michigan. A 23-roll set of microfilm of passenger and alien crew lists of vessels arriving at Detroit between 1946 and 1957 is available through the National Archives.

Naturalization Records: Naturalization was (and still is) a legal process used by immigrants to become U.S. citizens. In general, immigrants made application for citizenship to a court, observed a mandatory residency requirement, and took an oath of allegiance to the United States. The first U.S. naturalization act was passed in 1790 and specified that any free white person over the age of 21 who had lived in the United States for at least two years could apply for citizenship in "any common law court in any state where he or she had resided for at least one year."[180] Applicants had to convince the court that they were of good moral character and had to take an oath of allegiance to the United States.

In 1795, new legislation changed the naturalization process into a two-step procedure. Immigrants, who had lived in the United States at least two years and in their state or territory of application at least one year, filed their "Declaration of Intention," also known as "first papers." They then had to wait at least three years, for a total residency of five years, before filing their petition for citizenship, also known as their "second" or "final" papers. The process also included taking an oath of allegiance to the United States.

A naturalization act in 1798 lengthened the residency period to 14 years and the amount of time between the filing of first and second papers to five years, but it was repealed in 1802. The 1802 naturalization act was similar to the 1795 law. The residency period was five years in the United States and one year in the state or territory of residence, and the period between the filing of first and second papers was at least three years. In addition, the applicant had to renounce allegiance to any foreign powers, satisfy the court that they were of good moral character, and provide two witnesses who would testify, under oath, that the applicant had been a resident of the United States for the required time. "The 1802 act was the last major change in naturalization laws until 1906," with the exception of minor revisions, such as one that reduced the waiting period between first and second papers to two years.[181] Because Michigan didn't become a territory until 1805 and a state until 1837, the 1802 act and its later revisions was the law that most 19th-century Michigan immigrants used to become citizens.

In 1906, the Basic Naturalization Act standardized naturalization forms and established the U.S. Bureau of Immigration and Naturalization (renamed in 1933 the Immigration and Naturalization Service and today known as the U.S. Citizenship and Immigration Services). "The new agency became responsible for overseeing and supervising the courts in the naturalization of aliens and for keeping a duplicate of each court's final naturalization records."[182] The 1906 act also made knowledge of the English language mandatory for naturalization.

> The new forms included a declaration of intention to become a citizen, a petition for naturalization, and a certificate of naturalization. The new citizenship papers were expanded to include each applicant's age, occupation, personal description, date and place of birth, citizenship, present and last foreign addresses, ports of embarkation and entry, name of vessel or other means of conveyance, and date of arrival in the United States; also required were spouse's and children's full names with their respective dates and places of birth, and residence at the date of the document.[183]

Women and Citizenship: In early naturalization proceedings, there are few records for women. That's because between 1790 and 1922, wives of naturalized men were automatically granted citizenship (known as "derivative" citizenship) and information about the wife was rarely included in the man's naturalization records. "This provision applied to women regardless of their place of residence. Thus if a woman's husband left their home abroad to seek work in America, became a naturalized citizen, then sent for her to join him, that woman might enter the United States for the first time listed as a U.S. citizen."[184]

Under an 1855 law, an immigrant woman who married a U.S. citizen also automatically became a citizen. The flip side of this was that many American women who married immigrants after 1860 (when the law was modified) lost their citizenship, even if they never left the United States.[185] Many of these women eventually regained their citizen when their husbands naturalized or after the laws changed in 1936 (for women whose marriages had ended) or 1940 (for still married women).[186] After 1922, however, immigrant women had to apply for citizenship on their own, and American women who married immigrants did not lose their citizenship.

In addition, between 1804 and 1934, the widow of a man who had filed his declaration of intention but died before completing the naturalization process could become a citizen merely by taking an oath of allegiance. "Thus, among naturalization court records, one could find a record of a woman taking the oath, but find no corresponding declaration for her, and perhaps no petition."[187]

Children and Citizenship: Between 1790 and 1940, children under the age of 21 also were granted derivative citizenship at the time of the naturalization of their father. Information about these children, however, is rarely included in their father's papers. The 1804 law that granted citizenship to widows of men who had not completed the naturalization process also applied to the men's minor children. In addition, between 1824 and 1906 "minor aliens who had lived in the United States five years before their 23rd birthday could file both their declarations and petitions at the same time."[188]

Soldiers and Citizenship: An act in 1862 expedited naturalizations for soldiers from any war who had been honorably discharged from the U.S. Army. (These provisions were extended to honorably discharged five-year veterans of the U.S. Navy and U.S. Marine Corps in 1894.) It eliminated the requirement for the filing of first papers and shortened the residency period to one year.[189] A 1918 law allowed aliens serving in the U.S. armed forces during World War I to file a petition for naturalization without making a declaration of intention or proving five years of residency. "During World War I entire busloads of recruits were often driven to the local courthouse to become citizens."[190] Laws passed in 1919, 1926, 1940, and 1952 also continued preferential treatment for veterans.[191]

For more information on the naturalization process, see Schaefer's *Guide to Naturalization Records of the United States* (1997), Szucs' *They Became Americans: Finding Naturalization Records and Ethnic Origins* (1998), or online articles on naturalization records <www.archives.gov/research_room/genealogy/research_topics/naturalization_records.html> and women and naturalization <www.archives.gov/publications/prologue/summer_1998_women_and_naturalization_1.html>.

Records: Prior to 1906, most naturalization records have very little genealogical information, though there are exceptions. Most only show "the name, nationality, oath of allegiance, and date of admission."[192] Finding pre-1906 papers can be difficult because the naturalization laws did not specify which courts should engage in naturalization. "Many state and local courts naturalized for a while and then discontinued doing so because they wanted to reduce their workloads. Others continued to naturalize and still do."[193] There were no uniform standards for the records themselves, and many courts created their own naturalization forms or changed their forms from year to year. "As a consequence, before September 1906, the various federal, state, county, and local courts generated a wide variety of citizenship records that are stored in sundry courts, archives, warehouses, libraries, and private collections."[194] In some cases, naturalization records may have been misplaced or destroyed; in other cases, they may be mixed together with other court records. Complicating matters further is the fact that first and second papers did not have to be filed in the same court. In addition, not all immigrants went through the naturalization process. Between 1890 and 1930, only about 25 percent of foreign-born residents had been naturalized or taken the first step to naturalization by filing a declaration of intent.[195] "After 1906, the vast majority of naturalizations took place in federal courts, although some local courts continued to naturalize long after that date."[196]

Finding an ancestor's naturalization papers in Michigan may be a challenge – but it's not impossible.

- Many of Michigan's 83 counties still have naturalization records on file in their courts, but more than half of Michigan's counties have turned their records over to the State Archives of Michigan in Lansing. Indexes to more than 20 of these counties are online at the Archives' Web site. At this writing, the indexes are in PDF format and are not searchable. Counties with online indexes include Allegan, Antrim, Clare, Crawford, Delta, Dickinson, Eaton, Grand Traverse, Huron, Iosco, Kent, Lenawee, Mackinac, Macomb, Marquette, Mason, Newaygo, Ontonagon, Otsego, Ottawa, Sanilac, and Saint Clair. New indexes will be added to the Web site as they are completed. Researchers can find the indexes by visiting Michigan's History, Arts, and Libraries Web site <www.michigan.gov/hal> and selecting "Resources for Genealogists."
- The Burton Historical Collection in the Detroit Public Library has the "naturalization, or citizenship, papers of individuals who applied for and were granted citizenship at Detroit Recorders Court for the period 1852-1906."[197]
- The Great Lakes Regional Branch of the National Archives in Chicago has mid- to late-19th century and early 20th century naturalization records from several federal courts, including the U.S. Circuit Court, Eastern District, Detroit; U.S. District Court, Eastern District, Detroit; U.S. District Court, Western District, Grand Rapids; and U.S. District Court, Western District, Marquette. The Archives' Web site <www.archives.gov/facilities/il/chicago/naturalization_records.html> outlines the years and types of records available. Szucs' indexes *Naturalizations: Declarations of Intent and Final Oaths, Circuit Court, Eastern District of Michigan, Detroit* (1977) and *Naturalizations, Declara-*

tions of Intent and Final Oaths: District Court, Eastern District of Michigan, Detroit (1977) cover the years 1837 to 1903. These indexes also are available through Ancestry.com <www.ancestry.com>.

- Family History Centers have naturalization records on microfilm for many Michigan counties and the index for naturalization petitions of the U.S. District Court, Eastern District, Detroit (1880-1995).
- Many naturalization records have been indexed, abstracted, and published in books. Examples include Corwin's *Declaration of Intent, 1859-1890, Muskegon County, Michigan* (1998) and *Index of Naturalization Records at Alpena County Courthouse for the 26th Judicial Circuit, 1878-1978* (1980). Researchers should check the online card catalogs of such libraries as the Library of Michigan and Family History Centers for the availability of books in their areas of interest.
- Some naturalization records are available online, such as Tuscola County Naturalizations, 1850-1880 <www.usgennet.org/usa/mi/county/tuscola/nat/> or Ancestry.com's Iosco County, Michigan Naturalization Index, 1885-1910.
- After 26 September 1906, copies of naturalization records were forwarded to the Washington D.C. office of the U.S. Bureau of Immigration and Naturalization (renamed in 1933 the Immigration and Naturalization Service and today known as the U.S. Citizenship and Immigration Services). Since 1956, district offices have received these copies.[198] There is a District ISCIS Office in Detroit <uscis.gov/graphics/fieldoffices/detroit/aboutus.htm>.

Michigan Migration Project: The Michigan Migration Project <home.ix.netcom.com/~gsdownr/usgw/mimig.html>, part of the nationwide Migrations Project <www.migrations.org/>, allows researchers to post or search information about families who have migrated to or from Michigan. The Michigan page links to individual county pages or to information in the Migrations Project National Database. Information on individuals in the database includes the settlers' names, lifespans, birthplaces, migration steps, and the e-mail addresses of the researchers submitting the information. Additional notes also may be available. Individual county pages may include more detailed information, such as birth dates and places, death dates and places, and the sources of information for entries.

Migration information also may be available on MIGenWeb county sites, such as the one for Lenawee County <www.geocities.com/lenaweemi/migration.html>.

3 Vital Records

Vital records, as the name implies, are records of the vital or most important events in a person's life – birth, death, marriage, and divorce. Starting in 1867, Michigan required the registration of births, deaths, and marriages at the state-level. It became the ninth state in the country to have centralized vital records, and since that time more than 30 million vital records have been recorded with the state.[1] Some Michigan counties began keeping vital records prior to 1867. However, early records – whether on file with the state or county – are not always complete.

A Review of the Early Laws

Marriages: Marriages were the first public vital records to be recorded in Michigan. On 2 August 1805, Michigan's territorial governor and judges adopted an "Act Concerning Marriages," which was modeled after existing laws in Massachusetts and Virginia.[2] The 1805 act granted justices of the peace and ministers the authority to perform marriages, provided one of the parties to be married lived in the district where the justice of the peace or minister resided. Section 4 of the act also allowed religious societies with "peculiar regulations" to solemnize their own marriages. Persons who were already married could not marry. If the prospective bride or groom was under the age of 21, his or her father or guardian had to consent to the marriage. Ministers or justices of the peace who solemnized marriages were directed to forward to the clerk of the court in the district where the marriage took place a record of the marriage within 100 days of the ceremony. The clerk was to record the marriage in a book kept for that purpose and was then to annually return copies of these marriage records to the clerk of the Supreme Court of Michigan's territory.

On 31 October 1820, the territorial governor and judges passed an "Executive Act Regulating Marriages" that replaced the 1805 law.[3] It specified that men had to be at least 18 years old and women had to be at least 14 years old. However, men under age 21 and women under age 18 had to obtain the consent of their father in order to marry. If the father was dead or incapacitated, the bride or groom's mother or guardian could give consent. Men and women planning to marry could not be "nearer in kin than first cousin" and could not already be married.

The 1820 act further stated that justices of the peace "in his proper county" or ministers of the gospel in any part of the territory could perform marriage ceremonies. Quakers and Mennonites also were authorized to perform marriages.

Section 3 of the act said that notice of the impending marriage had to be given "either in writing affixed at some public place within the township where the female resides, at least 15 days before the day of marriage" or "publicly declared on two different days of public worship," the first to be at least 10 days previous to the marriage and within the county where the woman lived. A marriage license from the clerk of the county court where the woman lived could be used in lieu of this public notice. If either party needed consent to be married, the name of the parent or guardian who granted consent was to be listed on the license. The justice of the peace or minister was required to send to the county clerk in the county where the marriage took place a certificate of the marriage within three months of the ceremony. The clerk was to record the marriage in a book kept for that purpose.

The Legislative Council of the territory enacted another law regulating marriages on 12 April 1827.[4] It essentially was the same as the 1820 act, except notice of marriage was to be given within the township – rather than the county – where the prospective bride lived, and marriage licenses could be obtained from the township clerk, in addition to the county clerk, in the county where the woman lived. Laws passed in 1832 and 1833 were similar.

By 1838, the Revised Statutes of the State of Michigan said that men had to be at least 17 years old and women had to be at least 14 years old to marry.[5] Neither party was allowed to marry close blood relatives, and a "white" person was prohibited from marrying "a Negro or mulatto." (It wasn't until 1883 that marriages between "white persons and those wholly or in part of African descent" were legal.[6]) At least two witnesses had to be present at the ceremony. After the ceremony, the minister or justice of the peace performing the marriage was required to give a certificate of marriage to the parties, which was to include:

- Names, ages, and places of residence of the parties married
- Names and residences of at least two witnesses present at the marriage
- Time and place of marriage

A certificate of marriage also was to be returned to the county clerk within three months of the ceremony. The law further required the clerk or keeper of records for Quakers to annually send to the county clerk marriage returns for their meetings.

By 1846, Michigan had revised its statutes again. Marriage laws remained similar but specified that men had to be at least 18 years of age and women had to be at least 16 years of age to marry. The minister or justice of the peace performing the ceremony was not required to give a marriage certificate to the bride and groom but was to provide one "on request."[7]

Public Act 194 of 1867 set up a system of statewide registration of births, marriages, and deaths. For marriages, justices of the peace, ministers of the gospel, "all other persons authorized by law to solemnize marriages," and the clerks or keepers of records among Quakers were directed to keep records of marriages. The records were to include:

- Date and place of marriage
- Christian names and surnames of bride and groom
- Age and place of birth of each
- Residences of each at the time of marriage
- Occupation of the groom
- Name and official station of the person performing the marriage
- Names and residences of at least two witnesses present at the ceremony
- Date when such record was made

A certificate of marriage was to be delivered "on demand" to either the bride or groom. A record of the marriage also was to be delivered to the clerk of the county where the marriage took place within 90 days of the marriage. The clerk was to record the return of marriages in a book for that purpose. The marriages were to be recorded alphabetically, using both the name of the bride and groom, in the order received. In other words, clerks generally alphabetized last names by their first letter only and maintained separate lists for brides and grooms. Each year, on or before 1 November, the county clerk was to send a certified copy of all the marriages that had occurred in their county during the year preceding the first Monday in April to the Secretary of State. Once at the state level, the marriage returns were to be bound together in one or more volumes and indexed. In 1869, Public Act 125 added the requirement to record the "color" of the bride and groom.

It wasn't until 1887 that a law was passed requiring the issuance of marriage licenses. Public Act 128 required all parties intending to marry to obtain a marriage licenses from the county clerk "of the county in which either the man or woman resides." The license was issued after the parties to be married were questioned by the county clerk to see if they were legally entitled to be married. This affidavit was the basis for issuing the license. The license was to include for each of the parties:

- Full name
- Age
- Color
- Place of residence
- Place of birth
- Occupation
- Father's name and mother's maiden name, if known
- Number of times previously married

If the bride-to-be was a widow, the license was to include her maiden name. The license also was to include the date it was issued and the signature of the county clerk.

The clergyman or magistrate performing the ceremony was to fill out the certificate portion of the license with the time and place of the marriage, names and residences of two witnesses, and his own signature certifying that the licensed marriage took place. The clergyman or magistrate was to "separate the duplicate license and certificate and retain one-half for his own record." He was to return

Vital Record **Laws**

1805 – Territory of Michigan enacts its first marriage law

1812 – Territory passes its first divorce law

1867 – State of Michigan establishes a system for the registration of births, deaths, and marriages

1887 – State requires marriage licenses

1897 – Michigan sets up a method of reporting divorce statistics to the state

1897 – State requires death certificates

1905 – Michigan requires birth certificates; records must declare if births "legitimate" or "illegitimate"

1931 – Michigan introduces delayed birth registration

1945 – Courts seal original birth certificates at time of adoptions

1978 – State restricts the viewing and copying of all birth records; the term "illegitimate" is dropped from birth certificates

1997 – State allows birth records older than 110 years to be viewed or copied

2002 – State changes restriction on birth records to those less than 100 years old

the other half within 10 days to the issuing county clerk. Using the returned license and certificate, the county clerk was then to record in a book of registration the date and place of marriage, the names and residences of two witnesses to the marriage, and the name of the officiating clergyman or magistrate. All licenses and certificates were to be kept on file in the clerk's office, and as often as once every three months the clerk was to "make a faithful report to the Secretary of State of all licenses and certificates issued and received by him." Genealogists should note that the license had to be issued in the county of residence of either the bride or groom. Returns were to go to the county issuing the license. Therefore, it is possible for marriage records to be in a county other than the one in which the marriage took place.

Public Act 180 of 1897 set up a system of private or secret marriages for women "with child." Called "An Act to provide for the protection of the reputation and good name of certain persons," the law granted probate judges the authority to issue marriage licenses and to perform marriages in secret. The records were to be kept in a private probate file and also in a private register by the Secretary of State. The law, now known as "Marriages Without Publicity," is still on the books.[8]

Divorces: The first reference to divorce in Michigan territorial law was an act, passed on 10 January 1812, granting the Supreme Court of the territory jurisdiction over all cases of divorce and alimony.[9] Seven years later, the Michigan territorial governor and justices passed "An Act Concerning Divorce," on 30 November 1819.[10] It was patterned after laws in New York. The act allowed divorce from matrimony in cases of adultery. If the charges of adultery were denied, then the court could order a trial by jury. After the dissolution of a marriage it was lawful for the complainant (the party who brought the charges of adultery) to marry again "as though the defendant were actually dead." The defendant or the party convicted of adultery could not remarry until the complainant died. The court also could decree "a separation from bed and board" in cases of cruel and inhumane treatment or abandonment. A separation from bed and board, also known as a "limited divorce," might be for a specific time period only.

"An Act Concerning Divorce," passed 12 April 1827, was similar to the 1819 law. "An Act Concerning Divorce" passed 28 June 1832, added impotency as a cause for divorce.[11] It specified that the petitioner for divorce had to reside in Michigan territory for the previous three years. Petitions for divorce could be made to the Supreme Court of the territory or either of the Circuit Courts of the territory. The petition had to include the names and ages of the parties and the cause for divorce. The court could hear witnesses in open court or by deposition. Notice of the divorce petition had to be published in a newspaper in the territory. There could be a trial by jury, except in cases of impotency. "An Act Concerning Divorce," approved 4 April 1833, repealed the acts of 1827 and 1832, but its substance was similar to the 1832 law.[12]

Between June 1828 and March 1831 Michigan's Legislative Council granted divorces, even though it had "no statutory authority under federal or territorial law" to do so.[13] Because this was a more confidential route than going through the courts, petitioning the council for a divorce was a more popular option. During these three years the council granted 17 divorces, compared to only 22 granted by Michigan's Supreme Court during the three decades of Michigan's territorial period.[14]

By 1838, the Revised Statutes of the State of Michigan authorized divorce "from the bonds of matrimony" in the cases of adultery or impotency, desertion for five years, or if either party had been sentenced to hard labor in a prison, jail, or house of correction for life or for three years or more.[15] A divorce from "bed and board" could be granted in cases of extreme cruelty, desertion for three years, or if the husband did not support the wife. The petitioner for divorce had to be a resident of the state for the previous two years. The act authorized the circuit court or the court of chancery of the county in which one of the parties resided to handle divorce cases. The divorce petition had to include the names, ages, and residences of the parties and a cause for divorce. If the defendant in the divorce could not be found, the court could order that "a notice of the petition, or the petition itself, or the substance thereof" be published in one or more newspapers.

By 1846, the law had changed to allow divorces for cases of adultery, "when one of the parties was physically incompetent at the time of the marriage," when one of the parties was sentenced to imprisonment for three years or more, for desertion for two years, or when the husband or wife was "an habitual drunkard."[16] A divorce from "bed and board" forever or for a limited time could be decreed in cases of extreme cruelty, desertion for two years, or if the husband neglected to support his wife. To be eligible to petition for a divorce, the party had to live in the state for one year prior to the application "or unless the marriage was solemnized in this state, and the complainant shall have resided in this state from the time of such marriage to the time of exhibiting the petition or bill."

Public Act 9 of 1897 set up a system of reporting divorce statistics to the state. The law directed clerks of courts with divorce jurisdiction to annually report to the state statistics for divorces in their areas on or before 1 February. The report was to include divorces for the year ending 31 December. Clerks reported the following information of genealogical interest to the state:

- Name of each party
- Age of each party
- Number of children in the family
- Cause
- Gender of complainant
- Date and place where the marriage was performed

Only the divorce summaries were reported to the state. Details of the divorce can be found in the records of the court that handled the case.

Deaths: There was no requirement to report deaths prior to 1867. Public Act 194 of 1867, which set up a system of statewide registration of births, marriages, and deaths, directed the township supervisor or city assessor or supervisor to annually canvass their areas to record the births and deaths that took place the year preceding the first Monday in April. The supervisor or assessor was to return the results of their canvass to the county clerk within 30 days of completing the assessment. Each year, on or before 1 November, the county clerk was to send a certified copy of all the deaths that had occurred in their county during the year preceding the first Monday in April to the Secretary of State. Once at the state level, the deaths returns were to be bound together in one or more volumes and indexed.

The record of death was to state:

- Date of death
- Christian and surname of the deceased
- Gender
- Martial status
- Age in years, months, and days
- Place of death
- Disease or apparent cause of death
- Nativity of the deceased
- Occupation, if over 10 years of age
- Names and residence of parents, if under 10 years of age
- Date when record made

The supervisors or assessors were asked to "obtain the facts" of all births and deaths within their areas "from the heads of families, the keepers, overseers or superintendents of asylums, hospitals, jails, prisons, workhouses, almshouses,

houses of correction and similar institutions, the keepers of hotels, public and private boarding houses, and the masters or chief officers of steamboats and sail-vessels navigating any of the waters of [the] State, and touching at any port of entry." The supervisors and assessors were allowed to obtain information on births and deaths from any person who might have information about them. In 1869, Public Act 125 added the requirement to record the color of the deceased. It also changed the category for the decedent's parents to "residence of parents, if known" instead of only asking for the parents' names and residence if the decedent was under the age of 10.

It wasn't until 1897 that a law was passed requiring the issuance of death certificates. Public Act 217 of 1897 directed undertakers, householders, relatives, friends, managers of institutions, sextons, or other persons supervising the burial of a deceased person to fill out a death certificate. The certificate had to be signed by a relative or "some competent person acquainted with the facts," and the physician who attended the deceased had to fill in the cause of death. The law required the following facts about the decedent on a death certificate:

- Date of death, stating year, month, and day
- Full name
- Gender
- Age in years, months, and days, if known, or an approximate age if the exact age is not known
- Color
- Marital status
- If married, age at first marriage
- Parent of how many children and how many children living
- Place of death, giving ward, street, and number, if in a city
- Birthplace (state or country if not born in Michigan)
- Occupation
- Full names of both parents
- Birthplaces of both parents
- Proposed place and time of burial or place and route for removal of body
- Signature and address of reporter certifying the above facts
- Signature and address of undertaker
- Name of disease
- Immediate cause of death, together with contributory causes or complications, if any
- Duration of each cause
- Date last seen by medical attendant or fact of no medical attendance
- In violent deaths, statement whether death resulted from accident, suicide, or homicide
- Whether a post mortem was held and results thereof
- Signature and address of medical attendant, health officer, or coroner certifying the cause of death

The registrar of death in each township, village, or city was further directed to forward to the Secretary of State on the fourth day of each month all the certificates of death filed in his office during the preceding month. Once at the state level, the certificates were to be bound and indexed. The local registrars of death also were to send a transcript monthly to the county clerk of all the deaths in the preceding month.

In 1921, Public Act 170 transferred responsibility for vital records from the Secretary of State to the State Commissioner of Health. Public Act 343 of 1925, the first major revision of vital records law, created a State Bureau of Vital Statistics supervised by the State Department of Health.

Death records are generally recorded in the county of death, though they also may be recorded in the county of residence or in both counties. Some counties have separate out-of-county death indexes, and at least one county refers to these out-of-county death records as "foreign deaths."

Prior to 1897, when death certificates became mandatory, death records were frequently incomplete.

> Sometimes a friend or relative of the deceased duly reported the death to the township or village clerk; and sometimes that clerk duly reported the death to the county clerk, who was then expected to report county wide death statistics to the state. But often, this chain was never started or completed, so many died without an official record of their passing. The death records probably missed as many deaths as they recorded, and in an era of limited diagnostic skills, they no doubt often erred in listing an individual's true cause of death. (For example, when young children of teething age died, it was not uncommon for teething to be cited as the cause of death.)[17]

Births: The 1867 act that set up a system of statewide registration of births, marriages, and deaths required supervisors or assessors to gather information about births at the same time they canvassed their areas to gather information about deaths. The record of births were to include:

- Date of birth
- Name of the child (if any)
- Gender of the child
- Place of birth
- Christian and surname of both parents
- Residence and nativity of the parents
- Occupation of the father
- Date when record made

If the child had not yet been named, the law provided that the name could be received in the next annual canvass and included as belonging to a child previously reported.

It wasn't until 1905 that a law was passed requiring the issuance of birth certificates. Public Act 330 of 1905 directed the attending physician or midwife to file a certificate of birth with the local registrar within 10 days of the birth. If there was no attending physician or midwife, then it became the duty of the father of the child, householder, manager or superintendent of a public or private institution, or "other competent" person knowing the facts of birth to file the certificate with the local registrar within 10 days. The certificate was to contain the following information:

- Place of birth, including state, county, township, village, or city
- If the birth took place in a city, the ward, street, and house number
- If the birth took place in a hospital or other institution, the name was to be given rather than the street and number.
- Full name of the child. If the child died unnamed, then the words "died unnamed" was to be entered. If a living child hadn't been named by the time the certificate was filed, the space for name of child was to be left blank and was to be filled in later.
- Gender
- Whether twin, triplet, or other plural birth
- Whether legitimate or illegitimate
- Full name of father
- Residence of father
- Color or race of father
- Birthplace of father
- Age of father at last birthday, in years
- Occupation of father
- Maiden name of mother
- Residence of mother
- Color or race of mother
- Birthplace of mother
- Age of mother at last birthday, in years
- Occupation of mother
- Number of children of this mother
- Number of children of this mother now living
- Certificate of physician or attending midwife, including statement of year, month, day, and hour of birth, including signature, address, and date of signature. If there was no physician or midwife in attendance, the person filing the certificate was to draw a line through the words, "I hereby certify that I attended the birth of above child," and write "No physician or midwife."
- Exact date of filing in the office of registrar, with his signature

The registrar of births in each township, village, or city was further directed to forward to the Secretary of State on the fourth day of each month all the certificates of birth filed in his office during the preceding month, any delayed certificates for the preceding months, corrections of certificates previously transmitted, and supplemental statements regarding names of children who had not been named when their certificates were previously filed. Once at the state level, the certificates were to be bound and indexed. The local registrar of births was further directed to give a quarterly report of births in his area to the county clerk.

The 1905 act also provided for the correction of birth certificates and directed local registrars to make a complete list of births each April to be given to township supervisors or city assessors. Between April 10 and June 1, the supervisors or assessors were to "make diligent inquiry to ascertain whether any other births" had occurred in their townships, wards, or cities. If any births were discovered, they were to immediately fill out a birth certificate.

Public Act 343 of 1925 directed that birth certificates were to be filed within five days of births. Certificates of birth and death were required for all "still-births" that had reached the fifth month of pregnancy.

In 1931, Public Act 35 set up a system to register previously unreported births. The delayed birth registration could be done by applying to the probate judge in the county of residence or in the county of birth. The application had to be accompanied by the affidavit of two people. These records often appear in birth indexes with the notation "DR" for delayed record or delayed registration. Michigan law still allows late or delayed registration of births.[18]

Public Act 105 of 1933 stated that illegitimate births were to no longer be recorded in county records but were to be recorded by the State Vital Records Office in a closed file. It wasn't until 1978, with the second major revision of vital records law, that the term "illegitimate" was dropped from birth certificates. These births were to be recorded at both the state and county levels.

Because of problems with fraud, the state also took measures in 1978 to restrict the viewing and issuance of copies of birth certificates. Public Act 368 stated that copies of birth records can be issued only to:

- The individual named on the certificate
- The parents named on the certificate
- An heir of the individual on the certificate
- A legal representative or legal guardian of that individual
- A court of competent jurisdiction

To be considered an heir, the person requesting the copy must be related to the person named on the certificate and the person named on the certificate must be deceased. The person requesting the copy must state their relationship to the person named on the certificate and provide the individual's date and place of death when requesting the birth certificate.

Public Act 54 of 1997 lifted these restrictions somewhat by allowing birth certificates 110 years or older to be released to any applicant. This was followed by Public Act 544 of 2002 which allows birth certificates 100 years or older to be released to any applicant.

When searching for birth certificates, researchers should keep in mind that births were recorded in the county of birth rather than in the county of residence of the mother. Some counties did not have hospitals, so births may be recorded in a nearby county with a hospital. It also was a custom in many families for young brides to return to their parents' homes for the birth of their first child – even if that meant traveling from Detroit to the Upper Peninsula.[19]

A Word About Adoptions: Since 1945, the court that approved an adoption sealed the original birth record at the time of the adoption. The Michigan Department of Community Health can issue only a copy of the replacement birth record that indicates the name of the adopted child and the name(s) of the adoptive parent(s). The court that approved the adoption has a copy of the adoption decree and the original birth certificate. Adult adoptees can make a written request to the Michigan Department of Community Health to request the name of the court that finalized the adoption. (For more information about adoption, see Chapter 6.)

Locations of Records

State: The Michigan Department of Community Health <www.michigan.gov/mdch> in Lansing is the repository for birth, death, and marriage records from 1867 and divorce summaries from 1897. Anyone is eligible to receive a certified copy of a death, marriage, or divorce record, as long as they make their request in writing and pay the appropriate fees. Anyone also is eligible to receive a birth record that occurred at least 100 years ago. Birth records less than 100 years old can be issued only to the individual named on the certificate, either parent named on the record, a legal guardian, a legal representative of an eligible person, or any heir.

At this writing, certified copies of records from the Michigan Department of Community Health are $15 each; this fee includes a three-year search. Additional years searched per record request are $4 per year. Additional copies of the same record ordered at the same time are $5 each. If a record is not found, notice will be sent that the record is not on file. Checks or money orders must be made payable to the State of Michigan. To order records, use the appropriate application and send it to:

Vital Records Requests
P.O. Box 30721
Lansing, Mich. 48909

Applications are available online at the Michigan Department of Community Health Web site. Records also can be ordered online through VitalChek's Web site <www.vitalchek.com/>.

County: Marriage and divorce records are on file at the county level, generally from the date that the county's government was organized. Birth and death records usually begin in 1867. Researchers may visit county clerk's offices to view records. Copies of vital records also may be ordered by mail from county clerks. Search and/or copy fees vary from county to county, and the same access restrictions apply to birth records less than 100 years old. (See Chapter 10 for more details about county records.)

Cities and Townships: Some of the copies of early vital records kept by cities and townships have survived and can be found on microfilm or in printed sources, such as DAR records, or transcriptions, abstracts, and indexes prepared by individuals or genealogical societies. Some of these records are online at MIGenWeb county sites. Examples of these include:

- Index to the death register for Lake Township, Berrien County, 1919-1935 <www.usgennet.org/usa/mi/county/berrien/LakeD.htm>
- Death register for Coe Township, Isabella County, 1904-1907 <www.rootsweb.com/~miisabel/deathreg.html>
- Death register for Alamo Township, Kalamazoo County, 1897-1997 <www.rootsweb.com/~mikalama/alamo/alamodeaths.htm>
- Birth records for Lowell Township, Kent County, 1880 <www.rootsweb.com/~mikent/townships/lowell/births1880.html>
- Death record index for Blendon Township, Ottawa County, 1911-1951 <www.rootsweb.com/~miottawa/deaths/bldnbur/index.html>

Four Michigan Historical Records Survey volumes on birth, marriage, divorce, and death records held by governmental agencies in Michigan list the vital records on file with counties, cities, townships and villages as of the early 1940s.[20]

Some Michigan cities in Macomb, Oakland, and Wayne counties may still keep vital records.[21] In Detroit, for example, the City Health Department <www.ci.detroit.mi.us/health/vital/vital_r.htm> has birth records from 1893 and death records from 1897. That office can be contacted by writing:

Detroit Health Department
Herman Kiefer Health Complex
1151 Taylor St. Room 104 B
Detroit, Michigan 48202

Though Michigan cities are required by law to forward copies of their vital records to the state, researchers report finding records listed with cities that are not filed with the state. Additionally, researchers have found early vital records recorded in township records that were never forwarded to the county or state levels. The Newaygo County MIGenWeb site, for example, includes several of these "unrecorded" birth records for 1867 through 1883 <www.rootsweb.com/~minewayg/births.html>.

Library of Michigan: Indexes to the state's copy of vital records and some returns are available on microfilm at the Library of Michigan. These include a birth index (1867-1915); marriage index (1867-1921, 1950-1969) and returns (1867-1925); divorce index (1897-1969) and summaries (1897-1922); and death index (1867-1914) and returns (1867-1897). The marriage index between 1922 and 1949 has not been microfilmed because of the difficulty in microfilming the card file system that the state used at that time.[22] The marriage index from 1867 to 1921 is alphabetized by bride and groom, but from 1950 to 1969 the index is alphabetized by groom only. The divorce index is alphabetized by husband and wife through 1923 and by husband only after 1923.

State Archives of Michigan: Vital records on file at the State Archives are described in Archival Circular No. 19 <www.michigan.gov/documents/mhc_sa_circular19_49707_7.pdf>. These include the statewide birth index from 1867 to 1872; the statewide divorce index from 1897 to 1977 and divorce records from some counties; the statewide death index from 1867 to 1914 and death records from a few townships, counties, and the city of Lansing; and the statewide marriage index from 1867 to 1921, the statewide groom index from 1950 to 1969, and marriage records from the city of Dearborn and a few counties.

Family History Centers: The Church of Jesus Christ of Latter-day Saints has microfilmed the county's copies of many Michigan records. These can be rented for viewing at Family History Centers. For a complete list of microfilms available, visit the library's catalog at the Family Search Web site <www.familysearch.org/>.

Online: Indexes, transcriptions, abstracts, and databases of Michigan vital records can be found online. Examples of sites include:

- GENDIS, the Genealogical Death Indexing System, provides free online access to early death records. It is available through the Michigan Department of Community Health Web site <www.michigan.gov/mdch>. Data in GENDIS came from microfilmed death ledgers and was transcribed by genealogists from Michigan's local genealogical societies. The Abrams Foundation provided funding to the Michigan Genealogical Council for this project. At present, the database has more than 205,000 records from 1867 to 1885. Researchers can search records by decedent's name, father's last name, county of death, or year of death. Information returned includes death date, ledger page and record number, place and county of death, sex, race, marital status, age, cause, birthplace, occupation, father's name and residence, mother's name and residence, and date of record. Researchers can ask for returns to be sorted by decedent's name, father's last name, county of death, or date of death. GENDIS is updated regularly.
- Several Michigan counties, including Barry, Branch, Genesee, Grand Traverse, Macomb, Muskegon, Saginaw, and Washtenaw, have placed vital record indexes online. (See Chapter 10 for more details.)
- MIGenWeb <www.rootsweb.com/~migenweb> county sites often have indexes, abstracts, or transcriptions of vital records. Some sites, such as the Mackinac County MIGenWeb site <www.rootsweb.com/~mimackin/deathcert.html>, have placed digital images of vital records online.
- The Michigan Family History Network <www.mifamilyhistory.org/> has a number of free databases on its site, including the Early Michigan Births Index, Michigan Death Database, and Dibean's Michigan Marriage Collection.

- Rootsweb.com <www.rootsweb.com/> has a number of free user-contributed databases, including an index to deaths in Saint Clair County (1868-1974).
- Ancestry.com has a number of subscription-based databases, including Marriages – Michigan to 1850; Michigan Marriages, 1851-75 (including records from Branch, Hillsdale, Jackson, Kent, and Wayne counties); Oakland County, Michigan Vital Records, 1800-1917, taken from *Our Pioneers: Families of Early Oakland County, Michigan* (1888); and Michigan Vital Records: Deaths 1971-1996. (This death records database also is available on CD-ROM. See the description below.) These databases also are available through the library version of Ancestry.com that is available for free at most Michigan public libraries

CD-ROMs: Collections of vital records on CD-ROM are available for purchase. These include:

- Michigan and Wisconsin, 1830-1900 Marriage Index (from Genealogy.com) includes information on about 161,000 individuals from 30 Michigan counties including Allegan, Berrien, Branch, Cass, Cheboygan, Chippewa, Delta, Eaton, Genesee, Hillsdale, Ingham, Ionia, Isabella, Jackson, Kalamazoo, Kent, Lapeer, Livingston, Mackinac, Macomb, Monroe, Newaygo, Oakland, Saginaw, Saint Clair, Sanilac, Shiawassee, Van Buren, Washtenaw, and Wayne.
- Michigan Vital Records: Deaths 1971-1996 (from Ancestry.com) contains more than two million records from the Michigan Department of Vital and Health Records. The collection includes the full name of the decedent, birth and death dates, county and town of death, and county and town of residence. The database includes records from all Michigan counties.

Books: Several individuals and genealogical or historical societies have published transcriptions, abstractions, or indexes of vital records. Many are listed in the online card catalog for the Library of Michigan <www.michigan.gov/hal>, Allen County Public Library <www.acpl.lib.in.us/genealogy/index.html>, or the Family History Library <www.familysearch.org/>. Early divorce records can be found in the four-volume set, *Laws of the Territory of Michigan* (1871-1884), and the six-volume *Transactions of the Supreme Court of the Territory of Michigan* (1935-1940).

Death Without Official Michigan Record: The Michigan Genealogical Council is sponsoring a Death Without Official Michigan Record Project. The Council is accepting registrations for individuals who died in or before 1900 and left no official Michigan record. "Persons may be registered who lived in Michigan, had lived in Michigan and died elsewhere, died in Michigan and were not usual Michigan residents, or were children of lifetime Michigan residents," according to the Council's Web site. The Council is archiving this information, and researchers may access proof-of-death records by depositing an equal number of proof-of-death records. For more information, see the Council's Web site <www.rootsweb.com/~mimgc/death.htm>.

4
Alternative Sources for Vital Records

Official sources of vital records, particularly in the early years, are not always complete or accurate. "Unofficial" or alternative sources for vital records can help fill in these gaps or give clues for finding the official record. Churches, for example, often recorded burials, marriages, and baptisms. Cemetery tombstones usually list a birth and death date. Newspapers published obituaries and marriage, birth, and death notices. Military records and county histories sometimes provide birth and death information. In addition to providing vital records, these sources often go beyond the mere listing of dates, yielding information that can give researchers a clearer picture of their ancestors and their ancestors' lives.

Bible Records

Family Bibles are a good source for birth, death, and marriage records because it was, and often still is, the custom in many families to record information about family members in the Bible. The Daughters of the American Revolution have compiled many Bible records. (See the DAR section below.) Unpublished Bible records also may be found in collections of family papers in public libraries and at genealogical or historical societies. Researchers may even find family Bibles tucked away in an attic or at the home of a distant relative. Some Bible records have been transcribed and placed online. Examples include:

- Bible Records of Berrien County, Michigan <www.usgennet.org/usa/mi/county/berrien/bible.htm>
- Index to the Kalamazoo Valley Genealogical Society's Bible Records <www.rootsweb.com/~mikvgs/bible/biblindx.htm>
- Newaygo County's MIGenWeb site's Family Bibles page <www.rootsweb.com/~minewayg/fmbible.html>
- RootsWeb.com's county message boards (For more information on message boards, see Chapter 9.)

Diaries

Like Bible records, unpublished diaries may be found with collections of family papers in libraries, with societies, or in a researcher's very own home. The State Archives of Michigan, for example, has several unpublished diaries. Many of these are listed in Circular 61: Dairies, Daybooks, and Personal Journals <www.michigan.gov/documents/mhc_sa_circular61_49967_7.pdf>. The Michigan

Technological University Archives and Copper Country Historical Collections has the Brockway Diary Collection <www.lib.mtu.edu/mtuarchives/ms010brockwaydiary.aspx>, 31 diaries dating from 1866 to 1897.

Some diaries have been published. The Library of Michigan has compiled a research guide to Early Michigan Diaries and Autobiographies, and suggests such books as the *Diary of Captain Soren Kristiansen, Lake Michigan Schooner Captain, 1891-1893* (1981) or *Mary Austin Wallace: Her Diary, 1862; a Michigan Soldier's Wife Runs Their Farm* (1963). The Library of Michigan study guide is online <www.michigan.gov/hal>. Select "Publications and Products," then "Research Guides and Reading Lists."

Several published Michigan diaries also have been listed in bibliographies. For example, *American Diaries: An Annotated Bibliography of Published American Diaries and Journals* (1987) lists more than 5,000 diaries written between 1492 and 1980. The two-volume set is indexed by name, subject, and geographic area. Volume 1, which lists diaries written from 1492 to 1844, has more than 70 references to Michigan in its index, while Volume 2, which lists diaries written from 1845 to 1980, has more than 100 references to Michigan in its index. Compiled by Laura Arksey, Nancy Pries, and Marcia Reed, the volumes supercede "the previous authoritative work in this field ... William Matthews' *American Diaries: An Annotated Bibliography of American Diaries Written Prior to the Year 1861.*"[1] *The Published Diaries and Letters of American Women: An Annotated Bibliography* (1987) by Joyce D. Goodfriend lists seven references to diaries by Michigan women.

Some diaries, such as those found on the Kent County MIGenWeb site's Diaries and Letters page <www.rootsweb.com/~mikent/diaries/index.html>, have been transcribed and placed online.

Information from Others

Just as members of a researcher's immediate family can have helpful information in the form of family Bibles, diaries, records, or memories, so can distant cousins researching the same family lines. There are various ways of contacting these researchers. For example, societies may publish queries in their periodicals or libraries may maintain lists of researchers. The Lenawee County Library in Adrian, for example, keeps a Surname Exchange Book in which researchers can list the names and areas they are researching along with their contact information. Societies may publish books of members' charts or a listing of their research interests, such as the two volumes of *Ancestral Charts* by the Eaton County Genealogical Society (1998) or the seven-volume *Surname Directory* by the Oakland County Genealogical Society (1983-1999). Genealogical charts may be filed with libraries. In the past, for example, researchers who wanted to join the Detroit Society for Genealogical Research were required to submit their genealogical charts. "This has not been true for several years, but the society still maintains those charts and encourages its members to submit their charts even today."[2] An index to the names found on these charts is available at the Burton Historical Collection at the Detroit Public Library. There also are various methods of connecting with other researchers online. (See Chapter 9 for more.) In addition, there are genealogical projects that have a wealth of data available for researchers to utilize, and many of these are described below.

Michigan Pioneer Records: Starting in 1947, researchers submitted to the Library of Michigan more than 3,200 family group sheets with information about persons living in Michigan prior to 1880. These data sheets were bound in 38 volumes in the early 1960s, and an index on microfiche is available. The index includes other family members listed on the data sheet – not just the Michigan pioneers.

Michigan Family Register: Between 1969 and 1971, Ethel Williams established a Michigan Pioneer Register, which evolved from her work as editor and publisher of *Michigan Heritage.* "Correspondents researching the same families were put in touch with one another through her offices."[3] After Williams' death, her genealogical materials were donated to the Library of Michigan. The questionnaires for the Michigan Pioneer Register – consisting of handwritten and typed Family Group Sheets and Pedigree Charts – have been placed in nine volumes and are indexed. They also are available on microform.

Centennial Family Certificate Questionnaire: To celebrate the nation's bicentennial in 1976, the Michigan Genealogical Council issued Centennial Family Certificates to researchers who could prove that one of their ancestors lived in Michigan prior to 1877. The Library of Michigan has the 10,000 applications and an index on microform. The index is arranged alphabetically by ancestor and also by county and then alphabetically by ancestor.

Flint Genealogical Society Bicentennial Family Certificate Questionnaire: The Flint Genealogical Society issued Bicentennial Family Certificates in 1976. The questionnaires and supporting documentation have been microfilmed and are available at the Library of Michigan. The documentation includes such items as copies of vital records, pages from family Bibles and county histories, and handwritten letters from applicants. A surname index for the project is at the very end of the second roll of microfilm.

Sesquicentennial Pioneer Program: "As part of the impending celebration of the 150th anniversary of statehood in 1987, the Library of Michigan and the Michigan Genealogical Council designed a Sesquicentennial Pioneer program to honor people who could prove their ancestors were in Michigan by 1837, the year it became the 26th state."[4] An index to the 8,000 applications is on microfiche in the Library of Michigan, and the State Archives of Michigan has the original files submitted by researchers. These files are rich in documentation. Reporter Eric Freedman profiled more than 100 pioneers from this project in his book *Pioneering Michigan* (1992).

Michigan Surname Index: More than 100,000 surnames from about 1,000 members of Michigan genealogical societies are published in the Michigan Genealogical Council's two-volume *Michigan Surname Index* (1984-1989).

Each listing includes the name being researched; tentative or actual birth, death, and marriage dates and places, if known; spouse or other relative; and the contributor's code. An index of the contributors with their codes are at the back of each book; the index also lists the contributors' names and addresses. Researchers may correspond with the contributors or view the original cards on file at the Library of Michigan in Lansing. "The cards usually contain more data than can be abstracted on one printed line and are more revealing of family relationships than the abstracts."[5] One caveat: the index can include the names of individuals who did not live in Michigan because the index lists all surnames of ancestors being researched by Michigan society members, not just those who lived in Michigan.

Pioneer Certificate Programs: There are several local or county-level Pioneer Certificate Programs. Usually a researcher has to prove that an ancestor lived in a particular area at a particular time to receive a Pioneer Certificate. The documentation submitted by researchers to receive these certificates is sometimes available for other researchers to use.

The Herrick District Library, for example, awarded Pioneer Certificates <www.herrickdl.org/genealogy/pioneer.html> to individuals or families who proved that their ancestors lived in Holland, Michigan, as the first settlers of the town. The library's Pioneer Certificate File contains the genealogical records submitted to the Genealogy Department during the certification process. The Van Buren Regional Genealogical Society Pioneer Certificate Project <www.rootsweb.com/~mivbrgs/vbrgs.htm#pioneer>, begun in 1997, covers Allegan, Berrien, Cass, Kalamazoo, and Van Buren counties. The project archives are housed in the Local History Collection of the Van Buren District Library in Decatur and is available for public viewing.

Other pioneer certificate programs include Calhoun County's Pioneer Certificate Program <www.rootsweb.com/~micalhou/pioninst.htm>, Delta County's Genealogical Society Pioneer Certificate Project <www.grandmastree.com/society/pioneer.htm>, Grand Traverse Area Genealogical Society's Ancestral Family and Early Settler Certificates <www.rootsweb.com/~migtags/Certificates.htm>, and Muskegon County's Pioneer Certificate Program <www.rootsweb.com/~mimcgs/Pioneer.htm>. In addition, several pioneer programs took place around 2001 in conjunction with the 300th anniversary celebration of the founding of Detroit, including ones sponsored by the French Canadian Heritage Society of Michigan <habitant.org/fchsm/> and the Irish Genealogical Society of Michigan <www.rootsweb.com/~miigsm/>. Information from the Irish Genealogical Society of Michigan project was published in the book *Our Roots Began in Ireland* (2001).

Michigan Family Group Sheet Project: The Michigan Family Group Sheet Project <www.rootsweb.com/~migenweb/fgs> allows researchers to post their family group sheets online for others to use as resources. The family group sheets are organized by county and then alphabetically by name.

DAR Records

Michigan Chapters of the Daughters of the American Revolution <www.geocities.com/Heartland/Meadows/6543/> have transcribed and abstracted notes and information from many unpublished sources, including Bible, birth, cemetery, census, death, land, marriage, military, and probate records. These compilations, known as DAR Genealogical Records Committee Reports, are valuable sources of information. The DAR deposits copies of each of its books with the DAR Library in Washington, D.C. Michigan books also are deposited at the Burton Historical Collection at the Detroit Public Library and the Library of Michigan in Lansing. Some DAR records have been microfilmed by the Family History Library and are available through Family History Centers, and smaller libraries also may have copies of DAR records. The Benton Harbor Public Library, for example, reports having DAR cemetery records for all of Berrien County. The three-volume *Index to the First 37 Volumes of the Michigan DAR Bible and Pioneer Records* (1967) is a valuable key to unlocking these sources. A newer tool is the Genealogical Records Committee National Index, available on the DAR Web site <members.dar.org/dar/darnet/grc/grc.cfm>. The ongoing project is an every-name index for Genealogical Records Committee Reports. At present, there are more than 377,000 Michigan names in the database.

The DAR also has published the *Historical and Genealogical Record of the Michigan Daughters of the American Revolution* every 12 years since 1940. (A two-volume set, published in 1930, covers the years 1893 to 1930.) These books include an alphabetical listing of the Revolutionary War ancestors of the Michigan DAR members who have been admitted during the 12 years covered by the volumes. For a complete listing of DAR books, consult the DAR's Online Library Catalog <www.dar.org/library/onlinlib.cfm>. At present, there are more than 1,400 publications with Michigan in the title. In addition, DAR Lineage Books – many with Michigan references – can be searched through Ancestry.com.

Church and Synagogue Records

The first French settlers brought their Catholic faith with them to Michigan. In fact, the first permanent settlement in Michigan was a Catholic mission founded in 1668 by Jesuit Father Jacques Marquette at Sault Ste. Marie. Shortly after Detroit's founding in 1701, the first Roman Catholic Church in Michigan was established. Ste. Anne's registry dates from 1703, and it's the "second oldest continuously maintained parish of the Roman Catholic Church in the United States."[6] By the end of the 18th century, the "French-speaking Ste. Anne's in Detroit" was still the only Catholic Church in Michigan.[7] But by 1826 there were an estimated 7,000 Catholics, most of them French Canadians, and nine Catholic churches in the Territory of Michigan.[8]

Saint Patrick's of Washtenaw County's Northfield Township, established in 1831, was Michigan's first English-speaking Catholic parish. Renamed Saint Bridget's in 1837, the church reverted to Saint Patrick's in 1864 and "served as a magnet for Irish immigrants flowing into Michigan."[9] Because most Catholic priests in Michigan were from Europe, they tended to be more receptive to the many immigrants coming to Michigan. "Catholic services were conducted in Latin, but priests often delivered sermons and heard confessions in English, German, French, Italian, Chippewa, Potawatomi and other appropriate tongues."[10]

The first Protestant congregation in Michigan belonged to the Moravians and their Delaware Indian converts, who built a community near Mount Clemens during the Revolutionary War. (Most of this group moved to Canada at the end of the Revolutionary War.) A Congregational minister held religious services at Detroit as early as 1800; the first Methodist minister visited Michigan in 1803. "By 1817, a number of Protestant services were held in Michigan, but with no formal church building. A Methodist Church, built on the River Rouge in 1818, was the first Protestant church building in Michigan apart from [the] old Moravian Indian Mission built many years before."[11] By 1837, there were nearly 5,000 Methodists in Michigan, and churches had been built in Adrian, Ann Arbor, Coldwater, Detroit, Flint, Jackson, Kalamazoo, Marshall, Niles, Port Huron, and Ypsilanti. By 1865, the Methodist Church was the largest Protestant denomination in Michigan. "The huge number of frontier pioneers who became Methodists is directly attributable to the circuit riders, who were willing to go anywhere on the unsettled frontier for even the smallest of tasks."[12]

Other Protestant denominations active in early Michigan included the Baptists, Episcopalians, Lutherans, and Presbyterians.

> New churches were small, often with as few as four or five members. Some were interdenominational, organized according to the principles favored by the predominant group. ... Services were held in houses, outside, or, in more established communities, the school or courthouse. If a meeting house was built, frequently all the denominations shared it. Few churches could support a full-time minister in their early years. Therefore, preachers of all denominations usually rode circuits, stopping once every two or three weeks at a given community. If more than one minister served a particular town in this way, they scheduled their services for alternating weeks so as not to compete with each other.[13]

In larger cities, denominations might have two or more congregations divided by ethnicity, but in smaller communities different ethnic groups tended to worship together.[14] Pioneers frequently attended the church closest to home, whether or not this was the family's preferred faith. During the French regime, for example, many Protestants were baptized in the Catholic Church because there were no other churches available to perform the ceremony.[15] At other times settlers chose where they wanted to live based on the availability of their preferred church. "Quaker immigrants, for example, sought to settle together, and formed distinctive rural communities in southern Michigan."[16] Some settlers even moved from one Michigan community to another to live among others of their faith.

By 1884 there were nearly 3,000 church organizations from 30 different denominations in Michigan. The five largest denominations represented 60 percent of the state's church organizations. They were Methodist Episcopals (Methodists) with 738 organized churches, Baptists with 273, Roman Catholics with 249, Congregationalists with 248, and Evangelical Lutherans with 229.[17] The Methodists were evenly spread throughout Michigan, with congregations in 74 of Michigan's then 79 counties.[18] Baptists were in the majority in Jackson, Kent, Oakland, and Wayne counties, but they had at least one organization in 56 of the 79 counties.[19] Congregationalists "were spread thinly in 60 of Michigan's 79 counties, with the greatest number in southern Lower Peninsula counties, such as Eaton and Macomb, where New Englanders had settled."[20] Lutheran churches were in 52 of the 79 counties, with the most in counties where large numbers of Germans had settled, such as Berrien, Macomb, Monroe, Saginaw, Washtenaw, and Wayne.[21] Other large denominations included Presbyterian, Episcopal, United Brethren in Christ, Evangelical Association, and Free Methodist.

There were smaller numbers of Jews, Quakers, and Universalists. The Universalist Church organized at Ann Arbor in 1828, "and by 1850 seven Universalist churches were open in the state."[22] Quakers or Friends settled near Adrian and the first "monthly meeting" of Quakers in Michigan occurred there in 1831.[23] By 1843 there were "roughly 7,000 to 10,000 Quakers in the state," and by 1884 there were 21 Quaker meetings, most in southern Lower Michigan.[24]

Twelve German-Jewish immigrants met and formed Michigan's first Jewish congregation in Detroit on 22 September 1850.[25] Beth El, or House of God, was originally started as an Orthodox or Traditionalist congregation, but by the 1860s many members of the congregation were interested in the Reform movement in Judaism. "When the Traditionalists saw that they could not stem the tide toward Reform in Beth El, 17 of them withdrew in 1861 and organized the Shaarey Zedek (Gates of Righteousness) Society."[26] Shaarey Zedek later became one of the charter organizers of the Conservative movement. By 1880 membership at Temple Beth El was primarily German in origin, and membership in Shaarey Zedek was primarily Russia and Polish in origin.[27] As Jewish immigrants settled in other parts of Michigan, they organized Jewish congregations in such places as Jackson (1862), Kalamazoo (1865), Grand Rapids (1871), Bay City (1872), Traverse City (1885), and Saginaw (1890).[28] By 1906 membership in Jewish congregations totaled 1,530 and grew to 99,366 in 1936.[29]

The first Seventh-day Adventist Church to be established in Michigan was organized in Jackson in 1849. By 1855, it had moved to Battle Creek. By 1860, Battle Creek had become a center for the Seventh-day Adventist Church and the denomination set up its world headquarters there. In 1863, the denomination's spiritual leader, Ellen G. White, made "proper diet and health care central concerns of the Seventh-day Adventists."[30] These beliefs later inspired the development of Kellogg and Post breakfast cereals, both of which made Battle Creek famous.

The Amish, an orthodox sect that separated from the Mennonites in the late 17th century, first moved into Michigan from Indiana in 1895. They settled near White Cloud in Newaygo County. Other early Amish communities were established near Newberry in Luce County, Mio in Oscoda County, Spruce in Alpena County, West Branch in Ogemaw County, and Hope in Midland County. These settlements disbanded after several years. The first permanent Amish settlement in Michigan was established in 1910 in Centreville in Saint Joseph County. By 1955, however, there were fewer than 500 Amish in the state. Most of the Amish in Michigan today moved to the state since 1975.[31]

Also noteworthy is the fact that one of the first mosques in the United States was built in Highland Park, near Detroit, by Muslim immigrants in 1919. "By the 1990s an estimated 250,000 Muslims lived in the metropolitan Detroit area, plus some additional numbers in outstate areas, putting Islam on a par numerically with the largest of the state's Protestant Christian denominations."[32]

By 1942, there were 5,000 active churches, mosques, or synagogues in Michigan, representing 90 denominations.[33] (For information on James Jesse Strang's Mormon settlement on Beaver Island or the Israelite House of David in Berrien County, see Chapter 2.)

Records: Religious records vary in their content, depending on the denomination and/or the individual responsible for the records. Genealogists may find vital record information in records dealing with baptisms, marriages, burials, or other records that deal with individuals. Membership lists can serve as a type of community census, while council minutes and reports can yield other genealogical gems.

The location of religious records – particularly early records – again may depend on the denomination and/or individual responsible for the records. Religious records may still be with the congregation, or they may be with the heirs of an early pastor. If a church closed and merged with another, the new church may have the records of the closed church. Records may be located at a denomination's regional or state archives; or church record collections may be found at public or university libraries or museums. Because there is no central repository for all Michigan church records, it's impossible to make a blanket statement regarding the location of church records. There are, however, some large collections throughout the state.

- The Burton Historical Collection at the Detroit Public Library has a large collection of church records, particularly records of the Roman Catholic Church from Detroit and surrounding communities <www.detroit.lib.mi.us/burton/Records_Catholic_Church.htm>. Sacramental records of West Michigan Catholic parishes through 1900 are available on microfiche at the Grand Rapids Public Library <www.grpl.org/index.html> and Hackley Library in

Muskegon <hackleylibrary.org/>. In addition, diocese offices may have records of Catholic churches. (See Chapter 11 for more.)

- The Michigan Historical Collections at the Bentley Historical Library <www.umich.edu/~bhl/bhl/mhchome/denomhis.htm> on the North Campus of the University of Michigan in Ann Arbor has records from a number of Christian denominations within Michigan, including the Episcopal Church, Church of God in Michigan, Lutheran Church in America, United Church of Christ, and the United Presbyterian Church in the U.S.A. It also has a growing collection of records from African-American churches, primarily in the Ann Arbor and Detroit areas.
- Shipman Library at Adrian College <www.adrian.edu/library> has the Detroit Conference Methodist Archives. The Stockwell-Mudd Library at Albion College in Albion has the West Michigan Conference Archives of the United Methodist Church <www.albion.edu/library/specialcollections/metharch.asp>.
- Baptist records, including materials on the Michigan Baptist Convention, are deposited at the Kalamazoo College Library <www.kzoo.edu/is/library/>.
- Heritage Hall at Calvin College <www.calvin.edu/hh/> has records from the Christian Reformed Church in North America, and the Joint Archives of Holland <www.hope.edu/jointarchives/> has records from the Reformed Church in America.
- The Finnish-American Heritage Center <www.finlandia.edu/fahc.html> at Finlandia University in Hancock has church records from Finland and Finnish Churches in America, including those from Finnish Evangelical Lutheran churches.
- The Center for Adventist Research <www.andrews.edu/library/car/index.html> is located at the James White Library, Andrews University, Berrien Springs. It is one of the largest repositories of Seventh-day Adventist and Seventh-day Adventist-related materials.
- Rabbi Leo M. Franklin Archives of Temple Beth El <www.tbeonline.org/leofranklinarchives.htm> has "one of the most comprehensive congregational archives in the nation and the largest such collection in Michigan."[34]
- The Library of Michigan in Lansing has many church histories, directories, and transcribed and abstracted church records in its collection.
- Many public libraries report having church records in their collections. (See Chapter 11 for more.)

Though dated, the Inventory of the Church Archives of Michigan compiled by the Michigan Historical Records Survey may be a helpful tool for locating church and synagogue records. The Work Projects Administration program published 17 inventories of church archives between 1936 and 1942. They were:

- Jewish Bodies
- Protestant Episcopal Bodies, Diocese of Michigan
- Protestant Episcopal Church, Diocese of Western Michigan

- Protestant Episcopal Church, Diocese of Northern Michigan
- Dearborn Churches
- Presbyterian Churches in U.S.A., Presbytery of Detroit
- African Methodist Episcopal Church, Michigan Conference
- Evangelical, Michigan Conference
- Evangelical and Reformed Churches
- Churches of God, Michigan Assemblies
- Roman Catholic, Archdiocese of Detroit
- Presbyterian Church in U.S.A., Presbytery of Flint
- Directory of Churches and Religious Organizations, Greater Detroit 1941
- Vital Statistics Holdings of Church Archives, Michigan: Wayne County
- Salvation Army in Michigan
- Pilgrim Holiness, Michigan District
- Church of the Nazarene, Michigan District Assembly

Except for Volume 14, each of the above inventories gives a brief history of the denomination and of each individual congregation in Michigan. Included is the church's address, date founded, first clergyman, first church building, records that are available, and where they are located. In the volume about Churches of God, Michigan Assemblies, for example, there is a brief historical introduction to the four major types of Churches of God: those headquartered in Anderson, Indiana; Cleveland, Tennessee; Salem, West Virginia; and those that have A.J. Tomlinson as General Overseer. Then there is a listing of organizations and individual congregations in each of the four major categories.

The fourteenth church inventory – *Vital Statistics Holdings of Church Archives, Michigan: Wayne County* – lists about 1,000 churches in Wayne County representing more than 90 denominations. The book has a chapter on early church history in Michigan, followed by an alphabetical listing of individual churches, the type and dates of their records, and the location of the records. Last is a list of denominational depositories.

Another published volume of the Michigan Historical Records Survey that deals with church material is the *Calendar of the Baptist Collection of Kalamazoo College, Kalamazoo, Michigan* (1940). This is an inventory of Kalamazoo College's collection of materials about Baptist activities in Michigan. The college's collection includes records of early Michigan Baptist missionaries, the financial records of early Baptist churches and the Michigan Baptist State Convention, and records regarding the founding of Kalamazoo College.

Published volumes of the church archives inventory are available in several libraries, including the Library of Michigan. Some of the volumes also have been reprinted by Quintin Publications <www.quintinpublications.com/mi.html>. The Burton Historical Collection at the Detroit Public Library has several of the unpublished church inventories, including those for the American Lutherans; Church of Christ; Church of Christ, Scientist; Church of the Nazarene; Congregations of Christian Churches; Methodist; Free Methodists; Orthodox Romanian Eastern Churches; Salvation Army; United Lutheran; and United Presbyterian.[35]

Many church records have been microfilmed and are available through Family History Centers or other libraries. Other church records have been abstracted or transcribed and published in articles, books, or CDs.

- Some publications deal with individual congregations. *Marriage Records, Ste. Anne Church, Detroit, 1701-1850* (2001), for example, is a chronological listing of the records as they appear in the church register. It also includes the records from "exterior parishes [that] were under the jurisdiction [of] Ste. Anne Church."[36] The book includes alphabetical lists of brides and grooms. (Researchers should note that the first marriage recorded in the church register occurred in 1710, even though the register was started earlier.)
- Some publications deal with more than one congregation. Burton's *Michigan Quakers: Abstracts of 15 Meetings of The Society of Friends, 1831-1960* (1989), for example, includes abstracts from meetings in Calhoun, Cass, Grand Traverse, Lenawee, Ogemaw, Presque Isle, and Wayne counties.

Online sources for church records include USGenWeb's Church Records Project <www.rootsweb.com/~usgenweb/churches/mi.html> and individual MIGenWeb county Web sites. The Kent County MIGenWeb site, for example, includes Early Membership Rosters of the Vergennes Christian Church and an 1858 census of Saint Andrew's Parish among its many records on its church page <www.rootsweb.com/~mikent/churches/>. Church histories, such as the 1910 Detroit Catholic Churches Souvenir Album <freepages.genealogy.rootsweb.com/~detroitchurches> and the Cowden Lake Church of Christ Centennial Booklet (Montcalm County) <www.rootsweb.com/~mimontca/churches/CLChurch/clchurch.htm>, also can be found online.

Cemetery and Related Records

Cemetery records include those kept by the sexton, caretaker, or other person in charge of the cemetery and the information carved on tombstones. Tombstones, when they exist, can be important sources of genealogical data, listing the birth and death dates of the deceased and, in some cases, a birthplace, marriage date, or other clue. Some tombstones even display photographs or an engraving of the deceased. Unfortunately, not all graves in Michigan were marked. "First burials in most old cemeteries were made of necessity and without ceremony or fancy funerals. Graves of family members were marked with a wooden cross but most trappers, lumberjacks, and early settlers had no one to place even a simple marker."[37] Even in the 19th and 20th centuries, some families could not afford to purchase a tombstone. If graves were marked, weather or vandals may have damaged tombstones. Records kept by sextons or cemetery administrators, when available, may be as simple as a listing of lot ownership; or the records may be much more complete, including information about the deceased and other family members.

Researchers can find out where their ancestors are buried by checking such sources as death certificates, obituaries, or funeral home remembrance cards. To find the location of cemeteries, researchers with Internet access can consult Michigan Cemetery Sources <michigancemeteries.libraryofmichigan.org>. The Library of Michigan Web site identifies the location of more than 3,700 cemeteries in Michigan and lists compilations of published cemetery transcriptions located at the Library of Michigan. It is not, however, an every-name index for persons buried in Michigan cemeteries, though it does provides some links to cemetery transcriptions. Researchers can search the site by county, township, cemetery name, location, or keyword. Search results provide the cemetery name, location (including section number in the township, road or street, or the closest city), county, and township. If published cemetery transcriptions (tombstone readings and/or sexton's records) are available at the Library of Michigan, these are listed under the "view" category.

Michigan Cemetery Sources is an online version of two Library of Michigan print publications. *Michigan Cemetery Atlas* (1991) indexes Michigan burial sites and contains a map for each county with the cemeteries indicated by a number circled in red. The data used to compile the *Michigan Cemetery Atlas* came from the U.S. Geological Survey Topographical Map Series, 19th- and early 20th-century county plat maps, and materials from the defunct Michigan Cemetery Commission. *The Michigan Cemetery Source Book* (1994), a companion volume, includes a county-by-county listing of cemetery transcriptions found at the Library of Michigan. The Web site includes information received by the Library of Michigan since these books were published and is updated regularly.

The Michigan section of *Cemeteries of the U.S.: Guide to Contact Information for U.S. Cemeteries and Their Records* (1994) is not as complete as the *Michigan Cemetery Atlas,* but its information about the location of cemetery records is valuable. This guide is divided by state and then county and lists the following information on cemeteries: address, phone number, manager or sexton, number of years in operation, ownership or affiliation, facilities/services, and the location of cemetery records. The listing for Evergreen Cemetery in Genesee County, for example, says that the non-sectarian cemetery opened in 1823, is owned by Gerry Potter, and is open 24 hours a day for visitation. Office hours are 8 a.m. to 5 p.m. Mondays through Saturdays. Cemetery records are housed on site and are available for research with no appointment necessary.[38]

An older – but possibly helpful – publication is the *Michigan Cemetery Compendium* (1979). This book is divided by county and then by township and lists many – but not all – cemetery locations in the state. Other methods of finding cemetery locations include consulting county maps or checking with area libraries or historical/genealogical societies. The U.S. Geological Survey's GNIS Database <geonames.usgs.gov/pls/gnis/web_query.gnis_web_query_form> is another helpful online tool for finding cemeteries. Enter the name of the state and county on its search form and then select "cemetery" from the drop down menu for "feature type."

In addition to cemetery locations, tombstone transcriptions and photos of tombstones can be found online. MIGenWeb, for example, has listed many cemeteries on its cemeteries page <www.rootsweb.com/~migenweb/cemetery1.htm> and the Tombstone Transcription Project for Michigan <www.rootsweb.com/~cemetery/michigan.html> has tombstone transcriptions. The Michigan Tombstone Photo Project <www.rootsweb.com/~usgenweb/mi/tsphoto/index.htm>, an outgrowth of the Colorado Tombstone Photo Project, publishes photographs of Michigan tombstones. At present, there are photos from more than 350 cemeteries in more than 50 counties.

Other Web sites with Michigan cemetery information include:

- Cemetery Junction <www.daddezio.com/cemetery/junction/CJ-MI-NDX.html>
- Flint Genealogical Society Cemetery Index <www.rootsweb.com/~mifgs/cemindex/cemindex.html>
- Interment.net <www.interment.net/us/mi/index.htm>
- Kent County Michigan Master Cemetery List <www.rootsweb.com/~mikent/cemeteries>
- Leelanau (County) Cemetery Database <www.leelanau.com/cemetery>
- Macomb County Cemetery Master Index <offserv.libcoop.net/mtc/cemetery.asp>
- Michigan Cemetery Transcriptions <freepages.genealogy.rootsweb.com/~micemtranscriptions/>, includes information from Arenac and Montmorency counties
- Political Graveyard <politicalgraveyard.com/geo/MI/kmindex.html>

In at least one case, a cemetery director is willing to respond to requests by e-mail to look up information in the cemetery's database. Karl Crawford, director of Petoskey's Greenwood Cemetery (Emmet County's largest with more than 15,000 burials) and Petoskey's Saint Francis Catholic Cemetery (with about 2,500 burials) will consult the databases of the two cemeteries if he is provided with the name of the deceased and the approximate date of death. For more information, see Emmet County's Lookup Page <members.tripod.com/~deemamafred/emmlook.html>.

Another helpful online source is MI-CEMETERIES-L, a mailing list for anyone interested in locating and preserving historical information about Michigan cemeteries. Rootsweb.com sponsors the list <lists.rootsweb.com/index/usa/MI/misc.html>.

Funeral Home Records: Funeral home records also are a valuable source for death information. For a listing of funeral homes, see the *National Yellow Book Funeral Directors and Suppliers,* published yearly by Nomis Publications, the *American Blue Book of Funeral Directors,* published every two years by Kates-Boylston, or *The Red Book, the National Directory of Morticians,* all available in the reference section of many libraries. A version of *The Red Book* also is available online <www.funeral-dir.com/default.htm>. MIGenWeb's Funeral Home page <www.rootsweb.com/~migenweb/funeral1.htm>, Funeralnet.com

<www.funeralnet.com>, and USAFuneralHomesOnline.com <www.usa funeralhomesonline.com/> list the names and addresses for many Michigan funeral homes. Funeral home records are generally located with the funeral home, but they also may be found in libraries or with societies. For example, records of the Evert-Hunter Funeral Home in Alpena (1915-1940) and the Schnepp Funeral Home in Riverdale (1895-1915) are available on microfilm at the Library of Michigan. The Bentley Historical Library, Grand Rapids Public Library, and Three Rivers Public Library also are among those that report having funeral home records in their collections. (See Chapter 11 for more.) Some funeral home records are available online. Examples include:

- Funeral Home Memorial Folders for Arenac County <www.rootsweb.com/~miarenac/people/fhfolders.htm>
- Iosco County's Funeral Records <www.rootsweb.com/~miiosco2/iosco funeral.html>
- Rogers-Mohnke Funeral Home Records (Newaygo County) <www.rootsweb.com/~minewayg/RogersMohnkeFunHome.htm>

Burial Permits: In addition to tombstone transcriptions, sexton records, or funeral home records, burial permits are another source of death or funeral information. Starting in 1897, Michigan law required that "the body of no person whose death occurs in the State shall be interred, deposited in a vault or tomb or otherwise disposed of, or removed from the township, village or city in which the death occurred, until a permit for burial or removal shall have been properly issued by the clerk of the township, village or city in which the death occurs."[39] Known as "burial permits" or "burial transit permits," these records include such information as the name of the decedent, date and cause of death, place of burial, and name of undertaker. Some of these records have been microfilmed, published, or appear online. For example, a collection of Iron County Burial Transit Permits can be found through Roots.web <userdb.rootsweb.com/deaths/> and Burial Permits (1923-1976) for Goodwell Township in Newaygo County are available on microfilm at the Library of Michigan. Other online sources include:

- Grattan Township (Kent County) Burial Permits, 1926-1963 <www.rootsweb.com/~mikent/townships/grattan/burials.html>
- Iron River (Iron County) Burial Transit Permits <www.rootsweb.com/~miiron/Iron_River_Burial.htm>

Newspapers and Obituaries

The first newspaper in Michigan was short-lived. One issue of *The Michigan Essay or Impartial Observer* appeared in Detroit on 31 August 1809. It wasn't until eight years later, with the founding of the *Detroit Gazette* on 25 July 1817, that newspaper publishing in Michigan began to flourish. (The *Detroit Gazette* was an English-language newspaper, but some articles in the early issues were in French.)[40]

Between the years 1825 and 1835, nine different newspapers were published at Detroit. Detroit's *Democratic Free Press and Michigan Intelligencer,* first published on 5 May 1831, "continues today as the *Detroit Free Press,* Michigan's oldest newspaper."[41] The *Free Press* also was Michigan's first newspaper to be issued daily, starting in 1835. It was during this same time period that newspapers were first established outside Detroit. First there was the *Monroe Sentinel* started in 1825. Next came Ann Arbor's *Western Emigrant* in 1829 and Pontiac's *Oakland Chronicle* in 1830.

In 1833, the *Michigan Statesman and St. Joseph Chronicle* was established at White Pigeon. In 1835, the publisher moved the paper to Kalamazoo, changing its name to the *Kalamazoo Gazette* in 1837. Since the *Kalamazoo Gazette* is still being published, this makes it the oldest existing newspaper in Michigan outside Detroit.

Cities to start newspapers between 1834 and 1837 included Adrian, Centreville, Coldwater, Constantine, Grand Rapids, Jackson, Kalamazoo, Marshall, Mount Clemens, Niles, Port Huron, Saginaw, Saint Clair, Saint Joseph, Tecumseh, and Utica. During the 1840s newspapers were established in Battle Creek, Centreville, Coldwater, Flint, Howell, Lansing, Paw Paw, and Ypsilanti. The first Upper Peninsula newspaper, the *Lake Superior News and Miners' Journal,* was started at Copper Harbor in 1846 and was moved to Sault Ste. Marie in 1847. The *Northern Islander,* the first newspaper in Michigan's northern Lower Peninsula, was published on Beaver Island from 1850 to 1856.

The improvement of the postal service, development of the telegraph, and political partisan rivalry encouraged newspaper growth in Michigan. "By 1860 a total of eight Michigan newspapers were publishing daily editions; there were three bi-weeklies, one tri-weekly, and 96 weekly newspapers, as well as four religious periodicals and three literary magazines."[42] Many newspapers were short-lived. By 1885, for example, a "total of 253 newspapers had been started in Detroit."[43]

As early as 1844 a German-language newspaper had been established at Detroit; Holland had a Dutch-language newspaper by 1850; and more than 30 different Finnish newspapers appeared between 1876 and 1930. More than 30 French newspapers "appeared in Michigan at various times during the period 1809-1919."[44] There also were Swedish, Polish, and Italian foreign-language newspapers. "At the peak of publication of foreign language newspapers, there were 43 in Michigan representing nine languages other than English. At one time or another 17 different languages have been represented among these publications."[45] For more information on foreign-language newspapers in Michigan, researchers should consult Beets' article, "Dutch Journalism in Michigan" in the 1922 issue of *Michigan History;* Joyaux's articles, "French Press in Michigan: A Bibliography" in the September 1952 issue of *Michigan History* and "French Press in Michigan" in the June 1953 issue of *Michigan History;* Kistler's article, "The German Language Press in Michigan: A Survey and Bibliography" in the

September 1960 issue of *Michigan History;* Kolchmainen's article, "Finnish Newspapers and Periodicals in Michigan" in the Winter 1940 issue of *Michigan History;* and *Ethnic Newspapers and Periodicals in Michigan: A Checklist* (1978). The checklist includes periodicals published more than once per year through 1977 that were printed in English or non-English and produced for a specific ethnic readership. It includes 655 titles for 37 ethnic groups.

Other specialty newspapers were devoted to agriculture and religion. The *Western Farmer,* later renamed the *Michigan Farmer,* was established in 1841. Baptists started the *Michigan Christian Herald,* Michigan's first religious periodical, in 1842 in Detroit.[46]

Early newspapers tended to concentrate on publishing national and international news because many editors believed that local news was already known locally and did not need to be printed. Obituaries did, however, begin to appear in the latter part of the 19th century. In addition to obituaries, other items of genealogical interest in newspapers include marriage, death, and divorce notices; social events; real estate transfers; "gossip" columns; lists of unclaimed letters at post offices; and election reports.

Efforts to preserve Michigan newspapers have taken place for several years. The Library of Michigan and other leading libraries in the state, for example, initiated the Michigan Newspapers on Microfilm Project in March 1962. Today's Michigan Newspaper Project, one of 50 statewide projects of the U.S. Newspaper Program <www.neh.gov/projects/usnp.html>, began in 1993. Based at the Library of Michigan, the project consists of inventorying, cataloging, and microfilming all available Michigan newspapers. To date, the project has cataloged about 3,700 Michigan titles in 17 languages from 1809 to the present and microfilmed more than 3,000 titles.[47] The Library of Michigan owns at least one newspaper on microfilm from each county in Michigan. The Library of Michigan has most, if not all, Michigan newspapers that are available on microfilm. All newspaper titles are listed in the Library of Michigan's online catalog and on the Michigan Newspaper Project Web site (see below). Microfilmed newspapers are organized alphabetically by town, then by title, and then chronologically by date in the library's Newspaper Microfilm Room.

Another component of the Michigan Newspaper Project is the development of "a family history" for each newspaper. Online charts, available through the Library of Michigan's Web site, show title changes and mergers of Michigan newspapers. The "family histories" are alphabetical by the name of Michigan cities, and some are linked to the individual newspaper's entry in the card catalog. The family histories can help researchers identify the changing names of newspapers in their area of interest. The Newspaper Family Histories are available online <www.michigan.gov/hal>. Select "Resources for Genealogists," then "Michigan Newspaper Project," then "Michigan Newspaper Family Histories."

Other libraries in the state with large newspaper collections include Bentley Historical Library in Ann Arbor, Clarke Historical Library in Mount Pleasant, and the Detroit Public Library. Most libraries in the state usually have newspapers for their immediate area. In addition to libraries, newspapers can be found at museums or in the collections of historical or genealogical societies. Some newspaper offices keep back issues of their own newspaper. More than 90 Michigan newspapers now publish online editions, and many of these have archived the online edition, though in most cases the online archives only go back a few years. Abstracts, indexes, and even digital images of older Michigan newspapers also are available online. (See Chapter 9 for more.)

To determine whether a Michigan city had an early newspaper, consult the Library of Michigan's Newspaper Family Histories (see above) or check the Library of Michigan card catalog. The *Michigan Manual*, starting in 1863, lists newspapers published in the state. (See Chapter 7 for more about the *Michigan Manual*.) The annual *Gale Directory of Publications and Broadcast Media* (formerly IMS/Ayer Directory of Publications) lists newspapers (and magazines) that are currently being published and their date of establishment.

Newspaper Indexes: Most newspapers are not indexed at the time of publication, but some newspaper indexes have been created later and are available in print, on CD-ROM, or online. Published indexes are available for some of the larger newspapers including the *Bay City Times, Detroit Free Press, Detroit News, Flint Journal, Grand Rapids Press, Kalamazoo Gazette,* and the *Lansing State Journal*. (Most of these indexes start in the mid-20th century.) Libraries or local genealogical and historical societies have indexed many smaller newspapers. Researchers should consult the Library of Michigan's online card catalog or the library or society in their area of interest to find indexes. Another helpful source for locating indexes is Milner's *Newspaper Indexes: A Location and Subject Guide for Researchers* (3 volumes, 1977-1982).

Online indexes include:

- The Grand Rapids Public Library's *Grand Rapids Press* Index <www.grpl.org/resources/pressindex.html> has entries from 1982
- The Kalamazoo Public Library's Local/Community Information Database <www.kpl.gov/collections/LocalHistory/LocComInfoDatabase.aspx> indexes the *Kalamazoo Gazette* from 1972
- Macomb Newspaper Index <offserv.libcoop.net/mtc/news_database.asp> indexes *The Macomb Daily* from August 1994.
- The *Sault Ste. Marie Evening News* Index <student.lssu.edu/~library/> indexes this newspaper from 1991

Obituaries: Indexes, abstracts, and transcriptions of obituaries have been published or are available online. For published obituaries, researchers should consult the Library of Michigan's catalog, the library or society in their area of interest, or the appropriate MIGenWeb site. Jarboe's *Obituaries: A Guide to Sources* (1989) also lists 84 printed sources for Michigan obituaries. Some examples of online obituaries or obituary indexes include the following:

- Clarke Historical Library's Obituary Card Index (Isabella County) <207.75.101.12/obitsystem/obitview.asp>
- Iron County's *Diamond Drill* Obituary Index <www.rootsweb.com/~miiron/drill.htm>
- Kent County Obituaries 1920 to 2004 <data.wmgs.org/AboutObituaries.html> includes more than 460,000 items from Grand Rapids newspapers
- Macomb County Obituary Index <offserv.libcoop.net/mtc/obitindex.asp>
- Michigan Obituary Links <www.obitlinkspage.com/obit/mi.htm>
- Michigan Obituary Project <www.rootsweb.com/~usgenweb/obits/obitsmi.htm>
- Public Libraries of Saginaw Obituary Index <obits.netsource-one.net/> has more than 170,000 obituaries from the *Saginaw News* dating back to the 1800s

Military and Military-related Records

From the earliest days of Michigan's history, its residents have participated in military actions. These military engagements left records in the forms of rosters of military units, draft and discharge papers, citations, pensions, casualty lists, and membership files of veterans' organizations. In addition to information on an ancestor's military service, these records can include such items as birth dates and places, death dates and places, marital status, and a physical description of the soldier. Many Michigan military records have been published in books, on microfilm, or online.

One of the most recent books, Barnett and Rosentreter's *Michigan's Early Military Forces: A Roster and History of Troops Activated Prior to the American Civil War* (2003), is an exceptional source. The book identifies all known Michigan men who served in the Revolutionary War, Indian Wars, War of 1812, Black Hawk War, Toledo War, Patriot War, and the Mexican-American War – more than 7,000 soldiers in all. It includes the soldier's name, rank, military unit, service dates, and, in some case, remarks. Brief histories explain each of the conflicts, and bibliographies suggest further sources for study.

Unpublished records relating to Michigan soldiers are available at such places as the State Archives of Michigan, the National Archives in Washington, D.C., and the National Personnel Records Center in Saint Louis, Missouri.[48] Some veterans' discharge certificates are on file at county clerk's offices.

Online sources include the databases available through Ancestry.com <www.ancestry.com>, Michigan Family History Network <www.mifamilyhistory.org/>, sites sponsored by the MIGenWeb Project <www.rootsweb.com/~migenweb>, individual libraries, or societies. The Mount Clemens Public Library, for example, hosts the Macomb County Military Index <offserv.libcoop.net/mtc/military.asp>, which includes information on Macomb County soldiers serving in conflicts from the Civil War to the Korean War.

General guides to research in military records include Neagles' *U.S. Military Records: A Guide to Federal and State Sources, Colonial America to the Present*

(1994); Groene's *Tracing Your Civil War Ancestor* (1995); Schaefer's *The Great War: A Guide to the Service Records of All the World's Fighting Men and Volunteers* (1998), and Knox's *World War II Military Records: A Family Historian's Guide* (2003). General information about research in military records also is available online through the National Archives Web site <www.archives.gov/research_room/genealogy/research_topics/military.html>.

Michigan State Troops: Among the first laws passed in 1805 by Michigan's territorial government were acts that established a militia. "Compulsory enrollment was required of free, able-bodied males from ages 14 to 50. The commander-in-chief was authorized to organize the militia, provide for uniforms, appoint officers, set training or muster days, appoint courts martial, and conduct routine activities."[49] The commander-in-chief also was authorized to call out the militia in the cases of invasion, insurrection, or other occurrences. The Territorial Militia became the State Militia, also known as the "State Troops" or "Military Forces," shortly after Michigan achieved statehood. The Michigan Naval Brigade or Naval Reserve was first organized as part of the State Militia in 1893 and operated out of Benton Harbor, Detroit, Grand Rapids, Hancock, and Saginaw. "The State Militia was officially designated as the Michigan National Guard by Public Act 198 of 1893 and later became an integrated part of the United States Armed Forces by the National Defense Act of 1916."[50] The State Militia served at both the state and federal levels in various conflicts, including the War of 1812; the Black Hawk War, 1832; the Toledo War, 1835; the Mexican War, 1846-1848; the Civil War, 1861-1865; and the Spanish-American War, 1898-1899.

A large collection of unpublished military records relating to Michigan's State Militia can be found at the State Archives in Lansing. These include the Descriptive Rolls of Units Comprising the Michigan Military Establishment, 1838-1911. Information to be found in these Descriptive Rolls may include the soldier's name, rank, date and place of enlistment, and a physical description. Also at the State Archives are Civil War Regimental Service Records; Records of Sick, Disabled, Needy, and Deceased Civil War Soldiers From Michigan; Muster Out Rolls of Michigan Volunteers in the Spanish-American War, 1898; records of the State Veterans' Facility of Michigan from 1885-1960, which includes a register of inhabitants from 1885-1941; and Records of the Civil War Centennial Observance Commission, which includes the registration of Civil War veterans' graves in Michigan. A description of these records can be found in Browne and Johnson's *A Guide to the State Archives of Michigan: State Records* (1977) and also in four Archival Circulars.

- Circular No. 4: Military Records I: War Records <www.michigan.gov/documents/mhc_sa_circular04_49684_7.pdf>
- Circular No. 7: Military Records II: Post-war Records <www.michigan.gov/documents/mhc_sa_circular07_49691_7.pdf>
- Circular No. 20: Civil War Manuscripts <www.michigan.gov/documents/mhc_sa_circular20_49709_7.pdf>

• Circular No. 27: Military Records III: Local Records <www.michigan.gov/documents/mhc_sa_circular27_50001_7.pdf>

Revolutionary War: Michigan did not exist as a state or territory during the time of the Revolutionary War, and no battles were fought on its soil. The area was under British control, and the British often "called on Michigan men to recruit and lead Native people on expeditions against the Rebels."[51] British forces did not vacate Michigan at the end of the Revolutionary War, and the conflict continued as the Indian Wars of 1783 to 1796. British forces left Michigan in 1796. Barnett and Rosentreter have identified 365 Michigan men who served during the Revolutionary War and subsequent Indian Wars and list these in their book, *Michigan's Early Military Forces* (2003).

Information about men who served in the Revolutionary War prior to moving to Michigan can be found is such sources as Silliman's *Michigan Military Records* (1920), which includes a list of Revolutionary soldiers buried in Michigan; the Summer 1976 *Family Trails* article "American Revolutionary Soldiers in Michigan," which lists Revolutionary War soldiers and widows receiving pensions and soldiers buried in Michigan; and Curry's series of articles about "Michigan Revolutionary War Pension Payments," published in the Spring, Summer, Autumn, and Winter 1960 issues of *Michigan Heritage.* The Sons of the American Revolution, Michigan Society also has a list of Revolutionary War soldiers buried in Michigan on its Web site <www.sar.org/missar/search.htm>.

War of 1812: Unlike the Revolutionary War, several engagements of the War of 1812 took place in Michigan, including the bloody Battle of the River Raisin. Barnett and Rosentreter have identified 1,535 soldiers who fought in this war and list them in their book, *Michigan's Early Military Forces* (2003). The authors claim this roster can serve as a census substitute because it lists "practically every white male of fighting age in the Lower Peninsula."[52] Miller's *Soldiers of the War of 1812 Who Died in Michigan* (1962) and its supplement *Soldiers and Widows of the War of 1812 Who Died in Michigan* lists more than 3,400 veterans and widows of the War of 1812 who are buried in Michigan. However, these soldiers did not necessarily live in Michigan at the time of the war. In addition, Turner cautioned in her foreword that many of the records in her book had not been verified. (The information on War of 1812 soldiers and widows compiled by Turner also was published in a series of articles in *Michigan Heritage;* see the bibliography in this volume for publication dates.) For more information on Michigan's role in the war, see Hamil's *Michigan in the War of 1812* (1977).

Black Hawk War (1832): The last Indian War in the Old Northwest, the so-called Black Hawk War, took place outside the present boundaries of Michigan. It involved pursuing Sauk Chief Black Hawk and his Sauk and Fox warriors "through Illinois and Wisconsin until Black Hawk was captured and many of his followers were massacred while attempting to cross the Mississippi."[53] Barnett and Rosentreter have identified 1,838 soldiers who were involved in this engagement and list them in their book, *Michigan's Early Military Forces* (2003).

Toledo War (1835): The Toledo "War" was actually a border dispute between Michigan and Ohio for the possession of a 468-square-mile strip of land that included the mouth of the Maumee River. The quarrel, dating back to the early 19th century, became heated in 1835, and Michigan Territorial Governor Stevens T. Mason called out the militia. However, there were no fatalities during the clash and only one stab wound. The dispute was eventually settled by a compromise in which Michigan surrendered the Toledo Strip in exchange for the western three-quarters of the Upper Peninsula, about 13,000 square miles of mineral-rich land and "hundreds of miles of coastline on Lakes Michigan and Superior."[54] Barnett and Rosentreter have identified 1,181 soldiers who were activated for this conflict and list them in their book, *Michigan's Early Military Forces* (2003). For more information on this interesting chapter in Michigan's history, see George's *The Rise and Fall of Toledo, Michigan ... The Toledo War!* (1971).

Patriot Wars (1838-1839): Groups of armed American men, known as Patriots, attempted to "liberate" Canada from British rule in the aftermath of Canada's failed 1837 and 1838 rebellions against the governments of both Upper and Lower Canada (now Ontario and Quebec). In Canada, these citizen uprisings were known as the Mackenzie Rebellion and in the United States as the Patriot Wars. "Michigan, particularly the Detroit area, experienced extensive Patriot activity."[55] Barnett and Rosentreter have identified 437 soldiers who participated in these invasions and list them in their book, *Michigan's Early Military Forces* (2003).

Mexican War (1846-1848): When the U.S. Congress voted in 1845 to annex the Republic of Texas, Mexico broke diplomatic relations with the United States, and several skirmishes took place along the Mexico-Texas border. The United States sent in troops in April 1846 to safeguard American settlers, and those troops were attacked by Mexican forces. Congress responded by declaring war on Mexico on 13 May 1846. The war lasted until 1848, when the United States and Mexico signed the Treaty of Guadalupe Hidalgo. The United States received more than 500,000 square miles from Mexico. In addition to Texas, the area covered the present-day states of California, Nevada, and Utah and parts of Arizona, Colorado, New Mexico, and Wyoming.

"With approximately 350,000 citizens, Michigan sent over 1,500 to [the Mexican] war – more than many other states, including New York, which had nine times more people than Michigan. The war also left more Michiganians dead than in all previous wars combined."[56] Twenty-six soldiers died in combat in the Mexican War, while 329 others died from disease or accident. This compares to a total of 22 combat deaths in the Revolutionary War, Indian Wars, and War of 1812 combined.[57] Barnett and Rosentreter have identified 2,096 soldiers who were activated for the Mexican War and list them in their book, *Michigan's Early Military Forces* (2003). Lists of Mexican War soldiers from Michigan also can be found in Welch's *Michigan in the Mexican War* (1967) and *Joint Documents of the Senate and House of Representatives at the Annual Session of 1848* (1848).

Civil War (1861-1865): One month after President Abraham Lincoln called for Union volunteers to fight in the Civil War, the 798-member 1st Michigan Infantry Regiment arrived in Washington, D.C. "It was the first regiment from the western states to arrive at the national capital, which led to Lincoln reportedly exclaiming, 'Thank God for Michigan!'"[58] Throughout the war, some 90,000 Michigan men (and some women and boys) served in the Union forces, more than half of Michigan's men of military age. This total included 1,660 African Americans, 145 Native Americans, and a large number of immigrants.[59] The immigrants included 4,872 German, 3,929 Irish, 3,761 English, and 181 Jewish soldiers.[60]

The number of Jewish soldiers is noteworthy, given that there were only 150 Jewish families in Michigan at that time. Katz's *The Jewish Soldier From Michigan in the Civil War* (1962) includes biographical sketches and other information about these soldiers. The number of African-American soldiers from Michigan, most of them members of the 1st Michigan Colored Infantry Regiment, also was quite large considering that there were only about 7,000 African Americans in the state at that time. (However, about a quarter of Michigan's African-American troops came from Canada.) McRae's *Negroes in Michigan During the Civil War* (1966) includes a history and roster of the 1st Michigan Colored Infantry Regiment. Almost all of the Native Americans who served from Michigan were members of Co. K of the 1st Michigan Sharpshooters, one of the most famous Native-American units in the Union Army. The men were used in many battles from Spotsylvania to the Crater. This unit is profiled in a chapter in Hauptman's *Between Two Fires: American Indians in the Civil War* (1995).

Many Michigan boys also served as soldiers, and a few of these are profiled in Keesee's *Too Young to Die: Boy Soldiers of the Union Army, 1861-1865* (2001). Public Act 25 of 1861 allowed minors to be mustered into service "on the written consent of their parents or guardians." Those boys without parents or guardians could be mustered in "on the written consent of a justice of the peace" in the township or city where the boy resided. This law, passed in March 1861, paved the way for a plan to eliminate overcrowding and reduce discipline problems at the House of Correction of Juvenile Offenders in Lansing. Officials at the reform school offered reduced sentences to boys who agreed to join Michigan regiments, and nearly 100 boys took advantage of the offer. Information about these young soldiers, including their names, ages, units, mustered in and out dates, and comments, can be found in Thavenet's article, "The Michigan Reform School and the Civil War: Officers and Inmates Mobilized for the Union Cause" in the Spring 1987 issue of *The Michigan Historical Review.*

It's likely that many boys wishing to serve in the military did not go through the formality of seeking written permission from their parents, guardians, or justices of the peace. During the mid-19th century, individuals did not carry identification cards or have birth certificates so boys could easily lie about their ages, and physical exams were superficial. "If a boy looked big enough to carry a gun and if he wanted to fight, he was usually accepted with few questions."[61] That's also how several women were able to serve as soldiers. They dressed as men, changed their names, and circumvented the physical exam. It's not known how many Michigan women served as Civil War soldiers. The most famous was Sarah Emma Edmonds, who enlisted in the 2nd Michigan Infantry in 1861 as Franklin Thompson. Blanton and Cook have identified several others in their book, *They Fought Like Demons: Women Soldiers in the Civil War* (2002).

Most men volunteered to be soldiers, but a draft was instituted first by presidential order in 1862 and then by an act of Congress on 3 March 1863. The draft required men between the ages of 20 and 45 to enroll in the army. Drafted men could become exempt from military service for health or other reasons. In addition, a drafted man could hire a substitute to go in his place or pay a commutation fee of $300. In Michigan, 4,281 men were inducted into the army as a result of the draft, and nearly 2,000 others paid the $300 fee.[62] Michigan used bounty payments after 5 March 1863 to encourage men to volunteer for military service. Bounties attracted men from throughout the state and other areas, including Canada. Some men, however, became "bounty jumpers," enlisting and collecting bounties in several places.

"Michigan troops fought in all major engagements, from Bull Run, to Gettysburg and Vicksburg, to Sherman's march through Georgia and the Carolinas."[63] Michigan troops also captured Confederate President Jefferson Davis in May 1865. About 14,000 Michigan soldiers died during the Civil War, but about 10,000 of those died from disease (including measles, pneumonia, smallpox, and typhoid fever) rather than battle. Though most of Michigan's soldiers served with Michigan units, "an undetermined number" of Michigan men served with forces from other states, including Illinois, Indiana, Iowa, Kansas, Missouri, New York, Ohio, Pennsylvania, and Wisconsin.[64] For example, the Lafayette Light Guard, organized in Paw Paw, traveled to New York and became Company C of the 70th New York Infantry because they were unable to find a Michigan regiment in which to serve.[65] Some Michigan men served with the regular U.S. Army, and 600 Michigan men served in the Union Navy. For a brief introduction to Michigan's role in the war, see Williams' *Michigan Soldiers in the Civil War* (1994).

Records: One of the most important published sources of information on Michigan's Civil War soldiers is the 46-volume *Record of Service of Michigan Volunteers in the Civil War, 1861-1865* (also known as the "Brown Books"). This set, completed as a result of Public Act 147 of 1903, used records of the state and federal governments and other "authentic sources" to compile a "concise military history of each soldier or sailor so serving."[66] Volumes are organized by regiment, with the first 30 volumes covering the 30 infantry regiments. The next 10 volumes (31-41) cover the cavalry regiments; Volume 42, the light artillery regiment; Volume 43, the engineers; Volume 44, the sharpshooters; Volume 45, miscellaneous units (including those from out of state); and Volume 46, the 1st Colored Infantry. Volumes are alphabetical by name; a soldier's entire military history is placed with the unit where he served the longest. Information on reorganized regiments is included with the original regiment.[67] The Brown Books, however, do not include lists of principals (soldiers who should have served) and their substitutes. This information is available in the original records at the State Archives of Michigan. *Alphabetical General Index to Public Library Sets of 85,271 Names of Michigan Soldiers and Sailors Individual Records* (1915) is a master index to the series.

Other published sources include the following:

- *Annual Report of the Adjutant General of the State of Michigan* (1862-1866), includes regimental rosters, names of casualties, and discharge information
- Robertson's *Michigan in the War* (1882), a comprehensive history of Michigan's contribution to the war, includes biographies of commissioned officers and short histories of each regiment
- *The Roster of Union Soldiers 1861-1865: Michigan* (1998) is a printed copy of the National Archives' microfilmed *Index to Compiled Service Records of Volunteer Union Soldiers Who Served in Organizations from the State of Michigan*

Regimental histories are another good source of information for Civil War soldiers. Several have been published for units from Michigan, including:

- Anderson's *They Died to Make Men Free: A History of the 19th Michigan Infantry in the Civil War* (1994)
- Crawford's *The 16th Michigan Infantry* (2002)
- Herek's *These Men Have Seen Hard Service: The 1st Michigan Sharpshooters in the Civil War* (1998)
- Isham's *Historical Sketch of the 7th Regiment Michigan Volunteer Cavalry* (2000)

Other regimental histories can be found by checking the card catalog of the Library of Michigan, the Library of Congress <www.loc.gov/rr/main/uscivilwar/E514.html> or other libraries, or by checking Hydrick's *Guide to the Microfiche Edition of Civil War Unit Histories* (1994); part 4 inventories the histories available for Michigan. Some Web sites are devoted to histories of military units. The Old 4th Michigan Infantry <4thmichiganinfantry.com/>, for example, includes company rosters and pension records.

Letters, diaries, and other Civil War materials can be found in a number of libraries in Michigan. The State Archives, for example, has many of the official records, such as muster and descriptive rolls; some of these are described above under Michigan State Troops. The Archives also has bounty records from 1863 to 1865 – which includes the name, age, residence, and regiment of the soldier, and date and amount of payment – and Civil War manuscripts. Other Michigan libraries with Civil War materials include:

- Bentley Historical Library <www.umich.edu/~bhl/bhl/mhchome/cw/civilwar.htm>
- Clarke Historical Library <clarke.cmich.edu/civilwar/cwmain.htm>
- William L Clements Library <www.clements.umich.edu/Schoff.html>

Online sources of information include the following:

- Ancestry.com's <www.ancestry.com> Civil War Research Database, Civil War Pension Index, and Civil War Compiled Military Service Records Database
- Canadians in Michigan Regiments <pvtchurch.tripod.com/canucks/mich.html>
- Civil War Rosters: Michigan Links <www.geocities.com/Area51/Lair/3680/cw/cw-mi.html>
- Civil War Soldiers Buried in Michigan <www.mifamilyhistory.org/civilwar/interments/default.asp>
- Men of Co. K of the 1st Michigan Sharpshooters, a Native-American unit <members.aol.com/roundsky/company-k.html>
- Michigan in the Civil War <users.aol.com/dlharvey/cwmireg.htm> and <www.michiganinthewar.org/cwmireg.htm>
- Military Biographical Index <www.geocities.com/jjacks01>, a cumulative index to several Civil War sources, including Robertson's *Michigan in the War* (1882), the 46 volumes of *Record of Service of Michigan Volunteers in the Civil War, 1861-1865,* regimental histories, GAR publications, and more
- National Park Service's Civil War Soldiers and Sailors System <www.itd.nps.gov/cwss/index.html>, a database that contains basic facts about individual soldiers and sailors and information about regiments
- New York Veterans of the Civil War Who Moved to Michigan, July 1891 <www.usgennet.org/usa/ny/state/cw/cwindex.htm>
- Sons of Union Veterans of the Civil War: Department of Michigan <suvcw.org/mi/deptmi.htm>

Michigan Civil War Centennial Observance Commission: Michigan established a Civil War Centennial Commission in 1958 (later renamed the Civil War Centennial Observance Commission) as part of a nationwide effort to mark the 100th anniversary of the Civil War. Working through 1966, more than 30 subcommittees of the commission oversaw several projects, including dedicating and rededicating Civil War markers and monuments in Michigan and at national battlefields, preserving the state's Civil War flags, publishing 27 books and brochures about Michigan's role in the war, and registering the graves of Michigan Civil War veterans in 63 of Michigan's 83 counties. Many of the commission's books focused on how the Civil War affected culture, industries, religion, and agriculture. *Michigan Women in the Civil War* (1963), for example, dealt with the role of women in the war – whether they followed the troops or stayed at home. The Civil War Graves Registration and its index, available at the State Archives of Michigan, includes the name of the veteran, county of interment, name and location of cemetery, and in some instances, additional information such as enlistment and service records, place and date of birth and death, and additional remarks. The Civil War Graves Registration index cards also are on microfilm and are available through Family History Centers.

Spanish-American War (1898-1899): "Since the 1870s, native Cubans had been waging an unsuccessful fight for their freedom against Spanish colonial control."[68] In an attempt to put down the uprising, the Spanish military used a concentration camp system. That, plus the February 1898 destruction of the *USS Maine* (and the death of 260 of its sailors) in Cuba's Santiago Harbor caused many Americans to demand that the U.S. government take action. On 19 April 1898 the U.S. Congress adopted a war resolution that recognized the independence of Cuba, demanded that Spanish forces leave the island, and authorized the use of U.S. forces to put the resolution into effect. Spain responded by declaring war on the United States on 24 April 1898.[69] In just three months, Spain was defeated and agreed to get out of Cuba.

Among the unexpected results of the war was the United States' acquisition of the Philippines, Puerto Rico, and Guam. This was the last war in which the "states were the primary agency used to raise the nation's fighting forces."[70] Michigan supplied five infantry regiments, totaling 6,500 men, and 300 men from the state's naval reserves, but only the 33rd and 34th Regiments saw action in Cuba.[71] "In all, 209 Michiganians died during the Spanish-American War, though fewer than 20 were battle deaths."[72]

For more information on Michigan's role in the war, see Mehney's article, "The War With Spain," published in the May-June 2002 issue of *Michigan History.* Muster rolls for the regiments can be found in the book, *Michigan Volunteers of '98: A Complete Photographic Record of Michigan's Part in the Spanish-American War of 1898* (1898) and through the Michigan Family History Network Web site <www.mifamilyhistory.org/spanam/>. The online book, *A Souvenir of the 35th Michigan Volunteer Infantry* <www.memoriallibrary.com/MI/Military/SA35/>, includes information about that unit.

Punitive Expedition to Mexico (1916-1917): Members of Michigan's National Guard were among those military forces sent to guard the border with Mexico after Mexican revolutionary Pancho Villa and his men killed several Americans in Columbus, New Mexico, during a March 1916 raid. Villa's invasion was only the second foreign military attack on American soil since the War of 1812. President Woodrow Wilson reacted by ordering a punitive expedition into Mexico to capture Villa dead or alive. More than 100,000 U.S. troops were sent to the border by August 1916. By Feburary 1917, however, U.S. troops called it quits without punishing Villa, and very few skirmishes took place between Villa's and American forces. The State Archives of Michigan has the muster rolls for the units that served in this conflict and a card index that lists each soldier's name, rank, and unit. Many of these Michigan men went on to serve during World War I. For more information about this military engagement in

Mexico, see Yockelson's articles, "The United States Armed Forces and the Mexican Punitive Expedition," published in the Fall and Winter 1997 issues of *Prologue* and also available online <www.archives.gov/publications/prologue/fall_1997_mexican_punitive_expedition_1.html>.

World War I (1917-1919): World War I broke out in Europe in 1914, but the United States did not enter the war until 6 April 1917 after several American ships were destroyed by U-boat activity off the North American coast. The next month Congress approved the Selective Service Act, "authorizing registration and draft of all men between 21 and 30."[73] (The draft did not apply to the Navy or the Marine Corps because these were all-volunteer services.[74]) Between April 1917 and November 1918, more than 135,000 Michigan men served in the war. Of this number, about 5,000 died and another 15,000 were wounded. Several hundred additional Michigan men served in World War I in Canadian military regiments.[75]

> The Michigan unit that saw the most extensive and prolonged service during World War I was the Thirty-second, or Red Arrow, Division. Composed of units from the Michigan and Wisconsin National Guard, the Thirty-second began arriving in France in January 1918. From May until November 1918 the division saw almost constant combat.[76]

Virtually all of the World War I service records for U.S. Army personnel were destroyed in a 1973 fire at the National Personnel Records Center in Saint Louis, Missouri. However, U.S. Navy and Marine Corps service records were not lost, and alternative sources exist to "reconstruct" army records. For more information, see Knapp's article, "World War I Service Records," published in the Fall 1990 issue of *Prologue* and Yockelson's article, "They Answered the Call: Military Service in the United State Army During World War I, 1917-1919," published in the Fall 1998 issue of *Prologue.* Yockelson's article also is available online <www.archives.gov/publications/prologue/fall_1998_military_ service_ in_world_war_one.html>. World War I service records for Macomb County soldiers, taken from *Record of Macomb County Soldiers and Sailors in Service in the Great War* (1920) are available online <offserv.libcoop.net/mtc/wwirecords.asp>.

Draft registration cards: During World War I, there were three draft registrations. Nationwide, more than 24 million men born between 1872 and 1900 registered. This number amounted to about 98 percent of the men under age 46 in the United States or about 23 percent of the total population. In Michigan, there was a total registration of 873,383.[77] The draft registrations took place as follows:

- First registration, held 5 June 1917 for men born 6 June 1886 through 5 June 1896, registered all men between 21 and 31 years of age.
- Second registration, held 5 June 1918, registered men who had become 21 years of age since the last registration (men born 6 June 1896 through 5 June 1897) and those not previously registered. A supplemental registration, considered

part of the second registration, took place on 24 August 1918 for men who became 21 years of age after 5 June 1918 (those born 6 June 1897 through 24 August 1897) and those not previously registered.

- Third registration, held 12 September 1918 for men born 11 September 1872 through 12 September 1900, registered all men between 18 and 45 years of age who had not already registered.

The information collected in each registration differed somewhat, but generally included the man's full name, date and place of birth, race, citizenship, occupation, personal description, order and serial numbers assigned by the Selective Service System, and signature. The second registration asked for the father's birthplace, and the third registration asked for the name and address of next of kin. Blank copies of World War I Draft Registration Cards are available for viewing or printing through Ancestry.com <www.ancestry.com/save/charts/WWI.htm>.

Cards were arranged alphabetically by local draft boards; most boards filed the cards in one alphabetical list instead of three separate lists. There was one draft board per county, plus additional draft boards for each 30,000 people in each city or county with a population over 30,000. In Michigan, there were a total of 136 boards. Most counties in Michigan had one draft board, though nine counties had more than one. Detroit, the most populous area in the state, had 26 draft boards. Other Michigan cities with separate draft boards were Battle Creek, Bay City, Flint, Grand Rapids, Highland Park, Jackson, Kalamazoo, Lansing, and Saginaw. Draft registration cards for late registrants, Native Americans, prisoners, the insane, or others in hospitals were organized and microfilmed separately.

It's important to note that not all of the men who registered for the draft actually served in the military; they may have received an exemption, for example. Also, not every man who served in the military registered for the draft; they may have already been on active duty when the registrations took place. In addition, the draft registration cards do not have any information about military service.

Draft registration cards have been microfilmed and are available through the National Archives and Family History Centers. Other libraries, including the Library of Michigan, have microfilmed draft registration cards. At this writing, Ancestry.com has indexed about 1.2 million of the draft registration cards, including some from Michigan, and has announced plans to eventually post the digitized images of the cards. Other online sources for World War I draft registration cards include the Macomb County World War I Draft Registration Index <offserv.libcoop.net/mtc/draftindex.asp>.

For more information about World War I draft registration cards, see Newman's *Uncle, We Are Ready! Registering America's Men, 1917-1918 – A Guide to Researching World War I Draft Registration Cards* (2001). Newman's book includes a chart with a list of the draft boards in Michigan, including the number of men registered in each draft and the microfilm numbers for the records. Information about World War I Draft Registration Cards also is online at the

National Archives Web site <www.archives.gov/research_room/genealogy/military/wwi_draft_registration_cards.html>.

Miscellaneous Records: In 1923, the Daughters of the American Revolution in Michigan, in conjunction with county War Preparedness Boards, conducted a census of World War I veterans. Census forms were mailed to the veteran's last known address. Some forms were not returned; some returned forms were filled in more completely than others. Forms asked for personal information (including birth and death dates of the veteran, nationality, occupations before and after the war, and parents' names and addresses); military information (including rank, company, regiment, transfers, promotions, and discharge date); and family information (including marriage date, spouse's name, spouse's birth date and place, and children's names and birth dates). The census records and card index to the census are available at the State Archives of Michigan. The card index also has been microfilmed and is available at the Library of Michigan and through Family History Centers.

The federal government did not issue pensions to veterans of World War I, but some states, including Michigan, paid bonuses. Approved by the Michigan Legislature on 15 June 1921, the bonus equaled $15 per month for each month served. To qualify, the soldier had to have been a resident of Michigan serving in the military any time between 6 April 1917 and 1 August 1919. Bonus applications are available at the State Archives of Michigan. Applications include the veteran's name, address, race, place and date of birth; Army serial number; induction date and place; military duty; wounds received; overseas service dates; discharge date; total of bounty awarded, if any; date paid; and remarks. The bonus records are arranged by county and then alphabetically by name.

The State Archives of Michigan also has a card index of deserters from the draft, 1917 to 1918. This index also is available on microfilm through Family History Centers.

Casualty lists: A list of Michigan casualties in World War I can be found in Volume 2 of Haulsee's three-volume set, *Soldiers of the Great War* (1920). This volume also is online through Ancestry.com <www.ancestry.com> or RootsWeb.com <www.rootsweb.com/~michippe/gwarsoldier.htm>. Other online sources for World War I casualties include Macomb County Casualties of World War I <www.macomb.lib.mi.us/mountclemens/wwideath.htm>.

Polar Bear Expedition (1918-1919): Some 5,000 soldiers from the U.S. Army's 339th Infantry Regiment and support units (the 1st Battalion of the 310th Engineers, the 337th Field Hospital and Ambulance Company) were involved in an intervention in Archangel, Russia, near the end of World War I. The American soldiers, many of them from Michigan, joined an international force that had been sent to Northern Russia to prevent a German advance but ended up "fighting Bolshevik revolutionaries for months after the Armistice ended fighting in France."[78] The soldiers returned to Michigan in the summer of 1919. The Michigan Historical Collections at the University of Michigan's Bentley Historical

Library has a collection of the personal papers of the officers and enlisted men involved in this unusual military event. A searchable Polar Bear Database <141.211.39.65/polardbmain.html>, which lists the expedition's soldiers, is available on the library's Web site. The database may have the following information for each soldier: name; hometown; rank; company; regiment; branch; action (whether killed, attended reunion, or other information); medals, honors, or awards; burial information; or photographs. Coombs' *American Intervention in Northern Russia, 1918-1919, The Polar Bear Expedition: A Guide to the Resources in the Michigan Historical Collections* (1988) inventories the collection. Michigan Polonia's Polar Bears <mipolonia.net/polar_bears.htm> includes photographs and the 1927 Polar Bear Association Roster. More than 100 of the polar bears are buried in the White Chapel Cemetery in Troy.

Citizen's Military Training Camps: Prior to World War I, several Citizens' Military Training Camps provided college undergraduates with instruction in leadership and citizenship. Students attended at their own expense; one of the goals of the camps was to encourage young men to later enroll in the National Guard or Reserves. (Among the early camps was one that met in 1914 in Ludington, Michigan.)

The camps were reorganized as part of the National Defense Act of 1920, with the U.S. government providing funding for transportation, rations, and equipment. Ten of these reorganized camps met in 1921, including one at Fort Custer, near Battle Creek, Michigan. By 1929, a camp also met at Fort Brady, near Sault Ste. Marie, Michigan.

The camps were open to men 17 to 24 years of age, and they met for four weeks each summer with a sequence of training over four years. Regular Army officers provided instruction, and surplus World War I material was used for equipment. Training and discipline were similar to that of the regular army.

> [Men] lived in tents and barracks, marched, drilled, practiced on the rifle range, scouted, patrolled, had calisthenics, marksmanship and participated in athletics. They had mess and K.P. They had commissioned and non-commissioned officers and they had infantry, field artillery, engineering corps, signal corps and cavalry.[79]

Men who completed all four years of CMTC training became eligible for Reserve commissions.

The camps at Fort Custer published annual *Preparedness* volumes, similar to yearbooks, which included rosters of the men participating in the camps, photos, and other information. The Library of Michigan has volumes for 1922 through 1926. The volume for 1924 is online through the Michigan Family History Network <www.mifamilyhistory.org/ft-custer/>. It can be searched by name, company, or Michigan county. Newberry and Waldo's *History of Michigan Camps* (1929) has the rosters of Michigan men who participated in the 1929 camps at Fort

Custer; Fort Brady, near Sault Ste. Marie; Fort Sheridan, near Chicago; Camp McCoy, near Sparta, Wisconsin; and Fort Snelling, near Minneapolis.

World War II (1940-1945): More than 600,000 Michigan men and women served in the military during World War II. The first of these soldiers were inducted into the military in November 1940, two months after the U.S. Congress approved the nation's first peacetime draft. The United States officially entered World War II in December 1941, after the bombing of Pearl Harbor by Japanese forces. About 15,000 Michigan men and women died in the war. Service records for veterans of the U.S. Army, Navy, Marine Corps, and Coast Guard are located at the National Personnel Records Center in Saint Louis, Missouri, but they are protected by privacy laws and are only available to the veteran, if living, or the next of kin, if the veteran is deceased.

Draft registration cards: Six regular draft registrations took place during World War II as follows:

- The first took place on 16 October 1940, for men born on or after 17 October 1904, and on or before 16 October 1919
- The second was on 1 July 1941, for men born on or after 17 October 1919, and on or before 12 July 1920, and for those who had failed to register in the first registration
- The third was on 16 February 1942, for those men born on or after 17 February 1897, and on or before 31 December 1921
- The fourth took place on 27 April 1942, for those men born on or before 28 April 1877, and on or before 16 Feb. 1897
- The fifth took place on 30 June 1942, for those men born on or after 1 January 1922, and on or before 30 June 1924
- The sixth registration took place on 11-31 December 1942, for those men born on or after 1 July 1924, and on or before 31 December 1924, and also for men who reached their 18th birthday on or after 1 January 1943.

All but the fourth registration is protected under privacy laws; veterans, if living, or the next of kin, if the veteran is deceased, can request to view the information on the draft registration cards.[80] The fourth draft registration was for men between 45 and 65 years of age. "The military needed men with construction skills for the Navy Seabees. These men were not liable for military service."[81] These records are now open to the public, and Michigan's fourth draft registration cards are available at the Great Lakes Region Branch of the National Archives in Chicago.

Many World War II era newspapers published draft lists for their area; some of these lists – such as the ones for Isabella County <www.rootsweb.com/~miisabel/militaryWWII.htm> – have been transcribed and placed online.

Miscellaneous Records: Michigan paid bonuses to World War II veterans, but as of this writing, no index is available. Survivors of World War II soldiers were eligible to receive a beneficiary claim of up to $500 when the soldier was killed in action or died of service-related causes. Card indexes of beneficiary claims and claims rejected are available at the State Archives of Michigan.

"After a veteran was discharged, it was suggested that he file his discharge certificate at the county clerk's office, thereby protecting the document and allowing easy access if a copy was needed."[82] Some counties may still have these records on file.

The World War II Veterans Memorial <www.wwiimemorial.com/> has a user-contributed registry of Americans who played a part in the war effort, whether they served in the military or on the home front. Many of the individuals lived in Michigan.

Casualties: In 1946, the U.S. government released two lists of war dead. *State Summary of War Casualties: Michigan,* published by the Navy Department, lists 6,294 casualties from the Navy, Marine Corps, and Coast Guard. This book is arranged alphabetically by last name and includes the soldier's rank, branch of service, relationship and address of next of kin. The book can be found in the reference section of many libraries, and an online version is available through the National Archives Web site <www.archives.gov/research_room/arc/wwii/navy_marines_coast_guard_casualties/michigan.html> and Access Genealogy <www.accessgenealogy.com/navy/michigan/index.htm>. *World War II Honor List of Dead and Missing: Michigan,* published by the War Department, lists casualties of the U.S. Army and Army Air Force. It is arranged by county and then alphabetically by last name. Information includes the soldier's name, rank, military serial number, and cause of death. This book also is available in the reference section of many libraries, and an online version is available through the National Archives Web site <www.archives.gov/research_room/arc/wwii/army_aaf_honor_list/michigan.html> and Access Genealogy <www.accessgenealogy.com/worldwar/michigan/index.htm>. In addition, an online version of both books is available through the Michigan Family History Network Web site <www.mifamilyhistory.org/WWII>. This version is searchable and has added the county of residence for the soldiers listed in *State Summary of War Casualties: Michigan* (1946).

The Burton Historical Collection at Detroit Public Library also published a five-volume list of casualties, called *World War, 1939: Michigan Casualties* (1946). It includes casualties from 1943 to 1946 and lists the soldier's name, rank, hometown, and casualty date.

Korean War: From 1950 to 1953, about 250,000 Michigan men and women served in the Korean War. Lists of the more than 1,300 casualties from Michigan sorted alphabetically <www.archives.gov/research_room/research_topics/korean_war_casualty_lists/mi_alphabetical.html> and sorted by hometown <www.archives.gov/research_room/research_topics/korean_war_casualty_lists/mi_by_town.html> can be found on the National Archives Web site. The lists include the soldier's name, rank, branch of service, hometown, date of casualty, and category of casualty. Michigan paid bonuses to Korean veterans, and a card index to these claims is available at the State Archives of Michigan. The index includes names of veterans, regiments, addresses, and claim numbers. Survivors of Korean War soldiers also were eligible to receive a beneficiary claim of up to $500 when the soldier was killed in action or died of service-related causes. Card indexes of beneficiary claims and claims rejected are available at the State Archives.

Vietnam War: Between 1957 and 1975, more than nine million Americans served in Vietnam. About 402,000 soldiers were from Michigan, and of those, at least 2,654 died or went missing in action. Lists of Vietnam casualties from Michigan sorted alphabetically <www.michigan.gov/documents/Military_Personal_sorted_alpha_9542_7.pdf> and sorted by county of residence <www.michigan.gov/documents/MI_VN_Memorial_Names_by_County_9549_7.pdf> can be found on the State of Michigan's Web site. Michigan casualty lists sorted alphabetically <www.archives.gov/research_room/research_topics/vietnam_war_casualty_lists/mi_alphabetical.html> and by hometown <www.archives.gov/research_room/research_topics/vietnam_war_casualty_lists/mi_by_town.html> also can be found on the National Archives Web site. Both lists include the soldier's name, date of birth, date of death, hometown, service, and rank. The National Archives' lists also include place of death and type of casualty.

Michigan casualties also can be found on The Vietnam Veterans Memorial Wall Page <thewall-usa.com/> or The Virtual Wall <www.thevirtualwall.org>, Web sites that list the names of the soldiers on the Washington, D.C., Vietnam War memorial. Both sites give brief information about the soldiers' service, including their death date and place, and allow friends and relatives to post comments about them. Names of Michigan casualties also can be found on two monuments in Michigan. The Michigan Vietnam Memorial Monument, located in Lansing near the Library of Michigan, divides the state's casualty list by county. An alphabetical listing of casualties also is available at the monument and includes the soldier's name, rank, service, home of record, date of birth, and date of death. The Michigan Vietnam Memorial <vietmemorialmi.com/> in Mount Pleasant's Island Park lists casualties alphabetically.

Military Honors: Up until the time of the Civil War, there were no military medals. During the Civil War, the U.S. Congress established the Medal of Honor for the Navy in 1861 and the Medal of Honor for the Army in 1862. It was and is the highest military award for combat valor. In the 1880s, the Navy and the Marine Corps authorized Good Conduct medals. But it wasn't until the 20th century that the United States developed a military awards program. "In 1908 the United States authorized campaign medals, many retroactively, for the Civil War, Indian wars, War with Spain, the Philippine Insurrection and China Relief Expedition of 1900-1901."[83] The awarding of personal and campaign medals continues to this day.

Sources for information on Michigan soldiers who received military medals include the following:

- Silliman's *Michigan Military Records* (1920) includes information on more than 60 Michigan men, most of them Civil War soldiers, who received Medals of Honor. It lists biographical information, such as birth place and date; parents' names; spouse; and a summary of military service, including enlistment and discharge.

- Landrum's *Michigan in the World War: Military and Naval Honors of Michigan Men and Women* (1924) lists more than 1,000 military decorations for acts of gallantry performed during World War I, including the Medal of Honor, Distinguished Service Cross, Distinguished Service Medal, Naval Decorations, and Foreign Decorations. The book is divided by award, and lists the soldier's name, military unit, a summary of the military action leading to the award, the soldier's residence at enlistment, and in many cases, an emergency address, such as a parent's or sibling's address.
- *A Study in Valor: Michigan Medal of Honor Winners in the Civil War* (1966) was a publication of the Michigan Civil War Centennial Observance Commission. It recounts the military activities of the Michigan soldiers who received Medals of Honor.
- Bozich's *Michigan's Own: The Medal of Honor, Civil War to Vietnam War* (1987) includes biographical sketches and some portraits of 108 Michigan soldiers who received the Medal of Honor. The work reportedly corrects errors and omissions in the 1920 and 1966 publications listed above.[84]

Online sources for Medal of Honor information include the following:

- HomeOfHeroes.com's Medal of Honor Recipients Buried in Michigan <www.homeofheroes.com/moh/cemeteries/mi.html>
- U.S. Army Center of Military History Full-text Listings of Medal of Honor Citations <www.army.mil/cmh/Moh1.htm> is not a site specific to Michigan. It organizes the lists of awards by war and then by name.

In addition, the State Archives of Michigan has information on various honor rolls and medal winners. The items below are detailed in Circular No. 4: Military Records I – War Records <www.michigan.gov/documents/mhc_sa_ circular04_ 49684_7.pdf>.

- The Civil War Roll of Honor, a listing of deceased Michigan soldiers organized by regiment
- Applications for Spanish-American War medals
- Records of deceased World War I soldiers from Michigan, which include the soldier's name, military service, and death information
- Applications for World War I Victory Medals

Fraternal Organizations: Veterans organizations also can be sources of information about ancestors.

Mexican War Veterans Association: The records of the Michigan Chapter of the Mexican War Veterans Association were destroyed by fire in Ludington in July 1882. "The printed Proceedings of this group can be found in various major libraries around the state."[85]

Grand Army of the Republic: Founded in 1866, the Grand Army of the Republic was a fraternal group for honorably discharged Union soldiers, sailors, and marines. Michigan's first GAR post opened in 1867, and membership peaked in 1893 with 21,000 members. In all, 462 GAR posts were chartered in Michigan, and the last one closed in 1960.[86] Most Michigan towns and cities had at least one post. Detroit had six, including one with an all-African-American membership. The Sons of Union Veterans of the Civil War, consisting of men who descend from Union veterans, is the successor organization of the GAR.

The State Archives of Michigan has a number of records dealing with the GAR, including muster rolls, membership applications, and death rolls. These are detailed in Circular No. 7: Military Records II – Post-War Records <www.michigan.gov/documents/mhc_sa_circular07_49691_7.pdf> and *Finding Aid No. 15: Records of the Michigan Department of the Grand Army of the Republic 1861-1957 (Record Group 63-19)* (1966). The State Archives also has a card index of Michigan GAR members that includes the veteran's name and post number. It is alphabetical by name. The Library of Michigan has several volumes of the *Journal of the Annual Encampment of the GAR Department of Michigan* (1882-1948), which has information on the GAR annual meetings. Members of the Sons of Union Veterans of the Civil War - Michigan Department also are in the process of compiling a list of GAR records available, their locations, and the names of contacts for the records <suvcw.org/mi/garmi.html>. *Finding Aid No. 15* (mentioned above) includes lists of GAR posts, organized by post name, by city, and by county. The lists include the posts' dates of organization and disbandment. Other sources for lists of GAR posts are Sherman's *List of the Grand Army of the Republic Posts in Michigan, 1872-1948* (1994) and the Sons of Union Veterans of the Civil War Michigan Department Web site <suvcw.org/mi/mi.pdf >.

United Spanish War Veterans: The United Spanish War Veterans was organized in 1904 as an outgrowth of "a number of organizations formed by the men who fought in the Spanish-American War."[87] It was not as large as the Grand Army of the Republic. The State Archives of Michigan has applications for membership (which includes names of the veterans, ages, names and post numbers of camps), membership lists, and muster rolls. These are detailed in Circular No. 7: Military Records II – Post-War Records <www.michigan.gov/documents/mhc_sa_circular07_49691_7.pdf>. The State Archives also has a United Spanish War Veterans Master Card Index that includes the veteran's name, address, enlistment and discharge dates, rank, camp, and death date, and a Camp Index that includes the names of veterans, residences, ranks, and discharge dates.

Michigan Veterans' Facility: The Michigan Veterans' Facility, originally called the Michigan Soldiers Home, opened in Grand Rapids on 31 December 1886. It was established to care for honorably discharged Civil War veterans who were disabled or disadvantaged. In 1893, the home was opened to former nurses and the mothers, wives, or widows of honorably discharged veterans. "Wives and widows had to have been married to the veteran before 1 January 1875; and divorced wives or widows who had remarried were ineligible. A woman was also required to show that she was unable to earn her own living, had no relatives with sufficient ability to support her and was of good moral character."[88] After World War I, the home admitted veterans who had served during wars up to that time. Records of the Michigan Veteran's Facility, including registers of inhabitants and case files, are located at the State Archives of Michigan. The records are detailed in Circular No. 7: Military Records II – Post-war Records <www.michigan.gov/documents/mhc_sa_circular07_49691_7.pdf>. Published records include the *Biennial Report of the Board of Managers of the Michigan Soldiers' Home* (1887-1918), which lists residents and information about their ranks, units, and ages. For more information about the history of the facility, see Van Til's *Michigan Veteran's Facility Centennial: A Century of Caring* (1986). Online sources include:

- Deaths of Inmates of the Soldiers' Home <www.rootsweb.com/~mikent/baxter1891/soldiershome.html>
- Michigan Veterans' Facility <www.rootsweb.com/~mikent/veterans/>
- Michigan Veterans of the Civil War Buried at the Soldiers' Home <www.michiganinthewar.org/soldhme.htm>

Southwest Michigan Military Registry: The Van Buren Regional Genealogical Society is the sponsor of the Southwest Michigan Military Registry <www.rootsweb.com/~mivanbur/military.htm>, a project designed to record war or peacetime military service of anyone who ever lived in the Michigan counties of Allegan, Berrien, Cass, Kalamazoo, or Van Buren. Indexes to the county registers can be found on the project Web site and include the name of the soldier, war or service, date range, submission, and code. Registries are available for viewing at the Van Buren Regional Genealogical Society's collection, housed in the Local History Room of the Van Buren District Library in Decatur.

Veterans History Project: The Veterans History Project <www.loc.gov/folklife/vets/>, created by the U.S. Congress in 2000, is a national effort to collect and preserve audio- and video-taped oral histories of all men and women – military, civilian volunteer, support staff, or war industry workers – who participated in World War I, World War II, or the Korean, Vietnam, or Persian Gulf wars. In addition to oral histories, the project collects documentary materials such as letters, diaries, maps, photographs, or home movies. The Library of Congress' American Folklife Center oversees the effort in conjunction with local partners. Several organizations in Michigan, including the Michigan Oral History Association, are partners in the project. Materials collected will be preserved and made available to the public at the American Folklife Center Reading Room in Washington, D.C., or with some of the project's official partners. Selected examples of interviews and a register of veterans interviewed are available on the project's Web site. The register includes the name of the individual, branch of service, war, and service dates. In the future, information about "the nature and location of individuals' materials" also will be available on the Web site.[89]

Census Records and Substitutes: In addition to Michigan's census of World War I soldiers (mentioned earlier in this chapter), there were special veteran schedules taken as part of the regular federal and state censuses (described in Chapter 5). The U.S. government also prepared lists of men who received federal pensions for military service. The information on these lists vary from year to year but generally include the name of the veteran or beneficiary receiving the pension, the amount paid, date and/or reason placed on the pension roll, county of residence, rank, and military unit.

Only one Revolutionary War soldier in Michigan appeared on the 1813 Invalid Pensioners List, and three Michigan men appeared on an 1818 list of pensioners. Many more men were listed on the 1835 and 1883 lists. All of the lists have been printed, and some of them are available online. Published lists or indexes include Clark's *Index to Invalid U.S. Pension Records, 1801-1815* (1991), Clark's *Pension List of 1820* (1991), *The Pension Roll of 1835* (1992), *List of Pensioners on the Roll January 1, 1883* (1883), and Jackson's *Index to the List of Pensioners on the Roll, January 1, 1883* (1989). In addition, the 1835 pensioners for Michigan can be found in Silliman's *Michigan Military Records* (1920). Online sources include:

- 1813 Invalid Pensioners <www.arealdomain.com/dc1813.html>
- 1835 Michigan Territorial Pensioners <www.rootsweb.com/~miisabel/TerritorialPens.htm>
- Statewide List of Pensioners on the Roll 1883 <www.mifamilyhistory.org/civilwar/1883Pension/index.asp>
- 1883 List for Isabella County <www.rootsweb.com/~miisabel/govpen83.htm>
- 1883 List for Kent County <www.rootsweb.com/~mikent/pensioners1883>
- 1883 List for Muskegon County <www.rootsweb.com/~mimuskeg/83Pens.html>
- 1883 List for Ottawa County <www.rootsweb.com/~miottawa/military/1883pens.html>
- 1883 List for Presque Isle County <members.aol.com/alpenaco/presque/1883.htm>

Michigan Historical Collections

The Pioneer Society of the State of Michigan published their proceedings and other historical material in a series of 40 volumes – most between 600 and 700 pages – between 1877 and 1929. The titles of the volumes changed from year to year; some are called *Michigan Pioneer Collections* or *Michigan Pioneer and Historical Collections.* The series is commonly known as *Michigan Historical Collections.*

Because the indexes for the volumes are composed of authors and titles, a *Classified Finding List of the Collections of the Michigan Pioneer and Historical*

Society was started under the Work Projects Administration and finally published in 1952 by Wayne University Press in Detroit.

The finding list is first divided chronologically; material about the years 1600 to 1796 is in the first section, with material from 1796 to 1861 and 1861 to 1926 in the second and third sections. Each chronological section is divided topically: official papers; personal papers; reminiscences; special studies; maps, portraits, illustrations, and miscellaneous; and biographical sketches and genealogies. Each topical section is arranged alphabetically and lists the volume and page number in which the reference may be found. Biographical sketches and genealogies take up almost 100 pages of the 265-page finding list.

Many of these biographical sketches and genealogies are obituaries of Michigan pioneers. In addition to death dates, they often include the birth date and place of the pioneer, the year the pioneer moved to Michigan, and other interesting information. These obituaries are also called "Memorial Reports," or "report of the Memorial Committee." Some of these memorials can be found online at the following sites:

- Cass County <www.rootsweb.com/~micass/obituaries/mortality.htm>
- Michigan Family History Network <www.mifamilyhistory.org/memorials/default.asp>
- Kalamazoo County Pioneer Necrology Reports <www.rootsweb.com/~mikalama/obits/pindex.htm>
- Kent County Memorial Reports <www.rootsweb.com/~mikent/memorial reports/>

An annotated bibliography of Native American materials found in the *Michigan Historical Collections* can be found online through the Clarke Historical Library Web site <clarke.cmich.edu/nativeamericans/mphc/index.htm>. These materials are grouped into 17 categories, including the American Revolution, biographies, the fur trade, and treaties. In some cases, the bibliography links to digital images from the publications. Other online excerpts from *Michigan Historical Collections* include:

- Kalamazoo County 1876 county history <www.rootsweb.com/~mikalama/kalamazoo1876history.htm>
- History of the Moravian Settlement (Macomb County) <www.online-isp.com/~maggie/macomb/moravian.htm>
- Pioneer Society Collections, Muskegon County <www.rootsweb.com/~mimuskeg/PionSoc1.html>
- Early Saginaw Valley and Isabella County Extractions from the *Michigan Pioneer and Historical Collections* <www.rootsweb.com/~miisabel/mphc.htm>

In addition, nine complete volumes (8, 9, 10, 11, 12, 15, 16, 19, 20) of the *Michigan Historical Collections* can be found online free as part of the Pioneering the Upper Midwest: Books from Michigan, Minnesota, and Wisconsin, ca. 1820-

1910 <memory.loc.gov/ammem/umhtml/umhome.html> collection of the Library of Congress' American Memory Web site <memory.loc.gov/ammem/amhome.html>. The same volumes also are available through Ancestry.com <www.ancestry.com>.

County and Regional Histories

County histories, particularly those that feature biographical sketches of Michigan residents, can be a source of vital records and other interesting information about ancestors. At least one county history has been published for most of Michigan's 83 counties. *Portrait and Biographical Albums,* a type of county history that includes portraits and biographies of prominent citizens in a county, were popular in the late 1800s.

> Around 1880, histories of most of the counties of southern Michigan were published, which was part of a nation-wide program promoted by several publishing firms who cashed in on the historical interest that was generated in 1876 by the celebration of the centennial of the Declaration of Independence. More than any other group of citizens in the state, Michigan's farmers yielded to the temptation to pay to have their portraits and sketches of their farms appear in these volumes.[90]

In addition to printed volumes, county histories can be found on microfilm or microfiche and online. *County Histories of the Old Northwest, Series V: Michigan,* for example, is an 88-volume microfilm set that includes 269 state, regional, and county histories, plus separate indexes for 52 of the volumes that were created after the books' original publication dates. Some of these books are no longer available in print. *Reel Index to the Microform Collection of County and Regional Histories of the Old Northwest, Series V: Michigan* (1975) lists the titles on each of the reels and also lists the titles pertinent for each county. Many of these histories also are online as part of the Michigan County Histories Collection <www.hti.umich.edu/m/micounty/>. Other online sources for county histories include the following:

- Clarke Historical Library's Michigan Local History Resources <clarke.cmich.edu/online.htm>
- Mardos Memorial Library of Online Books and Maps <www.memoriallibrary.com/MI/>

Bibliographies of Michigan county histories include the following:

- *Sourcebook of Michigan Census, County Histories, and Vital Records* (1986) updates an earlier work: *Michigan County Histories: A Bibliography,* published in 1970 and updated in 1978
- *Guide to the Michigan Genealogical and Historical Collections at the Library of Michigan and the State Archives of Michigan* (1996) expands and updates the work above

Biographies

In addition to county and regional histories, biographical information can be found in a variety of books, such as the following:

- *American Biographical History of Eminent and Self-made Men: Michigan* (1878)
- *Bench and Bar of Michigan* (various editions)
- *The City of Detroit, Michigan, 1701-1922* (1922), Volumes 3 through 5 of the five-volume set are biographical
- Dunbar's *Michigan Through the Centuries* (1955), Volumes 3 and 4 of the four-volume set are biographical
- Edgar's *A History of Early Jewish Physicians in the State of Michigan* (1982) features 33 biographical sketches of Jewish doctors
- Farmer's *History of Detroit and Wayne County and Early Michigan: A Chronological Cyclopedia of the Past and Present* (1890), Volume 2 of the two-volume set is biographical
- Gibson's *Artists of Early Michigan: A Biographical Dictionary of Artists Native to or Active in Michigan* (1975) and Bentley, Helms, and Rospond's *Artists in Michigan, 1900-1976: A Biographical Dictionary* (1989)
- Johnson's *Black Medical Graduates of the University of Michigan (1872-1960 inclusive) and Selected Black Michigan Physicians* (1994)
- Lamport's *Michigan Poets and Poetry, with Portraits and Biographies* (1904) includes 20 biographical sketches and 13 portraits of Michigan poets
- *Men of Progress: Embracing Biographical Sketches of Representative Michigan Men With An Outline History of the State* (1900); an online version of this book is available through the American Memory collection Pioneering the Upper Midwest: Books from Michigan, Minnesota, and Wisconsin, ca. 1820 to 1910 <memory.loc.gov/ammem/umhtml/umhome.html>
- *Michigan: A Centennial History of the State and Its People* (1939) Volumes 3 through 5 of the five-volume set publish biographies of individuals who paid to be included in the set
- *Michigan Supreme Court Historical Reference Guide* (1998) has biographical sketches of Michigan Supreme Court Justices
- Moore's *History of Michigan* (1915), Volumes 3 and 4 of the set arebiographical
- Weddon's *First Ladies of Michigan* (1994), *Michigan Governors: Their Life Stories* (1994), and *Michigan Press Women: Today and Yesterday* (1996)
- Weeks' *Stewards of the State: The Governors of Michigan* (1991)

Online sources for biographical information include the following:

- Biographies are one of the general topics listed for each of RootsWeb.com's message boards <www.rootsweb.com>
- *The Book of Detroiters: A Biographical Dictionary of the Leading Living Men of the City of Detroit,* originally published in 1908 <www.usgennet.org/usa/mi/county/tuscola/det/dettoc.htm>

- Cass County Biographies <www.rootsweb.com/~micass/biographies/bios.htm>
- Michigan Biographies Project <www.jansdigs.com/Bios/bios.html> has more than 1,400 biographies online at this writing

Periodicals

Periodicals, particularly those published by genealogical or historical societies, often have transcribed records, family histories, and other valuable information for genealogists. Useful periodicals and periodical indexes for Michigan research include the following:

- *Michigan History Magazine* <www.michiganhistorymagazine.com> started publication in July 1917. It began as a quarterly academic journal, and in May 1978 it became a bimonthly popular-history magazine. It continues publishing to this day. Three separate indexes cover the years 1917 to 1941, 1942 to 1962, and 1963 to 1973. In addition, each volume has an index, starting in 1968. In 1995, the magazine also published a *Subject Guide to Michigan History Magazine 1978-1994.*
- *The Detroit Society for Genealogical Research Magazine* <www.dsgr.org/> has been published since 1937 by the Detroit Society for Genealogical Research. "The DSGR Magazine has a complete every name index. Cumulative indexes exist for Volumes 1-10; 11-15; 16-20; 21-25; and 26-30. Volumes 31 through current volumes are indexed annually by every name."[91] An annual subject index has been published since 1959.[92] Jackson's *Guide to the First Fifty Years of the Detroit Society for Genealogical Research Magazine* (1990) is intended to be a supplement to these indexes and lists such topics as family records and family histories, locality records, and queries and replies.
- *Michigan Heritage*, a quarterly, was published from 1959 to 1973 by the Kalamazoo Valley Genealogical Society. An annual index appears in the magazine.
- *Michigana,* a quarterly, has been published by the Western Michigan Genealogical Society since 1955. It specializes in original and unpublished material about western Michigan. "Beginning with Volume 9 it has been indexed annually; Volume 9 also contains a subject index of Volumes 1-9."[93]
- *The Flint Genealogical Quarterly* was published by the Flint Genealogical Society from 1959 to 1983. Specializing in Genesee and surrounding counties, it was indexed annually.
- *Timber Town Log,* a quarterly of the Saginaw Genealogical Society, has been published since 1971.
- *Family Trails* was originally published between 1967 and 1982 by the Michigan Department of Education, Bureau of Library Services. The 23 issues "focused on source material and ethnic studies in Michigan."[94] The Michigan Genealogical Council reprinted the 23 issues in 1983, first in six volumes, then in five volumes in a later reprint.
- An every-name index for *Generations* <www.rootsweb.com/~micalhou/generations.htm>, the newsletter of the Calhoun County Genealogical Society,

and images of the newsletter are available online. At present, the index covers 1988 (the year the society was established) to 1995.

- Quigley's *Index to Michigan Research Found in Genealogical Periodicals* (2nd ed., 1985) lists Michigan information in nearly 100 publications, including many published outside Michigan. An online version of Quigley's index is available <data.wmgs.org/AboutQuigley.html>.
- *Genealogical Periodical Annual Index:* The 40 volumes of *Genealogical Periodical Annual Index* indexes surnames, localities, topics, and book reviews published in English-language genealogy periodicals. Many of the entries pertain to Michigan.
- *PERSI:* Perhaps the most valuable tool to use to find Michigan references in periodicals is PERSI, the Periodical Source Index. It is the largest subject index to genealogical and historical periodical articles in the world, featuring nearly two million index entries from nearly 10,000 periodical titles. Visitors to any of the 14 Allen County Public Library facilities in Indiana can search PERSI for free at library computers. PERSI also is available on CD-ROM or through Ancestry.com as a subscription database. It also may be available through local libraries from HeritageQuestOnline.com. Because the Allen County Public Library owns a copy of every periodical indexed in PERSI, photocopies of articles listed in PERSI can be ordered from the Allen County Public Library Foundation, P. O. Box 2270, Fort Wayne, Ind. 46801-2270 <www.acpl.lib.in.us/database/graphics/order_form.html>. The current charge is $7.50 per each request, plus 20 cents per page copied. Only six articles can be requested at a time.

Indexes

Indexes help unlock other sources, such as county histories and periodicals. In addition to the periodical indexes listed above, valuable indexes for Michigan research include:

- *Michigan Biography Index:* The 10-volume *Michigan Biography Index,* compiled by Frances Loomis of the Detroit Public Library in 1946, indexes biographies of five lines or more from more than 300 books dealing with Michigan. The index does not include information from the 46 volumes of *Records of Services of Michigan Volunteers in the Civil War.* The index is part of the microfilm collection *County Histories of the Old Northwest, Series V: Michigan,* described in the County and Regional Histories section.
- *Pioneers From Massachusetts:* Flagg's *An Index of Pioneers from Massachusetts to the West* (1975) is an alphabetical list of more than 5,000 individuals who moved west from Massachusetts to a number of states, including Michigan. It is based on information from more than 70 Michigan county histories and includes such facts as the settler's name, date and town of birth, date of removal, and location of settlement.

5
Finding Families: Census Records and Their Substitutes

Census records – particularly the later schedules – directories, and other census substitutes are sources to use to find ancestors in their family units. Because families tended to live near relatives, researchers also may find their ancestor's siblings, aunts, uncles, and cousins living nearby when they scan census records and directories. Census records, directories, and census substitutes also help researchers find their ancestors in particular geographic locations, so that they can know where to search for land and other records.

Census Records

Early Censuses: Michigan residents were counted 19 times – 17 of those occasions in actual censuses – before Michigan became a state in 1837. The listings "are scattered, partial, and often limited by region, but when collected in one place, [they] present a complete picture of Michigan's residents" prior to statehood.[1] The French took the first Michigan census in 1710 in Detroit. The French, and later the British and Americans, took other Detroit-area censuses in 1743, 1750, 1762, 1765, 1768, 1779, 1782, and 1792. A census was taken at Fort Saint Joseph in 1780 and of Wayne County in 1796. There also are an 1802 tax list of Wayne County and an 1805 list of Detroit residents, both of which can serve in place of census records. An 1827 territorial census of Wayne County and federal censuses of 1810, 1820, and 1830 round out the list of available censuses for pre-statehood Michigan. (There also was an 1834 territorial census that survives for a few Michigan counties. Census takers were supposed to record the names of the heads of households in this census, but they didn't do so for any of Michigan's present-day counties.[2])

Of course, these early census records are not as detailed as later federal or state population schedules. The 1710 census, for example, lists only the last name of the male residents, except for one resident whose first and last names are recorded. The 1750 census lists the head of household, plus the number of women, boys over and under age 15, girls over and under age 15, and slaves. The 1762 census is a bit more detailed; it lists the age of the head of the household, birthplace if other than Canada, the amount of land he owned, his financial status, and the number of boys, girls, slaves, and hired help in his household. In addition to listing the number of men, women, children, and acres of land, the 1765 census also lists the number of horses, colts, bulls, cows, and calves. The 1796 census places the male head of household in an age category: "men over 50" or "men 16-50." None of these censuses list wives or children by name.

Russell's *Michigan Censuses 1710-1830 Under the French, British, and Americans* (1982) includes a full transcription of all of Michigan's pre-statehood censuses, plus the 1802 and 1805 census substitutes. The book gives a brief history of each census and lists where the censuses have been previously published. In many cases, the author also adds footnotes to clarify the identity of someone listed in a census. Her indexed book is an excellent guide to Michigan's early census records.

State and Territorial Censuses: Ten territorial and state censuses were taken in Michigan between 1827 and 1904. Unfortunately, only a few of these records exist. As early as 1884, Michigan's Secretary of State reported that the state's copies of the 1827, 1837, and 1845 censuses had disappeared.[3] Sometime after the 1940s, the state's copies of state censuses taken after 1854 – with the exception of the 1834 canvass because it had been placed in the governor's files – also disappeared. "The first, and most commonly accepted, version of how Michigan lost its censuses maintains that they were contributed to a paper drive early in World War II. The other account says that they were destroyed in the 1951 fire that burned much of the Lewis Cass Building."[4] The few census schedules that exist today are copies that had been deposited with county clerks at the time of the census and later found their ways to various libraries and archives. However, many of these surviving schedules are not complete.

State population schedules did not list all family members until 1884. Prior to that year, the censuses generally listed the heads of households, in some cases the heads' occupations, plus the number of other males and females in the households in various age categories. In 1884, census takers were "to identify the members of each family, their names, address, age, sex, color, place of birth (state or country of each citizen and his or her parents), occupation, marital status, physical and mental condition, literacy, and length of residence in Michigan."[5] An interesting feature of the 1884 census was a section that asked about former members of the household who were married within the census year but were no longer living in that household. The census asked for the age of the male or female involved, the month of the marriage, the name of the groom, place of the marriage, and the couple's present residence.

The 1894 census was almost identical to the 1884 census. One additional question asked residents how long they had lived in the United States. The 1904 census was similar, but also listed the physical characteristics of residents. In addition to population schedules, the state also took special censuses on such topics as agriculture, manufacturing, mortality, schools, and veterans.

For more information on territorial and state censuses, see Barnett's article, "State Censuses of Michigan: A Tragedy of Lost Treasures," published in the Summer-Fall 1978 issue of *Family Trails.* (For a list of the surviving state census records, see the chart at the end of this chapter.)

The State Archives of Michigan and the Library of Michigan have many of the surviving territorial and state census records. Archival Circular No. 9 <www.michigan.gov/documents/mhc_sa_circular09_49695_7.pdf> details the state census records available at the archives. The State Library of Michigan has a number of state population schedules on microfilm, along with abstracts and indexes of state census records. Several other libraries in the state may have copies of state census records in their genealogical or historical collections. Microfilmed state census records also are available through Family History Centers. Online sources for state or territorial census records include:

- Ancestry.com's <www.ancestry.com> database of 1894 census records for a number of counties, including Barry, Bay, Benzie, Dickinson, Emmet, Gratiot, Iosco, Ingham, Kalamazoo, Keweenaw, Lapeer, Menominee, Montcalm, and Washtenaw
- Barry County's 1894 census <www.rootsweb.com/~mibarry/census_ records .htm>
- Muskegon County's 1884 and 1894 censuses <freepages.genealogy. rootsweb. com/~muskegoncounty/Census/Index.htm>
- Saint Joseph County 's 1845 census <members.tripod.com/~tfred/ 1845census.html> or <www.rootsweb.com/~mistjose/census.htm>

Federal Population Schedules: The U. S. government has taken a census of its population every 10 years, starting in 1790. In 1790, however, the census was not taken in Michigan because it was under the jurisdiction of the British. At the time of the second U.S. census in 1800, Michigan was part of the Northwest Territory and those schedules have been lost, if they were taken at all.[6] Census records for only two of the four judicial districts existing at the time of the 1810 census have survived – those for Detroit and Michilimackinac, but both are incomplete.

The 1820 census counted residents in seven Michigan counties, including two that were later to become part of Wisconsin Territory: Brown and Crawford. The 1830 census enumerated residents in 16 counties, including three that were later to become part of Wisconsin Territory: Brown, Crawford, and Iowa. Residents in 32 counties were counted in the 1840 census, while residents in 43 counties were enumerated in the 1850 census. Sixty-two Michigan counties were represented in the 1860 census, 71 in 1870, 77 in 1880, and the current 83 counties in the 1900 and later censuses. In some cases, however, some Michigan censuses do not include counties that had been set off but did not yet have an organized local government. "As late as the 1870s, some of these counties are reported to have had no population, and in other cases inhabitants in unorganized counties were enumerated with their host county, although it is not clear how common this practice was."[7] (For more on county organization, see Chapter 10. For a list of the federal population schedules available for Michigan, see the chart at the end of this chapter.)

Prior to 1850, federal census records only list heads of households, with the other members of the household placed in age groupings. In 1850, all household members and their ages are listed, but family relationships are not specified until 1880. Starting in 1850, birthplaces are listed; starting in 1880, the birthplaces of the person's mother and father also are listed. The 1870 census was the first to count everyone, including former slaves and Native Americans living on reservations or treaty land. The race classification of "Indian," however, was not used until the 1880 census, and before then Native Americans may have been identified as "white," "black," or "mulatto."[8] The 1880 census was the first to ask about marital status and the first to report street names and house numbers. It also listed "all soldiers of the U.S. Army, civilian employees, and other residents at posts or on military reservations ... in the district in which they normally resided."[9]

The 1900, 1910, 1920, and 1930 censuses are quite detailed, listing such items as whether the person had been naturalized, the number of years the person had lived in the United States, the number of years married, and the number of children born. The 1900 census is the only one "to report the month and year of birth of each person," and the 1920 census is the only one to ask for the year a person was naturalized.[10] In 1910, census takers asked U.S-born men over age 50 and foreign-born men who came to the United States before 1865 if they were survivors of the Union or Confederate Army or Navy. In 1930, census takers asked veterans of U.S. military or naval forces to identify in which conflict they had served.

A 1954 law made all individual responses to the U.S. census confidential for 72 years; therefore, the 1940 census will not be released until 2012. However, some information from the 1940 through 2000 censuses can be requested from the U.S. Census Bureau. Researchers should consult the Census Bureau Web site <www.census.gov/genealogy/www/agesearch.html> and <www.census.gov/prod/2000pubs/cff-2.pdf > for more information.

1890 Census Reconstruction: Most of the 1890 census, including Michigan's population schedule, was lost due to a 1921 fire in the Commerce Building in Washington, D.C. Part of the census was damaged by fire and the rest was damaged beyond repair by water. The census was later destroyed by government order. In order to help fill the void left by the missing 1890 census, Ancestry.com <www.ancestry.com>, with the assistance of the National Archives and the Allen County Public Library in Fort Wayne, Indiana, announced plans in 2000 to "reconstruct" the 1890 census by placing in one searchable database a number of 1890-era sources. These include the remaining fragments of the 1890 census, Native American tribal censuses, state censuses, city and county directories, alumni directories, and voter registration lists. This database is available through Ancestry.com. Other efforts to reconstruct the 1890 census, such as Livingston County Genealogical Society's *1890 Residents of Livingston County, Michigan* (2000), may be available.

Special Schedules: In addition to population schedules, a number of special or "nonpopulation" schedules were taken at the state and federal levels. Many of these "include names of individuals and information not found in most other records."[11] The mortality schedules, for example, may contain death records not available from other sources. The agriculture and manufacturers' schedules may list persons who did not live in the area of the census, such as a farmer who owned a farm in one county and lived in another.

Agriculture Schedules (Federal): Agriculture schedules, which list information about farms and their production, are available for 1850, 1860, 1870, and 1880. The Census Bureau destroyed the agricultural schedules for 1900 and 1910 in 1918 to conserve space and reduce fire hazards. The 1850 through 1880 schedules have been microfilmed and are available at several libraries and archives, including the National Archives and the Library of Michigan. The original schedules are located at the State Archives of Michigan. The 1920 agricultural schedule for Jackson County, Michigan, is located at the National Archives.[12]

Agriculture Schedules (State): Agriculture schedules were taken by the state in the 1854, 1864, 1874, 1884, 1894, and 1904 censuses. Schedules survive for the following counties: Allegan (1894); Baraga (1884); Barry (1884); Bay (1884 and 1894); Clinton (1864); Dickinson (1894); Eaton (1854, 1864, and 1874); Emmet (1894); Hillsdale (1894); Houghton (1864); Ingham (1884 and 1894); Kent (1884 and 1894); Keweenaw (1884 and 1894); Leelanau (1884); Lenawee (1884 and 1894); Menominee (1884 and 1894); Newaygo (1864 and 1884); Ottawa (1894); Roscommon (1884); Sanilac (1864); and Washtenaw (1884 and 1894). Most of the agriculture schedules are located at the State Archives of Michigan, with a few located at other libraries in the state.

Civil War Veterans (State): Censuses of Civil War veterans were taken in 1888 and 1894. The 1888 census includes the name of the soldier, county of residence, rank, military unit, and post office address. This special census is available at the State Archives of Michigan. The 1894 census was published as *Census of the State of Michigan 1894: Soldiers, Sailors, and Marines Volume 3* (1896). It also can be found online through the Michigan Family History Network <www.mifamilyhistory.org/civilwar/1894VetsCensus/index.asp>. Both censuses include Civil War veterans then living in Michigan, not just those who served from Michigan.

Civil War Veterans (Federal): Although most of the 1890 federal census was destroyed in a 1921 fire in Washington, D.C., a portion of it dealing with Union Civil War veterans and their widows survived. This special schedule lists the name of the surviving soldier, sailor, marine, or his widow. It also lists the veteran's rank, company, regiment or vessel, date of enlistment, date of discharge, length of service, post office address, and whether he was disabled. "While this schedule never intended to count Confederate veterans or veterans from other wars, many were included on the schedules."[13] The census exists for all of Michigan's current counties, except Dickinson. It also exists for two defunct counties: Isle Royale and Manitou. It can be found online through the Michigan Family History Network <www.mifamilyhistory.org/civilwar/1890census/1890_paged_search.asp>. Census results for individual counties, such as the 1890 Special Veterans Census of Macomb County <offserv.libcoop.net/mtc/1890vets.asp>, also can be found online. Two printed indexes are available: Dilts' *1890 Michigan Census Index of Civil War Veterans or Their Widows* (1985) and Steuart's *Michigan 1890 Veterans Census Index* (1999).

DDD Schedules (Federal): The 1880 federal census was the only one to conduct a special census of "Defective, Dependent, and Delinquent Classes." Insane persons, idiots, deaf-mutes, blind persons, homeless children, prisoners, and pauper and indigent persons were counted in seven schedules. "The city, county, and state of residence that were reported in these schedules were supposed to be the individuals' residences when at home rather than the locations of institutions, hospitals, poorhouses, or prisons."[14] Michigan's schedules are located at the State Archives of Michigan. For more information on the DDD schedules, see Hatten's article, "The 'Forgotten' Census of 1880: Defective, Dependent, and Delinquent Classes," in the March 1992 issue of the *National Genealogical Society Quarterly.*

Manufacturers/Industry (Federal): As part of the 1850, 1860, 1870, and 1880 federal censuses, the U.S. government asked questions about manufacturers and their production. Questions included the name of the individual business owner, capital invested, average number of male and female employees, average monthly wage, and quantities, kinds, and values of annual production. The special census was called the Industry Schedule in 1850, 1860, and 1870. In 1880, it was named the Manufacturers Schedule. Microfilmed copies of the schedules are available at several libraries and archives, including the National Archives and the Library of Michigan. Some schedules have been abstracted or transcribed, such as Miller's *1860 United States Census, Muskegon County, Michigan: First Census of Muskegon County* (1985), which includes information from the mortality, agriculture, and industry schedules for that county.

Manufacturing (State): The state took manufacturing censuses in 1837, 1854, 1864, 1874, 1884, 1894, and 1904. Surviving schedules include Baraga (1894); Barry (1884 and 1894); Bay (1884 and 1894); Clinton (1864); Eaton (1854, 1864, and 1874); Emmet (1884 and 1894); Hillsdale (1884); Ingham (1884 and 1894); Isabella (1884 and 1894); Kent (1884); Keweenaw (1884 and 1894); Leelanau (1884); Lenawee (1884); Menominee (1884); Montcalm (1884); Newaygo (1864 and 1884); Roscommon (1884); Saint Clair (1884 and 1894); Saint Joseph (1884 and 1894); Sanilac (1864); Van Buren (Paw Paw Township, 1884); and Washtenaw (1884 and 1894). Most of the manufacturing schedules are located at the State Archives of Michigan, with a few located at other libraries in the state.

Military (State): Between 1862 and 1886, a census of white males between the ages of 18 and 45 was done annually to determine the number of men legally responsible to do military duty. Township and city assessors took the census, and the results were returned to county clerks, who then forwarded the lists to the state's Adjutant General on or before 1 July of each year. The census was started in response to the manpower needs of the Civil War and continued until an 1887 law made the census dependent upon a governor's order. "Though most of these canvasses of draft-eligible men have been destroyed, in rare instances some lists can still be found in the county clerks' offices."[15] Some of the lists, such as the ones for Bay County from 1862 through 1869 <www.mifamilyhistory.org/Bay/draftlist.htm>, may be found online.

Mortality Schedules (Federal): As part of the 1850, 1860, 1870, and 1880 federal censuses, a mortality schedule was taken. This was a list of deaths occurring in the 12 months prior to the census. The mortality schedules list the name, age, sex, and color of the deceased; marital status; place of birth; occupation; and month and cause of death. They are available on microfilm in a number of libraries, including the National Archives and the Library of Michigan. Several mortality schedules can be found online, including:

- 1880 for Baraga County <www.rootsweb.com/~mibaraga/1880_mortality.htm>
- 1860 and 1870 for Delta County <www.grandmastree.com/migenweb/census/census.htm>
- 1860 for Gratiot County <www.mfhn.com/gratiot/deaths/1860Mortality.asp>
- 1860 for Houghton County <www.mfhn.com/mortalitysch/houghton1860.asp>
- 1870 for Iosco County <www.rootsweb.com/~miiosco2/ioscomort.html>
- 1860 for Isabella County <www.mifamilyhistory.org/isabella/1860mortality.htm>
- 1850 for Kent County <www.rootsweb.com/~mikent/census/1850/mortality.html> and 1860 for Kent County <www.rootsweb.com/~mikent/census/1860/mortality.html>
- 1860 for Leelanau County <members.aol.com/VWilson577/Leemort.html>
- 1870 and 1880 for Manistee County <www.rootsweb.com/~mimanist/ManMortalitySchedules.html>
- 1870 for Menominee County <www.rootsweb.com/~mimenomi/1870mortality.htm>
- 1850 and 1860 for Saginaw County <www.mifamilyhistory.org/saginaw/census.asp>

Mortality Schedules (State): Mortality schedules were taken as part of the 1884 and 1894 state censuses in Michigan. The 1884 schedule asked for the name, age, sex, and color of the deceased; marital status; occupation; and date, place, and cause of death. The 1894 schedule asked similar questions, plus how long the deceased had lived in the country and whether the deceased was a Civil War veteran or a widow of a Civil War veteran. Mortality schedules survive for the following counties: Baraga (1884 and 1894); Barry (1884 and 1894); Bay (1884 and 1894); Dickinson (1894); Emmet (1894); Ingham (1884); Isabella (1884);

Kent (1884); Keweenaw (1884); Lenawee (1894); Livingston (1894); Menominee (1894); Muskegon (1884 and 1894); Newaygo (1884); Van Buren (Paw Paw Township, 1884); and Washtenaw (1884 and 1894). Most state mortality schedules are at the State Archives of Michigan, with a few at other libraries in the state.

Revolutionary War Veterans (Federal): The 1840 population schedule listed Revolutionary War veterans on page 2. Some men who received state or congressional pensions also were included.[16] The names of all of these pensioners were published in a book called *A Census of Pensioners for Revolutionary or Military Service* (1841). An index to this volume also has been published. The section for Michigan lists 91 men from 22 counties. In addition to the pensioner's name, the listing includes the man's age, township of residence, and the name of the head of the household in which he lives.

This special census is available online through USGenNet <www.usgennet.org/usa/topic/colonial/census/1840/1840mi.html>, Isabella County's MIGenWeb site <www.rootsweb.com/~miisabel/1840MichiganPensioners.htm>, the U.S. Census Bureau Web site <www2.census.gov/prod2/decennial/documents/1840c-01.pdf>, and Ancestry.com <www.ancestry.com>.

Additional information about federal nonpopulation schedules can be found online <www.archives.gov/research_room/genealogy/census/nonpopulation_census_records.html> through the National Archives Web site. Additional information about state nonpopulation schedules can be found in Barnett's article, "State Censuses of Michigan: A Tragedy of Lost Treasures," published in the Summer-Fall 1978 issue of *Family Trails.*

Census Indexes: Census indexes help researchers negotiate thousands of pages of records to find their ancestors. Indexes are especially useful when researchers are uncertain where their ancestors lived or if they lived in large cities. At least one statewide index has been published for each of the existing federal censuses in Michigan. In addition, county indexes exist for federal census records for various years for more than half of the counties in Michigan. Some indexes also exist for state census records. When more than one census index exists for a particular census or a particular area, researchers should consult all indexes in case their "ancestor was misread or missed entirely by one publisher but indexed correctly by another."[17]

Microfilm: As part of a Works Projects Administration program in the 1930s, the names and other key data about persons counted in the 1880, 1900, and 1920 censuses were copied onto file cards. "The cards for each of these censuses were alphabetically coded and filed by state under a system where all names sounding alike, regardless of spelling differences or errors (if they began with the same letter of the alphabet), would be interfiled."[18] This system is known as "Soundex indexing." In the 1960s, the Bureau of the Census created a Miracode index for the 1910 census for 21 states, including Michigan. The Miracode index uses the same Soundex codes; "the difference lies only in how the page number, enumeration number, and family number are reported on the index card."[19] The

Soundex and Miracode indexes have been microfilmed and are available at several libraries, including the Library of Michigan. Researchers should note that the 1880 Soundex is incomplete; it only lists heads of households with children 10 years of age or younger.

Books: Accelerated Indexing Systems was "the first commercial firm to mass-produce census indexes."[20] In the 1970s and 1980s, AIS created "indexes for every extant state and territorial census from 1790 through 1860, as well as some later years."[21] In 1984, AIS combined all of its computerized indexes into one microfiche publication, "Indexes to U.S. Censuses 1607-1906." For Michigan, it includes federal censuses through 1870, the 1827 territorial census, 1845 state census, 1837 state census for Kalamazoo County, 1840 pensioners list, and 1850 federal mortality schedule.

In addition to AIS indexes, several individuals, societies, and libraries have published census indexes in books. In 1991, for example, the Library of Michigan released the 10-volume *1870 Michigan Census Index.* (This index is now online.) Kemp's *The American Census Handbook* (2001) lists many indexes for federal and state censuses through 1920. (It also includes a few online indexes, but it does not include indexes published in periodicals.) For other listings, researchers should consult the genealogical or historical society in their areas of interest or the online card catalogs of such libraries as the Library of Michigan <www.michigan.gov/hal>, the Family History Library <www.familysearch.org/>, or the Allen County (Indiana) Public Library <www.acpl.lib.in.us/genealogy/index.html>.

Periodicals: Many census indexes have been published in genealogical or historical periodicals. Researchers should consult PERSI or other genealogical periodical indexes to find census indexes in their area of interest. (See Chapter 4 for more on PERSI.)

CD-ROMs: A number of genealogy vendors, including Genealogical Publishing Company <www.genealogical.com> and Ancestry.com <www.ancestry.com>, sell federal census indexes on CD-ROM. Particularly noteworthy is the 1880 U.S. Census and National Index on 56 CDs, available from the Family Search Web site <www.familysearch.org>. "It is an every-name index, divided into seven geographical regions and accompanied by a national index."[22]

Online: Census indexes can be found online on paid subscription sites, such as Ancestry.com, and on free Web sites, such as those affiliated with MIGenWeb <www.rootsweb.com/~migenweb>, societies, or libraries. Examples include:

- The Library of Michigan has placed a searchable index and the images of the 1870 federal census for Michigan online <envoy.libofmich.lib.mi.us/1870_census/>. The index is the online version of the 10-volume *1870 Michigan Census Index,* published by the Library of Michigan in 1991.
- The Family Search Web site <www.familysearch.org/> has their 1880 federal census index online. (This index also is available on CD-ROM.)
- The Mount Clemens Public Library has the 1930 federal census index for Macomb County online <offserv.libcoop.net/mtc/1930census.asp>

- The MIGenWeb site for Shiawassee County includes a 1930 census index for the county <www.usgennet.org/usa/mi/county/shiawassee/census.html>
- American Local History Network's Michigan Online Census Links <www.usgennet.org/usa/mi/state/micensus.html> links to several indexes and transcriptions
- Subscription site Ancestry.com <www.ancestry.com> has indexed several federal censuses, including 1850, 1860, 1870, 1880, 1920, and 1930, and subscription site Genealogy.com <www.genealogy.com> also has indexed several federal censuses, including 1860, 1870, 1900 and 1910.

Locations of Census Records: Researchers can find census records in a variety of formats, such as microfilm, print, or digital, and in a variety of locations, such as libraries, archives, historical or genealogical society collections, or online.

Microfilm: Census records for Michigan are available at several libraries and archives, including the Library of Michigan <www.michigan.gov/hal> and the Allen County (Indiana) Public Library <www.acpl.lib.in.us/genealogy/index.html>. Census records on microfilm also can be rented through the National Archives Microfilm Rental Program <www.archives.gov/publications/microfilm_catalogs/how_to_rent_microfilm.html>, Family History Centers <www.familysearch.org/>, and Heritage Quest <www.heritagequest.com/genealogy/microfilm/>. Genealogical vendors, such as Heritage Quest, also sell census microfilms.

CD-ROM: Some census records for Michigan have been published on CD-ROM and are available at libraries or for purchase from genealogical vendors, such as AllCensus <www.allcensus.com/stockmi.html>, Genealogy.com <www.genealogy.com>, and Heritage Quest <www.heritagequest.com>.

Print: Many census records have been abstracted or transcribed and printed in books or articles. For listings, researchers should consult some of the same sources that they would use to find census indexes: the genealogical or historical society in their areas of interest; the online card catalogs of such libraries as the Library of Michigan <www.michigan.gov/hal>, the Family History Library <www.familysearch.org/>, or the Allen County (Indiana) Public Library <www.acpl.lib.in.us/genealogy/index.html>; and PERSI or other genealogy periodical indexes.

Online: Transcriptions (copies), abstracts (summaries), and digital images of actual Michigan census records are available online on free Web sites and through paid subscription services. Examples include:

- The USGenWeb Census Project <www.us-census.org/states/michigan/> or <www.rootsweb.com/~census/states/michigan/> contains census data transcribed and proofread by volunteers. In some cases, there are also digital census images <www.rootsweb.com/~usgenweb/cen_mic.htm>, such as the 1910 census for Alger County <www.rootsweb.com/~usgenweb/mi/alger/census/1910/0000read.htm>.

- Many MIGenWeb <www.rootsweb.com/~migenweb> county sites have census records. The Kent County site, for example, includes a transcription of the county's 1850 census <www.rootsweb.com/~mikent/census/1850/index.html>.
- Census Online <www.census-online.com/links/MI/>, Census Finder <www.censusfinder.com/michigan.htm>, and CensusLinks <www.censuslinks.com/> feature links to online censuses, including those for the USGenWeb Census Project and MIGenWeb county sites.
- Transcriptions of the entire 1820 <www.members.tripod.com/~tfred/1820ind.html> and 1830 federal censuses of Michigan <www.rootsweb.com/~mikent/census/1830/> are available online.
- Digital images of the 1870 Michigan census are online <envoy.libofmich.lib.mi.us/1870_census/>, courtesy of the Library of Michigan.
- Patrons of the Family History Library and branch Family History Centers can view digital images of the 1880 U.S. federal census on site at no charge, thanks to an agreement between Ancestry.com's parent company, MyFamily.com, and The Church of Jesus Christ of Latter-day Saints.
- Digital images of Michigan census records are available by subscription from Ancestry.com <www.ancestry.com>, Genealogy.com <www.genealogy.com/uscensussub.html>, and HeritageQuest <www.heritagequest.com>.

For additional information about using census records in genealogical research, consult census guides such as Hinckley's *Your Guide to the Federal Census for Genealogists, Researchers, and Family Historians* (2002).

Directories

Directories – books with alphabetical lists of certain people or businesses – can be excellent census substitutes. Types of directories that may be valuable to genealogists include alumni, business or professional, city, and telephone.

Alumni Directories: Many high schools, colleges, and universities have published directories listing the students who have graduated from their institutions. Often directories are produced in conjunction with the school's centennial or other anniversary. The directories usually list such information as the students' names, graduation dates, spouses, children, professions, and current (as of the date of publication) addresses. Researchers can find these directories by contacting the school, college, or university, or by checking with area libraries or historical and genealogical societies.

Business and Professional Directories: Business and professional directories list individuals in specific businesses or professions for a certain year or years and may include additional information, such as the individual's address, graduation year, or school attended. *The Physicians', Dentists' and Druggists' Directory of Michigan* (1893), for example, is organized by profession and then by post office. It includes the individuals' names and in many cases their addresses and colleges attended. Ranney's *List of Regular Physicians Registered in Michigan* (1885) includes the doctors' names, residences, years in practice, schools attended, and graduation years. Michigan state gazetteer and business directories for various years (described in Chapter 6) list business owners in various communities. Directories can be found in libraries and, in some cases, online. Examples include:

- 1859 Grand Rapids (Kent County) Business Directory <www.rootsweb.com/~mikent/directories/business1859.html>
- Detroit College of Medicine Faculty, 1902 <members.aol.com/CensusResearch/PLS/Detroit.htm>
- Calhoun County Business Directory for 1869-1870 <www.rootsweb.com/~micalhou/County_Directory/TOC.htm>
- Kent County's Physicians, Dentists, Druggists Directory for 1893 and 1899 <www.rootsweb.com/~mikent/organizations/drsdent.html>

City and County Directories: The first city directory in Michigan appeared in 1837 and was called *Directory of the City of Detroit with Its Environs and Register of Michigan for the Year 1837.* The second, third, and fourth Detroit city directories appeared in 1845, 1846, and 1853. Johnston's *Detroit Directory and Business Advertiser for 1853* "marked the beginning of regular annual or biennial directory publishing for the city of Detroit."[23] The first city directory in Michigan to appear outside Detroit was published in 1859 in Grand Rapids. Grand Rapids city directories began appearing regularly in 1865.

In 1860, directories were printed for Ann Arbor, Kalamazoo, and Monroe. After the Civil War, directories began appearing in several other areas of the state. The first Upper Peninsula directory, published in 1873, was called *Beard's Directory and History of Marquette County with Sketches on the Early History of Lake Superior, its Mines, Furnaces, etc.*

The information to be found in city directories varies but usually includes a list of residents, their addresses, and occupations. A man's wife may be listed or a widow's former husband. Some directories list children, deaths for the previous year, and the city to which a former resident moved. The street addresses found in city directories can aid researchers in finding their ancestors in 1880 and later federal census records.

Public libraries and historical or genealogical societies may have city directories in their collections. Some have directories for their city or county only, while others have directories for areas throughout the state. The Bentley Historical Library, for example, has city directories from more than 100 Michigan communities <www.umich.edu/~bhl/bhl/mhchome/director.htm>. The Library of Michigan at Lansing has an extensive collection of city directories from throughout the state and directories from major U.S. cities prior to 1860 on microfiche and from 1860 to 1935 on microfilm. Many Michigan cities are included in the microfiche and microfilm collections. In addition, microfilmed city directories are available for rent from Family History Centers <www.familysearch.org>.

Some city directories have been reproduced on CD-ROM and are available for purchase from genealogy vendors, including Ye Olde Directory Shoppe <www.yeoldedirectoryshoppe.com/>. *City Directories: Northern Midwest, 1884-1898,* a CD-ROM available from Genealogical Publishing Company <www.genealogical.com> and other genealogy vendors, includes information from Michigan city directories for Alpena, Ann Arbor, Detroit, Grand Rapids, Jackson, Muskegon, and Saginaw. Researchers can search the CD by given name, surname, home address, or a number of other categories. Some city directories are available online:

- Ancestry.com <www.ancestry.com> has a number of Michigan city directories online, including those for Alpena (1887-1892), Ann Arbor (1886, 1888-1892), Detroit (1890), Ionia (1891), Muskegon (1887-1890), and Ypsilanti (1910).
- DistantCousin.com <distantcousin.com/Directories/> has information from several city directories in Michigan in a searchable database, including Detroit's 1837 directory, Alpena's 1920 directory, and Saginaw's 1923 directory. The site also includes digital images of the directories.
- Delta County: Index for the 1889 Escanaba and Gladstone Directory <www.grandmastree.com/society/directory/directory_index.htm>
- Gogebic Range City Directories 1888-1947 <mattsonworks.com/> has more than 150,000 names in its database of directories from Gogebic County, Michigan, and Iron County, Wisconsin. HTML versions of the directories also can be browsed.
- Ingham County: 1916-1921 Rural Directory for Ingham County <www.rootsweb.com/~miingham/RuralDirectory.html>
- Iron County: Directories of the Cities of Iron River, Crystal Falls, Stambaugh, and Iron County, 1913 <www.rootsweb.com/~miiron/city_directories.htm>
- Isabella County: Mount Pleasant City, Shepherd Village, and Isabella County Rural Directory, 1925-1926 <www.rootsweb.com/~miisabel/directory25.htm>
- Isabella County: Luedder's Historical and Pictorial City Directory of Mount Pleasant, 1930 <www.rootsweb.com/~miisabel/directory30.htm>
- Kalamazoo County: Augusta Directory, 1883 <www.rootsweb.com/~mikalama/augustadirectory.htm>
- Macomb County: Mount Clemens City Directory Master Index <offserv.libcoop.net/mtc/MCDirectory.asp>
- Mecosta County Farm Directory, 1918-1923 <www.rootsweb.com/~mimecost/farmdirectory.html>
- Midland County Directory, 1897 <www.mifamilyhistory.org/midland/1897directory.htm>
- Midland County: Luedders' 1929 Midland Directory <www.mifamilyhistory.org/midland/1929directory.htm>

- Ottawa County: Index to 1892 Farm Directory Records Allendale, Blendon, Georgetown, and Jamestown Townships <www.rootsweb.com/~miottawa/ottawa/1892dir/index.html>

City Directories of the United States of America <www.uscitydirectories.com/mi.htm> is attempting to identify all printed, microfilmed, and online directories and their locations. At this writing, however, the only Michigan repositories inventoried on the site are the Flint Public Library and the Grand Rapids Public Library. Other listings of city directories include Spear's *Bibliography of American Directories Through 1860* (1961), *City Directories of the United States, 1860-1901: Guide to the Microfilm Collection* (1984), and the Library of Congress' U.S. City Directories on Microfilm in the Microfilm Reading Room <www.loc.gov/rr/microform/uscity/mi.html>.

Telephone Directories: In 1877, the telephone "was introduced on an experimental basis in Detroit, Grand Rapids, Houghton, and several other communities."[24] The first telephone directory in Michigan was published on 13 September 1878 in Detroit and listed 124 customers (businesses and individuals) and their addresses. This first telephone book has been reproduced as *The Speaking Telephone!* (1941). Many libraries have telephone books for their geographic areas in their reference sections, but many are for more recent years.

Census Substitutes

In addition to directories, census substitutes include voter lists, petitions, church membership lists, lists of subscribers, and taxpayer lists. In fact, any list of residents from a particular geographic area for a certain time period can serve as a census substitute. Some census substitutes are discussed in other sections of this book. Other substitutes include:

Detroit Residents: Burton's *Cadillac's Village or Detroit Under Cadillac With List of Property Owners and A History of the Settlement 1701-1710* (1896) includes lists of Detroit's original colonists and a directory of Detroit, 1701 to 1710. The Detroit Society for Genealogical Research reprinted the volume in 1999. It is also available online <my.tbaytel.net/bmartin/cadillac.htm>.

Subscribers: Individuals who donated for the publication of atlases or county histories are often listed in the books they financially supported. Some newspapers also published lists of subscribers. Some of these lists can be found online.

- Patrons' List for 1889 Atlas of Gratiot County <www.mfhn.com/gratiot/atlas1889/db_paging.asp>
- Patrons' List for 1879 Atlas of Isabella County <www.rootsweb.com/~miisabel/1879patr.htm>
- Patrons of Ashland Township (Newaygo County) 1880 Atlas <www.rootsweb.com/~minewayg/AshPatron1880.htm>
- Patrons of Denver Township (Newaygo County) 1880 Atlas <www.rootsweb.com/~minewayg/DenPatron1880.htm>

Territorial Papers: Lists of petitioners, voters, and taxpayers from Michigan's territorial era can be found in *Territorial Papers of the United States* (1942-1945). (See Chapter 7 for more about this series of books.)

Voter Lists: Since the first election in 1792 when settlers on both sides of the Detroit River sent three representatives to the Parliament of Upper Canada, elections have taken place regularly in Michigan. Surviving voter lists can be an excellent census substitute. In Michigan's early history, however, usually only white males will be listed because they were often the only ones allowed to vote. In 1806, however, the Detroit City Council was to be elected "by those over 21 years old who had been residents for at least one year and had paid their taxes; thus a few women were qualified to vote."[25] By 1819, voters had to be "free, white males over the age of 21 who had been residents of the Territory a year and paid a county or territorial tax."[26] (Sometimes working on the territory's roads was accepted in lieu of the tax requirement.)

Under Michigan's Constitution of 1835, "every white male over the age of 21 who resided in Michigan at the time the constitution was ratified was qualified to vote."[27] New, white, male settlers had to live in the state for six months before being allowed the privilege. At that time, men did not have to be property owners to be eligible to vote. The State Constitution of 1850 granted the right to vote to male immigrants who had filed their first papers for naturalization and to "civilized" male Indians, that is, Native Americans who paid taxes and lived among the general population, rather than on reservations. It wasn't until 1870 that African-American males were eligible to vote in state elections, though they were able to vote in school elections in 1855 and some – particularly those with lighter skin – may have voted in county or city elections even earlier.[28]

Starting in 1867, female taxpayers were allowed to vote in school elections, and in 1908 women taxpayers were allowed "to vote on issues involving the expenditure of public money."[29] In March 1919, Michigan women were allowed for the first time to vote in statewide primary elections. Nationally, women received the right to vote in 1920 with the adoption of the 19th Amendment, and Native Americans became full U.S. citizens under the Snyder Act of 1924. This allowed Native Americans to vote in national elections.

Voter lists, also known as poll books or lists, can be found in a variety of places, including county histories and *Territorial Papers* (see above). The State Archives of Michigan has a large collection of voter records, and these are inventoried in Archival Circular No. 24 <www.michigan.gov/documents/mhc_sa_circular 24_49720_7.pdf >. Some voter records have been placed online. These include:

- Chippewa County 1870 voter lists <www.rootsweb.com/~michcgs/voters lists.html>
- Delta County 1881 registered voters <www.grandmastree.com/society/voter 1881.htm>
- Delta County: Escanaba Voters Registration Index (1932-1972) <www.grand mastree.com/society/voters/voter1932_index.htm>

- Iron River (Marquette/Iron County) First Voters List, 1882 <www.geocities.com/Heartland/Plains/5666/IronFirstSettlers>
- Kent County: Cannon Township Register of Electors, 1859-1882 <www.rootsweb.com/~mikent/townships/cannon/electors.html>
- Kent County: Cannon Township Vote Enrollment, 1906-1910 <www.rootsweb.com/~mikent/townships/cannon/vote.html>
- Midland County: Porter Township Poll Books, 27 August 1918 <www.mifamilyhistory.org/midland/Porterpoll.htm>
- Niles (Berrien County) registered voters, 16 October 1864 <www.usgennet.org/usa/mi/county/berrien/Niles1864.htm>
- Ottawa County: Georgetown Township Registered Voters, 1859-1878 <www.rootsweb.com/~miottawa/twprecords/Georgetw/voters/1859-78/index.html>
- Saginaw County's Chapin Township Poll Books <www.mifamilyhistory.org/saginaw/chapin/polls/default.asp> for 1906, 1910, and 1912.

State Population Schedules for Michigan Counties

COUNTY	1827	1834	1837	1845	1854	1864	1874	1884	1894	*Notes
Baraga								x	x	
Barry								x	x	
Bay								x	x	
Benzie								x	x	
Branch					x*		x			*Partial
Clinton						x				
Dickinson									x	
Eaton				x	x	x	x			
Emmet								x		
Gratiot									x	
Hillsdale								x*	x	*Partial
Houghton						x	x			
Ingham								x	x	

State Population Schedules for Michigan Counties

COUNTY	1827	1834	1837	1845	1854	1864	1874	1884	1894	*Notes
Iosco									x	
Jackson								x	x	
Kalamazoo			x				x	x	x	
Kent								x	x	
Keweenaw								x	x	
Lapeer								x	x	
Leelanau								x		
Lenawee				x				x	x	
Menominee								x	x	
Midland									x	
Monroe	x*		x*							*Partial
Montcalm								x	x	
Muskegon								x	x	

State Population Schedules for Michigan Counties

COUNTY	1827	1834	1837	1845	1854	1864	1874	1884	1894	*Notes
Newaygo						x		x	x	
Oakland				x						
Ottawa								x	x	
Roscommon								x		
St. Clair				x				x	x	
St. Joseph				x				x	x	
Sanilac						x*		x*	x*	*Partial
Van Buren				x				x*		*Partial
Washtenaw	x			x				x	x	
Wayne	x							x		

Note: The 1834 census survives for a few Michigan counties, but it does not list names or other genealogical data.

Sources: State Archives of Michigan Archival Circular No. 9, Michigan Genealogical Council's Guide to the Michigan Genealogical and Historical Collections at the Library of Michigan and the State Archives of Michigan (1996), and "Existing State Censuses of Michigan," Family Trails, Summer-Fall 1978.

Federal Population Schedules for Michigan Counties

COUNTY	1820	1830	1840	1850	1860	1870	1880	1900	1910	1920	1930
Alcona					x	x	x	x	x	x	x
Alger								x	x	x	x
Allegan			x	x	x	x	x	x	x	x	x
Alpena					x	x	x	x	x	x	x
Antrim					x	x	x	x	x	x	x
Arenac								x	x	x	x
Baraga							x	x	x	x	x
Barry			x	x	x	x	x	x	x	x	x
Bay					x	x	x	x	x	x	x
Benzie						x	x	x	x	x	x
Berrien		x	x	x	x	x	x	x	x	x	x
Branch			x	x	x	x	x	x	x	x	x
Brown	x	x									

Federal Population Schedules for Michigan Counties

COUNTY	1820	1830	1840	1850	1860	1870	1880	1900	1910	1920	1930
Calhoun			x	x	x	x	x	x	x	x	x
Cass		x	x	x	x	x	x	x	x	x	x
Charlevoix						x	x	x	x	x	x
Cheboygan					x	x	x	x	x	x	x
Chippewa		x	x	x	x	x	x	x	x	x	x
Clare						x	x	x	x	x	x
Clinton			x	x	x	x	x	x	x	x	x
Crawford (Wisconsin)	x	x									
Crawford							x	x	x	x	x
Delta					x	x	x	x	x	x	x
Dickinson								x	x	x	x
Eaton			x	x	x	x	x	x	x	x	x
Emmet					x	x	x	x	x	x	x

Federal Population Schedules for Michigan Counties

COUNTY	1820	1830	1840	1850	1860	1870	1880	1900	1910	1920	1930
Genesee			x	x	x	x	x	x	x	x	x
Gladwin					x		x	x	x	x	x
Gogebic								x	x	x	x
Grand Traverse					x	x	x	x	x	x	x
Gratiot					x	x	x	x	x	x	x
Hillsdale			x	x	x	x	x	x	x	x	x
Houghton				x	x	x	x	x	x	x	x
Huron				x	x	x	x	x	x	x	x
Ingham			x	x	x	x	x	x	x	x	x
Ionia			x	x	x	x	x	x	x	x	x
Iosco					x	x	x	x	x	x	x
Iowa		x									
Iron								x	x	x	x

Federal Population Schedules for Michigan Counties

COUNTY	1820	1830	1840	1850	1860	1870	1880	1900	1910	1920	1930
Isabella					x	x	x	x	x	x	x
Isle Royale							x				
Jackson			x	x	x	x	x	x	x	x	x
Kalamazoo			x	x	x	x	x	x	x	x	x
Kalkaska						x	x	x	x	x	x
Kent			x	x	x	x	x	x	x	x	x
Keweenaw						x	x	x	x	x	x
Lake						x	x	x	x	x	x
Lapeer			x	x	x	x	x	x	x	x	x
Leelanau					x	x	x	x	x	x	x
Lenawee		x	x	x	x	x	x	x	x	x	x
Livingston			x	x	x	x	x	x	x	x	x
Luce								x	x	x	x

Federal Population Schedules for Michigan Counties

COUNTY	1820	1830	1840	1850	1860	1870	1880	1900	1910	1920	1930
Mackinac			x	x	x	x	x	x	x	x	x
Macomb	x	x	x	x	x	x	x	x	x	x	x
Manistee					x	x	x	x	x	x	x
Manitou					x	x	x				
Marquette				x	x	x	x	x	x	x	x
Mason				x	x	x	x	x	x	x	x
Mecosta					x	x	x	x	x	x	x
Menominee						x	x	x	x	x	x
Michilimackinac	x	x									
Midland				x	x	x	x	x	x	x	x
Missaukee						x	x	x	x	x	x
Monroe	x	x	x	x	x	x	x	x	x	x	x
Montcalm				x	x	x	x	x	x	x	x

Federal Population Schedules for Michigan Counties

COUNTY	1820	1830	1840	1850	1860	1870	1880	1900	1910	1920	1930
Montmorency								x	x	x	x
Muskegon					x	x	x	x	x	x	x
Newaygo				x	x	x	x	x	x	x	x
Oakland	x	x	x	x	x	x	x	x	x	x	x
Oceana			x	x	x	x	x	x	x	x	x
Ogemaw						x	x	x	x	x	x
Ontonagon				x	x	x	x	x	x	x	x
Osceola					x	x	x	x	x	x	x
Oscoda						x	x	x	x	x	x
Otsego							x	x	x	x	x
Ottawa			x	x	x	x	x	x	x	x	x
Presque Isle					x	x	x	x	x	x	x
Roscommon							x	x	x	x	x

Federal Population Schedules for Michigan Counties

COUNTY	1820	1830	1840	1850	1860	1870	1880	1900	1910	1920	1930
Saginaw			x	x	x	x	x	x	x	x	x
St. Clair		x	x	x	x	x	x	x	x	x	x
St. Joseph		x	x	x	x	x	x	x	x	x	x
Sanilac				x	x	x	x	x	x	x	x
Schoolcraft				x	x	x	x	x	x	x	x
Shiawassee			x	x	x	x	x	x	x	x	x
Tuscola				x	x	x	x	x	x	x	x
Van Buren		x	x	x	x	x	x	x	x	x	x
Washtenaw		x	x	x	x	x	x	x	x	x	x
Wayne	x	x	x	x	x	x	x	x	x	x	x
Wexford						x	x	x	x	x	x

Sources: 1790-1890 Federal Population Censuses Catalog of NARA Microfilm, 1900 Federal Population Census Catalog of NARA Microfilm, 1910 Federal Population Censuses, 1920 Federal Population Censuses, and NARA 1930 Census Census Microfilm Locator <www.archives.gov/publications/genealogy_microfilm_catalogs.html>.

6
Land and Court Records

Land, probate, and court records are additional sources in which researchers may find direct or indirect evidence of family relationships. These records can help researchers trace the movement of their ancestors, to distinguish between families with the same surnames, and to discover the city, county, state, or country from which a Michigan pioneer moved. The records discussed in this chapter and the previous chapter also may include information about vital records, just as the sources discussed in Chapter 4 may include information about family relationships.

Land and Property Records

Michigan was a "public domain" state, which means the federal government disposed of the land in Michigan under the provisions of the Ordinance of 1785. Briefly, the Ordinance said that land grants could not be made to settlers until the Indian nations ceded their land to the United States and the land was then surveyed and divided into sections (parcels of land one-mile-square, containing 640 acres) and townships (parcels of land six-mile-square or 36 numbered sections). "Once a block of townships had been surveyed, a land district was proclaimed and lands then sold at government land offices."[1]

Acquiring Michigan's Land: Between 1795 and 1842 a series of 11 treaties were negotiated between the United States and Michigan-area Indian nations to acquire most of the 58,216 square miles that make up the present state of Michigan. In most Michigan treaties, the United States promised annuity payments and/or reserve lands for various tribes and/or individual land allotments. The United States also promised to provide teachers, agricultural experts, and blacksmiths to assist Native Americans in learning farming techniques and to educate Native American children. The treaties often guaranteed unrestricted passage and hunting and fishing rights on purchased lands that remained in public ownership. "Although most annuity payments promised in these treaties were eventually paid, many other treaty obligations were not fulfilled."[2] The full text of the following treaties, a land cessions map, and related information can be found online at Clarke Historical Library's Indian Treaties Web site <clarke.cmich.edu/treatyintro.htm>. Another source of information about treaties and land cessions is Royce's *Indian Land Cessions in the United States* (1971), found online at American Memory's Map Collections: 1500-2003

<memory.loc.gov/ammem/gmdhtml/gmdhome.html>. The book includes four maps of Michigan land cessions.

Greenville Treaty, 1795: This treaty "proclaimed the right of the United States to acquire Indian lands in Michigan through treaty and marked the first cessions of lands at Detroit and Michilimackinac."[3]

Detroit Treaty, 1807: Signed by Chippewa, Ottawa, Potawatomi, and Wyandot representatives, the treaty acquired the southeastern quarter of Michigan, including most of the Thumb region. The territory covered in this treaty includes the present-day counties of "Monroe, Lenawee, Wayne, Washtenaw, Macomb, Oakland, Livingston, Saint Clair, Lapeer and Genesee, and a portion of Jackson, Ingham, Shiawassee, Tuscola and Sanilac."[4]

Foot of the Rapids Treaty, 1817: In this agreement, also known as the Treaty of Fort Meigs, the United States acquired an area "corresponding roughly to the southern half of Hillsdale County."[5]

Saginaw Treaty, 1819: The Chippewas of Saginaw ceded six million acres or roughly one-third of the northeastern Lower Peninsula, including the Saginaw Bay area. The treaty also included provisions for "several special land grants to individuals."[6] For more information on the special land grants, see Barnett's article, "Land for Family and Friends: The Saginaw Treaty of 1819," in the September-October 2003 issue of *Michigan History.*

Sault Ste. Marie Treaty, 1820: The United States obtained 16 square miles near present-day Sault Ste. Marie. "This land is also included in the cession made by the Chippewas and Ottawas by the treaty of March 28, 1836, made at Washington."[7]

Chicago Treaty, 1821: The United States acquired "most of the land in the southwestern part of the Lower Peninsula south of the Grand River."[8] It includes the present-day counties of "Berrien, Cass, Saint Joseph, Branch, Hillsdale, Van Buren and Allegan, and also a part of Ottawa, Kent, Barry, Kalamazoo, Calhoun and Jackson."[9] About 30 individuals also received land grants through the treaty. For more information, see Barnett's article, "Private Land Grants in Michigan Awarded by the Treaty of 1821," published in the Winter 2004 issue of The Historical Society of Michigan's *Chronicle and Newsletter.*

Carey Mission Treaty, 1828: The United States gained a small portion of southwestern Lower Michigan south of the Saint Joseph River from the Potawatomies.

Chicago Treaty, 1833: "The United States agreed to purchase all remaining Potawatomi lands and to pay their outstanding debts and, in exchange, the Potawatomi agreed to remove west."[10] This included the land acquired through the Carey Mission Treaty in 1828.[11]

Washington Treaty, 1836: The treaty ceded the northwestern section of the Lower Peninsula and the Upper Peninsula east of the present-day city of Marquette. It also included all the islands in the Great Lakes bordering the ceded portion not included in previous treaties.[12]

Cedar Point Treaty, 1836: In this treaty, the Menominee surrendered portions of present-day Wisconsin and an area that roughly covers Michigan's Menominee County and surrounding counties in the Upper Peninsula.

LaPointe Treaty, 1842: The United States acquired the mineral-rich western portion of Michigan's Upper Peninsula.

Selling Michigan's Land: The first land office opened in Michigan at Detroit in 1804, but no land was sold until 1818. Land offices followed in 1823 in Monroe, in 1831 in White Pigeon, and in 1836 in Flint and Ionia. The White Pigeon Office moved to Kalamazoo (then known as Bronson) in 1834. The first land office in the Upper Peninsula opened at Sault Ste. Marie in 1848. Each land office was responsible for a certain segment of the public-domain land. Before public-domain land went on sale for the first time, announcements were made in the local newspapers for several months beforehand. The sale itself usually took place in the summer or fall. "On the designated date, parcels were auctioned to the highest bidders, usually in blocks of 80 or more acres. After the initial offering, any unsold property could be bought at the federal land office."[13]

> At the land offices the prospective buyer could obtain maps showing the sections available, with the letter 'S' marked on those sections or parts of sections that had been sold. It also was possible to obtain the surveyor's notes so as to get a general idea of the quality of the land. Almost invariably the buyer or someone representing him would proceed on foot or on horseback to look over the lands available, using maps and a compass to guide him. He then returned to the land office, and 'entered' the lands he wished to buy. He paid for them in silver, gold, bank notes, or drafts and was given a receipt. A record of the sale was then sent to Washington and after some delay (often a year or more) he would receive a 'patent,' signed by the President of the United States giving him title to the land he had purchased.[14]

At first, settlers were required to purchase a minimum of 160 acres at a cost of $2 an acre. The land could be paid for in four annual payments. In 1820, the U.S. Congress reduced the cost of the land to $1.25 per acre and the minimum purchase from 160 to 80 acres. In addition, the land had to be paid for in cash, rather than in installments. "This is the price for which most of the United States government land in Michigan was purchased."[15] Another land act in 1832 "allowed the sale of some lands in 40-acre parcels."[16] Some lands were sold for less than $1.25 per acre. Federal law in 1854, for example, stimulated the sale of lesser-quality lands by pricing it at 75 cents per acre, and Internal Improvement lands awarded to road contractors by the state often were resold for 40 cents per acre.[17]

Another source of cheap lands were those forfeited due to unpaid taxes. "The state disposed of tax-delinquent properties at sales. For the nominal sum of the taxes owed, a squatter could acquire a tax title deed, which did not convey the land he occupied outright, but gave the occupant rights to all improvements he had made on it."[18] However, the settler risked losing the land to the original owner who could reclaim it by repaying the back taxes, plus interest and the amount of the settler's improvements.

In some cases, settlers moved onto land before it was officially open to settlement – either it had not yet been secured by treaty or it had not yet been surveyed. The Act of Preemption of 1830, however, allowed these squatters or early settlers to petition to purchase the land. Squatting was one method settlers without cash used to acquire land. First, they located on unclaimed land. Then they placed it into production, and later purchased it through preemption with the proceeds of the land's production.

In addition to purchasing land, other ways in which early Michigan settlers could obtain a patent to public domain land was through Homesteading or redeeming military bounty land warrants. In 1862, President Abraham Lincoln signed the Homestead Act, which stated that a man or woman over 21 years of age who was a citizen of the United States or who had filed a Declaration of Intention to become a citizen was eligible to file an application to homestead on up to 160 acres of land. The settler could begin residency on the land after paying a $10 fee. After living on the land and improving it for a five-year period, the settler could apply for the land patent. Nearly 18,000 individuals and families settled more than 2.3 million acres of Michigan land in this way, much of it in the northern two-thirds of the state.[19] Laws passed in 1847 and later offered bounty land as a reward to soldiers who had served in previous wars. "All of these acts provided that a warrant for a quarter section (160 acres) of land, located on any part of the surveyed public domain, would be granted to those who qualified."[20]

Title to Section 16 in each township was given to the state by the federal government for the support of primary schools. These sections were then sold by the state and the proceeds used to create an endowment fund for schools. The federal government also granted other sections of land to the state for the support of universities, railroads, and other purposes.

Barnett's article, "Mapping Michigan's First Land Sales," published in the February 1999 issue of *Michigan Out-of-Doors,* features a color-coded map of Michigan's first land sales and another map showing when Michigan's public-domain land was first put on the market.

Land Patents: Land patents were documents transferring ownership or title of land from the government (public ownership) to individuals (private ownership). Patents do not have a lot of genealogical information (usually just the patentee's name and county or state of residence), but they are valuable because they place an individual in a particular location at a particular time. However, researchers should keep in mind that many settlers "bought land in several places and moved several times before settling permanently."[21] In other cases, the individual(s) owning land or paying taxes on it were not the individual(s) living on it.

In Michigan, most of the patents came from the federal government, but more than 55,000 patents were issued from the state – for lands that the federal government had granted to the state for the support of schools and other purposes. Federal patents issued prior to 1908 have been published on CD-ROM and are available for purchase from Ancestry.com <www.ancestry.com> or Genealogy.com <www.genealogy.com>. Pre-1908 federal patents also can be found online at the Bureau of Land Management General Land Office Records Web site <www.glorecords.blm.gov/>. Researchers can search patents by state and name (last name required, first name optional) and can view the following information:

- Patent description (including the patentee's name), details on the title transfer (including date of issue and land office), survey details (including number of acres), and document numbers
- Legal land description, including county, township, and range
- Document image in GIF, TIFF, or PDF formats

In addition, researchers have the option of ordering a certified copy of the federal patent from the Bureau of Land Management General Land Office Records Web site.

Information about patents issued by the State of Michigan can be found at the State Archives of Michigan. This includes land patents and certificates from 1847 to 1943. Land records located at the Archives are detailed in Circular No. 2: Land Records <www.michigan.gov/documents/mhc_sa_circular02_49679_7.pdf>. Archivists also are working on a land patent database project with the eventual goal of placing an index and/or the digital images of the state patents online.[22]

The Library of Michigan has the records of the first purchase of Michigan land from state and federal sales on microfilm, arranged by county, township, and range. Information from state and federal patents also have been transcribed, indexed, or abstracted and published in books or articles. Books dealing with the first purchase of land in Michigan include those for Barry, Eaton, Hillsdale, Ingham, Kalamazoo, Livingston, Marquette, Mason, Monroe, Oakland, Ogemaw, Presque Isle, Saginaw, Saint Clair, Shiawassee, Van Buren, and Wayne counties.

Other online sources for patents or records of first purchase include:

- Ancestry.com's Bureau of Land Management Land Records <www.ancestry.com/search/rectype/court/blm/main.htm>
- RootsWeb.com's User-contributed Land Records Database <userdb.rootsweb.com/landrecords/>
- Individual MIGenWeb county Web sites

Land-entry Case Files: Before individuals received their federal land patents to public-domain land, certain paperwork had to be completed for the government. The type of paperwork depended on the Act of Congress under which an individual was trying to acquire the federal land. Paperwork might include an application, receipts for payments, or affidavits of occupation. To be eligible for public-domain land, applicants had to be citizens of the United States or at least have declared their intention of becoming citizens, so applicants often had to provide proof of citizenship.[23] All of the paperwork generated by the acquisition of public-domain land can be found in land-entry case files, which are currently held at the National Archives. These files have not been microfilmed; in order to access them, researchers must fill out the appropriate form and provide the National Archives with the patentee, name of the state where the land is located, name of the land office, authority under which the land was acquired (such as Homestead Act, cash purchase), and document number. This information can be found on the patent. (More information about ordering land-entry case files can be found online at the Bureau of Land Management General Land Office Records Web site <www.glorecords.blm.gov/Visitors/Requests.asp#nara>.)

Subsequent Sales: Land sales and transfers from the first owners to subsequent owners are recorded in deeds, legal documents that transfer title of real property from one person to another. In Michigan, deeds are filed in the Register of Deeds Office in the county in which the land is located. Deed indexes usually are arranged by grantor (seller) and/or grantee (buyer). Deeds usually contain the names of the parties involved in the land transfer, the date of the transaction, and the purchase price. Deeds also may contain such information as the names of wives or children, the names of adjoining landowners, or the residences of the grantor and grantee. Types of deeds include warranty deeds in which owners guarantee that they have clear title to the land being sold; quitclaim deeds in which owners release their title or possible title to the land in question; and gift deeds in which property is transferred as a gift, often from parent to child.

Other Records: Though deeds are the most common land records, other land records researchers may find in Michigan include the following:

Surveyor Records: Before land could be sold, surveyors traveled throughout the territory and laid out Michigan's township system. Townships were six-mile square, with 36 one-square-mile sections in each township. "These sections were numbered continuously, with number one at the northeast corner of each township and number six at the northwest corner until number 36 was reached at the southeast corner."[24] (The only exceptions to this township system were tracts granted prior to American rule; these retained their original boundaries and most were located in Macomb, Monroe, Saint Clair, and Wayne counties. See Private Claims below for more.) The surveys began on 29 September 1815 and continued for more than 30 years. The surveyors' original notes and maps are located at the State Archives of Michigan and are detailed in Circular No. 5: Surveyors' Records <www.michigan.gov/documents/mhc_sa_circular05_49688_7.pdf>. These are seldom of interest to genealogists, "but for ancestors on the land prior to the survey, the surveyors' field notes may supply background descriptions of the area and sometimes specific, crude drawings of homes and outbuildings on the property."[25]

Tract Books: Tracts are parcels of property; tract books trace the first time tracts of land were transferred from public to private ownership. They contain legal descriptions of parcels, names, and addresses of purchasers of land, how the land was disposed of, and dates of patent. They are organized by land office and land description (county, township, and range). They list all applications for public-domain lands, "including land forfeitures, rejections, and cancellations" - not just those who completed the patent process.[26] Tract books can serve as an index to all of the land-entry case files at the National Archives. They have been microfilmed and are available through the National Archives and Family History Centers. The Library of Michigan also has microfilmed Tract Books, and the State Archives of Michigan has tract books from 1818, the year of first land sales in Michigan, to 1962. Plat and tract books from land offices in Michigan also are available at Bentley Historical Library's Michigan Historical Collections <www.umich.edu/~bhl/bhl/refhome/land.htm#landoffice>.

Land Ownership Maps: These maps list landowners and other information. (See Map section below for more.)

Mortgages: Much like today's secured loans, these were conditional transfers of title in which the landowners used their property to secure debts. When the debt was repaid, a deed of release returned complete title of the property to its owner. Mortgages are generally located in the county's Register of Deeds' Office; many have been microfilmed and are available through Family History Centers.

Sales of Land for Delinquent Taxes: When property owners failed to pay taxes, their land could be sold to pay for the back taxes. These sales records are generally located in the county's Treasurer's Office; many have been microfilmed and are available through Family History Centers. (See the Property Tax Records section below for more.)

Rural Property Inventories: During the Great Depression, rural property in most Michigan counties was inventoried. (See Chapter 7 for more.)

Private Claims: The federal government honored valid land titles given to settlers by the French or British governments prior to the United States taking possession of Michigan. These were known as "private land claims" and several were honored, primarily at Mackinac and Detroit. "In 1823 Congress passed new legislation which allowed for the filing of private claims based on occupancy before July 1812, rather than the earlier terminal date of 1796, providing the claimants had been friendly to the United States throughout the war [of 1812]."[27] As a result, some claims were filed for areas not occupied at the earlier date. Information about private land claims can be found in *American State Papers, Public Lands* (1994), nine volumes that cover the years 1789 to 1837. Each volume is indexed. *Grassroots of America* (1994) is an index to the series. The claims often give valuable genealogical data such as "ages of claimants; previous places of habitation; names of children, wives, and other relatives; exact location of claims; and the time period of 'cultivation and habitation.'"[28] Individual landowners as well as their heirs made claims.[29] Information on private land claims also can be found in the *Territorial Papers of the United States* (1942-1945). (See Chapter 7 for more on this series.) Private claim information, including surveys by Aaron Greely, 1809-1810; resurveys of private claims and concessions, 1807-1877; and private claim surveys in northern Michigan, 1823-1855, is located at the State Archives of Michigan. General information on private land claims can be found in Farmer's *History of Detroit and Wayne County and Early Michigan* (1890) and Reynolds' *Early Land Claims in Michigan* (1940).

Detroit's 1805 Fire: On 5 June 1805, a fire reduced Detroit to ashes in about six hours. At that time, Detroit had about 300 homes and 500 inhabitants. It was an important trading center and was scheduled to become the capital of the Territory of Michigan less than a month later, on 1 July 1805. Unfortunately, few of the French residents had written deeds to their land. On 21 April 1806, the U.S. Congress passed An Act to Provide for the Adjustment of Titles to Land in Detroit and the Territory of Michigan, and for Other Purposes. "According to the Act of 1806, every sufferer by the fire, above 17 years of age on the 11 of June, 1805, who lived in the city at the time of the fire, should be granted by the Governor and Judges [of the Michigan Territory] a lot not exceeding 5,000 square feet, where they judged most proper."[30] Every non-resident property owner also was to be given a lot of up to 5,000 square feet.[31] The Michigan Territory passed an Act on 13 September 1806 specifying the timeline for making claims under Congress' act. Persons living in Detroit at the time of the territorial act, for example, had six months from 13 September 1806 to make their claim. Others living within the Territory of Michigan but not within Detroit had one year, persons living outside Michigan but within the United States had 18 months, and persons living outside the United States had two years. A special land board was set up to review claims. Land board records from 2 June 1807 to 24 October 1808 have disappeared, but land board records from 24 October 1808 are contained in *Governor and Judges Journal: Proceedings of the Land Board of Detroit* (1915). An index to this volume can be found online <www.rootsweb.com/~miwayne/boardindex.htm >. In addition, a list of 62 Detroit landowners appeared in the article "List of Real Estate Owners and Values at the Time of the Detroit Fire in 1805," published in *Michigan Pioneer and Historical Collections* (1908), and more than 200 residents are listed in Russell's *Michigan Censuses 1710-1830 Under the French, British, and Americans* (1982). A list of French land claims in Wayne County also can be found online <www.geocities.com/michhist/landclaim.html>.

The 'Toledo Strip': Because of the border dispute with Ohio, known as the "Toledo War," land deeds for a five-to-eight-mile-wide portion of land in southern Michigan – known as the Toledo Strip – were recorded in both Michigan and Ohio counties in order to be considered valid. Monroe County deeds also may be recorded in Lucas County, Ohio; Lenawee County deeds in Fulton County, Ohio; and Hillsdale County deeds in Williams County, Ohio. (For more information on the Toledo War, see Chapter 4.)

Centennial Farms: The Michigan Historical Commission initiated a Centennial Farm Program in 1948 in which working farms of more than 10 acres owned by the same family for 100 years or more would be designated as Centennial Farms. The farms are given a green and yellow metal display marker, supplied by Michigan electrical utility companies, and farm owners receive Michigan Centennial Farm Certificates from the state. Since the program's inception, more than 6,000 farms have been certified as Centennial Farms, the oldest dating back to 1776. "The Michigan Historical Commission also established a Sesquicentennial Farm Program in 1990, to recognize, upon request, certified Centennial Farms that have been owned by the same family for 150 years or longer. There are 300 certified Sesquicentennial Farms in Michigan."[32] Most centennial farms are located in southern Lower Michigan, though a handful are in northern Lower Michigan and the Upper Peninsula.

To receive a Centennial Farm designation, the applicant must trace the current farm family back to the original owner of the farm and establish continuous ownership of the land by the same family. The proof of ownership submitted in Centennial Farm applications ranges in quality, according to the former Centennial Farm Coordinator Gilbert E. Apps. "With rare exceptions nothing in our files could be considered primary source proof of family relationship in the sense of the documentation normally required for genealogical research. In some cases, there's nearly no supporting documentation other than the line of descent. In many cases the records do remain a gold mine of secondary information that may be useful in guiding researchers to primary source documents. Some people have sent family histories, some have sent copies of deeds or tax statements, while others have provided photographs."[33]

The Centennial Farm Program is now overseen by the State Historic Preservation Office, located on the fifth floor of the Michigan Historical Center, 702 West Kalamazoo Street, Lansing. Centennial Farm records can be inspected by appointment during the office's normal business hours. Genealogists must schedule an appointment first by calling (517) 373-1630.[34]

Once designated as a Centennial Farm, farm owners are eligible for membership in the Michigan Centennial Farm Association, which was organized in 1957. In 1986, the Association published Wermuth's *Michigan's Centennial Family Farm Heritage, 1986: A Michigan Sesquicentennial History.* The book profiles more than 700 farms and their owners and includes an index of all Centennial Farms in Michigan at the time of publication.

Since 1958 the Michigan Historical Commission has published several Centennial Farm directories. These include the names and addresses of the centennial farm owners and the years the families purchased the farms. Lists of centennial farm owners also may be found in various issues of *Michigan History.* The March 1955 issue, for example, lists the 85 centennial farm marker recipients for 1953 and 1954. The list includes the name of the farm owner, the county and township in which the farm was located, the relationship to the original owner of the farm, and the date the original owner acquired the farm.

Online sources of information about Centennial Farms include the following:

- Arenac County Centennial Farms <www.rootsweb.com/~miarenac/places/farms.htm>
- Centennial Farms Grand Traverse County <hometown.aol.com/kingsley/gtcent.html>
- Kalkaska County Centennial Farms <hometown.aol.com/kingsley/kask farm.html>
- Centennial Farms Directory for Kent County – 1972 <www.rootsweb.com ~mikent/land/farms/centennial1972.html>
- Centennial Farms of Newaygo County <www.rootsweb.com/~minewayg/cenfarm.html>

Property Tax Records: Property tax/assessment rolls usually list the owners and legal descriptions of taxable property, total acreage, value of property, date of assessment, and the amount and kind of taxes (state, county, township, etc.) levied. Tax receipts list the person paying the taxes, the date the taxes were paid, and the amount collected. Property tax records usually begin after the county started keeping land records. These records are generally found in the County Treasurer's Office, Assessor's Office, or the Register of Deeds Office in the county in which the land was located. Many tax records have been microfilmed and are available through Family History Centers.

The State Archives of Michigan has a large collection of tax/assessment rolls for 45 Michigan counties. Several of the Archives' Regional Repositories, including Michigan Technological University and Western Michigan University, have tax rolls for 14 additional counties. The earliest of these tax records date back to 1831, but most of them are for the later part of the 19th century. Tax records at the State Archives and its Regional Repositories are detailed in Circular No. 1: Tax/Assessment Rolls <www.michigan.gov/documents/mhc_sa_ circular01_49677_7.pdf>. Tax/assessment rolls also may be found with smaller collections. The Shepherd Area Historical Society (Isabella County), for example, has assessment rolls for Coe Township for several years <www.mifamilyhistory.org/isabella/isaobit.html>.

Some tax records, such as Castle's *1888 Assessment Roll for Cass County, Michigan* (1997) or the *1877 Tax Assessment Roll, Odessa Township, Ionia County, Michigan* (2000), have been published; other tax records may be found online:

- Convis Township (Calhoun County) Tax Assessment Rolls for 1855 and 1866 <www.rootsweb.com/~micalhou/convis_tax.htm>
- Index to Georgetown Township (Ottawa County) Assessments, 1878-1879 <www.rootsweb.com/~miottawa/twprecords/Georgetw/assess/index.html>

Sales of Delinquent Land: Prior to 1882, it was difficult for the state to sell lands for back taxes "since tax-land buyers, during this period, must defend their titles by law suits against the first owners, a costly process, and often a complete loss."[35] The state often settled for selling these lands at a reduced price just to get rid of them. Knowing this, some landowners neglected to pay taxes for years and then purchased their lands back from the state with a clean title for a small sum at a tax sale.[36] A special tax commission at a special legislative session in 1882 passed a law requiring the state to secure "a 'court judgment' on each land title before it was offered for sale."[37] With good land titles, it became easier for the state to sell the delinquent land at appropriate prices, assisting settlement. For the genealogist, this means there may be additional court records available in connection with these parcels of property.

For general information about using land and tax records in genealogical research, see Hone's *Land and Property Research in the United States* (1997), Hatcher's *Locating Your Roots: Discover Your Ancestors Using Land Records* (2003), the chapter on land research in Greenwood's *Researcher's Guide to American Genealogy* (2000), the chapter on Land and Tax Records in *The Source: A Guidebook of American Genealogy* (1997), or RootsWeb's Guide to Tracing Family Trees <www.rootsweb.com/~rwguide/lesson29.htm>.

Maps and Gazetteers

Maps and gazetteers are two tools to help researchers place their ancestors in a geographical location. Gazetteers or place-name guides list geographical names in alphabetical order. They often describe communities and list when they were settled and by whom. Maps are visual representations of a geographical place. Depending on the type of map, they illustrate such items as towns, local cemeteries, property holdings, boundaries, railroads, roads and trails, and landscape features (rivers, swamps, etc.).

Land Ownership Maps: Perhaps the most common map used by genealogists, land ownership maps (also known as plat maps) show the names of landowners in a particular area and can include the locations of roads, streams, churches, and other features. The first land ownership map published in Michigan was John Farmer's 1855 "Map of Wayne County, Michigan, Exhibiting Names of the Original Purchasers and the Numbers of Acres in Each Tract."[38]

Shortly before the Civil War, representatives of Eastern firms sought Michigan subscribers to purchase their land ownership maps. "Nearly 1,000 customers had to be enrolled at about $5.00 each before a map could profitably be made, and one of the first East Coast publishers to obtain this number of patrons was Geil and Jones who had been canvassing Hillsdale County."[39] These single-sheet maps, also known as "wall maps," were nearly five or six square feet in size.

By 1900, nearly 50 maps of this type were published, most for counties in southern Lower Michigan. Most of the wall maps covered single counties, but several featured two or more counties. These are inventoried in Stephenson's *Land Ownership Maps: A Checklist of Nineteenth Century United States County Maps in the Library of Congress* (1967). The Library of Congress has reproduced these wall maps on microfiche, and the microfiche set is available at several libraries, including the Library of Michigan.

Nationwide, the publishing of single-sheet land ownership maps gave way to the publishing of county atlases during the late 1860s. These atlases included land ownership maps for each township in the county, illustrations, and possibly a historical or biographical section. In Michigan, the first county atlases appeared in 1872. "By 1930, at least one hundred and thirty-six plat atlases of Michigan counties had been published."[40] Atlases were published for all but six Lower Peninsula counties: Alcona, Crawford, Kalkaska, Oscoda, Otsego, and Roscommon. Only three Upper Peninsula counties – Delta, Houghton, and Menominee – had published atlases during this time period. The first *Atlas of the State of Michigan* was published in 1874. State and county atlases have been inventoried in Miles' *Michigan Atlases and Plat Books: A Checklist 1872-1973* (1975).

Many of the older atlases were not published with indexes. Several historical or genealogical societies have reprinted land ownership maps and atlases with indexes. Examples of these include:

- *Combined 1829-1929 Land Ownership Atlas of Branch County, Michigan: Showing Original Purchasers Starting in 1829, and Land Ownership in the Years of 1858, 1872, 1894, 1909, 1915 & 1929* (1996)
- *Combined Ingham County, Michigan 1874 and 1895 Atlases with Every Name Index* (1988)
- *Combined 1874, 1893, 1916 Atlases of Lenawee County, Michigan* (1997)
- *Atlases of Saginaw County, Michigan: 1877, 1896, 1916* (1992)
- *Combined 1859 Wall Map, 1875 Atlas, 1895 Plat Book Atlas, and 1915 Atlas of Shiawassee County, Michigan, Indexed* (2003)

County Boundaries: Records for a particular ancestor may appear in two or more counties – not because they moved but because the county's boundaries changed. Two tools to assist researchers in finding county boundaries are Thorndale and Dollarhide's *Map Guide to the U.S. Federal Censuses, 1790-1920* (1987) and Sinko's *Atlas of Historical County Boundaries: Michigan* (1997). Thorndale and Dollarhide's work shows Michigan boundaries at the time federal censuses were taken, compared to present-day boundaries. With detailed maps and explanation, Sinko's book is "the most detailed and comprehensive reference available on boundary changes."[41] Current boundaries of townships are depicted in Andriot's *Township Atlas of the United States* (1991). Online versions of Michigan county formation maps <www.negenealogy.com/mi/mi_maps/mi_cf.htm> and Michigan county census maps <www.negenealogy.com/mi/mi_maps/mi_cm.htm> also are available through the Northeastern Genealogy Online Web site <www.negenealogy.com/>.

Panoramas: Panorama or bird's-eye view maps were drawings of communities, "portrayed as if viewed from above at an oblique angle."[42] Popular in the late

19th and early 20th centuries, these were not drawn to scale nor were they always accurate. Still, they offer researchers an interesting perspective and show patterns of buildings and landscape features. More than 100 panoramas of Michigan cities and towns were produced. They have been inventoried in Hebert and Dempsey's *Panoramic Maps of Cities in the United States and Canada: A Checklist of Maps in the Collections of the Library of Congress, Geography and Map Division* (1984) and Cumming's *Preliminary Checklist of 19th Century Lithographs of Michigan Cities and Towns* (1969).

Fire Insurance Maps: Starting in the latter half of the 19th century, companies began creating special-purpose maps, known as fire insurance maps, that documented buildings in urban environments. Though several companies produced these maps, the Sanborn Company – founded in 1867 – produced most of them. Therefore, these maps are often referred to as Sanborn Fire Insurance Maps.

> These maps were used by insurance agents to determine hazards and risk in underwriting specific buildings. ... Size, shape, and construction of homes, businesses, farm buildings; locations of windows, doors, firewalls, roof types; widths and names of streets; property boundaries; ditches, water mains, sprinkling systems; and other details are clearly indicated.[43]

Some fire insurance maps also may include the names of major landowners.[44] More than 300 Michigan cities and towns have at least one fire insurance map; the earliest maps date from the 1880s. They are inventoried in *Fire Insurance Maps in the Library of Congress* (1981).

For more information about fire insurance maps, see Oswald's *Fire Insurance Maps: Their History and Applications* (1997) and the following Web sites:

- Sanborn Fire Insurance Maps <www.lib.berkeley.edu/EART/snb-intr.html> and the key for reading maps <www.lib.berkeley.edu/EART/images/sandkey.jpg>
- How to Read Sanborn Fire Insurance Maps <fisher.lib.virginia.edu/collections/maps/sanborn/web/details.html>

Finding Maps: In addition to the bibliographies mentioned above, Michigan maps are listed in the following publications:

- Streeter's *Michigan Bibliography* (1921) lists about 900 maps
- Karpinski's *Bibliography of the Printed Maps of Michigan, 1804-1880* (1931) lists about 1,000 maps
- Barnett's *Checklist of Printed Maps of the Middle West to 1900,* Volume 5 (1981) has information on more than 4,500 maps and updates Karpinski's book above

Several libraries in Michigan have map collections. For example, the Library of Michigan and Michigan Historical Collections at Bentley Historical Library

<www.umich.edu/~bhl/bhl/mhchome/atlases.htm> have large collections of land-ownership maps and atlases, and the State Archives of Michigan has some panoramas. Large collections of fire insurance maps can be found at the Library of Michigan, State Archives of Michigan, Detroit Public Library, and the University of Michigan Map Library <www.lib.umich.edu/maplib/sanborn/index.html>. Some maps and atlases can be found in the 88-volume microfilm set, *County Histories of the Old Northwest, Series V: Michigan.* (See Chapter 4 for more). Other maps and atlases can be found online. (See Chapter 9 for more.)

For general information about Michigan maps, see Barnett's articles, "Milestones in Michigan Mapping: Early Settlement" and "Milestones in Michigan Mapping: Modern Waymarks," published in the September-October and November-December 1979 issues of *Michigan History* and Clarke Historical Library's online exhibit, Mapping Michigan <clarke.cmich.edu/mpintro.htm>.

Gazetteers and Place-Name Guides: Settlements in Michigan have been given a variety of names; some reflect a geographic characteristic, ownership, or the origin of its first settlers, others incorporate Native American, French, or Finnish words. Some communities in Michigan have been known by three or four different names: "the name of the [railroad] station which was its shipping point; the original name chosen by the townspeople; the name assigned by the postal department; and the name used by the lumberjacks or owner of the lumber camp."[45] In some cases, settlers named new communities in northern Michigan after their old communities in southern Michigan to make them seem more like home. Multiple or duplicate community names can make it difficult for researchers to find their ancestors' hometowns, but gazetteers and place-name guides can help clear the confusion.

Gazetteers list all cities and communities in a state or region and the leading businesses and citizens in each. They also may list government resources and other information. Blois' *Gazetteer of the State of Michigan* (1838) was the first gazetteer published in the state. It was reprinted in 1839 and 1840. "State gazetteers for Michigan were published in 1856 and 1860. Beginning in 1863 Michigan State gazetteers appeared on a regular basis until 1931."[46] Titled *Michigan State Gazetteer and Business Directory,* these publications included such information as descriptions of communities and listings of business owners, postmasters, and churches. Some gazetteers also were published for specific areas of the state, such as the *Saginaw Valley and Lake Shore Business Gazetteer and Directory* (1873) and the *Van Buren County Gazetteer and Business Directory* (1869).

Place-name guides generally list in alphabetical order the names of places in particular locations and sometimes include additional information, such as dates of settlement. Romig's *Michigan Place Names: The History of the Founding and the Naming of More Than Five Thousand Past and Present Michigan Communities* (1986) includes information about when a community was first settled and by whom, when postal service began, and what were the major industries or commercial activities in the area. It also includes an index of personal names.

Meints' *Along the Tracks: A Directory of Named Places on Michigan Railroads* (1987) lists "passenger depots, freight houses, country flag stops, and any other places where passengers or freight are received or delivered."[47] Part One of the book is a continuous alphabetical list of places in the state and the counties in which they are located. Part Two is a list of places in the Lower Peninsula and Part Three is a list of places in the Upper Peninsula, both divided by county. Parts Two and Three include the township, section, and range number of the listed place.

There were hundreds of post offices in Michigan before 1845 and more than 1,000 by 1872. "Many of these were located in trappers' cabins near a trading post, in a country store, or in a farmer's house."[48] By 1965, more than 3,000 post offices had been discontinued. Post offices (and postmasters) are listed in several publications, including Ellis' *Michigan Postal History: The Post Offices, 1805-1986* (1993), Reed and Hennig's *Post Offices of Michigan* (1976), Priestley's *Michigan Territorial Post Offices* (1961), Wantz's *Post Offices of Newaygo County,* and Spooner's *Postoffices and Postmasters of Ottawa County* (1962), *Postoffices and Postmasters of Muskegon County* (1962), *Postoffices and Postmasters of Newaygo County* (1961), and *Postoffices and Postmasters of Oceana County* (1961). The four-reel set of microfilm, Record of Appointment of Postmasters 1832 to 30 September 1971, lists the dates of establishment and discontinuation of post offices, post office name changes, and the names and appointment dates of postmasters. This microfilm is available through the National Archives and at other libraries, including the Library of Michigan.

Michigan gazetteers and place-name guides can be found in several libraries in print or on microfilm. Some may be found online. (See Chapter 9 for more.)

Ghost Towns: There are hundreds, perhaps thousands, of "ghost towns" in Michigan, short-lived settlements that sprang up along a railroad or around a sawmill or mine. "Most ghost towns in Michigan have disappeared completely, due to ravages of nature or by the many fires that swept over northern Michigan after the timber was harvested. All evidence of many others lies buried beneath expressways and waters of rivers dammed up to obtain water power for electricity or to create artificial lakes."[49] Several books discuss Michigan's many ghost towns. Dodge published three volumes of *Michigan Ghost Towns* in the early 1970s. Volumes 1 and 2 (reprinted as one volume in 1990) deal with the Lower Peninsula, while Volume 3 discusses ghost towns of the Upper Peninsula. Dodge compiled his comprehensive books from a variety of sources, including county records, plat maps, gazetteers, legislative manuals, and business directories. The books include information about early settlers, postmasters, and businesses. Dodge said his books include places that may not even be considered an official town or a settlement. "They were named, either by someone who lived in the area, by a logging company, railroad company, or by the Post Office Department."[50] Wakefield's three volumes of *Ghost Towns of Michigan* (1994-2002) take a different approach to the subject by profiling a select number of towns with interesting tales. Ceasar's *Forgotten Communities of Central Michigan* (1978) focuses on Clinton, Gratiot, and Ingham counties. Online sources include:

- The Ghost Towns Web site <www.ghosttowns.com>
- MI-GHOSTTOWNS-L <lists.rootsweb.com/index/usa/MI/misc.html> is a mailing list for anyone with either a genealogical or historical interest in Michigan ghost towns
- Macomb County Extinct Towns, Railroad Stops, and Place Name Changes <www.libcoop.net/mountclemens/placename.htm> focuses on this southeastern Michigan county

Paper Towns: Unlike ghost towns, some towns were never established and merely existed on paper. Land speculators in the 1800s drew up town plans; divided their land tract into lots; created maps with drawings of homes, schools, and churches that didn't exist; advertised the towns; and even sold "city" lots – often at inflated prices – in an effort to draw settlers to their land holdings. "Many of them, on investigation, turned out to be a hollow stump in some deserted area miles from civilization."[51] Ingham County's Biddle City is an example of this sort of venture. Two men created the paper town in 1835 at the junction of the Grand and Red Cedar rivers. They then traveled to Lansing, New York, and sold lots located in the fictional community. In 1837, 16 New York farmers came to Michigan, expecting to find a thriving settlement. "Upon reaching their new homes, they found a heavily wooded, flooded area. To their further disappointment, the land they had purchased was owned by others."[52] Some of the individuals settled elsewhere in Michigan, while others returned to New York.

Michigan's Court System

Court records can be a rich source of genealogical information. Matters brought before the courts include both civil (private) and criminal (public) complaints.

> Criminal actions deal with the bringing of public offenders to justice. Crimes are defined and punishments are established by statute. Civil actions deal primarily with the protection of individual rights, and most civil actions have two parties (plaintiff and defendant) opposed to each other for the recovery of a right or the redress of a wrong, which the plaintiff claims to have suffered because of the acts of the defendant. It should be noted, however, that non-adversary proceedings, such as name changes, naturalizations, adoptions, and the like, may also have significant genealogical importance.[53]

Courts also deal with matters of probate, including appointing guardians for orphans and administrators for estates, ordering inventories and appraisements, and settling estates. There have been several courts of record in Michigan, including the Supreme Court, District Courts, Courts of Chancery, Circuit

Courts, Probate Courts, County Courts, and Justices' Courts. Some of these courts continue to this day, while others are defunct.

Supreme Court: The Supreme Court of Michigan was established in 1805, the same year that Michigan became a territory. The court's first session was held on 29 July 1805, and sessions were held at Detroit, the capital of the territory. "This court at first had original and exclusive jurisdiction in all cases involving the title to land, criminal cases punishable capitally, and cases of divorce and alimony; afterwards, of all cases beyond the jurisdiction of inferior courts, all cases wherein the United States was a party and all actions of ejectment," a lawsuit brought to remove someone who unlawfully occupied and claimed title to real property.[54] The supreme court also was required to hear appeals from lower courts in the territory. During the British occupation of Michigan during the War of 1812, the supreme court did not meet. After the war, cases that had been started before the war were abated.[55]

Michigan's 1835 State Constitution also provided for a supreme court. "It was given essentially the same powers, except chancery, that the supreme court and superior circuit courts of the territory exercised."[56] The supreme court was required to hold sessions at Detroit, Ann Arbor, and Kalamazoo. Starting in 1873, all sessions of the court were to be held in Lansing.

District Courts: In 1805, Michigan Territory was divided into four judicial districts: Detroit, Erie, Huron, and Michilimackinac. Judges of the supreme court were to preside over three districts courts – one each for Erie and Michilimackinac and one for Detroit and Huron. District courts were to have jurisdiction over "demands exceeding $20."[57] This district court system was abolished in 1810, and another district court system was set up in 1840 with the creation of the Wayne County District Court. In 1843, district courts also were established for Oakland, Washtenaw, and Jackson counties, but all four courts were dropped in 1846. The State Constitution of 1850 "provided that the counties of the Upper Peninsula and the islands appertaining thereto should constitute a separate judicial district," but this court was abolished in 1863.[58] Today's district court system was created in 1968 to replace the justice of the peace courts and circuit court commissioners.[59]

Justice Courts: In 1805, justices of the peace were given jurisdiction over "all claims or penalties not exceeding $20."[60] When an early district court system was abolished in 1810, justices were given jurisdiction to try all civil cases with claims less than $100. Later, this limit was raised to $300, and justices also were allowed to try criminal cases in which the fine did not exceed $100 or imprisonment in the county jail did not exceed three months.[61] "Each justice was legally required to keep a single-volume record of his work and to pass it to his successor when his term ended."[62] The district court system, created in 1968, replaced the justice of the peace courts.

County Courts: In 1815, an act was passed establishing county courts. However, at that time Wayne County was the only county in the territory, and the District of Michilimackinac was exempted from the act. County courts had jurisdiction in matters exceeding the jurisdiction of the justices' courts but not exceeding claims of $1,000.[63]

County courts in all the counties east of Lake Michigan were abolished in 1833, but the county court system in Wayne County continued until Michigan became a state. A new county court system was set up in 1846 for the counties of Wayne, Oakland, Washtenaw, and Jackson, but these were abolished in 1850.[64]

Probate Courts: In 1818, a court of probate was established in each county to probate estates. This court system continued when Michigan became a state. In certain cases, appeals could be made to the circuit or supreme court, but appeals only could be made to the circuit court after 1846. Michigan's State Constitution of 1909 also gave probate court jurisdiction over "all cases of juvenile delinquents and dependents."[65] (See below for more on probate records.)

Circuit Courts and Superior Circuit Courts: The establishment of circuit courts date back to 1824 when the three judges of the supreme court "were required to hold an annual term in each of the counties of Wayne, Monroe, Oakland, Macomb, and Saint Clair and were authorized to hold special sessions in Crawford, Brown, and Michilimackinac counties."[66] The next year, in 1825, circuit courts were established by name and were given the power to hear civil actions at law with demands in excess of $1,000, actions of ejectment, capital and non-capital criminal cases, and other cases not within the jurisdiction of other courts.

County courts in all of the counties east of Lake Michigan, except Wayne, were abolished in 1833. In their place, the Circuit Court of the Territory of Michigan was established. This circuit court was given jurisdiction over both chancery and common law cases and both criminal and civil cases. The early circuit courts were now known as superior circuit courts.

After Michigan became a state, the state was divided into three circuits, and the circuit courts had the same power as the territorial circuit courts, except in matters of chancery. When the chancery courts were abolished in 1846, matters of chancery also became the jurisdiction of circuit courts. Through the years, additional circuits were created, bringing the number of circuit courts to 40 by 1915. Today there are 57 circuit courts, divided along county lines, with some circuits covering more than one county.

Courts of Chancery: When Michigan became a state, equity or chancery and common law jurisdiction was "separated and vested in distinct courts."[67] Courts of chancery handled equity cases, those cases in which the rights of two parties conflicted. The courts of chancery heard cases in the circuits established at that time. The Revised Statutes of 1846 abolished the courts of chancery.

Municipal Courts: As early as 1909, many Michigan cities began to have municipal courts. They had jurisdiction over city ordinance violations, criminal jurisdiction formerly held by the justice courts, and civil jurisdiction in cases not exceeding $1,500. The act creating the district court system in 1968 abolished all but a few of the municipal courts.[68]

Court of Appeals: Established in 1963, the court of appeals hears both civil and criminal cases brought to it from lower courts. "Typical cases involve the constitutionality of a local tax, redistricting of the state legislature, medical malpractice, the issuance of bingo licenses, illegal search-and-seizure, product liability, assisted suicide, public liability in high-speed police chases, minimum-sentencing laws, utility rates set by the State Public Service Commission, the instructions given to a jury in a murder case or campaign finance laws."[69] Between 1975 and 1994 the court also heard appeals of guilty pleas in felony cases. Three-judge panels hear cases in Lansing, Detroit, Grand Rapids, and Marquette.[70]

Court of Claims: Established in 1979 as a function of the Judicial Circuit Court in Ingham County, the court of claims hears cases involving claims against the state or any of its departments, commissions, or institutions.[71]

Probate Law and Records

Michigan's probate law predates the establishment of its probate court system in 1818. "An Act Concerning Wills and Intestacies," passed 4 September 1805, specified that wills were to be recorded in the office of the clerk of the court of the district. The act also gave the district courts, any judge of the territory, or any clerk of the district court "power to take the proof of a will and grant a certificate of such probate." Distribution of an estate was not to be made until nine months after the death. If someone died without a will, then the estate was to go to the person's spouse. If there was no spouse, then the estate was to be distributed to "such as are next entitled to distribution, and are approved by the court or person granting the same."

An 1809 act specified that wills could be made by any person of legal age, which was 21 for men and 18 for women. Individuals could will their possessions "to and among his or her children, or otherwise, as he or she shall think fit." Other laws specified how estates were to be distributed when someone died without a will. For example, real estate was to go to a man's children or other blood kin; his widow was denied a share of his estate. Widows could have a portion of her husband's personal property, but most of it went to his children or other blood relatives. (See the section on Women and the Law below.)

Records: Probate records are the court records that deal with the distribution of an estate after an owner's death. Probate records include wills, bonds of executors or administrators, executor and administrator accounts or reports, inventories of personal property, appraisements, sale accounts, and more. The records also may include guardianship appointments. In Michigan, probate records before 1818 may be found in district court records, and after 1818 they may be found with probate court records. Many of Michigan's early probate records have been forwarded to the State Archives of Michigan or its regional depositories. These are inventoried in Archival Circular No. 6: Probate Court Records <www.michigan.gov/documents/mhc_sa_circular06_49689_7.pdf>. Some probate records, such as Druse and LeDuc's *Abstracts of the Early Probate*

Records of Ingham County, Michigan, 1838-1869 (1980), have been published. Others, such as the Delta County Probate Index, 1873-1975 <www.grandmastree.com/society/probate/probate_index.htm>, are available online.

Locations of Other Court Records

In addition to probate records, court records deal with a variety of matters, including naturalization (see Chapter 2 for more), divorce (see Chapter 3 for more), adoption, name changes, land transactions, taxation, and other civil matters as well as criminal cases. Court records include dockets (chronological abstracts of court actions and judgments), minutes (brief notes of court proceedings), court orders (full reports of court proceedings), and more.

Court records may be found in the office of the clerk of the court. Many circuit court records, for example, may be found with county clerks. Many older records have been microfilmed by the Family History Library and are available through Family History Centers. Some court records have been forwarded to the State Archives of Michigan or other repositories in the state. Circular No. 37: Circuit Court Records <www.michigan.gov/documents/mhc_sa_circular37_49972_7.pdf> describes the circuit court records on file at the State Archives. Some court records have been published. Examples include the following:

- The six-volume *Transactions of the Supreme Court of the Territory of Michigan* (1935-1940) summarizes the cases heard before that court between 1805 and 1836. The volumes are indexed and include information on naturalization proceedings and divorces.
- *Unreported Opinions of the Supreme Court of Michigan, 1836-1843* (1945) covers the early years of Michigan's statehood.
- Douglass' two volumes *Reports of Cases Argued and Determined in the Supreme Court of the State of Michigan* (1878), also known as *Douglass' Michigan Reports,* cover cases brought before the court between the January term 1843 and the January term 1847.
- The more than 450 volumes of *Michigan Reports: Cases Decided in the Supreme Court of Michigan* (1878-present) summarize cases brought before the state's Supreme Court, beginning with the January term of 1847. Volumes are indexed by subject, and the Table of Cases at the front of each book lists the cases alphabetically. However, there are no surname indexes. *Michigan Reports* can be found in large libraries, including law and university libraries.
- *Reports of Cases Determined in the Court of Chancery of the State of Michigan* (1845), also known as *Harrington's Chancery Reports,* contains all the decisions (that have been preserved) made by Elon Farnsworth between his appointment in 1836 and March 1842.
- *Reports of Cases Argued and Determined in the Court of Chancery of the State of Michigan* (1845), also known as *Walker's Chancery Reports,* covers cases heard by Chancellor Randolph Manning between June 1842 and March 1845.

- The more than 200 volumes of *Michigan Appeals Reports: Cases Decided in the Michigan Court of Appeals* (1967-present) are similar to *Michigan Reports,* except that they deal with cases heard before the state's Court of Appeals. Volume 1 begins with 1965.

A Word About Women and the Law

Married women in early Michigan had few rights; upon marriage their legal and financial status was essentially merged with the husband's. A married woman, for example, could not own property in her own name, even if she had owned it prior to marriage or had inherited it during marriage.

> Before 1844, the only situation in which a woman could regain the property she had brought into a marriage was in the case of a divorce awarded to her on the grounds of her husband's adultery. Even after her husband's death, a wife did not regain the property she had brought to the marriage unless it was willed to her by her husband.[72]

In 1844, however, Michigan was among the first states to pass an act to define and protect the rights of married women. Public Act 66, passed 11 March 1844, gave women limited control over property they had owned prior to marriage or had inherited during marriage. A women could not, however, "give, grant, or sell" her property without her husband's permission.[73] Public Act 168 of 1855 gave married women the right to contract, sell, transfer, mortgage, convey, devise, or bequeath their property "in the same manner and with the like effect as if she were unmarried."[74]

In the early 19th century – from 1811 to 1846 – the widow of a Michigan man who died without a will "inherited only a third of his personal property (or half if there were no children), and none of his real estate."[75] Even if the man had no children, his real estate descended to his other blood relatives – not his wife. If there were no blood relatives, his real estate reverted to the territory or state.

> Until 1846, therefore, a widow shared in any of her husband's real estate and in more than a third of his personal property only if he expressly granted her the privilege in his will. In 1846 the law was altered so that if there were no children to inherit, the estate passed to the widow for her use during her lifetime, after which it reverted to the husband's blood kin. Only if no blood kin were living at the time of the husband's death did his estate pass in full to his widow.[76]

It wasn't until 1909 that a widow was guaranteed a share of her husband's estate if he died intestate. "She received a third of his estate, his children two-thirds. If there were no children, the widow divided the estate evenly with her husband's parents."[77]

A married woman's earnings also belonged to her husband. It wasn't until 1911 with the passage of Public Act 196 that married women had the right to keep their own earnings.

Adoptions

Early adoptions in Michigan – like those in other states – were often informal; family members, friends, or neighbors took in children in need of parents. In some cases, female relatives "claimed the right to raise motherless children," even if the father was still alive and had legal custody, and "mothers assumed the right to 'bequeath' their children to relatives."[78] Some adoptions, however, were economically motivated. Some children, for example, may have been adopted for their value as laborers.

Nationwide, early adoption law developed to provide "a legal heir for the adoptive parent."[79] The first such law in Michigan was Public Act 26 of 1861, which established a method for adoptive parents to change the names of their adopted children and to make them their heirs. First, the law required the individual or individuals adopting a minor child to have permission from the child's surviving parent or parents for the adoption. If the child was an orphan, permission could be granted by the child's nearest of kin, principal officer of an orphan asylum, two superintendents of the poor, or "any authorized officers or agent of any institution, public or private, in this State or elsewhere, in whose care such orphan child may have been." If the child was older than 7 years, then the child also had to give his or her permission.

The law then directed the adoptive parent(s) and the person(s) giving permission for the adoption to write a statement declaring that the child had been adopted and the adoptive parent(s) intended to make the child "his, her, or their heir." The statement was to list the child's birth name and the new name the adoptive parent(s) desired the child to have. The statement was to be "acknowledged before any officer authorized by law to take acknowledgments of deeds" and later filed with the judge of probate in the county of residence of the adoptive parent(s).

The probate judge, if satisfied of the "good faith of such proceeding," was to enter an order in the journal of the probate court stating that the adoptive parents were now the legal parents of the child, and the judge was to list the new name of the adopted child.

Similar laws for adopting and changing the names of children were passed in 1887 and 1891, but the 1891 law also required the judge of probate to investigate the home of the adoptive parent(s) for "good moral character, and the ability to support and educate such child, and of the suitableness of the home."[80] Michigan was the first state in the nation to pass such a law requiring judicial review of the intended home for the adopted child.[81]

Starting in 1933, Michigan required records of adoption also to be filed with the State Department of Health. Public Act 105 of 1933 specified that the adoption record was to include the "new name of the child, the name of the foster parents, and the date and place of birth as nearly as may be known," but it was not to refer to the birth parents.[82] These adoption records were to be filed with the birth records of the state, and certified copies were to be issued upon request.

In 1945, adoption records were sealed. Public Act 324 of 1945 required all books, papers, and records of adoption proceedings to be kept in a separate file that was not to be open to inspection or copy except under court order. Adoption records remain sealed in Michigan today. However, the law allows the state's Family Independence Agency and courts to release certain "non-identifying" information to adult adoptees, biological parents, adult biological siblings, and adoptive parents of a minor child. This non-identifying information includes:

- Date, time, and place of birth of the adoptee, including the hospital, city, county, and state
- Description of the adoptee and the adoptee's birth family, including given first name of adoptee at birth and age and gender of sibling(s) of the adoptee

Identifying information includes the name of the child before adoption, the name of the biological parents before the termination of their parental rights, the names of biological siblings at the time of the termination, and the most recent name and address of each biological parent. Release of identifying information to the adult adoptee is handled differently, depending on when the rights of the biological parent(s) were terminated and whether the birth parents have filed statements of denial or consent with the Central Adoption Registry. The CAR is a file, maintained by the state's Family Independence Agency, with statements of consent or denial from biological parents or adult biological siblings about whether they want information about themselves released to adult adoptees who are searching for information about their birth families.

If the parental rights were terminated before 28 May 1945 or after 12 September 1980, adopt adoptees can obtain their name at birth and the names of their biological siblings at the time of the termination of parental rights as long as the birth parents have not filed a statement of denial with CAR. In addition, adoptees also can obtain identifying information about any birth parent that has not filed a statement of denial.

For adoptions that occurred on or after 28 May 1945 or before 12 September 1980, adult adoptees can obtain their name at birth, the names of their biological siblings at the time parental rights were terminated, and identifying information on both birth parents as long as both parents have filed statements of consent with CAR. If one parent has filed a statement of consent, adult adoptees can obtain their given name at birth, the names of their biological siblings at the time parental rights were terminated, and identifying information on the parent filing the statement of consent. In addition, adult adoptees can obtain the name of a birth parent that is deceased. For more information on the Central Adoption Registry or the release of identifying or non-identifying information, visit the Web site for Michigan's Family Independence Agency <www.michigan.gov/fia/> or MichiganSearching Online <www.michigansearching.com/>. (See Chapter 7 for information on orphanages and orphan train riders.)

7 Digging Deeper

Original papers, manuscripts, and business, institutional and legislative records can yield valuable genealogical data. However, many of these sources can be difficult to use or hard to locate, and it sometimes takes many hours of painstaking research to unearth worthwhile information. Generally, researchers should not dig into these resources until more traditional sources have been exhausted.

Manuscript Collections

Collections of unpublished manuscripts and papers relating to Michigan can be found in several libraries and archives in Michigan, including Bentley Historical Library in Ann Arbor <www.umich.edu/~bhl>, Burton Historical Collections in Detroit <www.detroit.lib.mi.us/burton/burton_index.htm>, Clarke Historical Library in Mount Pleasant <clarke.cmich.edu/>, Grand Rapids Public Library in Grand Rapids <www.grapids.lib.mi.us>, the Joint Archives of Holland <www.hope.edu/resources/arc>, the Library of Michigan in Lansing <www.michigan.gov/hal>, Michigan Technological University Archives and Copper Country Historical Collections in Houghton <www.lib.mtu.edu/mtuarchives/guide.aspx>, the State Archives of Michigan in Lansing <www.michigan.gov/hal>, Walter P. Reuther Library in Detroit <www.reuther.wayne.edu>, and the Western Michigan University Archives and Regional History Collection in Kalamazoo <www.wmich.edu/library/archives/>.

The types of records to be found in manuscript collections include genealogical notes and charts; diaries and memoirs; insurance, church, and school records; correspondence; photographs; scrapbooks and clippings; legal and business documents; and more. Generally, these are records created by individuals and private institutions. However, archives – especially the State Archives of Michigan – may have official public records, such as those usually found in county courthouses.

Guides have been written about several of these collections. These include Sprenger's *Guide to the Manuscripts in the Burton Historical Collection Detroit Public Library* (1985); Browne and Johnson's *A Guide to the State Archives of Michigan: State Records* (1977); *Guide to the Western Michigan University Regional History Collections* (1998); and *The Joint Archives of Holland: Guide to the Collections Holland Historical Trust, Hope College, Western Theological Seminary* (1989).

National and international databases that catalog manuscript holdings of archives and libraries include National Union Catalog of Manuscript Collections (NUCMC), National Inventory of Documentary Sources (NIDS), and Research Libraries Information Network (RLIN). Started in 1959, NUCMC "is a free-of-charge cooperative cataloging program operated by the Library of Congress."[1] NUCMC <www.loc.gov/coll/nucmc/nucmc.html> volumes were published annually between 1959 and 1993. These 29 printed volumes feature descriptions of more than 72,000 collections located in more than 1,400 repositories, including many from Michigan. The printed volumes of NUCMC (also available on microfilm) can be found in the reference department of many college and university libraries and large public libraries. The two-volume *Index to Personal Names in the National Union Catalog of Manuscript Collections, 1959-1984* (1987) and the three-volume *Index to Subjects and Corporate Names in the National Union Catalog of Manuscript Collections, 1959-1984* (1994) are valuable keys to unlocking this source.

In 1986, NUCMC began using Research Libraries Group (RLG) database, a nationwide database, to produce its published catalog. The RLG database has all NUCMC records since 1986. The NUCMC/RGL database can be searched online <lcweb.loc.gov/coll/nucmc/rlinsearch.html> for free.

NIDS is available on microfiche and CD-ROM, and RLIN <www.rlg.org/> is accessed at participating libraries. ArchivesUSA <archives.chadwyck.com/> is a subscription-based service, available in some libraries, that has more than 90,000 NUCMC records and more than 54,000 NIDS records. An excellent article describing the use of these three databases is Bell, Dwyer, and Henderson's article, "Finding Manuscript Collections: NUCMC, NIDS, and RLIN," published in the September 1989 issue of the *National Genealogical Society Quarterly.*

Though many collections are available for viewing only at the archives at which they are housed, some collections have been microfilmed and are available through interlibrary loan or from Family History Centers. Some collections can be found online. American Memory <memory.loc.gov/ammem/amhome.html>, for example, offers more than seven million digital items from more than 100 historical collections. Items in some collections relate to Michigan. Smaller organizations, such as the Shepherd Area Historical Society (Isabella County) <www.mifamilyhistory.org/isabella/isaobit.html>, may have placed some of their collections online. (See Chapter 9 for more details on online sources.)

Business Records

Business records may have information about employees; these records may be found with the business or they may be found in manuscript collections. Unfortunately, few companies between 1880 and 1930 "saved their records or offered them to archives."[2] Earlier records can be difficult to find as well. However, there are some exceptions.

Fur Trade: The French Canadian men who guided and paddled the canoes of the fur trade were known as "voyageurs," the French word for "travelers." The voyageurs signed labor contracts, known as engagements because the employee engaged "to labor for an employer for an agreed upon wage for a specific time span."[3] The voyageur or employee who signed an engagement was known as an "engagé," and the person who usually prepared the engagement was a notary. These engagements included the name of the voyageur and the names of the voyageur's parents, if he was a minor. Engagements also may include the names of witnesses, the residences of the voyageurs, and their occupations.

Both the French and British issued permits to fur traders to control the fur trade. These permits were known as "conges" during the French period and licenses during the British period. ("Coureur de bois" were fur traders who went into the wilderness without a license.) These permits usually included "the name of the official issuing the permit, the name of the person receiving it, the names of voyageurs in the canoes, the number of canoes, the destination, the cargo, the date issued, and the date registered."[4] Financial records of the fur trade also may include the name of employees.

Original manuscript materials relating to voyageurs and the fur trade can be found in the Archives nationale du Québec a Montreal <www.anq.gouv.qc.ca/>, the Library and Archives of Canada <www.collectionscanada.ca/>, Hudson Bay Company Archives <www.gov.mb.ca/chc/archives/hbca/about/hbca.html>, the Burton Historical Collection, the Minnesota Historical Society Collection <www.mnhs.org/index.htm>, and the State Historical Society of Wisconsin <www.wisconsinhistory.org/>. Some of the materials have been abstracted, indexed, and published. For example, Russell's *Michigan Voyageurs* (1982) lists more than 800 engagés from Samuel Abbott's Mackinac Notary Book, 1806 to 1818. However, these men were not necessarily local Mackinac men; they "were going from Mackinac to some point within the United States to spend the winter."[5] DuLong's article, "Engagements: Guide to Fur Trade Employment Contracts, 1670-1821," in the July 1989 issue of *Michigan's Habitant Heritage,* lists many other published sources. Nute's *The Voyageur,* originally published in 1931, includes much information about the voyageur's way of life.

Great Lakes Shipping: Several Web sites feature information about Great Lakes shipping. Downward Bound <www.mfhn.com/glsdb/> is devoted to those who worked in the Great Lakes Shipping trade. The site includes message boards, photographs, an index of articles found in the journal, *Inland Seas,* and more. It also includes information about the GLSHIPS-L mailing list. Historical Collections of the Great Lakes <www.bgsu.edu/colleges/library/hcgl/>, a site maintained by Bowling Green State University, includes the Great Lakes Ports and Personnel Online Databases. Maritime History of the Great Lakes <www.hhpl.on.ca/GreatLakes/> features a database of newspaper articles, including some from Detroit. Several hundred biographies of ship captains, found in Mansfield's *History of the Great Lakes* (1899), are online at the Ship Captain Biography Index <linkstothepast.com/

marine>. The Great Lakes Ship Masters Database <www.mifamilyhistory.org/glsdb/glship_index.htm> lists nearly 3,000 shipmasters.

Lumbering: According to John Cumming, former director of Clarke Historical Library, records of lumbering companies are rich – yet untapped – sources of genealogical information.[6] Clarke Historical Library in Mount Pleasant, Burton Historical Collections at Detroit Public Library, and Michigan Historical Collections at Bentley Historical Library in Ann Arbor are among those that have records of lumbering companies in their manuscript collections. These records may include correspondence, names of employees, and transactions between buyers and sellers. Online sources of lumbering records include:

- Abstracts from the ledgers of Alpena County's David McNeil Lumber Camp <www.rootsweb.com/~mialpena/HistDoc/david.htm>
- 1920 census of the Hebard Lumber Camp in Baraga County <www.genealogia.fi/emi/emi71me.htm>
- Logging in Muskegon – the Ryerson Family <www.rootsweb.com/~mimuskeg/Ryerson.html>
- Lumbering in the Fremont Area (Newaygo County) <www.rootsweb.com/~minewayg/fmtlumb.htm>

In addition, MILUMBERDAYS-L is a mailing list <lists.rootsweb.com/index/usa/MI/misc.html#MILUMBERDAYS> for those with a genealogical interest in Michigan's lumber industry.

Mining: Mining company records at Michigan Technological University's Copper County Historical Collections include personnel records, such as employment and medical information. MTU's Mining Company Collections <www.lib.mtu.edu/mtuarchives/overview.aspx#l7>, dates back to the 1840s and has records from three of the larger companies in the area: the Copper Range Company, the Quincy Mining Company <www.lib.mtu.edu/mtuarchives/ms001/ms001-intro.aspx>, the Calumet & Hecla Consolidated Mining Company, and others. The library has placed a Guide to Researching Copper Mining Companies online <www.lib.mtu.edu/mtuarchives/miningcompanyhistory.aspx>. Other sources of information about mining and mining records include:

- Archives of the Cleveland Cliffs Iron Mining Company <www.nmu.edu/olsonlibrary/archives/CCIintro.dwt>
- Calumet: Polish Miners in Michigan <mipolonia.net/calumet/calumet.htm>
- Collections at the State Archives of Michigan <www.michigan.gov/documents/mhc_sa_circular25_49722_7.pdf>
- A searchable database of Cornish miners who worked at the Calumet Hecla Mine <www.mifamilyhistory.org/ross_coll/>
- Michigan Technological University Mining History Links <www.mg.mtu.edu/hist.htm>
- Reports of County Mine Inspectors (see the Mining Accidents section in this chapter)

Labor Archives: The Walter P. Reuther Library at Wayne State University is home to the Archives of Labor and Urban Affairs. Among its holdings is a large collection of labor union newspapers. The Labor Archives of the Upper Peninsula <www.nmu.edu/www-sam/ais/archives/laborrecords.htm> is located at Northern Michigan University, and the University of Michigan-Flint Labor History Project <lib.umflint.edu/archives/labor.html> is located at the university's Genesee Historical Collections Center.

State Archives Collections: The State Archives of Michigan has a collection of business records that includes reports, minutes, daybooks, ledgers, and more. This collection is described in Circular No. 38: Business Records <www.michigan.gov/documents/mhc_sa_circular38_49970_7.pdf>. In addition, the State Archives has lists of licensed professionals in a number of occupations, including auctioneers, merchants, and peddlers. This collection is described in Circular No. 21: Licensed Professions <www.michigan.gov/documents/mhc_sa_circular21_49711_7.pdf>.

Lighthouses: With more than 3,200 miles of shoreline, it shouldn't come as a surprise that Michigan has more lighthouses than any other state in the United States. Today, more than 100 lighthouses dot Michigan's coastlines or are located on islands in the Great Lakes. Between 1825 – when the first lighthouse was completed – and 1983 – when the last manually operated lighthouse was automated – lighthouse keepers kept the lights lit throughout the night to warn ships away from rocks and other dangers. Originally, lighthouse keepers were political appointees; by 1896, they became members of the federal civil service. "In 1939, when the Lighthouse Service became a part of the U.S. Coast Guard, keepers who were then working had a choice of either retaining their civilian status or becoming members of the Coast Guard. After 1939 all newly employed individuals who worked with Great Lakes navigational aids were members of the Coast Guard."[7] There are several sources of information about lighthouse keepers:

- The National Archives <www.archives.gov/research_room/genealogy/research_topics/lighthouse_records.html> has many records about lighthouses and lighthouse keepers. Registers of Lighthouse Keepers, 1845-1912, for example, includes the names of lighthouse keepers and their assistants, their dates of appointment, location of the lighthouses, annual salaries, dates of resignation or discharge or death, and in some cases, places of birth. Michigan information is found in volume four of the six-reel set of microfilm. The Library of Michigan also has a copy of this microfilm.
- Great Lakes Lighthouse Research <home.att.net/~tatag/> maintains databases about Great Lakes Lighthouses and their keepers.
- Great Lakes Lighthouse Keepers Association <www.gllka.com/> has published *Living at a Lighthouse: Oral Histories from the Great Lakes* (1987). The book has excerpts from 10 interviews conducted between April 1985 and March 1986 as part of the organization's oral history project. The audiotapes

from the project were indexed and donated to the Wayne State University Folklore Archives, and a copy was given to the Lake Michigan Maritime Museum in South Haven. An *Index to the Great Lakes Lighthouse Keepers Association Oral History Tape Collection* (1986) also has been published.

- Clarke Historical Library's online exhibit "Beacons Shining in the Night: The Lighthouses of Michigan" <clarke.cmich.edu/lighthouses/index.htm> has much information about Michigan lighthouses.
- Lighthouse Getaway's Great Lakes Lighthouses <lighthousegetaway.com/lights/g_lakes.html> includes pictures and information about Michigan lighthouses.
- There are numerous books about lighthouses. Clifford's *Women Who Kept the Lights: An Illustrated History of Female Lighthouse Keepers* (2001), for example, includes a list of female lighthouse keepers in Michigan.
- The September-October 2003 issue of *Michigan History* magazine includes a list of the 49 female lighthouse keepers and assistant keepers in Michigan. The list includes the names of the lighthouses where they served and their dates of service.[8]

Institutional Records

Schools and Universities: Michigan was an early leader in education. In 1817, the territorial government passed an act setting up a complete system of education under centralized control. However, few schools were established under this plan, and in 1827 the territorial council abandoned the centralized concept and passed a law permitting townships to maintain schools. This law was similar to one passed in Massachusetts in 1647. "It provided that the citizens of any township having 50 householders should provide themselves with a school teacher, of good moral character, 'to teach the children to read and to instruct them in the English or French language as well as arithmetic, orthography, and decent behavior.'"[9] Townships with 200 householders were to hire a teacher who could teach Latin, English, and French. Other laws were passed in 1829 and 1833, but they "were not rigidly enforced, and most of the actual teaching during the territorial period was done in private schools opened for various lengths of time and then abandoned."[10]

Michigan's first state Constitution, adopted in 1835, established the office of Superintendent of Public Instruction, "the first state constitutional office of its kind in the United States."[11] A state school fund, resulting from the profits of the sale of Section 16 in each township, also was set up. For at least three months out of the year, schools were to be conducted. "By 1860 a total of 4,087 school districts had been formed in Michigan, and the number of teachers was 7,921. Even though not all schools were free, 75 percent of the children between the ages of 4 and 18 attended the public schools in 1860."[12]

A mandatory school attendance law, passed in 1871, required children between the ages of 8 and 14 to attend at least 12 weeks of school each year, including six consecutive weeks. This requirement was extended to four months in 1883. In

1905 the law changed again, requiring children between the ages of 7 and 16 to attend school for the entire academic year.

In 1841, the University of Michigan opened at Ann Arbor; by 1867, it was the largest university in the nation, with an enrollment of 1,255. In 1853, Michigan State Normal School (later Eastern Michigan University) opened at Ypsilanti as the state's first teachers' college. It also was the first state teachers' college west of New York. Just two years later, in 1855, Michigan Agricultural College (now Michigan State University) was established 10 miles east of Lansing, now East Lansing. In 1862, it received a grant of 240,000 acres from the U.S. government for the use or support of the college, making it the nation's oldest "land grant" college. It was also the first agricultural college in the nation.

Early private institutions of higher education included Kalamazoo College, formerly known as the Michigan and Huron Institute and Kalamazoo Literary Institute. It opened in 1836. Albion College, formerly Wesleyan Seminary, opened in 1842.

In 1852, Michigan Central College (now Hillsdale College) graduated its first female student. The college was the second in the nation to admit women. Both men and women attended Michigan State Normal School from the beginning, and female students were admitted to Michigan Agricultural College and the University of Michigan in 1870.[13]

The state opened the Michigan School for the Deaf in 1848 in Flint, and the Michigan School for the Blind opened in Lansing in 1880.

Native American Education: Prior to the mid-1800s, religious groups offered education to Native Americans, some through church-operated boarding schools. In 1857, the U.S. government granted the Mackinac Agency authority over Indian education in the State of Michigan. The Mackinac Agency was controlled by the Mission Society of the Methodist Episcopal Church.[14] Since the government's goal was to assimilate Native Americans, U.S. Interior Department officials thought it logical to entrust the education of Native Americans to church officials who would teach "the values of a culture based on a belief in one God, the inherent good of manual labor, and obedience, and personal accumulation of material wealth."[15] The Mackinac Agency set up a system of day schools which met from 9 a.m. to 4 p.m. weekdays to teach reading, writing, spelling, and arithmetic. By 1863, the Mackinac Agency had 30 day schools near Indian villages or reservations. After the Civil War, the Mackinac Agency day schools were often superior to public schools, leading "many white parents ... to send their children to Indian schools."[16]

However, government officials thought the schools a failure because they did not assimilate most Native American children. In the early 1880s, the government closed most day schools, expecting Native American youth to attend public schools. Many Native-American youths did not feel comfortable in the public school setting or were taunted by white children, and as a result, many parents withdrew their children from school. By 1887, the government had decided to open manual labor boarding schools. Three boarding schools were established in the state, and Native-American children were often taken from their families and sent to the following schools:

- The Catholic Otchippewa Boarding School at Baraga became a government contract school in 1888. It served the L'Anse and Vieux Desert bands of the Chippewa of Lake Superior.[17]
- Holy Childhood in Harbor Springs became a government contract school in 1889. It served Ottawa and Chippewa children.[18]
- The Bureau of Indian Affairs School at Mount Pleasant was owned and operated by the federal government from 1893 to 1933. It offered eight years of education and enrolled as many as 375 children on its 320-acre campus.[19]

After graduation from Michigan schools, many Native Americans continued their education at government schools located outside Michigan, including the Carlisle Indian Industrial School in Carlisle, Pennsylvania; Chilocco Training School in Chilocco, Oklahoma; the Genoa Government Indian School in Genoa, Nebraska; and Haskell Institute in Lawrence, Kansas. Some Native Americans who attended these schools did not move back to their homes in Michigan after graduation.

For more information on Native American education, see Clarke Historical Library's Native American Treaty Rights page <clarke.cmich.edu/indian/treatyeducation.htm> or Lesson 5 <hometown.aol.com/RoundSky/lesson5.html> of the Native American Research in Michigan Web site.

School records: School and university records include school board minutes, attendance records, school censuses, yearbooks, photographs, directories, newspapers and magazines, and applications for admission. They may be found in a variety of places, including the schools or universities, local libraries or archives, and university libraries and archives. Michigan sources for school and university records and information include the following:

- The State Archives of Michigan has school records, including school board minutes, attendance and grade books, and school directories, from at least 30 counties. The records are described in Circular No. 11: School Records 1 – Local Records <www.michigan.gov/documents/mhc_sa_circular11_49700_7.pdf>.
- The Library of Michigan has a collection of yearbooks, student directories, and other materials.
- Other public libraries in Michigan report having school yearbooks, school census records, and other school records. Researchers should check the library in the area of their interest to determine availability.
- Lists of schools, students, or teachers may be found in county or regional histories.
- Colleges and universities often have alumni associations that publish newspapers or bulletins with information about graduates.

- Colleges and universities also may publish alumni directories with information about former students. Some Michigan high schools also publish alumni directories.
- Records of the Mount Pleasant Indian School and Agency Student Case Files (1893 to 1946) are located at the Chicago branch of the National Archives <www.archives.gov/research_room/finding_aids/chicago/indian_school_files_rg75.html>.
- One Room Schools: Michigan's Educational Legacy <clarke.cmich.edu/schoolsintro.htm> is an online exhibit.
- Michigan Schools <www.rootsweb.com/~mivanbur/MichiganSchools.htm> lists one-room schools in the state.

Several Web sites feature school records. These include:

- Michigan Family History Network's Michigan School Records <www.mifamilyhistory.org/yearbooks/> features a database of more than 20,000 records from yearbooks and school censuses and also contains links to other sites with school records.
- DeadFred.com's School Annuals page <www.deadfred.com/annuals.html> has images from several Michigan yearbooks.
- Rootsweb.com's User-contributed Databases <userdb.rootsweb.com/regional.html#Michigan> have several lists of high school and university alumni.
- The Thirtieth Biennial Report of the Board of Trustees of the Michigan School of the Deaf (1911-1912) <www.memoriallibrary.com/MI/Genesee/Deaf/> lists the school's teachers and male and female students with their county of residence. It includes an all-name index.
- Mount Clemens (Macomb County) High School Yearbook Master Index <offserv.libcoop.net/mtc/mchsyearbook.asp>.
- Several MIGenWeb sites, including those for Ingham <www.rootsweb.com/~miingham/>, Isabella <www.mifamilyhistory.org/isabella/directories.htm> and Kent counties <www.rootsweb.com/~mikent/schools/index.html>, have school records

Poorhouses: The governor and judges of the Territory of Michigan passed the earliest law regarding the relief of paupers on 8 October 1805. "An Act for the Relief of the Poor" was modeled after laws in New Jersey. It allowed a pauper to petition three justices of the peace, "alleging that such person is destitute of support and is incapable of labor."[20] The justices were to investigate the claim and if they found it to be true, they could "grant to the pauper a certificate" and approve the pauper becoming a public charge. The law outlined a procedure for the marshal of the territory to "contract with the person offering the lowest terms for the support of such pauper; provided, that no contract be made for a greater sum than 25 cents for a day."

"An Act for the Support of the Poor," passed 1 February 1809, defined who was eligible for public support and set up the three-member panel known as the

Overseers of the Poor. This law was modeled after one in Vermont.[21] "An Act for the Relief of the Poor," passed 25 November 1817, allowed the children of the poor to be bound out to apprenticeships. This law repealed the 1805 act and was modeled after laws in Ohio.[22]

Further acts were passed in the next decade, but it wasn't until 1830 that the Legislative Council passed an act authorizing the establishment of poorhouses by county supervisors. The Wayne County Poorhouse, also known as Eloise, was established in 1832. It was the first county poorhouse in the state. (See the section on Eloise below.)

Public Act 148 of 1869 revised and consolidated all of the previous acts relating to the support and maintenance of the poor. Among its provisions, the law directed the county board of supervisors to select three Superintendents of the Poor, outlined the duties of these superintendents, set up a procedure for erecting a new county poorhouse, and required the education of pauper children between the ages of 5 and 18. After 1909, poorhouses or poor farms were renamed county infirmaries as required by Article VIII, Section 11 of the State Constitution of 1908. "Eventually all but one of the state's 83 counties built a poorhouse. ... In 1938 there were still 79 county infirmaries in Michigan, some with operating farms that had been the origin of the term 'poor farm.'"[23]

Unfortunately, not all poorhouse records have survived. In Van Buren County, for example, the poorhouse was established in 1866, but fire destroyed the building and records in 1884.[24] Patient Registers tend to be the best type of records for genealogical research, but other records may list patients by name. "For example, the cost of a coffin may be recorded in some sort of bookkeeping journal ... minutes of the Superintendent(s) may record the 'binding-out' (or indenturing) of children."[25]

Poorhouse records are available at the State Archives of Michigan. These records, detailed in Circular 22: Infirmaries, Sanatoria, Poor Homes <www.michigan.gov/documents/mhc_sa_circular22_49715_7.pdf>, include resident registers for Eaton County, 1859-1936; Gratiot County, 1886-1974; Ingham County, 1932-1937; Ionia County, 1876-1943; Isabella County, 1886-1948; Oceana County, 1887-1948; and Van Buren County, 1885-1905.

Abstracts of poorhouse records also have been published. They include the two-volume set, Benson's *Van Buren County Poorhouse/Infirmary Records: An Abstract of the Births, Deaths, Burials and General Register* (1995) and Sherman's *Index to Poor Farm Inmates, Iosco County, Michigan, 1874-1893* (1993). Some poorhouse records have been microfilmed and are available through Family History Centers. These include Kalamazoo County's Record of Inmates of the Poorhouse, 1885-1941, 1950 and Oceana County's Record of Inmates of the Poorhouse, 1887-1948.

The Poorhouse Story <www.poorhousestory.com/>, a clearinghouse for information about 19th century American poorhouses, has much information about Michigan poorhouses. The Web site includes photographs, historical notes, census records of poorhouse residents for various counties, lists of births and deaths at the Gratiot County Poor Farm, and a list of burials for the Shiawassee County Poor Farm.

Several other Web sites have poorhouse records and information. These include:

- Hillsdale County 1860 census of poor farm residents <www.rootsweb.com/~mihillsd/data/census/1860poorfarm.html>
- Isabella County Poor Farm Censuses <www.mifamilyhistory.org/isabella/poorfarm.htm>
- Kalamazoo County Poor Farm <www.rootsweb.com/~mikalama/countypoorhouse.htm>
- Index to Kent County's Maple Grove Poor Farm Record Book, 1895-1913, <www.rootsweb.com/~mikent/histories/poorfarm/bkindex.html>
- Mecosta County Poor House <www.rootsweb.com/~mimecost/mecostcoph.html>
- Oceana County Poor Farm, 1880 Census <www.rootsweb.com/~mioceana/1880CensusPoorFarm.htm>
- Sanilac County Poorhouse List, 1880 <www.poorhousestory.com/MI_SANILAC_1880Census.htm>

Mental Institutions: Prior to 1855, those in need of mental health care may have been sent to an institution in the East, such as the ones at Brattleboro, Vermont, or Utica, New York.[26] The Sisters at Saint Mary's Hospital in Detroit began to care for the mentally ill in 1855, and in 1860 they opened a separate facility, known as The Michigan State Retreat. This private institution was incorporated as Saint Joseph's Retreat in 1883.

Michigan's first state-sponsored mental health institution opened in 1859 in Kalamazoo as the Michigan Asylum for the Insane. Other state institutions included "Eastern Michigan Asylum at Pontiac, 1878; Northern Michigan Asylum at Traverse City, 1885; Michigan Asylum for Insane Criminals at Ionia, 1885; Michigan Home for Feebleminded and Epileptics at Lapeer, 1895; State Psychopathic Hospital at the University of Michigan, 1906; and the Michigan Farm Colony for Epileptics near Caro, 1914."[27] These asylums were renamed state hospitals by Michigan's Legislature in 1911.

The State Archives of Michigan has many early mental health records, including an index to individuals at Kalamazoo, 1859-1911; patient log books for Lapeer, 1895-1982; and a register of patients at Newberry, 1895-1910. However, Michigan law states that mental health patient records are closed to the public. According to the Archives Web site, "Academic Researchers who are not looking for records of a specific individual may contact the State Archives of Michigan at (517) 373-1415 to obtain a form entitled 'Contractual Agreement For The Release Of Confidential Mental Health Records For Legitimate Research Purposes.' This form can be completed and submitted for review and approval by the Department of Community Health."

Historic Asylums <www.historicasylums.com/>, which focuses on architectural preservation of historic mental health institutions, has much information about Michigan institutions.

A Word About "Eloise": The Wayne County Poorhouse, the first county poorhouse in the state, opened in 1832 at Gratiot and Mount Elliott Avenues in Hamtramck Township. It moved in 1839 to a new site on 280 acres in Nankin Township (now the City of Westland). Through the years it has been known by several names, including Wayne County House and Wayne County General Hospital and Infirmary, but the most common name associated with the complex is Eloise. This was the name of the post office in the facility, and the superintendents of the poor named the hospital after the post office in 1911.

"Eloise evolved into a self-supporting community with its own police and fire department, railroad and trolley stations, bakery, amusement hall, laundries, and a powerhouse. It even had a schoolhouse that was used for about 10 years."[28] In addition to being a poorhouse, Eloise also was a tuberculosis sanitarium, an infirmary and hospital, and a mental asylum. It accepted its first "insane" patients as early as 1841. Low-rent housing was available for staff, and about 20 percent of them lived on the grounds. "It was not uncommon for someone to meet his future spouse while working at Eloise and many children grew up on the grounds."[29]

The facility grew from 35 residents and 280 acres in 1839 to 902 acres, 75 buildings, and more than 10,000 patients, with the population peaking during the Great Depression. The last psychiatric patient left the facility in 1979, and the general hospital closed in 1984.[30] All but a few of the buildings have been demolished, and unfortunately most of Eloise's records were destroyed with the facility.[31] Tales of Eloise <www.talesofeloise.com/> is a Web site devoted to the complex and includes photos and other information about the facility, such as a searchable database of the names of insane patients as recorded in the 1860, 1870, 1900, and 1930 federal census reports. Histories of the institution include Keenan's *History of Eloise* (1913) and Ibbotson's *Eloise: Poorhouse, Farm, Asylum, and Hospital, 1839-1984* (2002).

Correctional Facilities: Michigan's first prison, the State Penitentiary at Jackson (then called Jacksonburgh in Jackson County) opened in 1839. It was modeled after a prison in Auburn, New York, and had individual cells for prisoners and space to work in groups during the day. The first building was wooden, but it was soon replaced with a structure that had stone walls. "A massive, medieval-like prison was built in the 1880s, which was replaced in the 1930s by a huge new facility which earned the dubious honor of being called the world's largest walled penal institution – it housed approximately 5,500 prisoners."[32] It has been known as the House of Correction, Michigan State Prison, Jackson State Prison, and since 1935 as the State Prison of Southern Michigan. The State House of Correction and Branch Prison at Marquette opened in 1889. The prisons at Jackson and Marquette were for men. "By about 1887 women convicted of felonies were sent to the Detroit House of Correction. Not until 1977 was a separate state prison for women opened near Ypsilanti."[33]

In 1877, the State House of Correction and Reformatory opened in Ionia for youthful first offenders. "Males between the ages of 16 and 25 who had been convicted of felonies were confined, employed, and disciplined here for purposes of punishment and reformation."[34] The institution's name was changed to the Michigan Reformatory in 1901.

In order to deal with an increase in juvenile crime and to stop imprisoning children in the Jackson prison, the House of Correction for Juvenile Offenders opened in Lansing in 1855. "Prior to 1861 youths of both sexes under 20 years of age were sentenced to it."[35] It was known by several names through the years: "Michigan State Reform School, 1859; Industrial School for Boys, 1893; Boys' Vocational School, 1925; and Boys' Training School, 1961."[36] The Michigan Reform School for Girls opened in Adrian in 1879. It housed girls between the ages of 7 and 20. It also had several name changes; after 1925, it was known as the Girls' Training School and later as the Adrian Training School.

Records for youthful offenders are closed, but most records relating to adults are open to the public. The State Archives of Michigan has records from the three major correctional facilities in Michigan: Ionia, Jackson, and Marquette. In addition, the State Archives has a prisoner index, 1839-1980. Arranged alphabetically by name, the index includes lengths and dates of sentences, identification numbers, and the counties where crimes occurred. It also may include escape attempts, paroles, or discharge dates. Some index cards have photographs of prisoners. This index also is available on microfilm through Family History Centers.

Additional prison records at the State Archives are described in Circular No. 3: Correctional Facilities <www.michigan.gov/documents/mhc_sa_circular03_49682_7.pdf>, and pardons, paroles, warrants, and extraditions are described in Circular No. 48 <www.michigan.gov/documents/mhc_sa_circular48_50005_7.pdf>. "Records of the Detroit House of Corrections from 1877 to 1983 are stored at the Burton Historical Collections in the Detroit Public Library."[37] Some criminal records also can be found online at the Skeletons in Michigan's Closets Web site <www.mifamilyhistory.org/skeletons/db_paging.asp>. Information about the history of Michigan prisons can be found on the Michigan Prison History page <www.ganginformation.com/myweb5/michiganprisonhistory.htm>.

Crimes and Criminals

"Throughout its history the Wolverine state produced a remarkable assortment of crooks and desperados, but Michigan's lumbering era bred outlaws, crime, and shady characters faster than Michigan swamps produce mosquitoes."[38] Northern Michigan rivaled – some would even say surpassed – the Wild West for its number of bandits and outlaws. Prohibition-era Detroit also had its share of violent gangs and mobsters.

Several books have been written about Michigan crime and criminals. These include Wakefield's *Butcher's Dozen: 13 Famous Michigan Murders* (1991); Powers' *Michigan Rogues, Desperados, Cut-throats* (2002); Barfknecht's *Murder, Michigan* (1983); Dodge's *Ticket to Hell: A Saga of Michigan's Bad Men* (1975); and Kavieff's *The Purple Gang: Organized Crime in Detroit 1910-1945* (2000) and *The Violent Years: Prohibition and The Detroit Mobs* (2001). Some information about crime and criminals, such as Pardons Granted by the Governor <www.rootsweb.com/~miingham/PardonsIndex.html>, can be found online.

The worst mass murder in Michigan history took place on 18 May 1927 in Clinton County's small town of Bath when a local resident bombed the Bath Consolidated School. "In all, 45 persons were killed, including 38 students and teachers."[39] The disaster in Bath is retold in Parker's *Mayday: The History of a Village Holocaust* (1980), Wilkins' *My Scrapbook on the Bath School Bombing of May 18th, 1927* (2002), and Hixson's article, "A May Day to Remember," published in the May-June 1999 issue of *Michigan History,* and the Bath School Disaster Web site <freepages.history.rootsweb.com/~bauerle/disaster.htm>.

Capital Punishment: Michigan abolished the death penalty for first-degree murder in 1846, becoming the first state in the United States – and the first government in the English-speaking world – to do so.[40] The last public hanging took place at Detroit on 24 September 1830. (A murderer was executed in Michigan on 8 July 1938, but his case fell under federal – rather than state – jurisdiction.) Chardavoyne's *A Hanging in Detroit* (2003) describes this final execution and also gives "a detailed account of farming, tavern life, and travel in early Detroit and describes the social life of the period."[41] A list of executions in Michigan also can be found online <users.bestweb.net/~rg/execution/MICHIGAN.htm>.

Coroners' Files

From the beginning of Michigan's history, provisions were made in the law to investigate suspicious deaths. In 1805, Michigan's territorial governor and judges granted marshals the authority to investigate deaths. Marshals were to "summon a jury of good and lawful men of the district" to investigate whether the deceased died "of felony, or of mischance or accident."[42] Fifteen years later, the territorial government established the office of coroner. "An Act Concerning Coroners," passed 28 November 1820, authorized the Governor of the Territory to appoint one coroner for each county. In addition to investigating suspicious deaths, the coroner was to perform the duties of the sheriff in certain situations. By 1838, Michigan law provided for two coroners to be elected in each of the organized counties for a term of two years. Public Act 181 of 1953 abolished the office of county coroner, replacing it with the office of county medical examiner. Some early coroner records are available at the State Archives of Michigan. These include:

- Genesee County coroners inquests (1905-1927)
- Houghton County record of inquests (1890-1967)

- Livingston County coroner's docket books (1927-1949)
- Mecosta County records of coroners inquests (1872-1889)
- Muskegon County coroners' inquest (1863 to 1920) coroners' inquests (1871, 1881, 1893-1932, 1939-1953)
- Saint Clair County inquest docket (1894 to 1966) of county coroner
- Saginaw County reports of coroner inquests (1861 to 1913)

Other coroners' records may be available on microfilm or at libraries. The Wayne County Coroners' Files (1870-1888), for example, are located at the Burton Historical Collection at the Detroit Public Library. "It is an alphabetically arranged file of cards listing information on people who died in Wayne County under circumstances that made it necessary for a coroner to be called in to the case. In each file, the name, residency, occupation, death date, age, birthplace, sex, race, and marital status of the deceased are listed."[43] Barry County's Coroner's Records, 1903-1908 are available on microfilm through Family History Centers. Some coroner records are filed with a county's circuit court records.

ERO Files

The Eugenics Record Office, a national project, was set up in 1910 in Cold Spring Harbor, New York, to study human genetics. Field workers went into mental institutions and patients' homes to gather data on human traits, and questionnaires were passed out in college classes. Materials in these records include name, birth date and birthplace, education, residences, date and place of marriage, total number of sons and daughters, occupations, diseases and illnesses, surgical operations, cause of death, height and weight, color of hair, complexion, and more. The records may span several generations in a single family. The ERO became inactive in 1944, but self-referred questionnaires were accepted at least until 1948. Michigan was one of the states involved in the project. "For genealogists, there is a wealth of documented material on many families bridging the late-eighteenth to late-nineteenth centuries, citing people who had personal knowledge of such significant family events as migrations from abroad and movements across the U.S. In many cases, this type of genealogical information is difficult if not impossible to come by."[44]

The Family History Library in Salt Lake City microfilmed the ERO files in the early 1990s. The surname/locality/trait index is on 247 microfilm reels and is available through Family History Centers across the country. "Photocopies of the records found in these indexes may be obtained only at the Family History Library [in Salt Lake City]."[45] For more information on this unique source, see Roderick, Anderson, Anderson, Joslyn, and Morris' article, "Files of the Eugenics Record Office: A Resource for Genealogists," published in the June 1994 issue of the *National Genealogical Society Quarterly*.

Orphans and Orphanages

Orphanages were established in Michigan as early as the 1830s. Saint Vincent's Catholic Orphan Asylum, for example, opened in 1834 in Detroit. "Among the associations which arose that were devoted to child welfare were the Michigan Children's Aid Society, founded in 1891, and the Children's Aid Society of Detroit, which developed in 1914 but was an outgrowth of two earlier societies, the Home for the Friendless, a Presbyterian women's organization formed in 1862 to care for the orphans of soldiers, and the Society for the Prevention of Cruelty to Children, established in 1893."[46] In addition to orphanages, children without parents often were placed in poorhouses. Online sources for Michigan orphanages include:

- Census records of orphanages in Michigan <freepages.genealogy.rootsweb.com/~orphanshome/censusrooms/uscensus/michigan/mistatep.htm>
- Detroit Diocese Orphan Asylums in the Early 1900s <www.rootsweb.com/~miwayne/orphanages.html>
- Detroit's First Asylums and Orphanages <www.geocities.com/genealogymi/asylum.html>
- Orphanages in Michigan Message Board available through Ancestry.com
- Shiawassee County's Orphanage: The Dorcas Home, Owosso <www.shiawasseehistory.com/dorcas.html>

The Orphan Train: Between 1854 and 1929, about 200,000 children, most of them from the New York Children's Aid Society, were "placed out" in homes throughout the West and the Midwest in an early form of foster care. The children, usually ages 3 to 16, were placed on trains in groups of 10 to 40 and traveled under the supervision of an adult agent. When the train stopped in a town, the children were shown to prospective parents. Children, who were not selected at the first stop, continued riding on the train to the next town and the next until they were selected. Children who were not selected by the time the train reached the end of its journey were returned to New York.

The first "Orphan Train," or "Baby Train" as it was sometimes called, arrived in Dowagiac, Michigan, in 1854. Forty-six children, ages 7 to 15 and of various nationalities, were on board.[47] By 1927, about 12,500 orphans, most from New York City and Boston, had been placed in more than 40 Michigan towns, including Adrian, Albion, Ann Arbor, Battle Creek, Bay City, Chelsea, Detroit, Fenton, Flint, Grand Rapids, Grass Lake, Holly, Jackson, Kalamazoo, Marshall, Midland, Olivet, Pontiac, Tecumseh, and Ypsilanti. Some of the children from Orphan Trains even found homes in Michigan's Upper Peninsula. Some of the children found happy homes, but others were only selected for their potential as laborers. Some of the boys ran away to the lumber camps in northern Michigan.

Starting in 1895, Michigan law required institutions to place a $1,000 bond with the county probate judge in the county of residence of each child resettled within the state. This was to ensure that the child did not "become a town, county or State charge, before it shall have reached the age of 21 years."[48] State law required the probate judge to investigate cases where children placed under this act were neglected or became a public charge.

"The Orphan Train in Michigan, 1854 to 1927," a video by Program Source International <www.program-source.com/modules.php?name=orphan_train>, details this chapter in Michigan's history. Video producers Al Eicher, and his son Dave, have collected 142 names of children placed in Michigan.[49] They can be contacted through their Web site. The Orphan Train Collection <www.orphantrainriders.com>, Web site of the Orphan Train Heritage Society of America, has much information about the topic, including arrival lists, compiled from books, magazines, and newspapers <www.orphantrainriders.com/ListFrame.html>. The site lists about 100 Michigan Orphan Train Riders.

British Home Children: "From 1869 to 1939 more than 100,000 abandoned, parentally surrendered, or orphaned children were rescued from the streets and slums of English and Scottish cities and sent to orphanages in British Empire countries, primarily Canada, to be claimed for adoption or employment."[50] With Michigan's proximity to Canada, it's possible that some of these British Home Children may have ended up in Michigan. Online sources of information about home children include:

- British Home Children <freepages.genealogy.rootsweb.com/~britishhomechildren/>
- British Home Children <charsnow.tripod.com/one.html>
- Home Children Database <www.collectionscanada.ca/02/020110_e.html>

Fraternal and Other Organizational Records

Fraternal orders or alliances, such as the Masons, the Odd Fellows, or the Grange, have a long history in the United States. Fraternal organizations first appeared in the early 1700s. In the late 1800s, fraternal organizations "were sprouting all over the American landscape."[51] By 1927, there were an estimated 800 fraternal orders with about 30 million members.

> By far the Masons were the most popular and most fraternal groups were patterned after the Masons. Some of these fraternal orders were open to everyone, and some were limited to certain specific special interest groups. For example, some fraternal orders were composed of members from a certain religious persuasion and some were composed of members of certain ethnic groups.[52]

Fraternal orders were created for social reasons, to provide life insurance, to sponsor immigration, and to help new immigrants adjust to their new homes.

In Michigan, British soldiers formed the first Masonic Lodge in Detroit in 1764, and the lodge was in existence until at least 1783. Because of anti-Masonic attitudes in the early 19th century, however, the Michigan Grand Lodge suspended activities in 1829. It wasn't until 1840 that a convention of Masons met in Mount Clemens to revive the organization.[53] The Michigan Masonic Home in Alma has the distinction of being one of the oldest Masonic homes in the Midwest. In 1885, Masons began fundraising for a home for aged and infirm Master Masons and their widows. The original building was dedicated in 1891 at Reed's Lake, near Grand Rapids. The home moved to the former Alma Sanitarium in 1910, and the present building was constructed in 1931.[54]

Other Michigan fraternal organizations include the following:

- The Michigan Odd Fellows Lodge No. 1 was organized at Detroit on 4 December 1843. Lodges in Monroe and Cassopolis soon followed. By the end of the Civil War, more than 100 lodges had been established in the state. The Odd Fellows Institute of Michigan was established in Lansing in 1871 to care for elderly Odd Fellows, their wives, widows, and orphans. The home relocated to Jackson in 1901.
- The Knights of Pythias was founded in Eagle Harbor in 1859 when schoolteacher Justus H. Rathbone wrote the original ritual.
- The oldest grand chapter in the world of the Order of the Eastern Star was organized at Adrian on 30 October 1867.
- The State Grange organized 15 April 1873, and the first State Grange meeting took place in Kalamazoo in January 1874. By 1875 the Grange had 616 chapters and more than 33,000 members.[55]
- The Knights of the Maccabees of the World, the first organization to offer fraternal life insurance in Michigan, was established on 11 June 1881.

Records of fraternal orders are private. Older records may be located at a local lodge, they may have been forwarded to a state lodge, or they may be found in archive collections. For example, the State Archives of Michigan has Lodge 422 Records for the Independent Order of Odd Fellows (1909-1913) and the minutes of the Grange of North Plains (1878-1884) in its collection of records of associations and organizations. These are described in Circular No. 40: Associations and Organizations <www.michigan.gov/documents/mhc_sa_circular40 _49968 _7.pdf>. Other records may have been lost or destroyed. Some records of the Grange, for example, were destroyed in a fire at the home of the organization's secretary in 1943.[56]

The Library of Michigan has a number of publications dealing with fraternal organizations, including *Proceedings Grand Chapter Order of the Eastern Star* for 1867 to 1957 and *Transactions of the Grand Lodge of Free and Accepted Masons of the State of Michigan at Its Annual Communication* (1841-1936), which include a listing of deaths of Freemasons and other information about Masons in Michigan. Conover's two volumes *Freemasonry in Michigan: A Comprehensive History of Michigan Masonry from Its Earliest Introduction in 1764* (1897-1898) includes histories of Michigan lodges and biographical sketches of Masons. The Library of Michigan also has several annual volumes of the *Proceedings of the Annual Session of the Michigan State Grange of Patrons of Husbandry* (1879-1900). These include lists of delegates and committee reports.

Some organization records also may be found online. Examples include:

- Members Grand Rapids Lodge No. 11 IOOF, 1889 (Kent County) <www.rootsweb.com/~mikent/organizations/gr11ioof1889.html>
- Grand River Lodge No. 34 of Free and Accepted Masons, 1902 Members (Kent County) <www.rootsweb.com/~mikent/organizations/masons/mason34.html>
- Organization of York Lodge, No. 410, Free and Accepted Masons, Grand Rapids (Kent County), Roll of Membership, 1922 <www.rootsweb.com/~mikent/organizations/masons/york410.html>
- Women's Relief Corps of Michigan, an auxiliary of the Grand Army of the Republic <www.mifamilyhistory.org/civilwar/wrc/default.asp>

For more information about fraternal organizations in Michigan, see volume two of Fuller's *Michigan: A Centennial History of the State and Its People* (1939). For general information about fraternal orders and alliances, see Schmidt's *Fraternal Organization* (1980) and "Fraternal Societies and Alliances," a chapter in Bremer's *Compendium of Historical Sources: the How and Where of American Genealogy* (1997 or current edition). Schmidt's book gives a description of every major fraternal group in the United States and Canada and includes lists of fraternal organizations by date of establishment, by geographic headquarters, and by ethnic and religious affiliation. Bremer's chapter includes a list of fraternal organizations and alliances. Yates' booklet *Researching Masonic Records: A Guide for Genealogists* (1998) gives an overview of Masonic records and suggestions for searching for them.

Ku Klux Klan: Unlike the Ku Klux Klan of the 1860s and 1940s, the Klan of the 1920s had more diverse objectives than anti-black sentiment and often depicted itself as a patriotic society. This helped the Klan spread from the South to other parts of the country. In the 1920s Michigan ranked eighth in Ku Klux Klan membership with at least 93 chartered "klaverns." "Although half of Michigan's 70,000 klansmen lived in the Detroit area, the Klan spread into every Michigan county south of Houghton Lake and into the eastern and western lakeside counties all the way to the tip of the Lower Peninsula. In the Upper Peninsula, at least two-thirds of the counties had some sort of klan organization."[57] Klan membership declined after the 1926 arrest and eventual conviction of a Muskegon Klan leader who mailed a bomb that killed three people. By 1929, the Klan "had nearly disappeared" from Michigan.[58]

Membership lists or membership cards rarely exist for the organization. However, the Ku Klux Klan Collection at Clarke Historical Library in Mount Pleasant has information documenting Klan activity in Mecosta County where at least 255 men joined the Ku Klux Klan in the 1920s. "The collection was created by Lewis D. Capen, who served as the Exalted Cyclops of the Mecosta Klan No.

28, 1926-1929. He then became Great Kaliff or Grand Titan, a leadership position over all the klans of Ionia and Mecosta counties and the towns of Petoskey, East Jordan, Hart, Manistee, Portland, and Muskegon."[59] Clarke Historical Library also has the membership cards of the Newaygo County Ku Klux Klan, 1923-1926. The Fremont Area District Library in Fremont also reports having the Newaygo County Ku Klux Klan membership cards on microfilm. Membership cards usually include such information as name, age, address, marital status, and occupation. Cards of foreign-born members include place of birth and citizenship status.[60] Michigan State University also has a Ku Klux Klan Collection in its library <www.lib.msu.edu/coll/main/spec_col/radicalism/klan.htm>.

Territorial Records

Territorial Papers: Petitions signed by Michigan residents, lists of voters and taxpayers, militia appointments and discharges, land claims of settlers, correspondence, and other information related to the governance of the Territory of Michigan can be found in volumes 10, 11, and 12 of the 28-volume series of *Territorial Papers of the United States* (1942-1945). These large volumes (about 1,000 pages each) contain transcribed records from the files of the U.S. Department of State, U.S. Department of War, and other Federal bodies. Edited by Clarence E. Carter, volume 10 covers the years 1805-1820, while volume 11 deals with 1820-1829, and volume 12 includes information from 1829-1837.

Earlier volumes dealing with the Northwest Territory (volumes 2 through 4) and the Indiana Territory (volumes 7 and 8) also may include information about Michigan residents. "State, county, and other local records accumulated during the territorial period, and preserved in county courthouses and state archives, are definitely excluded from the series, except insofar as such documents, for some reason, were forwarded to Washington, and then they became a part of the Federal Archives."[61]

Each volume is completely name indexed. The lists of petitioners, voters, and taxpayers are excellent census substitutes for early Michigan. In at least one case excerpts from *Territorial Papers of the United States* appear online. Lenawee County's MIGenWeb site includes information from the books that relate to that county <www.geocities.com/lenaweemi/territory.html>.

Territorial Laws: The four-volume set, *Laws of the Territory of Michigan* (1871-1884), reprints the acts passed by the territorial governor and judges or legislative council. Some of these acts involved individuals and deal with such items as divorce, pardons, payment for service as a hangman, permission to build a wharf on the Detroit River, or authorization to chose a guardian. The volumes are indexed.

Michigan Manual

The *Michigan Manual*, the state's official handbook, includes basic reference information about the state's history, governmental organizations, and institutions. It has been published every two years since 1836. Examples of information to be found in various editions of Michigan manuals include lists of banks, newspapers, post offices, and incorporated cities. Manuals also list the populations of Michigan counties, and some editions have maps of Michigan railroad routes.

Starting in 1873, *Michigan Manuals* included biographies of state officials. Two biographical directories have been based on the information in the manuals: Bingham's *Early History of Michigan, With Biographies of State Officers* (1888) and *Michigan Biographies* (2 volumes, 1924). Waterstreet's *Biography Index to the Michigan Manuals, 1923-1973* indexes the biographies by name, place of birth, and place of residence. Grabowski's *Lists of County Sheriffs of Michigan, 1869-1986* (1987) is a compiled list of sheriffs found in various volumes of Michigan manuals. It is divided by county and then chronologically and includes names and terms of office.

The Library of Michigan has editions of the *Michigan Manual*, dating back to 1836, with the volumes for 1836 to 1868 housed in the Rare Books Room. Many other libraries have various issues of the *Michigan Manual* in their reference sections. Current issues of the *Michigan Manual* also are available online through the Michigan Legislature site <www.michiganlegislature.org> in the Legislative Publications section. *Michigan Biographies* is available online through the American Memory collection Pioneering the Upper Midwest: Books from Michigan, Minnesota, and Wisconsin, ca. 1820 to 1910 <memory.loc.gov/ammem/umhtml/umhome.html>.

Depression-era Records

Civilian Conservation Corps: Between 1933 and 1942, the Civilian Conservation Corps gave unemployed men, most of them 17 to 28 years of age, an opportunity to work on conservation and reforestation projects for food, lodging, and a small income. During those years, 100,000 men worked in Michigan's more than 100 camps. "Some came from other states, among them Ohio, Indiana, Illinois, Pennsylvania, New York, and even Arkansas, but most were Michiganders."[62] Unfortunately, few records remain. Symon's *We Can Do It! A History of the Civilian Conservation Corps in Michigan: 1933-1942* (1983) includes the names of project superintendents, thumbnail histories of CCC camps, and personal recollections of men who served in the camps. The book is not indexed. The State Archives of Michigan has some CCC records, detailed in Circular No. 23: Depression-era Agencies <www.michigan.gov/documents/mhc_sa_circular23_49718_7.pdf>. These include:

- Applications for enrollment and discharges from Ionia County (1936-1941); Lapeer County (1933-1942); Monroe County (1934-1943); and Saint Clair County (1935-1942)
- Enumeration of CCC workers in Lake County (1933-1934)

In addition, CCC alumni have donated many photographs and artifacts to the Civilian Conservation Corps Museum, which is located in North Higgins Lake

State Park near Roscommon. The museum is located 15 miles south of Grayling on Roscommon Road.

Rural Property Inventories: During the Depression, Michigan's State Tax Commission and the Works Progress Administration (later Works Project Administration) joined forces to inventory parcels of land in the rural parts of Michigan. The inventory, the first of its kind in the nation, started in 1935 and continued until 1942. "Though the data entered on these records is now obsolete, the details they reveal serve to provide a remarkably sharp picture of the character of Michigan country life a half-century ago. The collected data describes lands; buildings; fences; crops; woodlands; means of communication; sources of heat and light; number of school district; legal description of the land; name of village, township and county wherein located; name and post office address of individual assessed; together with amount of acreage within certain classifications."[63] The inventories may include sketches of houses and property. About 1.5 million parcels of land in Michigan were examined during this project. Rural Property Inventories for most Michigan counties are available at the State Archives of Michigan and are listed in Circular No. 16: Rural Property Inventories <www.michigan.gov/documents/mhc_sa_circular16_49706_7.pdf>. The Rochester Hills Museum at VanHoosen Farm has copies of the Rural Property Inventories for Avon Township (Rochester Hills) and Rochester. The index for Grand Rapids Township, Kent County's Rural Property Inventory, 1939-1940 is available online <www.rootsweb.com/~mikent/townships/grandrapids/wpa/index.html>.

Historical Records Survey: Another Works Progress Administration (later Works Project Administration) program employed college graduates, teachers, writers, researchers, and other well-educated individuals in an archival survey of historical records. Between 1936 and 1942, thousands of workers surveyed "virtually every type of public record and a large number of private documents as well."[64] Nationwide, the Historical Records Survey published 2,000 volumes. In Michigan, 68 published volumes covered vital statistic holdings (see Chapter 3 for more), church archives (see Chapter 4 for more), county archives (see Chapter 10 for more), municipal and town archives, manuscript collections at the University of Michigan, and more. Though these volumes are dated, they can give clues about existing records. The published volumes are available at several libraries in Michigan, including the Library of Michigan. Several of the published volumes also have been reprinted by Quintin Publications <www.quintinpublications.com/mi.html>. Most of the unpublished material from the Historical Records Survey was deposited with the Michigan Historical Collections at the Bentley Historical Library at the University of Michigan. "A small amount [of the unpublished materials] was transferred to the Michigan State Library and the Detroit Public Library."[65] For a list of published volumes of interest to genealogists, see Heisey's *The W.P.A. Historical Records Survey Sources for Genealogists* (1988). For more information about the unpublished materials, see Hefner's *The WPA Historical Records Survey: A Guide to the Unpublished Inventories, Indexes, and Transcripts* (1980).

Land Exchange Files

Mackinac Island became Michigan's first state park in 1895. Since then, the state's Department of Natural Resources (DNR) has worked to develop a state park system. Many records of this development, including land exchange files, are available at the State Archives of Michigan. The DNR Park Land Exchange Files, 1877-1987 (Record Group 88-2) includes deeds, maps, photographs, appraisal reports, and land-exchange agreements. "The lands delineated in these records were not purchased but exchanged for land of equal value from other government or private holdings. These exchanges, initiated by a citizen's request, were approved on the grounds that the land the citizen desired to give to the state was better suited for the state's purposes than the land the citizen wished to acquire from the state."[66]

Disasters

Forest Fires: The four worst forest fires in Michigan's history are responsible for killing hundreds and leaving thousands homeless. The first recorded catastrophic fire occurred in October 1871, but that year is most often remembered for the Great Chicago Fire and the fire at Peshtigo, Wisconsin, which killed 600 people.[67] In Michigan, the 1871 fire was a series of blazes, rather than one large conflagration, that swept across the Lower Peninsula from Lake Michigan to Lake Huron. It also ate through parts of Menominee County in the Upper Peninsula. The fire started on 8 October. During the next 10 days about 40 towns and villages, including Holland and Manistee, were destroyed. Though the worst of the fires were out by 18 October, the fires were not completely out for nearly a month.[68] An estimated 200 people died, though some claim "an uncounted number of lumberjacks" also were lost in the inferno, and about 15,000 residents were left homeless.[69] The 1871 fire was "the most widespread of Michigan's forest fires."[70]

Fire again swept through Michigan in 1881, this time through the Saginaw Valley and Thumb areas, burning 2,000 square miles, killing from 200 to 300 people, and leaving more than 13,000 people homeless. Huron and Sanilac counties were hit particularly hard. In those counties, nearly two-thirds of the population was left homeless. The fire was so intense that sailors in ships seven miles offshore in Lake Huron reported that they were uncomfortable from the heat.[71] The week-long fire, peaking on 5 September, was "probably the worst disaster in Michigan's history relative to loss of life."[72] The fire also signaled the end of the lumber era in the Thumb and opened up the rich agricultural land for settlers.[73]

Metz, in Presque Isle County, was destroyed in less than three hours in a 1908 fire that took the lives of 43 people, including 16 who were attempting to flee by train. Most of those killed on the train were women and children. The Metz Fire ruined much more than the town after which it was named. The fire also raged in Alpena and Alcona counties, destroying an estimated 2.5 million acres. This makes the Metz Fire "one of the largest forest fires in the modern history of Michigan."[74]

In 1911, Michigan's last large forest fire "destroyed the sawmill towns of Au Sable and Oscoda" in Iosco County, and the unofficial death toll ranges from five to 20.[75] "Neither town rebuilt to its former stature after the fires," and the fire put an end to the lumber era in northeast Lower Michigan.[76]

More information about these fires and others can be found in several books and articles, including Sodders' *Michigan on Fire* (1997) and *Michigan on Fire 2* (1999); Lincoln and Donahue's *Fiery Trial* (1984); Schultz' *Walls of Flames* (1968); and Nagel's *The Metz Fire of 1908* (1979). The *Port Huron Times Herald* has written extensively about the 1881 Thumb Fire, and the 8 September 1881 issue of the *Huron Times* published a detailed account of the 1881 fire in Harbor Beach along with a list of people who had been killed by it. More than 600 fire victims listed in the 16 September 1881 issue of the *Huron County News* are included in RootsWeb.com's Newspaper Indexes <userdb.rootsweb.com/news/>. Other online sources include:

- The Great Fire of 1881 (Michigan) <freepages.family.rootsweb.com/~ptruckin/greatfire.html>
- Metz Fire of 1908 List of Victims <members.aol.com/alpenaco/presque/metzfire.htm>
- Sanilac County, Michigan - Fire Deaths of 1871 and 1881 <www.rootsweb.com/~misanila/history/fires.html>

In addition, the Presque Isle County Historical Museum reports having artifacts and files from the Metz fire (see page 338).

Mining Accidents: Miners died from such causes as falling rocks, machinery-related accidents, falls from ladders, explosions, cave-ins, and fires in the timbers that shored up the mines. In Michigan's copper mines, for example, 1,900 men died between the 1840s and 1960s, with more than half of those deaths occurring in the first two decades of the 20th century. Between 1905 and 1911, the copper region "averaged nearly 61 underground deaths per year, or more than one per week."[77] The rate of fatal injuries in the iron mines was higher.[78] Mine accidents usually killed only one or two men at a time.[79]

However, 51 men were killed in a 1926 cave-in at the Barnes-Hecker iron mine in Marquette County. It was the worst mining accident in Michigan's history. The disaster left 42 widows and 132 fatherless children. Friggens' *No Tears in Heaven: The 1926 Barnes-Hecker Mine Disaster* recounts the event. Originally published as an article in the May-June 1988 issue of *Michigan History,* the article has been reprinted as a booklet in 1988, 1998, and 2002. The 2002 edition is the only one to list the 51 men who died. In addition to the miner's full name, the listing includes his marital status, age, birthplace, family residence, and the number of his surviving children under the age of 16. The list also indicates if the miner's body was recovered.

The worst fatal accident in Michigan's Copper Country occurred on 7 September 1895 when 30 men and boys died of asphyxiation in the Osceola mine in northern Houghton County. A small fire had started at the 27th level of shaft No. 3, but the miners were not alarmed at first. The fire soon burned out of control, and the miners who had waited too long to escape were overcome by gas and smoke.[80]

In another serious accident, 27 miners died in a cave-in at Iron County's Mansfield Mine on 28 September 1893. The mine – 423-feet at its deepest – ran beneath and parallel to the Michigamme River. "It is generally believed that the disaster occurred when the fifth level of the mine caved in, allowing the levels above, and consequently the river, to crash down on the miners."[81] Eight iron miners died in an 1883 cave-in at the Keel Ridge Mine in Dickinson County.[82]

Many mining deaths, especially those occurring before 1900, did not make it into the newspapers or county death records; if newspapers did report accidents they "often garbled names or gave no names at all, saying two Swedes were injured in a premature blast, an Italian trammer suffered a broken leg when a rock fell, or a Frenchman had his leg broken in North Tamarack Mine."[83] Mine inspector reports are an alternative source for information about deaths as a result of mining accidents.

In 1887, Michigan passed a law authorizing county boards of supervisors in any of the counties in the Upper Peninsula with working mines to appoint a mine inspector and as many deputy inspectors as necessary. Among their duties, the law required the inspectors to visit each iron ore mine every 60 days and copper mines once per year, to investigate all accidents that caused death or injury, and to compile a report of all mine accidents. (The law later changed to require mine inspectors to visit all working mines every 60 days.[84])

Unfortunately for genealogists, the mine inspectors "almost wholly ignored the thousands of less-than-fatal accidents."[85] However, inspectors did a thorough job of reporting fatal accidents, summarizing what happened and the verdict of the coroner's jury, if any. The mining inspector reports include the miner's name, occupation, and nationality; date and type of accident; the name of the mine where the accident occurred; and a description of the accident. Some of the reports also include the marital status of the miner.

Mine inspector reports for Houghton County were published in separate volumes, while manuscript copies of some of the mine inspector reports for Ontonagon and Keweenaw counties can be found in the Michigan Technological University Archives. The J.M. Longyear Research Library in Marquette has the Marquette County reports from 1889 to the present, while the Library of Michigan has several volumes for Gogebic County. Some of these mine inspector reports also can be found online:

- Michigan Family History Network's Mining Accident Reports Web site <www.mifamilyhistory.org/mining/>
- Houghton County Report, 30 September 1891 to 30 September 1892 <www.sos.state.mi.us/history/museum/explore/museums/hismus/prehist/mining/accident.html>

Italian Hall Disaster: More than 500 children and 175 adults – families of striking copper miners – gathered on 24 December 1913 in the Italian Hall near Calumet in Houghton County to celebrate Christmas. As the children moved toward the stage, someone yelled, "Fire!" "In the panic that followed, 73 lost their lives, trampled in the stairway leading out as an avalanche of terrified men, women, and children cascaded down."[86] There was no fire, and it's unclear who yelled or why. Most of those who died – 60 of the 73 – were children, 2 to 16 years of age.[87] More than half of the dead were Finns.[88] A number of others were Croats and Slovenes. A list of those who died, most with ages and residences, can be found online <www.mfhn.com/houghton/rosscoll/ItalianHallpg2.htm>.

Diseases and Epidemics: From the earliest days of Michigan's history, settlers struggled against disease, and early death from disease was a common occurrence. During the winter of 1733-34, for example, "a great many people" at Detroit died of smallpox.[89] Several hundred soldiers at Detroit died of malaria in 1813, and 10 years later "typhoid fever forced the abandonment of Fort Saginaw."[90] The most common disease faced by Michigan pioneers was malaria, also known as the fever or ague. It was spread by mosquitoes and was so widespread that "as late as 1881 malaria was still believed to constitute over 50 per cent of the total sum of illness in the state."[91] Typhoid fever also was widespread. In 1886, one doctor estimated that at least 1,000 people died annually from the disease.[92] Diphtheria epidemics occurred regularly in Michigan, starting in 1865. In 1887, for example, a diphtheria epidemic struck Crofton in Kalkaska County and killed all but four or five of the town's children.[93] In 1847 and 1848 and again in 1872 and 1873 "Michigan was visited by an epidemic known as brain or spotted fever, or, as it was later called, cerebro-spinal meningitis."[94] Detroit was hit particularly hard in the earlier epidemic, and in the later epidemic it was severe in Monroe and Lenawee counties.

Smallpox took many lives, particularly among Native Americans. In 1752, for example, a smallpox epidemic at Detroit inflicted "heavy losses among the Potawatomi and the Ottawa and Wyandot."[95] Another epidemic in 1787-88 affected the Wyandot (Huron) at Detroit, and in 1801 smallpox was reported in Ottawa-Ojibwa villages on Little Traverse Bay of Lake Michigan. More than 300 Ojibwa in the Saginaw Valley died of smallpox in 1837.[96] In 1872, there were 302 deaths reported throughout the state from smallpox. This was the most smallpox deaths reported in any individual year between 1869 and 1884. Though many Native Americans and European settlers died from smallpox, it was less prevalent than many other diseases.

Cholera visited Michigan on several occasions. On 4 July 1832, several sick soldiers on their way to Chicago to fight against Black Hawk's uprising were taken off a ship docked at Detroit. "By morning, 11 were dead. The ship was sent away, but the city had already been infected."[97] Another troop transport infected soldiers at Fort Gratiot, at the present site of Port Huron. "Scared soldiers deserted, trying to escape the disease, but spreading it instead."[98] During the next two weeks, at least 46 people died, 28 at Detroit and 18 at Marshall. By the time the cholera epidemic ended in mid-August, 96 people had died.[99] Fear of the disease had caused many communities to post armed guards, allowing no one to pass in or out of their settlements.[100]

A second cholera epidemic hit Detroit in 1834, reportedly killing in August from 7 to more than 10 percent of the city's population of 3,500.[101] Cholera visited the state again in 1849 and 1850, and in Sandusky (located in Michigan's Thumb region), people panicked. "One-half of the population fled the city; in the month of July, 1849, alone, 350 deaths occurred from the disease in a population of 2,800."[102] The 1849-50 epidemic also was "particularly bad at Mackinac Island."[103] Kedzie's *The Cholera in Kalamazoo* (1961) recounts what happened on the west side of the state during the 1849-50 epidemic. Cholera visited Michigan again in 1852, 1853, 1854, and 1865. During the 1854 epidemic, about 1,000 people died in Detroit.

Scarlet Fever also was very common, resulting in hundreds of deaths each year. "In 1885, for example, there occurred in Michigan 356 outbreaks in 356 localities, 2,750 cases and 287 deaths; in 1886, 368 outbreaks were reported in 302 localities with 3,046 cases and 275 deaths."[104] The most reported deaths between 1869 and 1884 were 852 in 1870; other totals include 696 in 1871 and 673 in 1883. Part of the reason scarlet fever was so common was that some physicians, as late at 1871, thought the disease was not contagious and therefore didn't isolate patients.

Other diseases faced by pioneers included measles; whooping cough, which reached epidemic proportions in 1813-14; and tuberculosis. The Upper Peninsula was particularly hard hit by tuberculosis at the beginning of the 20th century, with about 300 people dying per year.[105] Michigan was the first state to pass a law providing for tax-paid hospitalization for tuberculosis patients. "The first state tuberculosis sanitarium was built at Howell in 1905. In subsequent decades other state sanitariums were opened at Gaylord, Kalamazoo, and Hancock, in addition to a tuberculosis unit at the University of Michigan Hospital, and 14 approved county, city, and private tuberculosis hospitals."[106] Some sanatoria records are available at the State Archives of Michigan <www.michigan.gov/documents/mhc_sa_circular22_49715_7.pdf>, but these are confidential and access to them must be approved by the Michigan Department of Public Health. The Central Upper Peninsula and Northern Michigan University Archives reports having patient records from the Morgan Heights Sanatorium, which was the first county sanatorium built in the state. It opened on 1 May 1911 in Marquette.

The influenza pandemic of 1918, also known as the Spanish flu or "La Grippe," took the lives of more than 6,300 Michigan residents, including about 1,000 soldiers at Fort Custer, located near Battle Creek. More than 600 of those soldiers died in October 1918. The flu took more lives of Michigan residents than deaths from World War I; the war resulted in 5,000 Michigan casualties.

Train Accidents: "From the 1840s to the beginning of the 20th century, accidents and hazards were commonplace in Michigan's railroads."[107] Employees, especially railroad brakemen, were killed or injured on the job. In 1873, for example, "the commissioner of railroads reported that 257 people had been killed in railroad accidents during the preceding years."[108] The majority of these had been employees, but passengers also were killed while getting on and off trains. Train collisions and derailments also killed passengers and employees. The state's worst train wreck, for example, took the lives of 33 Ionia County residents and seriously injured 100 others when two trains collided on 20 July 1907 near Salem in Washtenaw County <www.rootsweb.com/~miionia/train.htm>. In another two-train collision on 19 October 1893 near Battle Creek, 26 people were killed and dozens injured. Two Wallace Circus trains collided near Durand on 7 August 1903, killing 23 <www.usgennet.org/usa/mi/county/shiawassee/circus.html>. A listing of more than 20 fatal railroad wrecks can be found online <www.michiganrailroads.com/RRHX/Wrecks/WrecksMenu.htm>.

Great Lakes Shipwrecks: Unpredictable weather patterns on the Great Lakes have caused thousands of shipwrecks through the years. Swayze's Great Lakes Shipwreck File <greatlakeshistory.homestead.com/home.html> has information on more than 4,500 shipwrecks taking place between 1679 and 2001 on the Great Lakes. Swayze, who has studied Great Lakes shipwrecks for more than 15 years, claims it is "the most complete and accurate list of losses of Great Lakes commercial vessels in existence."[109] The searchable database includes basic information about the wrecks, including ship names, ship owners, and dates and places of loss.

At present, the site does not list the names of persons who have lost their lives in Great Lakes shipwrecks, but Swayze says he is compiling a list of more than 3,000 individuals who have died between 1799 and 2001 in these shipwrecks. This list includes the victim's name; gender; position, such as sailor or passenger; home or nationality; date of death; vessel; and location of the shipwreck.[110] At present, Swayze is not releasing the list, but he offers to look up specific names for researchers <greatlakeshistory.homestead.com/files/Geneal.htm>. He will not, however, do extensive research for family historians.

Swayze's Shipwreck File also is available for purchase on CD or in print, and ordering information is available on his Web site. For general information about researching Great Lakes Shipwrecks, see Kerstens' article, "Ship Wrecks on the Great Lakes," published in the January-February 2003 issue of *Ancestry.* There is also a list of sources to use in researching shipwrecks available on the U.S. Coast Guard Web site <www.uscg.mil/hq/g-cp/history/WEBSHIPWRECKS/SHIPWRECKGUIDE.html>.

The Titanic: Nearly 100 passengers on the Titanic were heading for Michigan when the luxury liner sank in April 1912. Forty of those Michigan passengers survived. Kohl's *Titanic, The Great Lakes Connections* (2000) tells their stories and includes a passenger list of the Great Lakes-bound travelers. The list includes the passenger's name, age, port boarded, class, destination, and death date. Draeger's article, "They Never Forgot: Michigan Survivors of the Titanic," published in the March-April 1997 issue of *Michigan History,* lists about 30 Michigan residents who were on board the Titanic.

Life in Michigan

From visiting museums to browsing through photographs, there are many tools to use to learn more about the lives of Michigan ancestors.

Museums: Through collections of artifacts, museums show what life was like for people in the past. The largest museum in the Michigan Historical Museum System is the Michigan Historical Museum <www.michigan.gov/museum>, located in the Michigan Library and Historical Center, 702 W. Kalamazoo St., two blocks west of the State Capitol, in Lansing. (It is located in the same building as the Library of Michigan and the State Archives of Michigan.) Its three floors of exhibits trace Michigan's history from pre-European settlement to the 20th century.

Nine other museums in the Michigan Historical Museum System include:

- Civilian Conservation Corps Museum near Grayling
- Father Marquette National Memorial in Saint Ignace
- Fayette Historic Townsite in Garden
- Fort Wilkins Historic Complex in Copper Harbor
- Hartwick Pines Logging Museum in Grayling
- Mann House in Concord
- Michigan Iron Industry Museum in Negaunee
- Sanilac Petroglyphs in Bad Axe
- Walker Tavern Cambridge in Junction/Brooklyn

Several museums in Michigan, including the Detroit Historical Museums <www.detroithistorical.org/>, are not affiliated with the Michigan Historical Museum System. For more information about Michigan museums, see the Michigan Museum Association Web site <www.michiganmuseums.org/index.html>. Several museums also are listed in Chapter 11 of this volume.

Living History: Another way researchers can learn about how their ancestors lived is through observing "living history" – the recreation or reenactment of what life was like for people in the past. This is done through demonstrations that use authentic clothes, equipment, weapons, and tools. In Michigan, there are several living history villages and forts including Fort Mackinac <www.mackinacparks.com/fortmackinac/> and the Henry Ford Museum and Greenfield Village <www.hfmgv.org/>. Reenactment groups in the state include Battery D, First Michigan Light Artillery <www.batteryd.com/>.

Social History: According to Katherine Scott Sturdevant, author of *Bringing Your Family History to Life Through Social History* (2000), social history is the study of ordinary people's everyday lives. "It is history from the bottom up instead of the top down, not focusing exclusively or primarily on the elite and famous," she says, adding it's the "best tool for reconstructing [an] ancestor's entire world."[111] Social historians use such sources as artifacts, correspondence, photographs, and oral histories. Many books have been written about the social history of Michigan. Some explore a particular region of the state, a certain ethnic group, or a specific occupational group. A sampling includes:

- Cleland's *Rites of Conquest: the History and Culture of Michigan's Native Americans* (1992)
- Fitzmaurice's *The Shanty Boy, or, Life in a Lumber Camp* (1970)
- Kent's *Fort Pontchartrain at Detroit: A Guide to the Daily Lives of Fur Trade and Military Personnel, Settlers, and Missionaries at French Posts* (2001)
- Lankton's *Cradle to Grave: Life, Work, and Death at the Lake Superior Copper Mines* (1991)
- Martin's *Call It North Country: The Story of Upper Michigan* (1986)
- Wilson's *Black Eden: The Idlewild Community* (2002)
- Wytrwal's *The Polish Experience in Detroit* (1992)
- The Making of America Web sites have books and journal articles about social history online. (See Chapter 9 for more.)

Women's History: Several books and projects deal exclusively with the history of women in Michigan. They include:

- *Birchbark Belles: Women on the Michigan Frontier* (1993)
- Bush's *First Lady of Detroit: The Story of Marie-Thérese Guyon, Mme. Cadillac* (2001)
- Greater Grand Rapids Women's History Council <www.ggrwhc.org/>
- Harley and MacDowell's *Michigan Women: Firsts and Founders* (1992, 1995)
- *Historic Women of Michigan: A Sesquicentennial Celebration* (1987)
- *Michigan History* focused on Michigan women in its November-December 2002 issue
- Michigan Women's Historical Center and Hall of Fame <www.michigan womenshalloffame.org>
- Motz's *True Sisterhood: Michigan Women and Their Kin, 1820-1920* (1983), a social history of women in Michigan
- Women's History Project of Northwest Michigan <www.whpnm.org>
- Women's Voices: Early Years at the University of Michigan <www.hti. umich.edu/w/womv>

Oral Histories: Oral histories, true stories told in the words of the individuals who lived through them, are another way to learn more about what life was like in the past. Several Michigan libraries have oral histories in their collections. Some oral histories have been published, and some are online. In addition, the Michigan Oral History Association <www.h-net.org/~oralhist/moha/> publishes a journal and sponsors conferences. Sources for oral histories include the following:

- Michigan Women's Historical Center and Hall of Fame Oral Histories <www.michiganwomenshalloffame.org/pages/oralhistories.htm>
- Moon's *Untold Tales, Unsung Heroes: An Oral History of Detroit's African American Community, 1918-1967* (1994)
- Rosemond's *Reflections: An Oral History of Detroit* (1992)
- Sanders' *Bronze Pillars: An Oral History of African-Americans in Flint* (1995)
- *The Tree That Never Dies: Oral History of the Michigan Indians* (1978)

Travel Narratives: Early explorers and settlers of Michigan often kept records of their journeys. "Hundreds of narratives, composed by individuals of various nationalities, dispositions, and types, describing all sections of the Midwest, have been preserved from as early as the year 1634."[112] Some of these, such as *George Croghan's Journal of His Trip to Detroit in 1767* (1939), have been published in single volumes. Other travel narratives have been compiled into series or appear in periodicals. For example, the 32-volume *Early Western Travels, 1748-1846* (1904-1907) include travel narratives from the area of present-day Michigan. Volumes 31 and 32 are a detailed index to the series. Hubach's *Early Midwestern Travel Narratives: An Annotated Bibliography, 1634-1850* (1998) lists many other travel narratives relating to Michigan. Some travel narratives can be found online, such as Swan's *Journal of a Trip to Michigan in 1841* (1904) available through the American Memory collection Pioneering the Upper Midwest: Books from Michigan, Minnesota, and Wisconsin, ca. 1820 to 1910 <memory.loc.gov/ammem/umhtml/umhome.html> or Ancestry.com.

Jesuit Relations: Much information about New France, which included the area of present-day Michigan, can be found in the 73-volume *Jesuit Relations and Allied Documents: Travels and Explorations of the Jesuit Missionaries in New France, 1610-1791,* edited by Reuben Gold Thwaites. These missionaries were among the first Europeans to travel to New France, and they kept detailed records of their journeys. Volumes 72 and 73 are an index to the set. The *Jesuit Relations* also can be found online <puffin.creighton.edu/jesuit/relations/> and can be purchased as a two-volume CD set from Quintin Publications <www.quintinpublications.com/>.

Memoirs: In the late 1800s, many of Michigan's early pioneers wrote down their memories of settling the state. Many of these works were published in 1876, the year of the nation's centennial. "Among the best-known memoirs are those of William Nowlin, which he recorded in *The Bark Covered House*."[113] Nowlin's book, which includes illustrations, recounts the family's trip from New York on the steamboat *Michigan,* their journey to Dearborn over the Chicago Road, and other details. It can be found online through the American Memory collection Pioneering the Upper Midwest: Books from Michigan, Minnesota, and Wisconsin, ca. 1820 to 1910 <memory.loc.gov/ammem/umhtml/umhome.html>. Other memoirs in this collection include Williams' *A Child of the Sea and Life Among the Mormons* (1905) and Mevis' *Pioneer Recollections: Semi-historic Sidelights on the Early Days of Lansing* (1911).

Quiltmaking: Quilts, according to those who study them, are more than just bed-coverings. "Personal or family history, art, community life, religious beliefs and practices, business and political history, and more are gleaned from these textiles, their makers and their owners."[114] Quilts may even suggest a pattern of migration by reflecting the techniques and styles from specific regions.

The Michigan Quilt Project <www.museum.msu.edu/glqc/mqp.html>, begun in 1984, is part of a national movement to document and preserve quilting history. Under the direction of the Michigan State University Museum, more than 300 "significant historical and contemporary" Michigan quilts have been photographed and the history of the quilts, their owners, and makers have been recorded.[115] "Each quilt was given its own inventory number and file. This information is stored at the Michigan State University Museum's Traditional Arts Research Collections Area where it is available, by appointment, to those interested in doing research, education, and exhibition projects."[116]

The first project of the Michigan Quilt Project was the 1987 book and exhibit titled, *Michigan Quilts: 150 Years of a Textile Tradition.* The book profiles more than 200 quilts and their makers and includes color photographs of the quilts and quilters. Another book stemming from the project is *African American Quiltmaking in Michigan* (1997), which examines the "history and meaning of quilting within Michigan African American communities."[117] Additional information about quilts can be found online at the Great Lakes Quilt Center <www.museum.msu.edu/glqc/index.html>.

Michigan's Weather: From damaging winds to early freezes, the weather affected Michigan ancestors. For example, the five-month winter of 1835-36, known as the "Starving Time," resulted in near-famine conditions in parts of Michigan. Another five-month winter in 1842-43 also was difficult for settlers.[118] In July 1936, a heat wave with seven days of 100-plus degree weather took the lives of 750 people statewide; almost half of the deaths took place in Detroit.[119] Keen's *Michigan Weather* (1993) includes interesting facts about the state's weather. For example, Keen's book says Michigan's first recorded tornado occurred in Detroit in February 1834. The deadliest tornado occurred on 8 June 1953, in Genesee and Lapeer counties, killing 116 people.[120] Of special interest to genealogists will be the 17-page timeline of Michigan weather events. Some of these weather events also are listed on Ronnie August's Web page, "Michigan Weather and Our Ancestors" <www.rootsweb.com/~mikent/histories/weather.html>.

Photographs: Historical pictures can show what life was like in the past. Photographs can be found in collections at libraries, archives, or societies, or they can be published in books or online. The largest collection of historical photographs about Michigan in Michigan is located at the State Archives of Michigan.

Described in Circular No. 31: Photography <www.michigan.gov/documents/mhc_sa_circular31_50007_7.pdf>, the collection consists of more than 300,000 images. It is divided into a general photo collection, a biography collection, special collections, and a negative collection. An index to the Archives' portrait collection can be found online <www.michigan.gov/hal>. Select "Our Agencies," then "Michigan Historical Center," and "State Archives of Michigan." The Burton Historical Collection at the Detroit Public Library has 250,000 images in its photo collection; many other libraries and archives in Michigan have photo collections. Some libraries have put some of their images online. These include:

- Charlevoix County Photos by Bob Miles <www.charlevoix.lib.mi.us/main-m.htm>
- Grand Century, photos of Grand Rapids <www.grpl.org/coll/grandintro.html>
- Historical Images of Battle Creek <www2.willard.lib.mi.us/>
- Saginaw Images <www.saginawimages.org/>

Other online sources for Michigan photographs include the American Memory Web site <memory.loc.gov/ammem/amhome.html>. (See Chapter 9 for more details.) Books with Michigan photographs include the "Images of America" and "Postcard History" series, published by Arcadia Publishing (see below), and *Michigan Remembered: Photographs From the Farm Security Administration and the Office of War Information, 1936-1943* (2001).

Michigan in Fiction: Descriptions of life in Michigan's past also can be found in fiction. In some cases, writers of Michigan fiction were "historical participants who had utilized fiction as a medium to records their experiences."[121] Bibliographies of Michigan fictions include:

- Andrews' *Michigan in Literature* (1992)
- Beasecker's *Michigan in the Novel 1816-1996: An Annotated Bibliography* (1998)
- Massie's *From Frontier Folk to Factory Smoke: Michigan's First Century of Historical Fiction* (1987)
- Michigan Authors and Illustrators Database <mel.org/miai/miai.html> includes information about authors and illustrators born in Michigan, who live in Michigan, or who have written books about or set in Michigan.

Publishers: Several academic and regional publishers produce books about Michigan and the Great Lakes. These include:

- Arcadia Publishing <www.arcadiapublishing.com>, a leading publisher of regional and local history, currently has more than 100 titles about Michigan, including several from their "Images of America" and "Postcard History" series
- Michigan State University Press <msupress.msu.edu/> publishes the series "Discovering the Peoples of Michigan" and many other books about Michigan and the Great Lakes

- Wayne State University Press <wsupress.wayne.edu/glb/glb.htm> publishes the Great Lakes Books Series
- Program Source International <www.program-source.com/ > has produced several Michigan town video histories
- University of Michigan Press <www.press.umich.edu/> publishes books about Michigan and the Great Lakes

Records in Canada

Many of Michigan's early residents came from Canada – either directly or after staying there for several years after immigration from the eastern United States or another country. For most of Michigan's history, Michigan and Canadian residents have easily traveled back and forth between the two areas. In addition, the French and then later the British governed early Michigan. In the 1770s, for example, the British administered Michigan "as part of the province of Quebec."[122] Up until 1789, serious crimes and disputes were sent to Montreal or Quebec for trial, and for several years after that time they were dealt with at various courts in Sandwich (now Windsor), Ontario.[123] For these reasons, information about Michigan residents may be found in Canada. There are many excellent guides to Canadian research, including the following:

- *French Canadian Sources: A Guide for Genealogists* (2002)
- Baxter's *In Search of Your Canadian Roots: Tracing Your Family Tree in Canada* (2000)
- DuLong's *French-Canadian Genealogical Research* (1995)
- Merriman's *Genealogy in Ontario: Searching the Records* (1996)

Helpful Web sites include:

- 1871 Census of Ontario <db.library.queensu.ca/census/>
- 1901 Census of Canada <www.archives.ca/02/020122_e.html>
- Canada GenWeb <www.rootsweb.com/~canwgw/>
- Canadian County Atlas Digital Project <digital.library.mcgill.ca/countyatlas/search.htm>
- National Archives of Canada Genealogy Research Tips <www.archives.ca/02/020202_e.html>
- Ontario Cemetery Finding Aid <www.islandnet.com/ocfa/homepage.html>, a database of more than two million burials
- Our Roots: Canada's Local Histories Online <www.ourroots.ca/e/intro1.asp>, more than 4,000 books searchable by title, author, or keyword

In addition, Riddell's *Michigan Under British Rule: Law and Law Courts 1760-1796* (1926) reprints court records relating to the present-day area of Michigan that were filed in Canada.

8
People of Michigan

Michigan has a rich cultural heritage. From its original Native American inhabitants to the early French explorers, from the former slaves who came to Michigan via the Underground Railroad to the European and Middle Eastern settlers, Michigan's population includes a wide variety of ethnic and racial backgrounds. "Over the last 400 years at least 75 ethnic groups coming from 150 countries have given the state one of the most ethnically diverse populations in the United States."[1]

Immigration Patterns

The first residents of Michigan, of course, were Native Americans, primarily members of six tribal groups. French explorers and settlers were the first Europeans to locate in Michigan, and up until the end of the 19th century, most of Michigan's settlers were from northwestern and central Europe, Canada, or the northeastern United States. Then in the early 20th century, immigrants from southern and eastern Europe as well as residents from the southern United States poured into Michigan. "Peoples from Latin America, Asia, and virtually all other parts of the world" followed later in the 20th century.[2]

Michigan Becomes the "Third New England": Until the early 1820s most of Michigan's European settlers – more than 6,000 out of about 9,000 – were French in background.[3] But starting in 1800 families of English Protestant ancestry – Yankees – primarily from Vermont, New Hampshire, and Massachusetts, along with New Yorkers, began to settle in southern Michigan. "The largest numbers came from western New York, but were largely the descendants of Yankees who had settled in [that] region after the American Revolution."[4] This area of New York had long been known as the Second New England.

Between 1820 and 1824 "several waves of Yankee settlers flowed into [Michigan's] Washtenaw, Lenawee, and Hillsdale counties"; they tended to avoid areas where the French "were already entrenched."[5] After the opening of the Erie Canal in 1825, Yankees flooded southern Michigan from Monroe to Berrien counties. In fact, during most of the 1830s Michigan "was the most popular destination for westward-moving pioneers."[6] In the late 1830s, for example, the number of settlers from western New York moving into the Grand Rapids area prompted promoters to refer to that city as the "Rochester of the West."[7] "The Erie Canal contributed greatly to the predominantly Yankee make-up of Michigan's settlement between the 1820's and 1850."[8] The State of Michigan even became known as the Third New England.

Most Yankees came to Michigan for the inexpensive farmland, though many young men from Maine came to the state in the 1840s and 1850s for the lumber industry. Other Yankees started small businesses. They had heard about Michigan from "guidebooks, travelers' diaries and journals, newspapers, letters and word of mouth."[9] They brought with them strong values and a desire to transplant their institutions and preserve New England patterns of life. Michigan's township system, for example, was modeled after both New England and New York styles of local government. "Many southern Michigan communities bear names commonly found in New England," and many towns with their orderly streets and homes even resembled New England communities.[10] Yankees tended to be "evangelical Protestants, especially Presbyterians, Congregationalists, and Baptists."[11] They built churches, schools and colleges; formed temperance clubs; and promoted anti-slavery societies. Michigan's Yankee residents influenced the state's leadership in education and in "the antislavery crusade and other reforms of the 1840s and 1850s."[12]

It is estimated that "New Englanders and their descendants comprised over two-thirds of the state's population in 1838."[13] By 1850 about 41 percent of Michigan's residents had come from New York or New England, with the majority of those – 133,756 – from New York.[14] At that time Michigan settlers from the Northeast outnumbered settlers from the South 45 to 1, and they totaled more than 64 percent of the settlers not born in Michigan.[15] "As late as 1860, about a quarter of Michigan's population were native 'York staters,' while a sizable number had been born in the New England states proper."[16] Many more were the children and grandchildren of early Yankee pioneers; others with New England ancestry had lived elsewhere before moving to Michigan. (See "Phased Migration" in Chapter 2.) "As a result of the early immigration from New York and New England, Michigan probably has a larger percent of original New England stock than has any other State in the Union."[17] The common place of origin of these early settlers "helped shape the character of institutions in Michigan communities."[18] As a result, the descendants of Michigan's first Yankees do not have a separate ethnic identity, and the British and Canadians with British ancestry were easily assimilated into Michigan's Yankee culture.

Michigan Attracts Foreigners: Foreign-born settlers, many of them German and Irish, had started to move to Michigan by the 1830s. Yet on the eve of the Civil War, only about 20 percent of Michigan's residents were foreign-born. That number had increased from 13 percent in 1850. "Almost half of the foreigners [in 1860] came from the British Isles, primarily from Ireland and England; about a quarter came from Germany, and most of the remainder came from Canada."[19] Between 1860 and 1900, about 700,000 individuals – more than half of them from foreign lands – moved to Michigan for jobs in mills, mines, and factories. By 1890 more than 25 percent of Michigan's total population was foreign-born, most of them from Canada with the second largest number – 135,509 – from Germany.[20] Detroit's population grew from 80,000 in 1870 to 286,000 in 1900 when Detroit had the "largest percentage of non-English-speaking population in [the] nation – 11.98 percent."[21] The Upper Peninsula, particularly the copper and iron mining areas, also attracted large numbers of foreign-born settlers. "By 1920 Mackinac County was the only Upper Peninsula county that had less than one-half of its population of foreign-born stock."[22]

By the turn of the 20th century, more than 22 percent of Michigan's residents were foreign-born and about 61 percent of Michigan's residents had foreign ancestry, with the five most numerous countries of origin being Germany, Canada, the United Kingdom, Ireland, and Poland. "These five countries of origin accounted for 46 percent of the total foreign stock in Michigan. Ranking just below the first five were people with origins in Scandinavia – the Swedes, Norwegians, and Danes."[23]

Immigrants from Canada and northwestern and central Europe continued to move into the state in the 20th century, but the majority of Michigan's new immigrants came from southern and eastern Europe – at least until the 1920s when federal legislation established national origin quotas for immigration.[24] Many were attracted to jobs in the auto industry. Poles, for example, became the dominant ethnic group in Detroit. "By 1930, despite restrictions on immigration that had been enforced for some time, Poles constituted the largest foreign-born group in Detroit, numbering 66,113."[25] Other eastern and southern European groups moved into the state, including Greeks, Hungarians, Italians, Rumanians, Russians, and South Slavs. Later, people from the Middle East, Latin America, and Asia moved to Michigan.

In addition, black and white workers from the American South came to Michigan in the early 20th century as part of the Great Northern Migration, "the largest internal migration in North American history."[26] Most came to work in the auto – and later defense – industries. "Between 1910 and 1920, Michigan's black population more than tripled, rising from 17,115 to 60,082."[27] There were more than 169,000 African Americans in the state by 1930, with 120,000 of those living in Detroit.[28] Several thousand Southern whites, most born in Arkansas, Kentucky, Missouri, and Tennessee, also moved to Michigan.

By 1930 a large number of Michigan's ethnic groups had come to the state only in the last 30 to 40 years.

> Italians and Russians outnumbered the Dutch, Swedes, and Irish. Many emigrated from Albania, Czechoslovakia, Hungary, Yugoslavia, Romania, Greece, Russia, and Mexico. Armenians, Chaldeans, Macedonians, and Arabs added to the mix. By 1973 Detroit hosted the largest Macedonian and Arabic-speaking communities in North America. The Poles, however, became Michigan's most prominent 'new' ethnic group of the 20th century, and were second in number only to the Canadians.[29]

Some of Michigan's ethnic groups are discussed in further detail below. Other sources that focus on the people of Michigan include *Ethnic Groups in Michigan* (1983), Graff's *The People of Michigan* (1974), and Vander Hill's *Settling the Great Lakes Frontier: Immigration to Michigan, 1837-1924* (1970). In addition, Michigan State University Press <www.msupress.msu.edu> is publishing a series of books called "Discovering the Peoples of Michigan." At this writing, more than 10 books have been published about various groups in the state.

Michigan's First Residents

At the time the first Europeans explored the Great Lakes area, about 15,000 Native Americans lived within the current geographical boundaries of Michigan. They included the Chippewa (Ojibwa), Menominee, Miami, Potawatomi, and Ottawa (Odawa) – all of the Algonquian linguistic group – and the Huron (Wyandot) of the Iroquoian linguistic group. Though the word "tribe" is typically used to describe different groups of Native people, researchers should note that the concept of "tribe" had little meaning to Michigan's first residents. Native people tended to identify more closely with others who shared their language and/or with smaller groups, such as clans or kin groups.[30] The Ottawa, for example, "were organized into four, or possibly more, large families (clans) who thought of each other as relatives."[31] In addition, Native people tended to share or use land, rather than "own" it; as a result, geographic boundaries between Native groups were often fluid.

Tribal Groups: The three major groups of Native people in Michigan were the Chippewa (Ojibwa), Ottawa (Odawa), and Potawatomi, who had "a loose association known as 'the three fires.'"[32] The three groups had a common language and cultural traditions and "expressed their relationship in family terms."[33] The Chippewa were known as the "Elder Brother," the Ottawa as the "Next Older Brother," and the Potawatomi as the "Younger Brother." Later, as European settlement encroached upon Native lands, the three groups worked together "for purposes of common defense."[34] The Chippewa (Ojibwa), Ottawa (Odawa), and Potawatomi continue to be the major tribal groups in Michigan today, with the Chippewa being the largest. Individuals of Native American descent live throughout the state, with large populations on and near reservations or trust lands and in Detroit and other large cities. Researchers should note that some Native Americans in Michigan today are not descendants of Michigan tribes; in fact, one source claims that Native Americans from more than 30 different North American groups live throughout the state.[35]

Chippewa (Ojibwa): The Ojibwa of Sault Ste. Marie was the first group of Native people "sighted by Europeans on Michigan soil."[36] Many lived along the southern shore of Lake Superior. The popular name "Chippewa" is a corruption of the name "Ojibwa," "Ojibwe," or "Ojibway." Other names for this group include "Saulters," a French label, and "Anishinabe," an Algonquian word that translates to "first man" or "original man." In the late 17th century, the Chippewa began visiting the Lake Huron coast of the Lower Peninsula and later established villages between the Straits of Mackinac and Detroit. They soon became the predominant Native group in eastern Michigan, with large settlements in the Saginaw Valley, near Detroit, and at the Straits of Mackinac.[37] In the 1830s epidemics of cholera and smallpox among the Saginaw-Chippewa communities reduced their population to "a third of their original size, and survivors scattered to Canada and elsewhere in Michigan."[38]

Huron (Wendat or Wyandot): At the time of French contact in the 17th century, the Wendat lived along the south shore of Lake Superior and later at the Straits of Mackinac with the Ottawa.[39] The French named them "Huron," after their hairstyle. One group of Huron moved to the Detroit area in 1701 after the conclusion of the Iroquois Wars.[40] They became known as the "Wyandot," a version of their name, "Wendat." An 1809 act of Congress gave the Wyandot a tract of land in southeastern Michigan, but Michigan Governor Lewis Cass later negotiated a treaty with them to give up this land in exchange for "a tract of 4,996 acres along the Huron River in Wayne County."[41] The Wyandot later moved into Ohio, and in an 1842 treaty "relinquished all their claims to land in Michigan."[42] They later moved to Wyandotte County, Kansas, and still later to northeastern Oklahoma, where they lost their tribal organization and identity.[43]

Menominee: At the time of French contact, some Menominee lived in the central Upper Peninsula, near the Menominee River and numbered about 3,000, but most Menominee lived in the area of present-day Wisconsin.[44]

Miami: In the late 17th century, the Miami lived in southwestern Michigan, near the Saint Joseph and Kalamazoo rivers.[45] In 1703, the Miami were among the 2,000 or so Native people who had moved to the Detroit area at the invitation of Cadillac, but the main part of their settlement in Michigan was still on the Saint Joseph River.[46] Later in the 18th century, they were "displaced southward into Indiana."[47]

Ottawa (Odawa): In the late 17th century, the Ottawa lived at the Straits of Mackinac. By the early 18th century, they had moved along the shores and among the islands of northern Lake Huron and numbered about 3,000 people.[48] "Later the main portion of the tribe settled at Waganakisi (L'Arbre Croche). It was from this area that they began to spread in many directions, with the main body settling on the east shore of Lake Michigan as far south as the Saint Joseph River."[49] A smallpox epidemic swept through the Grand River valley in 1835, killing an unknown number of Ottawa and causing others to flee.[50] Some Ottawa later fled to Canada to avoid being removed to Kansas, but most escaped this fate "when the Treaty of Washington in 1836 reserved five tracts of land, totaling 142,000 acres, in northern Michigan" for the Chippewa and Ottawa tribes.[51] "In 1850 the Ottawas were offered Michigan citizenship, and a year later the Michigan legislature petitioned the U.S. government to grant them permanent residency in Michigan."[52] Citizenship and the right to vote was granted only if the Ottawa renounced their tribal affiliation, but in this way, many of the Ottawa avoided dispersal and removal.[53]

Potawatomi: In the late 17th century, Potawatomi from the present-day area of Wisconsin migrated "south and eastward around the end of Lake Michigan" and, along with the Miami, lived near Fort Saint Joseph in Berrien County.[54] "By the end of the 18th century, the Potawatomi, including a segment of this tribe known as the Mascoutens or 'little prairie people,' occupied the southwestern and central part of the Lower Peninsula where they were sometimes joined by their old Wisconsin neighbors, the Sauk and Fox."[55] Between 1838 and 1840 some Potawatomi were removed west, but most were able to stay in Michigan. Others moved to Walpole Island, a Canadian island in Lake Saint Clair.

Native People and the French: The French "co-existed fairly harmoniously" with the Native people in Michigan.[56] The French used Native Americans in the fur trade, for example, and in return gave them various goods of European manufacture. "Even the zealous efforts of the missionaries and the French desire to save souls did not seriously disrupt the Indian people. They were baptized by the thousands and were faithful in their attendance at Mass to please the French."[57] Unfortunately, Native Americans became dependent on European technology, particularly guns, and this made them "vulnerable to European control."[58]

Shortly after Detroit was established in 1701, about 2,000 Huron, Miami, Ottawa, and Chippewa people moved to the Detroit area at the invitation of the French. This was the "biggest change in Indian settlement patterns in the upper lakes since the Iroquois attacks ... 60 years earlier."[59] By 1703 most of the Native people living near Michilimackinac had moved to Detroit, forcing the Jesuits to abandon their Saint Ignace mission. The French cultivated friendships with Native groups in an effort to use them in the fur trade and as a military buffer against "hostile groups like the Iroquois."[60]

Native People and the British: For the most part, Native Americans considered themselves allies of the French and not "vanquished enemies of the British."[61] British policies, such as those that "made it difficult for native people to acquire the firearms, powder, and shot that they had become dependent upon for hunting," angered Native Americans.[62] Eventually these policies and the general attitude of the British toward Native Americans led to the siege of Detroit in 1763 by Chief Pontiac, an Ottawa leader, and Ottawa, Potawatomi, Chippewa, and Huron warriors. (See Chapter 2 for more.) Many Native Americans, however, allied with the British against the United States during the War of 1812.

Native People and the Americans: Under the government of the United States, Native Americans lost possession of almost all of their land in Michigan and were forced to adapt to a new way of life. Some stayed in rural areas and supported themselves through such activities as commercial fishing, lumbering, or farming. Others moved to cities to work in manufacturing. Many Native Americans in the early 20th century found themselves without "marketable skills in a rapidly evolving and increasingly complex society," and they constantly struggled against poverty.[63]

Treaties and Removal: In 1807 Native Americans owned almost all of the land in Michigan, but "57 years later they held only 32 square miles – less than a single township."[64] Americans had acquired Native land through various treaties and other efforts, such as pressuring Native people to sell their land in order to pay debts. (For more on land treaties, see Chapter 6.)

National policy in the early 19th century was to remove Native Americans east of the Mississippi River – including those in Michigan – to lands west of the Mississippi River, but most of Michigan's Native Americans were able to stay in the state. One source says only 651 Native Americans were ever removed from Michigan, though other sources place the number higher. "Most [of those removed] were Potawatomi in southern Michigan; some were Chippewa and possibly a few Ottawa."[65] The Potawatomi were first moved to Missouri opposite Fort Levenworth; then two years later to Iowa, near Council Bluffs; and finally to Kansas. "Here many of the descendants of these Michigan Potawatomi continue to live to the present day, although an additional relocation of some of this group was made later in the 19th century to what is now Oklahoma."[66] In addition, some who moved west later returned to Michigan.

Some Native Americans were able to stay in Michigan due to treaty provisions. An 1854 treaty, for example, granted the Chippewas the right to stay in Michigan, and an 1855 treaty assured the Chippewas and Ottawas that they could not be removed.[67] Devout Catholic and Potawatomi leader Leopold Pokagon was able to "get an exemption in the Treaty of 1833 that allowed him and his band [of 250] to remain on the lands he had obtained in Silver Creek Township, Cass County."[68] Other Native Americans saved annuity money to purchase lands, such as those at L'Arbre Croche and Grand River.[69] In one case, Michigan residents near Athens in Calhoun County purchased a small tract of land for the settlement of Native Americans, and in another case Catholic Bishop Frederic Baraga purchased land in Baraga County and deeded it to the Chippewas to prevent their removal west.[70]

Some Native Americans left the state on their own, moving to the Manitoulin Islands in Canada or just across the Saint Clair or Detroit rivers into Lower Canada (Ontario); others moved from southern Lower Michigan to the Upper Peninsula to avoid being removed.

Reservations: By the middle of the 19th century, a new Indian policy emerged in the United States. Instead of removing Native Americans west, the U. S. government attempted to concentrate Indians "on small reservations within their own territories, where they could be protected from undesirable influences and effectively exposed to education, Christianity, the domestic arts, and agriculture."[71] In Michigan, lands had been set aside or "reserved" in some of the early treaties. In the Saginaw Treaty of 1819, for example, reserve land was set aside for the Saginaw Chippewas, but the government later purchased this land in 1837. Today there are 12 federally recognized tribes in Michigan; most of them have reservation or trust land. They include:

- Bay Mills Chippewa Indian Community in Chippewa County's Brimley <www.baymills.org>
- Grand Traverse Bay Band of Ottawa and Chippewa Indians in Leelanau County's Suttons Bay <www.gtb.nsn.us>
- Hannahville Potawatomi Indian Community in Menominee County's Wilson <www.hannahville.com>
- Huron Potawatomi-Nottawaseppi Huron Band of Potawatomi in Kalamazoo County's Fulton
- Keweenaw Bay Indian Community in Baraga County <www.ojibwa.com/>
- Lac Vieux Desert Band of Lake Superior Chippewa Indians in Gogebic County's Watersmeet <www.lvdtribal.com/>
- Little River Band of Odawa Indians in Manistee County
- Little Traverse Bay Band of Odawa Indians in Emmet County's Petoskey
- Match-e-be-nash-she-wish Band of Potawatomi Indians of Michigan in Allegan County's Dorr
- Pokagon Band of Potawatomi Indians in Cass County's Dowagiac <www.pokagon.com>
- Saginaw Chippewa Indian Tribe in Isabella County <www.sagchip.org>
- Sault Ste. Marie Tribe of Chippewa Indians in Chippewa County's Sault Ste. Marie <www.sootribe.org>

Schools: Schools were set up to help assimilate Native Americans. (For more information, see Chapter 7.)

Records: There are a number of excellent books about the history and culture of Michigan's native people. These include:

- *Atlas of Great Lakes Indian History* (1987)
- Cleland's *A Brief History of Michigan Indians* (1975), *The Place of the Pike: A History of the Bay Mills Indian Community* (2001), and *Rites of Conquest: The History and Culture of Michigan's Native Americans* (1992)
- Clifton, Cornell, and McClurken's *People of The Three Fires: The Ottawa, Potawatomi, and Ojibway of Michigan* (1986)
- Kubiak's *Great Lakes Indians: A Pictorial Guide* (1999)

In addition, a number of records and resources are helpful for researchers tracing Native American ancestry. These include annuity rolls, census records, and land records. Many records are specific to a particular "tribe" or "band" of Native Americans, so researchers must first know the tribal affiliation of their ancestors. Researchers can often find this by starting their family research with the present and working their way back in time, instead of jumping first into Native American records. Researchers should also note that some of the records described below may not be available for every tribe or for every year. In addition, this is not an exhaustive list of Native American records.

Federal Censuses: Native Americans who did not live on reservations or treaty land were counted for the first time in the 1860 census, and all Native Americans were counted for the first time in the 1870 census. However, some Native Americans, such as those living in 1850 in Allegan County's Wayland Township <members.aol.com/RoundSky/1850.html>, may have been counted in earlier censuses. In addition, the race classification of "Indian" was not used until the 1880 census, so Native Americans in earlier censuses (and some later ones) may have been identified as "white," "black," or "mulatto."

The 1900 and 1910 censuses included special "Indian" schedules. "Indians answered the same questions as the general population," plus several additional ones including Indian name, individual's tribe, parents' tribes, degree of white blood, whether taxed, whether living in polygamy, and whether living in a fixed or moveable dwelling.[72] These schedules are found with the general population schedules or at the end of enumeration districts or counties.

State Censuses: Native Americans were counted in Michigan's state censuses for 1874, 1884, and 1894.[73] Unfortunately, many state census records have been lost or destroyed. (See Chapter 5 for more.)

Indian Censuses (1885-1940): The U.S. Congress required Indian agencies to take an annual census of residents living on Indian reservations between 1885 and 1940. "The tribal census collection is not complete. It neither includes every reservation nor every year."[74] Indian censuses in Michigan include those for Bay Mills School (Chippewa Indians) for 1909, 1910, 1911, 1913, 1914, and 1915, and Mackinac (Chippewa Indians) for 1902-1903, 1910, and 1915 to 1927. The censuses are available on microfilm through the National Archives and at other libraries, including the Library of Michigan. A surname index is available online for the Bay Mills School census <members.aol.com/RoundSky/baymills.html>. Enrollment records later replaced the annual census lists.

Annuity Rolls (1848-1940): Treaties often guaranteed a certain amount of money or goods paid on a regular basis, usually to the heads of families. Annuities were usually paid annually or quarterly, and the annuity rolls list the names of tribal members eligible for payment. Sometimes these lists also included the ages and genders of family members. Several annuity rolls have survived and are available in print or on microfilm. Lantz' *Ottawa and Chippewa Indians of Michigan, 1855-1868* (1993), for example, reprints an 1855 roll of Ottawas and Chippewas within the Michigan Indian Agency; 1857 roll of Chippewas of Sault Ste. Marie; 1857 and 1858 rolls for the Chippewas of Swan Creek and Black River; 1857, 1859, 1864, and 1865 rolls for Grand River Ottawas; 1865 roll for Chippewas of Saginaw, Swan Creek, and Black River; and the 1868 roll for Ottawas and Chippewas. Lantz also has compiled lists of *Ottawa and Chippewa Indians of Michigan, 1870-1909* (1991) and *The Potawatomi Indians of Michigan, 1843-1904* (1992). Some annuity lists, such as the 1846 list for Lake Superior Chippewa Indians <www.baylisslib.org/1846annuity.html>, can be found online.

Durant Roll: "Shortly before the turn of the 20th century the Michigan Odawa and Ojibwe descendants of the bands that were party to the 1855 treaty sued the federal government for money they believed was still owned them under the treaty."[75] They won their case, but before money could be distributed a census was taken of those entitled to the benefit. Bureau of Indian Affairs Special Agent Horace B. Durant came to Michigan and compiled a list or roll of individuals descended from the bands that signed the treaty. The roll, completed in 1908, listed "all persons who were enumerated in the 1870 census and their known descendants, living on 4 March 1907."[76] It included 5,644 members of the Grand River, Grand Traverse, Mackinac, and Sault Ste. Marie bands of the Ottawa (Odawa) and Chippewa (Ojibwe) and lists their "Durant roll number, Indian name, English name, relationship to head of the household, age, sex, tribal band, residence, and remarks."[77] Durant's field notes includes genealogical information to determine eligibility. A supplement roll, completed in 1910, lists "the names of children born after March 4, 1907, and prior to August 1, 1908."[78] The Durant roll is available on microfilm through the National Archives and several other libraries, including the Library of Michigan. Abstracts and indexes of the Durant roll as well as additional information also can be found online:

- Durant Index – Grand Traverse Band <members.aol.com/VWilson577/durant-gtb.html>
- Durant Introduction <members.aol.com/RoundSky/durant-intro.html>
- Ottawa and Chippewa of Michigan, including the 1870 Census, 1908 Durant Roll, and 1910 Durant Supplemental Roll <www.rootsweb.com/~mimackin/ottchipp.htm>
- Surnames from the Durant Roll – Sault Ste. Marie Band <members.aol.com/RoundSky/ssm-durant.html>

Land Records: Treaties sometimes allotted parcels of land to individual Native Americans. Though many "allotments were lost as a result of land fraud," some were later recorded as land patents.[79] (See Chapter 6 for more about land patents.) Cleland's *The Place of the Pike: A History of the Bay Mills Indian Community* lists 64 allotments at Iroquois Point distributed as a result of an 1855 treaty. An index of land patents resulting from the 1855 treaty with the Sault Ste. Marie, Grand River, Grand Traverse, Little Traverse, Mackinac, and other bands of Chippewas also can be found online <members.aol.com/roundsky/reserve.html>. Lockwood's *Indian Patents Issued in Leelanau County from Allotment Lists in the National Archives* (1978) also lists land patents.

Records of interest to researchers with Native American ancestry can be found in a variety of archives and libraries:

- The National Archives <www.archives.gov/research_room/genealogy/research_topics/native_american_records.html> and the National Archives' Great Lakes Region Facility in Chicago have Native American records <www.archives.gov/facilities/il/chicago/holdings_guide_02.html#75>.
- The Library of Michigan has microfilmed Indian census records among its many sources.

- Clarke Historical Library <clarke.cmich.edu/nativeamericans/index.htm> claims to have "the most complete collection in the state regarding Michigan's first people."[80]
- Mackinaw City Library <members.aol.com/RoundSky/jacob.html> has census records, annuity rolls, and other Native American genealogical information.
- The History Department at the Bay Mills Indian Community has a number of documents, photographs, maps, and "a complete genealogy of all of the major Bay Mills families from the late 18th century until modern times."[81]
- The Ziibiwing Cultural Society (see page 376) has census, annuity, and allotment records.

For additional information about researching Native American ancestry in Michigan, see Wilson's *Native American Research in Michigan: A Genealogical Guide* (1997). An online version of this book also is available <hometown.aol.com/roundsky/introduction.html>. Other online sources to assist researchers with Native American roots include the following:

- Native Genealogy: People of the Three Fires <www.rootsweb.com/~minatam/>
- Native Americans <www.rootsweb.com/~mimacki2/native_americans.html>
- NISHNAWBE-L <lists.rootsweb.com/index/usa/MI/misc.html #NISHNAWBE>, a mailing list for anyone researching Native Americans in Michigan or Wisconsin or the fur traders connected with them

Other Ethnic Groups in Michigan

French and French-Canadians: The French and French-Canadians – descendants of Canada's first French settlers – were the earliest Europeans in Michigan. They garrisoned military outposts, assisted missionaries in their efforts to convert Native people to Christianity, but most, however, were active in the fur trade. Permanent French Canadian settlers, primarily farmers known as habitants, started coming to the state in the early 18th century with the founding of Detroit by French military officer Antoine de Lamothe Cadillac. Cadillac wanted to encourage permanent settlement, so he granted small plots of land within the fort and outside of it on both sides of the Detroit River; many of these plots became known as "strip" or "ribbon" farms because they were about 500 feet wide along the river front and a half-mile or more in depth.[82] It was several years, however, before Detroit became a desirable location for settlers. "By 1750 the population of Detroit was 483 inhabitants plus transient voyageurs, Indians, and soldiers."[83] Between 1749 and 1752 more than 50 Quebec families moved to Detroit enticed by government notices promising free land and supplies for settlers.[84] By 1760, when France turned control of Detroit over to the British, there were about 2,000 inhabitants "scattered along the river on both sides for several miles."[85]

Most of Michigan's early settlers were French-Canadian, rather than French, and during the French period of Michigan's history most of the French-Canadian settlers came from the Montreal area.[86] "Only a few settlers who came to Detroit were born in France; for the most part these were former soldiers."[87] In addition to Detroit, Michilimackinac was an important French-Canadian settlement. "While Michilimackinac remained exclusively a fur trading post, Detroit became the most developed settlement west of Montreal."[88] Near the end of the 18th century, Monroe became "the third most important French Canadian settlement in Michigan."[89] The first era of French-Canadian immigration to Michigan ended in 1796, the same year the Americans gained control of Michigan. At that time, about 80 percent of Michigan residents were French-Canadian; some, however, fled from Michigan to Canadian communities, including Windsor and Amherstburg.[90]

A second wave of French-Canadian immigration to Michigan, lasting for nearly 100 years, started in 1840 and peaked between 1880 and 1890.[91] This second wave had tampered off by 1910 and "virtually ended with the Depression."[92] These French-Canadian settlers came primarily for opportunities in lumbering and mining, though some came to farm, and they tended to settle in "isolated towns and rural areas."[93] They generally came alone or with their families – not in groups like the Germans or Dutch. The Saginaw Valley and the Keweenaw Peninsula were two significant locations of French-Canadian settlement.[94]

Some French-Canadians came directly from Canada; others migrated to the state after living for a while in New England or New York. "Others had resided for a while in the Kankakee-Bourbonnais area of Illinois or the Green Bay-Manitowoc area of Wisconsin before drifting to Michigan."[95] Descendants of the first wave of settlers in Detroit also were among the new French-Canadian immigrants. By 1850 there were about 20,000 French-Canadians in Michigan, more than half had been born in Canada; this number increased to nearly 88,000 in 1900.[96]

At the turn of the 20th century nearly 60 percent of the foreign-born French-Canadians were living in eight counties: Alpena, Bay, Saginaw, and Wayne in the Lower Peninsula and Delta, Houghton, Marquette, and Menominee in the Upper Peninsula. Large concentrations of French-Canadians also were located in the cities of Cheboygan, Ludington, Manistee, and Muskegon and in the counties of Huron, Sanilac, and Tuscola.[97] Though Michigan had the largest settlement of French-Canadians in the Midwest, less than 4 percent of Michigan's total population in 1900 was foreign-born French-Canadians or children of French-Canadian parents.[98] In just 80 years French Canadians had gone from being the most numerous European group in Michigan to "a small minority."[99] By the 1920s little remained of French-Canadian culture in Michigan.[100] When opportunities in mining and lumbering waned in Michigan, some French-Canadians moved on to Wisconsin, Minnesota, or further west to Montana, Colorado, or Arizona to follow the industries. Others moved to Detroit to work in the auto industry; still others returned to Canada. Today Michigan has the fourth largest French-American and second largest French-Canadian population in the United States, with 489,240 persons of French ancestry and 191,699 persons of French-Canadian ancestry.[101]

Métis: The French word "Métis," meaning a person of mixed blood, was used to describe those of French and Native American ancestry. Cadillac, the founder of Detroit, first recommended that French habitants marry Native Americans "believing that miscegenation would win the Indians' loyalty and further their Christianization."[102] Later, marriages took place to facilitate trade relations or simply because of the regular interaction between French traders and Native American women. Fur traders, for example, often wintered near or in Native American settlements. "Typically, a French Canadian man took an Indian woman as his wife, more often married by tribal custom than a French religious ceremony."[103] Some of these alliances were short-lived, but the resulting children often took their father's name and were "acknowledged and cared for by him."[104] It also wasn't unusual for a French man to wed a Native American woman, even if he already had a wife in Canada.[105] By bridging two cultures, Métis men and women played an important role in the fur trade, often serving as interpreters or in other positions. Through the years, the Métis have blended in with their Native American or French Canadian families. "There is no strong, independent ethnic identity of Métis in Michigan."[106]

Sources: Several resources are available to assist Michigan researchers with French-Canadian ancestry:

- DuLong's *French Canadians in Michigan* (2001) gives an overview of French-Canadian settlement in the state, and Lamarre's *The French Canadians of Michigan: Their Contribution to the Development of the Saginaw Valley and the Keweenaw Peninsula, 1840-1914* (2003) focuses of those two regions.
- Early Catholic church records, such as those from Ste. Anne's Church in Detroit, are important sources of information for French-Canadian settlers. Other early Catholic records include "The Mackinac Register of Marriages, 1725-1821," published in Volume 18 of the *Wisconsin State Historical Society Collections;* "Mackinac Register of Baptisms and Interments, 1695-1821," published in Volume 19 of the *Wisconsin State Historical Society Collections;* and "The St. Joseph Baptismal Register" for 1720 to 1773, published in Volume 13 of the *Mississippi Valley Historical Review.* The Mackinac Register also has been reprinted by Quintin Publications <www.quintinpublications.com/mi.html> in book form and on CD, and the volumes of the *Wisconsin State Historical Society Collections* in which it appears are available online through Pioneering the Upper Midwest: Books from Michigan, Minnesota, and Wisconsin, ca. 1820 to 1910 <memory.loc.gov/ammem/umhtml/umhome.html>.
- Denissen's *Genealogy of the French Families of the Detroit River Region, 1791-1936* (1987) has information on more than 1,100 French families in the Detroit area.
- Lajeunesse's *The Windsor Border Region, Canada's Southernmost Frontier: A Collection of Documents* (1960).

- The French-Canadian Heritage Society of Michigan <fchsm.habitant.org> publishes *Michigan's Habitant Heritage* <fchsm.habitant.org/toc.htm>.
- Acadian and French-Canadian Genealogy <habitant.org>.
- Early French Families of Detroit <www.geocities.com/histmich/french familys.html>.
- French Canadian Voyageurs and Métis <www.rootsweb.com/~mimacki2/ voyageurs_and_metis.html>.
- Métis Women in the Fur Trade at Mackinac <www.rootsweb.com/~mimacki2/ women_in_the_fur_trade.html>.

Non-French Canadians: Because of Michigan's proximity to Canada, many of the state's foreign settlers have been Canadian-born. It's estimated, for example, that at least one of every four persons researching Michigan ancestry today will find a direct Ontario connection.[107] In 1850, 25 percent of Michigan's foreign immigrants were Canadians. This amount increased to 30 percent by 1870. "At [that] time they constituted the largest group of foreign-born people entering the state and outnumbered other foreign immigrant groups after this time as well."[108]

It is difficult, however, to determine how many Canadian residents in Michigan were not of French ancestry until the 1890 U.S. census, "the first to distinguish between French and English-speaking Canadians."[109] At that time there were more than 63,000 English-speaking Canadian men in Michigan, and that number had grown to more than 66,000 English-speaking Canadian men by 1900.[110] The total number of English-speaking Canadian men, women, and children in 1900 in Michigan was 151,915, "more than a ten-fold increase over 1850."[111] Most of these Canadians were from Ontario and "were predominantly of English, Irish, Scots, and German descent."[112] Some of these immigrants had lived in Ontario only for a short time, while others had lived in Canada for many years. A number of Loyalists, Americans who had supported the British during the American Revolution, also had settled in Ontario and "some of their descendants subsequently moved from Ontario to Michigan."[113]

Canadians came to Michigan for many of the same reasons as other immigrants – for land and jobs. In addition, in the late 1830s many Canadians came to Michigan due to their country's unsettled political conditions. During the Civil War, some Ontario men moved to Michigan to become soldiers; some were motivated by adventure, others by enlistment bonuses. "Some Ontario residents left in groups to found settlements in Michigan," such as the Canadian Settlement in Keene Township, Ionia County.[114] Most, however, came alone or with their immediate families. By 1900 there were large concentrations of Canadians in Bay, Chippewa, Huron, Kent, Saginaw, Saint Clair, Sanilac, Tuscola, and Wayne counties, but Canadians also lived in every Michigan county.[115] Unlike French Canadians, however, non-French Canadians "have left few written records of their immigrant experiences," and those of British and Scots ancestry easily assimilated into Michigan's culture.[116]

British: The term "British" is used to identify residents from Great Britain, which includes England, Scotland, Wales, Ulster or Northern Ireland, and, before the 20th century, also the Republic of Ireland. Therefore, all English are British but not all British are English.[117]

English: English settlers have been in Michigan since the first British soldiers, fur traders, and merchants came to Michigan in the late 18th century. American culture, however, has been heavily influenced by English culture, so it is easy for English immigrants to assimilate into American culture. As a result, it is difficult to pinpoint dates of arrival or geographic locations of settlement for English immigrants in Michigan. Census records show that by 1870 there were more than 35,000 English-born residents in Michigan. This number increased to more than 44,000 in 1880 and 55,000 in 1890.[118] The City of Detroit had 7,168 English settlers in 1890, more than half of which had arrived since 1870.[119] "Throughout the state's history, many Englishmen have made their way to Michigan seeking employment. Often these immigrants were single men. ... Many married soon after arriving in Michigan and settled down to family life."[120] Residents of Cornwall, England, came to Michigan in significant numbers starting in the mid-19th century to work in Michigan's Upper Peninsula mines (see below).

Scots: Scots, residents of Scotland, also known as "Scotch" or "Scottish," were among the first British soldiers, fur traders, and merchants in Michigan. The Scots, for example, "were dominant in the establishment and management of the North West Company, the American Fur Company, and the Hudson's Bay Company, all of which operated in the Great Lakes region on both sides of what is now the U.S.-Canadian border."[121] Scots later came to the state to farm or work in the lumber industry; some came directly from Scotland, others by way of Canada or the eastern United States. The Scottish names and birthplaces of "a significant number of 'Yankees,'" for example, suggest that many had originated in Scotland.[122] Some Scottish lumberjacks from Ontario were seasonal residents of Michigan, working in Michigan's lumber industry and then returning home in the off-season.

Scots settled throughout Michigan, easily assimilating into Michigan's culture. Though they did not feel the need "to cluster in ethnic communities," there may have been some Scottish settlements in the Thumb area of the state.[123] Chandler Township in Huron County, for example, was known as the "Scotch Settlement" in the 1870s. Argyle in Sanilac County was settled by "Scots from Ontario."[124]

Scots came to Michigan in increasing numbers in the 20th century for opportunities in the auto industry. "By the 1920s the greatest concentration of Scots in the state was in the metropolitan Detroit area."[125] Accurate statistics on the number of Scots in Michigan are "difficult to come by and often unreliable" because Scots were often identified as British, Canadians, or Yankees.[126] According to the 2000 U.S. census, however, Michigan has the fourth largest Scottish-American population in the United States, with 224,803 persons of Scottish ancestry.[127]

Scots Irish: Descendants of the Lowland Scots who had been exiled to Ireland in the early 17th century became known as the "Scots Irish" or "Scotch Irish," though they were sometimes identified simply as "Irish." Scots Irish also were among the early settlers of Michigan. Scots Irish from Ontario, for example, settled Kinross in Chippewa County.[128] They also were among the Southern whites that came to Michigan as part of the Great Northern Migration in the early 20th century.[129]

Irish: The first Irish in the area of present-day Michigan arrived during the French regime. "Early records of Mackinac and Detroit reveal evidence of a small Irish population in the 1720s."[130] About 30 Irish persons lived in Michigan by 1778, and there were 55 by 1800.[131] The Irish – both Catholic and Protestant – began arriving in significant numbers in the early 19th century. By 1840 there were an estimated 4,000 to 5,000 Irish persons or persons of Irish ancestry living in Michigan; that number increased to more than 42,000 by 1870, "with major settlements in Wayne, Houghton, Kent, and Marquette counties."[132] Most Irish pioneers came to Michigan in search of work. They found jobs in mining and lumbering; they dug canals and built railroad lines; and they farmed, fished, and practiced other trades.

One of the first regions settled by Irish immigrants was the Union Lake area of Oakland County, originally known as "the Dublin area."[133] Settlers first moved there around 1830. As early as 1835 "unskilled Irish workers came to Grand Rapids ... to dig the canals along the Grand River."[134] By 1846 there was a significant Irish community in Grand Rapids.[135] Other Irish communities included Ann Arbor's Kerrytown, Lenawee County's Irish Hills, and Hubbardston, founded in 1849 on the Ionia-Clinton county line. Irish fishermen, many from County Donegal, moved to Beaver Island in Lake Michigan in the 1850s; "about a third of the island's year-round population of 400 people claim Irish heritage today."[136] By the mid-19th century, the Irish also could be found "in most of the Upper Peninsula's mining communities."[137] Many Irish miners, however, moved to the copper mining region near Butte, Montana, by the 1920s.[138]

The Irish began moving to Detroit in serious numbers in the 1820s, and by the early 1830s the Irish parish, Most Holy Trinity Catholic Church, had been established. By 1850 about one out of every seven people in Detroit was Irish; "the Irish ranked first among Detroit's nationality groups," but the Germans soon outnumbered the Irish.[139] Detroit's Eighth Ward became known as Corktown, because of the large number of immigrants from Ireland's Cork County. By the 1880s Corktown had about 1,000 Irish families, most from "Kerry, Cork, Limerick, Tipperary, and Connaught."[140]

Many of Michigan's Irish entered the state by way of Canada or had lived first on the East Coast, including New York and Boston.[141] Unlike the East Coast, Irish potato famine immigrants did not flood Michigan in the 1840s, primarily because many could not afford to travel inland. However, other Irish moved from the East Coast to escape discrimination.[142]

Researchers should note that not every person in Michigan with an Irish surname was Irish. At least one source reports that Irish logging camp foremen often renamed Swedes or other foreign-born workers with Irish names. "The name went down on the records for posterity, and some of their descendants are known by these names yet today."[143]

Cornish: Miners originally from Cornwall first came to Michigan in the mid-19th century. During the first half of the 19th century, the copper mines in Cornwall, a small peninsula in southwestern England, "were among the richest in the world and the workers in these mines undoubtedly the best underground miners in the world."[144] The first Cornish in Michigan came from the lead mines in southwestern Wisconsin or from Canada.[145] Later, they came directly from Cornwall, in many cases recruited by the mine companies.

By 1844 there were about 20 Cornish working near Copper Harbor. Thousands more came in the years that followed, most to work in the copper mines in Houghton and Keweenaw counties. "Smaller groups of Cornishmen settled in the iron ore districts of Marquette-Ishpeming, Iron Mountain, Iron River and on the Gogebic Range at Bessemer, Wakefield and Ironwood."[146] The Cornish became so well established in the mining districts "that by 1882 one writer stated, 'almost all the captains, superintendents and shift bosses were Cornish.'" Many Cornish families moved from mine to mine, so by the 1880s a Cornish couple might have a family with children born in Cornwall, southwestern Wisconsin, the Keweenaw Peninsula, and the iron ranges of Michigan.[147]

Though most Cornish worked in mining, some were ministers of the Methodist faith, and others ran small businesses. When mining fell on hard times in the early 20th century, many Cornish moved to Detroit, Lansing, or Grand Rapids to work in manufacturing or migrated to western states to work in mining.

Many of the Cornish had English surnames, so they were often listed as English or British in official records. "However, the Cornish were originally Celtic," and some have Celtic surnames, such as those that start with "Tre," "Poll," or "Pen."[148]

Welshmen: Though "never a prominent ethnic group in Michigan," many Welshmen settled in the Upper Peninsula mining communities or in Detroit.[149] Many of the miners "migrated from the anthracite coal mining regions of Pennsylvania rather than directly from Wales."[150] At least one Welshmen was in Detroit in the early 19th century. John R. Williams, author of Detroit's Charter, was the city's first mayor in 1825.[151] A Welsh community later developed near Grand River and Chicago Avenues, and in 1919 the Welsh United Presbyterian Church organized in Detroit.[152]

Manxmen: Several residents of the Isle of Man, "formerly an English protectorate in the Irish sea," came to Michigan's Upper Peninsula to work in the iron mines.[153] Several had worked in the Colorado lead mines before coming to Michigan. "During the peak years of the mining operations on the Marquette Range there were perhaps 12 to 15 Manx families living in the Ishpeming area."[154]

Sources: Several resources are available to assist Michigan researchers with British or Irish roots:

- Rowse's *The Cousin Jacks: The Cornish in America* (1969) includes biographical information about a number of Michigan's Cornish residents and a listing of Celtic surnames.
- The Dick and June Ross Collection: Cornish to Michigan <www.mfhn.com/houghton/rosscoll/> has a number of records relating to Cornish immigrants, including vital records, cemetery transcriptions, obituaries, naturalizations, and Calumet and Hecla Mining Employment Card Transcriptions <www.mifamilyhistory.org/ross_coll/>.
- Forrester's *Scots in Michigan* (2003) provides an overview of Scottish immigration to Michigan.
- The Irish Genealogical Society of Michigan <www.rootsweb.com/~miigsm/> published *Our Roots Began in Ireland* (2001), a surname registry with surnames sorted alphabetically, by location in Ireland, by locations settlers lived prior to coming to Michigan, and by residences within Michigan.
- IRISH-MI-L <lists.rootsweb.com/index/usa/MI/misc.html #IRISH-MI> is an e-mail list for anyone researching Irish ancestry in Michigan. The companion Web site, Irish in Michigan <home.carolina.rr.com/ninah/irishmi/index.htm>, features a surname registry and a list of Irish individuals in Michigan's 1850 and 1870 mortality schedules.
- McGee's *The Passing of the Gael* (1975) has information about the Irish in western Michigan.

African Americans: African Americans, both slave and free, lived in Michigan from the state's earliest days. The French often brought black slaves into their Canadian colonies and may have brought slaves into the present-day area of Michigan as early as 1688. Some historians believe at least one African man was in Detroit in the early 18th century.[155] "One famous independent African American explorer, Jean Baptiste Point Du Sable, was held by the British as a political prisoner at Fort Michilimackinac in 1780."[156] In 1796 several free blacks lived in Detroit, and both African and Native slaves were "noted in the records."[157] Most slaves were used as laborers, house servants, or carriage drivers; "a few were given educations and became trusted employees."[158] That's not to say that some slaves weren't mistreated, but their treatment was often less severe than in other parts of the United States.

In the late 18th and early 19th centuries slavery in Michigan was subject to two conflicting laws. In 1793, while the British still controlled Michigan, the House of Assembly of Upper Canada (now Ontario) passed a law prohibiting the importation of slaves from either the United States or British colonies. The law further ruled that slaves in Upper Canada, including the area of present-day Michigan, would remain in slavery until death. Their children born after the passage of this new law would be freed at age 25, and that group's children would be born free.[159]

However, the Northwest Ordinance, passed by the United States in 1787 to govern the Northwest Territory, prohibited slavery and "involuntary servitude." When Michigan passed from British to American control in 1796, it became part of the Northwest Territory. Yet treaties governing the change in governments "guaranteed that citizens would not lose any property rights."[160]

In 1807 Michigan's Territorial Supreme Court tackled the dilemma and ruled that slaves born before 1793 would remain slaves and their children born after 31 May 1793 would be slaves only until age 25. "However, anyone born in Michigan after the American occupation in 1796 automatically was free."[161] In addition, runaway slaves from Canada did not have to be returned to their masters, but runaway slaves from other states in the United States were to be returned. In 1810 there were about 300 slaves in the Detroit area, but the practice of slavery gradually faded from Michigan life.[162] By 1837 – when Michigan entered the Union as a free state – there were only three slaves in the state and more than 200 free African Americans.[163]

Like many states, however, Michigan passed a series of laws designed to discourage the migration of African Americans to the Territory. In 1827, for example, Michigan had passed "An Act to regulate Blacks and Mulattoes and to punish the kidnapping of such persons." Otherwise known as the "Black Code," the law required African Americans to possess a certificate of freedom, to register themselves and their children with the clerk of the county court in the county where they lived, and to post a $500 bond guaranteeing good behavior. In practice, however, few African Americans registered with their county clerk or posted bond, and the Black Code was rarely enforced. Other laws prohibited African Americans from voting or marrying white spouses. Despite these laws, Michigan in the early 19th century became a strong antislavery state.

The movement of escaped slaves across the Detroit River into Canada dates back at least until 1815, and Michigan's first antislavery organization – the Logan Female Anti-Slavery Society – was founded in Lenawee County in 1832 by Quaker Elizabeth M. Chandler. Quakers were in the forefront of antislavery agitation; they helped form the Michigan Antislavery Society in 1836, the same year a Quaker preacher brought the first fugitive slaves into Cass County via the Underground Railroad. The Underground Railroad was a loosely organized group of people and organizations that helped escaping slaves move north, often to Canada. Underground Railroad "stations" where fugitive slaves and their conductors rested were "no more than 15 to 20 miles apart."[164]

Because of its proximity to Canada, Michigan was an important gateway to freedom. Underground Railroad routes included ones from Toledo to Detroit, Toledo to Adrian to Detroit, Saint Joseph to Detroit, Chicago to Detroit, Muskegon to Detroit, Chicago to the Upper Peninsula, and Detroit to Saginaw Bay.[165] "An established route ran from Niles through Cassopolis, Schoolcraft, Climax, Battle Creek, and along the old Territorial Road to Detroit or northward to Port Huron."[166] It's estimated that more than 30,000 slaves escaped into Canada via Michigan between 1842 and 1862, the years the Underground Railroad was most active.[167] Some escaped slaves settled in Michigan, but they accounted for only about 5 percent of the total African-American population in pre-Civil War Michigan, perhaps only 350 people.[168]

Several times slave owners, usually from Kentucky, came to Michigan to reclaim their "property," but Michigan residents often assisted the fugitive slaves through legal means, subterfuge, force, or intimidation. One of the most famous cases involved Adam Crosswhite and his family, who had escaped to Calhoun County and settled near Marshall in 1844. Three years later slave catchers arrived at his house, but a crowd of about 100 irate Marshall residents, carrying clubs and knives, soon foiled their attempt. Also in 1847 the same group of Kentucky slave catchers came to Cass County, but they soon found themselves "surrounded by crowds of angry farmers armed with clubs, scythes, and other farm implements."[169]

Incidents like these helped encourage the U.S. government to pass the 1850 Fugitive Slave Act that required citizens to assist in the recovery of fugitive slaves and denied a fugitive's right to a trial by jury. The act encouraged many slave catchers to kidnap any blacks, regardless of whether they were runaway slaves. As a result, many African Americans, both fugitive slaves and those who had been born free, moved to Canada to avoid the possibility of returning to slavery. Michigan responded in 1855 by passing a Personal Liberty Law that "would effectively strip the detested 1850 federal Fugitive Slave Act of much of its effectiveness in Michigan."[170] The new law, for example, gave those accused of being fugitive slaves the right to a trial by jury and directed prosecuting attorneys to defend all persons accused of being escaped slaves. All costs for defense were to be paid by the state, and local jails could not be used to hold suspected fugitive slaves. The law also punished those falsely accusing another of being a fugitive slave by imprisoning them for three to five years. Persons "wrongfully and maliciously" seizing an African American in an attempt to return them to slavery could be fined from $500 to $1,000 or imprisoned for five years.[171]

With the passage of this law Michigan became even more of a refuge for fugitive slaves, but by far most black settlers in pre-Civil War Michigan had been born free. Free African Americans from New England, for example, arrived in Michigan in the 1820s and 1830s. "Many were New Yorkers and settled in Washtenaw County near the present city of Ann Arbor."[172] By 1840 there were 70 free African Americans in Washtenaw County, the second largest number of African Americans in any Michigan county.[173] "Many quasi-freed blacks were sent or brought north by masters who were also their fathers."[174]

Before the Civil War, most free African Americans lived in Detroit or Wayne County, but the largest rural black settlement in early Michigan was in Cass County in southwestern Michigan. The community grew from one African American in 1830 to more than 1,000 in 1860. In fact, Cass County had the second greatest number of African Americans in Michigan in 1860, 20 percent compared to Wayne County's 25 percent.

Free African Americans from Ohio, Indiana, Illinois, and other areas of the United States started coming to Cass County in 1845. Many of them had lived for years in these states before moving on to Michigan. Several of the families from Logan County, Ohio, had originated in Northampton County, North Carolina. Forty-seven freed slaves from Cabell County, Virginia, also moved to Cass County in 1849. "Sampson Saunders, a planter of that county (which fronts on the Ohio River in what was to become West Virginia), had died some time before this, and had provided by will that his slaves should be freed and that his executors might expend $15,000 in establishing homes for them in a free community."[175] Cass County was selected because of the availability of inexpensive land and the number of friendly abolitionists, many of them Quaker, in the area. About two-thirds of the African-American settlers in Cass County lived in Calvin and Porter Townships. They purchased land; built homes, schools, and churches; and farmed or established businesses.[176]

By the 1850s African Americans had established communities in other areas of southern Lower Michigan, including Niles and Saint Joseph in Berrien County, Battle Creek and Marshall in Calhoun County, Fayette in Hillsdale County, Kalamazoo in Kalamazoo County, and Adrian in Lenawee County.[177] They lived in 33 of Michigan's 41 counties, and a few African Americans had started moving into the mining and lumbering areas of the Upper Peninsula and northern Lower Peninsula.

In the 1860s most of Michigan's African Americans lived in the southeastern counties of Macomb, Monroe, Oakland, Saint Clair, Washtenaw, and Wayne or Michigan's southwestern counties of Allegan, Berrien, Cass, Saint Joseph, and Van Buren. The two areas had 71 percent of Michigan's total African-American population, with the rest scattered "in either the agricultural villages in southcentral Michigan or in the forest and mining regions in the northern counties."[178] For example, about 65 African Americans from Ohio, Canada, and elsewhere moved in 1861 into Mecosta County's Wheatland Township in central Lower Michigan.[179] This was the nucleus of a community that was to spread throughout Mecosta and Isabella counties and to grow to nearly 1,200 by 1900. More than 100 African Americans also lived in the Upper Peninsula during the 1860s. Michigan's free black population rose from 261 in 1830 to 6,799 in 1860.[180]

During the early part of the Civil War, the Michigan legislature passed a law prohibiting the enlistment of African Americans in the state's militia. Many of Michigan's African Americans enlisted elsewhere. In early 1863, for example, "200 men were enlisted in Detroit for the 54th Massachusetts Colored Infantry."[181] In August 1863 – more than two years after the start of the Civil War – African Americans were mustered into the First Michigan Colored Infantry, later renamed the 102nd Regiment of the United States Colored Troops. Throughout the war 1,660 African Americans, some from Canada and other parts of the United States, served with this unit,

By 1880, there were 15,100 African Americans in Michigan, more than half lived in rural communities. In the late 19th century, however, African Americans began moving to cities in increasing numbers. "By 1910, a majority (71 percent) of Michigan blacks lived in urban areas."[182] Michigan's African-American population increased dramatically before and during World War I and World War II as southern rural blacks – most from Alabama, Arkansas, Florida, Georgia, Louisiana, Mississippi, South Carolina, and Texas – moved to industrial centers in Michigan as part of the Great Northern Migration. Michigan's African-American population increased nearly tenfold between 1910 and 1930, rising to 169,453. It increased to more than 200,000 by 1940, and during the decade of the 1940s the rate of increase of Michigan's African-American population was "higher than that of any other state."[183]

Michigan's "Black Eden": Perhaps the most unique African-American community in Michigan was Lake County's Idlewild. "Because resort facilities across the country were segregated, in 1912 four white couples purchased a 2,700-acre parcel of land and secured land rights for two sections near Idlewild Lake in rural Michigan to establish a vacation community for African Americans."[184] It evolved into a prosperous resort and summer retreat for residents of major Midwestern cities, including Chicago, Cleveland, Detroit, Fort Wayne, and Gary, but it also attracted African Americans from other U.S. and Canadian cities and from as far away as Alberta, Canada, and Roxbury, Massachusetts.[185] "The great days of Idlewild were the late 1920s through the 1960s. It was estimated that on July 4, 1959, no fewer than 25,000 people, both white and black, visited Idlewild. It was known then as the Las Vegas of Michigan."[186] Entertainers to perform at Idlewild included Sammy Davis Jr., Sarah Vaughn, the Four Tops, Jackie Wilson, Della Reese, B.B. King, and Aretha Franklin. The year-round African-American population of Lake County jumped from about a dozen in 1920 to nearly 400 in 1930 and more than a 1,000 in 1950.[187] Many black-owned businesses developed near the resort.

Sources: Several resources are available to assist Michigan researchers with African-American roots:

- Books with general information about African Americans in Michigan include Walker, Wilson, and Cousins' *African Americans in Michigan* (2001) and Larrie's *Black Experiences in Michigan History* (1975).
- More information about Idlewild can be found in Walker and Wilson's *Black Eden: The Idlewild Community* (2002) and Stephens' *Idlewild: The Black Eden of Michigan* (2001).
- Banner's *The Black Pioneer in Michigan* (1973) focuses on Flint and Genesee County.
- McRae's *Negroes in Michigan During the Civil War* (1966) includes a history and roster of the First Michigan Colored Infantry Regiment.
- *The Michigan Manual of Freedmen's Progress* (1915), reprinted in 1968 and 1985 as *Negroes in Michigan History*, details African-American life in Michigan between 1863 and 1915. It includes lists and details about African-

American professionals, politicians, business owners, property owners, and Civil War soldiers. The book was originally published for the Lincoln Jubilee Exposition in Chicago; the reprint volumes include an index.

- *1895 Afro-American Journal and Directory of Adrian, Michigan* lists the names and address of 184 African Americans who lived in Adrian in 1895. It also includes photographs and short biographies of some men and women. A copy of the directory is at the Lenawee County Historical Museum.[188]
- Michigan People of Color <www.rootsweb.com/~miafamer/index.html>.
- MICHIGAN-AFAM-L is a mailing list for anyone researching African-American ancestry in Michigan. MI-FREEDMEN-L is a mailing list for anyone with a genealogical interest in Freedmen in Michigan, including African Americans. For more information, see RootsWeb.com's list of Michigan mailing lists <lists.rootsweb.com/index/usa/MI/misc.html>.
- Johnson's Detroit City Directory of "Colored" People 1857-1858 <www.geocities.com/michdetroit/1857direct.html>.
- Index of African Americans Listed in Local and Michigan Newspapers Found at the Grand Rapids Public Library, 1830-1935 <www.rootsweb.com/~mikent/ethnic/AfrAmer/index.html>.
- Negro Settlers Michigan Historic Site (Mecosta and Isabella counties) <www.rootsweb.com/~mimecost/oldsettlers.html>.
- Negro Settlers of Michigan (Mecosta and Isabella counties) <www.oldsettlersreunion.com/>.

Germans: Few Germans moved to Michigan before the early 19th century. They were primarily "adventurers, missionaries, soldiers under the British flag, and other rugged individuals of German descent," but many of these individuals died without leaving a record of their lives.[189] Michael Yax and his wife, Catherine Herkinee, are credited with being the first German-born man and woman to live in Michigan. Ottawas had captured the couple and their child, probably somewhere in Kentucky, and brought them to Detroit in 1751 to be ransomed by French authorities. Yax and his family settled in the Detroit area to farm.[190] Other Germans, including the Moravians who lived near Mount Clemens at the time of the Revolutionary War, trickled into the state in the following years.

Starting around 1830, a missionary effort to convert Native Americans and German settlers motivated the first major wave of German migration to Michigan. Thirty-four families from Wurttemberg, Germany, had settled near Ann Arbor in Washtenaw County to become farmers. Fredrich Schmid, the first German Lutheran missionary in Michigan, arrived in Ann Arbor in 1833, using the existing community as a base to launch his 50-year missionary career. Schmid traveled throughout Michigan, starting churches and attempting to convert Native Americans to Lutheranism. Meanwhile, the Germans at Ann Arbor sent letters to family and friends in Germany, praising the opportunities in Michigan and prompting chain migration to the area. "By 1850 approximately 4,102 German-born pioneers were listed in the U.S. Census for Washtenaw County."[191]

While traveling in the Thumb region of the state, Schmid "came across the area that was to become the focus for the second German missionary center in Michigan."[192] In 1845, Frankenmuth was established 16 miles south of Saginaw by leader Fredrich August Craemer, five farm families, and two single men from Bavaria.[193] In 1846, another 90 immigrants from Bavaria came to Frankenmuth. Emil Baierlein joined Craemer in 1847, and he became "the most outstanding Lutheran missionary in the Saginaw Valley" by learning the Chippewa language and trying to understand the Native culture.[194] Other German Lutheran communities established in the Saginaw Valley were Frankentrost in 1847, Frankenlust in 1848, and Frankenhilf in 1850. Of the four communities, Frankenmuth retained its unique German character. "Until 1905 everyone in Frankenmuth was of German birth or descent except one Welshman and one Indian, and ... these two spoke German fluently."[195] Even today, Frankenmuth is a popular tourist attraction and is known as "Michigan's Little Bavaria."

In addition to the settlements in the Saginaw Valley, Schmid also established German Lutheran churches and communities in "Detroit, Monroe, Lansing, Grand Rapids, Saginaw, Waterloo, Chelsea, Bridgewater, Northfield, Saline, Ypsilanti, Plymouth, Jackson, and Wayne."[196] German Catholics also were active in missionary work in Michigan. They established Westphalia in 1836 in Clinton County. (See "Covenanted Communities" in Chapter 2.)

The second wave of German migration came after the 1848 revolutions in Germany. The country's political problems, along with crop failures in the late 1840s and 1850s, prompted more than one million Germans to immigrate to the United States. Thousands came to Michigan due to the state's established German settlements and Michigan's efforts to recruit German settlers. (See "Recruitment Efforts" in Chapter 2.) Between 1850 and 1890, Germans "constituted the largest ethnic minority group entering Michigan."[197] By 1860 about five percent of Michigan's population of 749,113 was German, by 1880 Germans were the largest foreign-born group in Detroit, and by 1890 nearly seven percent of Michigan's population of more than two million was German.[198] Wayne County in 1890 had the largest group of Germans with 43,000.[199] By 1920, about 18 percent of Michigan's population "claimed German birth or ancestry."[200] Germans had settled in every county, but the largest concentrations were in Berrien, Kent, Macomb, Monroe, Saginaw, Saint Clair, Washtenaw, and Wayne counties.[201] During this second wave of migration, Germans settled many communities including Ora et Labora in Huron County in 1857 (see "Covenanted Communities" in Chapter 2); Chocolay Township near Marquette in 1862; and Forestville in Sanilac County in 1873.

Early German settlers came from Bavaria, Dusseldorf, Saxony, Westphalia, and Wurttemberg. Most became farmers. In the late 19th century, many German immigrants did not have enough money to purchase land so they moved to cities for industrial jobs, to booming lumber towns along the Saginaw River, or into the Upper Peninsula to work in copper or iron ore mines. "Many immigrants were single males seeking to avoid conscription into the Prussian armies during the years of German unification."[202] In addition to Prussia, late 19th century German immigrants came from Baden, Bavaria, Hesse, Mecklenburg, and Saxony.

Germans from Russia: Between 1763 and 1861, thousands of Germans moved to the Volhynia and Volga territories of Russia at the invitation of Catherine the Great, the German-born ruler of Russia. By the 1870s, problems between these Germans and their Russian neighbors prompted the Germans to migrate.[203] In the late 19th century, many immigrants from Volga settled in the Saginaw area, especially Sebewaing. "They introduced sugar beets to the valley and many became prosperous farmers."[204] Immigrants from Volhynia settled in southwestern Michigan, and it is estimated that Berrien County today has "the largest concentration of Germans from Volhynia in North America."[205]

Germans in Detroit: By 1833, there were two large German congregations in Detroit, one Catholic and one Protestant. Many of the Detroit Germans stayed in the city only long enough to earn money to buy farmland outside the city. Detroit's German community grew substantially after 1848. "Germantown developed in the center of the city along Broadway and Gratiot Avenue."[206]

Sources: Several resources are available to assist Michigan researchers with German ancestry:

- Kilar's *Germans in Michigan* (2002) gives an overview of German migration to the state
- Russell's *The Germanic Influence in the Making of Michigan* (1927) includes a list of Civil War officers from Michigan and deceased World War I soldiers from Michigan who were of German descent
- Zehnder's *Teach My People the Truth! The Story of Frankenmuth, Michigan* (1970)
- Frankenmuth Historical Association (see pages 402-403)
- The American Historical Society of Germans from Russia <www.ahsgr.org/> has chapters in Saginaw and Southwest Michigan (see pages 358 and 404)

Dutch: Most of the Dutch who came in the first wave of immigration to west Michigan were Seceders (and also Calvinists), members of a group that had separated from the state church of the Dutch government. Their desire for religious freedom coupled with the Netherlands' depressed economy in the mid-19th century prompted the Seceders' immigration to the United States.

Albertus C. Van Raalte and other leaders in the Seceders movement wrote the "Principles of the Society for the Dutch Emigration to the United States of North America" in 1846. "The 'Principles' set out in some detail the religious, educational, social, and political ideas that were to govern Van Raalte's Kolonie."[207] Originally, Van Raalte had planned to settle in Wisconsin, but once in the United States he was persuaded to examine sites in Michigan's Allegan, Kent, and Ottawa counties. Van Raalte thought the east end of Black Lake (present-day

Lake Macatawa) in Ottawa County "was the ideal location for his Kolonie."[208] On 9 February 1847 Van Raalte and six followers arrived at the Old Wing Mission near Black Lake. This marked the settlement of the Kolonie at Holland, which was to become "a focal point for Dutch Protestant emigration to America."[209] In just six months as many as 700 or 800 settlers arrived, and as early as September 1847 three other villages with about 1,700 settlers were established near Holland.

During the next few years, more Dutch settlers arrived; many of them traveled in groups, some as large as 200.[210] Intact congregations with their own clergyman tended to settle their own communities near Holland and name them after "the province or town where most of the first settlers originated."[211] Reverend Cornelius Van der Meulen and his more than 400 followers, for example, settled Zeeland in 1847 and named it after their home province of Zeeland in the Netherlands.[212] In addition to Zeeland, the Dutch had established communities at Drenthe, Graafschap, Overisel, and Vriesland by 1849, and more than a dozen Dutch communities had sprouted in Ottawa and Allegan counties by the end of the century. "People continued to speak in their regional dialects, and formed villages that were virtual transplants from the rural provinces of the Netherlands."[213]

By 1860 Holland had grown to nearly 2,000 residents, and 10 years later it had a population of nearly 2,400. In 1871, Holland was one of the many communities destroyed by the October forest fires that swept Michigan. More than 200 homes, five churches, three hotels, five docks and warehouses, and 45 miscellaneous buildings – about half of the community – were destroyed. However, only one of the community's residents was killed, and very few people left the colony permanently. The Dutch settlers soon rebuilt Holland.[214] "If anything, the fire served to weld the people into a more tightly-knit community."[215]

Even though most of the Dutch Calvinists settled in and near Holland, many also lived in Grand Rapids, Kalamazoo, and Muskegon. Some moved from Van Raalte's Kolonie for jobs in lumber camps and factories and others came directly from the Netherlands. The Dutch first started coming to Muskegon in 1850.[216] About 2,000 people of Dutch birth or ancestry lived in Grand Rapids as early as 1860 and that number grew to 10,000 by 1890.[217] Ten years later 40 percent of Grand Rapids' population was of Dutch birth or ancestry, and this was "the largest proportion of Dutch in any American city over 25,000 population."[218]

A party of 30 Dutch immigrants, led by Paulus Den Bleyker, moved to Kalamazoo in 1850. Some Dutch immigrants moved to Kalamazoo after being recruited for work by Dewing and Sons Company, producers of sashes, doors, blinds, and lumber. The Kalamazoo Dutch also are credited with developing Michigan's nationally known celery industry. "From the 1860's on, Dutch farmers in and around Kalamazoo, as well as in other Dutch settlements of southwestern Michigan, drained and cleared previously worthless muck bogs and made fortunes in celery growing."[219]

The Holland Kolonie also "birthed" daughter colonies, expanding into five adjacent counties and as far north as Missaukee County by 1880. "By 1900 the

Hollanders had even reached the Upper Peninsula."[220] The first Dutch community north of Grand Rapids was Newaygo County's Fremont (formerly Fremont Center), settled in 1867. Other northern Michigan Dutch communities included Antrim County's Atwood (1882-83); Missaukee County's Vogel Center (1868), Falmouth and Moddersville (ca. 1868), and Lucas (1882); and Oceana County's New Era (1878).[221] "A short-lived Dutch settlement in Mason County was given the unlikely name of Craw Wingle."[222]

The church was the center of activities in Dutch communities. At first the churches affiliated with the Dutch Reformed Church in America, later the Reformed Church in America (RCA), but in the late 1850s religious differences led to the creation of the Christian Reformed Church (CRC). Both denominations, however, have "common origins in the Reformed Church of the Netherlands."[223] Most Dutch communities supported both RCA and CRC churches. The larger Dutch community also supported systems of higher education for both denominations. "Hope College (founded in 1866) and Western Theological Seminary (founded in 1884), located in Holland, provided the Midwestern RCA with many of its church and community leaders."[224] The CRC founded Calvin College and Seminary in Grand Rapids in 1876.

The Dutch Calvinists tended to remain within their tightly knit communities or to migrate only to other Dutch settlements, maintaining their sense of "Dutchness" for many generations. "Few immigrant groups, if any, have clustered more than the Dutch."[225] Dutch Catholics, however, tended to settle throughout the state and tended to assimilate much more quickly. They first came to Bay City and Detroit in the 1850s.[226] "Dutch Catholics readily worshipped and intermarried with Catholics of other nationalities, especially Germans, Belgians, and Irish."[227]

More than 2,500 Dutch immigrants had arrived in Michigan by 1850 and more than 6,000 by 1860.[228] By 1870 there were more than 12,000 Dutch immigrants in Michigan, about 10,000 of them living on the west side of the state, and an additional 30,000 second-generation Dutch.[229] The second wave of Dutch immigration got underway in the 1880s and was prompted by the need for skilled labor in Grand Rapids. Many of these immigrants were joining family and friends already living in west Michigan.[230] By 1900 there were 30,406 Dutch immigrants in Michigan and many thousands more with Dutch ancestry. Today Michigan has the largest Dutch-American population in the nation with more than 4.5 million persons of Dutch ancestry.[231] More than half of Michigan's Dutch live in western Michigan.[232]

Sources: Several resources are available to assist Michigan researchers with Dutch ancestry:

- Ten Harmsel's *Dutch in Michigan* (2002) gives an overview of Dutch migration to Michigan.
- Swierenga's *Dutch Households in U.S. Population Censuses, 1850, 1860, 1870: An Alphabetical Listing by Family Heads* (1987, 3 volumes) lists entries for all counties with more than 50 Dutch residents. For Michigan, this includes the counties of Allegan, Barry, Bay, Berrien, Calhoun, Kalamazoo, Kent,

Missaukee, Montcalm, Muskegon, Newaygo, Oakland, Oceana, Ontonagon, Ottawa, Saginaw, Van Buren, and Wayne.

- The Dutch in Kalamazoo <www.rootsweb.com/~mikalama/dutchin.htm>.
- Heritage Hall at Calvin College <www.calvin.edu/hh/> has records from the Christian Reformed Church in North America, and the Joint Archives of Holland <www.hope.edu/jointarchives/> has records from the Reformed Church in America.

Belgians (Belgiums): Though Belgians were among the early ethnic groups in Michigan, their numbers have not been as great as those of other nationalities. However, compared to other states Michigan today has a large concentration of Belgians. In 2000, there were 53,135 persons of Belgian heritage counted in Michigan by the U.S. census, the second largest concentration of the 360,642 Belgians in the United States. Wisconsin was the only state with more Belgians with 57,808.[233]

Belgians first came to Michigan in the 1830s. In 1833 "a Flemish priest, Fr. Desielle, was working among the Potawatami Indians in southwest Michigan."[234] (Flemish was the language spoken in Flanders, one of the two regions in Belgium.) Also in 1833 two other Belgian priests established the first Catholic college in Detroit. By 1840 there were more than 200 Belgians in Detroit; many worked as brick-makers.[235] Our Lady of Sorrows Church, formerly St. Ann's Catholic Church, served Detroit-area Belgians since 1857.[236] In addition to the Detroit area, Belgians settled in Jackson, Lenawee, Macomb, and Monroe counties; many of them became successful farmers. Other Belgians came into the state to work in Upper Peninsula copper and iron mines. Many Belgians, for example, settled in the iron mining communities of Norway and Vulcan in Dickinson County.[237]

By 1900 there were 2,647 individuals born in Belgium in Michigan.[238] In the early 20th century, the auto industry prompted Belgian immigration, and the number of Belgians in Michigan increased to 10,501 in 1920 and 13,931 in 1930.[239] In 1930, Detroit had the largest Belgian settlement in the United States.[240]

Sources: Several resources are available to assist Michigan researchers with Belgian roots:

- Belgium Roots Project: Michigan <belgium.rootsweb.com/usa/mi/index.html>
- Genealogical Society of Flemish Americans <welcome.to/gsfa>
- Sabbe and Buyse's *Belgians in America* (1960) has information about Belgian settlements in Michigan and includes several biographical sketches

Scandinavians: Scandinavians are immigrants who came from any of the Scandinavian countries, usually defined as Denmark, Finland, Iceland, Norway, and Sweden. They were often attracted or recruited to the state for jobs in lumbering or mining, and they usually came directly from Europe to Michigan rather than from older Scandinavian settlements in the United States. (Some, however, may have worked several weeks or months as laborers in Boston or New York in order to earn money for transportation to Michigan.[241]) Once in Michigan, many saved their money to buy farmland, either in Michigan or farther west. Scandinavians settled predominantly in the western sections of the Lower Peninsula and in the Upper Peninsula.

Swedes: There were only seven Swedes in Michigan in 1850, but by the end of the 19th century they were one of the most numerous Scandinavian groups, numbering about 27,000 in 1890.[242] The first Swedes in the state were Elias Hedstrom, a cabinet-maker, and his wife, Sarah, who arrived in Detroit in 1841. By 1872, however, there were only a few Swedes in Detroit.

The first large Swedish settlements took place in Kent and Muskegon counties. In 1853, several Swedish families from the province of Smaland settled in Alpines, located about six miles south of Sparta in Kent County. The group reportedly came from Boston to Detroit around 1850 and lived in Plymouth, near Detroit, for three years before moving to Alpines.[243] Lisbon, another Swedish settlement located west of Sparta, was settled around the same time.

Swedes established more than a dozen communities in western Michigan in the 1860s and 1870s in Berrien, Manistee, Mason, and Oceana counties, in addition to Kent and Muskegon counties. Many worked in the lumber industry. "In 1866, 72 individuals founded the Swedish Evangelical Lutheran Mamrelund Congregation of Lisbon, Kent County, the first Swedish Evangelical Church in the state."[244] In 1870, Swedes were recruited to Osceola County. (See "Recruitment Efforts" in Chapter 2.) Lesser numbers of Swedes settled on the eastern side of the Lower Peninsula, primarily in Alpena, Bay, Iosco, and Saginaw counties. They likely worked in the lumber industry.

Opportunities in iron and copper mining attracted Swedes to the Upper Peninsula. Swedes from the province of Skone founded Skanee, located 18 miles north of L'Anse in Baraga County, in 1871.[245] Swedes lived in most Upper Peninsula counties, but they were concentrated in Gogebic, Houghton, Marquette, and Menominee counties.[246] By 1880, for example, 2,597 Swedes lived in Marquette County.[247] By the end of the 19th century, 90 percent of the 500 residents of Bates Township in western Iron County were native or first-generation Swedes.[248] Ishpeming in Marquette County, Iron River in Iron County, and Iron Mountain in Dickinson County also were major Swedish settlements.[249] Today Michigan has the fifth largest Swedish-American population in the United States with 161,301 persons of Swedish ancestry.[250]

Finns: Though a few Finns lived in Detroit starting as early as 1852, the migration of Finns to Michigan usually dates from 1864 "when a small number of Finns, working in the copper mines of northern Norway, were lured by Quincy Copper Mine agents, and joined Norwegian miners in a voyage to America."[251] When the group arrived at Hancock, Union Army recruiters convinced all but two of the Finns to become soldiers. More Finns, including some from the "central provinces and the Torneo River valley in Sweden" continued to arrive in the Copper Country.[252] It's estimated that 1,000 Finns lived on the northern half of the Keweenaw Peninsula by 1873.[253] Starting in the 1870s, Finns also moved into the iron mining towns of the Upper Peninsula, including those in Gogebic, Iron, Marquette, and Ontonagon counties. "By 1911, one-quarter of the workers on the Gogebic Iron Range were Finns."[254] Altogether, there were nearly 18,000 Finns in the Upper Peninsula, along with more than 20,000 others from Scandinavian countries, by the start of the 20th century.[255]

In 1896, Finnish immigrants established Suomi College and Theological Seminary (now Finlandia University) in Hancock. It is the only higher education institution founded by Finnish Americans and the only private university in Michigan's Upper Peninsula. It was originally started to train ministers for Finnish Evangelical Lutheran Churches and "to educate Finnish youth, specifically to give the children of Finnish immigrants an opportunity to study the literature, history, and fine arts of Finland."[256] Today, Finlandia University is home to the Finnish-American Heritage Center <www.finlandia.edu/fahc.html>, which houses "the most comprehensive Finnish-American archival collection in the world" (see page 312 for more).[257]

Finns moved into Lower Peninsula lumber towns in the late 1860s. By 1868, for example, Finns worked in sawmills at Muskegon and in the 1870s in the sawmills and lumber camps near East Tawas and Oscoda on the east side of the state.[258] By 1880 Finns also were working in the lumber camps and sawmills near Ludington in Mason County, at Black Lake in Eaton County, and at Howard City in Montcalm County. "The largest concentration was at White Cloud [in Newagyo County], where in the autumn of 1879 there were an estimated 100 Finns and two Finnish restaurants."[259] Many of these lumberjacks were Swedish-speaking Finns.

Jacob E. Saaren, a New York Finn and land agent, developed a community for Finns in Manistee County starting in 1899 "at a railroad crossing originally known as Manistee Crossing."[260] The town was renamed Kaleva in 1900 after a famous Finnish epic, the town's streets were given Finnish names, and in 1901 a Finnish-language newspaper came to the area. Finns from the Upper Peninsula and from other states as far west as Wyoming and California came to Kaleva to farm and start small businesses. By 1911, more than 900 Finnish members were recorded in the town's Evangelical Lutheran Church. Kaleva remained a predominantly Finnish community until the 1950s.

In addition to Kaleva, other Lower Peninsula cities with large Finnish communities were Lake City and Jennings in Missaukee County, East Tawas and Tawas City in Iosco County, and Detroit in Wayne County. Even so, in the late 19th century and early 20th century there were fewer Finns in the Lower Peninsula of Michigan than in the Upper Peninsula. "In fact, there were 30 times as many Finns in the Upper as in the Lower Peninsula."[261] In 1920 Finns were concentrated in the Lower Peninsula counties of Iosco, Kent, Manistee, Muskegon, and Wayne, but they lived in every county of the Upper Peninsula. The largest concentrations were in the western Upper Peninsula, especially Houghton, Gogebic, and Marquette counties. Statewide by 1930 there were more than "27,000 native-born

Finns and nearly 75,000 Michigan citizens of Finnish descent."[262] Today Michigan has the largest Finnish-American population in the United States with 101,351 persons of Finnish ancestry.[263]

Norwegians: In 1850 most Scandinavian-born people in the United States were Norwegian, some 12,678 out of a total of 18,074.[264] However, Michigan only had 86 Norwegians, and by 1860 that number had grown only to 384.[265] Though few in numbers, the Norwegians were the first Scandinavians to come to Michigan "in any considerable number."[266] They were attracted by the employment opportunities in lumbering, mining, shipping, and later, manufacturing, particularly the auto industry. Some were recruited to the state or came after seeing letters written by Norwegians who praised the opportunities available in Michigan.

The first permanent Norwegian settlement in Michigan was established in 1847 or 1848 in Muskegon County. By 1850, 27 of the 86 Norwegians listed in the census lived in Muskegon Township. Muskegon County continued to have the greatest concentration of Norwegian settlers in western Michigan, with 641 Norwegians numbered in the county in 1880.[267] In addition to Muskegon County, Norwegians settled in several of the nearby western Michigan counties, including Allegan, Benzie, Kent, Leelanau, Manistee, Mason, Mecosta, Montcalm, Newaygo, Oceana, Osceola, and Wexford. Norwegians in the Lower Peninsula also settled in Alpena, Bay, Berrien, and Wayne counties. Opportunities in mining drew Norwegians to the Upper Peninsula starting in the 1860s, and settlers concentrated in Delta, Houghton, and Marquette counties.

After saving some money, many Norwegians "went farther west to take up farms in Wisconsin, Minnesota, Iowa, Kansas, Nebraska, the Dakotas, and beyond."[268] Many, however, stayed in Michigan. By 1880, there were 4,112 Norwegians in Michigan, and 10 years later there were nearly 8,000.[269]

Danes: By 1850, there were only 13 Danes in the state, most living near the Great Lakes.[270] In 1853, Christian Jensen, Americanized as "Johnson," arrived in Montcalm County. He was the earliest permanent Danish settler recorded in the interior of Michigan. Jensen wrote home to friends and family in Denmark, and more Danish settlers came to the county. "By 1870 a large Danish settlement was well established [in Montcalm County], with centers at Gowen, Trufant, Greenville, and later, Edmore."[271] By 1930, nearly 2,500 Danish-Americans lived in Montcalm County.[272]

Danish settlers spread out into other western Michigan counties, including Kent, Manistee, Mason, Mecosta, Muskegon, Newaygo, and Oceana. By 1880, Danish Lutheran Churches had been established in Big Rapids and Morley in Mecosta County; Coral, Greenville, and Trufant in Montcalm County; Ludington in Mason County; Manistee in Manistee County; and Holton and Muskegon in Muskegon County. In 1882, a Danish college known as the Ashland Folk School was established in Ashland Township in Newaygo County.[273]

Starting in the 1860s, Danes also immigrated to the Upper Peninsula to work in the iron mines. By 1870, 207 Danes lived in Marquette County.[274] Danes also moved to Menominee and Delta counties for opportunities in lumbering.

Icelanders: Few Icelanders came to Michigan and most of those who did came after World War II. "The latest arrivals [were] Icelandic women who married American soldiers stationed in Iceland after World War II."[275]

Scandinavians in Detroit: Scandinavian communities in early Detroit were not very large. The first Finn, Alex Lampi, came to Detroit in 1852, but by 1871 there were only eight Finnish families in the city.[276] Few Swedes lived in Detroit until the 20th century when a number of "highly skilled Swedish engineers, technicians, and tool and die makers" came directly from Sweden to work in the auto industry.[277] The auto industry also attracted many Norwegians and Danes and prompted many Finns to move from the Upper Peninsula or to move directly from Finland to Detroit. By 1930 about 9,000 Finnish immigrants and first-generation Finns lived in the Detroit-area, along with 13,500 Swedes, about 5,000 Norwegians, and about 5,000 Danes.[278]

Sources: Several resources are available to assist Michigan researchers with Scandinavian roots:

- Feddersen's *Scandinavians in Michigan With Special Reference to Detroit and Environs* (1968) includes biographies of Scandinavians and information on Scandinavian churches and organizations
- Holmio's *History of the Finns in Michigan* (2001)
- Finnish-American Heritage Center <www.finlandia.edu/fahc.html>
- The Finnish of Houghton and the Upper Peninsula <www.mfhn.com/houghton/finn/>
- *They Made a Difference: Highlights of the Swedish Influence on Detroit and Michigan* (1976)
- Qualey's *Norwegian Settlement in the United States* (1970) features a chapter about Michigan
- Vesterheim Museum's Norwegians in the Civil War Database <www.vesterheim.org/CivilWar/db/index.html> has references to several Michigan men.
- The Digital Archives of the National Archives of Norway <digitalarkivet.uib.no/cgi-win/wc/webcens.exe?slag=meny&kategori=1&emne=7&spraak=e> features several free databases, including Norwegians living in Michigan according to the 1880 U.S. census and Norwegians living in the United States according to the 1850 U.S. census

Czechoslovaks: Czechoslovaks is a term that came about after 1918 when the Czechs and Slovaks united to form the Czechoslovak Republic. Czechs, also known as Bohemians, arrived in Michigan in the mid-19th century, while the Slovaks first came to Michigan later in the 19th century.

Czechs (Bohemians): By the 1850s Czechs lived in Detroit and northern Michigan's Leelanau County. In Detroit, Czech Catholics lived near Saint Mary's Parish on Saint Antoine and Monroe Streets. "By 1857, the city's first Czech organization, a cultural society named 'Slovanska Lipa,' was established."[279] Czechs settled the North Unity colony at Good Harbor in Leelanau

County in 1855, and Czechs later moved into northern Leelanau County and Antrim County. In the 1860s, a number of Czechs settled in the Saginaw Valley on the east side of the state and in New Buffalo in southwestern Michigan's Berrien County. In addition to being farmers, "many of these early settlers were shoemakers, tailors, bakers, woodworkers, and other types of craftsmen."[280] Some Czechs worked in lumbering or mining in the Upper Peninsula, "but their numbers were not great contrasted with other nationalities there."[281] By 1870, there were nearly 1,200 Czechs in the state and more than 2,100 in 1900.[282] In the early 20th century, Czechs were recruited to work in the sugar beet fields of the Saginaw Valley and in other areas of the state, including Lenawee, Monroe, Washtenaw, and Wayne counties, because of their familiarly with the crop in their home country.[283] Czechs later moved to Detroit, Saginaw, Flint, and Lansing for opportunities in the auto industry.

Slovaks: Slovaks came to Michigan in the late 19th century, establishing communities in the iron mining districts of the Upper Peninsula, working in the sugar beet fields of the Lower Peninsula's Saginaw Valley, or farming in northern Michigan.[284] "Soon after the turn of the [20th] century, thousands of Slovaks from abroad or from Pennsylvania and Ohio flocked to the cities of lower Michigan particularly Detroit, Muskegon, Flint, Saginaw and Lansing."[285] Most worked in the auto industry.

Jews: Jewish immigrants came to Michigan as early as 1761, but by the start of the Civil War there were only 151 Jewish families in the state, about half of them from the Detroit area.[286] The first known Jewish settler in Michigan was Ezekiel Solomon, a German-born trader who came to Fort Michilimackinac in 1761. Solomon, who first supplied British troops and later developed a fur trade, was joined by several of his trading partners, including Chapman Abraham. Abraham, another German-born trader who had come to Montreal from England, moved on to Detroit in 1762, becoming the first Jewish resident of that city.[287] Solomon, Abraham, and other Jews from Montreal traded with the Native Americans, and some supported the British during the Revolutionary War.

Jewish immigrants continued to come into Michigan during the next 100 years, though not in very large numbers. Starting around 1840, Jews moved across southern Lower Michigan, establishing communities in several Michigan cities. German Jews, for example, settled in Ann Arbor and Ypsilanti during the 1840s because of the size of the German community already there. In 1848, the first Jewish cemetery in Michigan was dedicated in Ann Arbor. Other Jews moved to Jackson in 1842, Kalamazoo in 1844, Lansing in 1849, and Grand Rapids in 1852. "There are many records of Jews in Three Rivers, Adrian, Sandwich (now Windsor, Ontario), Monroe, and Detroit before 1850."[288]

In the latter part of the 19th century, several Jews followed the lumber and mining industries, setting up general stores or peddling goods in northern Lower Michigan and the Upper Peninsula. Palestine, a Jewish farming community, was established in Huron County in 1891. (See Chapter 2 for more.) Jewish communities were established in other areas, including Alpena, Hancock, Iron Mountain,

Marquette, Muskegon, Petoskey, and Traverse City. Grand Rapids, Bay City, and Saginaw had the largest Jewish communities; each had more than 1,000 Jewish residents by 1917.

Jews in Detroit: By 1850, 51 Jews lived in Detroit. Most had been born in Germany, and one reason they came to Detroit was because of the size of the city's German population.[289] Twelve of these German-Jewish immigrants met and formed the first Jewish congregation in Detroit on 22 September 1850.[290] (See Chapter 4 for more information on Jewish congregations.) In the 1860s, an increasing number of Eastern European Jews, mostly Polish, began coming to Detroit.[291]

After 1881, Detroit's Jewish population grew tremendously due to the mass migration to the United States of eastern European Jews fleeing poverty and oppression. "Detroit's Jewish population ... [grew] from 1,000 in 1880 to 10,000 in 1900 to about 34,000 by 1914, with Russian Jews constituting over 75 percent of the total."[292] Between 1920 and 1940, Detroit's Jewish population increased to 85,000.[293]

Many Jews had lived elsewhere in the United States before coming to Detroit. Unlike other immigrant groups, Jews did not come to Detroit primarily for opportunities in the automobile industry. "Far more Jewish men worked in retail and wholesale establishments and in the sales, clerical, or peddling lines than in any other field of enterprise."[294]

Sources: Several resources are available to assist Michigan researchers with Jewish roots:

- Cantor's *Jews in Michigan* (2001) gives an overview of Jewish migration to the state, Rockaway's *The Jews of Detroit: From the Beginning, 1762-1914* (1986) focuses on Detroit, and Devlin's *Muskegon's Jewish Community: A Centennial History, 1888-1988* (1988) focuses on Muskegon
- Katz's *The Jewish Soldier From Michigan in the Civil War* (1962)
- *Michigan Jewish History,* a journal published by the Jewish Historical Society of Michigan
- Jewish Genealogical Society of Michigan <www.jgsmi.org>
- International Association of Jewish Genealogical Societies Cemetery Project - Michigan <www.jewishgen.org/cemetery/northamerica/michigan.html>
- Irwin I. Cohn Michigan Jewish Cemetery Index <www.thisisfederation.org/Cemetery/default.asp>
- Temple Beth El's Rabbi Leo M. Franklin Archives <www.tbeonline.org/leofranklinarchives.htm>

Italians: When the French first explored Michigan, Italy did not exist as a nation. Italians who wanted to come to the New World often traveled to France first and came under the French flag. "A number of Italians in Michigan's colonial past came as administrators, chroniclers, explorers, fur traders, and soldiers."[295] Many of these Italians' names became "frenchified," and it is often difficult to determine their Italian origin.[296] The first, and perhaps best known, Italian in Michigan was Alfonso Tonti, officially known as Alphonse de Tonty. Tonty was

Cadillac's second-in-command when Detroit was established in 1701. He served as governor or commandant at Detroit from 1704 to 1706 and again from 1717 to 1728. His daughter, Therese, was the first European child born in Michigan.

It wasn't until the mid-19th century that Italian immigrants began arriving in noticeable numbers in Michigan. Many came to work in the iron and copper mines in Gogebic, Houghton, Marquette, and Menominee counties in the Upper Peninsula. "In 1860 the earliest Italians – Joseph and Vitale Coppo, Joseph Gatan, Bart Quello – were mining in the Hancock area."[297] They had come to the Upper Peninsula from the Canavese area of Piedmont by way of Canada. Soon chain migration brought thousands of other Italians, many of them single men without their families, to the Upper Peninsula. In 1890, about 3,000 Italians lived in Michigan, but 2,386 of those lived in the Upper Peninsula.[298] (Another 340 worked in Detroit, with the rest living in Flint, Grand Rapids, Saginaw, Macomb County, and Oakland County.)[299] "[By] 1910 there were some 10,000 Italians living in the Copper County alone."[300] Calumet and Iron Mountain had the two largest Italian communities. Between 1890 and 1930, many Italians in the Upper Peninsula moved to Detroit due to labor unrest in the mining industries and increased opportunities in Detroit's auto industry.

Many of the Italians in the Upper Peninsula came from northern Italy. In Houghton County, for example, they came from Piedmont, especially from Canavese north of Turin; Lombardy; and Luca in Tuscany. In Gogebic County, they came from Piedmont, Tyrol, Abruzzi, and Sicily, while those in Menominee County came primarily from the province of Venice. Other northern Italian provinces represented in the Upper Peninsula included Abruzze, Calabria, and Umbria. However, the Italians in Ishpeming in Marquette County tended to come from southern Italy.[301]

Michigan cities in the Lower Peninsula with early Italian communities included Flint, Pontiac, Lansing, Muskegon, Saginaw, and Grand Rapids, where many Italians migrated from the coal-mining region of Pennsylvania to work in the Grand Rapids area plaster quarries.

Italians in Detroit: In 1855, there were about a dozen Italians in Detroit, most from northern Italy. More immigrated from Genoa and Lombardy, and in 1883, several Sicilians came to Detroit from Cleveland. They had worked as fruit merchants and quickly opened similar businesses in Detroit. By 1897, there were 207 Italian families – 1,103 adults and 630 children – in Detroit, most of these Lombards and Sicilians.[302] By 1910 there were about 8,000 Italians in Detroit and 16,000 in 1920.[303] "In 1930, out of 43,087 Italians in the state, 73 percent resided in Wayne County and only 11 percent in the mining counties."[304] Detroit's "Little Italy" was located along Gratiot Avenue, and another Italian community was near Gratiot and Harper.[305]

Sources: Several resources are available to assist Michigan researchers with Italian roots:

- Magnaghi's *Italians in Michigan* (2001) gives an overview of Italian settlement throughout the state, and Magnaghi's *Miners, Merchants, and Midwives: Michigan's Upper Peninsula Italians* (1987) focuses on the Upper Peninsula

- Vismara's article, "Coming of the Italians to Detroit," published in the January 1918 issue of *Michigan History* magazine, has much information about Detroit's early settlers
- Italians of the Upper Peninsula of Michigan <www.mfhn.com/houghton/ItaliansRice> has census records and other information

South Slavs: South Slavs, residents of the former provinces of Yugoslavia, first started coming to Michigan in significant numbers in the late 19th century. They left their land "to escape overpopulation, a shortage of land, high taxes, and a political situation that offered no hope for national self-determination."[306] They came to Michigan primarily for jobs. Accurate statistics on South Slavs are difficult to find because "many South Slavs told the census takers that they were Austrians or Hungarians."[307] (They also are referred to as Yugoslavs or Jugoslavs.)

Slovenes: The first Slovene in Michigan was Frederic Baraga, the first Catholic bishop of the Upper Peninsula. He left his home in Slovenia in 1830 to come to the Upper Great Lakes to minister to Native Americans. Among his accomplishments, he developed the first Ojibwa (Chippewa) language dictionary and served as the first bishop of the Diocese of Marquette from 1853 to 1868.

Other Slovenes came to Hancock in 1858 and later to Calumet, both in Houghton County. "Most worked in the mines, while others labored at unskilled jobs and saved their money to go into business ventures."[308] A larger number of Slovenes came in the early 1880s to work in the Upper Peninsula copper and iron mines. By the end of the 19th century, for example, from 5,000 to 6,000 Slovenes lived in Calumet.[309]

In addition, skilled Slovenian woodworkers were recruited from Pennsylvania to work in the lumber industry. Sixty-five young men arrived in Alger County in 1906. They later founded Traunik, a farming community with a peak population of 500 in the 1930s.[310] The 1910 U.S. census also listed Slovenes in other lumber communities in Marquette.[311]

In the early 20th century, many Upper Peninsula Slovenes moved to the Lower Peninsula or other states to farm or work in industry. "The first known Slovenian in Detroit was Joseph Feletich, who opened a saloon in 1903."[312] In the 1920s, the auto industry attracted Slovenes to the Detroit area, some from the "coal mining regions of Pennsylvania, Kansas, and Illinois," and many settled in Highland Park.[313]

Croats: Croats arrived in Michigan's Upper Peninsula in the 1870s to work in the copper and iron mines. "By the turn of the century, 10,000 Croats were living in [Houghton County's] Calumet, the largest Croatian mining colony in the United States."[314] Other Croats lived in Gogebic County. As the copper industry waned in the early 20th century, many Croats moved to other areas of Michigan to work in farming or industry. The first Croats arrived in Detroit in 1890; in 1923 the Croats founded Saint Jerome's Catholic parish.[315] Also in the early 20th century, Croats from Pennsylvania or Ohio migrated "to Manistique, Munising, Escanaba, and Hermansville in Michigan's Upper Peninsula in order to work in the burgeoning logging camps and lumber mills."[316]

Serbs: Serbs moved to the Upper Peninsula's Gogebic County in the 1890s to work in iron mines or to start small businesses. Others moved to Detroit for manufacturing opportunities. "By 1908 Detroit's East Side included about 3,000 Serbs."[317]

Macedonians: Macedonians, often recorded as immigrants from Turkey, Serbia, Bulgaria, or Greece, came to the Detroit area in the early 20th century to work in the auto industry. Others opened "Polish bakeries" in Hamtramck.[318] Today, Detroit "is home to the largest Macedonian community in the United States" and Michigan has the largest number of Macedonians in the United States with 7,801.[319]

Bosnian Muslims: Bosnian Muslims from the republic of Bosnia-Herzegovina first came to Michigan in the 20th century. Today, Michigan's Polish neighborhood of Hamtramck in Detroit "is second to Chicago in the number of Bosnian refugees; Madison Heights and Dearborn also boast large Bosnian settlements."[320]

Sources: For more information on Michigan's South Slavs, see Cetinich's *South Slavs in Michigan* (2003).

Poles: Though Poles have lived in Michigan since the late 18th century, their numbers didn't exceed 5,000 until 1880. Between 1880 and 1920, the largest wave of Polish immigration hit Michigan. By 1920, nearly 104,000 Polish-born residents lived in the state. This number does not include the children and grandchildren of Polish immigrants or those who may have been recorded as Russians, Prussians, or Austrians, a practice that was common between 1796 and 1918 when Poland did not exist as an independent country. By 1960, there were more Michigan residents of Polish ancestry than of any other European nationality.[321] Today, Michigan has the third largest Polish-American population in the United States with 854,844 Polish residents.[322]

Francis and Genevieve Godek, the first Poles "officially listed as residents of Michigan," were married in Ste. Anne's Church in Detroit in 1762.[323] Other Poles trickled into the state, and by the 1830s the first Polish neighborhood was established in Muskegon. The first Polish resident of Grand Rapids arrived in 1853, and by 1869 about a dozen Polish families lived in that city. Grand Rapids' Polish community quickly grew to become one of the largest concentrations of Poles in Michigan.

In 1856, five Poles from Canada founded Parisville in Huron County, the first Polish settlement in Michigan. "The Parisville settlement was only the second Polish settlement in America."[324] Polish immigrants later moved to other Thumb-area communities, including Kinde, Port Austin, Rapson, and Ubly.

Between 1855 and 1860, Poles came to Bronson in Branch County to work on construction crews building the railroad from Detroit to Chicago. "Local historians state that railroad crews building the lines in opposite directions met in Bronson and since their work was completed, they simply stayed at this 'meeting point.'"[325] A Polish parish, Saint Mary's, was established by 1867.[326]

In the 1870s a group of Polish settlers in Alpena County founded the second Polish community in Michigan, Posen. "The Polish settlers of this area spoke both

German and Polish since their homeland was the German-occupied part of Poland, called Poznan in Polish but Posen in German."[327] Polish immigrants also settled in five other northeast Michigan communities: Alpena, Cheboygan, Metz, Mullet Lake (Riggsville), and Rogers City.

Also in the 1870s "about 200 Polish families lived south of Bay City and worked in the local sugar beet fields."[328] Thirty years later, Bay City had the largest Polish community outside Detroit. Other Polish communities in the Saginaw Valley included those in Bridgeport, Carrollton, Pinconning, Saginaw, and Standish.

In the late 19th century, the northwestern Lower Peninsula had at least five Polish communities, including those at Boyne Falls, Cedar, Elmira, Gaylord, and Larks Lake. The largest settlement was at Gaylord with about 250 Polish families.[329] Other communities on the west side of the state with a number of Polish residents included Hilliards in Allegan County, Belmont in Kent County, Muskegon in Muskegon County, Freesoil and Ludington in Mason County, and Manistee in Manistee County.

Poles also moved into the Upper Peninsula to work in the copper and iron mines. They first came to Calumet in 1872, later establishing the largest Polish settlement in the Upper Peninsula. At least 24 additional Polish communities were established in the Upper Peninsula, including Atlantic Mine, Baraga, Bessemer, Cedar River, DeTour, Eagle Harbor, Escanaba, Fayette, Hancock, Houghton, Iron Mountain, L'Anse, Laurium, Mass City, Munising, Nadeau, Norway, Ontonagon, Republic, Sault Ste. Marie, Spalding, Stephenson, Vulcan, and Wakefield.[330]

Many of the early Polish settlers in the state came to Michigan from Illinois, Massachusetts, New York, Ohio, and Pennsylvania. Some, for example, came from the coal mining regions of Pennsylvania to work in the coal mines southwest of Saginaw.

The Polish immigrants' lives revolved around the Catholic church. A total of 94 Polish parishes were established in Michigan, 41 in the Detroit area. "Sts. Cyril and Methodius Seminary opened in Detroit in 1886 to train Polish-speaking priests."[331] It moved to Orchard Lake in 1909 and was the only seminary like it in the United States.

Because Polish surnames were unfamiliar to Michigan's early residents, some Polish immigrants responded by shortening their names or translating them into English. "Kowalski, the most common Polish surname, became Smith while Jaworowicz became Mapleton. Others were Anglicized; Walker for Walkowiak, Preston for Przekopowski, and Jarvis for Jaworski. ... The majority, however, retained their 'ski,' 'cki,' and 'wicz' endings and endured the problems."[332]

Poles in Detroit: Poles moved to Detroit as early as 1855, and by 1871 there were enough Polish residents to establish Saint Albertus, Detroit's first Polish parish.[333] By 1882, there were only 1,200 Poles in Detroit, but that number had grown to 35,000 by 1892, and more than 100,000 in 1914.[334] Poles were moving to Detroit for industrial jobs and were replacing Detroit's German laborers. "The Polish settlers found employment chiefly in building railways, paving streets, digging sewers and laying water pipes."[335] Later they were attracted to opportunities in the auto industry. By 1916, for example, Poles were the largest ethnic group working for Ford Motor Company. Many Polish women and girls found work. "By 1915 most of Detroit's cigars were made by unskilled Polish born women and girls, many quite young."[336]

Before 1900, most of Detroit's Polish residents lived on the east side of Detroit; after 1900 many Polish immigrants moved to Hamtramck, an independent community surrounded by Detroit. The population of Hamtramck rose from more than 3,500 in 1910 to more than 48,000 in 1920, and 60,000 in 1928.[337] In 1930 about 80 percent of Hamtramck's residents were Polish born or of Polish descent.[338] That same year, about 25 percent of all the Poles in American – 300,870 of 1,268,583 – lived in Detroit.[339]

Sources: Several resources are available to assist Michigan researchers with Polish ancestry:

- Badaczewski's *Poles in Michigan* (2002) gives an overview of Polish settlement in Michigan
- Treppa's *An Index to Detroit's Polonia in the Michigan Catholic, 1872-1900* (1981)
- *Parisville Poles: First Polish Settlers in U.S.A.?* (1977)
- Detroit Area Polonia and the City of Hamtramck Genealogical Web site <www.rootsweb.com/~miwayne/hamtramck.htm>
- The J. William Gorski Polish Genealogy and Historical Collection, focusing on Polish history and genealogy in Michigan, is located at the Library of Michigan
- Polish Genealogical Society of Michigan <www.pgsm.org>
- Michigan Polonia <www.mipolonia.net> and its companion mailing list MI-POLISH-L <lists.rootsweb.com/index/other/Ethnic-Polish/MI-POLISH.html>
- The Polish Legacy in Cedar, Michigan <www.leelanauhistory.org/projects/polishlegacy>
- First Polanders to Homestead in Presque Isle County <members.aol.com/alpenaco/presque/1stpoles.htm>

20th Century Immigrants

During the late 19th and early 20th centuries the country of origin of an increasing number of immigrants to Michigan changed from the nations of northwestern and central Europe to the nations of eastern and southern Europe as well as to other parts of the world.

Albanians: Albanian immigrants, both Orthodox Christian and Muslim, "first came to Michigan from New England and New York in the second decade of the 20th century."[340] They originated from the towns of southern Albania. In this early period of immigration, they may have been "recorded as Greeks or Turks or as nationals of the country from which they sailed."[341] Albanians settled primarily in Macomb, Oakland, and Wayne counties. For more information, see Trix's *The Albanians in Michigan* (2001).

Armenians: Though some Armenians were in Michigan at the end of the 19th century, most came in the early 20th century and settled in urban areas, including Detroit, Flint, and Grand Rapids. By 1909, there was an Armenian community in Detroit.[342] Many men worked in factories or opened small businesses, such as shoe repair shops, dry cleaners, or grocery stores.[343] Some Armenians came to Michigan after living for a while in New England. The 1920 U.S. census counted 2,498 Armenian-born residents in Michigan.[344] Today, Michigan has the fifth largest Armenian-American population in the United States, with more than 15,000 of the nation's nearly 400,000 persons of Armenian ancestry.[345]

Asians: A few Chinese, coming by way of the west coast of the United States, settled in Michigan as early as 1872.[346] By 1940, however, Michigan had only 12,388 residents who were natives of any part of Asia.[347]

Asian Indians: Asian Indian immigrants first started coming to Michigan, some by way of California, in the 1920s. Many worked in the auto industry. For more information, see Helweg's *Asian Indians in Michigan* (2002).

Arabs: Arabic-speaking people, mostly from Syria and Lebanon, first started moving to Michigan in the 1880s and settled primarily in Detroit, Grand Rapids, and Lansing. "The first Arabs to arrive in the Detroit area were reportedly a few merchants who stopped to dispose of unsold wares on their return to the Middle East from the Columbian Exposition of 1892-1893 in Chicago. They were followed by immigrants, primarily single Lebanese men, who had settled first in New York and Boston."[348] There were about 50 Arabs in Detroit by 1900, but the number of Arabs increased, starting in 1908, because of opportunities in the auto industry. "[Lansing's automaker] Ranson Olds became well known for his employment of immigrants from the Holy Lands, and by the '20s the Ford Rouge plant was responsible for making Dearborn one of the few cities in the United States with an Arab settlement."[349] Many single men worked until they saved enough money to return home to be married or to send for their families "starting a chain migration by which many extended families, and even entire villages, settled in the Detroit area."[350] By 1973, Detroit had "the largest Arabic-speaking community in North America."[351] Today Metropolitan Detroit is still home to one of the largest and most diverse Arab communities in the United States. It includes both Christians and Muslims and people who immigrated from or can trace their ancestry to a number of countries, including Egypt, Iraq, Lebanon, Palestine, Syria, and Yemen. Detroit also is home to a large community of Chaldeans, a Catholic minority from Iraq that started arriving in Detroit in the early 20th century. "Most of these immigrants came from a single village in the northern part of Iraq – Telkaif."[352]

Bulgarians: Bulgarians began coming to Detroit around 1904 to work in the auto industry. They also had settled in Battle Creek by 1907 where they worked as tailors, barbers, or shoemakers.[353] The 1920 U.S. census recorded 1,692 Bulgarian-born residents in Michigan.[354] By the 1930s Detroit had the largest settlement of Bulgarians in the United States.[355]

Greeks: Michigan's 1900 U.S. census recorded only 134 Greek-born residents, but this number may be misleading because many Greeks entering the United States from Turkey, Italy, or other countries were counted as natives of those countries.[356] By 1910 there were nearly 1,200 Greek-born residents in Michigan.[357] "The opportunities for developing small businesses offered by a large city probably first attracted Greeks to Detroit, but when Henry Ford began [in 1914] to pay a wage of $5 a day many came to the city from other parts of the country."[358] This included railroad construction workers from Colorado, Iowa, and Kentucky.[359] Many Greeks opened their own businesses, and by the 1930s there were about 3,500 Greek businesses in Detroit. This included 2,000 restaurants and 150 grocery stores.[360] Greeks settled throughout the state, though the largest concentration was in Detroit. By 1920, there were more than 7,000 Greek-born residents in Michigan.[361] The Berrien County Historical Association, in cooperation with other organizations, is studying "the settlement patterns and history of the Greeks who resided or vacationed in Berrien County."[362] For more information about this project, see the Preservation of American Hellenic History Web site <www.pahh.com/bcha/>.

Hungarians: Hungarians first started coming to Michigan in the 1880s and worked in manufacturing in southeastern Michigan, in the lumber industry of northern Lower Michigan, in the sugar beet industry of the Saginaw Valley, or the mines of the Upper Peninsula. There were less than 1,000 Hungarians in the state in 1890. The migration of Hungarians to Michigan – including some Hungarian Jews who first settled in New York, Pennsylvania, or Ohio – picked up by 1898.[363] By 1900 there were more than 2,000 Hungarians in the state, more than 11,000 in 1910, and more than 22,000 in 1920.[364] Most of the Hungarians settled in the Detroit area, particularly Delray. "By 1930 the city of Detroit had a Hungarian population of 23,311 and was the fourth-largest center of Hungarian settlement in the United States (after New York, Cleveland, and Chicago)."[365] For more information, see Huseby-Darvas' *Hungarians in Michigan* (2003).

Lithuanians: Lithuanians first came to Michigan in the late 19th century to work as manual laborers or in the lumber or mining industries. Several settled in Grand Rapids as early as 1860, where they worked in the furniture factories.[366] Lithuanians settled in Detroit as early as 1886. They later were attracted to the city for the auto industry. "Most of the early arrivals in Detroit came from the coal-mining districts of Pennsylvania, Oklahoma, and Kentucky, but some were immigrants directly from Europe who left their country following the Russian revolution of 1905."[367] By 1920, more than 5,000 Lithuanian-born residents lived in Michigan.[368] An index of Lithuanians listed in the 1920 census in Michigan, as well as a number of other databases of Michigan records, can be found online through the Lithuanian Global Genealogical Society Web site <www.lithuaniangenealogy.org/databases/index.html>.

Mexicans: Fewer than 100 Mexicans were living in Michigan in 1910. In 10 years, however, that number increased more than tenfold. "While the census of

1920 found that there were 1,268 Mexicans in Michigan, historians estimate that the number was really well over 4,000 in Detroit alone."[369] Mexicans and Mexican Americans, primarily from Texas, came to Michigan for opportunities in agriculture and industry. Mexicans and Mexican Americans began arriving in 1915 in the Thumb area to work in the sugar beet industry, "which eventually paid for the transportation of tens of thousands of Mexicans and Mexican Americans into the state."[370] Others moved to Detroit to work in the auto industry. "Ford soon became the largest employer of Mexicans, with some 1,000 workers at the River Rouge plant alone."[371] In addition, railroad companies transferred many of their Mexican employees to Detroit to do the work previously done by men off fighting in World War I. Adding to the number of Mexicans and Mexican Americans in Michigan were the migrant farm workers who came to harvest fruit and vegetable crops, and in some cases, stayed on as permanent residents. During the Depression of the 1930s, more than 12,000 Mexicans in Michigan returned to Mexico through repatriation programs. Among those going to Mexico were several "Anglo-American women married to Mexican men."[372] When Michigan's economy picked up in the 1940s, Mexicans and Mexican Americans again settled in Michigan, some under the Bracero Program, which "allowed for the temporary or seasonal use of imported Mexican labor in various sectors of the economy."[373] For more information, see Alvarado and Alvarado's *Mexicans and Mexican Americans in Michigan* (2003) and Badillo's *Latinos in Michigan* (2003).

Romanians: Romanians began coming to Michigan around 1904, most settling in the Detroit area, and by 1920 there were 6,331 Romanians in Michigan.[374] Between 1920 and 1926, thousands of Romanians moved to Detroit from Cleveland attracted by jobs in the auto industry. "This influx gave Detroit the largest Romanian population of any city in the United States."[375] There were more than 11,000 Romanians in the state by 1930.[376] Today Michigan has the fourth largest Romanian-America population in the United States with 26,857 persons of Romanian ancestry.[377]

Russians: Few Russians, both Jews and Orthodox Christians, lived in Michigan in the early 19th century. Only 25 Russians, for example, were counted in Michigan's 1850 U.S. census. By 1890, there were nearly 12,000 Russians in the state and nearly 38,000 by 1910. "A few Slavic Russians reached Detroit as early as 1901, but the greater number came in 1912 and 1913."[378] Many had first settled in New York or the coal-mining districts of Pennsylvania before coming to Detroit to work in the auto industry. By 1920, there were 45,313 Russians in Michigan.[379]

Turks: European and Asian Turks came to Detroit, starting in 1890. "By 1910 there were 561 people from Asia Turkey in the city, while only 125 from the European sector settled there."[380]

Ukrainians: Ukrainians, some from other parts of the United States, first came to Michigan in the late 19th century. The first group of Ukrainians in Detroit came in 1904 from the Pittsburgh area.[381] More Ukrainians came to Michigan after World War II. For more information, see Stefaniuk and Dohrs' *Ukrainians of Detroit* (1979).

9
Michigan Online

The Internet, a worldwide network of computer networks, is another resource available for Michigan genealogical research. Information on the World Wide Web (commonly known as the Web) includes library catalogs; databases of genealogy records; digital images of books, censuses, maps, newspapers, and photographs; transcriptions and abstracts of vital records; and more. E-mail can be used for person-to-person communication or discussion lists. Many excellent guides about online genealogy have been written, so the focus of this chapter will be online Michigan sources and resources. One note of caution: the Internet is merely a tool to use for research. Information found online is no more – or no less – accurate than information found in other sources. Genealogical researchers should always evaluate information found online with the same critical eye they use for information found in printed or other "offline" sources. Whenever possible, researchers should view the original version of the record they find online.

Communication

E-mail: Electronic mail, perhaps the most familiar resource on the Internet, allows one person to send a written message via computer to another person. It can be delivered in a matter of hours (sometimes even minutes), making it an excellent method of person-to-person communication. Genealogists often use e-mail to share research with others.

Mailing Lists: Discussion on various genealogy topics can take place via e-mail through mailing lists. Lists are available for most of Michigan's counties as well as on several topics, such as African-American research in Michigan or Irish genealogy in Michigan. In order to participate in a list's discussion, individuals must subscribe to the list. Subscribers receive a copy of each message sent to the list. When subscribers respond to the list, a copy of their message is sent to every other subscriber on the list. Some lists have more "traffic" – messages per day – than others. More than 100 mailing lists deal with Michigan genealogy topics. Descriptions of these lists can be found in several places, including:

- Genealogy Resources on the Internet – Michigan Mailing Lists <www.rootsweb.com/~jfuller/gen_mail_states-mi.html>
- Rootsweb.com Michigan Mailing Lists <lists.rootsweb.com/index/usa/MI/>
- Yahoo! Groups' Michigan Mailing Lists <dir.groups.yahoo.com/dir/Family_Home/Genealogy/By_Location/U.S._States/Michigan>

Many lists have online archives that store past messages for viewing or searching, and in most cases, researchers do not have to subscribe to the list to use the archives. Archives for RootsWeb.com-sponsored lists, for example, can be found through the site's list page <lists.rootsweb.com/index/usa/MI/>. Researchers can follow the links to the desired list and then browse or search the archives.

Message Boards: Message boards or bulletin boards are online message areas. They are similar to bulletin boards or message boards at a local grocery store in that the messages stay at one location; researchers must visit the message board to read and post messages. Researchers do not have to be a subscriber to participate in the exchange. Some messages found on message boards, such as Rootsweb.com's Great Lakes Shipping Board, also are available via a mailing list. In addition to the Great Lakes Shipping Board, RootsWeb.com <boards.rootsweb.com/> sponsors message boards for all of Michigan's counties, plus a few societies. Messages can be viewed chronologically, by "thread" or message subject, or sorted by general topics, such as biographies; Bible, birth, cemetery, census, death, marriage, military, and pension records; deeds; immigration information; obituaries; and wills. In addition, individual message boards or all of the message boards can be searched for a name or term. An advanced option allows researchers to search for message authors or subjects or to narrow their search to a particular time frame. Genealogy.com also has a Michigan Genealogy Forum <genforum.genealogy.com/mi/>.

Queries: Researchers often publish queries, messages that ask other persons questions about their family lines. Traditionally, queries have been published in genealogical newsletters or magazines, but now they also can be published online through mailing lists or message boards. In fact, queries are one of the general topics listed for each of RootsWeb.com's message boards.

Lookups and Research Exchange: The Internet also makes it easier for genealogists who need assistance looking up information at a distant courthouse, cemetery, or library to find someone who's willing to give them help. In most cases, "lookups" are done by volunteers who expect nothing other than perhaps reimbursement for expenses. With "research exchange," volunteers generally offer to look up the information in exchange for research done in the home area of the person making the request. Places for researchers to connect for lookups or research exchange include the following:

- Geneasearch's Michigan Lookups <geneasearch.com/lookups/mi.htm>
- MIGenWeb county sites often list volunteers willing to assist others
- MIGenWeb's Michigan Lookups <www.rootsweb.com/~migenweb/mi-lookups.html>
- MIGenWeb's Michigan Research Exchange allows researchers to register <www.rootsweb.com/~migenweb/research.htm> to give help or to view the list of those offering help <www.rootsweb.com/~migenweb/postedexchange.htm>
- Random Acts of Genealogical Kindness <www.raogk.org/michigan.htm>

- RootsWeb.com's message boards include "lookups" as one of their topics
- RootsWeb.com's mailing list MI-NEWSPAPER-L was set up to facilitate lookups in Michigan newspapers, and MI-CENSUS-LOOKUP-L was established to assist researchers with requests for checking census records.

Research

The World Wide Web, the multimedia portion of the Internet, organizes text, graphics, sound, video, and animation into individual Web sites. Each Web site has an address, also known as a Uniform Resource Locator or URL. Each document or "page" on a Web site is linked to other pages via hypertext links, most often indicated by underlined words on the page or graphics that change color when a mouse passes over them. Researchers can move seamlessly from page to page and site to site by using the computer's mouse to click on these links. Many Web sites have been mentioned in other chapters of this book, so the following list is not a comprehensive inventory of Michigan resources online. Instead, it is intended to give researchers some examples of the types of resources available by computer.

General Sites: Genealogists should be familiar with the following Web sites, regardless of their geographical area of interest:

- American Memory from the Library of Congress <memory.loc.gov/ammem/amhome.html> offers more than seven million digital items from 100 historical collections. Some of the collections that relate to Michigan will be discussed below.
- Cyndi's List of Genealogy Sites on the Internet <www.cyndislist.com/> offers more than 230,000 categorized and cross-referenced links; several thousand links deal with Michigan <www.cyndislist.com/mi.htm>.
- Family Search <www.familysearch.org/>, the Web site of the Church of Jesus Christ of Latter-day Saints, includes several free databases and the catalog of the Church's Family History Library System.
- RootsWeb.com <www.rootsweb.com> is the oldest and largest free genealogy site. It is supported by Ancestry.com <www.ancestry.com>, a subscription-based site. RootsWeb hosts the Michigan Genealogy on the Web (MIGenWeb) project and includes a page with links to several Michigan sources <www.rootsweb.com/roots-l/USA/mi/index.html>. Ancestry.com includes a number of databases of Michigan records.

Books Online: Many Web sites have placed books online, either digital images of the actual book or HTML pages of the book's text. Some sites have indexed previously unindexed books and placed the indexes online:

- Some libraries have placed books online. Clarke Historical Library <clarke.cmich.edu/online.htm>, for example, has several books online, including county histories and the *Michigan State Gazetteer and Business Directory for 1860.*

- County Web sites affiliated with the American History and Genealogy Project, American Local History Network, or MIGenWeb often have online books. Examples of these include:
  - *1892 Portrait and Biographical Album of Genesee, Lapeer, and Tuscola Counties* <www.usgennet.org/usa/mi/county/tuscola/book/>
  - Books Online, Kent County, Michigan <www.rootsweb.com/~mikent/books/>
  - *History of Genesee County, Michigan, Her People, Industries, and Institutions* (1916) <www.usgennet.org/usa/mi/county/lapeer/gen/>
  - *History of Gratiot County, Michigan* (1913) <www.mfhn.com/gratiot/tucker/index-1.html>
  - *History of Manistee County, Michigan* (1882) <www.rootsweb.com/~mimanist/1882ManHist.html>
- The Digital General Collection <www.hti.umich.edu/g/genpub/> of the University of Michigan Digital Library Production Service's Digital Library Collections and Publications <www.hti.umich.edu/cgi/c/collsize/collsize> includes atlases, county histories, city directories, and other books of interest to Michigan genealogists, such as Russell's *The Germanic Influence in the Making of Michigan* (1927).
- The Making of America Web sites, a joint project of the University of Michigan <moa.umdl.umich.edu> and Cornell University <moa.cit.cornell.edu/moa>, is "a digital library of primary sources in American social history from the antebellum period through reconstruction."[1] The University of Michigan site has more than 100 books with Michigan in the title.
- Mardos Memorial Library of Online Books and Maps includes several county histories and other books about Michigan <www.memoriallibrary.com/MI/>.
- Michigan County Histories Collection <www.hti.umich.edu/m/micounty/> has a number of county histories online. (See Chapter 4 for more.)
- Pioneering the Upper Midwest: Books from Michigan, Minnesota, and Wisconsin, ca. 1820 to 1910 <memory.loc.gov/ammem/umhtml/umhome.html>, an American Memory collection <memory.loc.gov/ammem/amhome.html>, features digitized page images and transcribed, searchable text from 138 books. More than 50 books deal with Michigan and include biographies, local histories, memoirs, and more.
- RootsWeb.com's User-contributed Book Indexes Database includes information from some Michigan books <userdb.rootsweb.com/bookindexes/>.
- Web sites affiliated with societies also may have books or book indexes. An example is Delta County Genealogical Society's Surname Index of the *History of the Upper Peninsula of Michigan* (1883) <www.grandmastree.com/society/uphistory.htm>.

Censuses and City Directories: Transcriptions, abstracts, indexes, and digital images of census records and city directories are available through many Web sites. (See Chapter 5.)

Databases: Databases are collections of information organized in such a way that they can be easily searched for specific facts. For example, a database of marriages for a particular county may be arranged so that it can be searched by the name of the bride or groom or by the date of the event. It also may allow researchers to scan marriage entries alphabetically or chronologically. Many genealogical databases are available via the Internet; some are free, while others may require a subscription fee.

Subscription Sites: Ancestry.com <www.ancestry.com> offers more than 100 databases specific to Michigan, including family and local histories, vital records, census records, military records, directories, and more. Ancestry.com charges a subscription fee. At this writing, however, AncestryPlus – a version of Ancestry.com created for libraries – can be used for free at most Michigan libraries. Other subscription-based sites include HeritageQuest Online <www.heritagequestonline.com/>, available for free at some libraries, and Genealogy.com <www.genealogy.com>.

Free Sites: Several free databases also are available to researchers:

- County Web sites affiliated with the American History and Genealogy Project, American Local History Network, or MIGenWeb often have databases. These sites are described below under the Projects section.
- GENDIS, the Genealogical Death Indexing System, provides free online access to early Michigan death records. (See Chapter 3 for more.)
- The Michigan Family History Network <www.mifamilyhistory.org> has a number of free databases on its site, including vital, military, and school records.
- RootsWeb.com's User-contributed Databases <userdb.rootsweb.com/regional.html#Michigan> includes nearly 70 databases of alumni lists, vital records, book indexes, church and cemetery records, and more.
- Sites affiliated with libraries or societies often have databases.

Governmental Units: The State of Michigan's official Web site <www.michigan.gov> has links to state departments and other information. Of particular interest to genealogists will be the site's History, Arts, and Libraries section <www.michigan.gov/hal>, which links to the Library of Michigan, State Archives of Michigan, and other information for family history researchers, such as naturalization indexes, the Michigan 1870 census index and images, and Michigan cemetery sources. (These resources are described more fully in earlier chapters.) Several county's also have Web sites, some with access to vital record indexes. (See Chapter 10 for more.)

Libraries: Many libraries in Michigan have Web sites that include online catalogs, finding aids, collection descriptions, photographs, or databases of genealogical information. (See Chapter 11 for more.)

Maps: Digital images of maps can be found on a variety of Web sites. Several examples are listed below. In addition, some libraries may have a subscription to Digital Sanborn Maps <sanborn.umi.com>.

- American Memory's Map Collections: 1500 to 2004 <memory.loc.gov/ammem/gmdhtml/gmdhome.html> includes maps from more than 30 Michigan communities
- 1901 Atlas of Gratiot County <www.mfhn.com/gratiot/atlas/default.asp> and 1914 Atlas of Gratiot County <www.mfhn.com/gratiot/Chadwick1914/>
- Isabella County Plats <www.mifamilyhistory.org/isabella/township.html>
- Kent County Plat Maps <www.rootsweb.com/~mikent/platmaps/>
- Lake County, Farm Plat Book, 1930s <www.rootsweb.com/~milake/Plat_Map/plat_map.htm>
- 1875 Map of Macomb County, with Notes on the Founding and Early Settlers of the Townships and Villages <www.libcoop.net/mountclemens/1875map.htm>
- 1879 Atlas of Mecosta County <www.rootsweb.com/~mimecost/1879Atlas.htm>
- Michigan Digital Map Library <www.rootsweb.com/~usgenweb/maps/michigan/>
- Michigan Family History Network's Maps of Michigan <www.mifamilyhistory.org/mfhn_maps/> and Michigan Place Names <www.mifamilyhistory.org/mi_places/>
- 1872 Oakland County Plat Atlas Maps <www.memoriallibrary.com/MI/Oakland/PLATS/index.htm>
- Perry-Castaneda Library Map Collection: Michigan Maps <www.lib.utexas.edu/maps/michigan.html>
- 1895 U.S. Atlas: Michigan <www.livgenmi.com/1895/MI/>
- U.S. Gazetteer <www.census.gov/cgi-bin/gazetteer>

Newspapers: Digital images of newspapers, transcriptions or abstracts of newspaper articles, and newspaper indexes can be found online. Ancestry.com's Historical Newspapers Collection, for example, has digital images of a few Michigan newspapers. The OldenTimes.com's Old Michigan News <theoldentimes.com/old_news_mi.html> has digital images of selected articles from selected newspapers. Michigan Newspaper Abstracts <www.newspaperabstracts.com/michigan/index.shtml> features newspaper items from newspapers dated prior to 1931. It is divided by county, year, and then newspaper item. NewsLink: Michigan Newspapers <newslink.org/minews.html> and 50states.com's Michigan Newspapers <www.50states.com/news/michigan.htm> feature links to present-day online editions of newspapers.

Photographs: Many Web sites, such as those affiliated with libraries, societies, or MIGenWeb, features photographs of Michigan people and events:

- Among the American Memory collections with Michigan photographs are America from the Great Depression to World War II: Photographs from the FSA-OWI, 1935 to 1945 <memory.loc.gov/ammem/fsowhome.html>; Taking the Long View: Panoramic Photographs, 1851-1991 <memory.loc.gov/ammem/pnhtml/pnhome.html>; and Touring Turn-of-the-Century America: Photographs from the Detroit Publishing Company 1880 to 1920 <memory.loc.gov/ammem/detroit/dethome.html>

- Saginaw County, Michigan, Photographs <freepages.genealogy.rootsweb.com/~evansandobertein/saginaw.htm>

Projects: Several organizations and individuals have placed Michigan documents and data online. Most, but not all, of these projects have been designed specifically for family history researchers:

AHGP: The American History and Genealogy Project <www.ahgp.org/> is a network of independent Web sites devoted to history and genealogy. There is a state-level page for Michigan <www.ahgp.org/deb/mi/> and several county-level pages.

ALHN: The American Local History Network <www.alhn.org/> serves as a hub for freely accessible, independent historical and genealogical Web sites that are maintained by volunteers. There is a state-level page for Michigan <www.usgennet.org/usa/mi/state/> and several county-level pages.

The Making of Modern Michigan: The Making of Modern Michigan: Digitizing Michigan's Hidden Past <mmm.lib.msu.edu/> is a new project with the goal of placing online historical materials such as local histories, maps, oral histories, photographs, and other documents.

The Michigan Family History Network <www.mifamilyhistory.org> offers a number of free databases on its site, including the Early Michigan Births Index, Michigan Death Database, Dibean's Michigan Marriage Collection, Great Lakes Passenger Lists, Michigan School Records, and more. At this writing, the site has more than 200,000 genealogical records.

MIGenWeb: Michigan Genealogy on the Web <www.rootsweb.com/~migenweb/> is part of the USGenWeb Project <www.usgenweb.org/>, a volunteer effort to place genealogical data online. USGenWeb began in 1996 as an outgrowth of the Kentucky Comprehensive Database Project, also known as the KyGenWeb Project. Volunteers coordinate each state-level and county-level page in the USGenWeb Project. In Michigan, most counties have a county-level page, and there are several state-level projects, such as the Michigan Tombstone Photo Project and the Michigan Research Exchange, on the state-level page. At the county level, the amount of information varies, but many sites include vital records, county and township histories, census and land records, county maps and directories, obituaries, biographies, queries, surname registries, photographs, and more. Some of the county-level pages in the MIGenWeb project serve as county-level pages in the American Local History Network <www.alhn.org/> or the American History and Genealogy Project <www.ahgp.org/>.

Societies: Historical and genealogical societies often have Web sites that feature information about the society as well as record transcriptions and other information. (See Chapter 12 for more.)

Michigan Counties

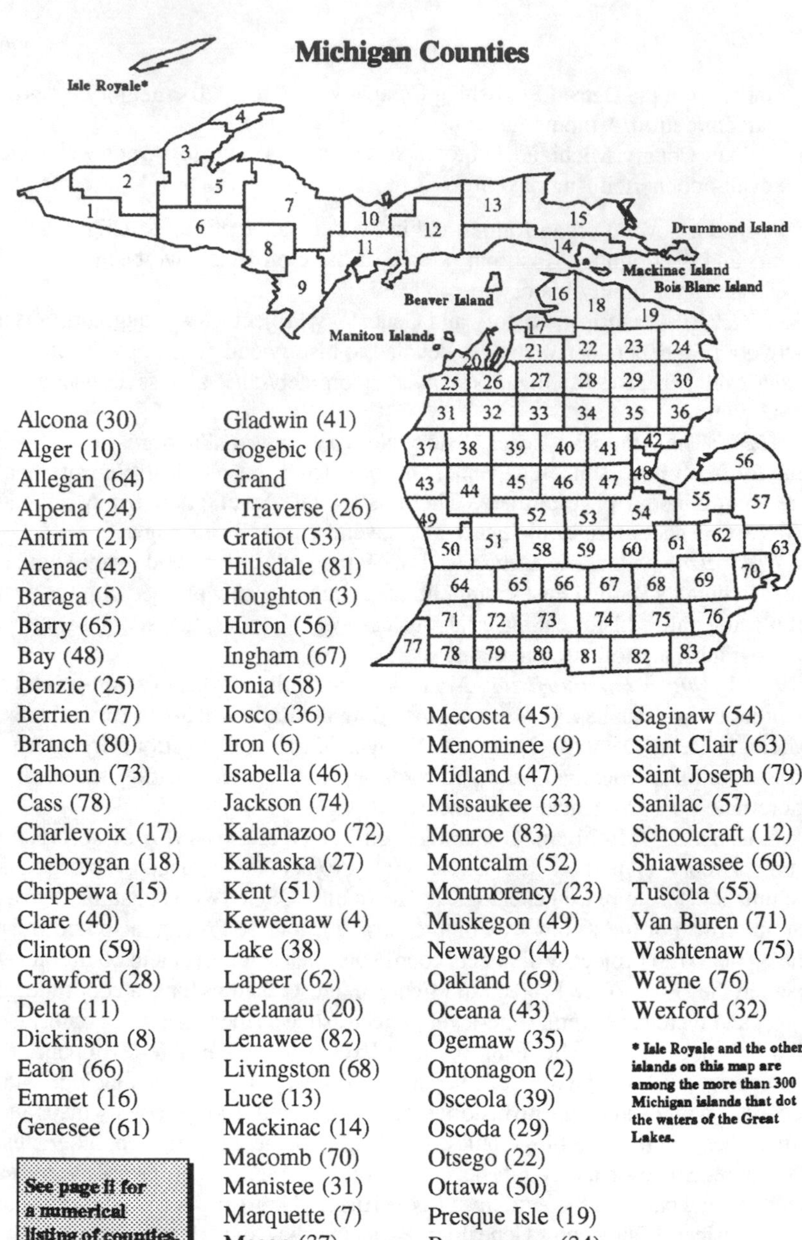

Alcona (30)
Alger (10)
Allegan (64)
Alpena (24)
Antrim (21)
Arenac (42)
Baraga (5)
Barry (65)
Bay (48)
Benzie (25)
Berrien (77)
Branch (80)
Calhoun (73)
Cass (78)
Charlevoix (17)
Cheboygan (18)
Chippewa (15)
Clare (40)
Clinton (59)
Crawford (28)
Delta (11)
Dickinson (8)
Eaton (66)
Emmet (16)
Genesee (61)
Gladwin (41)
Gogebic (1)
Grand Traverse (26)
Gratiot (53)
Hillsdale (81)
Houghton (3)
Huron (56)
Ingham (67)
Ionia (58)
Iosco (36)
Iron (6)
Isabella (46)
Jackson (74)
Kalamazoo (72)
Kalkaska (27)
Kent (51)
Keweenaw (4)
Lake (38)
Lapeer (62)
Leelanau (20)
Lenawee (82)
Livingston (68)
Luce (13)
Mackinac (14)
Macomb (70)
Manistee (31)
Marquette (7)
Mason (37)
Mecosta (45)
Menominee (9)
Midland (47)
Missaukee (33)
Monroe (83)
Montcalm (52)
Montmorency (23)
Muskegon (49)
Newaygo (44)
Oakland (69)
Oceana (43)
Ogemaw (35)
Ontonagon (2)
Osceola (39)
Oscoda (29)
Otsego (22)
Ottawa (50)
Presque Isle (19)
Roscommon (34)
Saginaw (54)
Saint Clair (63)
Saint Joseph (79)
Sanilac (57)
Schoolcraft (12)
Shiawassee (60)
Tuscola (55)
Van Buren (71)
Washtenaw (75)
Wayne (76)
Wexford (32)

*** Isle Royale and the other islands on this map are among the more than 300 Michigan islands that dot the waters of the Great Lakes.**

See page ii for a numerical listing of counties.

10 Counties and Their Records

Shortly after Michigan became a territory, Gov. William Hull divided Michigan into four judicial districts: Detroit, Erie, Huron, and Michilimackinac. Created on 3 July 1805, these districts approximately covered the following areas: "District of Michilimackinac, the area north of the southwest part of Saginaw Bay; Huron, south from the southwest part of Saginaw Bay to five miles north of the old citadel in Detroit; Detroit, from here south to the Huron River of Lake Erie; Erie, from the Huron River south to the territorial boundary."[1] The four districts extended westward to Lake Michigan.

"While not counties in name, these districts served as the geographical units used for the 1810 federal census of Michigan territory and during the first 10 years of territorial government carried out many typical county functions through a system of district courts, justices of the peace, district marshals, and probate officers."[2] Erie and Michilimackinac each formed a judicial district, and Huron and Detroit were combined into a third one.[3]

County government in Michigan started in 1815 with the creation of Wayne County, but the districts continued as "judicial districts until at least 1818."[4] By 1820, however, the district system had been fully replaced by the county system; the 1820 federal census of Michigan Territory used counties as their geographical units.

When many Michigan counties were created they had few or no permanent residents, so a county government was not organized at that time. The county boundaries were laid out in advance of settlement to encourage settlers to move in and to ease the transition into regular government.[5]

> Until the population grew to the point where an unorganized county could begin to carry out its official functions, it was attached to a fully organized county. Inhabitants of the unorganized county would have to go to the host county to probate wills, enter land transactions, and conduct any other county business.[6]

This is an important fact for genealogists to keep in mind, especially since this "unorganized" status of many counties lasted anywhere from a few months to a few decades. Plus, attachments often changed. "It is possible for records on an individual living in an unorganized county to be found in several different host counties, even though that person never moved."[7] Alcona County, for example, remained unorganized from its creation in 1840 until its organization in 1869 and was attached to four counties during those 29 years. Crawford County remained unorganized for 39 years and was attached to five counties. Similarly, Oscoda County was attached to five different counties during the 41 years between its creation and organization. Many other Michigan counties were attached to two or more counties between their creation and organization.

Complicating matters further is the fact that counties could be attached for various reasons "including 'judicial purposes,' 'civil and municipal purposes,' 'judicial and municipal purposes,' and so forth."[8] Sometimes unorganized counties remained totally unorganized, while in others "all or part of the unorganized county became part of a civil township under the jurisdiction of the host county."[9] *Evolution of Michigan Townships,* published in 1972, can help researchers determine when a township was created and from which township(s) it came.

In addition, four of Michigan's counties – Isle Royale, Manitou, Omeena, and Wyandot – were eliminated and absorbed by other counties. Three Michigan counties – Arenac, Charlevoix, and Ogemaw – were created, eliminated, and then re-created. Eighteen others had their names changed, 16 of them in 1843. These were Aischum to Lake; Anamickee to Alpena; Cheonoquet to Montmorency; Kanotin to Iosco; Kautawaubet (also spelled Kautawbet) to Wexford; Kaykakee to Clare: Keskkauko (also spelled Keshkauko or Reshkauko) to Charlevoix; Meegisee to Antrim; Mikenauk to Roscommon; Negwegon (also spelled Neewago) to Alcona; Notipekago (also spelled Nontipekago) to Mason; Okkuddo (also spelled Okkudo) to Otsego; Shawono (also spelled Shawano or Shawona) to Crawford; Tonedagana to Emmet; Unwattin to Osceola; and Wabassee to Kalkaska. Around 1850, Michilimackinac was changed to Mackinac, and in 1863, Bleeker was changed to Menominee.

Two county names were used more than once. The name "Crawford County" was used twice – first for a county created in 1818 that later became part of Wisconsin and then for Michigan's present-day Crawford County, created in 1840.

The name "Wayne County" was used twice before its present incarnation, first by the Northwest Territory and then by the Indiana Territory. On 15 August 1796, Wayne County was created by the Northwest Territory from Hamiliton in Ohio, Knox in Indiana, and non-county area. This Wayne County included all of the Lower Peninsula of present-day Michigan, the eastern part of the Upper Peninsula, and parts of present-day Illinois, Indiana, Ohio, and Wisconsin.[10] It was eliminated on 1 March 1803 when the Northwest Territory was eliminated. However, on the same day Indiana Territory created a Wayne County from Knox in Indiana, Saint Clair in Illinois, and "the former Northwest Territory north of Ohio."[11] Except for the western portion of the Upper Peninsula, it included nearly all of present-day Michigan. This Wayne County was eliminated on 30 June 1805 when Michigan Territory was created. Michigan's current Wayne County was created on 21 November 1815.

County Records

Records found at the county level include land and court (described in Chapter 6) and births, deaths, marriages, and divorces (described in Chapter 3). Birth and death records generally date from 1867, and land, court, divorce, and marriage records usually date from the county's organization. Earlier records may be on file in the county to which an unorganized county was attached. Generally, the County Clerk's Office keeps track of birth, death, and marriage records. Circuit court records, including naturalizations and divorces, may be found with the County Clerk or the Circuit Court Clerk. Land records are generally found with the Register of Deeds Office, while probate records are usually found with the Probate Court Office or Probate Judge's Office.

In-person research can be done in many counties, but researchers should write or call ahead for current policies and the times that the records will be available for genealogical research. Some counties store older records offsite, and it may take a few days or more to move them to the county courthouse to be available for inspection. Many county clerk offices have days or times that are busier than others due to court activity, and clerks appreciate it if genealogists avoid those days.

When visiting a Michigan county courthouse, researchers may be asked to present identification, such as a driver's license, and to sign a statement that they agree to abide by certain rules for inspecting records. Generally, the rules prohibit researchers from using ink pens, photocopy machines, or cameras. They prohibit the tracing of records. They require that records be handled with care and that they remain in the area designated by the county official. Rules prohibit smoking, eating, or drinking when viewing the records or indexes. Rules also state that the inspection of fragile or valuable records, or those being arranged, may be restricted.

Many clerks also will respond to written queries, though some reported that they would not. Copy and/or search fees may be charged. When writing to a county clerk, be brief but be sure to list all pertinent names and dates. Always include a self-addressed stamped envelope and appropriate fees for copies or searches. Some counties have placed record indexes online to assist researchers in ordering records. These include the following:

- **Barry County** <www.barrycounty.org/Departments/Clerk.htm> has indexes of births previous to 1903 and deaths and marriages through 2003. The birth index provides the name and year of birth and the book and page number where the full record can be found. The death index provides the name of the decedent, year of death, date the death was recorded, and the liber (book) and page where the full death record can be found. The marriage index provides the name of the bride and groom, the record date, and the book and page number where the full record can be found.
- **Branch County's** <co.branch.mi.us/deathsearch.taf> death index, which includes records from 1867, provides the name of the decedent and the date of death. It can be searched by name and year of death or by name only, or researchers can view all deaths for a given month and year.

- **Emmet County's** marriage index <www.co.emmet.mi.us/clerk/marriage input.asp> and death index <www.co.emmet.mi.us/clerk/deathinput.asp> include records from 1867. The death index can be searched by last name or month and year of death and returns the name of the deceased, death date, place of death, and the book and page number of the record. The marriage index can be searched by the last name of the bride or groom or the month and year of the marriage. It returns the names of the bride and groom, the marriage date, and the book and page number of the record.
- **Genesee County** <www.co.genesee.mi.us/vitalrec> provides indexes for death records from 1930 and marriage records from 1963. The death index includes the date of death and the volume and page number for the record, and the marriage index includes the marriage date, the names of the bride and groom, and the volume and page number of the record.
- **Grand Traverse County** <www.co.grand-traverse.mi.us> offers death and marriage indexes, dating back to 1853 for marriages and 1867 for deaths. The death index provides the name of the decedent, date of death, and the book and page number where the full record can be found. The marriage index provides the name of the bride and groom, year of marriage, the license number, and the liber (book) and page where the full record can be found.
- **Macomb County's** Database Direct <www.macomb.mcntv.com> provides access to the county's central databases. It includes a death records index from 1904 to date, though at this writing deaths before 1960 may not be complete. Search results list the name of the decedent and date and county of death.
- **Muskegon County's** Genealogical Death Indexing System <www.co.muskegon .mi.us/clerk/websearch.cfm> eventually will include all death records from 1867 to 1965. Members of the Muskegon County Genealogical Society are entering the records into a database. The index provides the name of the decedent, the year of death, and the liber (book) and page number where the full death record can by found.
- **Saginaw County's** <saginawcounty.com/clerk/search/index.html> marriage and death certificates are available from 1995 to date. Marriage certificates provide the name and residence of the bride and groom and the names of the parents of each, while death certificates provide the name of the deceased, the decedent's birth and death dates, and the name of the decedent's mother and father.
- **Washtenaw County** <secure.ewashtenaw.org/ecommerce/vitalrecord/vr Home.do> has indexes for death and marriage records. At this writing the death index goes back to 1960 and the marriage index to 1965, but county officials say they are constantly adding older records to the databases. The death index includes the name of the decedent, the decedent's birth and death dates, a residence code, and a local file number. The marriage index includes the name of the bride and groom, the marriage date, and a local file number. Certified copies of marriage and death records can be ordered online.

Other sources for county records include the following:

- Some circuit court <www.michigan.gov/documents/mhc_sa_circular37_49972_7.pdf>, naturalization <www.michigan.gov/documents/mhc_sa_circular10_49699_7.pdf>, probate <www.michigan.gov/documents/mhc_sa_circular06_49689_7.pdf>, and vital records <www.michigan.gov/documents/mhc_sa_circular19_49707_7.pdf> have been transferred to the State Archives of Michigan. In addition, indexes to naturalization records at the State Archives may be found online. (See Chapter 2 for more information on naturalization records.)
- Many county records have been microfilmed by the Family History Library in Salt Lake City and may be rented for research at Family History Centers. The Family History Library's catalog is online <www.familysearch.org>. (See Chapter 11 for more information on Family History Centers.)
- Many county records have been indexed, abstracted, or transcribed by genealogical or historical societies or individuals. These have been printed or appear online on Web sites sponsored by MIGenWeb, societies, or libraries. Some sites, such as the Cheboygan County MIGenWeb Site, include digital images of vital records <www.rootsweb.com/~micheboy/vrcertsproj.shtml>. (See Chapter 9 for more information about online sources. Library card catalogs will list print sources.)

Between 1936 and 1942 the Michigan Historical Records Survey, a program of the Work Projects Administration, began compiling an inventory of the records of all Michigan counties and some cities. Inventories for the following 12 counties were published and can be found in many libraries: Alger, Alpena, Baraga, Bay, Calhoun, Cheboygan, Genesee, Iosco, Iron, Jackson, Marquette, and Muskegon. (The inventories for Alpena, Bay, and Calhoun also are available on CD through Quintin Publications <www.quintinpublications.com/mi.html>).

Inventories for the rest of Michigan's counties were not completed by the time the project was abandoned. The notes, correspondence, rough drafts of inventories, and other materials for these unpublished inventories were deposited with the Michigan Historical Collections at the Bentley Historical Library, located on the North Campus of the University of Michigan in Ann Arbor.

The published guides are valuable because they list and describe all records kept by the county. This includes everything from vital, land, and court records to records kept by the offices of the sheriff, coroner, treasurer, school commissioner, health department, and social welfare board. The unpublished inventories also are valuable, though the 107 boxes of loose papers may prove to be intimidating.

Another helpful source for locating county records is the Michigan County Clerk's Directory. Originally published in 1994 and last updated in 2001, the directory lists information about records available in county clerk offices. The directory is available online through the State of Michigan's History, Arts, and Libraries Web site <www.michigan.gov/hal>. Select "Resources for Genealogists."

Former Michigan Counties

Information about early Michigan can include the names of counties that are no longer part of present-day Michigan.

Brown County was created and organized on 3 December 1818 from non-county area in present-day Wisconsin and Michigan. The seat was at Fox River. When Wisconsin Territory was created from Michigan Territory on 3 July 1836, Brown County became a Wisconsin county and was eliminated from Michigan Territory. The northeast portion of Brown County that fell in present-day Michigan (portions of present-day Gogebic, Iron, Dickinson, Marquette, and Menominee counties) became non-county area.

Crawford County was created and organized on 3 December 1818 from non-county area in present-day Minnesota and Wisconsin. The seat was at Prairie du Chien. When Wisconsin Territory was created from Michigan Territory on 3 July 1836, this Crawford County was eliminated from Michigan Territory and became part of Wisconsin. However, there is a different county named Crawford in present-day Michigan.

Des Moines County was created and organized 1 October 1834 from non-county area in present-day Iowa. No county seat was established. When Wisconsin Territory was created from Michigan Territory on 3 July 1836, the county was eliminated from Michigan and became part of Wisconsin Territory. It is now part of the state of Iowa.

Dubuque County was created and organized on 1 October 1834 from non-county areas in present-day Iowa, Minnesota, North Dakota, and South Dakota. The seat was established at Dubuque. When Wisconsin Territory was created from Michigan Territory on 3 July 1836, the county was eliminated from Michigan. It is now a part of the state of Iowa.

Forest County was organized in 1913 from Cheboygan and Presque Isle counties. It was subject to a referendum, which was voted down.

Iowa County was created 1 January 1830 from the Crawford County in present-day Wisconsin. It was organized on the same day, with the county seat established at Mineral Point. When Wisconsin Territory was created from Michigan Territory on 3 July 1836, Iowa County was eliminated from Michigan. It is now part of Wisconsin.

Isle Royale County, which consisted of the Lake Superior island of Isle Royale, was created 4 March 1875 from Keweenaw County. It was organized on the same day, with the seat established at Island Mine. On 13 March 1885, the county was deorganized and attached to Houghton County for judicial purposes. Then on 9 April 1897, the county was eliminated and absorbed by Keweenaw County. The Keweenaw County MIGenWeb site has more information about Isle Royale County <www.mfhn.com/keweenaw/isleroyal.html>.

Manitou County was created from Emmet and Leelanau (which was attached to Grand Traverse) on 12 February 1855. Manitou County was organized on the same day. It was named after the Manitou Islands, which formed part of the county, and the county seat was established at Saint James on Beaver Island, which formed another part of the county. On 16 March 1861, the county was attached to Mackinac for meetings of the district court. Attachment was changed to Leelanau County in 1865 for meetings of the circuit court. Manitou County was eliminated and absorbed by Charlevoix and Leelanau counties on 4 April 1895. Population at this time was 917. Some naturalization records (1870-1894) have survived and are at the State Archives of Michigan. Transcripts of census records also can be found online <members.aol.com/vwilson577/manitou.html>.

Milwaukee County was created 6 September 1834 in present-day Wisconsin from Brown and Iowa counties. At its creation, it was attached to Brown for judicial purposes. Milwaukee County was organized on 7 September 1835, with its seat established at Milwaukee. When Wisconsin Territory was created from Michigan Territory on 3 July 1836, Milwaukee County was no longer a part of Michigan. It is now in the state of Wisconsin.

Omeena County was created on 1 April 1840 from Michilimackinac (now Mackinac County). It was attached to Michilimackinac for judicial purposes and never fully organized. Omeena County was eliminated and absorbed by Grand Traverse County on 3 February 1853.

Washington County was created in 1867 from Marquette County. "Residents of Marquette County protested so loudly that the legislature backed off and rescinded the act, returning the area to its former location in Marquette County."[12]

Wyandot County was created 1 April 1840 from Michilimackinac (now Mackinac County) and attached to Michilimackinac for judicial purposes. Wyandot County was eliminated and absorbed by Cheboygan County on 29 January 1853. It was never fully organized.

Alcona County Clerk
106 Fifth St.
P.O. Box 308
Harrisville, Mich. 48740-0308
Telephone: (989) 724-6807

Creation: First named Negwegon, the county was created on 1 April 1840 from non-county area attached to Saginaw. Negwegon was renamed Alcona on 8 March 1843.[13]

Attachments: At its creation, Alcona was attached to Michilimackinac for judicial purposes. It was later attached to Cheboygan in 1853, Alpena in 1857, and Iosco in 1858.

Organization: County government was organized on 12 March 1869.

Townships: Alcona, Cadedonia, Curtis, Greenbush, Gustin, Harrisville, Hawes, Haynes, Mikado, Millen, and Mitchell.[14]

Records begin on the following dates: Probate, 1868; birth, marriage, divorce, death, land, naturalization, 1869; and civil court, 1872.[15]

In-person research: Researchers can inspect vital records from 10 a.m. to noon and 1 to 3 p.m. Tuesdays, Thursdays, and Fridays. Researchers must provide identification and are asked to register for each visit. Researchers may view birth records only upon the clerk's discretion.

Written queries: No search fee. Copies are $1; certified copies are $5.

American History and Genealogy Project and American Local History Network: <www.geocities.com/Heartland/Plains/5666/Alcona.html>

MIGenWeb: <www.rootsweb.com/~mialcona/index.htm>

Alger County Clerk
101 Court St.
Munising, Mich. 49862

Telephone: (906) 387-2076

Creation: Alger was created and organized on 17 March 1885 from Schoolcraft, with the first seat at Autrain. "The county seat was moved to Munising in 1901 or 1902."[16]

Townships: Au Train, Burt, Grand Island, Limestone, Mathias, Munising, Onota, and Rock River.

Records begin on the following dates: Birth, death, land, 1884; divorce, court, probate, naturalization, 1885; and marriage, 1887.

American History and Genealogy Project and American Local History Network: <www.geocities.com/Heartland/Plains/5666/Alger.html>

MIGenWeb: <www.rootsweb.com/~mialger>

Allegan County Clerk
113 Chestnut St.
Allegan, Mich. 49010

Telephone: (269) 673-0200

Web site: <www.allegancounty.org>

Creation: Allegan was created on 2 March 1831 from Barry (which was attached to Kalamazoo) and non-county areas attached to Cass and Kalamazoo.

Attachments: It was attached to Kalamazoo in 1833.

Organization: County government was organized on 7 September 1835.

Townships: Allegan, Casco, Cheshire, Clyde, Dorr, Fillmore, Ganges, Gunplain, Heath, Laketown, Lee, Leighton, Manlius, Martin, Monterey, Otsego, Overisel, Salem, Saugatuck, Trowbridge, Valley, Watson, and Wayland.

Records begin on the following dates: Land, 1833; marriage, 1835; court and probate, 1836; divorce, 1850; and birth and death, 1867. Naturalization records (1850-1956) are at the State Archives of Michigan.

In-person research: Researchers can inspect records from 8:30 a.m. to 4:30 p.m. on Tuesdays, Wednesdays, and Thursdays.

Written queries: Will answer. Copies are $7 for the first copy and $3 for each additional copy of the same record.

MIGenWeb: <www.rootsweb.com/~miallega>

Alpena County Clerk
720 W. Chisholm St., Suite #2
Alpena, Mich. 49707-2453
Telephone: (989) 354-9520
Fax: (989) 354-9644
Web site: <www.alpenacounty.org/alpcnty/index.htm>

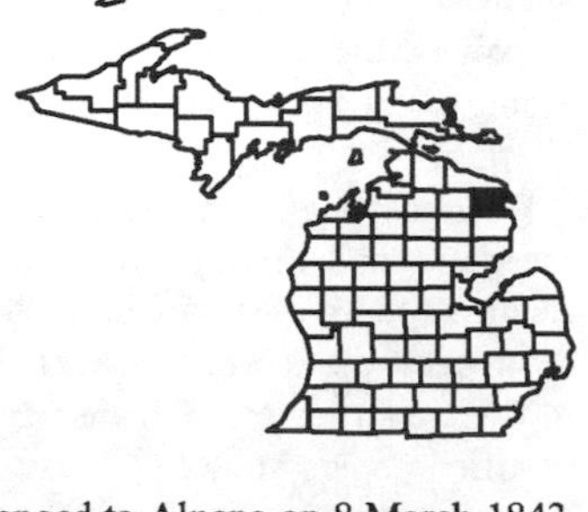

Creation: First called Anamickee, the county was created on 1 April 1840 from Michilimackinac (now Mackinac) and non-county area attached to Saginaw. The county's name was changed to Alpena on 8 March 1843.

Attachments: Alpena was attached to Michilimackinac for judicial purposes at its creation, and in 1853 it was attached to Cheboygan.

Organization: County government was organized on 7 February 1857, with the seat established at Fremont (now Alpena).

Townships: Alpena, Green, Long Rapids, Maple Ridge, Ossineke, Sanborn, Wellington, and Wilson.

Records begin on the following dates: Land and probate, 1858; civil court, 1860; naturalization, 1867; birth and marriage, 1869; and divorce and death, 1871.

In-person research: Researchers may inspect records from 10 a.m. to 2 p.m. Mondays through Fridays.

Written queries: Searches are $1 for each year selected and includes a search of one year before and one after. "In other words, if someone picks 1985 to be searched, we will search 1984-1986." Certified copies are $8 for the first one and $4 for additional copies of the same record ordered at the same time.

MIGenWeb: <www.rootsweb.com/~mi alpena/>

Antrim County Clerk
203 E. Cayuga St.
P.O. Box 520
Bellaire, Mich. 49615
Telephone: (231) 533-6353
Fax: (231) 533-6238
E-mail: <coclerk05@torchlake.com>
Web site: <www.antrimcounty.org>

Creation: First named Meegisee, the county was created 1 April 1840 from Michilimackinac (now Mackinac). Its name was changed to Antrim on 8 March 1843.

Attachments: At its creation, Antrim was attached to Michilimackinac for judicial purposes, and in 1853 it was attached to Grand Traverse.

Organization: County government was organized on 11 March 1863, with the seat established at Elk Rapids. Seat was changed to Keno (now Bellaire) in 1879.

Boundaries: In 1865, Antrim gained a small area from Grand Traverse, then lost about 110 square miles to the re-creation of Charlevoix in 1869. It gained a small area from Kalkaska in 1881.

Townships: Banks, Central Lake, Chestonia, Custer, Echo, Elk Rapids, Forest Home, Helena, Jordan, Kearney, Mancelona, Milton, Star, Torch Lake, and Warner.

Records begin on the following dates: Land, 1853; probate, 1863; birth, marriage, and divorce, 1866; and death and civil court, 1867. Naturalization records (1863-1955) are at the State Archives of Michigan.

In-person research: No restrictions.

Written queries: Will answer. Searches are $5. Certified copies are $10, non-certified copies are $2.

American Local History Network and MIGenWeb: <www.online-isp.com/~maggie/antrim/>

Arenac County Clerk
120 North Grove St.
P.O. Box 747
Standish, Mich. 48658
Telephone: (989) 846-4561
Fax: (989) 846-9194

Creation: Arenac was created twice, the first time on 2 March 1831 from non-county areas attached to Oakland. Arenac was eliminated and absorbed by Bay in 1857 and then re-created on 21 April 1883 from Bay "with different boundaries from those Arenac originally had in 1831."[17]

Attachments: Arenac was attached to Saginaw for judicial purposes from 1836 to 1857.

Organization: Arenac was organized at the time of its second creation on 21 April 1883. The first seat was established at Omer. Today's county seat is Standish.

Townships: Adams, Arenac, Au Gres, Clayton, Deep River, Lincoln, Mason, Moffatt, Sims, Standish, Turner, and Whitney.

Records begin on the following dates: Land, 1845; birth, marriage, divorce, death, probate, and civil court, 1883. Naturalization records (1883-1956) are at the State Archives of Michigan.

In-person research: Preferred days and times are 8:30 a.m. to 5 p.m. Mondays, Wednesdays, and Fridays. "Will assist on other days, staff permitting."

Written queries: Will answer. Certified copies are $5 for the first one and $2 for each additional copy of the same record ordered at the same time.

MIGenWeb: <www.rootsweb.com/~miarenac/index.htm>

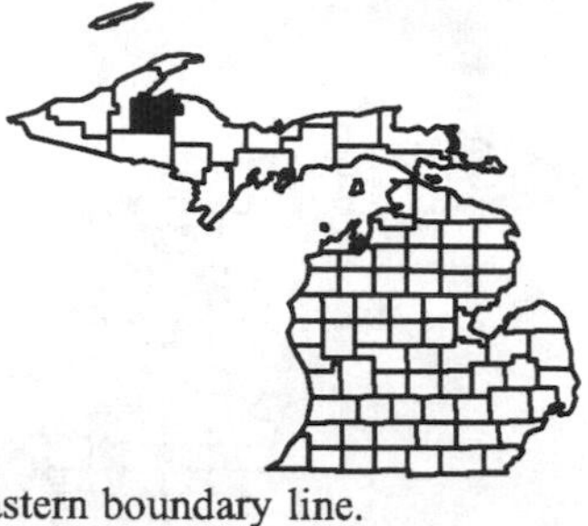

Baraga County Clerk
16 North Third St.
L'Anse, Mich. 49946
Telephone: (906) 524-6183

Creation: Baraga was created from Houghton on 19 February 1875.

Organization: County government was organized at the time of its creation.

Boundaries: In 1885, Baraga exchanged area with Houghton, straightening Baraga's eastern boundary line.

Townships: Arvon, Baraga, Covington, L'Anse, and Spurr.

Records begin on the following dates: Land, 1861; birth, death, 1874; marriage, divorce, court, probate, and naturalization, 1875.

American Local History Network: <www.usgennet.org/usa/mi/county/baraga>

MIGenWeb: <www.rootsweb.com/~mibaraga>

Barry County Clerk
220 W. State St.
Hastings, Mich. 49058
Telephone: (269) 945-1285
Fax: (269) 945-0209
Web site: <www.barrycounty.org>

Creation: Barry was created on 29 October 1829 from non-county areas attached to Lenawee and Oakland.

Attachments: Barry was attached to Saint Joseph in 1829 and Kalamazoo in 1830.

Organization: County government was organized on 15 March 1839, with the seat established at Hastings.

Boundaries: Barry lost about 140 square miles to the creation of Allegan in 1831.

Townships: Assyria, Baltimore, Barry, Carlton, Castleton, Hastings, Irving, Johnstown, Maple Grove, Orangeville, Prairieville, Rutland, Thornapple, Woodland, and Yankee Springs.

Records begin on the following dates: Divorce, 1825; land, 1834; marriage, 1839; civil court, 1847; naturalization, 1851; probate, 1862; and birth and death, 1867.

In-person research: Researchers can inspect records from 9 a.m. to 4 p.m. Mondays, Tuesdays, Wednesdays, and Fridays. "We have very limited space. We allow one person for one hour – first come, first served."

Written queries: Will answer.

American Local History Network: <www.usgennet.org/usa/mi/state/orphan/barry>

MIGenWeb: <www.rootsweb.com/~mibarry>

Bay County Clerk
515 Center Ave., Suite 101
Bay City, Mich. 48708-5122
Telephone: (989) 895-4280
Fax: (989) 895-4284
Web site: <www.co.bay.mi.us>

Creation: After a three-year court battle, Bay was created from portions of Midland and Saginaw counties and all of Arenac on 20 April 1857. Arenac was eliminated.

Organization: County government was organized on the same day the county was created, with the seat established at Bay City.

Boundaries: Bay gained a small portion (about 20 square miles) from Saginaw in 1871, gained Charity Island from Huron in 1880, and gained another 20 square miles from Saginaw in 1881. Bay lost its northern portion in 1883 when Arenac was recreated.

Townships: Bangor, Beaver, Frankenlust, Fraser, Garfield, Gibson, Hampton, Kawkawlin, Merritt, Monitor, Mount Forest, Pinconning, Portsmouth, and Williams.

Records begin on the following dates: Land, 1835; marriage and probate, 1857; birth and death, 1867; divorce, 1869; and civil court, 1883. Naturalization records (1858-1966) are at the State Archives of Michigan.

In-person research: "Records are available Monday through Friday (with the exception of legal holidays) between the hours of 2 p.m. and 4 p.m."

Written queries: Will answer. "Records prior to 1930 we type and certify at a cost of $10.25 for the first copy and $2 for additional copies (ordered at the same time). Also, when possible, [photo] copies can be requested at a rate of $4.50 each."

American History and Genealogy Project and American Local History Network: <www.usgennet.org/usa/mi/county/bay>

MIGenWeb: <www.mifamilyhistory.org/bay>

Benzie County Clerk
448 Court Place
P.O. Box 377
Beulah, Mich. 49617
Telephone: (231) 882-9671
Fax: (231) 882-5941
Web site: <www.benziecounty.com>

Creation: Benzie was created 27 February 1863 from Leelanau.

Attachments: At its creation, Benzie was attached to Grand Traverse for civil and municipal purposes.

Organization: County government was organized on 30 March 1869, with the seat established at Frankfort. The seat was changed to Benzonia in 1872, back to Frankfort by 1895, to Honor by 1908, and finally to Beulah by 1916. Beulah remains the county seat.

Townships: Almira, Benzonia, Blaine, Colfax, Crystal Lake, Gilmore, Homestead, Inland, Joyfield, Lake, Platte, and Weldon.

Records begin on the following dates: Land, 1854; birth and death, 1868; marriage and civil court, 1869; divorce and probate, 1870; and naturalization, 1871.

In-person research: Office hours are 8 a.m. to noon and 1 p.m. to 5 p.m. "Closed during the noon hour."

Written queries: Will answer. Certified copies are $5 for the first copy and $2 for each additional copy purchased at the same time. "If the request is very lengthy, we will charge search fees based on wages."

American Local History Network: <members.aol.com/vwilson577/benzie-alhn.html>

MIGenWeb: <www.grandtraverseregion.com/benzie/>

Berrien County Clerk
Berrien County Administration Center
701 Main St.
Saint Joseph, Mich. 49085
Telephone: (269) 983-7111, ext. 8233
Fax: (269) 982-8667
E-mail: <records@berriencounty.org>
Web site: <www.berriencounty.org>

Creation: Berrien was created 29 October 1829 from unattached non-county area and non-county area attached to Lenawee.

Attachments: On 4 November 1829 Berrien was attached to Cass for administrative and judicial purposes.

Organization: County government was organized on 1 September 1831, with the seat established at Niles. The seat was changed to Newburyport by 1832, to Berrien Springs in 1837, and to today's Saint Joseph by 1894.

Townships: Bainbridge, Baroda, Benton, Berrien, Bertrand, Buchanan, Chikaming, Coloma, Galien, Hagar, Lake, Lincoln, New Buffalo, Niles, Oronoko, Pipestone, Royalton, Saint Joseph, Sodus, Three Oaks, Watervliet, and Weesaw.

Records begin on the following dates: Land and marriage, 1831; probate, 1832; civil court, 1833; divorce, 1835; naturalization, 1836; and birth and death, 1867.

In-person research: "We have a Genealogy Department at 5054 Saint Joseph Ave., Stevensville, that is open for genealogy research on Mondays from 8:30 a.m. to 12:30 p.m. and Fridays 12:30 p.m. to 4:30 p.m. This is for walk-in service only."

Written queries: Mail requests should be sent to the address above. Certified copies are $13 for the first copy and $4 for additional copies of the same record ordered at the same time.

American Local History Network: <www.usgennet.org/usa/mi/county/berrien>

MIGenWeb: <www.rootsweb.com/~miberrie/index.htm>

Branch County Clerk
Courthouse
31 Division St.
Coldwater, Mich. 49036
Telephone: (517) 279-4306
Web site: <co.branch.mi.us>

Creation: Branch was created on 29 October 1829 from non-county area attached to Lenawee.

Attachments: On 4 November 1829 Branch was attached to Saint Joseph for administrative and judicial purposes.

Organization: County government was organized on 1 March 1833, with the seat established at Branch. In 1842 it was moved to Coldwater.

Townships: Algansee, Batavia, Bethel, Bronson, Butler, California, Coldwater, Gilead, Girard, Kinderhook, Matteson, Noble, Ovid, Quincy, Sherwood, and Union.

Records begin on the following dates: Land, 1831; marriage and probate, 1833; naturalization, 1847; civil court and divorce, 1848; and birth and death, 1867.

In-person research: Researchers may view records from 9 a.m. to 3 p.m. Mondays through Thursdays.

Written queries: Will answer. "Search fee is $1 per year with a $3 minimum. Includes handwritten information – no copies. Certified copies are $15."

American History and Genealogy Project and American Local History Network: <www.geocities.com/TheTropics/1050/index.html>

MIGenWeb: <www.rootsweb.com/~migenweb/branch/branch.html>

Calhoun County Clerk
315 West Green St.
Marshall, Mich. 49068
Telephone: (269) 781-0716
Fax: (269) 781-0721
Web site: <co.calhoun.mi.us>

Creation: Calhoun was created 29 October 1829 from non-county areas attached to Lenawee and Oakland.

Attachments: On 4 November 1829 Calhoun was attached to Saint Joseph for administrative and judicial purposes, and on 1 October 1830 it was attached to Kalamazoo for judicial purposes.

Organization: County government was organized on 1 April 1833, with the seat established at Marshall.

Townships: Albion, Athens, Battle Creek, Bedford, Burlington, Clarence, Clarendon, Convis, Eckford, Emmett, Fredonia, Homer, LeRoy, Lee, Marengo, Marshall, Newton, Pennfield, Sheridan, and Tekonsha.

Records begin on the following dates: Naturalization, 1832; land, 1833; probate, 1834; marriage, 1836; civil court, 1847; and birth, divorce, and death, 1867. Naturalization records (1892-1980) are at the State Archives of Michigan.

In-person research: No restrictions.

Written queries: Will answer. "We only do a three-year search." Certified copies are $10 each for the first one and $5 for each additional copy of the same record ordered at the same time.

MIGenWeb: <www.rootsweb.com/~micalhou/index.htm>

Cass County Clerk
120 North Broadway
P.O. Box 355
Cassopolis Mich. 49031-1398
Telephone: (269) 445-4420
Web site: <www.casscountymi.org/>

Creation: Cass was created 29 October 1829 from non-county area attached to Lenawee.

Organization: Cass was organized on 4 November 1829, with the seat at Geneva. It moved to Cassopolis in 1834.

Boundaries: On 3 March 1831, Cass lost a small area to Saint Joseph.

Townships: Calvin, Jefferson, LaGrange, Marcellus, Mason, Milton, Newberg, Ontwa, Penn, Pokagon, Porter, Silver Creek, Volinia, and Wayne.

Records begin on the following dates: Probate and land, 1829; marriage, 1830; divorce and civil court, 1831; naturalization, 1856; and birth and death, 1867.

In-person research: Researchers may view records from 9 a.m. to 4 p.m. Wednesdays and Thursdays.

Written queries: Will answer. No search fee. Copy fee is $1 per page. "Some of the journals can't be [photocopied], so we charge $10 for a certified copy."

MIGenWeb: <www.rootsweb.com/~micass/>

Charlevoix County Clerk
203 Antrim St.
Charlevoix, Mich. 49720
Telephone: (231) 547-7200
Fax: (231) 547-7217
E-mail: <clerk@charlevoixcounty.org>
Web site: <www.charlevoixcounty.org>

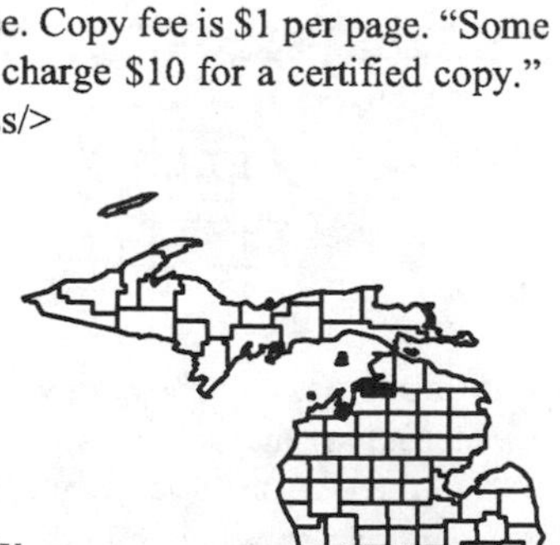

Creation: First named Keskkauko, the county was created from Michilimackinac (now

Mackinac) on 1 April 1840. On 8 March 1843, its name was changed to Charlevoix. The county was absorbed by Emmet on 29 January 1853. Charlevoix was re-created from Emmet, Antrim, and Otsego (which was attached to Antrim) on 2 April 1869. The "boundaries were different from those Charlevoix originally had in 1840."[18]

Attachments: Between 1840 and 1853, Charlevoix was attached to Michilimackinac for judicial purposes.

Organization: County government was organized on the same day of its re-creation, 2 April 1869, with the seat established at Charlevoix. In 1884, the county seat was moved to East Jordan. The county's government moved again in 1885 to Boyne City, but the Registrar of Deeds stayed in East Jordan. Two years later Boyne City became the official county seat, but in 1897 it was moved back to Charlevoix.[19]

Boundaries: Charlevoix gained part of Manitou when it was eliminated on 4 April 1895. This included the islands of Beaver, Garden, Gull, Hat, High, Hog, Squaw, Trout, and Whiskey. On 6 April 1896 Charlevoix lost about 50 square miles to Emmet.

Townships: Bay, Boyne Valley, Chandler, Charlevoix, Evangeline, Eveline, Hayes, Marion, Melrose, Norwood, Peaine, Saint James, South Arm, and Wilson.

Records begin on the following dates: Land and civil court, 1857; birth, 1867; marriage, death, 1868; divorce, 1869; and probate, 1872. Naturalization records (1855-1956) are at the State Archives of Michigan.

In-person research: "We allow the public to research on Mondays through Fridays 9 a.m. to 5 p.m. We also are open through the lunch hour."

Written queries: Certified copies are $5, "which is the only type of record we provide. We answer queries by informing customers if we have a certain record and that if they wish a copy they must provide a check for a $5 fee."

MIGenWeb: <www.rootsweb.com/~micharle/charlevx.htm>

Cheboygan County Clerk
870 South Main St.
P.O. Box 70
Cheboygan, Mich. 49721
Telephone: (231) 627-8847

Creation: Cheboygan was created on 1 April 1840 from Michilimackinac (now Mackinac).

Attachments: At its creation, Cheboygan was attached to Michilimackinac.

Organization: Cheboygan was organized on 29 January 1853. The seat was established at Duncan and was changed by 1857 to Cheboygan.

Boundaries: On 29 January 1853, Cheboygan lost to Emmet and gained all of Wyandot, which was eliminated. On 28 March 1873, Cheboygan lost about 30 square miles to Presque Isle.

Townships: Aloha, Beaugrand, Benton, Burt, Ellis, Forest, Grant, Hebron, Inverness, Koehler, Mackinaw, Mentor, Mullett, Munro, Nunda, Tuscarora, Walker, Waverly, and Wilmot.

Records begin on the following dates: Land and probate, 1854; birth, marriage, and death, 1867; naturalization, 1878; and divorce and civil court, 1884.

In-person research: Hours are 8:30 a.m. to 5 p.m. Mondays through Fridays. "Because space is limited, we only allow two researchers at a time."

Written queries: Will answer. All copies prior to 1934 are $10 for the first copy and $3 for each additional copy of the same record. After 1934, photocopies are $1, and certified copies are $10 for the first one and $3 for each additional copy of the same record ordered at the same time.

MIGenWeb: <www.rootsweb.com/~micheboy>

Chippewa County Clerk
319 Court St.
Sault Ste. Marie, Mich. 49783
Telephone: (906) 635-6300

Creation: Chippewa was created on 1 February 1827 from Michilimackinac (now Mackinac) and included parts of present-day Minnesota and Wisconsin.

Organization: County government was organized on the same day as the county's creation, with the seat established at Sault Ste. Marie.

Townships: Bay Mills, Bruce, Chippewa, Dafter, Detour, Drummond, Kinross, Pickford, Raber, Rudyard, Soo, Sugar Island, Superior, Trout Lake, and Whitefish.

Boundaries: On 3 July 1836, Chippewa lost to the creation of Wisconsin Territory. On 9 March 1843 it exchanged land with Michilimackinc and lost to the creation of Marquette, Ontonagon, and Schoolcraft. On 1 May 1875, the boundary between Chippewa and Mackinac was redefined with no change, and on 1 March 1887, Chippewa lost to the creation of Luce.

Records begin on the following dates: Marriage and land, 1826; probate, 1828; naturalization, 1846; civil court, 1860s; birth and death, 1869; and divorce, 1891. Naturalization records (1847-1985) are at the State Archives of Michigan.

In-person research: Researchers may view records from 9:30 a.m. to 11:30 a.m. and 1:30 p.m. to 3:30 p.m. on Tuesdays, Wednesdays, and Thursdays.

Written queries: Will answer. "Our office requires a $5 fee made payable to the County Clerk for each individual's search."

American History and Genealogy Project and American Local History Network: <www.geocities.com/Heartland/Plains/5666/Chippewa.html>

Chippewa County History and Genealogy Network: <www.jansdigs.com/Chippewa/index.html>

MIGenWeb: <www.rootsweb.com/~michippe/>

Clare County Clerk
225 West Main St.
P.O. Box 438
Harrison, Mich. 48625
Telephone: (989) 539-7131

Creation: First called Kaykakee, the county was created from Michilimackinac (now Mackinac) and non-county area attached to Saginaw on 1 April 1840. On 8 March 1843, its name was changed to Clare.

Attachments: At its creation, Clare was attached to Saginaw for judicial purposes. The attachment was changed to Midland on 29 January 1858 and Isabella on 11 February 1859. On 22 March 1869, the western portion of Clare was attached to Mecosta for judicial and municipal purposes.

Organization: County government was organized on 16 March 1871, with the seat established at Farwell. "In July 1877 embittered Clare town residents burned the county courthouse in Farwell to protest corruption in county government."[20] In 1879, the seat was changed to Harrison.

Townships: Arthur, Franklin, Freeman, Frost, Garfield, Grant, Greenwood, Hamilton, Hatton, Hayes, Lincoln, Redding, Sheridan, Summerfield, Surrey, and Winterfield.

Records begin on the following dates: Land, 1855; birth, 1870; marriage, divorce, death, and civil court, 1871; and probate, 1872. Naturalization records (1871-1965) are at the State Archives of Michigan.

In-person research: Researchers may view records from 9 a.m. to 3 p.m. Mondays through Fridays. "You are more than welcome to come in and search the records at no charge on your own."

Written queries: Will answer. Requires a $30 deposit. "You will be charged the lowest employee's salary for the search, minimum of a quarter hour." If the search requires more time, researchers will be billed the difference. If money is left over from the deposit, it will be refunded. Certified copies of death and marriage records are $10. Certified copies of divorce records are $10, plus $1 per page.

MIGenWeb: <www.rootsweb.com/~miclare/index.htm>

Clinton County Clerk
100 E. State St. Suite 2600
P.O. Box 69
Saint Johns, Mich. 48879-0069
Telephone: (989) 224-5140
Fax: (989) 224-5102
Web site: <www.clinton-county.org>

Creation: Clinton was created from non-county area attached to Kalamazoo on 2 March 1831.

Attachments: On 4 April 1836, Clinton was attached to Kent, and on 18 March 1837, it was attached to Shiawassee.

Organization: Clinton was organized on 12 March 1839, with the seat established at DeWitt. The seat was changed to Saint Johns by 1857.

Townships: Bath, Bengal, Bingham, Dallas, DeWitt, Duplain, Eagle, Essex, Greenbush, Lebanon, Olive, Ovid, Riley, Victor, Watertown, and Westphalia.

Records begin on the following dates: Land, 1836; marriage and divorce, 1839; probate, 1840; naturalization, 1850s; civil court, 1860s; and birth and death, 1867.

In-person research: Hours are 8 a.m. to 5 p.m. weekdays. "It is necessary to close from noon to 1 p.m. on occasion. Only one genealogist is allowed to work in the office at a time due to limited space. A two-hour time limit may be necessary due to various circumstances."

Written queries: Will answer. There is a $10 fee per name for a three-year search.

American History and Genealogy Project and American Local History Network: <www.usgennet.org/usa/mi/county/clinton>

MIGenWeb: <www.rootsweb.com/~miclinto/index.htm>

Crawford County Clerk
200 West Michigan Ave.
Grayling, Mich. 49738
Telephone: (989) 348-2841
Web site: <www.crawfordco.org>

Creation: First called Shawono, the county was created from Michilimackinac (now Mackinac) and non-county area attached to Saginaw on 1 April 1840. On 8 March 1843, its name was changed to Crawford.

Attachments: On the day of its creation, the county was attached to Michilimackinac for judicial purposes. The attachment changed to Cheboygan on 29 January 1853, to Iosco on 29 January 1858, to Antrim on 11 March 1863, and to Kalkaska on 27 January 1871.

Organization: County government was organized on 22 March 1879, with the seat first established at Pere Cheney and later at Grayling.

Townships: Beaver Creek, Frederic, Grayling, Lovells, Maple Forest, and South Branch.

Records begin on the following dates: Land, 1863; birth, marriage, and death, 1873; probate, 1879; and divorce and civil court, 1881. Naturalization records (1879-1964) are at the State Archives of Michigan.

In-person research: Hours are 8:30 a.m. to 4:30 p.m.

Written queries: Will answer.

American History and Genealogy Project and American Local History Network: <www.geocities.com/Heartland/Plains/5666/Crawford.html>

MIGenWeb: <www.rootsweb.com/~micrawfo/>

Delta County Clerk
310 Ludington St.
Escanaba, Mich. 49829
Telephone: (906) 789-5105
Fax: (906) 789-5196

Creation: Delta was created from Michilimackinac (now Mackinac) and non-county area on 9 March 1843.

Attachments: At its creation, Delta was attached to Michilimackinac for judicial purposes.

Organization: County government was organized on 12 March 1861, with the seat established at Masonville. It moved to Escanaba in 1864.

Boundaries: On 12 March 1861, Delta gained from Schoolcraft but lost to non-county area. About 10 years later, on 15 April 1871, its boundaries were clarified "to include Big Summer Island, Saint Martin's Island, Gull Island, and Poverty Island."[21]

Townships: Baldwin, Bark River, Bay de Noc, Brampton, Cornell, Ensign, Escanaba, Fairbanks, Ford River, Garden, Maple Ridge, Masonville, Nahma, and Wells.

Records begin on the following dates: Land and probate, 1843; birth, marriage, death, and divorce, 1867; and civil court, 1869. Naturalization records (1866-1955) are at the State Archives of Michigan.

Written queries: Will answer. No search fees. Copies are $6 each.

MIGenWeb: <www.grandmastree.com/migenweb/>

Dickinson County Clerk
705 S. Stephenson Ave.
P.O. Box 609
Iron Mountain, Mich. 49801
Telephone: (906) 774-2573

Creation: Dickinson was created on 21 May 1891 from Iron, Marquette, and Menominee. It was the last county created in Michigan.

Organization: Dickinson was organized at its creation, with the seat established at Iron Mountain.

Townships: Breen, Breitung, Felch, Norway, Sagola, Waucedah, and West Branch.

Records begin on the following dates: Birth, marriage, death, divorce, land, civil court, and probate, 1891. Naturalization records (1891-1970) are at the State Archives of Michigan.

American Local History Network: <www.geocities.com/Heartland/Plains/5666/Dickinson.html>

MIGenWeb: <www.rootsweb.com/~midickin/>

Eaton County Clerk
1045 Independence Blvd.
Charlotte, Mich. 48813
Telephone: (517) 485-6445
Web site: <www.eatoncounty.org/Main.htm>

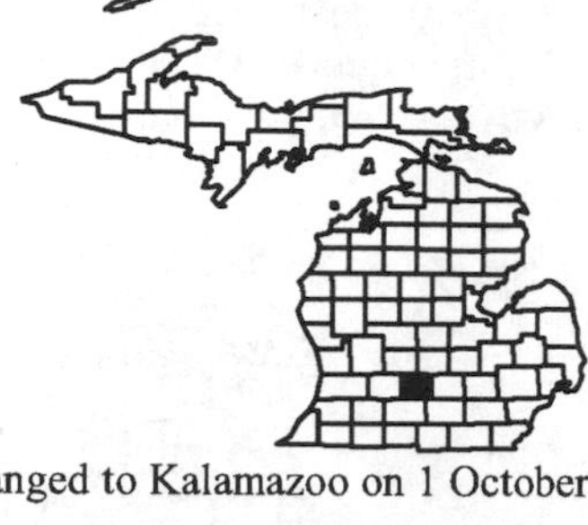

Creation: Eaton was created on 29 October 1829 from non-county area attached to Oakland.

Attachments: On 4 November 1829, Eaton was attached to Saint Joseph for administrative and judicial purposes. The attachment changed to Kalamazoo on 1 October 1830.

Organization: Eaton was organized on 29 December 1837, with the seat established at Bellevue. Seat was changed to Charlotte in 1840.

Townships: Bellevue, Benton, Brookfield, Carmel, Chester, Delta, Eaton Rapids, Eaton, Hamlin, Kalamo, Oneida, Roxand, Sunfield, Vermontville, Walton, and Windsor.

Records begin on the following dates: Land and probate, 1835; marriage, 1838; divorce and civil court, 1847; and birth and death, 1867. Naturalization records (1836-1959) are at the State Archives of Michigan.

MIGenWeb: <www.rootsweb.com/~mieaton/eatonmn.htm>

Emmet County Clerk
County Building
200 Division St.
Petoskey, Mich. 49770
Telephone: (231) 348-1702
Web site: <www.co.emmet.mi.us>

Creation: First called Tonedagana, the county was created on 1 April 1840 from Michilimackinac (now Mackinac). On 8 March 1843, its name was changed to Emmet.

Attachments: At its creation, Emmet was attached to Michilimackinac.

Organization: County government was fully organized on 29 January 1853, with the seat established at Little Traverse. By 1867, the seat was changed to Charlevoix. It was changed again in 1869 to Harbor Springs and to Petoskey in 1902.

Boundaries: On 29 January 1853, Emmet gained from Cheboygan, gained Beaver Island from Mackinac, and gained all of Charlevoix when Charlevoix was eliminated. On 12 February 1855, Emmet lost to the creation of Manitou, and on 2 April 1869, Emmet lost to the re-creation of Charlevoix. Emmet gained about 50 square miles from Charlevoix on 6 April 1896.

Townships: Bear Creek, Bliss, Carp Lake, Center, Cross Village, Friendship, Little Traverse, Littlefield, Maple River, McKinley, Pleasant View, Readmond, Resort, Springvale, Wawatam, and West Traverse.

Records begin on the following dates: Land, 1843; marriage, 1856; probate, 1857; birth, death, and civil court, 1867; and divorce and naturalization, 1875.

Written queries: Will answer. Searches are $4 per year.

MIGenWeb: <www.rootsweb.com/~miemmet>

Genesee County Clerk
900 S. Saginaw St.
Flint, Mich. 48502
Telephone: (810) 257-3225
Web site: <www.co.genesee.mi.us>

Creation: Genesee was created on 28 March 1835 from Lapeer, Saginaw, and Shiawassee (which was attached to Oakland) counties.

Attachments: At its creation, Genesee was attached to Oakland.

Organization: County government organized on 4 April 1836, with the seat established at Flint.

Boundaries: On 31 March 1843, Genesee gained about 150 square miles from Lapeer.

Townships: Argentine, Atlas, Burton, Clayton, Davison, Fenton, Flint, Flushing, Forest, Gaines, Genesee, Grand Blanc, Montrose, Mount Morris, Mundy, Richfield, Thetford, and Vienna.

Records begin on the following dates: Land, 1819; naturalization, 1820; marriage and civil court, 1835; probate, 1836; birth and death, 1867; and divorce, 1871. Naturalization records (1838-1965) are at the State Archives of Michigan and also at the Genesee Historical Collections Center, University of Michigan-Flint Library.

Michigan Local History Network: <www.usgennet.org/usa/mi/county/genesee/genesee>

MIGenWeb: <www.rootsweb.com/~migenese/index.html>

Gladwin County Clerk
401 West Cedar Ave.
Gladwin, Mich. 48624-2088
Telephone: (989) 426-7351

Creation: Gladwin was created on 2 March 1831 from non-county areas attached to Kalamazoo and Oakland.

Attachments: Gladwin was attached to Saginaw on 2 March 1836 for judicial purposes. The attachment changed on 12 February 1855 to Midland.

Organization: County government was organized on 18 April 1875, with the seat established at Gladwin (formerly Cedar).

Townships: Beaverton, Bentley, Billings, Bourret, Buckeye, Butman, Clement, Gladwin, Grim, Grout, Hay, Sage, Secord, Sherman, and Tobacco.

Records begin on the following dates: Land, 1855; birth, marriage, divorce, death, and probate, 1875; and civil court, 1880. Naturalization records (1875-1964) are at the State Archives of Michigan.

In-person research: Hours are 8:30 a.m. to 4:30 p.m. weekdays. Researchers "should call ahead to make sure we do not have any court trials or major meetings that would cause our office to be extra busy."

Written queries: "Search fee is $2 per name, if no copies are requested. If copies are requested, the search fee is waived." Only certified copies are issued. Copies are $7 each and $3 for each additional copy of the same record ordered at the same time.

American Local History Network: <www.usgennet.org/usa/mi/county/gladwin>

MIGenWeb: <www.rootsweb.com/~migladwi/>

Gogebic County Clerk
200 North Moore St.
Bessemer, Mich. 49911
Telephone: (906) 663-4518
Fax: (906) 663-4660
E-mail: <gpelissero@gogebic.org>
Web site: <www.gogebic.org>

Creation: Gogebic was created from Ontonagon on 7 February 1887.

Organization: Gogebic was organized on the day of its creation, with the seat established at Bessemer.

Townships: Bessemer, Erwin, Ironwood, Marenisco, Wakefield, and Watersmeet.

Boundaries: The U.S. Supreme Court settled a boundary dispute between Michigan and Wisconsin regarding the southern and western boundaries of Gogebic in Wisconsin's favor in 1926.

Records begin on the following dates: Birth, death, and marriage, 1886; and divorce, probate, land, and civil court, 1887. Naturalization records (1887-1980) are at the State Archives of Michigan.

In-person research: Hours are 8:30 a.m. to noon and 1 p.m. to 4:15 p.m. Researchers must present identification and register.

Written queries: "Genealogical researches are not a top priority in our office. We work on them when there is a free moment. When we do, there is no search charge. We do charge for copies of vital records – $7 for the first copy and $2 for each additional copy of the same record."

American Local History Network: <www.angelfire.com/mi2/gogebic>

MIGenWeb: <www.rootsweb.com/~migogebi>

Grand Traverse County Clerk
400 Boardman Ave.
Traverse City, Mich. 49684
Telephone: (231) 922-4760
Web site: <www.co.grand-traverse.mi.us>

Creation: Grand Traverse was created on 7 April 1851 from Omeena, which was attached to Mackinac.

Organization: Grand Traverse was organized on the day of its creation, with the seat established at Traverse City.

Boundaries: On 3 February 1853, Grand Traverse gained all of Omeena, and Omeena was eliminated. On 18 March 1865, Grand Traverse lost a small area to Antrim.

Townships: Acme, Blair, East Bay, Fife Lake, Garfield, Grant, Green Lake, Long Lake, Mayfield, Paradise, Peninsula, Union, and Whitewater.

Records begin on the following dates: Land, 1842; marriage, probate, 1853; birth, 1856; divorce, civil court, 1857; and death, 1867. Naturalization records (1853-1981) are at the State Archives of Michigan.

In-person research: Hours are 8:30 a.m. to noon and 2 p.m. to 4:30 p.m. weekdays.

Written queries: Will not answer.

American Local History Network: <members.aol.com/VWilson577/GT-ALHN.html>

MIGenWeb: <www.grandtraverseregion.com/grandtraverse>

Gratiot County Clerk
214 East Center St.
P.O. Drawer 437
Ithaca, Mich. 48847
Telephone: (989) 875-5215
Web site: <www.co.gratiot.mi.us/>

Creation: Gratiot was created on 2 March 1831 from non-county area attached to Kalamazoo.

Attachments: On 2 March 1836, Gratiot was attached to Saginaw for judicial purposes. On 19 March 1845, the southwestern portion of Gratiot was attached to Clinton for administrative and judicial purposes.

Organization: County government was organized on 3 February 1855, with the seat established at Ithaca.

Townships: Arcada, Bethany, Elba, Emerson, Fulton, Hamilton, Lafayette, New Haven, Newark, North Shade, North Star, Pine River, Seville, Sumner, Washington, and Wheeler.

Records begin on the following dates: Land, 1847; marriage and probate, 1855; and birth, divorce, death, and civil court, 1867. Naturalization records (1857-1956) are at the State Archives of Michigan.

In-person research: Researchers may view records from 10 a.m. to noon and 1 p.m. to 3 p.m. Tuesdays and Wednesdays.

Written queries: Will not answer.

MIGenWeb: <www.mfhn.com/gratiot/>

Hillsdale County Clerk
Courthouse Room 1
29 North Howell St.
Hillsdale, Mich. 49242
Telephone: (517) 437-3391
Web site: <www.co.hillsdale.mi.us/>

Creation: Hillsdale was created on 29 October 1829 from unattached non-county area and non-county area attached to Lenawee, including "part of the disputed strip west of Lake Erie that also was claimed by Ohio but controlled by Michigan."[22]

Attachments: On 4 November 1829, Hillsdale was attached to Lenawee for administrative and judicial purposes.

Organization: County government was organized on 11 February 1835, with the seat established at Jonesville. In 1843, the seat was changed to Hillsdale.

Boundaries: When Michigan became a state in 1837, the boundary dispute was settled in favor of Ohio.

Townships: Adams, Allen, Amboy, Cambria, Camden, Fayette, Hillsdale, Jefferson, Litchfield, Moscow, Pittsford, Ransom, Reading, Scipic, Somerset, Wheatland, Woodbridge, and Wright.

Records begin on the following dates: Marriage, probate, land, 1835; divorce, 1844; civil court, 1846; and birth and death, 1867. Naturalization records (1846-1930) are at the State Archives of Michigan.

In-person research: No restrictions.

Written queries: "There is no charge for genealogical searches, if the requests are small in number." Certified copies are $13, typed copies are $8, and photocopies are $4.

MIGenWeb: <www.rootsweb.com/~mihillsd/county.html>

Houghton County Clerk
401 E. Houghton Ave.
Houghton, Mich. 49931
Telephone: (906) 482-1150

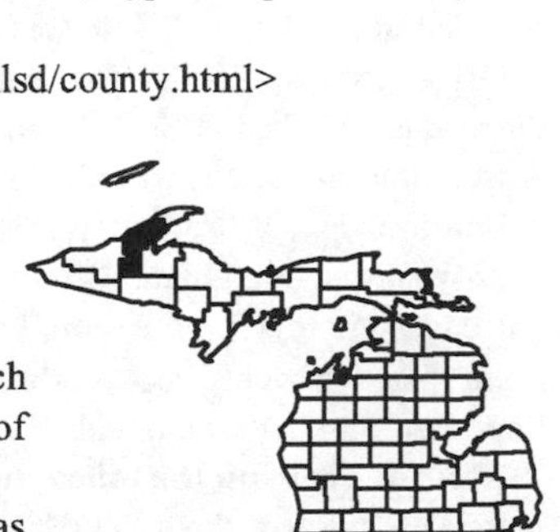

Creation: Houghton was created on 19 March 1845 from Marquette and Ontonagon, both of which were attached to Chippewa.

Attachments: At its creation, Houghton was attached to Chippewa.

Organization: County government was organized on 18 May 1846, but the seat was not established until 1852 when Houghton was chosen.

Boundaries: On 3 April 1848, Houghton's boundaries were redefined with no change. On 17 January 1853, Houghton lost to Ontonagon. In 1861, Houghton lost more than 500 square miles to Keweenaw, gained more than 1,000 square miles from Marquette and Ontonagon, and lost more than 200 square miles to Marquette. Houghton lost to the creation of Baraga on 17 February 1875 and exchanged with Baraga on 12 March 1885.

Townships: Adams, Calumet, Chassell, Duncan, Elm River, Franklin, Hancock, Laird, Osceola, Portage, Quincy, Schoolcraft, Stanton, and Torch Lake.

Records begin on the following dates: Marriage, land, civil court, naturalization, and divorce 1848; birth and death, 1867; and probate, 1872. Divorce records (1865-1976) are located at the Michigan Technological University Archives. Non-certified copies are $2.

In-person research: "We have limited space, four people maximum. Appointments are appreciated. Please call (906) 482-1150."

Written queries: Will answer. Search fee, including one copy, is $8.

American Local History Network: <www.usgennet.org/usa/mi/county/houghton>

MIGenWeb: <www.mfhn.com/houghton/>

Huron County Clerk
250 E. Huron Ave.
County Building, Room 201
Bad Axe, Mich. 48413
Telephone: (989) 269-8242

Creation: Huron was created on 1 April 1840 from Sanilac County (which was attached to Lapeer and Saint Clair).

Attachments: At its creation, Huron was attached to Saginaw. The attachment was changed to Saint Clair in 1844 and Saniliac in 1850. In 1853, the western part of Huron was attached to Tuscola.

Organization: County government was organized on 25 January 1859, with the seat established at Sand Beach. By 1864, the seat had been changed to Port Austin, and in 1872 it was changed to Bad Axe (originally Bad Axe Corners).

Boundaries: On 1 January 1880, Huron lost Charity Island to Bay.

Townships: Bingham, Bloomfield, Caseville, Chandler, Colfax, Dwight, Fairhaven, Gore, Grant, Huron, Lake, Lincoln, McKinley, Meade, Oliver, Paris, Pointe Aux Barques, Port Austin, Rubicon, Sand Beach, Sebewaing, Sheridan, Sherman, Sigel, Verona, and Winsor.

Records begin on the following dates: Land, 1837; probate, 1861; and birth, marriage, divorce, death, and civil court, 1867. Naturalization records (1864-1961) are at the State Archives of Michigan.

In-person research: Hours are 9 a.m. to 4:30 p.m. weekdays, but "assistance is limited from 11:30 a.m. to 1:30 p.m."

Written queries: Will answer. "No search fee, but if a copy is requested, there is a $10 fee. Certified copies are all we issue."

American Local History Network: <www.usgennet.org/usa/mi/county/huron>

MIGenWeb: <www.rootsweb.com/~mihuron/>

Ingham County Clerk
Courthouse
315 S. Jefferson St.
P.O. Box 179
Mason, Mich. 48854
Telephone: (517) 676-7201
Fax: (517) 676-7254
Web site: <www.ingham.org>

Creation: Ingham was created on 29 October 1829 from Shiawassee (which was attached to Oakland), Washtenaw, and non-county area attached to Oakland.

Attachments: On 4 November 1829, Ingham was attached to Washtenaw for administrative and judicial purposes. By October 1837, it was attached to Jackson for judicial purposes.

Organization: County government was organized on 4 June 1838, with the seat established at Mason.

Townships: Alaiedon, Aurelius, Bunker Hill, Delhi, Ingham, Lansing, Leroy, Leslie, Locke, Meridian, Onondaga, Stockbridge, Vevay, Wheatfield, White Oak, and Williamston.

Records begin on the following dates: Probate and land, 1835; marriage, 1837; civil court, 1838; divorce, 1839; and birth and death, 1867. Naturalization records (1845-1985) are at the State Archives of Michigan.

In-person research: Hours are 8:30 a.m. to 4 p.m. weekdays. "Limited to two hours per genealogist per day. Limit of two genealogists at one time."

Written queries: Will answer.

American Local History Network: <www.usgennet.org/usa/mi/county/ingham>

MIGenWeb: <www.rootsweb.com/~miingham/index.htm>

Ionia County Clerk
100 Main St.
Ionia, Mich. 48846
Telephone: (616) 527-5300
Web site: <www.ioniacounty.org>

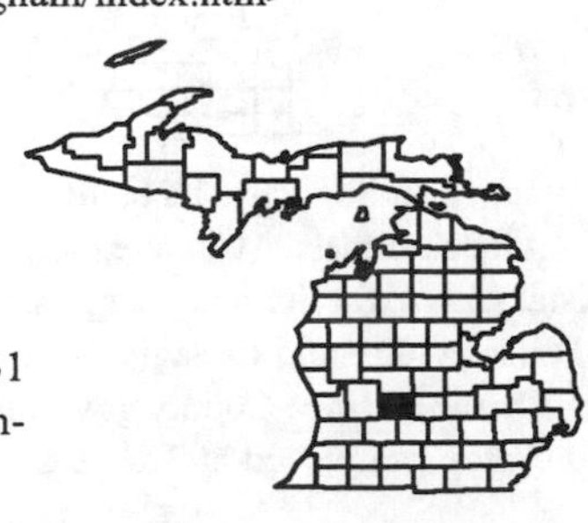

Creation: Ionia was created on 2 March 1831 from Michilimackinac (now Mackinac) and non-county area attached to Kalamazoo.

Attachments: On 4 April 1836, Ionia was attached to Kent.

Organization: County government was organized on 3 April 1837, with the seat established at Ionia.

Townships: Berlin, Boston, Campbell, Danby, Easton, Ionia, Keene, Lyons, North Plains, Odessa, Orange, Orleans, Otisco, Portland, Ronald, and Sebewa.

Records begin on the following dates: Land, 1833; marriage and probate, 1837; civil court, 1845; divorce, 1858; probate, 1865; and birth and death, 1867. Naturalization records (1835-1959) are at the State Archives of Michigan.

In-person research: Hours are 8:30 a.m. to noon and 1 to 5 p.m. weekdays. "On Mondays and Fridays we normally have a heavier Circuit Court schedule which could cause some counter congestion if too many genealogists are working. Therefore, avoiding these two days might be to your – as well as – our advantage. We ask that as much as possible working with the indexes be completed prior to asking for the actual records." Staff members must conduct research in birth and divorce records due to restrictions. "We are continually in the process of purging old files to make room for new, so all that remains of many older files is the final decree/judgment." Staff try to accommodate requests for copies while the genealogist is in the office, "however, on occasion time and/or staff is at a premium so we appreciate it if a list can be left and we then forward copies by mail."

Written queries: "All mail requests are honored in a timely fashion. As a general rule, you should receive a response within a week or two at the latest, though there may be exceptions." Genealogy record copies are $1 per page. Certified copies are $10 each and $3 for each additional copy of the same record.

American History and Genealogy Project and American Local History Network: <www.usgennet.org/usa/mi/county/ionia1>

MIGenWeb: <www.rootsweb.com/~miionia/index.html>

Iosco County Clerk
422 Lake St.
P.O. Box 838
Tawas City, Mich. 48764
Telephone: (989) 362-3497
Fax: (989) 362-1444
E-Mail: <IOSCO-CO@MIQVF.ORG>

Creation: First named Kanotin, Iosco was created on 1 April 1840 from non-county area attached to Saginaw. Its name changed to Iosco on 8 March 1843.

Attachments: At its creation, Iosco was attached to Michilimackinac (now Mackinac) for judicial purposes. Then it was attached to Cheboygan on 29 January 1853 and to Saginaw on 3 February 1853.

Organization: County government was organized on 16 February 1857, with the seat established at Tawas City.

Boundaries: On 7 March 1867, Iosco gained all of Ogemaw when Ogemaw was eliminated. Then on 28 March 1873, Iosco lost to the recreation of Ogemaw.

Townships: Alabaster, Au Sable, Baldwin, Burleigh, Grant, Oscoda, Plainfield, Reno, Sherman, Tawas, and Wilber.

Records begin on the following dates: Land, 1840; marriage, 1858; civil court, divorce, and probate, 1859; and birth and death, 1867. Naturalization records (1859-1974) are at the State Archives of Michigan.

In-person research: Researchers may view records from 10 a.m. to noon and 2 p.m. to 4 p.m. weekdays. "Due to limited space, a maximum of two people will be allowed in the genealogy area. Researchers are not allowed to search birth records."

Written queries: Will answer. Searches are $5 and include one copy of the record, if found. Additional copies of the same record ordered at the same time are $2 each. Send money orders payable to the Iosco County Clerk.

MIGenWeb: <www.rootsweb.com/~miiosco2/index.html>

Other: Researchers can submit their family surnames to a Genealogical Name Registry for Iosco County.

Iron County Clerk
Courthouse
2 South Sixth St.
Crystal Falls, Mich. 49920-1413
Telephone: (906) 875-3221
Web site: <www.iron.org>

Creation: Iron was created on 3 April 1885 from Marquette and Menominee counties.

Organization: Iron was organized at its creation. Seat was first established at Iron River and changed to Crystal Falls by 1887.

Boundaries: On 21 May 1891, Iron lost more than 100 square miles to the creation of Dickinson, and on 22 May 1891, it gained almost 300 square miles from Marquette. The U.S. Supreme Court settled an early 20th century border dispute with Wisconsin in Wisconsin's favor in 1926.

Townships: Bates, Crystal Falls, Hematite, Iron River, Mansfield, Mastodon, and Stambaugh.

Records begin on the following dates: Land, 1855; birth, marriage, death, 1884; probate, 1886; and civil court and divorce, 1895. Naturalization records (1881-1956) are at the State Archives of Michigan.

In-person research: "Birth records are not open to the public."

Written queries: Will answer.

American Local History Network: <www.geocities.com/Heartland/Plains/5666/Iron.html>

MIGenWeb: <www.rootsweb.com/~miiron>

Isabella County Clerk
200 North Main St.
Mount Pleasant, Mich. 48858
Telephone: (989) 772-0911 ext. 260
Fax: (989) 772-6347
Web site: <www.isabellacounty.org>

Creation: Isabella was created on 2 March 1831 from Michilimackinac (now Mackinac) and non-county area attached to Kalamazoo.

Attachments: On 2 March 1836, Isabella was attached to Saginaw for judicial purposes. Then on 3 April 1837, the western half of Isabella was attached to Ionia for judicial purposes. On 1 April 1840, the western half of Isabella was re-attached to Saginaw for judicial purposes. Isabella was attached to Midland on 12 February 1855.

Organization: Isabella County was organized on 11 February 1859, with the seat established at Mount Pleasant.

Townships: Broomfield, Chippewa, Coe, Coldwater, Deerfield, Denver, Fremont, Gilmore, Isabella, Lincoln, Nottawa, Rolland, Sherman, Union, Vernon, and Wise.

Records begin on the following dates: Land, 1838; marriage and probate, 1859; naturalization, 1861; birth and death, 1867; and civil court and divorce, 1880.

In-person research: Hours are 8 a.m. to 4:30 p.m. weekdays. There is a limit of two researchers at one time and a limit of two hours if someone is waiting. Researchers are required to show identification.

Written queries: Will answer "only if exact dates are known." Copy fee is $10.

American Local History Network: <www.usgennet.org/usa/mi/county/isabella>

MIGenWeb: <www.mifamilyhistory.org/isabella/>

Jackson County Clerk
312 S. Jackson St.
Jackson, Mich. 49201
Telephone: (517) 788-4265
Fax: (517) 788-4601
Web site: <www.co.jackson.mi.us/>

Creation: Jackson was created on 29 October 1829 from Washtenaw and non-county areas attached to Lenawee and Oakland counties.

Attachments: Jackson was attached to Washtenaw for administrative and judicial purposes on 4 November 1829.

Organization: County government was organized on 1 August 1832, with the seat established at Jackson.

Townships: Blackman, Columbia, Concord, Grass Lake, Hanover, Henrietta, Leoni, Liberty, Napoleon, Norvell, Parma, Pulaski, Rives, Sandstone, Spring Arbor, Springport, Summit, Tompkins, and Waterloo.

Records begin on the following dates: Civil court, 1830s; land, 1830; probate, 1832; marriage, 1833; naturalization, 1839; divorce, 1847; and birth and death, 1867.

MIGenWeb: <www.rootsweb.com/~mijackso/jackson.htm>

Kalamazoo County Clerk
201 W. Kalamazoo Ave.
Kalamazoo, Mich. 49007
Telephone: (269) 383-8840
Web site: <www.kalcounty.com/>

Creation: Kalamazoo was created on 29 October 1829 from non-county areas attached to Lenawee and Oakland.

Attachments: On 4 November 1829, Kalamazoo was attached to Saint Joseph.

Organization: Kalamazoo was fully organized by 1 October 1830, with the seat established at Kalamazoo.

Townships: Alamo, Brady, Charleston, Climax, Comstock, Cooper, Kalamazoo, Oshtemo, Pavilion, Prairie Ronde, Richland, Ross, Schoolcraft, Texas, and Wakeshma.

Records begin on the following dates: Divorce, 1800s; land, 1824; marriage, 1831; probate, 1833; naturalization, 1834; civil court, 1847; and birth and death, 1867. Naturalization records (1839-1967) are at the Western Michigan University Archives.

In-person research: Can be done "when a genealogy volunteer is present, normally every afternoon and Friday mornings. Please call the office (269-383-8840) to check that a genealogy volunteer will be present at the time desired."

Written queries: Will answer. "No fee if they are brief requests."

MIGenWeb: <www.rootsweb.com/~mikalama>

Kalkaska County Clerk
605 North Birch St.
Kalkaska, Mich. 49646
Telephone: (231) 258-3304

Creation: First called Wabassee, the county was created from Michilimackinac (now Mackinac) on 1 April 1840. Wabassee was renamed Kalkaska on 8 March 1843.

Attachments: At its creation, Kalkaska was attached to Michilimackinac for judicial purposes. Attachment was changed to Grand Traverse on 3 February 1853 and to Antrim on 11 March 1863.

Organization: Kalkaska was fully organized 27 January 1871, with the seat established at Kalkaska.

Boundaries: Kalkaska lost a small area to Antrim on 12 March 1881.

Townships: Bear Lake, Blue Lake, Boardman, Clearwater, Cold Springs, Excelsior, Garfield, Kalkaska, Oliver, Orange, Rapid River, and Springfield.

Records begin on the following dates: Land, 1853; birth, marriage, death, divorce, civil court, 1871; and probate, 1874.

MIGenWeb: <www.grandtraverseregion.com/kalkaska>

Kent County Clerk
County Administration Building
300 Monroe Ave., N.W.
Grand Rapids, Mich. 49503-2288
Telephone: (616) 336-3550
Fax: (616) 336-2885
Web site: <www.accesskent.com>

Creation: Kent was created on 2 March 1831 from Michilimackinac (now Mackinac) and non-county area attached to Kalamazoo.

Organization: On 4 April 1834, part of Kent was organized as the Township of Kent. It "may have been attached to Kalamazoo for administrative and judicial purposes."[23] By 4 April 1836, Kent was fully organized. County seat was established at Grand Rapids.

Boundaries: On 1 April 1840, Kent gained territory from Oceana.

Townships: Ada, Algoma, Alpine, Bowne, Byron, Caledonia, Cannon, Cascade, Courtland, Gaines, Grand Rapids, Grattan, Lowell, Nelson, Oakfield, Plainfield, Solon, Sparta, Spencer, Tyrone, and Vergennes.

Records begin on the following dates: Land, 1835; naturalization, 1840; marriage, 1845; birth, divorce, civil court, and death, 1867; and probate, 1898. Naturalization records (1860-1929) are at the State Archives of Michigan.

In-person research: Researchers may inspect records from 8 a.m. to 5 p.m. Tuesdays, Wednesdays, and Thursdays. There is a limit of two researchers at a time and a two-hour daily limit "if others request access or unless researchers from out of state have made prior arrangements."

Written queries: Will answer. Copies are $7 for the first copy and $3 for each additional copy of the same record.

American History and Genealogy Project and American Local History Network: <www.usgennet.org/usa/mi/county/kent>

MIGenWeb: <www.rootsweb.com/~mikent>

Keweenaw County Clerk
HC1, Box 607
Eagle River, Mich. 49924
Telephone: (906) 337-2229

Creation: Keweenaw was created from Houghton on 11 March 1861.

Organization: Keweenaw was organized on 1 August 1861, with the seat established at Eagle River.

Boundaries: On 4 March 1875, Keweenaw lost to the creation of Isle Royale, but on 9 April 1897, it regained all of Isle Royale when the county was eliminated.

Townships: Allouez, Eagle Harbor, Grant, and Sherman.

Records begin on the following dates: Land, 1849; divorce and civil court, 1861; probate, 1866; and birth, marriage, and death, 1867. Naturalization records (1862-1954) are at the State Archives of Michigan. Many of the county's records also are at the Michigan Technological University Archives.

In-person research: No restrictions.

Written queries: $3 per copy and search.

American Local History Network: <www.usgennet.org/usa/mi/county/keweenaw>

MIGenWeb: <www.mfhn.com/keweenaw>

Lake County Clerk
800 Tenth St., Suite 200
Baldwin, Mich. 49304 
Telephone: (231) 745-2725

Creation: First named Aishcum, the county was created on 1 April 1840 from Michilimackinac (now Mackinac). Aishcum was renamed Lake on 8 March 1843.

Attachments: At its creation, Lake was attached to Ottawa. Attachment was changed to Mason on 13 February 1855, to Newaygo on 17 February 1857, and back to Mason on 29 January 1858. On 26 March 1867, the eastern third of Lake was attached to Mecosta and the remainder of the county was still attached to Mason. On 22 March 1869, the eastern half of the county was attached to Osceola and the western half of Lake remained attached to Mason.

Organization: County government was organized on 16 March 1871, with the seat first established at Chase, the oldest village in the county, and later moved to Baldwin in 1875. The residents of Chase resented the courthouse being moved to Baldwin and refused to give up the county records. In a conflict that some call a "battle," 60 armed Baldwin residents came to Chase on May 1, 1897, and "broke into a shed that housed a safe with the courthouse records, loaded it aboard the flatcar and took it back to Baldwin."[24]

Townships: Chase, Cherry Valley, Dover, Eden, Elk, Ellsworth, Lake, Newkirk, Peacock, Pinora, Pleasant Plains, Sauble, Sweetwater, Webber, and Yates.

Records begin on the following dates: Land, 1862; birth, marriage, and death, 1870; civil court, 1871; probate, 1872; and divorce, 1874. Naturalization records (1872-1955) are at the State Archives of Michigan.

In-person research: No restrictions.

Written queries: Will answer. Certified copies are $7 for the first copy and $3 for each additional copy of the same record. Regular copies are $1 each.

MIGenWeb: <www.rootsweb.com/~milake>

Lapeer County Clerk
255 Clay St.
Lapeer, Mich. 48446
Telephone: (810) 667-0366
Web site: <www.county.lapeer.org>

Creation: Lapeer was created on 10 September 1822 from a small portion of non-county area attached to Oakland and parts of Oakland and Saint Clair.

Attachments: At its creation, Lapeer was attached to Oakland for administrative and judicial purposes.

Organization: Lapeer was fully organized by 2 February 1835, with the seat established at Lapeer.

Boundaries: Lapeer lost more than 100 square miles to the creation of Genesee on 28 March 1835 and lost another 150 square miles to Genesee on 31 March 1843. On 19 March 1845 Lapeer lost about 20 square miles to Tuscola, and on 13 February 1855, Lapeer exchanged land with Tuscola.

Townships: Almont, Arcadia, Attica, Burlington, Burnside, Deerfield, Dryden, Elba, Goodland, Hadley, Imlay, Lapeer, Marathon, Mayfield, Metamora, North Branch, Oregon, and Rich.

Records begin on the following dates: Land, 1830; marriage, 1831; divorce and civil court, 1835; probate, 1838; and birth and death, 1867. Naturalization records (1840-1956) are at the State Archives of Michigan.

In-person research: "No research (allowed) on the second and fourth Wednesday mornings each month."

Written queries: Will answer. Copies are $10 for the first copy and $3 for each additional copy of the same record requested at the same time.

American History and Genealogy Project and American Local History Network: <www.usgennet.org/usa/mi/county/lapeer>

MIGenWeb: <www.rootsweb.com/~milapeer>

Leelanau County Clerk
301 East Cedar St.
P.O. Box 467
Leland, Mich. 49654
Telephone: (231) 256-9824
FAX: (231) 256-8295
E-mail: <clerk@leelanaucounty.com>
Web site: <www.leelanaucounty.com>

Creation: Leelanau was created on 1 April 1840 from Michilimackinac (now Mackinac).

Attachments: At its creation, Leelanau was attached to Michilimackinac for judicial purposes. On 3 February 1853, Leelanau was attached to Grand Traverse for judicial and municipal purposes.

Organization: Leelanau was fully organized by 27 February 1863. County seat was first established at Northport and changed to Leland by 1882.

Boundaries: Leelanau lost about 30 square miles to Manitou at its creation on 12 February 1855. Leelanau lost about 300 square miles to the creation of Benzie on 27 February 1863. When Manitou was eliminated on 4 April 1895, Leelanau gained part of that county, including North and South Manitou Islands.

Townships: Bingham, Centerville, Cleveland, Elmwood, Empire, Glen Arbor, Kasson, Leelanau, Leland, Solon, and Suttons Bay.

Records begin on the following dates: Land, 1847; birth, marriage, divorce, and death, 1867; naturalization, 1870; probate, 1876; and civil court, 1879.

In-person research: "There is no genealogy on court days. Only one person can research records at a time due to space constraints. Certain times of the year require genealogy to be at limited hours of the day. It is best to call in advance."

Written queries: Search fee is $5. "Certified copy will be issued for this fee, if the record is located. We only issue certified copies of vital statistics, even for genealogical purposes. Birth information more recent than 100 years needs proof of death before any information will be released and then only according to the law."

American Local History Network: <members.aol.com/vwilson577/lee-alhn.html>

MIGenWeb: <members.aol.com/vwilson577/leelanau.html>

Lenawee County Clerk
425 North Main St.
Rex B. Martin Judicial Building, 3rd Floor
Adrian, Mich. 49221
Telephone: (517) 264-4599
Web site: <www.lenawee.mi.us>

Creation: Lenawee was created on 10 September 1822 from Monroe, including "part of the disputed strip west of Lake Erie that also was claimed by Ohio but controlled by Michigan."[25]

Attachments: At its creation, Lenawee was attached to Monroe for administrative and judicial purposes.

Organization: On 31 December 1826, the county was fully organized, with its seat established at Tecumseh. In 1838, the seat was changed to Adrian.

Boundaries: When Michigan became a state in 1837, the boundary dispute was settled in favor of Ohio.

Townships: Adrian, Blissfield, Cambridge, Clinton, Deerfield, Dover, Fairfield, Franklin, Macon, Madison, Medina, Ogden, Palmyra, Raisin, Ridgeway, Riga, Rollin, Rome, Seneca, Tecumseh, and Woodstock.

Records begin on the following dates: Probate and land, 1827; marriage and divorce, 1852; birth and death, 1867; and civil court, 1870. Naturalization records (1853-1982) are at the State Archives of Michigan.

In-person research: Researchers may view records from 9:30 a.m. to 11:30 a.m. and 1:30 p.m. to 3:30 p.m. Tuesdays through Fridays.

Written queries: Will answer. Certified copies are $10 and $3 for each additional copy of the same record ordered at the same time.

MIGenWeb: <www.geocities.com/lenaweemi>

Livingston County Clerk
200 East Grand River
Howell, Mich. 48843-2399
Telephone: (517) 546-0500
Fax: (517) 546-4354
E-mail: <countyclerk@co.livingston.mi.us>
Web site: <www.co.livingston.mi.us>

Creation: Livingston was created on 21 March 1833 from Shiawassee (which was attached to Oakland) and Washtenaw.

Attachments: At its creation, part of Livingston was attached to Shiawassee and part was attached to Washtenaw.

Organization: Livingston was fully organized on 4 April 1836, with its seat established at Howell.

Townships: Brighton, Cohoctah, Conway, Deerfield, Genoa, Green Oak, Hamburg, Handy, Hartland, Iosco, Marion, Oceola, Putnam, Tyrone, and Unadilla.

Records begin on the following dates: Land, 1834; marriage, 1836; probate and civil court, 1837; divorce and naturalization, 1847; birth and death, 1867.

In-person research: Hours are 8:30 a.m. to 4 p.m. Researchers must present identification and register.

Written queries: Will answer. "The fee to search for a record for an unknown year is $10. One copy of a record is $10. Additional copies of the same record ordered at the same time are $5 each. Please send checks drawn on Michigan banks or a money order payable to: Livingston County Clerk."

American History and Genealogy Project and American Local History Network: <www.livgenmi.com>

MIGenWeb: <www.rootsweb.com/~miliving/>

Luce County Clerk
County Government Building
407 W. Harrie St.
Newberry, Mich. 49868
Telephone: (906) 293-5521

Creation: Luce was created on 1 March 1887 from Chippewa and Mackinac.

Organization: Luce was fully organized at its creation, with the seat established at Newberry.

Townships: Columbus, Lakefield, McMillan, and Pentland.

Records begin on the following dates: Land, 1861; birth, marriage, and death, 1886; divorce and civil court, 1887; and probate, 1888. Naturalization records (1887-1955) are at the State Archives of Michigan.

In-person research: Researchers may view records on Mondays, Wednesdays, Thursdays, and Fridays, "unless our vault is extremely busy and then we restrict time."

Written queries: Will not answer.

MIGenWeb: <www.rootsweb.com/~miluce>

Mackinac County Clerk
100 North Marley St.
Saint Ignace, Mich. 49781
Telephone: (906) 643-7300

Creation: First named Michilimackinac, the county was created on 3 December 1818 from non-county area and Wayne. Around 1850, Michilimackinac was renamed Mackinac, but "this change was never officially adopted by the legislature and both names were used interchangeably through the 1840s."[26]

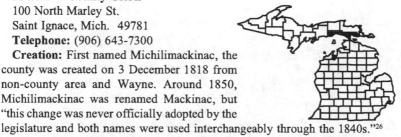

Organization: The county was organized at its creation, with the seat established at Mackinac. In 1882, the seat was changed to Saint Ignace.

Boundaries: At its creation, Mackinac included parts of present-day Minnesota and Wisconsin, most of Michigan's present-day Upper Peninsula and south into Michigan's southern Lower Peninsula. On 13 April 1821, part of Mackinac in the Lower Peninsula reverted to non-county status and was attached to Oakland for administrative and judicial purposes. On 10 September 1822, more of Mackinac in the Lower Peninsula reverted to non-county status and was attached to Monroe for administrative and judicial purposes.

Mackinac lost to the creation of Chippewa on 1 February 1827 and lost again on 2 March 1831 to the creation of Ionia, Isabella, Kent, Montcalm, Oceana, and Ottawa. Mackinac lost to the creation of Wisconsin Territory on 3 July 1836. It lost again on 1 April 1840 to Oceana and also to the creation of 24 counties: Alpena, Antrim, Charlevoix, Cheboygan, Clare, Crawford, Emmet, Kalkaska, Lake, Leelanau, Manistee, Mason, Mecosta, Missaukee, Montmorency, Newaygo, Omeena, Osceola, Oscoda, Otsego, Presque Isle, Roscommon, Wexford, and Wyandot.

On 9 March 1843, Mackinac exchanged with Chippewa and lost to the creation of Delta, Marquette, Ontonagon, and Schoolcraft. Mackinac lost Beaver Island to Emmet on 29 January 1853. On 1 May 1875, the boundary between Mackinac and Chippewa was redefined with no change. Mackinac lost its last territory on 1 March 1887 with the creation of Luce.

Townships: Bois Blanc, Brevort, Clark, Garfield, Hendricks, Marquette, Moran, Newton, Portage, and Saint Ignace.

Records begin on the following dates: Marriage, late 1700s; land, 1785; civil court and divorce, 1808; probate, 1821; and birth and death, 1873. Naturalization records (1821-1964) are at the State Archives of Michigan.

In-person research: Office hours are 8:30 a.m. to 4:30 p.m. weekdays. "Summer is a very busy time for us. Some days we don't have time for research. Fall and winter are slow; it's a better time for genealogy."

Written queries: Will answer. Searches are free. Certified copies are $7 each and $3 for each additional copy of the same record ordered at the same time.

American Local History Network: <www.rootsweb.com/~mimacki2/page1.html>

MIGenWeb: <www.rootsweb.com/~mimackin>

Macomb County Clerk
40 North Main St., 1st Floor
Mount Clemens, Mich. 48043
Telephone: (586) 469-5213
Web site: <www.co.macomb.mi.us>

Creation: Macomb was created on 15 January 1818 from Wayne.

Organization: Macomb was organized on the day of its creation. On 11 March 1818, its seat was established at Mount Clemens.

Boundaries: Macomb lost to the creation of Oakland on 28 March 1820 and to the creation of Saint Clair on 8 May 1821. Macomb gained from Saint Clair on 10 September 1822 and 31 March 1833.

Townships: Armada, Bruce, Chesterfield, Clinton, Harrison, Lake, Lenox, Macomb, Ray, Richmond, Shelby, and Washington.

Records begin on the following dates: Land and civil court, 1818; marriage, 1819; probate 1825; divorce, 1847; and birth and death, 1867. Naturalization records (1820-1985) are at the State Archives of Michigan.

In-person research: Researchers may inspect genealogy records from 9:30 a.m. to 11:30 a.m. Tuesdays, Wednesdays, and Thursdays. Researchers must present identification, such as a driver's license or state identification. "Only indexes for death records can be viewed from 1867 through 1933. Death records from 1934 through 1958 are stored off-site, and there is a two-day delay for these records to be shipped to our office. Death records filed in our office are from 1958 to present and can only be verified by a Deputy Clerk by computer. Death records from 1958 to present are not available for viewing, but a certified copy can be obtained. Birth records are not open to public inspection, except those from 1867 through 1899. Records from 1900 to present can be obtained if the person is deceased and proof of death can be shown with proof of their relationship to the deceased. Marriage records from 1819 through 1925 are open for inspection. Indexes for marriage records from 1819 through 1962 can be viewed. Records from 1926 to present are not open for viewing, but a certified copy can be obtained."

Written queries: Will answer. Certified copies are $10 and $3 for each additional copy of the same record ordered at the same time.

American Local History Network and MIGenWeb: <www.online-isp.com/~maggie/macomb>

Manistee County Clerk
415 Third St.
Government Center
Mainistee, Mich. 49660
Telephone: (231) 723-4575

Creation: Manistee was created on 1 April 1840 from Michilimackinac (now Mackinac).

Attachments: At its creation, Manistee was attached to Michilimackinac for judicial purposes. The attachment changed to Ottawa on 25 March 1846 and to Grand Traverse on 3 February 1853.

Organization: Manistee was fully organized on 13 February 1855, with the seat established at Manistee.

Boundaries: Manistee lost to Wexford on 27 March 1873 and gained from Wexford on 22 March 1881.

Townships: Arcadia, Bear Lake, Brown, Cleon, Dickson, Filer, Manistee, Maple Grove, Marilla, Norman, Onekama, Pleasanton, Springdale, and Stronach.

Records begin on the following dates: Land, 1853; marriage, civil court, and probate, 1855; divorce, 1856; naturalization, 1857; and birth and death, 1867.

In-person research: "Some restrictions as to the documents themselves."

Written queries: Will answer. Search fee is $5. Certificates are $10 for records before 1950 or for birth records, $1 if after 1950 and/or non-birth record.

American History and Genealogy Project and American Local History Network: <www.geocities.com/Heartland/Plains/5666/Manistee.html>

MIGenWeb: <www.rootsweb.com/~mimanist/Index.html>

Marquette County Clerk
Courthouse
234 W. Baraga Ave.
Marquette, Mich. 49855
Telephone: (906) 225-8151
Web site: <www.co.marquette.mi.us>

Creation: Marquette was created on 9 March 1843 from non-county area and Chippewa and Michilimackinac (now Mackinac).

Attachments: At its creation, Marquette was attached to Chippewa for judicial purposes. On 18 May 1846, Marquette was attached to Houghton.

Organization: County government was fully organized on 1 December 1851, with the seat established at Marquette.

Boundaries: Marquette lost to the creation of Houghton on 19 March 1845. The county's boundaries were redefined with no change on 3 April 1848. Marquette lost to Houghton on 12 March 1861 and then gained from Houghton on 16 March 1861. Marquette gained from non-county area on 28 March 1873. Marquette gained from Schoolcraft on 26 March 1875, but lost to Menominee on 26 April 1877, lost to the creation of Iron on 3 April 1885, lost to the creation of Dickinson on 21 May 1891, and lost to Iron on 22 May 1891.

Townships: Champion, Chocolay, Ely, Ewing, Forsyth, Ishpeming, Marquette, Michigamme, Negaunee, Powell, Republic, Richmond, Sands, Skandia, Tilden, Turin, Wells, and West Branch.

Records begin on the following dates: probate, 1840; marriages, 1850; land, 1851; divorce and civil court, 1852; and birth and death, 1867. Naturalization records (1852-1971) are at the State Archives of Michigan.

Written queries: Will answer. "$10 per record, $2 per search."

American History and Genealogy Project and American Local History Network: <www.geocities.com/Heartland/Plains/5666/Marquette.html>

MIGenWeb: <www.mifamilyhistory.org/marquette>

Mason County Clerk
304 E. Ludington Ave.
Ludington, 49431

Telephone: (231) 843-7999

Creation: First called Notipekago, the county was created on 1 April 1840 from Michilimackinac (now Mackinac). Notipek-ago was renamed Mason on 8 March 1843.

Attachments: At its creation, Mason was attached to Ottawa for judicial purposes.

Organization: County government was organized on 13 February 1855, with the seat established at Burr Caswell Farm. By 1861, the seat was changed to Lincoln, and by 1874, it had moved to Ludington.

Townships: Amber, Branch, Custer, Eden, Freesoil, Grant, Hamlin, Logan, Meade, Pere Marquette, Riverton, Sheridan, Sherman, Summit, and Victory.

Records begin on the following dates: Land, 1840; probate, 1855; birth, marriage, death, divorce, and civil court, 1867. Naturalization records (1870-1969) are at the State Archives of Michigan.

Written queries: Will answer. Certified copies, $7; non-certified copies prior to 1933, $5; and non-certified copies after 1933, $3.

MIGenWeb: <www.rootsweb.com/~mimason/county.html>

Mecosta County Clerk
400 Elm St.
Big Rapids, Mich. 49307
Telephone: (231) 796-2505

Creation: Mecosta was created on 1 April 1840 from Michilimackinac (now Mackinac) and Oceana, which was attached to Kent.

Attachments: At its creation, Mecosta was attached to Kent for judicial purposes. On 17 February 1857, Mecosta was attached to Newaygo.

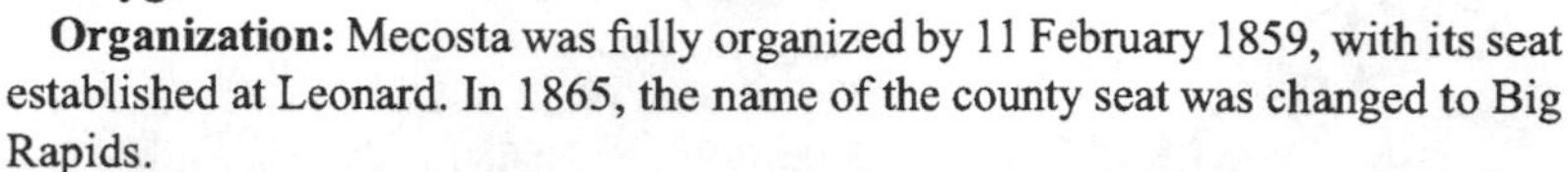

Organization: Mecosta was fully organized by 11 February 1859, with its seat established at Leonard. In 1865, the name of the county seat was changed to Big Rapids.

Boundaries: Mecosta lost to Montcalm on 11 February 1859.

Townships: Aetna, Austin, Big Rapids, Chippewa, Colfax, Deerfield, Fork, Grant, Green, Hinton, Martiny, Mecosta, Millbrook, Morton, Sheridan, and Wheatland.

Records begin on the following dates: Probate, 1820; land, 1855; civil court and marriage, 1859; and birth, death, and divorce, 1867. Naturalization records (1859-1956) are at the State Archives of Michigan.

MIGenWeb: <www.rootsweb.com/~mimecost/index.html>

Menominee County Clerk
Courthouse
839 Tenth Ave.
Menominee, Mich. 49858
Telephone: (906) 863-9968 or (906) 863-9969
Fax: (906) 863-8839
Web site: <www.menomineecounty.com>

Creation: First named Bleeker, the county was created on 15 March 1861 from non-county area. Bleeker was renamed Menominee on 19 March 1863.

Attachments: At its creation, Menominee was attached to Marquette for judicial and other purposes.

Organization: Menominee was fully organized by 19 March 1863, with its seat established at Menominee.

Boundaries: The county's boundaries were redefined with no change on 28 March 1873. Menominee gained a small portion of non-county area on 10 March 1875, and on 26 April 1877 Menominee gained from Marquette but lost to non-county area. Menominee lost to the creation of Iron on 3 April 1885 and the creation of Dickinson on 21 May 1891.

Townships: Cedarville, Daggett, Faithorn, Gourley, Harris, Holmes, Ingallston, Lake, Mellen, Menominee, Meyer, Nadeau, Spalding, and Stephenson.

Records begin on the following dates: Land, 1850; civil court and divorce, 1861; marriage and naturalization, 1863; birth and death, 1867; and probate, 1868.

In-person research: No restrictions.

Written queries: Will answer. "Regular copies are 20 cents a page. Certified copies are $10 each."

MIGenWeb: <www.rootsweb.com/~mimenomi>

Midland County Clerk
220 West Ellsworth St., 1st Floor
Midland, Mich. 48640
Telephone: (989) 832-6739
Fax: (989) 832-6680
E-mail: <kholcomb@co.midland.mi.us>
Web site: <www.co.midland.mi.us>

Creation: Midland was created on 2 March 1831 from Saginaw (which was attached to Oakland) and non-county areas attached to Kalamazoo and Oakland.

Attachments: On 2 March 1836, Midland was attached to Saginaw.

Organization: Midland was fully organized on 3 July 1855, with its seat established at Midland.

Boundaries: Midland lost to the creation of Bay on 20 April 1857. On 28 March 1873, the county's boundaries were redefined with no change.

Townships: Edenville, Geneva, Greendale, Homer, Ingersoll, Jasper, Jerome, Larkin, Lee, Lincoln, Midland, Mills, Mount Haley, Porter, and Warren.

Records begin on the following dates: Civil court, 1839; probate, 1850; marriage, land, and naturalization, 1855; death, 1866; birth, 1867; and divorce, 1877.

In-person research: No restrictions.

Written queries: Will answer. "First certified copy of a birth, death, or marriage record is $10. Additional copies made at the same time of the same record are $5."

MIGenWeb: <www.mifamilyhistory.org/midland>

Missaukee County Clerk
111 S. Canal St.
P.O. Box 800
Lake City, Mich. 49651
Telephone: (231) 839-4967

Creation: Missaukee was created on 1 April 1840 from Michilimackinac (now Mackinaw).

Attachments: At its creation, Missaukee was attached to Michilimackinac for judicial purposes.

The attachment was changed to Grand Traverse on 3 February 1853, to Manistee on 29 January 1858, and to Wexford on 30 March 1869.

Organization: Missaukee was fully organized by 11 March 1871,with the seat established at the home of Perley Palmer. By 1873, the seat had been changed to Lake City.

Townships: Aetna, Bloomfield, Butterfield, Caldwell, Clam Union, Enterprise, Forest, Holland, Lake, Norwich, Pioneer, Reeder, Richland, Riverside, and West Branch.

Records begin on the following dates: Land, 1859; birth and death, 1870; marriage, probate, and naturalization, 1871; and divorce and civil court, 1872.

In-person research: No restrictions.

Written queries: Will answer. Certified copies are $5, photocopies are $1.

MIGenWeb: <www.mifamilyhistory.org/missaukee/>

Monroe County Clerk
106 East First St.
Monroe, Mich. 48161
Telephone: (734) 240-7020
Fax: (734) 240-7046
Web site: <www.co.monroe.mi.us>

Creation: Monroe was created on 14 July 1817 from Wayne County, including "part of the disputed strip west of Lake Erie that also was claimed by Ohio but controlled by Michigan."[27]

Organization: The county was organized at its creation. Its seat was established at Monroe on 1 September 1817.

Boundaries: On 10 September 1822, Monroe lost to Wayne and to the creation of both Lenawee and Washtenaw counties. When Michigan became a state in 1837, the boundary dispute was settled in favor of Ohio.

Townships: Ash, Bedford, Berlin, Dundee, Erie, Exeter, Frenchtown, Ida, La Salle, London, Milan, Monroe, Raisinville, Summerfield, and Whiteford.

Records begin on the following dates: Probate, 1800; civil court, 1805; land, 1806; marriage, 1818; death, 1867; birth, 1874; and divorce, 1897. Naturalization records (1849-1929) are at the State Archives of Michigan.

In-person research: Researchers may view records from 9 a.m. to 4:30 p.m. Tuesdays and Thursdays. "First come, first served."

Written queries: Will answer. Search fee is $8 for five years. Copies are "$1 for plain copy and $8 for certified." Accepts cash and money orders only. No personal checks.

American History and Genealogy Project and American Local History Network: <www.usgennet.org/usa/mi/county/monroe>

MIGenWeb: <www.geocities.com/Athens/4105>

Montcalm County Clerk
211 W. Main St.
P.O. Box 368
Stanton, Mich. 48888
Telephone: (989) 831-7339
Fax: (989) 831-7474
Web site: <www.montcalm.org>

Creation: Montcalm was created on 2 March 1831 from Michilimackinac (now Mackinac) and non-county area attached to Kalamazoo.

Attachments: On 3 April 1837, Montcalm was attached to Ionia for judicial purposes.

Organization: By 20 March 1850, Montcalm was fully organized. Its seat was first established at Greenville and was changed to Stanton by 1860.

Boundaries: Montcalm gained from Mecosta on 11 February 1859.

Townships: Belvidere, Bloomer, Bushnell, Cato, Crystal, Day, Douglass, Eureka, Evergreen, Fairplain, Ferris, Home, Maple Valley, Montcalm, Pierson, Pine, Reynolds, Richland, Sidney, and Winfield.

Records begin on the following dates: Land, 1838; marriage, 1851; probate, 1855; civil court, 1860s; divorce, 1865; and birth and death, 1867. Naturalization records (1852-1955) are at the State Archives of Michigan.

In-person research: Hours are 8 a.m. to noon and 1 p.m. to 5 p.m. "Only one person allowed at a time."

Written queries: Will answer. Copies are $10.

MIGenWeb: <www.rootsweb.com/~mimontca/index.htm>

Montmorency County Clerk
12265 M-32
P.O. Box 789
Atlanta, Mich. 49709
Telephone: (989) 785-8022

Creation: First called Cheonoquet, the county was created on 1 April 1840 from Michilimackinac (now Mackinac) and non-county area attached to Saginaw. Cheonoquet was renamed Montmorency on 8 March 1843.

Attachments: At its creation, Montmorency was attached to Michilimackinac for judicial purposes. It was later attached to Cheboygan on 29 January 1853 and Alpena on 7 February 1857.

Organization: Montmorency was fully organized by 21 May 1881, with the seat established at Hillman. By 1893, the seat had been changed to Atlanta.

Townships: Albert, Avery, Briley, Hillman, Loud, Montmorency, Rust, and Vienna.

Records begin on the following dates: Birth, marriage, and death, 1881 (indexes only); divorce and civil court, 1940; and probate and land, 1943. Most records were lost in a 1942 courthouse fire.

In-person research: Researchers should call ahead first.

Written queries: Will answer "some, if only one or two names. No search fee at this time, but it is being looked into. Copies of vital records are $2 each or $5 for certified copies."

American Local History Network: <www.usgennet.org/usa/mi/county/montmorency>

MIGenWeb: <www.rootsweb.com/~mimontmo>

Muskegon County Clerk
Michael E. Kobza Hall of Justice
990 Terrace St.
2nd Floor
Muskegon, Mich. 49442
Telephone: (231) 724-6221
Fax: (231) 724-6262
E-mail: <clerk@co.muskegon.mi.us>
Web site: <co.muskegon.mi.us>

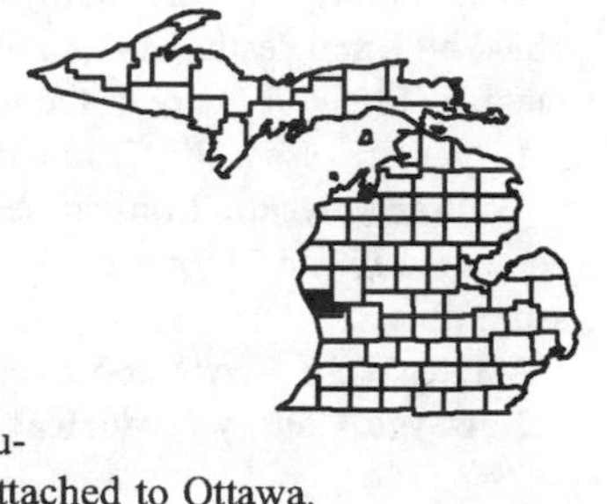

Creation: Muskegon was created on 4 February 1859 from Ottawa and non-county area attached to Ottawa.

Organization: Muskegon was organized at its creation, with the county seat established at Muskegon.

Townships: Blue Lake, Casnovia, Cedar Creek, Dalton, Egelston, Fruitland, Fruitport, Holton, Laketon, Montague, Moorland, Muskegon, Ravenna, Sullivan, White River, and Whitehall.

Records begin on the following dates: Land, 1839; marriage, probate, and civil court, 1859; birth, death, and divorce, 1867. Naturalization records (1850-1980) and divorce records (1894-1936) are at the State Archives of Michigan.

American Local History Network: <www.usgennet.org/usa/mi/county/muskegon>

MIGenWeb: <www.rootsweb.com/~mimuskeg>

Newaygo County Clerk
1087 Newell St.
P.O. Box 885
White Cloud, Mich. 49349-0885
Telephone: (231) 689-7235
Fax: (231) 689-7241
E-mail: <laurie@co.newaygo.mi.us>
Web site: <www.countyofnewaygo.com>

Creation: Newaygo was created on 1 April 1840 from Michilimackinac (now Mackinac) and Oceana, which was attached to Kent.

Attachments: At its creation, Newaygo was attached to Kent for judicial purposes. On 25 March 1846, part of Newaygo was attached to Ottawa.

Organization: Newaygo was fully organized by 27 June 1851. The seat was first established at Newaygo and was changed to White Cloud (formerly Morgan Station) by 1879.

Townships: Ashland, Barton, Beaver, Big Prairie, Bridgeton, Brooks, Croton, Dayton, Denver, Ensley, Everett, Garfield, Goodwell, Grant, Home, Lilley, Lincoln, Merrill, Monroe, Norwich, Sheridan, Sherman, Troy, and Wilcox.

Records begin on the following dates: Land, 1840; marriage, 1850; divorce, 1854; birth and death, 1867; probate, 1880; and civil court, 1893. Naturalization records (1855-1966) are at the State Archives of Michigan.

In-person research: "Limited space; first come, first served."

Written queries: Limited search. "Not many names at a time." Certified copies are $7 and $3 for each additional copy of the same record purchased at the same time.

MIGenWeb: <www.rootsweb.com/~minewayg>

Newaygo County Historical Archives: <ncha.ncats.net/html/index.html>

Oakland County Clerk
1200 North Telegraph Rd., Building 12 East
Pontiac, Mich. 48341

Telephone: (248) 858-0571

Web site: <www.co.oakland.mi.us>

Creation: Oakland was created from Macomb on 28 March 1820.

Organization: Oakland was organized at its creation, with the seat established at Pontiac.

Boundaries: Oakland lost to the creation of Lapeer, Shiawassee, and Washtenaw on 10 September 1822.

Townships: Addison, Avon, Bloomfield, Brandon, Commerce, Farmington, Groveland, Highland, Holly, Independence, Lyon, Milford, Novi, Oakland, Orion, Oxford, Pontiac, Rose, Royal Oak, Southfield, Springfield, Waterford, and White Lake.

Records begin on the following dates: Land, 1821; probate, 1822; divorce and civil court, 1826; marriage and naturalization, 1827; and birth and death, 1867.

American Local History Network: <www.usgennet.org/usa/mi/county/genesee/oakland>

MIGenWeb: <www.ameritech.net/users/mwheeler1/MIOakland.html>

Oceana County Clerk
100 State St.
P.O. Box 653
Hart, Mich. 49420
Telephone: (231) 873-4835

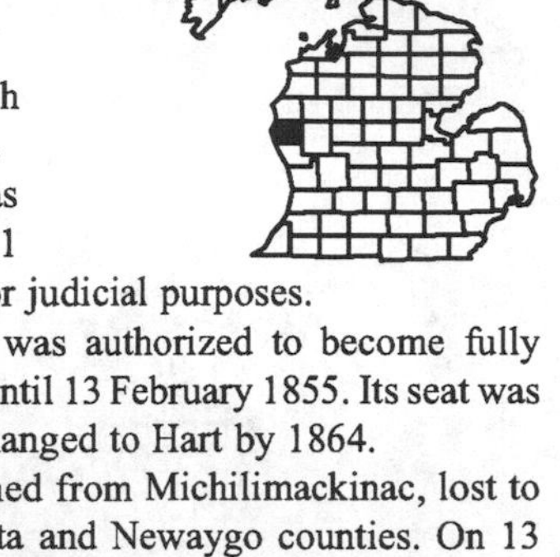

Creation: Oceana was created on 2 March 1831 from Michilimackinac (now Mackinac).

Attachments: On 3 April 1837, Oceana was attached to Kent for judicial purposes, and on 1 April 1840 Oceana was attached to Ottawa for judicial purposes.

Organization: On 7 April 1851, Oceana was authorized to become fully organized but did not become fully organized until 13 February 1855. Its seat was first established at Whiskey Creek but was changed to Hart by 1864.

Boundaries: On 1 April 1840, Oceana gained from Michilimackinac, lost to Kent, and lost to the creation of both Mecosta and Newaygo counties. On 13 February 1855, the southern portion of Oceana reverted to non-county status and remained attached to Ottawa for judicial purposes.

Townships: Benona, Claybanks, Colfax, Crystal, Elbridge, Ferry, Golden, Grant, Greenwood, Hart, Leavitt, Newfield, Otto, Pentwater, Shelby, and Weare.

Records begin on the following dates: Land, 1846; naturalization, 1856; marriage, 1857; divorce, probate and civil court, 1859; and birth and death, 1867.

In-person research: There is limited space.

Written queries: Free searches. Certified copies only. Cost is $7 for the first one and $3 for each additional copy of the same record ordered at the same time.

MIGenWeb: <www.rootsweb.com/~mioceana/index.html>

Ogemaw County Clerk
806 West Houghton Ave.
West Branch, Mich. 48661
Telephone: (989) 345-0215

Creation: Ogemaw was created on 1 April 1840 from non-county area attached to Saginaw. However, Ogemaw was eliminated and absorbed by Iosco County on 7 March 1867, and then it was re-created from Iosco County on 28 March 1873.

Attachments: At its first creation, Ogemaw was attached to Michilimackinac (now Mackinac) for judicial purposes. It was later attached to Cheboygan on 29 January 1853 and Iosco on 29 January 1858. At its second creation, Ogemaw was attached to Iosco for judicial and municipal purposes.

Organization: Ogemaw was fully organized by 27 April 1875, with its seat established at West Branch.

Townships: Churchill, Cumming, Edwards, Foster, Goodar, Hill, Klacking, Logan, Mills, Ogemaw, Richland, Rose, and West Branch.

Records begin on the following dates: Land, 1853; marriage, death, civil court, and naturalization, 1876; divorce and probate, 1877; and birth, 1879.

In-person research: Viewing of birth records is restricted as per state law.

Written queries: Will answer queries for deaths and marriages. Copies are 50 cents.

MIGenWeb: <www.rootsweb.com/~miogemaw>

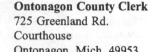

Ontonagon County Clerk
725 Greenland Rd.
Courthouse
Ontonagon, Mich. 49953
Telephone: (906) 884-4255

Creation: Ontonagon was created on 9 March 1843 from Chippewa and Michilimackinac (now Mackinac) counties.

Attachments: At its creation, Ontonagon was attached to Chippewa for judicial purposes. It was later attached to Houghton on 18 May 1846.

Organization: Ontonagon was fully organized by 17 January 1853, with the seat established at Ontonagon.

Boundaries: Ontonagon lost Isle Royale to the creation of Houghton on 19 March 1845. On 3 April 1848, the county's boundaries were redefined with no change. Ontonagon gained from Houghton on 17 January1853, but lost to Houghton on 12 March 1861. Ontonagon also lost more than 1,000 square miles to the creation of Gogebic on 7 February 1887.

Townships: Bergland, Bohemia, Carp Lake, Greenland, Haight, Interior, Matchwood, McMillan, Ontonagon, Rockland, and Stannard.

Records begin on the following dates: Land, 1850; marriage, 1851; probate, 1853; civil court and divorce, 1854; and birth and death, 1868. Naturalization records (1848-1953) are at the State Archives of Michigan.

American Local History Network: <www.usgennet.org/usa/mi/county/ontonagon>

MIGenWeb: <www.rootsweb.com/~miontona/index.htm>

Osceola County Clerk
301 West Upton St.
P.O. Box 208
Reed City, Mich. 49677-0208
Telephone: (231) 832-6196

Creation: First named Unwattin, the county was created on 1 April 1840 from Michilimackinac (now Mackinac). Unwattin was renamed Osceola on 8 March 1843.

Attachments: At its creation, Osceola was attached to Ottawa. It was later attached to Mason on 13 February 1855, to Newaygo on 17 February 1857, and to Mecosta on 11 February 1859.

Organization: Osceola was fully organized by 17 March 1869, with the seat established at Hersey. By 1927, the seat had been changed to Reed City.

Townships: Burdell, Cedar, Evart, Hartwick, Hersey, Highland, Le Roy, Lincoln, Marion, Middle Branch, Orient, Osceola, Richmond, Rose Lake, Sherman, and Sylvan.

Records begin on the following dates: Land, 1853; birth, marriage, and death, 1869; divorce, probate, and civil court, 1870; and naturalization, 1874.

In-person research: Open from 9 a.m. to 4:30 p.m. Tuesdays through Fridays.

Written queries: Will not answer.

MIGenWeb: <www.rootsweb.com/~miosceol>

Oscoda County Clerk
311 Morenci St.
P.O. Box 399
Mio, Mich. 48647

Telephone: (989) 826-1100

Creation: Oscoda was created on 1 April 1840 from Michilimackinac (now Mackinac) and non-county area attached to Saginaw.

Attachments: At its creation, Oscoda was attached to Michilimackinac. It was later attached to Cheboygan on 29 January 1853, to Alpena on 7 February 1857, to Iosco on 29 January 1858, and to Alcona on 12 March 1869.

Organization: Oscoda was fully organized by 10 March 1881, with the seat established at Union Corners. By 1884, the seat had been change to Mio.

Townships: Big Creek, Clinton, Comins, Elmer, Greenwood, and Mentor.

Records begin on the following dates: Land, 1850; birth, 1880; marriage, death, divorce, probate, and civil court, 1881; and naturalization, 1906.

In-person research: No restrictions.

Written queries: Will answer. "No fees unless party requests copy of document."

MIGenWeb: <www.rootsweb.com/~mioscod2/index.html>

Otsego County Clerk
225 West Main St.
Gaylord, Mich. 49735

Telephone: (989) 732-6484

Web site: <www.otsego.org/gov/county/countygov.htm>

Creation: First named Okkuddo, the county was created from Michilimackinac (now Mackinac) on 1 April 1840. Okkuddo was renamed Otsego on 8 March 1843.

Attachments: At its creation, Otsego was attached to Michilimackinac fc judicial purposes. It was later attached to Cheboygan on 29 January 1853, t Alpena on 29 January 1858, and to Antrim on 11 March 1863.

Organization: Otsego was fully organized by 12 March 1875, with its sea established at Otsego Lake. In 1877, the seat was changed to Gaylord.

Boundaries: Otsego lost to the re-creation of Charlevoix on 2 April 1869.

Townships: Bagley, Charlton, Chester, Corwith, Dover, Elmira, Haye Livingston, and Otsego Lake.

Records begin on the following dates: Land, 1863; birth, marriage, death, an civil court, 1875; probate, 1876; and divorce, 1877. Naturalization records (1875 1956) are at the State Archives of Michigan.

In-person research: Researchers may view records from 9 a.m. to noon an 1 p.m. to 3:30 p.m. Wednesdays, Thursdays, and Fridays.

Written queries: Will answer, but requests are "not a priority." Search fee i $1 per name. Copies are $8 for the first one and $4 for each additional cop ordered at the same time. "All copies are certified."

MIGenWeb: <www.rootsweb.com/~miotsego/index.html>

Ottawa County Clerk
414 Washington St.
Room 301
Grand Haven, Mich. 49417
Telephone: (616) 846-8310
Web site: <www.co.ottawa.mi.us>

Creation: Ottawa was created on 2 Marc 1831 from Michilimackinac (now Mackina and non-county area attached to Cass.

Attachments: On 4 April 1836, Ottawa w attached to Kent for judicial purposes.

Organization: Ottawa was fully organized by 29 December 1837, with its se established at Ottawa. In 1863, the name of the seat was changed to Grand Have

Boundaries: On 4 February 1859, Ottawa lost to the creation of Muskegor

Townships: Allendale, Blendon, Chester, Crockery, Georgetown, Grar Haven, Holland, Jamestown, Olive, Park, Polkton, Port Sheldon, Robinso Spring Lake, Tallmadge, Wright, and Zeeland.

Records begin on the following dates: Land, 1834; civil court, 1839; probat 1844; marriage, 1847; divorce, 1863; birth, 1866; and death, 1867. Naturalizatic records (1852-1962) are at the State Archives of Michigan.

In-person research: Hours are 8 a.m. to 5 p.m. weekdays. "There is a limit how many people may do research at a time."

Written queries: Will answer. "We do not charge for a search. We only iss certified copies of the record, if they want one, which is $10."

MIGenWeb: <www.rootsweb.com/~miottawa>

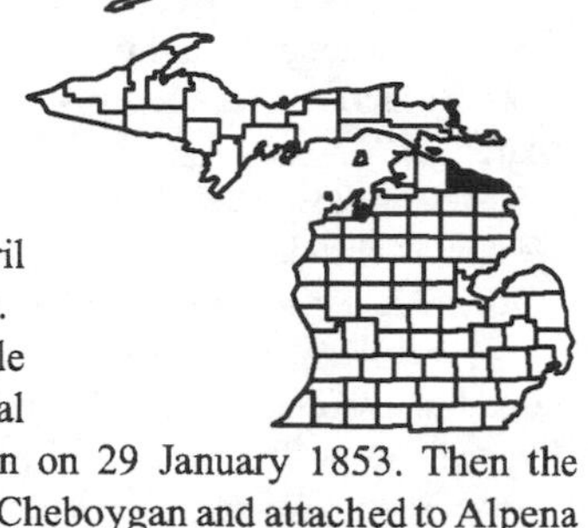

Presque Isle County Clerk
151 East Huron Ave.
P.O. Box 110
Rogers City, Mich. 49779
Telephone: (989) 734-3288

Creation: Presque Isle was created on 1 April 1840 from Michilimackinac (now Mackinac).

Attachments: At its creation, Presque Isle was attached to Michilimackinac for judicial purposes. It was later attached to Cheboygan on 29 January 1853. Then the eastern part of Presque Isle was detached from Cheboygan and attached to Alpena on 7 February 1857, and the western portion of Presque Isle was detached from Cheboygan and attached to Alpena on 29 January 1858.

Organization: Presque Isle was fully organized by 31 March 1871. Rogers (later Rogers City) and Crawfords Quarry "each claimed a right to the county seat, each built a courthouse, and for a time the county had two governments."[28] In 1875, the county was reorganized, and Rogers (later Rogers City) became the county seat.

Boundaries: On 28 March 1873, Presque Isle gained from Cheboygan.

Townships: Allis, Bearinger, Belknap, Bismarck, Case, Krakow, Metz, Moltke, North Allis, Ocqueac, Posen, Presque Isle, Pulawski, and Rogers.

Records begin on the following dates: Land, 1855; birth, death, and probate, 1871; marriage, civil court, and naturalization, 1872; and divorce, 1874.

In-person research: "We ask that everyone makes an appointment."

Written queries: Will answer. Certified copies are $8 for the first one and $3 for additional copies of the same record ordered at the same time. Photocopies are $1.

MIGenWeb: <members.aol.com/presqisle/>

Roscommon County Clerk
500 Lake St.
P.O. Box 98
Roscommon, Mich. 48653
Telephone: (989) 275-5923
Fax: (989) 275-8640
E-mail: <clerk@roscommoncounty.net>
Web site: <www.roscommoncounty.net>

Creation: First named Mikenauk, the county was created on 1 April 1840 from Michilimackinac (now Mackinaw) and non-county area attached to Saginaw. Mikenauk was renamed Roscommon on 8 March 1843.

Attachments: At its creation, Roscommon was attached to Michilimackinac for judicial purposes. It was later attached to Cheboygan on 29 January 1853 and to Midland on 29 January 1858.

Organization: Roscommon was fully organized by 20 March 1875, with the seat established at Houghton Lake. Three years later it was moved to Roscommon.

Boundaries: The county's boundaries were redefined with no change on 28 March 1873.

Townships: Au Sable, Backus, Denton, Gerrish, Higgins, Lake, Lyon, Markey, Nester, Richfield, and Roscommon.

Records begin on the following dates: Land, 1852; birth, death, and probate, 1874; marriage, divorce, and civil court, 1875; and naturalization, 1876. Naturalization records (1911-1921) are at the State Archives of Michigan as part of the Records of the Roscommon County Clerk, 1879-1931, collection.

In-person research: No restrictions. Hours are 8:30 a.m. to 4:30 p.m. weekdays.

Written queries: Will answer. "If the search is quite extensive, it may be turned over to the Roscommon County Genealogical Society."

MIGenWeb: <www.rootsweb.com/~miroscom>

Saginaw County Clerk
Saginaw County Governmental Center
111 S. Michigan Ave., Room 101
Saginaw, Mich. 48602
Telephone: (989) 790-5251
Fax: (989) 790-5254
Web site: <www.saginawcounty.com/>

Creation: Saginaw was created on 10 September 1822 from Saint Clair and non-county area attached to Oakland.

Attachments: At its creation, Saginaw was attached to Oakland for administrative and judicial purposes.

Organization: Saginaw was fully organized by 9 February 1835, with the seat established at Saginaw.

Boundaries: Saginaw lost to the creation of Midland on 2 March 1831 and lost to the creation of Genesee on 28 March 1835. It also lost to the creation of Bay on 20 April 1857. Saginaw lost an additional 20 square miles to Bay on 15 April 1871 and another 20 square miles to Bay on 3 June 1881.

Townships: Albee, Birch Run, Blumfield, Brady, Brant, Bridgeport, Buena Vista, Carrollton, Chapin, Chesaning, Frankenmuth, Fremont, James, Jonesfield, Kochville, Lakefield, Maple Grove, Marion, Richland, Saginaw, Saint Charles, Spaulding, Swan Creek, Taymouth, Thomas, Tittabawassee, and Zilwaukee.

Records begin on the following dates: Land, 1823; marriage, 1835 (but "limited" records prior to 1867); civil court, 1843; probate, 1857; birth and death, 1867; and divorce, 1886. Naturalization records (1852-1966) are at the State Archives of Michigan.

In-person research: "Space for research for about five people open during regular office hours."

Written queries: Will answer. Search fee is $3 per year for "record searches over six years. All return mail requests also require an additional $1 to cover mailing costs." Certified copies for births, deaths, and marriages are $10 each and $4 for each additional copy of the same record requested at the same time. Divorce record/judgments are $1 per page and $10 for certification, if required.

American Local History Network: <www.usgennet.org/usa/mi/county/saginaw>

MIGenWeb: <www.mifamilyhistory.org/saginaw>

Saint Clair County Clerk
201 McMorran Blvd.
Room 204
Port Huron, Mich. 48060
Telephone: (810) 985-2200
Fax: (810) 985-4796
E-mail: <mdunn@stclaircounty.org>
Web site: <www.stclaircounty.org>

Creation: Saint Clair was created on 8 May 1821 from Macomb.

Organization: Saint Clair was organized at its creation, with the seat established at Saint Clair. In 1871, the seat was changed to Port Huron.

Boundaries: On 10 September 1822, Saint Clair lost to Macomb and lost to the creation of Lapeer, Saginaw, Sanilac, and Shiawassee counties. Saint Clair lost additional territory to Macomb on 31 March 1833 and lost to Sanilac on 3 April 1848.

Townships: Berlin, Brockway, Burtchville, Casco, China, Clay, Clyde, Columbus, Cottrellville, East China, Emmett, Fort Gratiot, Grant, Greenwood, Ira, Kenockee, Kimball, Lynn, Mussey, Port Huron, Riley, Saint Clair, and Wales.

Records begin on the following dates: Land, 1821; probate, 1828; civil court and divorce, 1833; marriage, 1834; birth, 1867; and death, 1868. Naturalization records (1843-1982) are at the State Archives of Michigan.

In-person research: Researchers may view records from 9:30 a.m. to 2:30 p.m. "with staff help. You may stay until 4 p.m. if you do not require help."

Written queries: Will answer. Search fee is $5 for every 10 years searched. Birth, death, and marriage copies are $7 for the first copy and $3 for additional copies of the same record ordered at the same time. Divorces are $1 per page, plus an additional $10 for certification. Pay by personal check (Michigan banks only) or money order made to Saint Clair County Clerk. Enclose a stamped self-addressed envelope with all requests.

American History and Genealogy Project and American Local History Network: <www.usgennet.org/usa/mi/county/stclair>

MIGenWeb: <www.rootsweb.com/~mistclai/index.html>

Saint Joseph County Clerk
Courthouse
125 West Main St.
P.O. Box 189
Centreville, Mich. 49032-0189
Telephone: (269) 467-5500

Creation: Saint Joseph was created on 29 October 1829 from non-county area attached to Lenawee.

Organization: Saint Joseph was fully organized by 4 November 1829, with its seat established at White Pigeon. In 1831, the seat was changed to Centreville.

Boundaries: On 3 March 1831, Saint Joseph gained a small area from Cass.

Townships: Burr Oak, Colon, Constantine, Fabius, Fawn River, Florence, Flowerfield, Leonidas, Lockport, Mendon, Mottville, Nottawa, Park, Sherman, Sturgis, and White Pigeon.

Records begin on the following dates: Land, 1830; marriage and probate, 1832; civil court, 1842; divorce, 1850; naturalization, 1854; and birth and death, 1867.

In-person research: No restrictions. Hours are 8 a.m. to 5 p.m.

Written queries: Will answer. "The search fee is $10 for a 10-year search and a certified copy, if found. Fees are $10 for the first certified copy and $3 for additional copies of the same record ordered at the same time. We will only accept money orders."

MIGenWeb: <www.rootsweb.com/~mistjose>

Sanilac County Clerk
Courthouse Room 203
60 West Sanilac Ave.
Room 203
Sandusky, Mich. 48471
Telephone: (810) 648-3212
Fax: (810) 648-5466
Web site: <www.sanilaccounty.net>

Creation: Sanilac was created on 10 September 1822 from Saint Clair and non-county area attached to Oakland.

Attachments: At its creation, Sanilac was attached to Oakland for administrative and judicial purposes. It was later attached to Saint Clair on 12 April 1827. The western portion of Sanilac was attached to Lapeer on 28 March 1836. The western portion was reattached to Saint Clair on 1 April 1840.

Organization: Sanilac was fully organized by 31 December 1849. Its seat was first established at Lexington and was changed to Sandusky by 1880.

Boundaries: Sanilac lost to the creation of both Huron and Tuscola counties on 1 April 1840. Sanilac gained from Saint Clair on 3 April 1848.

Townships: Argyle, Austin, Bridgehampton, Buel, Custer, Delaware, Elk, Elmer, Evergreen, Flynn, Forester, Fremont, Greenleaf, Lamotte, Lexington, Maple Valley, Marion, Marlette, Minden, Moore, Sanilac, Speaker, Washington, Watertown, Wheatland, and Worth.

Records begin on the following dates: Civil court, 1831; land, 1834; probate, 1857; birth, marriage, and death, 1867; and divorce, 1898. Naturalization records (1850-1965) are at the State Archives of Michigan.

In-person research: "We ask researchers to conduct their work Tuesdays through Fridays from 8:30 a.m. to 4 p.m. The reason is we have court in Circuit and Family and do not have staff available to assist researchers."

Written queries: Will answer. Search fee is $10 per name, "if no information or dates are provided." Copy fee is $15 for the first copy and $4 for each additional copy of the same record ordered at the same time.

American History and Genealogy Project and American Local History Network: <www.usgennet.org/usa/mi/county/sanilac>

MIGenWeb: <www.rootsweb.com/~misanila>

Schoolcraft County Clerk
300 Walnut St.
Room 164
Manistique, Mich. 49854
Telephone: (906) 341-3618
Web site: <www.manistique.org/government/countyofficials.html>

Creation: Schoolcraft was created on 9 March 1843 from Chippewa and Michilimackinac (now Mackinac) counties.

Attachments: At its creation, Schoolcraft was attached to Chippewa for judicial purposes. It was later attached to Houghton on 18 May 1846 and to Marquette on 1 December 1851.

Organization: Schoolcraft was fully organized by 23 March 1871, with the seat established at Onota. The seat was changed to Manistique by 1882.

Boundaries: The county's boundaries were redefined with no change on 3 April 1848. Schoolcraft lost to Delta on 12 March 1861 and then gained the non-county area attached to Delta on 18 January 1862. Schoolcraft lost to Marquette on 26 March 1875 and also lost to the creation of Alger on 17 March 1885.

Townships: Doyle, Germfask, Hiawatha, Inwood, Manistique, Mueller, Seney, and Thompson.

Records begin on the following dates: Birth, marriage, and death, 1870; land, 1871; probate, 1874; and divorce and civil court, 1881.

Written queries: "No search fee at this time." Only certified copies are issued. Cost is $10 for the first copy and $3 for additional copies of the same record ordered at the same time.

MIGenWeb: <www.rootsweb.com/~mischool>

Shiawassee County Clerk
208 N. Shiawassee St.
Corunna, Mich. 48817
Telephone: (989) 743-2242
Fax: (989) 743-2241
Email: <clerk@shiawassee.net>
Web site: <www.shiawassee.net>

Creation: Shiawassee was created on 10 September 1822 from Oakland and Saint Clair and non-county area attached to Oakland.

Attachments: At its creation, Shiawassee was attached to Oakland for administrative and judicial purposes. It was later attached to Genesee on 4 April 1836.

Organization: Shiawassee was fully organized by 18 March 1837, with its seat established at Corunna.

Boundaries: Shiawassee lost to the creation of Ingham on 29 October 1829, lost to the creation of Livingston on 21 March 1833, and lost to the creation of Genesee on 28 March 1835.

Townships: Antrim, Bennington, Burns, Caledonia, Fairfield, Hazelton, Middlebury, New Haven, Owosso, Perry, Rush, Sciota, Shiawassee, Venice, Vernon, and Woodhull.

Records begin on the following dates: Land, 1836; probate, 1837; divorce and civil court, 1848; naturalization, 1854; and birth, marriage, and death, 1867.

In-person research: Hours are 8 a.m. to 5 p.m. weekdays. "Some of the civil court files are not kept in-house and might take one to two weeks for retrieval."

Written queries: Will answer.

MIGenWeb: <www.rootsweb.com/~mishiawa/>

Tuscola County Clerk
440 North State St.
Caro, Mich. 48723
Telephone: (989) 672-3780
Fax: (989) 672-4266
Web site: <www.tuscolacounty.org>

Creation: Tuscola was created on 1 April 1840 from Sanilac, which was attached to Lapeer.

Attachments: At its creation, Tuscola was attached to Saginaw for judicial purposes.

Organization: Tuscola was fully organized by 2 March 1850, with its seat established at Vassar. By 1860, the seat had been changed to Caro.

Boundaries: Tuscola gained from Lapeer on 19 March 1845. Tuscola exchanged with Lapeer on 13 February 1855.

Townships: Akron, Almer, Arbela, Arela, Columbia, Dayton, Denmark, Elkland, Ellington, Elmwood, Fairgrove, Fremont, Gilford, Indianfields, Juniata, Kingston, Koylton, Millington, Novesta, Tuscola, Vassar, Watertown, Wells, and Wisner.

Records begin on the following dates: Land, 1848; divorce, probate, and civil court, 1850; marriage, 1851; and birth and death, 1867. Naturalization records (1857-1965) are at the State Archives of Michigan.

In-person research: "We have people come in to look up records for genealogy Mondays through Thursdays, 8 a.m. to noon and 1 p.m. to 4:30 p.m. We only have room for one person at a time to do this."

Written queries: Will answer. "As of right now there is no search fee. Cost for a copy of our record is $13 for the first copy and additional copies issued at the same time of the same records are $5 each. Verification of facts is $4."

American History and Genealogy Project and American Local History Network: <www.usgennet.org/usa/mi/county/tuscola>

MIGenWeb: <www.rootsweb.com/~mituscol>

Van Buren County Clerk
Courthouse
212 Paw Paw St., Suite 101
Paw Paw, Mich. 49079
Telephone: (269) 657-8218
Fax: (269) 657-8298

Creation: Van Buren was created from non-county area attached to Lenawee on 29 October 1829.

Attachments: On 4 November 1829, Van Buren was attached to Cass for administrative and judicial purposes.

Organization: Van Buren was fully organized by 3 April 1837, with its seat established at Paw Paw.

Townships: Almena, Antwerp, Arlington, Bangor, Bloomingdale, Columbia, Covert, Decatur, Geneva, Hamilton, Hartford, Keeler, Lawrence, Paw Paw, Pine Grove, Porter, South Haven, and Waverly.

Records begin on the following dates: Marriage and land, 1836; civil court, divorce, and probate, 1837; naturalization, 1846; and birth and death, 1867.

In-person research: "Van Buren County Clerk will allow inspection of indexes of marriages, death and divorce records on a first come first served basis on Tuesday and Wednesday of each week from 10:30 a.m. to 3 p.m., unless prior arrangements for appointed time are made. Space permits only two people researching at one time. Birth indexes are not available for public inspection. We will, however, verify a birth record if it is on file in our office."

Written queries: Will answer. Search fee is $1 per liber (book), per name. "Upon written request and payment of search fee, we can verify the following facts: name or names of the individual to whom the vital record pertains, the nature of the event, the date of the event, place of the event, date of the filing." Certified copies are $7 for the first copy and $3 for each additional copy of the same record purchased at the same time.

American Local History Network: <www.usgennet.org/usa/mi/county/vanburen>

MIGenWeb: <www.rootsweb.com/~mivanbur/Mivanbur.html>

Washtenaw County Clerk
101 East Huron St.
P.O. Box 8645
Ann Arbor, Mich. 48107
Telephone: (734) 996-3055
Web site: <www.ewashtenaw.org/>

Creation: Washtenaw was created on 10 September 1822 from Monroe, Oakland, and Wayne.

Attachments: At its creation, Washtenaw was attached to Wayne for administrative and judicial purposes.

Organization: Washtenaw was fully organized by 31 December 1826, with Ann Arbor established as the seat.

Boundaries: Washtenaw lost to the creation of both Ingham and Jackson counties on 29 October 1829 and lost to the creation of Livingston on 21 March 1833.

Townships: Ann Arbor, Augusta, Bridgewater, Dexter, Freedom, Lima, Lodi, Lyndon, Manchester, Northfield, Pittsfield, Salem, Saline, Scio, Sharon, Superior, Sylvan, Webster, York, and Ypsilanti.

Records begin on the following dates: Marriage and probate, 1827; divorce, land, and civil court, 1835; and birth and death, 1867. Naturalization records (1830-1985) are at the State Archives of Michigan.

In-person research: Researcher may view records from 9 a.m. to 4 p.m. Tuesdays, Wednesdays, and Thursdays.

Written queries: Will answer "if they are requesting specific records. We do not do the research for them. Copies are $13 for the first copy and $4 for each additional copy of the same record purchased at the same time."

MIGenWeb: <www.rootsweb.com/~miwashte>

The Making of Ann Arbor: <moaa.aadl.org/>

Wayne County Clerk
c/o Birth and Death Records Division
or Marriage Records Division
201 Coleman A. Young Municipal Center
Detroit, Mich. 48226
Telephone: (313) 224-5535
or (313) 224-5520
Fax: (313) 224-5364
Web site: <www.waynecounty.com>

Creation: Wayne was created on 21 November 1815 from non-county area, including "part of the disputed strip west of Lake Erie that also was claimed by Ohio but controlled by Michigan."[29]

Organization: Wayne was organized at its creation, with the seat established at Detroit.

Boundaries: On 18 October 1816, Wayne gained the non-county area known as the Michilimackinac District. Wayne lost to the creation of Monroe on 14 July 1817, to the creation of Macomb on 15 January 1818, and to the creation of Michilimackinac (now Mackinac) on 3 December 1818. On 10 September 1822, Wayne gained from Monroe but lost to the creation of Washtenaw. When Michigan became a state in 1837, the boundary dispute was settled in favor of Ohio.

Townships: Brownstown, Canton, Grosse Ile, Grosse Pointe, Huron, Northville, Plymouth, Romulus, Sumpter, and Van Buren.

Records begin on the following dates: Land, 1703; probate, 1797; naturalization, 1815; marriage and civil court, 1818; and birth and death, 1867. Naturalization records (1837-1942) are at the State Archives of Michigan.

American Local History Network: <www.geocities.com/histmich/index.html>

MIGenWeb: <www.rootsweb.com/~miwayne>

Wexford County Clerk
437 East Division St.
Cadillac, Mich. 49601
Telephone: (231) 779-9453

Creation: First named Kautawaubet, the county was created on 1 April 1840 from Michilimackinac (now Mackinac). Kautawaubet was renamed Wexford on 8 March 1843.

Attachments: At its creation, Wexford was attached to Michilimackinac for judicial purposes. It was later attached to Grand Traverse on 3 February 1853 and to Manistee on 13 February 1855.

Organization: Wexford was fully organized by 30 March 1869, with the seat established at Sherman. "Clam Lake (now Cadillac), settled a few years later, coveted the distinction, and a county-seat war of unusual duration and bitterness, lasting for a decade, was waged. In 1881, the county seat was moved to Manton, but later that same year the records were removed by force to Cadillac, which became the county seat in 1882."[30]

Boundaries: Wexford gained about 30 square miles from Manistee on 27 March 1873 but lost the same area to Manistee on 22 March 1881.

Townships: Antioch, Boon, Cedar Creek, Cherry Grove, Clam Lake, Colfax, Greenwood, Hanover, Haring, Henderson, Liberty, Selma, Single, Slagle, South Branch, Springville, and Wexford.

Records begin on the following dates: Naturalization, 1850; marriage, 1864; birth and death, 1867; and divorce, probate, land, civil court, and criminal, 1869.

Written queries: Search fee is $5 for first three years, $2 for each additional year.

American Local History Network and MIGenWeb: <www.rootsweb.com/~miwexfor>

Michigan Counties at a Glance

COUNTY	FIRST NAMED	CREATED	ATTACHED	ORGANIZED	PARENT COUNTIES
Alcona	Negwegon	1840	Yes	1869	Non-county area
Alger		1885	No	1885	Schoolcraft
Allegan		1831	Yes	1835	Barry, non-county area
Alpena	Anamickee	1840	Yes	1857	Mackinac, non-county area
Antrim	Meegisee	1840	Yes	1863	Mackinac
Arenac		1831/1883	Yes	1883	Non-county area/Bay
Baraga		1875	No	1875	Houghton
Barry		1829	Yes	1839	Non-county area
Bay		1857	No	1857	Arenac, Midland, Saginaw
Benzie		1863	Yes	1869	Leelanau
Berrien		1829	Yes	1831	Non-county area
Branch		1829	Yes	1833	Non-county area
Calhoun		1829	Yes	1833	Non-county area

Michigan Counties at a Glance

COUNTY	FIRST NAMED	CREATED	ATTACHED	ORGANIZED	PARENT COUNTIES
Cass		1829	No	1829	Non-county area
Charlevoix	Keskkauko	1840/1869	Yes	1869	Mackinac/Emmet, Antrim, Otsego
Cheboygan		1840	Yes	1853	Mackinac
Chippewa		1827	No	1827	Mackinac
Clare	Kaykakee	1840	Yes	1871	Mackinac, non-county area
Clinton		1831	Yes	1839	Non-county area
Crawford	Shawono	1840	Yes	1879	Mackinac, non-county area
Delta		1843	Yes	1861	Mackinac, non-county area
Dickinson		1891	No	1891	Iron, Marquette, Menominee
Eaton		1829	Yes	1837	Non-county area
Emmet	Tonedagana	1840	Yes	1853	Mackinac
Genesee		1835	Yes	1836	Lapeer, Saginaw, Shiawassee
Gladwin		1831	Yes	1875	Non-county area

Michigan Counties at a Glance

COUNTY	FIRST NAMED	CREATED	ATTACHED	ORGANIZED	PARENT COUNTIES
Gogebic		1887	No	1887	Ontonagon
Grand Traverse		1851	No	1851	Omeena
Gratiot		1831	Yes	1855	Non-county area
Hillsdale		1829	Yes	1835	Non-county area
Houghton		1845	Yes	1846	Marquette, Ontonagon
Huron		1840	Yes	1859	Sanilac
Ingham		1829	Yes	1838	Shiawassee, Washtenaw, non-county area
Ionia		1831	Yes	1837	Mackinac, non-county area
Iosco	Kanotin	1840	Yes	1857	Non-county area
Iron		1885	No	1885	Marquette, Menominee
Isabella		1831	Yes	1859	Mackinac, non-county area
Jackson		1829	Yes	1832	Washtenaw, non-county area
Kalamazoo		1829	Yes	1830	Non-county area

Michigan Counties at a Glance

COUNTY	FIRST NAMED	CREATED	ATTACHED	ORGANIZED	PARENT COUNTIES
Kalkaska	Wabassee	1840	Yes	1871	Mackinac
Kent		1831	Maybe	1836	Mackinac, non-county area
Keweenaw		1861	No	1861	Houghton
Lake	Aishcum	1840	Yes	1871	Mackinac
Lapeer		1822	Yes	1835	Oakland, St. Clair, non-county area
Leelanau		1840	Yes	1863	Mackinac
Lenawee		1822	Yes	1826	Monroe
Livingston		1833	Yes	1836	Shiawassee, Washtenaw
Luce		1887	No	1887	Chippewa, Mackinac
Mackinac	Michilimackinac	1818	No	1818	Wayne, non-county area
Macomb		1818	No	1818	Wayne
Manistee		1840	Yes	1855	Mackinac
Marquette		1843	Yes	1851	Chippewa, Mackinac, non-county area

Michigan Counties at a Glance

COUNTY	FIRST NAMED	CREATED	ATTACHED	ORGANIZED	PARENT COUNTIES
Mason	Notipekago	1840	Yes	1855	Mackinac
Mecosta		1840	Yes	1859	Mackinac, Oceana
Menominee	Bleeker	1861	Yes	1863	Non-county area
Midland		1831	Yes	1855	Saginaw, non-county area
Missaukee		1840	Yes	1871	Mackinac
Monroe		1817	No	1817	Wayne
Montcalm		1831	Yes	1850	Mackinac, non-county area
Montmorency	Cheonoquet	1840	Yes	1881	Mackinac, non-county area
Muskegon		1859	No	1859	Ottawa, non-county area
Newaygo		1840	Yes	1851	Mackinac, Oceana
Oakland		1820	No	1820	Macomb
Oceana		1831	Yes	1855	Mackinac
Ogemaw		1840/1873	Yes	1875	Non-county area/Iosco

Michigan Counties at a Glance

COUNTY	FIRST NAMED	CREATED	ATTACHED	ORGANIZED	PARENT COUNTIES
Ontonagon		1843	Yes	1853	Chippewa, Mackinac
Osceola	Unwattin	1840	Yes	1869	Mackinac
Oscoda		1840	Yes	1881	Mackinac, non-county area
Otsego	Okkuddo	1840	Yes	1875	Mackinac
Ottawa		1831	Yes	1837	Mackinac, non-county area
Presque Isle		1840	Yes	1871	Mackinac
Roscommon	Mikenauk	1840	Yes	1875	Mackinac, non-county area
Saginaw		1822	Yes	1835	St. Clair, non-county area
St. Clair		1821	No	1821	Macomb
St. Joseph		1829	No	1829	Non-county area
Sanilac		1822	Yes	1849	St. Clair, non-county area
Schoolcraft		1843	Yes	1871	Chippewa, Mackinac
Shiawassee		1822	Yes	1837	Oakland, St. Clair, non-county area

Michigan Counties at a Glance

COUNTY	FIRST NAMED	CREATED	ATTACHED	ORGANIZED	PARENT COUNTIES
Tuscola		1840	Yes	1850	Sanilac
Van Buren		1829	Yes	1837	Non-county area
Washtenaw		1822	Yes	1826	Monroe, Oakland, Wayne
Wayne		1815	No	1815	Non-county area
Wexford	Kautawaubet	1840	Yes	1869	Mackinac

Source: *Michigan Atlas of Historical County Boundaries,* compiled by Peggy Tuck Sinko and edited by John H. Long, 1997.

11 Genealogical Collections

Libraries, museums, and archives often have genealogical or historical collections that feature many or all of the sources described in previous chapters of this book. The largest genealogical/historical collection at a Michigan public library is the Burton Historical Collection at the Detroit Public Library <www.detroit.lib.mi.us/burton/burton_index.htm>, located at 5201 Woodward Ave. in downtown Detroit. Opened in 1915, the collection's emphasis is on Detroit and Michigan. It includes 400,000 books, 50,000 microfilms, 250,000 photographs, and 12 million pieces in the manuscript collections. Examples of their holdings include naturalization records for 1852 to 1906 from the Recorder's Court for the City of Detroit; Wayne County coroner's files for 1870 to 1888; and John Farmer's 1855 Map of Wayne County, Michigan, the first county landownership map published in Michigan. Oldenburg's *A Genealogical Guide to The Burton Historical Collection Detroit Public Library* (1988) discusses the library's many sources, and Sprenger's *Guide to the Manuscripts in the Burton Historical Collection Detroit Public Library* (1985) describes almost 2,400 manuscript collections cataloged prior to October 1978. The library's catalog is online. (See pages 346-347 for more.)

The Abrams Foundation Historical Collection at the Library of Michigan in Lansing is "one of the 10 largest genealogy collections in the country."[1] It has more than 100,000 items, including more than 3,000 titles of Michigan newspapers, Michigan vital record indexes and records, and the first purchase of Michigan land from federal and state sales, all on microfilm. The library's catalog is online. In addition, the library publishes a newsletter, the *Abrams Collection Genealogy Highlights,* which describes sources available at the library. Published several times a year, the newsletter's back issues are available on the library's Web site. The Library of Michigan is located in the Michigan Library and Historical Center, 702 W. Kalamazoo St., Lansing, which also houses the State Archives of Michigan and the Michigan Historical Museum.

The State Archives is Michigan's official depository for state records. "Its holdings, numbering over one hundred million items, fall into five basic categories: state government records, local government records, maps, photographs, and private manuscripts."[2] Items of interest to genealogists include tax assessment rolls, naturalization records, and military records, among others. Many of the State Archives' holdings are listed in the Library of Michigan's catalog. In addition, the State Archives has published more than 50 Archival Circulars that describe its holdings, and these also can be found online.

Print sources that describe the holdings of the State Archives include Browne and Johnson's *A Guide to the State Archives of Michigan: State Records* (1977); a number of finding aids, published in the 1960s and 1970s; and the Michigan Genealogical Council's *Guide to the Michigan Genealogical and Historical Collections at the Library of Michigan and the State Archives of Michigan* (1996). The more than 20 finding aids cover such topics as the *Records of the Michigan Military Establishment, 1838-1941* (1962) and the *Records of the Grand Army of the Republic, Michigan Department, 1876-1945* (1966). They are listed in Appendix IV of Browne and Johnson's guide and also can be found in the Library of Michigan catalog. Browne and Johnson's book lists information about state departments and agencies and descriptions of their records available at the Archives. The Michigan Genealogical Council's guide lists federal and state census records; county and local histories; atlases; newspapers on microfilm; vital records; cemetery records; land records; probate records; and additional records, such as naturalization records, for each county. More details about Michigan's state library and archives can be found in the Ingham County section on page xx.

Many local government records also can be found at one of the state's regional depositories. Known as the Regional Depository System, the State Archives has entered into agreements with local archival depositories to store local governmental records that have been transferred to the State Archives in facilities closer to the origins of the records. These depositories and the counties they cover include the following:

- **Central Upper Peninsula and Northern Michigan University Archives** <www.nmu.edu/olsonlibrary/archives/index.htm> in Marquette covering Alger, Delta, Dickinson, Marquette, Menominee, and Schoolcraft counties (see pages 328-329)
- **Central Michigan University's Clark Historical Library** <clarke.cmich.edu/> in Mount Pleasant covering Clare, Gladwin, Gratiot, Isabella, and Midland counties (see page 317)
- **Detroit Public Library's Burton Historical Collections** <www.detroit.lib.mi.us/burton/burton_index.htm> covering the city of Detroit (see pages 346-347)
- **Michigan Technological University Archives and Copper Country Historical Collections** <www.lib.mtu.edu/mtuarchives/guide.aspx> in Houghton covering Baraga, Gogebic, Houghton, Iron, Keweenaw, and Ontonagon counties (see pages 312-313)
- **Oakland University's Kresge Library** <www.kl.oakland.edu>, 2200 N. Squirrel Rd., Rochester covering Oakland County
- **Western Michigan University Archives and Regional History Collections** <www.wmich.edu/library/archives/index.php> in Kalamazoo covering Allegan, Barry, Berrien, Branch, Calhoun, Cass, Kalamazoo, Kent, Muskegon, Ottawa, Saint Joseph, and Van Buren counties (see page 320)

The second largest genealogical collection in the country is about 50 miles from Michigan's southern border. The Reynolds Historical Genealogy Department at the Allen County Public Library <www.acpl.lib.in.us/genealogy/index.html> in Fort Wayne, Indiana, has holdings for the entire United States and some foreign countries. However, its emphasis is on Midwestern local history, including Michigan. Its collection of nearly 600,000 items is the largest at a public library in the country (see pages 349-350).

Family History Centers of the Church of Jesus Christ of Latter-day Saints (Mormons) allow researchers access to the church's enormous Family History Library at Salt Lake City, Utah. Researchers can rent for a small fee microfilms from Salt Lake City of such items as county, church, cemetery, land, and naturalization records. There are 38 Family History Centers in Michigan. Because volunteers staff these centers, hours may vary and volunteers are not able to respond to mail inquiries. The Family History Library's catalog is online at the FamilySearch Web site <www.familysearch.org/> and includes many sources for Michigan. At this writing, Family History Centers are located in Adrian, Ann Arbor, Battle Creek, Benton Harbor, Big Rapids, Bloomfield Hills, Cadillac, Cheboygan, Clarkston, Escanaba, Flint, Gaylord, Grand Blanc, Grand Rapids, Harvey, Hastings, Houghton, Howell, Jackson, Jonesville, Kalamazoo, Kingsford, Lansing, Ludington, Midland, Mount Pleasant, Muskegon, Owosso, Petoskey, Riverview, Rochester Hills, Roseville, Saint Clair, South Haven, Sturgis, Traverse City, West Branch, and Westland. The FamilySearch Web site has a current list of addresses and hours for these centers.

Although large collections have much to offer, researchers shouldn't overlook smaller collections, particularly if they are located in the area they are studying. Most Michigan libraries offer visitors free access to AncestryPlus, the library version of Ancestry.com, or other databases. Researchers who can't visit Michigan's libraries in person can still visit them from home through the Internet. Many libraries have Web sites with online catalogs, finding aids, collection descriptions, photographs, or databases of genealogical records. Some of these resources are listed below.[3]

On the **Web**

The Library of Michigan and the State Archives of Michigan have provided genealogist with a number of online resources, such as:

1870 Michigan census index and images
Michigan cemetery sources
Michigan county clerk's directory
Michigan naturalization record indexes

These sources can be found through the state's Web site <www.michigan.gov/hal>. Select "Resources for Genealogists."

Alcona County

Alcona County Library
312 W. Main St. (M-72)
P.O. Box 348
Harrisville, Mich. 48740-0348
Telephone: (989) 724-6796
Fax: (989) 724-6173
Web site: <www.alcona.lib.mi.us/harrisville.htm>

Hours: Open 10 a.m. to 7 p.m. Mondays through Thursdays; 10 a.m. to 5 p.m. Fridays; and 10 a.m. to 2 p.m. Saturdays.

Genealogical/historical collection: About 1,000 volumes. Microfilm and CDs do not circulate. Includes databases; Federal census records for Alcona County; cemetery records; county or local history books; newspapers; and periodicals (genealogical or historical).

Items in this collection that may not be found in others include locally produced books on the cemeteries of Alcona County.

Written queries: "If dates are given, we will look up some obituaries. No set cost; cost depends on the amount of copies and staff time spent researching."

Allegan County

Herrick District Library
300 S. River Ave.
Holland, Mich. 49423-3247
Telephone: (616) 355-3709
Fax: (616) 355-3083
E-mail: <genealogy@llcoop.org>
Web site: <www.herrickdl.org/genealogy/index.html>

Hours: Open 9 a.m. to 9 p.m. Mondays through Thursdays; 9 a.m. to 5 p.m. Fridays and Saturdays; and 2 to 5 p.m. Sundays (except summers).

Genealogical/historical collection: This is reported to be the largest collection of Dutch resources east of the Mississippi River. Consists of 4,000 books, 200 CDs, and two online computers. Most books are for in-house use. About 100 books circulate. Includes federal census records for Michigan and other states; state census records for 1884 and 1894; cemetery records; county or local history books; church records; city directories; DAR records; family genealogies; land records; maps or atlases; military records; local newspapers; periodicals (genealogical or historical); vital records; and Filby's passenger ships indexes.

Items in this collection that may not be found in others include "600,000 obituaries from Muskegon, Grand Rapids, Holland, Kalamazoo, Fremont, South Bend, Grand Haven, Allegan."

Written queries: Will answer. Fee is $15 per hour.

Other: "The purpose of the Herrick District Library's Genealogy Collection is to collect resources that will document the history of Holland area families as well as assist families from other parts of Allegan and Ottawa counties." The library has an online Surname Index <www.herrickdl.org/genealogy/indices/AB.html> for some of the sources in the genealogy collection.

Barry County

Delton District Library
330 N. Grove St.
P.O. Box 155
Delton, Mich. 49046
Telephone: (269) 623-8040
Fax: (269) 623-6740
E-mail: <ddl@mei.net>
Web site: <www.deltonlib.org>

Hours: Open 10 a.m. to 5 p.m. Mondays, Wednesdays, and Fridays; 10 a.m. to 8 p.m. Tuesdays and Thursdays; and 9 a.m. to 1 p.m. Saturdays.

Genealogical/historical collection: The "small" collection is for in-house use only. Includes databases; 1870 federal census records for Michigan; cemetery records; county or local history books; church records; family genealogies; maps or atlases; and obituaries.

Items in this collection that may not be found in others include "*Years Gone By* by Prosper Bernard, a locally written and published history of the area; some old church records on index cards; and many obituaries on index cards dating back to early 1900s."

Written queries: Will answer. "There is no cost for our services if the query is simple, but copies are 15 cents per page, plus postage."

Bay County

Bay City Branch Library
708 Center Ave.
Bay City, Mich. 48708-5949
Telephone: (989) 893-9566
Fax: (989) 893-9799
Web site: <baycountylibrary.org/bbc.htm>

Hours: Open 9 a.m. to 9 p.m. Mondays through Thursdays; 9 a.m. to 5 p.m. Fridays and Saturdays; and 1 p.m. to 4 p.m. Sundays (September through May).

Genealogical/historical collection: 56 feet of shelving for books, plus microforms. Includes databases (AncestryPlus); federal census records for Michigan; state census records for Bay County; county or local history books; city directories; family genealogies; maps or atlases; and newspapers.

Written queries: Will answer. Cost includes copy charges of 25 cents per page, plus postage.

Benzie County

Benzonia Public Library
891 Michigan Ave.
P.O. Box 445
Benzonia, Mich. 49616-0445
Telephone: (231) 882-4111
Fax: (231) 882-4111

Hours: Open 11 a.m. to 5 p.m. Mondays, Wednesdays, and Fridays; Tuesdays and Thursdays; 11 a.m. to 7 p.m.; and 11 a.m. to 3 p.m. Saturdays.

Genealogical/historical collection: Some materials only can be used in the library. Includes county or local history books; "a few" family genealogies; land records; and newspapers.

Items in this collection that may not be found in others include back issues of the area weekly newspaper. "It dates back to 1888 and is bound by year. There is an alphabetical index of most names found in the paper."

Written queries: Will answer for "cost to cover time and materials."

Berrien County

Benton Harbor Public Library
213 E. Wall St.
Benton Harbor, Mich. 49022-4499
Telephone: (269) 926-6139
Fax: (269) 926-1674
E-mail: <bhlibrary@yahoo.com>
Web site: <www.geocities.com/bhlibrary>

Hours: Open 9 a.m. to 8 p.m. Mondays and Wednesdays; 9 a.m. to 6 p.m. Tuesdays, Thursdays and Fridays; and 9 a.m. to 5 p.m. Saturdays.

Genealogical/historical collection: About 600 volumes. Includes federal census records for Berrien County; cemetery indexes; county or local history books; city directories; family genealogies; maps or atlases; and newspapers.

Items in this collection that may not be found in others include *Herald-Palladium* and *News-Palladium* newspapers on microfilm dating back to October 1868 and *Berrien Roots* on CD, an index of marriage (1832-1929) and death records (1867-1929) maintained at the 1839 Courthouse Museum in Berrien Springs.

Written queries: "The base cost for obituary research is $3 for searching up to three obituaries, if the day, month, and year are known. The charge is applied regardless of the success of the search. An individual may request up to six obituaries per month, if an exact date, month, and year are provided for each item. If only the month and year are known, the cost is $3 per search. Names of individuals and businesses may be looked up in the Benton Harbor-Saint Joseph city directories dating back to the 1890s. The cost is the same as the obituaries – $3 for searching and copying up to three listings, if names and years are given. A maximum of six listings per month may be ordered. Newspaper articles may be ordered for a base fee of $8, plus $1 per article for up to 10 articles if the day, month, and year are known. Staff will be unable to search unless an exact date is given. The staff reserves the right to refuse a newspaper research request if time is a limiting factor."

Berrien Springs Community Library
215 W. Union St.
Berrien Springs, Mich. 49103
E-mail: <bslibrary@qtm.net>
Web site: <www.bsclibrary.org>
Hours: Open 10 a.m. to 8 p.m. Mondays through Thursdays; 10 a.m. to 6 p.m. Fridays; and 10 a.m. to 4 p.m. Saturdays.

Genealogical/historical collection: About 400 volumes, half owned by the Berrien County Genealogical Society. Library books circulate; society books do not. The collection includes databases; federal census records for Michigan; cemetery records; county or local history books; family genealogies; maps or atlases; newspapers; periodicals (genealogical or historical); and the Berrien County marriage record index (1831-1902) and death record index (1867-1919).

Items in this collection that may not be found in others include the *Berrien Springs Journal Era* newspaper on microfilm (1873-1973). Hard copies of the *Journal* are available from 1972 to the present.

Written queries: Will answer for "a minimal charge of $2 or a voluntary donation."

Fort Miami Heritage Society
708 Market St.
Saint Joseph, Mich. 49085
Telephone: (269) 983-1191
Fax: (269) 983-1274
Web site: <www.fortmiami.org>
Hours: Open 9 a.m. to 5 p.m. Tuesdays through Fridays by appointment.

Genealogical/historical collection: "Our total collection includes approximately 300 books, 200 cubic feet of paper records, 50 maps, and 1,000 photographs. Access to the collection is by appointment only." It includes county or local history books; city directories; maps or atlases; original papers, manuscripts, diaries; periodicals (genealogical or historical); and oral histories.

Items in this collection that may not be found in others include "a number of oral histories of the Saint Joseph/Benton Harbor area, conducted by the Fort Miami Heritage Society. We have a number of rare books related to Michigan history, and particularly to the history of the Saint Joseph/Benton Harbor area."

Written queries: "At this time, there is no charge for research services."

Mary's City of David
1158 E. Britain Ave.
P.O. Box 187
Benton Harbor, Mich. 49023-0187
Telephone: (269) 925-1601
Fax: (269) 925-2154
E-mail: <info@maryscityofdavid.org>
Web site: <www.maryscityofdavid.org>
Hours: Open 1 p.m. to 5 p.m. weekdays.

Genealogical/historical collection: Restricted access. Includes newspapers; original papers, manuscripts, diaries; and vital records.

Items in this collection that may not be found in others include original photographs and literature imprints.

Written queries: Will answer. "Costs are dependant on time usage and volume of materials requested."

Other: This is the largest collection of original photographs and literature spanning 200 years, 1792-1992, particular to Mary's City of David, the Israelite House of David as reorganized by Mary Purnell in 1930.

North Berrien Historical Museum
300 Coloma Ave.
Coloma, Mich. 49038-9724

Genealogical/historical collection: Includes county or local history books; family genealogies; and maps or atlases.

Niles District Library
620 E. Main St.
Niles, Mich. 49120-2620
Telephone: (269) 683-8545
Fax: (269) 683-0075
E-mail: <LH-gene@nileslibrary.com>
Web site: <www.nileslibrary.com/localhistory.htm>

Hours: Open 9 a.m. to 8 p.m. Mondays through Thursdays and 9 a.m. to 5 p.m. Fridays and Saturdays.

Genealogical/historical collection: Collection does not circulate. Includes databases; federal census records for Michigan; county or local history books; city directories; maps or atlases; newspapers; periodicals (genealogical or historical); tax lists; and vital records.

Items in this collection that may not be found in others include "local newspapers on microfilm, local high school yearbooks, and an index to obituaries in the Niles newspapers."

Written queries: "Limited research services are available. If an exact date of death is known, an obituary will be copied for $2. Other research is done for $6 per hour."

Three Oaks Township Public Library
3 N. Elm St.
Three Oaks, Mich. 49128
Telephone: (269) 756-5621
Fax: (269) 756-3004
E-mail: <enieman@qtm.net>
Web site: <quicksitebuilder.cnet.com/threeoaks/>

Hours: Open 10 a.m. to 6 p.m. Mondays, Wednesdays, and Fridays; 10 a.m. to 8 p.m. Tuesdays and Thursdays; and 10 a.m. to 4 p.m. Saturdays.

Genealogical/historical collection: "We have one of the largest local collections in the area." Includes databases; federal and state census records; cemetery records; county or local history books; a few city directories; DAR records; family genealogies; land records; maps or atlases; military records; newspapers; and tax lists.

Items in this collection that may not be found in others include "the newspaper archive back to 1894 and the only index to the names in the *History of Berrien County* by Judge Orville Coolidge."

Written queries: Will answer. "Cost can vary."

Other: "We have a volunteer genealogist every Friday afternoon from 1 p.m. to 4:30 p.m."

Branch County

Branch District Library
10 E. Chicago St.
Coldwater, Mich. 49036-1615
Telephone: (517) 278-2341
Web site: <www.brnlibrary.org/>

Hours: Open 10 a.m. to 8 p.m. Mondays; 9 a.m. to 8 p.m. Tuesdays through Thursdays; 9 a.m. to 5 p.m. Fridays; and 9 a.m. to 4 p.m. Saturdays.

Genealogical/historical collection: More than 500 books, tapes and microfilms. "Most of the items are to be used in the Holbrook Heritage Room only. Some of our books may be checked out for seven days." Includes databases; federal census records for Michigan and a few other states; state census records; cemetery records; county or local history books; some church records; city directories; some DAR record books; family genealogies; land records; maps or atlases; military records; newspapers; original papers, manuscripts, diaries; periodicals (genealogical or historical); and death indexes.

Items in this collection that may not be found in others include "a large collection of materials on the history of Coldwater and Branch County, Michigan."

Written queries: Will answer. "We do not charge for queries other than 15 cents per photocopy or computer copy, 25 cents for microfilm copies, and we also charge for postage."

Union Township Library
221 N. Broadway
Union City, Mich. 49094
Telephone: (517) 741-5061
Fax: (517) 741-5061
E-mail: <union@brnlibrary.org>
Web site: <www.brnlibrary.org/bru.html>

Hours: Open 9:30 a.m. to 5 p.m. Tuesdays; 11:30 a.m. to 7 p.m. Wednesdays; 9:30 a.m. to 4:30 p.m. Fridays; and 9:30 a.m. to noon Saturdays.

Genealogical/historical collection: "Minimal" collection for in-house use only. Includes cemetery records; county or local history books; and city directories.

Written queries: Will not answer.

Calhoun County

Marshall District Library
124 W. Green St.
Marshall, Mich. 49068
Telephone: (269) 781-7821
Fax: (269) 781-7090

Hours: Open 10 a.m. to 8:30 a.m. Mondays through Wednesdays; 10 a.m. to 5:30 p.m. Thursdays and Fridays; and 10 a.m. to 3 p.m. Saturdays.

Genealogical/historical collection: About 100 books for in-house use only. Includes federal census records for Calhoun County; cemetery records; county or local history books; church records; city directories; family genealogies; land records; and newspapers.

Items in this collection that may not be found in others include "Marshall newspapers on microfilm back to 1838."

Written queries: Will answer. "Must send the request in writing with money for photocopies (at least 25 cents per page) and a self-addressed stamped envelope. Dates are required as our microfilm is not indexed."

Willard Library
7 W. Van Buren St.
Battle Creek, Mich. 49017-3080
Telephone: (269) 968-8166
Web site: <www.willard.lib.mi.us>

Genealogical/historical collection: 9,500 items. Includes databases (immigration and census); all federal census records for Michigan (including 1930) and some for other states; state census records; cemetery records; county or local history books; city directories; DAR records; family genealogies; probate and land records (for Calhoun County, on microfilm); maps or atlases; newspapers; original papers, manuscripts, and diaries; periodicals (genealogical or historical); and vital records (Calhoun County's death and marriage records, on microfilm).

Items in this collection that may not be found in others include "news index since 1852 and the Dorothy Martich Black History Photo Archive."

Written queries: Will answer.

Other: Willard Library's Historical Images of Battle Creek <www2.willard.lib.mi.us> includes photographs of Battle Creek homes and buildings; photographs from Battle Creek's history; and the Dorothy Martich Black History Photo Archive.

Cass County

Cass District Library
319 M-62 North
Cassopolis, Mich. 49031-1099
E-mail: <cass@cass.lib.mi.us>
Web site: <cass.lib.mi.us/>

Hours: Open 9 a.m. to 8 p.m. Mondays through Thursdays; 9 a.m. to 6 p.m. Fridays; and 9 a.m. to 3 p.m. Saturdays.

Genealogical/historical collection: "No materials can leave the building." Collection includes federal census records for Michigan; cemetery records for Cass County; county or local history books; family genealogies; maps or atlases; newspapers (local from 1872); and vital records (birth and death records on microfilm from 1867 and marriage records on microfilm from 1830).

Written queries: Will answer for cost of copies and postage.

Southwestern Michigan College Museum
58900 Cherry Grove Rd.
Dowagiac, Mich. 49047
Telephone: (269) 782-1378
Fax: (269) 782-1460
Web site: <www.smc.cc.mi.us/museum/exhibit.htm>

Hours: Open 10 a.m. to 5 p.m. Tuesdays, Thursdays, Fridays, and Saturdays; and 10 a.m. to 8 p.m. Wednesdays.

Genealogical/historical collection: "16,000 artifacts with minimal genealogical resources. Must make an appointment with the curator of history." Includes federal census records for Michigan; county or local history books; city directories; maps or atlases; newspapers; and original papers, manuscripts, and diaries.

Written queries: Will answer specific requests. Search fee is $25 per hour, plus 15 cents per photocopy.

Other: "Our museum primarily houses artifacts and has little in its collections for use in genealogy. There are newspapers and directories, but few land records and letters. We do have files on some of the prominent families of Cass County."

Charlevoix County

Boyne District Library

201 E. Main St.

Boyne City, Mich. 49712

Fax: (231) 582-2998

E-mail: <boynecl@northland.lib.mi.us>

Web site: <nlc.lib.mi.us/members/boyne_c.htm>

Hours: Open 9 a.m. to 8 p.m. Mondays through Thursdays and 9 a.m. to 5 p.m. Fridays and Saturdays.

Genealogical/historical collection: Small collection for in-house use only includes federal census records for Michigan; Antrim and Charlevoix county cemetery records; county or local history books; church records ("two for Boyne City"); city directories; family genealogies; genealogical periodicals; maps or atlases; newspapers; and vital records (birth and death).

Items in this collection that may not be found in others include city directories for Boyne City, 1934 and 1940; East Jordan, 1941; and Charlevoix, 1940.

Written queries: Will answer. "If it is a small search, it's free. Otherwise, we would probably give it to the genealogy society."

Other: "The local newspaper is on microfilm until 1960. After that, they are housed at City Hall."

Charlevoix Public Library

109 W. Clinton St.

Charlevoix, Mich. 49720-1399

Telephone: (231) 547-2651

Fax: (231) 547-0678

E-mail: <info@charlevoixlibrary.org>

Web site: <www.charlevoixlibrary.org/genealogy.htm>

Hours: Open 10 a.m. to 8 p.m. Mondays through Thursdays; 10 a.m. to 5 p.m. Fridays; and 10 a.m. to 3 p.m. Saturdays.

Genealogical/historical collection: Many volumes for in-house use only. Includes county/local history books; city directories; and newspapers.

Written queries: Will answer.

Other: The library's Web site includes photographer and historian Bob Miles' materials about Charlevoix County <www.charlevoix.lib.mi.us/main-m.htm> and the highlights of Charlevoix County history (1869-1906) from Rosa Nettleton's book <www.charlevoix.lib.mi.us/main-n.htm>. Nettleton's book is searchable.

Chippewa County

Bayliss Public Library

541 Library Dr.

Sault Ste. Marie, Mich. 49783

Telephone: (906) 632-9331

Fax: (906) 635-0210

E-mail: <bayref@uproc.lib.mi.us>

Web site: <www.uproc.lib.mi.us/bpl/>

Hours: Open 9 a.m. to 9 p.m. Tuesdays and Thursdays; 9 a.m. to 5:30 p.m. Wednesdays and Fridays; 9 a.m. to 1 p.m. Saturdays (in the summer); and 9 a.m. to 4 p.m. Saturdays (in the winter).

Genealogical/historical collection: The Judge Joseph H. Steere Room is open by appointment. Four researchers are allowed in the room at one time. There also are three microfilm machines that can be used without appointment. Collection includes databases; federal census records for Michigan; state census records; cemetery records; county or local history books; church records; city directories; family genealogies; maps or atlases; newspapers; original papers, manuscripts and diaries; periodicals (genealogical or historical); vital records; photographs; CDs; Durant Rolls; high school yearbooks; telephone books; and obituary notebooks.

Items in this collection that may not be found in others include Sault Ste. Marie history, manuscript collections, and photographs.

Written queries: "Queries answered by Reference Librarian when possible. List of local professional genealogists also is available."

Other: The library's Web site has abstracts of Chippewa County marriages <www.baylisslib.org/marriages.html>, Chippewa County death records <www.baylisslib.org/deaths.html>, the 1846 Annuity List for Lake Superior Chippewa Indians <www.baylisslib.org/1846annuity.html>, cemetery transcriptions <www.baylisslib.org/cemtrans.html>, and other genealogical information.

Clare County

Harrison Community Library

105 W. Main St.
Harrison, Mich. 48625

Telephone: (989) 539-6711

Fax: (989) 539-6301

Web site: <www.geocities.com/Athens/ithaca/4577/>

Hours: Open 10 a.m. to 7:30 p.m. Mondays through Thursdays; and 10 a.m. to 5 p.m. Fridays and Saturdays.

Genealogical/historical collection: 12 linear feet (12 archival boxes), plus 12 Princeton files for in-house use only. Includes databases; federal census records for Michigan; cemetery records; county or local history books; city directories; family genealogies; maps or atlases; military records; newspapers; original papers, manuscripts and diaries; historical photographs; and artifacts of early Harrison.

Written queries: "We will check newspapers on microfilm and mail copies of obits."

Emmet County

Petoskey Public Library
451 E. Mitchell St.
Petoskey, Mich. 49770-2623
Telephone: (231) 347-4211
Fax: (231) 348-8662
E-mail: <library@petoskeylibrary.org>
Web site: <www.petoskeylibrary.org>

Hours: Open 10 a.m. to 8 p.m. Mondays through Thursdays; 10 a.m. to 5 p.m. Fridays; and 9:30 a.m. to 3 p.m. Saturdays.

Genealogical/historical collection: Includes cemetery records (six volumes); county or local history books; city directories; genealogical periodicals; maps or atlases; newspapers (200 rolls of local newspapers on microfilm).

Written queries: Will answer. "Usually it's free unless extraordinary depth is required." Copies are 15 cents per page. Postage is extra.

Genesee County

Flint Public Library
1026 E. Kearsley St.
Flint, Mich. 48502-1994
Telephone: (810) 232-7111
Web site: <flint.lib.mi.us/genealogy/index.html>

Hours: Open 9 a.m. to 9 p.m. Mondays through Thursdays and 9 a.m. to 6 p.m. Fridays and Saturdays.

Genealogical/historical collection: "28,957 items in the Genealogical, Michigan History, and Local History Collection and 380 rolls of census microfilm" for in-house use only. Includes databases; federal census records for Michigan and other states; state census records; cemetery records; county or local history books; church records; city directories; DAR records; family genealogies; land records; maps or atlases; military records; newspapers; periodicals (genealogical or historical); and vital records.

Items in this collection that may not be found in others include "the Genesee Biography File, many local history scrapbooks, and a local obituary index. We have indexes for all of the Flint/Genesee County history books."

Written queries: Will answer. "Fees quoted on request. SASE appreciated."

Other: "The collection at the Flint Public Library has a great deal on the local area as well as materials from New England, New York, Ohio, and Pennsylvania. We have the census on microform for the Province of Ontario, Canada, as well as the Ontario Vital Records Index also on microform. Obituaries that appeared in the Flint newspapers are indexed for the last 100 years. The library has most of the early city directories for Flint either in print or in microform. We also hold copies of the cemetery readings, published by the Flint Genealogical Society."

Sloan Museum
Buick Gallery and Research Center/Perry Archives
303 Walnut St.
Flint, Mich. 48503
Telephone: (810) 237-3440
E-mail: <sloan@flintcultural.org>
Web site: <www.sloanmuseum.com/index.html>

Genealogical/historical collection: "The archives are not open to the public, but researchers can view the information in our reading room by appointment by calling (810) 237-3440." Collection includes cemetery records; county or local history books; city directories; DAR records; family genealogies; land abstracts; maps or atlases; military records; newspapers; original papers, manuscripts, diaries; city tax lists from 1892; and funeral home records.

Items in this collection that may not be found in others include Genesee County Circuit Court Records, 1872-1970s.

Written queries: Will answer.

University of Michigan-Flint
Frances Willson Thompson Library
Genesee Historical Collections Center, Room 227
Flint, Mich. 48502
Telephone: (810) 762-3402
Web site: <lib.umflint.edu/archives>

Hours: Open 1 p.m. to 5 p.m. weekdays and 6 p.m. to 9 p.m. Wednesdays.

Genealogical/historical collection: 300 cubic feet for in-house use only. Includes federal census records for Michigan; cemetery records; county or local history books; church records; city directories; maps or atlases; newspapers; and naturalization records for Genesee County.

Items in this collection that may not be found in others include manuscript collections.

Written queries: Will answer "normally at no cost."

Gladwin County

Gladwin County Library
555 W. Cedar Ave.
Gladwin, Mich. 48624
Telephone: (989) 426-8221
Web site: <www.gladwinlibrary.org/>

Hours: Open 9 a.m. to 8 p.m. Mondays through Thursdays and 9 a.m. to 5 p.m. Fridays and Saturdays.

Genealogical/historical collection: Small collection for in-house use only. Includes state census records; county or local history books; maps or atlases; and newspapers.

Written queries: Will answer. Cost is 15 cents per copy, plus postage.

Hillsdale County

Friends of Mitchell Research Center
22 N. Manning St.
Hillsdale, Mich. 49242-1624

Genealogical/historical collection: 15,000 items for in-house use only. Includes databases; federal census records for Hillsdale County; cemetery records; county or local history books; church records; city directories; DAR records; family genealogies; land record index; maps or atlases; military records; newspapers; original papers, manuscripts and diaries; periodicals (genealogical or historical); vital records; school records and yearbooks; and Hillsdale College records.

Written queries: Will answer requests by mail. Include "necessary information to help find answers quickly." Cost goes up when more time is spent on request.

Other: "We plan to add to our collection of family pictures, historic buildings, and events." There also are plans to add archival items as space permits.

Houghton County

Finlandia University
Finnish-American Historical Archives
601 Quincy St.
Hancock, Mich. 49930-1882
Telephone: (906) 487-7347
Fax: (906) 487-7557
Web site: <www.finlandia.edu/fahc.html>
Hours: Open 8 a.m. to 4:30 p.m. weekdays.

Genealogical/historical collection: More than 20,000 items for in-house use only. "Electronic scanning is forbidden." Includes county or local history books; family genealogies; newspapers; original papers, manuscripts, diaries; periodicals (genealogical or historical); and church records from Finland and Finnish Churches in America.

Items in this collection that may not be found in others include Finnish language newspapers and periodicals and photographs.

Written queries: Will answer. "One hour research for $15 prepaid. Send request through standard mail."

Other: "The Finnish-American Historical Archives has the distinction of housing the most comprehensive Finnish-American archival collection in the world." The Archives is part of the Finnish-American Heritage Center, which includes a theater, art gallery, and museum.

Michigan Technological University
Copper Country Historical Collection
1400 Townsend Dr.
Houghton, Mich. 49931-1295

Telephone: (906) 487-2505
Fax: (906) 487-2357
E-mail: <copper@mtu.edu>
Web site: <www.lib.mtu.edu/mtuarchives/overview.aspx>
Hours: Open 1 p.m. to 5 p.m. weekdays.

Genealogical/historical collection: 10,000 linear feet for in-house use only. Includes databases; federal census records for Michigan; state census records; cemetery records; county or local history books; church records; city directories; family genealogies; land records; maps or atlases; newspapers; original papers, manuscripts and diaries; periodicals (genealogical or historical); tax lists; photographs; and some non-current public records, including tax, circuit court, and naturalization.

Items in this collection that may not be found in others include copper mining company employee records.

Written queries: "We will do simple searches (under one hour) for $10. We refer more extensive requests to a list of local researchers for hire."

Other: "We are a general regional history collection housing information about communities, industries, businesses, and people, primarily in Houghton and Keweenaw counties but also in Baraga, Ontonagon, Gogebic, and Iron counties." The archive's Web site includes cemetery transcriptions <www.lib.mtu.edu/mtuarchives/cemetery/ms027.aspx>.

Huron County

Bad Axe Public Library
200 S. Hanselman St.
Bad Axe, Mich. 48413-1479
Web site: <main.badaxelibrary.org/bapl/>

Genealogical/historical collection: 50 books, cemetery records, and newspapers on microfilm from 1867 to present for in-house use only. Collection also includes federal census records for Huron County; county or local history books; church records; family genealogies; and maps or atlases.

Items in this collection that may not be found in others include Huron County newspapers.

Written queries: Will not answer.

Huron City Museums
7995 Pioneer Dr.
Port Austin, Mich. 48467
Telephone: (989) 428-4123
Fax: (989) 428-4123
E-mail: <huroncity@centurytel.net>
Web site: <www.huroncitymuseums.org/>

Genealogical/historical collection: Museums are closed in the winter. "Private collection of diaries, letters, ledgers – 16 steel cases, 12,000 volumes of

On the Web

The Library of Michigan publishes *Abrams Collection Genealogy Highlights,* a newsletter that focuses on the library's resources. Back issues are available through HAL, the State of Michigan's History, Arts, and Libraries site <www.michigan.gov/hal>. Select "Publications and Products," then "Newsletters," and then *"Abrams Collection Genealogy Highlights."* Recent newsletters focused on:

- Genealogy Research with Michigan State Census Records
- Michigan Cemetery Sources
- 1930 Federal Census Research
- Michigan Local Histories and Biographies
- Naturalization Resources
- Michigan Civil War Research
- Genealogical Research With Military Records
- Research in the Old Northwest
- Michigan Documents
- Genealogical Research With Maps and Atlases
- Immigration and Passenger Lists
- 50 Best Michigan Genealogical Resources

books." Includes family genealogies; land records; maps or atlases; newspapers; original papers, manuscripts and diaries; ledgers; business records; and photographs.

Items in this collection that may not be found in others include "original papers, manuscripts, and ledgers of the Hubbards of Connecticut and William Lyon Phelps."

Written queries: Will not answer.

Other: "Our collection is not large and covers a specific family group. The oldest letters date back to about 1816."

Ingham County

Capital Area District Library, Main Library
401 S. Capitol Ave.
Lansing, Mich. 48843
Telephone: (517) 367-6363
Fax: (517) 367-6333
Web site: <www.cadl.org>

Genealogical/historical collection: Closed stacks. Includes county or local history books; city directories; newspapers; and tax lists.

Written queries: Will answer "as time provides." Please send a SASE.

Catholic Diocese of Lansing
1500 E. Saginaw St., Suite 2
Lansing, Mich. 48906-5550
Telephone: (517) 485-9902
Fax: (517) 484-8880
Web site: <www.dioceseoflansing.org/>
Hours: Open 9 a.m. to 4 p.m. Tuesdays.

Genealogical/historical collection: Includes parish history books; church records; newspapers (*Catholic Weekly,* 1954-1991, and *Catholic Times,* 1991-present); and original papers, manuscripts and diaries.

Items in this collection that may not be found in others include "materials relating to bishops, clergy and parishes at the Diocese of Lansing."

Written queries: Will answer.

Library of Michigan
Abrams Foundation Historical Collection
702 W. Kalamazoo St.
P.O. Box 30007
Lansing, Mich. 48909-7507
Telephone: (517) 373-1300
Fax: (517) 373-5853
E-mail: <librarian@michigan.gov>
Web site: <www.michigan.gov/hal>
Hours: Open 8 a.m. to 6 p.m. weekdays; 9 a.m. to 5 p.m. Saturdays; and 1 p.m. to 5 p.m. Sundays.

Genealogical/historical collection: More than 100,000 items for in-house use only. Includes databases; federal census records for Michigan and other states; state census records; cemetery records; county or local history books; church records; city directories; DAR records; family genealogies; land records; maps or atlases; military records; newspapers; original papers, manuscripts and diaries; periodicals (genealogical or historical); tax lists; vital records; microfiche indexes to the Michigan Centennial and Sesquicentennial Project Files; and Michigan Pioneer Records.

Items in this collection that may not be found in others include "Michigan cemetery readings; the first purchase of Michigan land from federal and state sales; Michigan vital records; all U.S. and Canadian census records; most state census records that survived; a small manuscript collection; a large collection of Michigan materials, including state documents; a large collection of National Archive materials; and the UMI Genealogy and Local History Collection."

Written queries: "We will only do a limited amount of research due to staffing and time restrictions. We do not do extensive research. There is no charge. SASE is nice but not required. Do not send money."

Other: "The State Archives is housed in the same building but with different hours, requirements, address, and management. You must contact the archives separately. We subscribe to AncestryPlus, Heritage Quest Online, and other electronic databases." The library's Web site includes an index and images of the 1870 Michigan census <envoy.libraryofmichigan.org/1870_census> and Michigan Cemetery Sources <michigancemeteries.libraryofmichigan.org>, an online version of the *Michigan Cemetery Atlas* (1991) and the *Michigan Cemetery Source Book* (1994).

State Archives of Michigan
Michigan Historical Center
702 W. Kalamazoo St.
P.O. Box 30740
Lansing, Mich. 48909
Telephone: (517) 373-1408
Fax: (517) 241-1658

On the **Web**

The State Archives of Michigan has prepared a number of Archival Circulars – or finding aids – on a variety of topics. They are available online through HAL, the State of Michigan's History, Arts, and Libraries site <www.michigan.gov/hal>. Select "Publications and Products" and then "Research Guides and Reading Lists." Circulars of interest to genealogists include:

Account Books and Ledgers
Associations and Organizations
Business Records
Census Records
Circuit Court Records
Civil War Manuscripts
Correctional Facilities
Depression-era Agencies
Diaries, Daybooks, and Personal Journals
Election Records
Infirmaries, Sanatoria and Poor Homes
Land Records
Licensed Professions
Manuscript Records
Mental Health Records
Military Records
Rural Property Inventories
School Records
Tax/Assessment Rolls
Vital Records

E-mail: <archives@michigan.gov>
Web site: <www.michigan.gov/hal>
Hours: Open 10 a.m. to 4 p.m. weekdays. "Advance appointments are not required, but they may make research visits more worthwhile."

Genealogical/historical collection: For in-house use only. Some medical records are confidential. Holdings fall into five basic categories: "state government records, local government records, maps, photographs, and private manuscripts." Includes land records; maps or atlases; military records; original papers, manuscripts, and diaries; and tax lists. Documents date back to 1792.

Items in this collection that may not be found in others include "Michigan probate and circuit court records, Michigan naturalization records, and Michigan prison records."

Written queries: "Brief inquiries received by letter, e-mail, and telephone will be promptly handled at no charge to the researcher." Check the Archives' Web site for a listing of other research fees.

Other: Archives established in 1913. The archives' Web site includes indexes to naturalization records for several Michigan counties and a Michigan County Clerk's Directory.

University Archives and Historical Collections
Michigan State University Libraries
101 Conrad Hall
East Lansing, Mich. 48824-1327
Telephone: (517) 355-2330
Web site: <www.msu.edu/unit/msuarhc>

Historical collection: Historical collections are approximately 3,000 feet, and the university archives is more than 25,000 feet. Includes original papers, manuscripts, and diaries. All items in this collection are one-of-a-kind.

Written queries: Will not answer.

Ionia County

Hall-Fowler Memorial Library
126 E. Main St.
Ionia, Mich. 48846-1630
E-mail: <ion@llcoop.org>
Web site: <ionia.llcoop.org/>

Genealogical/historical collection: Small collection for in-house use only. Includes state census records for Ionia County; cemetery records; county or local history books; city directories; family genealogies ("a few donated copies"); maps or atlases; and newspapers.

Written queries: "Will search and photocopy on a limited basis. We must have specific dates. Cost is 25 cents per copy and a legal-sized self-addressed stamped envelope. If the request appears to be time consuming, then we refer them to a professional researcher."

Isabella County

Central Michigan University
Clarke Historical Library
250 Preston St.
Mount Pleasant, Mich. 48859
Telephone: (989) 774-3352
Fax: (989) 774-2160
Web site: <clarke.cmich.edu/>
E-mail: <clarke@cmich.edu>

Genealogical/historical collection: "The historical collection focuses on the history of Michigan and the Old Northwest Territory. The library also serves as the archives of its parent institution, Central Michigan University. The historical collection includes more than 65,000 volumes, 2,500 manuscript collections, 11,000 reels of microfilm, 16,000 visual images, and 3,000 maps." Collection is non-circulating with closed stacks. Includes federal census records for Michigan; state census records; cemetery records; county or local history books; church records; city directories; DAR records; family genealogies; land records; military records; a large collection of microfilmed newspapers; original papers, manuscripts, and diaries; and vital records.

Other: The library's Web site includes the full text of several Michigan county histories <clarke.cmich.edu/online.htm>.

Jackson County

Jackson District Library – Carnegie Branch
244 W. Michigan Ave.
Jackson, Mich. 49201-2275
Telephone: (517) 788-4087
E-mail: <reference@jackson.lib.mi.us>

Web site: <www.jackson.lib.mi.us>

Hours: Open 9:30 a.m. to 8:30 p.m. Mondays through Thursdays; 9:30 a.m. to 6 p.m. Fridays; and 9:30 a.m. to 5 p.m. Saturdays from September through May. From June through August, open 9:30 a.m. to 7 p.m. Mondays through Thursdays; 9:30 a.m. to 6 p.m. Fridays; and 9:30 a.m. to 1:30 p.m. Saturdays.

Genealogical/historical collection: More than 1,000 volumes for in-house use only. Includes databases; federal census records for Michigan; state census records; cemetery records; county or local history books; church records; city directories; DAR records; family genealogies; land records; maps or atlases; military records; newspapers; periodicals (genealogical or historical); and vital records.

Items in this collection that may not be found in others include "*Jackson Citizen Patriot* on microfilm; birth, death, and marriage index for Jackson County; and photo archive."

Written queries: Will answer. "Mail request to Reference Department with SASE and donation to cover copy costs and research time."

Kalamazoo County

Comstock Township Library

6130 King Highway
P.O. Box 25
Comstock, Mich. 49041-0025
Telephone: (269) 345-0136
Fax: (269) 345-0138
Web site: <www.comstocktownshiplib.org>

Hours: From Labor Day to Memorial Day, open 10 a.m. to 9 p.m. Mondays through Thursdays; 10 a.m. to 6 p.m. Fridays; and 10 a.m. to 4 p.m. Saturdays. From Memorial Day to Labor Day, open 10 a.m. to 8 p.m. Mondays through Thursdays; 10 a.m. to 6 p.m. Fridays; and 10 a.m. to 4 p.m. Saturdays.

Genealogical/historical collection: "Modest-sized" collection for in-house use only. Includes state census records; cemetery records; a county or local history book; and city directories.

Items in this collection that may not be found in others include "a local obituary file and a newspaper clipping file about local people."

Written queries: Will answer at no cost.

Galesburg Memorial Library

188 E. Michigan Ave.
Galesburg, Mich. 49053
Telephone: (269) 665-7839
Fax: (269) 665-7839

Hours: Open 10:30 a.m. to 4:30 p.m. Tuesdays, Thursdays, and Fridays; noon to 8 p.m. Wednesdays; and 10 a.m. to 2 p.m. Saturdays.

Genealogical/historical collection: In-house use only. Includes cemetery records; county or local history books; city directories; family genealogies; maps or atlases; and newspapers.

Items in this collection that may not be found in others include scrapbooks, information on General William R. Shafter, 'Pecos Bill,' who was born in Galesburg, and the Alphadelphia Association.

Written queries: Will answer as time permits.

Kalamazoo Public Library
Clarence L. Miller Family History Room
315 S. Rose St.
Kalamazoo, Mich. 49007-5270
Telephone: (269) 553-7808
Fax: (269) 342-0414
Web site: <www.kpl.gov>

Hours: Open 9 a.m. to 9 p.m. Mondays through Thursdays; 9 a.m. to 6 p.m. Fridays; 9 a.m. to 5 p.m. Saturdays; and 1 p.m. to 5 p.m. Sundays. Call ahead for summer hours.

Genealogical/historical collection: About 5,000 volumes, 2,000 photos, and 100 drawers of vertical file materials about local people and institutions. "All materials are non-circulating; some rare or fragile items are in closed storage." Includes databases; all federal census records for Michigan and some for other states ("through 1850 we have New York, Connecticut, Massachusetts, Vermont, New Hampshire, and Pennsylvania"); cemetery records; county or local history books; church records; city directories; DAR records; family genealogies; land records; maps or atlases; military records; newspapers; original papers, manuscripts, diaries ("minimal"); periodicals (genealogical or historical); vital records; newsletters; annual reports; photographs; and an extensive clipping file.

Items in this collection that may not be found in others include "extensive clipping files and photographs on local subjects; 36-volume Meader Collection of local biographies; and 27 volumes of clippings on local servicemen in World War I and World War II."

Written queries: "We answer brief questions free, do photocopying at 20 cents per page and prints from film at 30 cents per page, plus postage. We refer lengthier questions to private searchers."

Other: "We have an index to local newspapers, magazines, and other materials, about 1.5 million citations, searchable on our Web site."

McKay Memorial Library
105 S. Webster St.
Augusta, Mich. 49012
Telephone: (269) 731-4000
Fax: (269) 731-5323
E-mail: <marlib@tdsnet.com>

Genealogical/historical collection: Collection focuses on local history since 1800s. "Most items do not circulate, but items can be copied." Includes a few cemetery records; county or local history books; a few family genealogies; maps or atlases; military records; newspapers; original papers, manuscripts, and diaries; and school records.

Written queries: Will answer. Copies are 15 cents each.

Western Michigan University
Archives and Regional History Collections
111 East Hall, East Campus
Kalamazoo, Mich. 49008-5307
Telephone: (269) 387-8490
Fax: (269) 387-8484
E-mail: <arch_collect@wmich.edu>
Web site: <www.wmich.edu/library/archives/index.php>

Hours: Open 8 a.m. to 5 p.m. Tuesdays through Fridays and 9 a.m. to 4 p.m. Saturdays from September to June. During July and August, open 10 a.m. to 4 p.m. weekdays.

Genealogical/historical collection: 20,000 linear feet. Includes databases; federal and state census records; cemetery records; county or local history books; church records; city directories; DAR records; family genealogies; land records; maps or atlases; military records; newspapers; original papers, manuscripts, and diaries; periodicals (genealogical or historical); tax lists; and circuit court records.

Items in this collection that may not be found in others include county government records for southwestern Michigan. "The Regional History Collections is designated by the Michigan Historical Commission as a repository for public records of 12 counties in southwest Michigan, including Allegan, Barry, Berrien, Branch, Calhoun, Cass, Kalamazoo, Kent, Muskegon, Ottawa, Saint Joseph, and Van Buren. Records from county, township, city and village governmental agencies are on deposit from the State Archives and include tax records, court records and township minutes."

Written queries: "Limited to 30 minutes or as staff time permits."

Kent County

Diocesan Archives
Diocese of Grand Rapids
660 Burton St., S.E.
Grand Rapids, Mich. 49507-3290
Telephone: (616) 243-0491
Web site: <www.dioceseofgrandrapids.org/>

Hours: By appointment only.

Genealogical/historical collection: "Requests for information must be received by U.S. mail." Collection features "various parish, institutional, and sacramental records from 1850 to present." Includes cemetery records; county or local history books; church records; city directories; maps or atlases; newspapers; original papers, manuscripts, and diaries; periodicals (genealogical or historical); and vital records.

Items in this collection that may not be found in others include "correspondence and sacramental records generated by the Catholic Church."

Written queries: Will answer. There is a $10 to $20 per hour research fee "in certain circumstances." Certificates of sacramental records issued for $5 each.

Other: "Sacramental records of West Michigan Catholic parishes through 1900 are available on microfiche at the Grand Rapids Public Library and Hackley Library in Muskegon. Certain older records are in the process of being translated, transcribed, and indexed."

Grand Rapids Public Library
111 Library St., N. E.
Grand Rapids, Mich. 49503-3268
Telephone: (616) 988-5400
E-mail: <localhis@grpl.org>
Web site: <www.grpl.org>

Genealogical/historical collection: 30,000 books, 300 manuscript collections; more than one million photographs and negatives for in-house use only. Emphasis is on Grand Rapids and Kent County, but the collection covers all of Michigan. Includes databases; federal census records for Michigan; some state census records; cemetery records; county or local history books; church records; city directories; DAR records; family genealogies; land records; maps or atlases; newspapers; original papers, manuscripts, and diaries; periodicals (genealogical or historical); photos; funeral home records; and real estate listing cards for house histories.

Items in this collection that may not be found in others include "a collection of 900,000 negatives, the 'Robinson' Collection."

Written queries: Will answer for $25 per hour, plus cost of photocopies.

Other: The library's Web site includes an index to the *Grand Rapids Press* <www.grpl.org/resources/pressindex.html> and the Grand Rapids Photo Archive <www.grpl.org/coll/grhsty_spcoll/HistMain.html >.

Calvin College
Hekman Library
Heritage Hall
3207 Burton St., S.E.
Grand Rapids, Mich. 49546-4301
Web site: <www.calvin.edu/hh>
Hours: Open 8 a.m. to 5 p.m. weekdays.

Genealogical/historical collection: 350 cubic feet. Includes some databases; church records; family genealogies; newspapers; original papers, manuscripts, and diaries; and baptismal and marriage records.

Items in this collection that may not be found in others include "membership records of Christian Reformed Church in North American congregations."

Written queries: Will not answer.

Lapeer County

Lapeer County Library deAngeli Branch
921 W. Nepessing St.
Lapeer, Mich. 48446-1699
Telephone: (810) 664-6971
Web site: <www.library.lapeer.org>
Hours: Open 9 a.m. to 5 p.m. weekdays.

Genealogical/historical collection: 751 titles for in-house use only. Includes databases; federal census records for Michigan and other states; state census records; cemetery records; county or local history books; church records; city directories; family genealogies; genealogical periodicals; maps or atlases; newspapers; and original papers, manuscripts, and diaries.

Items in this collection that may not be found in others include Lapeer County obituary and historical files and ancestor charts for local families.

Written queries: Will do "limited searches." Makes referrals to the Lapeer County Genealogical Society (see page 380).

Leelanau County

Leelanau Historical Museum
203 E. Cedar St.
Leland, Mich. 49654
Telephone: (231) 256-7475
Fax: (231) 256-7650
E-mail: <info@leelanauhistory.org>
Web site: <www.leelanauhistory.org>
Hours: By appointment.

Genealogical/historical collection: 5,000 photographs, 500 books, plus manuscripts and documents. There are restrictions on some items. Collection includes county or local history books; city directories; maps or atlases; newspapers; and original papers, manuscripts, and diaries.

Items in this collection that may not be found in others include special collections on James B. Hendrix, Stephen Hutchinson, and other Leelanau County people and topics.

Written queries: Will answer written requests, including those via e-mail, for projects that take less than an hour. "We have no research staff to establish a paid service."

Other: "Our collection is limited to materials related to Leelanau County."

Lenawee County

Adrian College
Shipman Library
110 S. Madison St.
Adrian, Mich. 49221-2575

Telephone: (517) 264-3828

Web site: <www.adrian.edu/library>

Hours: The Adrian College and Detroit Conference Methodist Archives are open by appointment only. The college library is open during the school year from 8 a.m. to 11 p.m. Mondays through Thursdays; 8 a.m. to 5 p.m. Fridays; 10 a.m. to 5 p.m. Saturdays; and noon to 11 p.m. Sundays. The library is open May through August from 8 a.m. to 4 p.m. weekdays.

Genealogical/historical collection: Includes databases; federal census records for Michigan and Ohio; county or local history books; and church records.

Written queries: "Standard reference queries answered at no cost."

Adrian Public Library

143 E. Maumee St.

Adrian, Mich. 49221-2703

Telephone: (517) 265-2265

Fax: (517) 265-8847

Web site: <adrian.lib.mi.us>

Hours: Open 10 a.m. to 9 p.m. Mondays, Tuesdays, and Thursdays; 10 a.m. to 5:30 p.m. Wednesdays and Fridays; and 9:30 a.m. to 5 p.m. Saturdays. During June, July, and August the library closes at 8 p.m. on Mondays, Tuesdays, and Thursdays.

Genealogical/historical collection: About 4,500 volumes for in-house use only. No photocopying allowed. Collection includes federal census records; state census records for 1845, 1884, and 1894; cemetery records; county or local history books; church records; city directories; family genealogies; maps or atlases; military records; newspapers; and original papers, manuscripts, and diaries.

Items in this collection that may not be found in others include state censuses for Lenawee County and local genealogies.

Written queries: Will answer requests for "basic searching." The library charges for photocopies or microfilm copies and postage.

Hudson Museum

219 W. Main St.

Hudson, Mich. 49247

Hours: Open 1 p.m. to 4 p.m. Mondays and Wednesdays; noon to 3 p.m. Saturdays; and by appointment.

Genealogical/historical collection: Small collection includes cemetery records; county or local history books; city directories; family genealogies; maps or atlases; military records; original papers, manuscripts, and diaries; tax lists; vital records; and photographs.

Items in this collection that may not be found in others include "a few diaries from Civil War men; some local family stories; and photographs of people and places in the area."

Written queries: Cost is $5, plus photocopies.

Lenawee County Library
4459 W. U.S. 223
Adrian, Mich. 49221-9461
Telephone: (517) 263-1011
Web site: <www.lenawee.lib.mi.us/>
Hours: Open 10 a.m. to 9 p.m. Mondays and10 a.m. to 6 p.m. Tuesdays through Saturdays.

Genealogical/historical collection: In-house use only. Includes databases; federal census records for Lenawee County; cemetery records; county or local history books; Quaker records; city directories; family genealogies; genealogical periodicals; maps or atlases; and newspapers.

Items in this collection that may not be found in others include local newspapers: *Addison Courier* and *Tri-County Advertiser* (17 July 1885-21 January 1960); *Blissfield Advance* (1877-5 September 1946); and *Morenci Observer* (4 January 1923-19 July 2000).

Written queries: "We can check indexed volumes. Please be as specific as possible. We can check the newspapers if we have an approximate date for the event. We ask for a donation to cover the costs of the copies and the postage."

Other: "Our collection focuses on Lenawee County. There are a few items from neighboring counties. We have a 'Surname Exchange Book' in which researchers may place the names they are researching in the area, the area being researched, and how to contact the researcher."

Tecumseh Public Library
Clara Waldron Historical Room
215 N. Ottawa St.
Tecumseh, Mich. 49286-1564
Telephone: (517) 423-2238
Web site: <www.tecumseh.lib.mi.us/>
Hours: Open 10 a.m. to 8 p.m. Mondays through Thursdays and 10 a.m. to 5 p.m. Fridays and Saturdays.

Genealogical/historical collection: In-house use only. "Nothing may be photocopied without permission from the Reference Librarian." Includes federal census records for Lenawee County; cemetery records; county or local history books; church records; city directories; DAR records; family genealogies; land records; maps or atlases; newspapers; original papers, manuscripts, and diaries; periodicals (genealogical or historical); tax lists; and vital records.

Items in this collection that may not be found in others include high school yearbooks dating back to 1913; scrapbooks and ledgers; more than 600 photographs and slides; black and white silent films of the Tecumseh area made by Leon Rosacrans between 1927 and 1950; and oral history videotapes.

Written queries: "For a small donation to the library, our Historical Room Coordinator and our Historical Room Volunteer will research genealogical queries on a limited basis and without a deadline."

Other: "The collection primarily includes material on the city of Tecumseh and the area covering the Tecumseh School District. Subjects include the history of the area's settlement and growth, government, schools, churches, clubs, businesses, architecture, and individuals important to Tecumseh's history and development."

Livingston County

Howell Area Archives
c/o Howell Carnegie District Library
314 W. Grand River Ave.
Howell, Mich. 48843
E-mail: <archives@howelllibrary.org>
Web site: <howelllibrary.org/>
Hours: Open 1 p.m. to 5 p.m. Wednesdays, Fridays, and Saturdays.

Genealogical/historical collection: More than 500 boxes for in-house use only. Includes federal census records for Michigan; cemetery records; county or local history books; city directories; DAR records; family genealogies; land records; maps or atlases; military records; tax lists; and obituaries.

Items in this collection that may not be found in others include "land records (abstracts), family genealogies, obituaries, maps, original county and city records, and tax lists."

Written queries: Will answer for a "minimal" donation to cover copy costs and postage.

Other: "We have many one-of-a-kind records, more than 20,000 obituaries for our county, and extensive cemetery lists. The information is primarily on Livingston County."

Fowlerville District Library
131 Mill St.
P.O. Box 313
Fowlerville, Mich. 48836-0313
Telephone: (517) 223-9089
Fax: (517) 223-0781
E-mail: <library131@yahoo.com>

Hours: Open from 9:30 a.m. to 5 p.m. Mondays, Wednesdays, and Fridays; 9:30 a.m. to 7 p.m. Tuesdays and Thursdays; and 10 a.m. to 2 p.m. Saturdays.

Genealogical/historical collection: "Small" collection of books, pictures, and newspaper clippings is for in-house use only. Includes federal and state census records; cemetery records; county or local history books; church records; city directories; family genealogies; land records; maps or atlases; military records; original papers, manuscripts, and diaries; vital records; and obituaries.

Written queries: Will answer for "mailing costs, phone costs, and copier costs."

Mackinac County

Mackinac Island Public Library
Main St.
Box 903
Mackinac Island, Mich. 49757
Telephone: (906) 847-3421
Fax: (906) 847-3368
E-mail: <mipl2@sault.com>

Hours: Open 11 a.m. to 5:30 p.m. Tuesdays through Saturdays during the winter. Open 11 a.m. to 8:30 p.m. Mondays and Fridays and 11 a.m. to 5:30 p.m. Tuesdays, Wednesdays, and Saturdays during the summer.

Genealogical/historical collection: Small collection must be viewed in the Rosa Webb Room. Includes 1860 federal census records; Mackinac County cemetery records; county or local history books; Ste. Anne's church records on CD; and a "very limited" number of newspapers.

Written queries: Will not answer.

Saint Ignace Public Library
6 Spring St.
Saint Ignace, Mich. 49781-1606
Telephone: (906) 643-8318
Fax: (906) 643-9809
E-mail: <cindy@uproc.lib.mi.us>
Web site: <www.uproc.lib.mi.us/sti>

Genealogical/historical collection: Collection consists of "file box with local family genealogies, 40 books, and papers on microfilm" for in-house use only. Collection includes state census records; cemetery records; county or local history books; church records; family genealogies; and newspapers.

Items in this collection that may not be found in others include "local family genealogies."

Written queries: Will answer. Copies are 25 cents each.

Macomb County

Mount Clemens Public Library
150 Cass Ave.
Mount Clemens, Mich. 48043-2297
Telephone: (586) 469-6200
Fax: (586) 469-6668
Web site: <www.libcoop.net/mountclemens>

Hours: Open 9 a.m. to 9 p.m. Mondays through Thursdays; 9 a.m. to 5 p.m. Fridays and Saturdays; and 1 p.m. to 5 p.m. Sundays (school year only).

Genealogical/historical collection: 3,000 volumes and 1,500 reels of microfilm. Includes databases; federal and state census records; cemetery records;

county or local history books; church records; city directories; DAR records; family genealogies; maps or atlases; military records; newspapers; periodicals (genealogical or historical); and vital records.

Written queries: "Queries answered by volunteer; $5 for initial search. Cost for additional search negotiable with client."

Other: The library's Web site includes an every-name index for the 1930 census for Macomb County <offserv.libcoop.net/mtc/1930census.asp>, Macomb County Cemetery Master Index <offserv.libcoop.net/mtc/cemetery.asp>, Macomb County Obituary Index <offserv.libcoop.net/mtc/obitindex.asp>, Macomb County Military Index <offserv.libcoop.net/mtc/military.asp>, a World War I Draft Registration Index for Macomb County <offserv.libcoop.net/mtc/draftindex.asp>, World War I Service Records for Macomb County <offserv.libcoop.net/mtc/wwirecords.asp>, an Honor Roll of Men Who Lost Their Lives in Service During World War I <www.libcoop.net/mountclemens/wwideath.htm>, the 1890 Special Veterans Census of Macomb County <offserv.libcoop.net/mtc/1890vets.asp>, a Mount Clemens City Directory Master Index <offserv.libcoop.net/mtc/MCDirectory.asp>, and more.

Roseville Public Library
29777 Gratiot Ave.
Roseville, Mich. 48066
Telephone: (586) 445-5407
Fax: (586) 445-5499
Web site: <www.libcoop.net/roseville>

Hours: Open 9 a.m. to 9 p.m. Mondays through Thursdays; 9 a.m. to 5 p.m. Fridays; 9 a.m. to 5 p.m. Saturdays (September through June).

Genealogical/historical collection: Many items, such as reference and microfilm, cannot be checked out. Includes databases; federal census records for Michigan; state census records; cemetery records; county or local history books; a few city directories; family genealogies; genealogical periodicals; land records; maps or atlases; military records; and newspapers (*Roseville Record*).

Items in this collection that may not be found in others include historic Roseville photographs and Erin Township records on microfilm.

Written queries: Will not answer. "But the Roseville Historical and Genealogical Society does. Send inquires to the RHGS c/o of the Roseville Public Library." (Also see pages 385-386.)

Saint Clair Shores Public Library
22500 Eleven Mile Rd.
Saint Clair Shores, Mich. 48081-1399
Telephone: (586) 771-9020
Fax: (586) 771-8935
E-mail: <bieniekc@libcoop.net>
Web site: <www.libcoop.net/stclairshores>

Hours: Open 9 a.m. to 9 p.m. Mondays through Thursdays; 9 a.m. to 5 p.m. Fridays; and 9 a.m. to 5 p.m. Saturdays (between Labor Day and Memorial Day).

Genealogical/historical collection: 5,000 volumes in the Michigan/Great Lakes Collection and 200 volumes of genealogy for in-house use only. Includes databases (AncestryPlus); cemetery records; county or local history books; church records; Detroit city directories; DAR records; family genealogies; maps or atlases; newspapers; and periodicals (genealogical or historical).

Items in this collection that may not be found in others include "oral histories, family histories, and local photographs."

Written queries: Will answer. "No charge."

Manistee County

Manistee County Library
95 Maple St.
Manistee, Mich. 49660
Telephone: (231) 723-2519
Fax: (231) 723-8270

Hours: Open 10 a.m. to 8 p.m. Mondays through Wednesdays; 10 a.m. to 5 p.m. Thursdays and Fridays; and 10 a.m. to 3 p.m. Saturdays.

Genealogical/historical collection: About 1,000 volumes total. "General 'How to,' etc., may be checked out. Reference collection has been removed from public access. Researchers must ask for each item." Includes federal census records for Michigan; county or local history books; city directories; some family genealogies; maps or atlases; and newspapers.

Written queries: Will answer for $5, plus copy charges of 25 cents per page.

Marquette County

Bishop Baraga Association and Archives
347 Rock St.
Marquette, Mich. 49855
Telephone: (906) 227-9117
Fax: (906) 225-0437
E-mail: <edelene@dioceseofmarquette.org>
Web site: <www.dioceseofmarquette.org/>

Hours: Open by appointment.

Genealogical/historical collection: Includes cemetery and church records.

Written queries: Will answer. "Written requests preferred."

Other: "All our records are not centrally located. Each parish is responsible for their records and makes their own policy as to whether or not they will conduct research."

Central Upper Peninsula and Northern Michigan University Archives
1401 Presque Isle Ave.
Marquette, Mich. 49855

Telephone: (906) 227-1225
Fax: (906) 227-1333
E-mail: <mrobyns@nmu.edu>
Web site: <www.nmu.edu/www-sam/ais/archives>
Hours: Open 8 a.m. to 5 p.m. weekdays.

Genealogical/historical collection: 1,000 cubic feet. Restricted use. Collection includes databases; county or local history books; church records; city directories; land records; newspapers; original papers, manuscripts, and diaries; and tax lists.

Items in this collection that may not be found in others include "Morgan Heights Sanitorium Patient Records."

Written queries: Will answer. Cost is $10 per hour after the first half hour. Photocopies are 10 cents each, and microfilm copies are 25 cents each.

Peter White Public Library
217 N. Front St.
Marquette, Mich. 49855
Telephone: (906) 228-9510
Fax: (906) 226-1783
Web site: <www.uproc.lib.mi.us/pwpl>

Hours: Open 9 a.m. to 9 p.m. Mondays through Thursdays; 9 a.m. to 6 p.m. Fridays; 10 a.m. to 5 p.m. Saturdays; and 1 p.m. to 5 p.m. Sundays (September through May).

Genealogical/historical collection: About 5,000 volumes for in-house use only. Includes databases; federal census records for Michigan and other states; cemetery records; county or local history books; church records; city directories; DAR records; family genealogies; land records; maps or atlases; military records; newspapers; and periodicals (genealogical or historical).

Items in this collection that may not be found in others include "newspaper clipping file of local interest, *Mining Journal* newspaper on microfilm, *Ishpeming Iron Ore* newspaper on microfilm, 426 15-minute radio scripts on 'Historical Highlights'; and local high school and Northern Michigan University yearbooks."

Written queries: Will answer if "not too extensive." Copies are $1 per page.

Other: "Marquette Genealogical Society Collection is housed in the Peter White Library and is available for use by public."

Mason County

Mason County Historical Society Research Library
Historic White Pine Village
1687 Lakeshore Dr.
Ludington, Mich. 49431
Telephone: (231) 843-4808
Fax: (231) 843-7089
E-mail: <info@historicwhitepinevillage.org>
Web site: <www.historicwhitepinevillage.org>

Hours: Open 11 a.m. to 4 p.m. Tuesdays through Fridays.

Genealogical/historical collection: "Extensive" collection includes databases; federal census records; cemetery records; county or local history books; church records; city directories; family genealogies; land records; maps or atlases; military records; newspapers; original papers, manuscripts, and diaries; periodicals (genealogical or historical); tax lists; vital records; scrapbooks; and photographs. Items may not be scanned.

Items in this collection that may not be found in others include "Mason County archival history."

Written queries: Will answer for $10 for the first half hour and $15 an hour thereafter. Copies of obituaries are $5; duplicates of photos are $14 for an 8 x 10; other copies are 30 cents each.

Other: The library's Web site has a Guide to the Archives and Artifacts of the Historic White Pine Village <www.historicwhitepinevillage.org/research/archive.asp>, a database of more than 45,000 records.

Menominee County

Spies Public Library
940 First St.
Menominee, Mich. 49858
Telephone: (906) 863-2900
Fax: (906) 863-5000
E-mail: <splill@uproc.lib.mi.us>
Web site: <www.uproc.lib.mi.us/spies>

Hours: Open 9 a.m. to 5 p.m. Mondays, Fridays, and Saturdays and 9 a.m. to 9 p.m. Tuesdays through Thursdays in the winter. In the summers, open 9 a.m. to 5 p.m. Mondays and Fridays; 9 a.m. to 9 p.m. Tuesdays; 9 a.m. to 6 p.m. Wednesdays and Thursdays; and 9 a.m. to noon Saturdays.

Genealogical/historical collection: 750 volumes for in-house use only. Includes databases; federal census records; state census records; cemetery records; county or local history books; city directories; maps or atlases; and newspapers.

Items in this collection that may not be found in others include local history.

Written queries: Will answer for copy fees and postage.

Midland County

Grace A. Dow Memorial Library
1710 W. Saint Andrews Rd.
Midland, Mich. 48640-2698
Telephone: (989) 837-3430
Fax: (989) 837-3468
E-mail: <gadml@midland-mi.org>
Web site: <www.midland-mi.org/gracedowlibrary>

Hours: Open 9 a.m. to 7 p.m. weekdays; 10 a.m. to 2 p.m. Saturdays.

Genealogical/historical collection: In-house use only. Includes federal census records; state census records; cemetery records; county or local history books; church records; city directories; family genealogies; land records; maps or atlases; newspapers; and periodicals (genealogical or historical).

Items in this collection that may not be found in others include indexes for Midland County censuses 1900, 1910, 1920, and 1930.

Written queries: Cost is $5 for five copies from books in the library.

Other: "We have a genealogy computer with more than 200 disks."

Monroe County

Milan Public Library
151 Wabash St.
Milan, Mich. 48160
Telephone: (734) 439-1240
Fax: (734) 439-5625
E-mail: <milanweb@monroe.lib.mi.us>
Web site: <woodlands.lib.mi.us/milan>

Hours: Open 10 a.m. to 8 p.m. Mondays through Thursdays; 10 a.m. to 6 p.m. Fridays; and 10 a.m. to 4 p.m. Saturdays.

Genealogical/historical collection: About 400 items for in-house use only. Includes databases (AncestryPlus); federal census records for Michigan; cemetery records; county or local history books; church records; family genealogies; genealogical periodicals; maps or atlases; newspapers; and vital records.

Items in this collection that may not be found in others include "local newspapers and compilations of local news (weddings, births, deaths) indexed by name."

Written queries: Will answer. "Donations encouraged."

Monroe County Historical Museum
126 S. Monroe St.
Monroe, Mich. 48161
Telephone: (734) 240-7787
Fax: (734) 240-7788
Web site: <co.monroe.mi.us/Museum/>

Hours: Open 10 a.m. to 5 p.m. Wednesdays through Sundays. Closed 1 p.m. to 1:30 p.m. each day for lunch.

Genealogical/historical collection: 1,000 linear feet. Some items cannot be photocopied. Includes federal census records for Michigan; cemetery records; county or local history books; church records; city directories; DAR records; family genealogies; maps or atlases; military records; original papers, manuscripts, and diaries; tax lists; vital records; and obituaries.

Items in this collection that may not be found in others include "obituaries from Monroe County newspapers and scrapbooks."

Written queries: Will answer. "The first half hour of research is free. After that it's $11 per hour, plus photocopies. Photocopies are 25 cents per page."

Muskegon County

Hackley Public Library
316 W. Webster Ave.
Muskegon, Mich. 49440
Telephone: (231) 722-7276
Web site: <hackleylibrary.org/>

Muskegon County Museum
430 W. Clay Ave.
Muskegon, Mich. 49440-1002
Telephone: (231) 722-0278
Fax: (231) 728-4119
E-mail: <info@muskeonmuseum.org>
Web site: <www.muskegonmuseum.org>
Hours: Open by appointment only with the archivist.

Genealogical/historical collection: More than 1,000 cubic feet of archival collections. "Some collections are not available for public use." Includes databases; cemetery records; county or local history books; church records; city directories; DAR records; family genealogies; maps or atlases; newspapers; original papers, manuscripts, and diaries; periodicals (genealogical or historical); tax lists; photographs of local people and places; school yearbooks; and scrapbooks.

Items in this collection that may not be found in others include "local photographs; organizational collections; collections from businesses, factories, banks, and churches; scrapbooks; ledgers; tax assessment record books for city of Muskegon (1860-1916); more than 200 Willard Gebhart landscape design projects from 1940 to 1970; Edwin Valentine architectural papers, including plans and modifications for more than 100 buildings (1925-1980); and Casnovia Township records, including school census, voter registrations, and property taxes (1859-1980)."

Written queries: Will answer. "Minimal expenses for making copies. Must be for personal use."

Newaygo County

Fremont Area District Library
Local History – Genealogy Room
104 E. Main St.
Fremont, Mich. 49412-1246
Telephone: (231) 928-0253
Fax: (231) 924-2355
Web site: <fadl.ncats.net/localhistory.html>

Hours: Open 9:30 a.m. to 8:30 p.m. Mondays through Wednesdays; 9:30 a.m. to 5:30 p.m. Thursdays and Fridays; and 9:30 a.m. to 1:30 p.m. Saturdays.

Genealogical/historical collection: About 800 printed items, plus microfilm and "a growing database" for in-house use only. Includes databases; federal census records for Michigan and other states; state census records; cemetery records; county or local history books; family genealogies; plat maps; maps or atlases; newspapers; periodicals (genealogical or historical); and Newaygo County one-room schoolhouse records.

Items in this collection that may not be found in others include Newaygo County Ku Klux Klan membership cards on microfilm and the Harry L. Spooner Collection. "Harry Spooner was an editor, educator, and historian. He kept many records over the years on Newaygo County area history. Lumbering, Native Americans, Trading Posts are just a few examples. He has included information on the families and the natural history of the area. We are currently putting the contents of this collection on disk for easy patron use. An index is available."

Written queries: Will answer. "Limited searches. No fee."

Other: "We are currently putting a searchable database online. It can be accessed through our Web page. It is being updated monthly. It contains births, marriages, anniversaries, and deaths taken from Newaygo County papers and from items donated, such as obituaries and funeral cards. We have several photos being scanned and put on disk for patrons' use."

Oakland County

Baldwin Public Library
300 W. Merrill St.
Birmingham, Mich. 48009
Telephone: (248) 647-1700
Fax: (248) 644-7297
E-mail: <question@baldwinlib.org>
Web site: <www.baldwinlib.org>

Hours: Open 9:30 a.m. to 9 p.m. Mondays through Thursdays; 9:30 a.m. to 5:30 p.m. Fridays and Saturdays; and noon to 5 p.m. Sundays.

Genealogical/historical collection: Materials are for in-house use only. "We take identification for certain materials, such as county atlases, city directories, and yearbooks." Collection includes databases; federal census records for Oakland County; cemetery records; county or local history books; city directories; DAR records; maps or atlases; military records ("a list of names of service men and women from World War II"); newspapers; periodicals (genealogical or historical); and high school yearbooks.

Items in this collection that may not be found in others include the *Birmingham-Bloomfield Eccentric,* the local newspaper, on microfilm from 1878 to present. The paper covers Birmingham, Beverly Hills, Bingham Farms, Bloomfield Hills, Bloomfield Township, Bloomfield Village, Franklin, and Southfield Township. It's indexed from 1878 to 2000 and includes subject and biographical indexes. The index for 2000 to present is in progress. The library also has *Acorns to Oaks,* the Oakland County Genealogical Society Quarterly, from 1978 to present. There's a cumulative index to the first 20 volumes.

Written queries: Will answer brief queries. "No charge, but we cannot do extensive research. We appreciate a SASE. Donations are gratefully accepted."

Central Archives of Polonia
Orchard Lakes Schools
3535 Indian Trail
Orchard Lake, Mich. 48324
Telephone: (248) 683-0412
Hours: Open 9 a.m. to 4:30 p.m. weekdays.
Genealogical/historical collection: Small collection ("one bookshelf") includes church records; family genealogies; maps or atlases; newspapers; original papers, manuscripts and diaries; and periodicals (genealogical or historical).
Written queries: Will not answer.

Farmington Community Library
32737 W. Twelve Mile Rd.
Farmington Hills, Mich. 48334-3302
Telephone: (248) 553-0300
Fax: (248) 553-3228
Web site: <www.farmlib.org>
Genealogical/historical collection: More than 600 lineal feet for in-house use only. Some closed stacks. Collection includes databases; federal census records for Michigan; cemetery records; county or local history books; church records; city directories; DAR records; family genealogies; land records; maps or atlases; newspapers; original papers, manuscripts, and diaries; periodicals (genealogical or historical); tax lists; and photographs.

Items in this collection that may not be found in others include "information on Farmington area residents and a photograph collection of approximately 1,500 images, some unidentified."

Written queries: Will answer "on a limited basis."
Other: "The Heritage Collection at the Farmington Community Library provides access to resources of interest to individuals who wish to study local, county, and state history. The development of the collection is done cooperatively by the Farmington Community Library, Farmington Historical Society, Farmington Genealogical Society, and other interested groups, such as the Farmington Historical Commission and the Farmington Hills Historical Commission."

Milford Township Library
1100 Atlantic St.
Milford, Mich. 48381
Telephone: (248) 684-0845
Fax: (248) 684-2923
Web site: <milford.lib.mi.us>
Hours: Open 9:30 a.m. to 8 p.m. Mondays through Thursdays; 9:30 a.m. to 5 p.m. Fridays and Saturdays; and 12:30 p.m. to 5 p.m. Sundays (September to May).

Genealogical/historical collection: 1,000 volumes, many for in-house use only. Includes databases; federal census records for Michigan; cemetery records; county or local history books; church records; city directories; DAR records; family genealogies; maps or atlases; military records; newspapers; and periodicals (genealogical or historical).

Items in this collection that may not be found in others include the *Milford Times* from 1871 to 2002 and Milford High School yearbooks.

Written queries: Will answer "on a limited basis. We will start you on your search and point you to resources."

Rabbi Leo M. Franklin Archives of Temple Beth El
7400 Telegraph Rd.
Bloomfield Hills, Mich. 48301
Telephone: (248) 851-1100, ext. 3137
Fax: (248) 851-1187
E-mail: <franklinarchives@tbeonline.org>
Web site: <www.tbeonline.org>
Hours: Open 9 a.m. to 5 p.m. weekdays.

Genealogical/historical collection: Records date back to Temple Beth El's founding in 1850. Includes about 500 family files and collections; cemetery (Woodmere, Lafayette, and Beth El Memorial Park), congregational, school, and membership records; family genealogies; newspapers; original papers, manuscripts and diaries; and lifecycle events.

Items in this collection that may not be found in others include original manuscript collections of families.

Written queries: "Will fill requests up to 30 minutes. Fee for longer requests."

Other: "Temple Beth El, Detroit's first Jewish congregation, is home to one of the most comprehensive congregational archives in the nation and the largest such collection in Michigan. Advance appointments are not required but may make research visits more worthwhile. Tours are available for groups by arrangement." The archive's Web site includes photographs and Collection Guides.

Rochester Hills Museum
1005 Van Hoosen Rd.
Rochester Hills, Mich. 48306
Telephone: (248) 656-4663
Fax: (248) 608-8198
E-mail: <rhmuseum@rochesterhills.org>
Web site: <www.rochesterhills.org/museum.htm>
Hours: Open 1 to 4 p.m. Wednesdays through Saturdays.

Genealogical/historical collection: "Call to make an appointment. All items must remain on the premises. Instructions will be given by staff upon arrival." Includes local cemetery records; county or local history books; maps or atlases; newspapers; and original papers, manuscripts and diaries.

Items in this collection that may not be found in others include "information/historical documents of the greater Rochester Hills community."

Written queries: Cost "to be determined as each case presents itself."

Other: "Our focus is on the Taylor-Van Hoosen families, the establishment of Stoney Creek Village, farming, and local history between 1817 and 1952." The Web site <www.rochesterhills.org/museum/wwtwonames.htm> includes a listing of the names on the Rochester World War II Honor Roll Monument.

Royal Oak Public Library
222 E. Eleven Mile Rd.
P.O. Box 494
Royal Oak, Mich. 48068-0494
Web site: <www.ci.royal-oak.mi.us/library/index.html>

Genealogical/historical collection: Several hundred volumes for reference use only. Includes federal census records for "three Michigan counties"; county or local history books; city directories; maps or atlases; and newspapers.

Items in this collection that may not be found in others include historical files on Royal Oak.

Written queries: Will answer.

Troy Public Library
510 W. Big Beaver Rd.
Troy, Mich. 48084-5289
Web site: <www.libcoop.net/troy>

Hours: Open 10 a.m. to 9 p.m. Mondays through Thursdays; 10 a.m. to 6 p.m. Fridays and Saturdays; and 1 p.m. to 6 p.m. Sundays.

Genealogical/historical collection: 250 linear feet for in-library use only. Includes federal and state census records; cemetery records; county or local history books; family genealogies; and periodicals (genealogical or historical).

Written queries: Answers "only slightly or as time permits."

Ogemaw County

Ogemaw District Library
107 W. Main St.
P.O. Box 427
Rose City, Mich. 48654-0427
Telephone: (989) 685-3300
Fax: (989) 685-3647

Genealogical/historical collection: In-house use only. Includes databases; federal census records for Michigan; cemetery records; county or local history books; church records; city directories; family genealogies; land records; maps or atlases; newspapers; original papers, manuscripts and diaries; periodicals (genealogical or historical); and vital records.

Written queries: "It depends if we have the staffing to answer requests."

West Branch Public Library
119 N. Fourth St.
West Branch, Mich. 48661
Telephone: (989) 345-2235
Fax: (989) 345-8735

Genealogical/historical collection: 1,000 items, most for in-house use only. Includes federal census records for Ogemaw County; cemetery records; county or local history books; church records; family genealogies; newspapers (1923-present); original papers, manuscripts and diaries; and periodicals (genealogical or historical).

Written queries: Will answer brief queries for copies and postage. "Extensive research is referred to the Ogemaw County Historical Society."

Osceola County

Evart Public Library and Museum
104 N. Main St.
Evart, Mich. 49631
Telephone: (231) 734-5542
Fax: (231) 734-5542

Hours: Open 9 a.m. to 4:30 p.m. Mondays, Tuesdays, and Thursdays; 9 a.m. to 6 p.m. Wednesdays; and 9 a.m. to noon Saturdays.

Genealogical/historical collection: About 30 linear feet of books for in-house use only. Includes federal census records for Michigan; cemetery records; county or local history books; church records; family genealogies; land records; maps or atlases; military records; newspapers; original papers, manuscripts and diaries; periodicals (genealogical or historical); tax lists; and vital records.

Items in this collection that may not be found in others include the weekly issues of the *Evart Review* from 1872 to 2000 on microfilm and a large photograph collection.

Written queries: "No cost to answer queries, but we do appreciate a self-addressed stamped envelope."

Otsego County

Diocese of Gaylord
611 North St.
Gaylord, Mich. 49735
Telephone: (989) 732-5147
Web site: <www.dioceseofgaylord.org/diocese/archives.html>

Ottawa County

Loutit District Library
407 Columbus St.
Grand Haven, Mich. 49417
Telephone: (616) 842-5560

Fax: (616) 847-0570

E-mail: <gdhjb@llcoop.org>

Web site: <www.loutitlibrary.org/>

Hours: Open 9 a.m. to 9 p.m. Mondays through Thursdays; 9 a.m. to 6 p.m. Fridays; 9 a.m. to 5 p.m. Saturdays; and 1 p.m. to 5 p.m. Sundays (during the winter).

Genealogical/historical collection: 1,800 books, plus census records and periodicals for in-house use only. Fragile items cannot be photocopied. Includes databases; federal census records for Michigan and "a few" other states; state census records; cemetery records; county or local history books; church records; city directories; family genealogies; maps or atlases; military records; newspapers; original papers, manuscripts, and diaries; periodicals (genealogical or historical); tax lists; vital records; and immigration records of Dutch and Germans to America.

Written queries: Will answer.

Presque Isle County

Onaway Library
20774 State St.
P.O. Box 742
Onaway, Mich. 49765

Telephone: (989) 733-6621

Hours: Open 10 a.m. to 2 p.m. Mondays through Fridays, plus 2 p.m. to 7 p.m. Tuesdays through Thursdays.

Genealogical/historical collection: For in-house use only. Includes state census records; cemetery records; county or local history books; church records; city directories; family genealogies; genealogical periodicals; military records; and original papers, manuscripts and diaries.

Items in this collection that may not be found in others include local history.

Written queries: Will answer. "$10 fee, plus copies."

Presque Isle County Historical Museum
176 W. Michigan Ave.
P.O. Box 175
Rogers City, Mich. 49779

Telephone: (989) 734-4121

Hours: Archives open by appointment from June to October. Call in advance. Closed in winter.

Genealogical/historical collection: Two file drawers. Includes databases; cemetery records; family genealogies and biographies; "limited" maps or atlases; and a 1903 plat book of Alpena, Montmorency, and Presque Isle counties, listing original homesteaders.

Items in this collection that may not be found in others include 1908 Metz Fire artifacts and files about the 1958 sinking of the *Carl D. Bradley*.

Written queries: "The curator is the only person here. Will answer questions on an incidental basis, but we do not offer a service per se."

Saginaw County

Chesaning Public Library
227 E. Broad St.
Chesaning, Mich. 48616-1501
Telephone: (989) 845-3211
Web site: <valley.vlc.lib.mi.us/~chelib/>

Hours: From Labor Day to Memorial Day, open from 10 a.m. to 5:30 p.m. Mondays and Fridays; 10 a.m. to 8 p.m. Tuesdays and Thursdays; and 10 a.m. to 2 p.m. Saturdays. From Memorial Day to Labor Day, open from 10 a.m. to 5:30 p.m. Mondays, Tuesdays, and Fridays and 10 a.m. to 8 p.m. Thursdays.

Genealogical/historical collection: Most materials are for in-house use only. Includes databases; federal census records for Michigan; cemetery records; county or local history books; church records; city directories; DAR records; family genealogies; maps or atlases; military records; newspapers; original papers, manuscripts, and diaries; periodicals (genealogical or historical); and tax lists.

Items in this collection that may not be found in others include "family history records and local newspapers."

Written queries: Will answer.

Hoyt Main Library/Saginaw Public Library
Eddy Historical Collection
505 Janes Ave.
Saginaw, Mich. 48607-1285
Telephone: (989) 755-9827
E-mail: <plosgene@saginawlibrary.org>
Web site: <www.saginawlibrary.org>

Hours: Open 9 a.m. to 9 p.m. Mondays through Thursdays; 9 a.m. to 5 p.m. Fridays and Saturdays; and 1 p.m. to 5 p.m. Sundays (October through April).

Genealogical/historical collection: More than 15,000 books, microfilms, and periodicals for in-house use only. Includes databases; federal census records for Michigan and other states; state census records; cemetery records; county or local history books; church records; city directories; DAR records; family genealogies; land records; maps or atlases; military records; newspapers; original papers, manuscripts, and diaries; periodicals (genealogical or historical); tax lists; vital records; Michigan and Saginaw sheet music; and the Saginaw Genealogical Society Ancestor Files.

Items in this collection that may not be found in others include the Saginaw City Cemetery database and Dr. Richard Mudd's collection of books on the Lincoln Assassination and Civil War era.

Written queries: Will answer. "Donations solicited."

Other: The library's Web site includes an index of more than 125,000 obituaries from the *Saginaw News,* dating back to the 1800s <obits.netsource-one.net/> and Saginaw Images Online, a database of historical photographs and information <www.saginawimages.org/>.

Rauchholz Memorial Library
1140 N. Hemlock Rd.
Hemlock, Mich. 48626-8613
Telephone: (989) 642-8621
Fax: (989) 642-5559
E-mail: <rauchholz@hotmail.com>
Web site: <www.richlandtownship.com/library1.htm>

Hours: Open 9 a.m. to 5 p.m. Mondays, Tuesdays, and Fridays; 1 p.m. to 8 p.m. Wednesdays and Thursdays; and 10 a.m. to 2 p.m. Saturdays (fall and winter).

Genealogical/historical collection: One file drawer for in-house use only. Includes *Richland Township Sons and Daughters* booklet and pioneer records of Richland Township.

Written queries: "We check to see if we have a folder of their family name."

Other: "We sell copies of the *Richland Township Sons and Daughters* booklet for $3."

Saint Clair County

Saint Clair County Library
210 McMorran Blvd.
Port Huron, Mich. 48060
Telephone: (810) 987-7323
Fax: (810) 987-7327
E-mail: <reference@sccl.lib.mi.us>
Web site: <www.sccl.lib.mi.us/>

Hours: Open 9 a.m. to 9 p.m. weekdays and 9 a.m. to 5:30 p.m. Saturdays.

Genealogical/historical collection: For in-house use only. "Michigan Room appointment recommended; staff must be present." Includes databases; federal census records for Michigan; state census records; cemetery records; county or local history books; church records; city directories; DAR records; family genealogies; land records; maps or atlases; military records; newspapers; "very few" original papers, manuscripts, and diaries; periodicals (genealogical or historical); and vital records.

Written queries: Will answer for $20 per hour, plus copy fees.

Saint Joseph County

Sturgis Public Library
255 North St.
Sturgis, Mich. 49091-1433
Telephone: (269) 659-7224
Fax: (269) 651-4534
Web site: <ci.sturgis.mi.us/library.htm>

Hours: From Labor Day to Memorial Day, open from 9:30 a.m. to 8 p.m. Mondays through Wednesdays; 9:30 a.m. to 5:30 p.m. Thursdays and Fridays;

and 9:30 a.m. to 2 p.m. Saturdays. From Memorial Day to Labor Day, open 9:30 a.m. to 8 p.m. Thursdays; 9:30 a.m. to 5:30 p.m. Tuesdays, Wednesdays, and Fridays; and 9:30 a.m. to 12:30 p.m. Saturdays.

Genealogical/historical collection: "Patrons sign in upon arrival." Collection includes databases; federal census records for Michigan and other states; state census records; cemetery records; county or local history books; church records; city directories; DAR records; family genealogies; land records; maps or atlases; military records; newspapers; periodicals (genealogical or historical); tax lists; and vital records.

Items in this collection that may not be found in others include family histories of people connected to Saint Joseph County.

Written queries: Will answer requests via e-mail or postal service for 25 cents per photocopy, plus a donation for research time.

Three Rivers Public Library
920 W. Michigan Ave.
Three Rivers, Mich. 49093-2137
Telephone: (269) 273-8666
Fax: (269) 279-9654
Web site: <www.threeriverslibrary.org>
Hours: Open 10 a.m. to 9 p.m. weekdays; 10 a.m. to 5 p.m. Saturdays and Sundays.

Genealogical/historical collection: 1,500 items including databases; federal census records for Michigan and other states; state census records; cemetery records; county or local history books; church records; city directories; DAR records; family genealogies; genealogical periodicals; land records; maps or atlases; military records; newspapers; original papers, manuscripts, and diaries; and vital records. "Maps and land records are in locked cabinets and must be researched in the presence of library personnel."

Items in this collection that may not be found in others include local cemetery and funeral home records.

Written queries: Will answer. "Extensive queries are done by a volunteer who charges based upon the request."

Other: The library's Web site has reproduced portions of the book *Three Rivers: The Early Years* <www.threeriverslibrary.org/history.htm>.

Sanilac County

Sandusky District Library
55 E. Sanilac Ave.
P.O. Box 271
Sandusky, Mich. 48471-0271
Telephone: (810) 648-2644
Fax: (810) 648-1904
E-mail: <gnartker@sandusky.lib.mi.us>
Web site: <www.sandusky.lib.mi.us>

Hours: Open 9:30 a.m. to 7 p.m. weekdays and 9:30 a.m. to 2:30 p.m. Saturdays.

Genealogical/historical collection: "Largest collection of materials in our county." In-house use only. Includes databases; federal census records for Sanilac County; state census records; cemetery records; county or local history books; church records; city directories; family genealogies; maps or atlases; newspapers; periodicals (genealogical or historical); obituary file; photo file; and naturalization index of papers housed at the State Archives.

Items in this collection that may not be found in others include the naturalization index and state census records for Sanilac County.

Written queries: Will answer "simple requests only." No charge.

Shiawassee County

Shiawassee District Library
502 W. Main St.
Owosso, Mich. 48867-2687
Telephone: (989) 725-3134
E-mail: <info@sdl.lib.mi.us>
Web site: <sdl.lib.mi.us/>

Hours: Open 10 a.m. to 9 p.m. Mondays through Thursdays; 1 to 5 p.m. Fridays; and 10 a.m. to 5 p.m. Saturdays. From October to April, open Sundays from 1 to 5 p.m. From June to August, open 10 a.m. to 5 p.m. Fridays and 10 a.m. to 2 p.m. Saturdays.

Genealogical/historical collection: In-house use only. Includes databases; federal census records for Michigan; cemetery records; county or local history books; city directories; family genealogies; and newspapers.

Written queries: "Requests must be mailed or e-mailed. Copying costs over $1 will be billed."

Other: The library's Web site has the Shiawassee County Surname Index <www.sdl.lib.mi.us/surname/>.

Tuscola County

Mayville Area Museum of History and Genealogy
2124 Ohmer Road
P.O. Box 242
Mayville, Mich. 48744
Telephone: (989) 843-7185
E-mail: <dutchess@tds.net>

Hours: Open 10 a.m. to 4 p.m. Fridays and Saturdays, from Memorial Day Weekend until the second Saturday after Labor Day.

Genealogical/historical collection: "Fairly large collection about local families" for in-house use only. Includes 1880 federal census records for Tuscola County; cemetery records; county or local history books; some church records; some DAR records; family genealogies; some land records; maps or atlases;

"minimal" military records; newspapers; original papers, manuscripts, and diaries; and tax lists.

Items in this collection that may not be found in others include "donated items from the homes and businesses of local families."

Written queries: Will answer for a donation, plus 10 cents per copy.

Other: "We have just moved a one-room schoolhouse to our site and will be restoring this for future use."

Van Buren County

Marialyce Canonie Great Lakes Research Library

Michigan Maritime Museum
91 Michigan Ave.
South Haven, Mich. 49090

Telephone: (269) 637-9156

E-mail: <info@michiganmaritimemuseum.org>

Web site: <michiganmaritimemuseum.org>

Hours: Open 1 p.m. to 5 p.m. Tuesdays through Thursdays or by appointment.

Genealogical/historical collection: "The emphasis of the library is Great Lakes maritime history, especially that of Michigan." 2,000 volumes, plus periodicals, photographs, postcards, maps, and videos for in-house use only. Also includes databases; county or local history books; and periodicals (genealogical or historical).

Written queries: Will answer for $20 per hour, plus photocopying costs.

Other: "The library (and museum curatorial center) inhabit the old lighthouse keeper's house."

Van Buren District Library

200 N. Phelps St.
Decatur, Mich. 49045

Telephone: (269) 423-4771

Fax: (269) 423-8373

Web site: <www.youseemore.com/VanBuren/>

Hours: Open 9 a.m. to 8 p.m. Mondays through Thursdays; 9 a.m. to 5 p.m. Fridays; and 9 a.m. to 3 p.m. Saturdays.

Genealogical/historical collection: 3,500 volumes, plus a manuscript and photo collection and several special collections for in-house use only. Includes databases; federal census records for Michigan; state census records; cemetery records; county or local history books; church records; city directories; DAR records; family genealogies; land records; maps or atlases; military records; newspapers; original papers, manuscripts, and diaries; periodicals (genealogical or historical); tax lists; vital records; photographs; and special collections.

Written queries: Will answer "brief lookup requests only. Longer requests referred to private researcher."

Other: "The collection is co-owned by the library and the Van Buren Regional Genealogical Society (see pages 407-408). The collection is regional, including the Michigan counties of Allegan, Berrien, Cass, Kalamazoo, Van Buren, and Saint Joseph. It's strong in Michigan history and general and northeast genealogy."

Washtenaw County

Bentley Historical Library
Michigan Historical Collections
1150 Beal Ave.
Ann Arbor, Mich. 48109-2113
Telephone: (734) 764-3482
Fax: (734) 936-1333
E-mail: <bentley.ref@umich.edu>
Web site: <www.umich.edu/~bhl>

Hours: Open 9 a.m. to 5 p.m. weekdays all year and 9 a.m. to 12:30 p.m. Saturdays from September to April.

Genealogical/historical collection: For in-house use only. Includes federal census records for Michigan; state census records; cemetery records; county or local history books; church records; city directories; family genealogies; land records; maps or atlases; newspapers; original papers, manuscripts, and diaries; periodicals (genealogical or historical); and tax lists.

Items in this collection that may not be found in others include "Washtenaw County records, Dolph Funeral Home records, and University of Michigan student information, especially from the 19th century."

Written queries: Will answer. "One hour of free research."

Other: The library's Web site includes the Bentley Image Bank, images from the library's collections, and the Polar Bear Database <141.211.39.65/polardbmain.html>, a compiled roster of the soldiers who participated in the American military intervention in Russia at the end of World War I. Many of these soldiers were Michigan residents.

Chelsea District Library
Mailing Address:
221 S. Main St.
Chelsea, Mich. 48118-1267
Temporary Location:
500 Washington St., Building 400
Chelsea, Mich. 48118
Telephone: (734) 475-9732
Fax: (734) 475-6190
E-mail: <chel@chelsea.lib.mi.us>
Web site: <chelsea.lib.mi.us>

Hours: Open 10 a.m. to 9 p.m. Mondays through Thursdays; 10 a.m. to 6 p.m. Fridays; and 10 a.m. to 5 p.m. Saturdays during the academic year. Open 10 a.m. to 8 p.m. Mondays through Thursdays; 10 a.m. to 6 p.m. Fridays; and 10 a.m. to 3 p.m. Saturdays.

Genealogical/historical collection: 100 items for in-house use only. Includes databases; cemetery records; county or local history books; family genealogies; genealogical periodicals; maps or atlases; military records; newspapers; and original papers, manuscripts, and diaries.

Items in this collection that may not be found in others include the Family Index Collection <chelsea.lib.mi.us/familyindex.htm>, formerly known as the Obituary File, for those who died in Chelsea and the surrounding areas. The collection has more than 65,000 entries.

Written queries: Will not do research. Will look up obituaries. "Limited to three lookups each time."

Ypsilanti District Library
5577 Whittaker Rd.
Ypsilanti, Mich. 48197
Telephone: (734) 482-4110
Web site: <www.ypsilibrary.org/>

Hours: Open 10 a.m. to 9 p.m. Mondays through Thursdays; 10 a.m. to 6 p.m. Fridays and Saturdays; and 1 p.m. to 5 p.m. Sundays (September through May).

Genealogical/historical collection: About 300 books, plus microfilm, photos, clippings, and periodicals for in-house use only. Includes databases; state census indexes; county or local history books; city directories; DAR records (Michigan 1893-1930); maps or atlases; military records; newspapers; and periodicals (genealogical or historical).

Items in this collection that may not be found in others include "Ypsilanti newspapers on microfilm back to 1864."

Written queries: Will not answer. "We direct users to the sources available here."

Other: "The Michigan/Ypsilanti Room is located on the second floor behind the Reference Desk. It not only contains the library's collection of books, maps, photographs, and clippings about our area but also has a computer that can access both the library's collection and the Internet and a microfilm reader/printer for the use of genealogists studying census records and old newspapers."

Wayne County

Archdiocese of Detroit
Archives Department
1234 Washington Rd.
Detroit, Mich. 48226-1875
Telephone: (313) 237-5846
Fax: (313) 237-5791
E-mail: <archives@aod.org>
Web site: <www.archdioceseofdetroit.org>

Hours: By appointment only.

Genealogical/historical collection: "There is no on-site genealogical research. Inquiries are redirected to the main Detroit Public Library. The same original records are available on microfilm for public use." Archives has more than 800 volumes of original church registers for closed parishes only; county or local history books; church records; maps or atlases; original papers, manuscripts, and diaries; and vital records.

Items in this collection that may not be found in others include "photos of individual churches and pastors who may have served there and biographical information on Catholic priests serving the Detroit area."

Written queries: Will answer. "Limited research service usually to provide guidance/advice about alternative sources for information. Written inquiry required either by letter or e-mail. No set fee, only a stamped, self-addressed envelope."

Bacon Memorial District Library
45 Vinewood St.
Wyandotte, Mich. 48192-5221
Telephone: (734) 246-8357
Fax: (734) 282-1540
Web site: <wyandotte.lib.mi.us>

Hours: Open 10 a.m. to 9 p.m. Mondays through Thursdays and 10 a.m. to 5 p.m. Fridays and Saturdays.

Genealogical/historical collection: 500 books, 10,000 paper items, 1,000 microfilm rolls, plus 8,000 photos for in-house use only. Collection focuses on Wyandotte. Includes federal census records for Michigan; cemetery records; county or local history books; church records; city directories; family genealogies; genealogical periodicals; maps or atlases; newspapers; original papers, manuscripts, and diaries; and vital records.

Items in this collection that may not be found in others include 8,000 historical photos of the area <wyandotte.lib.mi.us/vewebsite/index.htm> and an index of the local newspapers back to 1882.

Written queries: Will answer. "A half-hour search is $5. For anything more involved, contact us first for information on how to proceed."

Burton Historical Collection
Detroit Public Library
5201 Woodward Ave.
Detroit, Mich. 48202-4093
Telephone: (313) 833-1480
E-mail: <dporemba@detroit.lib.mi.us>
Web site: <www.detroit.lib.mi.us/burton/burton_index.htm>

Hours: Open noon to 8 p.m. Tuesdays and Wednesdays and 10 a.m. to 6 p.m. Thursdays, Fridays, and Saturdays.

Genealogical/historical collection: 400,000 books, 50,000 microfilms, 250,000 photographs; and 12 million pieces in the manuscript collections. Includes federal census records for Michigan and other states; state census records; cemetery records; county or local history books; church records; city directories;

DAR records; family genealogies; land records; maps or atlases; military records; newspapers; original papers, manuscripts, and diaries; periodicals (genealogical or historical); tax lists; and vital records. There are restrictions on copying.

Items in this collection that may not be found in others include "original sources from Filby."

Written queries: Will answer.

Other: Non-Detroit residents may be asked to purchase a library card.

Northville District Library
212 W. Cady St.
Northville, Mich. 48167-1560
Web site: <northville.lib.mi.us/>

Genealogical/historical collection: About 45 shelf feet of general genealogy books and publications, about 100 books on local history, and local newspapers on microfilm from 1869 to present, most for in-house use only. Includes databases; federal census records for the "local area only"; cemetery records; county or local history books; church records; city directories; a few family genealogies; maps or atlases; newspapers; a few original papers, manuscripts, and diaries; and periodicals (genealogical or historical).

Items in this collection that may not be found in others include local history.

Written queries: Will answer "if not too labor-intensive. More in-depth searches may be given to local genealogical society members." The society members may charge a fee. (See page 414.)

Other: "Nearly all locally relevant sources are indexed in a database. The newspaper is also indexed from 1869 to 1917 and 1990 to 1995."

Plymouth Historical Museum
155 S. Main St.
Plymouth, Mich. 48171
Telephone: (734) 455-8940
Fax: (734) 455-7747
E-mail: <director@plymouthhistory.org>
Web site: <www.plymouthhistory.org/>

Hours: Open 1 p.m. to 4 p.m. Wednesdays, Thursdays, Saturdays, and Sundays.

Genealogical/historical collection: Closed stacks. Must have an archivist present, plus there's a $5 research fee. The collection concentrates on Plymouth and the surrounding areas and includes databases; federal census records for Michigan; cemetery records; county or local history books; church records; city directories; DAR records; family genealogies; land records; maps or atlases; military records; newspapers; original papers, manuscripts, and diaries; periodicals (genealogical or historical); tax lists; and vital records.

Written queries: "Cost is $10 for one request, plus the cost of copies."

River Rouge Historical Museum
10600 W. Jefferson Ave.
River Rouge, Mich. 48218
Telephone: (313) 842-4713
E-mail: <dmswek1234@aol.com>
Hours: Open noon to 4 p.m. Sundays or by appointment.

Genealogical/historical collection: "Small genealogical" collection includes federal census records for Michigan ("local area only, 1900, 1920, 1930"); county or local history books; "limited" church records; city directories; family genealogies; land abstracts; maps or atlases; military records; newspapers (1930-1980s); and vital records ("published sources").

Items in this collection that may not be found in others include materials on ship-building; collections of memorabilia on organizations, local businesses, and local government; and family photos.

Written queries: Will answer for a donation to the museum.

Trenton Veterans Memorial Library
2790 Westfield Rd.
Trenton, Mich. 48183
Web site: <www.trenton.lib.mi.us/>

Genealogical/historical collection: 600 to 700 items for in-house use only. Includes cemetery records; county or local history books; church records; city directories; reports; school research papers; and yearbooks from the local high school.

Items in this collection that may not be found in others include local history.

Written queries: Will answer.

Wayne State University
Walter P. Reuther Library
5401 Cass Ave.
Detroit, Mich. 48202
Telephone: (313) 577-4024
Fax: (313) 577-4003
Web site: <www.reuther.wayne.edu/>

On the **Web**

To find other libraries in Michigan, researchers can check the Michigan Interactive Library Directory <envoy.libofmich.lib.mi.us/isapi/4disapi.dll/directory/search.html>. The directory lists information about 2,000 libraries and library organizations in the state. Researchers can search the site by such items as category, library name, or city. Results provide the addresses and contact information for the libraries or organizations and links to their sites.

Hours: Open 11 a.m. to 6:45 p.m. Mondays and Tuesdays and 9 a.m. to 4:45 p.m. Wednesdays through Fridays.

Genealogical/historical collection: "Sizeable" collection for in-house use only. Includes newspapers; original papers, manuscripts, and diaries; and periodicals (genealogical or historical).

Items in this collection that may not be found in others include labor union newspapers, university-related materials, and original papers.

Written queries: "Anything taking 15 minutes or longer, a graduate student researcher has to be hired. Rate of pay is $15 per hour. One must contact the researcher personally."

Other: "Genealogy is not our mainstay. However, university records and labor union newspapers are used extensively for this type of research."

Wexford County

Cadillac-Wexford Public Library
411 S. Lake St.
Cadillac, Mich. 49601
Telephone: (231) 775-6541
Fax: (231) 775-1749
Web site: <www.cadillaclibrary.org/>

Hours: From Memorial Day to Labor Day, open 8:30 a.m. to 8:30 p.m. Mondays and Wednesday; 8:30 a.m. to 5:30 p.m. Tuesdays, Thursdays, and Fridays; and 8:30 a.m. to 12:30 p.m. Saturdays. From Labor Day to Memorial Day, open 8:30 a.m. to 8:30 p.m. Mondays through Thursdays and 8:30 a.m. to 5:30 p.m. Fridays and Saturdays.

Genealogical/historical collection: 300 volumes, most for in-house use only. Includes federal census records for Michigan; state census records; cemetery records; county or local history books; city directories; "very few" family genealogies; land records; maps or atlases; newspapers (from 1970 only); and periodicals (genealogical or historical).

Items in this collection that may not be found in others include city directories and local history.

Written queries: "We refer them to the genealogy organization."

Out-of-State

Allen County Public Library
Fred J. Reynolds Historical Genealogy Department
Permanent Location:
900 Webster St.
Fort Wayne, Ind. 46802
Temporary Location:
200 E. Berry St.
Fort Wayne, Ind. 46802

Telephone: (260) 421-1225
Fax: (260) 422-9688
Web site: <www.acpl.lib.in.us/genealogy>
Hours: Open 9 a.m. to 9 p.m. Mondays through Thursdays; 9 a.m. to 6 p.m. Fridays and Saturdays; and 1 p.m. to 6 p.m. Sundays (between Labor Day and Memorial Day).

Genealogical/historical collection: Nearly 600,000 items of books and microtext. "Largest genealogy collection in a public library in the country." Includes databases; all federal population schedules for all states, 1790-1930; several state-level censuses, including Michigan; cemetery records; county or local history books; church records; city directories (30,000 Polk directories from 1964 to present; directories on microfiche for 240 cities, 1785-1860; and directories on microfilm for 79 cities, 1861-1935); DAR records; more than 38,000 family genealogies; land records; maps or atlases; military records; newspapers; original papers, manuscripts, and diaries; periodicals (genealogical or historical); tax lists; vital records; and passenger lists.

Items in this collection that may not be found in others include "many family and local county histories for North American geographic areas that one would be hard pressed to find in many other places."

Written queries: "We offer a fee-based information service."

Other: "The department holds the largest English-language genealogy and local history periodical collection in the world with more than 3,200 current subscriptions and more than 4,100 titles." PERSI, the Periodical Source Index, is compiled by library staff members. (See page 96 for more on PERSI.)

National Archives and Records Administration
Great Lakes Region
7358 S. Pulaski Rd.
Chicago, Ill. 60629-5898
Telephone: (773) 581-7816
Fax: (312) 353-1294
E-mail: <chicago.archives@nara.gov>
Web site: <www.nara.gov/regional/chicago.html>
Hours: Open 8 a.m. to 4:15 p.m. weekdays. "For additional hours, call or check our Web site."

Genealogical/historical collection: NARA's Chicago facility has historical records from federal agencies and courts in Illinois, Indiana, Michigan, Minnesota, Ohio, and Wisconsin. Records of interest to Michigan researchers include naturalization records from U.S. District Courts at Marquette, Grand Rapids, Detroit, and Bay City; bankruptcy, civil and criminal records of the U.S. District Courts at Marquette, Grand Rapids, Kalamazoo, Bay City, Detroit, and Flint; World War I draft registration cards, 1917-1918; World War II draft registration cards for Michigan men born on or between April 28, 1877, and Feb. 16, 1897; and Native American census rolls.

Other: Researchers are advised to call or e-mail before visiting.

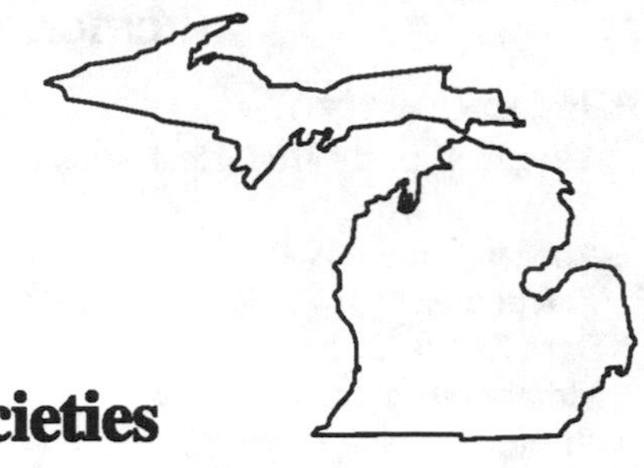

12
Historical and Genealogical Societies

Genealogical and historical societies can be rich sources of information and assistance. Some offer to answer queries or to do research (generally for a small fee or donation), while others maintain archives, museums, or libraries. Some societies publish newsletters or magazines in which researchers can place queries. Other societies publish abstracts or transcriptions of records or local history books. Many have Web sites that include such items as photographs, surname indexes, cemetery or census transcriptions, or abstracts of vital records. Best of all, most societies do not require individuals to be members to make use of their services and resources. Joining a society, however, is an excellent way for researchers to network with people who share similar interests.

Many of Michigan's genealogical and historical societies are listed in this chapter.[1] Other sources of information for Michigan societies include:

- *The Ancestry Family Historian's Address Book* (2003, or current edition)
- Cyndi's List of Michigan Societies and Groups <www.cyndislist.com/mi.htm#Societies>
- *Directory of Historical Organizations in the United States and Canada* (2002, or current edition)
- *Genealogist's Address Book* (1998, or current edition)
- *Handybook for Genealogists* (2002, or current edition)
- Historical Society of Michigan's list of Local Societies and Historical Organizations <www.hsmichigan.org/societies.php>
- Michigan Genealogical Council's list of Member Societies <www.rootsweb.com/~mimgc/member.htm>
- MIGenWeb's list of Genealogical and Historical Societies <www.rootsweb.com/~migenweb/migensoc.htm>
- Society Hall <www.familyhistory.com/societyhall/>

One note of caution: before purchasing any of the publications listed below or visiting a society's library, museum, or archives, contact the society for its current policies, library or museum hours, or publication prices.

Alger County

Alger County Historical Society
P.O. Box 201
Munising, Mich. 49862

Allegan County

Allegan County Historical Society
13 Walnut St.
Allegan, Mich. 49010
Telephone: (616) 673-8292 or (616) 673-4853
Date founded: 1952
Membership dues: $5
Number of members: 130

Purpose: "To encourage historical study and research, to collect and preserve historical material connected with the county of Allegan, and to house such material where it may be displayed and made accessible."

Library/archives: The society also refers researchers to the Allegan Public Library, 331 Hubbard St., Allegan, 49010, (616) 673-4625, <web.triton.net/a/allegan>.

Publications: Several books are available, including atlases and atlas indexes for Allegan County for 1864, 1873, 1895, and 1913.

Research service: "We refer all requests to a very qualified researcher. Her prices are very reasonable."

Holland Genealogical Society
c/o Herrick District Library
300 River Ave.
Holland, Mich. 49423
Date founded: 1974
Membership dues: $18
Number of members: 70

Library/archives: The society's holdings are at the Herrick District Library (see pages 300-301).

Magazine/newsletter: Members receive *Family Ties,* published three times a year. Some back issues also are available for purchase.

Research service: $15 per hour. One-hour minimum.

Holland Historical Trust
31 W. 10th St.
Holland, Mich. 49423-3101
Telephone: (616) 394-1362
Fax: (616) 394-4756
E-mail: <hollandmuseum@hollandmuseum.org>
Web site: <hollandmuseum.org>
Date founded: 1986
Membership dues: $20 to $1,000
Number of members: 860

Library/archives: Located at the address above, holdings include a Dutch heritage collection and local history.

Museum: The Holland Museum, located at the address above, is open 10 a.m. to 5 p.m. Mondays through Saturdays and 2 p.m. to 5 p.m. Sundays. Closed Tuesdays.

Publications: Several books are available, including *Dutch Immigrant Memoirs and Related Writings* and *Dutch in Michigan.*

Research service: Yes.

Then and Now Historical and Genealogical Society
532 N. Main St.
Wayland, Mich. 49348-1043
Telephone: (269) 792-9970
Fax: (269) 792-0809
E-mail: <barbhugh@accn.org>
Web site: <www.thenandnowsociety.0catch.com/>
Date founded: 1996
Membership dues: $8 single; $10 family
Number of members: 35
Purpose: "Preservation of records."

Library/archives: The society's collection is located in the Dorr Elementary School #316, located on 18th St., two blocks south of 142nd St. in Dorr. The library is open Wednesdays from 1 p.m. to 5 p.m.

Magazine/newsletter: Members receive a quarterly newsletter.

Publications: *1864 Atlas of Allegan County,* $30.

Research service: Donation required.

Alpena County

Northeast Michigan Genealogical Society
c/o Jesse Besser Museum
491 Johnson St.
Alpena, Mich. 49707

Antrim County

Bellaire Area Historical Society
202 N. Bridge St.
P.O. Box 646
Bellaire, Mich. 49615
Telephone: (231) 533-8631
Date founded: 1973
Membership dues: $7
Number of members: 75

Purpose: "To preserve the history of the area and maintain a museum relative to same."

Museum: Bellaire Area Historical Museum, located at the address above, has displays of pictures and artifacts from 1865 to 1965.

Publications: The society sells books by local authors, including *Pioneer Notes* and *Antrim Steamers.*

Research service: "Two of our members do research for the persons we receive requests from. They are on their own, but usually share any donations they receive for their work."

Elk Rapids Area Historical Society
401 River St.
P.O. Box 2
Elk Rapids, Mich. 49629
Telephone: (231) 264-5692
Date founded: 1972
Number of members: 120

Purpose: "To bring together those people interested in history, especially the history of our community."

Museum: The Elk Rapids Museum, located at the address above, is open 2 p.m. to 4 p.m. Saturdays and Sundays in the winter and 1 p.m. to 4 p.m. Tuesdays, Thursdays, Saturdays, and Sundays in the summer. "The museum features many articles and artifacts pertaining to the history of Elk Rapids. There are many books and pictures, many of them for sale."

Publications: Several books are for sale, including the *Elk Rapids Town Hall Centennial Booklet,* $2 postpaid.

Research service: Yes.

Helena Township Historical Society
10670 Coy St.
P.O. Box 204
Alden, Mich. 49612
Telephone: (231) 331-4274
Date founded: 1989
Membership dues: $10
Number of members: 90

Purpose: "To establish and maintain a historical museum in the Alden Depot."

Museum: The museum is open Memorial Day to Labor Day from 1 p.m. to 4 p.m. Thursdays through Sundays or by appointment.

Publications: Local historical books.

Research service: No cost.

Mancelona Area Genealogy Society
P.O. Box 103
Mancelona, Mich. 49659
Telephone: (231) 587-0503
Fax: (231) 587-0503 (not always available)
E-mail: <edcripmd@torchlake.com>
Date founded: 1994

Membership dues: $10, individuals; $25, lifetime

Number of members: 90

Purpose: "To promote the history of the area and pride through meetings, the book *Mancelona in the 20th Century,* and a recently acquired building for a museum."

Museum: The old Antrim Iron Company Store was donated in October 2002 to be a museum.

Publications: *Mancelona in the 20th Century,* $40, plus $5 postage. Profits to go toward museum.

Research service: "We are planning [a research service] or offer purchase of our book, *Mancelona in the 20th Century,* which has a 'Who's Who' of 280 families."

Arenac County

Arenac County Historical Society

304 Michigan Ave.
P.O. Box 272
Au Gres, Mich. 48703

Telephone: (989) 876-6399

Date founded: 1970

Membership dues: $10 individuals; $15 couples/families

Number of members: 200

Purpose: "A non-profit educational organization to preserve history and to establish and operate a museum."

Library/archives: "We do not have a public library at the museum. Everything in our museum and archives has been donated so we have limited resources." Resources include Arenac County cemetery records; some township assessment and election records; and some school records.

Museum: Yes.

Research service: "We do limited research. This is an all-volunteer organization. We do research by appointment as time permits."

Bay County

Bay County Genealogical Society of Michigan

P.O. Box 1366
Bay City, Mich. 48706-0366

Telephone: (989) 684-6819

E-mail: <theakergen@chartermi.net>

Web site: <www.rootsweb.com/~mibcgs/bay_co_web_5/Page_1x.html>

Date founded: 1968

Membership dues: $10, individuals; $12, families

Number of members: About 130.

Purpose: "To assist and encourage members in their genealogical research; to assist others by collecting and preserving genealogical and historical data; to cooperate with other genealogical societies; to assist area libraries in expanding their genealogical sections."

Library/archives: The society has holdings at the Bay County Public Library (see page 301).

Museum: Bay County Historical Museum, located at 321 Washington Ave., Bay City, Mich. 48708, has various displays throughout the year. There also is a small library with limited hours. Call (989) 893-5733.

Magazine/newsletter: Members receive *The Clarion,* a quarterly newsletter.

Publications: Several publications are available including cemetery transcriptions and obituary indexes for the *Bay City Times.*

Research service: "Limited to volunteer members. Cost is negotiable."

Other: "An area resources booklet is being developed that is targeted specifically to genealogists and others doing research in the Bay County area."

Saginaw River Marine Historical Society
Dept. W
P.O. Box 2051
Bay City, Mich. 48707
Telephone: (989) 686-1895
Date founded: 1990
Membership dues: $10, $20, $300
Number of members: 225

Purpose: "To preserve and interpret the maritime history of the Saginaw River and its connecting waterways."

Magazine/newsletter: Members received the newsletter, *MODOC Whistle.*

Research service: "Cost depends on the amount of material needed."

Other: "Programs on maritime history available to schools or civic organizations."

Benzie County

Benzie Area Historical Society
6941 Traverse Ave.
P.O. Box 185
Benzonia, Mich. 49615
Telephone: (231) 882-5539
Fax: (231) 882-5539
E-mail: <museum@t-one.net>
Membership dues: $25, senior citizens; $35, regular
Number of members: 513

Purpose: "To collect two- and three-dimensional artifacts pertaining to Benzie County."

Library/archives: Holdings include old newspapers.

Museum: The Benzie Area Historical Museum (archives and museum) is open 10 a.m. to 4 p.m. Tuesdays through Saturdays May through December. It is also open Mondays in June, July, and August and can be opened by appointment.

Magazine/newsletter: Members receive the quarterly, *Benzie Heritage.*
Research service: $15 per hour, plus postage and copy costs.

Berrien County

Berrien County Genealogical Society

P.O. Box 8808
Benton Harbor, Mich. 49023-8808
Telephone: (219) 429-6335
E-mail: <bcgensoc@gtm.net>
Web site: <w3.qtm.net/bcgensoc/index.htm>
Membership dues: $15
Number of members: 140

Purpose: "To stimulate interest in genealogy, to acquire and share genealogical materials, to preserve records of ancestors in Berrien County, and to assist genealogists with educational meetings."

Library/archives: The society's holdings are at the Berrien Springs Community Library (see page 303).

Magazine/newsletter: Members receive *Past Finder,* a monthly.

Publications: Several books are available, including cemetery transcriptions and *Historical Sketches of Berrien County,* Vol. 3, $5.95, Vol. 4, $7.95, plus $4 shipping.

Research service: Yes.

Other: "We have monthly meetings and beginner's genealogy classes. We have Pioneer Certificate kits for sale. This program is focused around Berrien County pioneers and has an annual potluck."

Berrien County Historical Association

313 N. Case St.
P.O. Box 261
Berrien Springs, Mich. 49103
Telephone: (269) 471-1202
Fax: (269) 471-7412
E-mail: <info@berrienhistory.org>
Web site: <www.berrienhistory.org>
Date founded: 1967
Membership dues: $20, individuals; $30, families
Number of members: 350

Purpose: "To operate the 1839 Courthouse Square in Berrien Springs as a museum and to interpret the history of Berrien County."

Museum: Located at the address above, research hours are 9 a.m. to 4 p.m. weekdays. An appointment is required. "Holdings include original Berrien County marriage certificates (1831-1929), death records (1867-1929), probate court estate files (1831-1935), probate court estate files for minor children (1834-1906), and miscellaneous records. We do not have birth records."

Publications: *Historical Sketches of Berrien County,* volumes 3 and 4, $7.95 each (volumes 1 and 2 being reprinted); *Millennial Visions and Earthly Pursuits: the Israelite House of David,* $8.95; and *Lost on the Lakes: Shipwrecks of Berrien County, Michigan.* Publication details are online <www.berrienhistory.org/giftshop/gsindex.html>.

Research service: $20 per hour plus photocopy fees. "If researchers already know what documents they wish photocopied, we will photocopy and mail them at a set fee of $3 each for marriage and death records and $10 each for probate court files."

Four Flags Area Genealogical Society
P.O. Box 414
Niles, Mich. 49120
E-mail: <FourFlagsGen@aol.com>
Web site: <www.fourflagsgenealogicalsociety.com/index.html>

Southwest Michigan Chapter, AHSGR
c/o Paul Koehler
1468 Saint Joseph Circle
Saint Joseph, Mich. 49085-9707
Telephone: (269) 428-0483
E-mail: <pkoe662885@aol.com>
Date founded: 1970
Membership dues: $10, local; $50, national
Number of members: About 100

Purpose: "To bring together people interested in the history and culture of Germans from Russia; to promote understanding and preservation of the heritage."

Magazine/newsletter: Members receive local chapter newsletter.

Written queries: "Inquiries should be handled by e-mail."

Other: Most resources are available through the society's International Headquarters AHSGR, 631 D St., Lincoln, Neb. 68502.

Calhoun County

Calhoun County Genealogical Society
P.O. Box 879
Marshall, Mich. 49068
Web site: <www.rootsweb.com/~micalhou/ccgs.htm>

Marshall Historical Society
107 N. Kalamazoo Ave.
Marshall, Mich. 49068
Telephone: (269) 781-8544
Fax: (269) 789-0371
E-mail: <dircherie@cablespeed.com>
Web site: <www.marshallhistoricalsociety.org>
Date founded: 1961

Membership dues: $10 and up
Number of members: 285
Purpose: "To preserve, protect, and promote Marshall's historical heritage."

Cass County

Cass County Historical Commission
24010 Hospital St., Apt. 105
Cassopolis, Mich. 49031-9690
Telephone: (269) 445-9016
Date founded: 1974
Membership: Appointed by the County Board of Commissioners
Number of members: 9
Purpose: "To encourage and promote interest in the history of Cass County."
Museum: Historic Newton Home is located at 20689 Marcellus Highway, and the Brick School is located on M-62 South Cassopolis.

Publications: Several books are available, including *1860 Map of Cass, Berrien and Van Buren County, Michigan,* $15, plus $2.25 shipping; *1872 Atlas of Cass County, Michigan,* $15, plus $2.25 shipping; *History of Cass County, From 1825 to 1875,* $25, plus $5 shipping; and *History of Cass County, Michigan,* $30, plus $5 shipping. Publications also are available at the Cass District Library (see page 307) and Dowagiac Public Library.

Research service: "Only on a volunteer basis."

Charlevoix County

Beaver Island Historical Society
P.O. Box 263
Saint James, Mich. 49782
Telephone: (231) 448-2254
E-mail: <history@beaverisland.net>
Web site: <beaverisland.net/history>
Date founded: 1956
Membership dues: $10 or $200
Number of members: 408
Library/archives: The Beaver Island Historical Society Archives.

Museum: The Mormon Print Shop Museum and The Marine Museum <www.beaverisland.net/History/Museums/index.htm>.

Magazine/newsletter: *Journal of Beaver Island History,* Vol. 1 (1976), Vol. 2 (1982), Vol. 3 (1988), Vol. 4 (1998), and Vol. 5 (2002), $12 each. Details are online <www.beaverisland.net/History/Books-Maps/index.htm>.

Research service: "We expect material expenses to be reimbursed."

Charlevoix County Genealogical Society
P.O. Box 7
Boyne City, Mich. 49712

Telephone: (231) 582-9602
Date founded: 1970s
Membership dues: $10 per year
Number of members: 32
Web site: <www.rootsweb.com/~micharle/cx-03.htm>

Library/archives: The society's holdings are at the Boyne District Library (see page 308). "Emphasis on and a good collection of local history of Charlevoix County. We also gather as much information as possible about surrounding areas."

Publications: Several books are available, including several cemetery transcriptions and *Plat Book of Charlevoix County, 1901,* $16, plus postage. See the society's Web site <www.rootsweb.com/~micharle/cx-05.htm> for more information.

Research service: "One hour free for new members. Minor lookups free."

Other: The society has an ongoing project of indexing old area newspapers and has an obituary file of all obituaries published in Charlevoix and Emmet county newspapers since the early 1980s.

Cheboygan County

Cheboygan County Genealogical Society

P.O. Box 51
Cheboygan, Mich. 49721
Web site: <www.rootsweb.com/~miccgs/CCGSmainx.html>
Date founded: 1979
Membership dues: $10 per year (April to April)
Number of members: 104
Purpose: "Genealogy awareness, preservation, education."

Magazine/newsletter: Members receive the quarterly, *Cheboygan Rivertown Roots.*

Publications: *Cemetery Recordings of Cheboygan County, Michigan.*

Research service: Cost depends "on the individual taking on the query."

Historical Society of Cheboygan County

P.O. Box 5005
Cheboygan, Mich. 49721

Research Service: Research requests are referred to the Cheboygan County Genealogical Society (see above).

Chippewa County

Bay Mills-Brimley Historical Research Society

P.O. Box 273
Brimley, Mich. 49715
Telephone: (906) 248-3487
Web site: <www.baymillsbrimleyhistory.org>
Date founded: 1981

Membership dues: $7.50
Number of members: About 100
Purpose: "To preserve the history of the Bay Mills-Brimley area and to operate a small museum."
Museum: Wheels of History, a museum located on M-221 at Depot St. in Brimley, is open 10 a.m. to 4 p.m. Saturdays and Sundays May 15 to June 15 and Labor Day to October 15 and 10 a.m. to 4 p.m. Wednesdays through Sundays June 15 to Labor Day.
Publications: *Brief History of Brimley Bay Mills Area,* $4, and *Lighthouse Memories,* $3.

Chippewa County Genealogical Society
P.O. Box 1686
Sault Sainte Marie, Mich. 49783
Web site: <www.rootsweb.com/~michcgs/index.html>

Chippewa County Historical Society
P.O. Box 342
Sault Sainte Marie, Mich. 49783
Telephone: (906) 635-7082
Fax: (906) 635-9280
E-mail: <cchs@sault.com>
Web site: <www.rootsweb.com/~micchs/>
Date founded: 1919
Membership dues: $20, individuals; $10, seniors
Museum: A "small display area" is located on the lower level of 409 Ashmun St.
Publications: *Chippewa County: Memories of the 20th Century,* $10.

Drummond Island Historical Society
P.O. Box 293
Drummond Island, Mich. 49726
Telephone: (906) 493-5746
Date founded: 1940
Membership dues: $10, individuals; $15, families; $100, lifetime
Number of members: 86
Library/archives: "We have some birth and death certificates back to 1910."
Museum: Open 1 p.m. to 5 p.m. daily June to mid-October.
Publications: *History of Drummond Island* and *Island of the Manitou.*

Clare County

Clare Historical Society
109 5th St.
Clare, Mich. 48617
Date founded: 1993
Membership dues: $10 per year

Number of members: About 40

Purpose: "Collection of historical objects of all kinds, manner and nature; to obtain real, personal and mixed property; to present exhibits, pageants, erect markers, sponsor or engage in activities related to Clare County."

Library/archives: "We have a limited local archives in our museum, but as of this writing there are no set times. Appointments only."

Publications: *Spikehorn,* the life story of John E. Spikehorn Meyers.

Research service: "Very limited. Some members do limited research on a personal desire to be helpful. There is no set fee."

Harrison Area Genealogical Society
P.O. Box 796
Harrison, Mich. 48625
Web site: <www.rootsweb.com/~miclare/harrison.htm>

White Pine Historical Society
2865 E. Rock Rd.
Clare, Mich. 48617
Telephone: (989) 386-7178
Fax: (989) 386-7178 (let it ring four times)
Date founded: 1977
Membership dues: $5 per year
Purpose: "To research history."
Publications: *Michigan's Timber Battleground* and *Michigan's Heartland.*

Clinton County

Clinton County Historical Society
P.O. Box 174
Saint Johns, Mich. 48879
Web site: <www.dewittlibrary.com/CCHS/>
Date founded: 1974
Membership dues: $10, individuals; $15, families
Number of members: 100

Library/archives: "The Archives of the Clinton County Historical Society is located at 16101 Brook Rd., DeWitt Township Community Center, Lansing, Mich. 48906. Volunteers are there to give research assistance from 9 a.m. to 4 p.m. on Mondays and Tuesdays and 2 p.m. to 6 p.m. on Thursdays and Fridays." Holdings include census records and cemetery transcriptions; and newspapers, church histories, scrapbooks, Grange records, pioneer records, town histories, atlases, tax rolls, family histories, photographs, and directories.

Museum: "The Paine-Gillum-Scott Museum is located on the west side of the Courthouse Square in Saint Johns, Mich. It is open from 1 to 4 p.m. Sundays and from 2 to 7 p.m. Wednesdays April 1 to Dec. 31. The 1860 historic house has six rooms of period furniture and seven rooms of exhibits and artifacts."

Publications: Several books are available, including *Historical Date Book of Clinton County,* $5, plus $1 postage; *Past and Present of Clinton County, Michigan,* $40, plus $5 postage; and *1864 Plat Map of Clinton County, Michigan,* $5, plus $2 postage. For more information, see the society's Web site.

Research service: Inquiries can be sent to the Genealogists of Clinton County (see below).

Elsie Historical Society
c/o Elizabeth Hess
Box 125
Elsie, Mich. 48831
Web site: <www.rootsweb.com/~migratio/elsiehiso/elsiehistsoc.html>

Genealogists of the Clinton County Historical Society
P.O. Box 23
Saint Johns, Mich. 48879-0023
Telephone: (517) 482-5117
E-mail: <ccgensoc@yahoo.com>
Web site: <www.dewittlibrary.com/CCHS/>
Membership dues: $10, individuals; $15, couples
Number of members: More than 100

Purpose: "To preserve Clinton County historical and genealogical materials and to make them accessible to researchers."

Archives: See the Clinton County Historical Society listing above.

Magazine/newsletter: Members receive *Clinton County Trails,* a quarterly newsletter.

Publications: Several books available, including *Cemeteries in Clinton County, Michigan,* $1, plus 50 cents postage; *1840 Federal Census, Clinton County, Michigan,* $5, plus $1 postage; and *1940 Rural Directory of Clinton County, Michigan,* $7.50, plus $2 postage. For more information, see the society's Web site.

Research service: $6 per hour

Other: The society's Web site offers searchable databases of Clinton County marriages (1863-1940), births, and deaths.

Delta County

Delta County Genealogical Society
P.O. Box 442
Escanaba, Mich. 49829-0442
Telephone: (906) 786-1893
Web site: <grandmastree.com/society/>
Date founded: 1980
Membership dues: $7, individuals; $10, families
Number of members: 60
Purpose: "Researching and compiling county records."

Library/archives: The society's holdings, totalling more than 1,000 items, are housed at the Escanaba Public Library, 400 Ludington St., Escanaba, 49829, (906) 786-7323. Hours are 9 a.m. to 8: 30 p.m. Mondays through Thursdays and 10 a.m. to 5 p.m. Fridays and Saturdays. "A member of the society will be on hand in the library one day each week to offer assistance. You may contact the library as to what day this assistance is available."

Magazine/newsletter: Members receive a quarterly newsletter.

Research service: "Our society does not have staff available to do research. Anyone needing research assistance from the Delta County area may contact volunteers listed at the Delta County Genealogical Society Web page."

Other: The society's Web site offers several databases, including a Birth Record Index (1867-1915); Hospital Patient Records (1897-1914); Marriage Records (1862-1927); Divorce Index (1883-1949); and a Probate Record Index (1873-1975).

Garden Peninsula Historical Society
P.O. Box 202
Garden, Mich. 49835
Telephone: (906) 644-2165
Web site: <www.dsisd.k12.mi.us/bigbay/GPHS.htm>
Date founded: 1975
Membership dues: $5
Number of members: 78

Purpose: "Preserve the local history and genealogical records of the peninsula as well as display and protect artifacts."

Museum: The museum archives has the history of 400 pioneer families and up-to-date cemetery records for the area. It is open from 11 a.m. to 3 p.m. Wednesdays through Sundays during the summers. Requests for information will be answered year-round.

Magazine/newsletter: Members and donors receive *The Peninsula Historian,* a newsletter published three times a year.

Publications: Several books are available, including *A History of the Garden Peninsula,* $25, plus $4 postage and *Our Heritage,* $30, plus $4 postage.

Research service: Donation requested, plus 25 cents per copy.

Other: "Our materials are listed on the Internet through the Library of Congress at <lcweb.loc.gov/coll/nucmc>."

Dickinson County

Dickinson County Genealogical Society
c/o Dickinson County Library
401 Iron Mountain St.
Iron Mountain, Mich. 49801
Date founded: 1977
Membership dues: $10 per year

Number of members: 50

Purpose: "To promote genealogical research."

Library/archives: Holdings in the Dickinson County Library include census (Upper Peninsula and northern Wisconsin) and newspaper microfilms.

Magazine/newsletter: Members receive *Dickinson Diggings,* published four times per year.

Eaton County

Bellevue Area Historical Society

212 N. Main St.
Bellevue, Mich. 49021

Telephone: (269) 763-9049

Date founded: 1976

Membership dues: $10, individuals; $15, families

Number of members: 125

Museum: The Bellevue Memorial Museum shares facilities with the Bellevue Township Library.

Magazine/newsletter: Members receive a quarterly newsletter.

Publications: *1983 Pictorial History,* $5.

Research service: Will do research for cost or donations.

Other: "We maintain the Bellevue Personal History Archives, alphabetized obituaries, births, marriages, etc."

Eaton County Genealogical Society

100 W. Lawrence Ave.
P.O. Box 337
Charlotte, Mich. 48813-0337

Web site: <www.rootsweb.com/~miecgs/index.htm>

Grand Ledge Area Historical Society

P.O. Box 203
Grand Ledge, Mich. 48837-0203

Telephone: (517) 627-4949

Fax: (517) 627-5170

Web site: <www.gdledgehistsoc.org/>

Date founded: 1975

Membership dues: $15, $30, $45

Number of members: 150

Purpose: "To preserve the history of Grand Ledge and make it available to the public and schools through the archives, publications, and the museum."

Library/archives: The society's archives are housed at the Grand Ledge Public Library, 131 E. Jefferson St., Grand Ledge. Includes birth and death records, cemetery records, photos, and information about "people, businesses, groups, town, homes, schools."

Museum: Located at 118 W. Lincoln St., Grand Ledge.
Publications: Several publications are available.
Research service: Yes

Emmet County

Emmet County Genealogical Society
P. O. Box 2476
Petoskey, Mich. 49770
Web site: <members.tripod.com/~deemamafred/ecgs.html>

Little Traverse Historical Society
P.O. Box 162
Petoskey, Mich. 49770
Web site: <members.tripod.com/~deemamafred/lths.html>

Genesee County

Clio Area Historical Association
P.O. Box 295
Clio, Mich. 48420
Telephone: (989) 871-2213
E-mail: <fdclevenger@tds.net>
Date founded: 1976
Membership dues: $5
Number of members: 95

Purpose: "To preserve the history of the Clio area and pass it on to future generations."

Library/archives: Genealogy Hall is open from 1 p.m. to 3 p.m. the first Monday of the month or on the second if the first falls on a holiday; also open by appointment. Holdings include land, death, and cemetery records; histories of Thetford and Vienna townships and Clio; and Genesee County censuses.

Museum: The museum is open from 1 p.m. to 3 p.m. Thursdays and Sundays May through September. Closed October through April, except by appointment.

Publications: *Down Memory Lane,* reminisces of early Clio.
Research service: Will do research for "cost of copies."

Flint Genealogical Society
P.O. Box 1217
Flint, Mich. 48501-1217
Telephone: (810) 694-1445
Web site: <www.rootsweb.com/~mifgs/>
Date founded: 1956
Membership dues: $17, individuals; $20, families
Number of members: More than 400

Library/archives: The society has more than 8,000 items at the Flint Public Library (see page 310). "A book of library holdings is available for $12." The society also has holdings at the Perry Archives (see page 311).

Publications: Several books are available, including census indexes. More information is available online <www.rootsweb.com/~mifgs/fgspubs.html>.

Research service: $10 per hour, plus 10 cents per copy.

Other: The society's Web site includes a cemetery index and a "Red Book Index," an index of death records (1867-1930).

Flushing Area Historical Society
431 W. Main St
P.O. Box 87
Flushing, Mich. 48433
Telephone: (810) 478-0814
Web site: <flushinghistorical.org>
Date founded: 1975
Membership dues: $3, individuals; $5, couples; $2, seniors; $150, lifetime
Number of members: About 500

Purpose: "The purpose of the historical society is to capture the history of the Flushing area. The museum showcases many artifacts of the area."

Museum: "Address all mail to the P.O. Box listed above. The museum is open 1 p.m. to 4 p.m. Sundays May to the first week in December. It is closed all holiday weekends. In addition, volunteers are usually working from 9 a.m. to noon Tuesdays. The museum is a restored 1888 railroad depot and contains memorabilia of the Flushing area and railroad items. Displays of general interest are changed yearly. Holdings of genealogical interest include: *Flushing Observer* (newspaper) 1883 to 1980; Flushing area obituary file (incomplete), approximately 5,000 names; all cemetery index books for the Flushing area; atlases and plat maps for Genesee County 1876 to 1916; Flushing High School Year Books (not all years); and *Flushing Sesquicentennial,* volumes 1-3."

Publications: *Flushing Sesquicentennial,* volumes 2 and 3. For more information, see the society's Web site <flushinghistorical.org/shop.html>.

Research service: "We offer research services limited to the materials at the museum. We do not set a fee, but a minimum donation of $10 is suggested for a one- or two-name search. If several photocopies are made and/or the research takes more than an hour, the cost would increase."

Other: "We have large photo and postcard collections of the area, but these are not cataloged or available at the present time."

Grand Blanc Heritage Association
203 E. Grand Blanc Rd.
Grand Blanc, Mich. 48439-1303
Telephone: (810) 694-7274
Date founded: 1972

Membership dues: $10, individuals; $15, families

Purpose: "To preserve the history of our community and surrounding area."

Museum: The Heritage Museum, located at the address above, is owned by the city of Grand Blanc and operated by volunteers of the association. It is open 10 a.m. to 2 p.m. Wednesdays or by special arrangement. (Closed July, August, and December.) Holdings include books, newspapers, pictures, diaries, ledgers, and public records.

Magazine/newsletter: Members receive five newsletters per year.

Publications: Books available include census transcriptions.

Research service: "No cost. Donations welcome."

Montrose Area Historical Society
144 E. Hickory St.
P.O. Box 577
Montrose, Mich. 48457
Telephone: (810) 639-6644
E-mail: <telemusm@gfn.org>
Web site: <www.gfn.org/telemusm>
Date founded: 1980
Membership dues: $5, individuals; $7, families
Number of members: 90

Library/archives: "We offer books, obituaries, newspapers, and other items pertaining to the history of the Montrose area." Call the number above to schedule an appointment for research.

Museum: The Montrose Historical and Telephone Pioneer Museum, located at the address above, is one of five telephone museums in the United States and the only one in Michigan. It has one of the largest displays of antique phones and related equipment. The museum also has a large changing display of artifacts of the Montrose area, including household and outdoor equipment. The displays are changed about every four months. The museum is open from 1 p.m. to 5 p.m. Saturdays and Sundays April through December and 1 p.m. to 5 p.m. Sundays January through March.

Magazine/newsletter: *The Memory Lane Gazette* is published four times a year. Cost is $6 per year.

Gogebic County

Gogebic Range Genealogical Society
P.O. Box 23
Ironwood, Mich. 49938
Web site: <www.gogebicroots.com/>
Date founded: 2000
Membership dues: $12
Number of members: 100

Purpose: "Preserve the history of and promote genealogy in the Gogebic Range (Gogebic County, Mich., and Iron County, Wis.)."

Magazine/newsletter: Members receive a newsletter.

Research service: "$2 per obituary lookup, based on the names listed on our Web site."

Other: "We maintain a well-developed Web site. The site contains access to local directories (Ironwood), obituary lists, military service members of various wars, and other information of interest to those conducting family research." Membership is required to access certain areas of the Web site.

Grand Traverse County

Grand Traverse Area Genealogical Society
P.O. Box 2015
Traverse City, Mich. 49685
Telephone: (231) 995-9388
Web site: <www.rootsweb.com/~migtags/gtag.htm>
Date founded: 1979
Membership dues: $10, individuals; $15, families
Number of members: 75

Purpose: "Genealogy in Antrim, Benzie, Grand Traverse, Kalkaska, and Leelanau counties."

Library/archives: Holdings are located at the Traverse Area District Library, 610 Woodmere Ave., Traverse City. Includes more than 1,000 books and 100 reels of microfilm.

Newsletter: *Kinship Tales,* published four times a year, has genealogical news, information, and free queries. Single issues are $3 each.

Publications: Several books are available, including cemetery records and census indexes. For more information, see the society's Web site <www.rootsweb.com/~migtags/Cemetery.htm>.

Research service: "One hour free for new members; $10 per hour for others."

Other: The society offers an Ancestral Family Certificate to anyone who can prove descent from an ancestor who lived in Antrim, Benzie, Grand Traverse, Kalkaska, or Leelanau counties prior to 1900. It also offers an Early Settler Certificate to those who can prove their ancestor was in one of these counties prior to 1860.

Gratiot County

Gratiot County Historical and Genealogical Society
P.O. Box 73
Ithaca, Mich. 48847
Web site: <www.rootsweb.com/~migratio/gchgs/index.html>

Houghton County

Cooper Range Historical Society
P.O. Box 148
South Range, Mich. 49963

Telephone: (906) 482-6125
Web site: <www.pasty.com/crhm>
Date founded: 1988
Membership dues: $10, individuals; $15, families; $150, lifetime
Number of members: 300

Purpose: "To preserve the historical heritage of the mines and the surrounding communities: Atlantic Mine, South Range, Baltic, Trimountain, Painesdale, Winona, Toivola, Donken, Redridge, Beacon, Hill, Edgemere, and Freda. Our mission is to help create a sense of life during the copper mining era."

Museum: The Copper Range Historical Museum, located at 44 Trimountain Ave., South Range, is open noon to 4 p.m. Mondays through Saturdays June through mid-October. Cost is $1 per visit for non-members.

Magazine/newsletter: Publishes three newsletters annually.

Houghton County Historical Society
53102 Highway M-26
P.O. Box 127
Lake Linden, Mich. 49945
Telephone: (906) 296-4121
Fax: (906) 296-9191
Date founded: 1968
Membership dues: $20
Number of members: 400
Purpose: Museum and research

Library/archives: Office and research centers are open 9:30 a.m. to 1:30 p.m. "Everything is run by volunteers. Donations expected." The facility has files and newspapers from 1898 to 1974.

Museum: Open 10 a.m. to 4 p.m. Mondays through Saturdays and noon to 4 p.m. Sundays.

Publications: The society has published several books of local history.

Huron County

Pigeon Historical Society
59 S. Main St.
Pigeon, Mich. 48755
Telephone: (989) 453-3864
Date founded: 1976
Membership dues: $5
Number of members: 40
Purpose: "To promote history in the Pigeon area."

Museum: The society's museum is located at the address above in a 95-year-old depot. It's open from noon to 4 p.m. weekdays and 10 a.m. to noon Saturdays during June, July, and August. "We have 4,000 artifacts from our area."

Ingham County

Historical Society of Michigan

1305 Abbott Rd.

East Lansing, Mich. 48823

Telephone: (517) 324-1828

Fax: (517) 324-4370

E-mail: <hsm@hsmichigan.org>

Web site: <www.hsmichigan.org>

Date founded: 1828

Membership dues: $35, regular; $30, seniors

Purpose: "As Michigan's oldest cultural institution, the Historical Society of Michigan preserves and illuminates the state's long and diverse heritage from the arrival of the first Native American to the present day."

Magazine/newsletter: Members receive *Michigan Chronicle,* a quarterly newsletter, and *Michigan Historical Review,* a semi-annual journal of Michigan history.

Publications: *Michigan History Directory,* $19.95, plus $3 shipping. (Michigan residents should add 6 percent sales tax.)

Ingham County Genealogical Society

P.O. Box 85

Mason, Mich. 48854

Telephone: (517) 374-8178

E-mail: <icgs@ingcogenesoc.org>

Web site: <www.ingcogenesoc.org>

Date founded: 1995

Membership dues: $10, individuals; $15, families

Number of members: 115

Purpose: "Preserve and make available research of genealogical records of our members, publish materials of interest and use to genealogists, encourage and assist the study of family history, promote the exchange of knowledge, encourage the deposit of genealogical records, and cooperate with other genealogical groups, societies, and libraries."

Library/archives: The society's collection is housed in the Mason Library, 145 W. Ash St., Mason, and includes many Ingham County resources.

Magazine/newsletter: Members receive the ICGS newsletter, published four times per year.

Publications: Several publications are available, including vital record and funeral home records on CD, newspapers on microfilm, and photographs. See the society's Web site <www.ingcogenesoc.org/icgsorderform.html> for more information.

Other: The society's Web site has an index to the *Ingham County Democrat,* 1901 to 1910.

Mason Area Historical Society
200 E. Oak St.
P.O. Box 44
Mason, Mich. 48854
Telephone: (517) 676-9837
E-mail: <mahsmuseum@aol.com>
Web site: <www.masonmuseum.com/>
Date founded: 1998
Membership dues: $8, individuals; $15, families; $25, patrons; $125, lifetime
Purpose: "To preserve local artifacts and history."

Museum: Located at the corner of Barnes and Oak streets, the Mason Area Historical Museum is open noon to 4 p.m. Tuesdays, Thursdays, and Saturdays. (Closed Tuesdays in January and February.) Holdings include more than 1,000 books about Michigan and local history, clippings, photographs, and oral history tapes.

Publications: *Pink School,* $5; *Mason Yesterday and Today,* $6.95; and *A Walk Through Time,* 50 cents.

Michigan Genealogical Council
P.O. Box 80953
Lansing, Mich. 48908-0953
Web site: <www.rootsweb.com/~mimgc>
Date founded: 1972
Number of members: 78 genealogy societies

Purpose: "To locate, preserve, publish, and deposit in suitable repositories records of value to genealogists and to initiate activities which encourage and assist those involved in genealogical research."

Library/archives: "Our meetings are held at the Library of Michigan (see page 315), and we work cooperatively with them and the State Archives of Michigan (see page 315-316)."

Magazine/newsletter: A newsletter is published quarterly. Cost is $10 per year.

Other: "We have a seminar of general interest to all genealogist, usually every other year. We keep a calendar of upcoming seminars of our member societies listed on our Web site. We fund and research the Michigan Death Index that is published on the Web <www.mdch.state.mi.us/pha/osr/gendisx/search2.htm>. We also have a Michigan Death Without Record Project. Details are on our Web site <www.rootsweb.com/~mimgc/death.htm>."

Mid-Michigan Genealogical Society
P.O. Box 16033
Lansing, Mich. 48901-6033
Web site: <www.rootsweb.com/~mimmgs>
Date founded: 1967

Membership dues: $10, individuals; $15, families

Number of members: 225

Purpose: "To preserve and make available for genealogical research the records of our members; to encourage and assist the study of family history; to promote the exchange of knowledge and to encourage the deposit of genealogical records; to cooperate with other societies and to assist the area libraries in expanding and publicizing their genealogical holdings; to publish materials of interest and use to genealogists."

Library/archives: "Resource materials donated to MMGS are passed on to the Library of Michigan (see page 315)."

Magazine/newsletter: Members receive a newsletter three times a year.

Publications: Several books and booklets are available, including *Evolution of Michigan Townships,* $7, plus $1.10 shipping; cemetery transcriptions; *Combined Ingham County, Michigan, 1874 and 1895 Atlas,* $35 hardcover or $28 softcover, plus $3 shipping; and a six-volume *Index to Ingham County, Michigan, 1894 Census,* $7 for each book or $35 for the set of six, plus $2.50 shipping. See the society's Web site <www.rootsweb.com/~mimmgs/mmgspubl.html> for more information.

Research service: "Fee is $10 per hour and includes standard copy costs, postage, etc."

Ionia County

Ionia County Genealogical Society

13051 Ainsworth Rd.
Route 3
Lake Odessa, Mich. 48849
Web site: <www.rootsweb.com/~miionia/icgshome.htm>

Ionia County Historical Society

P.O. Box 1776
Ionia, Mich. 48846
Telephone: (616) 527-3369
Fax: (616) 527-4252
Date founded: 1974
Membership dues: $20
Number of members: More than 50.

Library/archives: "We offer our sources to anyone who wants to come research. We have Ionia High School annuals, city directories, and other Ionia sources." Holdings are located at Hall Fowler Memorial Library (see page 317).

Publications: The society has a few publications about Ionia.

Lake Odessa Area Historical Society

839 Fourth Ave.
Lake Odessa, Mich. 48849

Telephone: (616) 374-8420 or (517) 566-7317
Date founded: 1968
Membership dues: $12
Number of members: About 150
Purpose: "To preserve the history of the Lake Odessa area; and to preserve and restore the Lake Odessa Depot/Museum."
Archives: Yes
Museum: Yes
Magazine/newsletter: The *Bonanza Bugle,* published four times per year, is $12.
Research service: "The only searches are by volunteers."

Iosco County

AuSable-Oscoda Historical Society and Museum
P.O. Box 679
Oscoda, Mich. 48750
Telephone: (989) 739-2782
Fax: (989) 739-2782
Date founded: 1976
Membership dues: $10 yearly. Membership is required to use the society's services/resources.
Number of members: 65
Archives: Located at the museum. Resources include a postcard file that is open to the public.
Museum: Located at 114 E. River Rd., the museum is open 11 a.m. to 4 p.m. Saturdays and noon to 4 p.m. Sundays during the spring and fall. In the summer, it is open 11 a.m. to 5 p.m. Fridays and Saturdays and noon to 5 p.m. Sundays.
Publications: Books include *Death Records 1850-1950* and a number of books on news accounts and remembrances. A book list is available by writing to the P.O. address above.

Huron Shores Genealogical Society
c/o Elaine Johnston
1909 Bobwhite St.
Oscoda, Mich. 48750
Telephone: (989) 739-5791

Iron County

Crystal Fall Museum Society
17 N. Fourth St.
Box 65
Crystal Falls, Mich. 49920
Telephone: (906) 875-4341

Date founded: 1982

Membership dues: $10

Number of members: 50

Purpose: "To protect, maintain, and restore local history."

Library/archives: The Library, located in the museum, has copies of the local newspaper, the *Diamond Drill,* from 1887 to 1996. "Some weekly issues are missing."

Museum: The Harbour House Museum, located at the address above, is open 11 a.m. to 4 p.m. Tuesdays through Saturdays Memorial Day through Labor Day. Exhibits include a restored turn-of-the-century home setting, a local logging and mining room, a women's interest room, an Ojibwe Indian Room, and a children's antique toy room.

Research service: "A donation of $5 is asked for an obituary." A more difficult request may cost more.

Iron County Historical Society

P.O. Box 272
Caspian, Mich. 49915

Telephone: (906) 265-2617

E-mail: <icmuseum@up.net>

Web site: <ironcountymuseum.com>

Date founded: 1962

Membership dues: $5, seniors; $15-$24, contributing; $25-$99, patrons; $100, benefactors; and $1,000, lifetime.

Number of members: More than 150

Purpose: "To collect artifacts and material on Iron County."

Library/archives: The holdings at the Cultural Center (see the address and hours below) include 51,000 obituary cards, 8,000 photographs, 8,000 maps, about 300 oral history interviews, and more than 160 archival boxes of materials.

Museum: The Iron County Museum and Park, the largest outdoor museum in Michigan's Upper Peninsula, features 22 buildings, including a Cultural Center, homestead, logging camp, logging miniatures, two art galleries, Victorian home and school, iron mining memorial room, and more. Located one mile east of Highway M-189 on Brady Ave. in Caspian, the museum is open 8:30 a.m. to 2 p.m. weekdays in May; 9 a.m. to 5 p.m. Mondays through Saturdays and 1 p.m. to 5 p.m. Sundays in June, July, and August; and 10 a.m. to 4 p.m. Mondays through Saturdays and 1 p.m. to 4 p.m. Sundays in September.

Publications: Several books are available, including *They Came to Iron County,* $6.50, plus $1.50 postage; *The History of Iron County,* $6.50, plus $2 postage; and *Iron County Historical Sites and Landmarks,* $14, plus $3 postage. For more information, see the society's Web site <www.ironcountymuseum.com/giftshop.html>.

Research service: $25 per hour

Isabella County

Genealogical Society of Isabella County
523 N. Fancher
Mount Pleasant, Mich. 48858
Web site: <www.rootsweb.com/~migsic/>

Ziibiwing Cultural Society
6853 Pickard St.
Mount Pleasant, Mich. 48858
Telephone: (989) 775-4121
Fax: (989) 772-1208
Web site: <www.sagchip.org/ziibiwing/index.htm>
Date founded: 1993
Membership dues: None

Purpose: "To enlighten and educate tribal and community members and all other people of the world to the cultural heritage and history of the Saginaw Chippewa Indian Tribe."

Library/archives: Located at the address above, the archives is open by appointment only during normal business hours, 8 a.m. to 5 p.m. weekdays. Holdings include annuity rolls for 1857, 1858, 1859, 1861, 1864, 1865, 1866, and 1867; 1908 Durant Roll; 1939 Isabella County census roll; 1939 Saginaw Chippewa Census roll; 1939 Pinconning-Saganing Census Roll; and allotment rolls for 1883, 1885, and 1891.

Museum: The museum, opened in 2004, features changing and permanent exhibits.

Research service: "ZCS encourages researchers to come in person to do their work, but if they must rely solely on telephone, fax or e-mail, a research fee will be charged after 30 minutes of staff time at the rate of $35 an hour."

Jackson County

Grass Lake Area Historical Society
P.O. Box 53
Grass Lake, Mich. 49240
Telephone: (517) 522-4485
Date founded: 1972
Membership dues: $5
Number of members: 70

Purpose: "To inform, to honor, to educate."

Museum: Coe House Museum is a restored Victorian house and is open by appointment. Call (517) 522-4485 or (517) 522-5141. Grass Lake Depot is a restored depot and is open by appointment. Call (517) 522-4332 or (517) 522-4660. Collections include ledgers, scrapbooks, notes, club minutes of the area, news clippings about the area from 1890s to present, World War I and World War II uniforms, and Civil War information on Michigan only.

Jackson County Genealogical Society
c/o Jackson District Library
244 W. Michigan Ave.
Jackson, Mich. 49201-2275
Web site: <www.rootsweb.com/~mijackso/jcgs.htm>

Kalamazoo County

Kalamazoo Valley Genealogical Society
P.O. Box 405
Comstock, Mich. 49041
Web site: <www.rootsweb.com/~mikvgs/>

Schoolcraft Historical Society
16278 Prairie Ronde
Schoolcraft, Mich. 49087
Date founded: 1976
Membership dues: $9, individuals; $10, families; $100, lifetime.
Number of members: About 75
Purpose: "To preserve and promote the local historical aspects of the community."
Museum: The Schoolcraft Underground Railway House, 613 Cass St., Schoolcraft, does not have regular hours, but tours are available on request. "The restored home serves as a meeting place and a museum of local history."
Publications: *So I'm Told,* a history of the Schoolcraft area in the 19th century.

The Searchers
c/o Pierson
14300 "V" Ave.
Vicksburg, Mich. 49097
Telephone: (269) 778-3712
Date founded: 1978
Membership dues: "As needed."
Number of members: 2

Vicksburg Historical Society
300 N. Richardson St.
P.O. Box 103
Vicksburg, Mich. 49097
Telephone: (269) 649-1733
Web site: <www.rootsweb.com/~mivhs/>
Membership dues: $5, families; $10, contributing; $25, sustaining; $50, patrons
Number of members: 73
Purpose: "To preserve and present the history of the Greater Vicksburg area, including school, business, and family histories."

Museum: The Vicksburg Museum, located at the address above, is open from 1 p.m. to 3 p.m. Tuesdays and from 1 p.m. to 4 p.m. Saturdays. "The museum has 20,000 items relating to the history of the greater Vicksburg area and includes artifacts, photographs, documents, and family histories. The museum is housed in a 1905 train station. It is part of a historic village that includes a 1910 one-room school, letterpress printing museum, and a 1930s farmhouse. For those doing family history research, we ask for a copy of the completed project for our archives. There is a charge for photocopies and computer copies. Floppy disks may be purchased on site."

Magazine/newsletter: Members receive *The Review,* a quarterly newsletter.

Publications: *Glimpses of a 19th Century Village,* $9 softcover or $13 hardcover.

Kalkaska County

Kalkaska Genealogical Society
P.O. Box 353
Kalkaska, Mich. 49646
Web site: <users.rootsweb.com/~mikgs/KGS.htm>

Kent County

Byron Center Historical and Genealogy Society
2508 Prescott St., S. W.
P.O. Box 20
Bryon Center, Mich. 49315-0020
Telephone: (616) 878-0888
Date founded: 1978
Membership dues: $10 per year
Number of members: 220

Purpose: "Organizing a historical and genealogical society for gathering and preserving the history of Byron Township and its families."

Museum: Located at the address above, the museum is open 1 p.m. to 3 p.m. and 5 p.m. to 7 p.m. Mondays or by appointment. Holdings include the general history of Byron in articles and books, cemetery records, school annuals, some church records, an obituary file, and family histories.

Magazine/newsletter: Members receive *Timekeeper Magazine,* or it is $3 per year.

Publications: Several books are available, including *Byron Township Sesquicentennial Album,* $15; *A Century of Progress,* $30; and *1860 Byron Township Census, Kent County,* $10.

Research service: "Need to cover copy charges and postage."

Caledonia Historical Society
P.O. Box 110
Caledonia, Mich. 49316
Web site: <www.angelfire.com/mi/CaledoniaHistory/index.html>

Cedar Springs Historical Society
60 Cedar St.
P.O. Box 296
Cedar Springs, Mich. 49319
Telephone: (616) 696-3335
E-mail: <csmuseum@wingsisp.com>
Date founded: 1967

Membership dues: $10. Membership is required to use the society's resources but not its services.

Number of members: 200

Library/archives: Open from 10 a.m. to 5 p.m. Wednesdays.

Publications: *Railroads of Cedar Springs Area,* $14.95; *History of Solon Township,* $18; and *History of Lincoln Lake,* $30.

Research service: $7.50 per hour.

Lowell Area Historical Association
325 W. Main St.
Lowell, Mich. 49331
Telephone: (616) 897-7688
E-mail: <history@lowellmuseum.org>
Web site: <www.lowellmuseum.org/>
Date founded: 1989

Membership dues: $10, individuals; $20, families; $35, businesses; or $100, patrons

Number of members: 231

Purpose: "To collect, preserve, and present the history of the Lowell area."

Library/archives: Open by appointment. Holdings include obituary file and local citizen and business file.

Museum: Open 1 p.m. to 4 p.m. Tuesdays, Saturdays, and Sundays and 1 p.m. to 8 p.m. Thursdays.

Western Michigan Genealogical Society
c/o Grand Rapids Public Library
111 Library St., N.E.
Grand Rapids, Mich. 49503-3268
E-mail: <wmgs@wmgs.org>
Web site: <www.wmgs.org/>

Other: The society's Web site features several databases, including Kent County School Records, Kent County Obituaries, and the 1860 Kent County Census.

Keweenaw County

Keweenaw County Historical Society
HC-1 Box 265L
Eagle Harbor, Mich. 49950

Telephone: (906) 289-4990
Web site: <www.keweenawhistory.org>
Date founded: 1981
Membership dues: $15
Number of members: 831
Purpose: "Save Keweenaw County history."
Museum: Museums include Eagle Harbor Lighthouse and Museums, Phoenix Church, Rathbone Schoolhouse, Central Mine, and the Bammert Blacksmith Shop. "No library, only museum artifacts."
Publications: Several are listed on the society's Web site <www.keweenawhistory.org/publications.html>.
Magazine/newsletter: Members receive a quarterly newsletter.

Lapeer County

Lapeer County Genealogical Society
P.O. Box 353
Lapeer, Mich. 48446
Date founded: 1980
Membership dues: $15 per year
Number of members: 110
Purpose: Research
Library/archives: The society's Research Center is located in the Lapeer County Historical Society Museum (see below). Materials include census records (1840-1930), Lapeer newspapers on microfilm (1879-1959), family histories, and cemetery records. For an appointment, contact <alhart@intouchmi.com>.
Museum: The Lapeer County Historical Society Museum, located at 518 W. Nepessing St., Lapeer, is open 10 a.m. to 3 p.m. Wednesdays and Saturdays.
Publications: Several books are available, including cemetery transcriptions, Mayfield Township assessment records; marriage abstracts; and indexes to land owners in 1863, 1874, and 1893.
Research service: Requests should be sent to the address above.

Leelanau County

Grand Traverse Lighthouse Museum
15500 N. Lighthouse Point Rd.
P.O. Box 43
Northport, Mich. 49670
Telephone: (231) 386-7195
Fax: (231) 386-7195
E-mail: <info@grandtraverselighthouse.com>
Web site: <www.grandtraverselighthouse.com>
Date founded: 1985
Membership dues: $15, individuals; $25, families

Number of members: 225

Purpose: "To effectively restore, maintain, and develop the GTLH property, in cooperation with other concerned agencies, for the enjoyment of the public and to enhance knowledge and understanding of the area's history and cultural heritage."

Museum: The museum is open from noon to 4 p.m. daily in May, from 10 a.m. to 7 p.m. daily from June 1 to Labor Day, from noon to 4 p.m. daily Labor Day to October, and on the weekends only in November. Holdings include "lighthouse and maritime history and genealogical history of the lightkeepers."

Publications: *Grand Traverse Lighthouse* and *Savor the Treasure,* a sesquicentennial publication about the history of the lighthouse that includes a list of keepers, assistant keepers, and Coast Guard personnel who worked at the lighthouse. For more information, see the society's Web site <www.grandtraverselighthouse.com/giftshop.shtml>.

Leelanau Historical Society/Leelanau Historical Museum
203 E. Cedar St.
P.O. Box 246
Leland, Mich. 49654
Telephone: (231) 256-7475
Fax: (231) 256-7650
E-mail: <info@leelanauhistory.org>
Web site: <www.leelanauhistory.org>
Date founded: 1957
Number of members: 600

Purpose: "Preservation, documentation, and interpretation of the history of Leelanau County."

Archives: The archives is open by appointment year round. "Staff available Monday through Friday 10 a.m. to 4 p.m. year round. Collections relate to Leelanau County."

Museum: Located at the address above, the museum is open 10 a.m. to 4 p.m. Tuesdays through Saturdays during the summer and 10 a.m. to 4 p.m. Fridays and Saturdays or by appointment in the winter.

Publications: There is a bookstore on the premises, specializing in local history.

Lenawee County

Lenawee County Family Researchers
c/o Corresponding Secretary
519 Company St.
Adrian, Mich. 49221-2007
Web site: <geocities.com/genieyorks/LenCoFamRes.html>

Lenawee County Genealogical Society
P.O. Box 511
Adrian, Mich. 49221

Date founded: 1977

Membership dues: $8.50, individuals; $10, families

Number of members: 65

Publications: Several books are available, including *Index to Naturalization in Lenawee County* and *Graduates of Adrian High School 1857-1901.*

Research service: Donation requested after information received.

Lenawee County Historical Society
110 E. Church St.
P.O. Box 511
Adrian, Mich. 49221

Telephone: (517) 265-6071

Date founded: 1923

Dues: $15, individuals; $25, families

Number of members: 650

Purpose: "To aid in the discovery, collection, and preservation of every variety of material illustrative of the history of Lenawee County and the State of Michigan."

Archives: Located at the museum, the archive has "business, educational and government records, photographs and postcards, maps, an ever-growing genealogical file of information, and personal documents such as letters."

Museum: Located at address above, the museum is open 1 p.m. to 5 p.m. Tuesdays through Fridays and 1 p.m. to 4 p.m. Saturdays year round and other times by appointment.

Publications: "Lots of books and booklets. No list is available. The best way to keep informed is through our newsletter which we publish five times a year."

Livingston County

Green Oak Township Historical Society
P.O. Box 84
Brighton, Mich. 48116

Telephone: (248) 437-8461

E-mail: <jowilliams@aol.com>

Date founded: 1974

Membership dues: $15, individuals; $20, families; $40, patrons/businesses; $250, lifetime

Number of members: 150

Purpose: "Our mission is to collect and disseminate the history of Green Oak Township and relate how in turn our history relates to the history of our state and nation to promote a better appreciation of our American heritage."

Publications: Several books are available, including *Yesteryears of Green Oak 1830-1930* and *Green Oak Plat Maps,* and *Then There Were Parties in the Woods,* a collection of tapes from "old timers memories."

Research service: "We charge $15 per hour with one hour payable in advance."

Other: "The society has begun collecting family histories of those people who settled and lived in Green Oak Township."

Livingston County Genealogical Society
P.O. Box 1073
Howell, Mich. 48844-1073
Telephone: (517) 545-0903
Fax: (517) 545-0464
E-mail: <milcgs@hotmail.com>
Web site: <www.rootsweb.com/~milcgs/>
Date founded: 1982
Membership dues: $10, individuals; $13, couples
Library/archives: The society's holdings are in the Howell Area Archives at the Howell Carnegie Library (see page 325).
Publications: Several books are available, including cemetery transcriptions, census records, *Index of Probate Records Livingston County, Michigan, 1838-1888,* $6; *First Land Owners, Livingston County, Michigan,* $16.50; and the *Bicentennial History of Pinckney, Michigan,* $14. For more information, see the society's Web site <www.rootsweb.com/~milcgs/lcgs1d.htm>.
Research service: "Some query service is available."

Luce County

Luce County Historical Society
P.O. Box 41
Newberry, Mich. 49868
Telephone: (906) 293-5709
Date founded: 1975
Membership dues: $5
Number of members: About 150
Purpose: "To maintain a museum and to preserve artifacts of local history."
Museum: The Luce County Historical Museum, located at 411 W. Harris St., Newberry, is a "handsome Queen Anne-style building, constructed in 1894 as the Sheriff's residence and jail." It has the original cells, kitchen, dining room, bedrooms, double parlors, arts and crafts room, old-fashioned schoolroom, unique bottle collection, and more. Genealogical materials include newspapers, obituaries, books, high school yearbooks, photographs, maps, and documents. The museum is open from 2 p.m. to 4 p.m. Tuesdays through Thursdays July 4 to Labor Day or by appointment.
Publications: Several books are available, including church histories, *Luce County: A History Commemorating Newberry Centennial,* $14; and *Past Years,* a history of Luce County, $25.

Mackinac County

Luce-Mackinac Genealogical Society
P.O. Box 113
Engadine, Mich. 49827-0113
Web site: <www.rootsweb.com/~miluce/luce-mac.htm>
Membership dues: $6.50 per year; $25 for five years; $75 for a lifetime membership
Publications: Several books are available, including ones on early settlers, cemetery records, and *Newberry News* death notices. For more information, see the society's Web site <www.rootsweb.com/~miluce/publicat.htm>.
Research service: Limited

Macomb County

Macomb County Genealogical Group
c/o Mount Clemens Public Library
150 Cass Ave.
Mount Clemens, Mich. 48043
Web site: <www.libcoop.net/mountclemens>

New Baltimore Historical Society
51065 Washington
New Baltimore, Mich. 48047
Telephone: (586) 725-4755
E-mail: <ejllanne@cs.com>
Web site: <www.newbaltimorehistoricalsociety.org/>
Date founded: 1975
Membership dues: $10, individuals; $15, families; $20, organizations; and $100, lifetime
Number of members: 170
Purpose: "Preserve and maintain historical records, archives of the Anchor Bay area; maintain and operate the museum; offer workshops for children and adults; and provide monthly programs for the public."
Museum: Grand Pacific House Museum, located at the address above, is open noon to 2 p.m. Wednesdays and Saturdays. "In addition to the 1881 hotel building that contains rooms of the period, we have a resource room containing books, files, maps, AV materials, and an extensive obituary file for the Anchor Bay area."
Magazine/newsletter: Members receive a monthly newsletter.
Publications: Books include the two-volume *History of New Baltimore.*
Research service: "Free or minimal price, depending on the number of copies and/or mailing expenses. Donations graciously accepted."

Richmond Area Historical and Genealogical Society
P.O. Box 68
Richmond, Mich. 48062

Telephone: (586) 727-3001

E-mail: <ubatrans@klondyke.net>

Web site: <www.klondyke.net/ubatrans>

Date founded: 1990

Membership dues: $7, individuals; $10, families

Number of members: 77

Purpose: "Our purpose is to bring together people interested in the history and genealogy of the Richmond area. We are trying to discover and collect and preserve historical and genealogical material from the area and make it available to others. We also want to encourage and instruct members in genealogical research."

Library/archives: "We have records of the Richmond area (Richmond Township, City of Richmond, Casco Township, Columbus Township, and Lenox Township). Records can be searched by appointment."

Publications: *Saint Matthew United Church of Christ, Adair, Michigan, 1899-1999* and *Lenox Burial Grounds.*

Research service: "We will search our records."

Romeo Historical Society

132 Church St.
P.O. Box 412
Romeo, Mich. 48065

Telephone: (586) 752-4111

Web site: <www.libcoop.net/romrhs>

Date founded: 1961

Membership dues: $18

Number of members: 75

Purpose: "To promote, document, and preserve Romeo history."

Museum: The Bancroft Museum, located at the address above, is open from 1 p.m. to 3 p.m. the second and fourth Sundays of the month.

Publications: *A Tour of Historic Romeo,* $6.

Roseville Historical and Genealogical Society

c/o Roseville Public Library
29777 Gratiot Ave.
Roseville, Mich. 48066-2279

Telephone: (586) 445-5407

Date founded: 1989

Membership dues: $10, individuals; $15, families

Number of members: 125

Library/archives: "The Roseville Public Library has a Michigan History Room with many resources available, including the 1930 Michigan census on microfilm and other census microfilms for Macomb County and Michigan. Appointments must be made for archival material; the archivist is available on Tuesdays." (Also see page 327.)

Magazine/newsletter: Members receive a monthly newsletter.

Research service: "Research is available on a limited basis. Donation is appreciated, plus SASE."

Sons of the American Revolution
Michigan Society
22031 L'Anse St.
Saint Clair Shores, Mich. 48081
Telephone: (586) 294-3509
Web site: <www.sar.org/missar/>
Date founded: 1890
Membership dues: $25
Number of members: 307 in Michigan; 25,000 total

Purpose: "Patriotic, educational. To find and preserve records of our ancestors of the Revolutionary War."

Library/archives: SAR Library, 1000 S. Fourth St., Louisville, Ky. 40203. "Large genealogical collection, census records, pension records. E-mail: <library@sar.org>."

Magazine/newsletter: *SAR Magazine,* issued quarterly, is $10 per year.

Publications: See the society's national Web site <www.sar.org/> for books and CDs available.

Research service: "Copies of member applications available from the National Society, SAR, for $5."

Other: In addition to 50 state societies, there are chapters in Canada, France, Germany, and Mexico.

Sterling Heights Genealogical and Historical Society
P.O. Box 1154
Sterling Heights, Mich. 48311-1154
Telephone: (586) 254-2127
E-mail: <shghs_info@yahoo.com>
Web site: <www.rootsweb.com/~mishghs>
Date founded: 1980
Membership dues: $10
Number of members: 46

Purpose: "To encourage and assist members in genealogical and historical research; to promote the exchange of knowledge among members; to compile, prepare, and preserve historical and genealogical records; and to cooperate with other genealogical and historical societies."

Magazine/newsletter: Members receive *The Ancestral Tree,* a quarterly.

Publications: *Transcription of Sterling Grove Cemetery,* $4.95.

Tri-County Genealogical Society
21715 Brittany Ave.
Eastpointe, Mich. 48021-2503

Telephone: (586) 774-7953
E-mail: <rferrari@comcast.net>
Date founded: 1983
Membership dues: None
Number of members: 25
Purpose: "To help adoptees find their families and do genealogy research to find their families' roots and to make their pasts part of the present."
Research service: "We charge $250, plus expenses, such as [researching and copying] marriage, divorce, or death records and [making] telephone calls."
Other: "This is just a small operation with mainly two people doing much of the research, but I can and do have help from other members when needed."

Manistee County

Kaleva Historical Society
14551 Wuoski Ave.
Box 252/311
Kaleva, Mich. 49645
Telephone: (231) 362-2080
E-mail: <bottlehouse@kaltelnet.net>
Date founded: 1969
Membership dues: $10 per year
Number of members: About 150
Purpose: Education
Museum: The Bottlehouse Museum has family histories as well as artifacts. Open noon to 4 p.m. Saturdays and Sundays.

Manistee County Historical Museum/Society
425 River St.
Manistee, Mich. 49660
Telephone: (231) 723-5531
Web site: <www.rootsweb.com/~mimanist/Page63.html>

Marquette County

Marquette County Genealogical Society
116 W. Spring St.
Marquette, Mich. 49855
Web site: <members.aol.com/MQTCGS/MCGS/mcgs.html>

Marquette County Historical Society
J.M. Longyear Research Library
213 N. Front St.
Marquette, Mich. 49855
Telephone: (906) 226-3571
Web site: <www.marquettecohistory.org>

Date founded: 1918

Membership dues: Individuals, $20

Number of members: 600

Purpose: "For historical research; to collect and preserve books, records, documents, papers, photographs, maps, relics, and other items of historical value in a museum; to prepare records, biographies, and other papers."

Library/archives: The J. M. Longyear Research Library, located at the address above, is open 10 a.m. to noon and 1 p.m. to 5 p.m. weekdays and the third Thursday of every month until 9 p.m. There is a $5 research fee per project for adults, $2 per university student, and free for society members or students in secondary schools. The library specializes in the history of the Lake Superior region and has more than 15,000 titles. "Library holdings include books, manuscripts, biographical and pamphlet files, maps, and photographs on regional and local history. The genealogical collection includes a 70,000-name biography file, federal and state censuses, city and county directories from 1873 to present, cemetery records, mine reports, yearbooks, scrapbooks, and newspapers."

Museum: The Marquette County History Museum, located at the address above, is open 10 a.m. to 5 p.m. weekdays and the third Thursday of every month until 9 p.m. The museum has a permanent gallery of local history and two other galleries that change exhibits yearly. Admission is $3 per adult.

Magazine/newsletter: Members receive *Harlow's Wooden Man,* published quarterly.

Publications: For books, see the society's Web site.

Research service: "$15 per hour, plus copying and shipping costs. Payment is required before research is initiated."

Mason County

Mason County Historical Society

Historic White Pine Village
1687 S. Lakeshore Dr.
Ludington, Mich. 49431

Telephone: (231) 843-4808

Fax: (231) 843-7089

E-mail: <info@historicwhitepinevillage.org>

Web site: <www.historicwhitepinevillage.org>

Date founded: 1937

Membership dues: $35 and up

Number of members: 600

Purpose: "To foster a deeper understanding of and appreciation for Mason County history; to collect, preserve, and present for viewing historically important artifacts, archives, and buildings of the inhabitants of Mason County; to stimulate and encourage the interpretation of Mason County's past through publications, educational programs, and related historical activities; to cooperate with appropriate individuals, organizations, and institutions of the local and state levels in projects and activities which promote and sustain a general interest in history and preservation."

Library/archives: The Research Library of White Pine Village, located at the address above, is open 11 a.m. to 4 p.m. Tuesdays through Fridays. Holdings include photographs, maps, scrapbooks, family histories, city and county directories, biographies, obituaries, and newspapers. "A guide to our archives can be found on our Web site." Daily usage fee is $5 per visit for non-members and free to members.

Museum: Historic White Pine Village is a community of 21 buildings on 23 acres, including Rose Hawley Museum; Maritime, Lumbering, and Museum of Music; an old-fashioned ice cream parlor; and a chapel overlooking Lake Michigan.

Publications: Books include *Mason County Pictorial History* and *Centennial Farms of Mason County.*

Research service: "$10 for the first half hour and $15 per hour after the first half hour; $5 per obituary, plus postage and research time. Copies are 20 cents each for members and 30 cents each for non-members. Photo scans printed on regular paper are $5 each for members and $6 each for non-members. Photographs are $9 each for 4 x 5, $11 each for 5 x 7, and $14 each for 8 x 10. "All research requests being mailed are subject to postage, shipping, and handling charges determined at the time of shipment."

Mecosta County

Mecosta County Genealogical Society
P.O. Box 1068
Big Rapids, Mich. 49307
Web site: <www.rootsweb.com/~mimecost/mecgen.html>

Midland County

Midland County Genealogical Society
c/o Grace A. Dow Library
1710 W. St. Andrews Dr.
Midland, Mich. 48640
Web site: <www.rootsweb.com/~mimgs>
Date founded: 1970
Membership dues: $14, individuals; $17.50, couples
Number of members: 115

Purpose: "To further genealogical interest by joining together people; by gathering, recording, and preserving historical and family records; by encouraging each other in the proficiency of genealogical research."

Library/archives: The society's holdings are located at the Grace A. Dow Library (see pages 330-331). Society volunteers are available from 1 p.m. to 4 p.m. weekdays.

Magazine/newsletter: Members receive *Pioneer Record,* a quarterly. It also can be purchased for $6 per year.

Publications: *Midland County Obituary Index, 1872-1927,* $20, plus $3 shipping, and *Midland County Obituary Index 1928-1950,* $20, plus $3 shipping. Other publications are listed on the society's Web site <www.rootsweb.com/~mimgs/publications.htm>.

Research service: "Requests by mail are preferred. Research done by qualified MGS volunteers. Copying fee for obits for up to five individuals is a $5 donation. Doing limited research is at least a $3 donation. More extensive research is $5 per hour."

Other: The local LDS Family History Center has all federal census microfilms 1850 to 1930 for Midland and surrounding areas, plus many other Michigan sources.

Midland County Historical Society
Midland Center for the Arts
1801 W. Saint Andrews Dr.
Midland, Mich. 48640
Telephone: (989) 631-5931
Fax: (989) 631-7890
Web site: <www.mcfta.org/historical_society/index.htm>
Date founded: 1952
Membership dues: $25, individuals; $35, families; $20, seniors
Number of members: 400
Purpose: "To preserve and present the history of Midland County."

Archives: "The files are not complete, but we do have pictures and some family histories." The archives is located at Studio 7 of the Midland Center for the Arts at the address above and is open 9 a.m. to 5 p.m. weekdays.

Publications: Includes *Salt of the Earth,* a history of Midland County; *The Dow Story;* and *The Papers of Herbert H. Dow.*

Sanford Historical Society
P.O. Box 243
Sanford, Mich. 48657
Telephone: (989) 687-9048 (weekends only)
Date founded: 1970
Membership dues: $10
Number of members: 151
Purpose: "To maintain the Sanford Centennial Museum."
Library/archives: Yes

Museum: The Sanford Centennial Museum, located at 2234 Smith St., is open 1 p.m. to 5 p.m. Saturdays and Sundays Memorial Day to Labor Day. The museum is housed in an old school built in 1910. Several other buildings and items are on the grounds, including a general store, Flint and Pere Marquette Depot, tool shed with antique farm implements, log cabin, blacksmith shop, bunkhouse, Jerome Township Hall, Clare Bailey Chapel, and a train.

Magazine/newsletter: Members receive a newsletter seven times per year.

Publications: *Upper Tittabawassee Boon Towns,* $14.95, plus $3 postage.

Research service: "Very limited."

Missaukee County

Missaukee County Historical Society

P.O. Box 93

Lake City, Mich. 49651

Web site: <www.mifamilyhistory.org/missaukee/histsoc.htm>

Membership dues: $5

Purpose: "To keep area history available."

Library/archives: "The Lake City District Library, 210 S. Canal St., Lake City, has most local newspapers on microfilm."

Museum: "The local museum is currently a 100-plus-year-old log cabin, located three miles south of Lake City on S. Morey Rd. at Highway M-55 and M-66." Summer hours are 2 p.m. to 5 p.m. Saturdays and Sundays. Closed Labor Day to Memorial Day. Also open by appointment.

Monroe County

Genealogical Society of Monroe County

P.O. Box 1428

Monroe, Mich. 48161

Telephone: (734) 279-2196

Web site: <www.angelfire.com/mi3/monroecountycems/gsmc.htm>

Date founded: 1977

Membership dues: $15

Number of members: About 200

Purpose: "Preserve records, help researchers, education of research, hold eminars and workshops."

Library/archives: The GSMC Archives is located at the Historical Museum, 26 S. Monroe St., Monroe. It is open 10 a.m. to 5 p.m. Wednesdays and 10 a.m. o noon the first Saturday of the month. Holdings are mostly for Monroe County, ut there is also information on other counties, including some out of state.

Magazine/newsletter: Members receive *GSMC Record.* Otherwise, it is $1 per opy.

Research service: Individuals should send group sheets or pedigree charts vith request. No cost, but donations accepted.

Milan Area Historical Society

Hack House

61 W. Second St.

Milan, Mich. 48160

Telephone: (734) 439-7522
Date founded: 1972
Membership dues: $10
Number of members: 50
Purpose: "To preserve Milan's past for Milan's future."
Library/archives: Society's holdings are housed at the Milan Public Library (see page 331).
Publications: *Ancient and Modern Milan,* $10, plus $3 shipping, and *Way Back When,* $10, plus $3 shipping.

Muskegon County

Muskegon County Genealogical Society
c/o Hackley Public Library
316 W. Webster Ave.
Muskegon, Mich. 49440
Telephone: (231) 722-7276, ext. 233
E-mail: <mcgs1972@msn.com>
Web site: <www.rootsweb.com/~mimcgs>
Date founded: 1972
Membership dues: $15, individuals; $18, families
Number of members: 106

Purpose: "To assemble and educate individuals interested in preserving family history; to assist members of the society and the public in genealogical investigation and compilation of family histories; to carry on projects of a genealogical nature; and to cooperate in the location, preservation, publication and deposit in the Hackley Public Library records of value to the genealogical community."

Library/archives: The society's holdings are located at the Hackley Library <www.hackleylibrary.org>, 316 W. Webster Ave., Muskegon, and include Muskegon County records, newspapers on microfilm, family histories, census records, land records, and city directories.

Magazine/newsletter: Members received *Family Tree Talk,* published quarterly.

Publications: Several books are available, including *Atlas of Muskegon and Ottawa Counties - 1864,* $10, plus $2.50 shipping; *Fruitland Township Genealogical Records,* $10, plus $3.25 shipping; and *History of Muskegon and Ottawa County, 1882,* $15, plus $3.25 shipping. See the society's Web site for more information.

Research service: $20 for the first two hours and $10 for each additional hour.

Other: The society offers Pioneer Certificates. Contact the society or visit its Web site for guidelines and applications. The society's Web site has cemetery transcriptions and other research data.

Newaygo County

Newaygo County Genealogical Society
1038 E. Wilcox Ave.
P. O. Box 68
White Cloud, Mich. 49349
Telephone: (616) 689-6631
Fax: (616) 689-6699
Web site: <www.rootsweb.com/~minewayg/society.html>

Oakland County

Clarkston Community Historical Society
6495 Clarkston Rd.
Clarkston, Mich. 48346
Telephone: (248) 922-0270
Fax: (248) 625-2499
E-mail: <info@clarkstonhistorical.org>
Web site: <www.clarkstonhistorical.org>
Date founded: 1972
Membership dues: $25 to $500
Number of members: 250
Purpose: "Dedicated to the preservation of local history."
Museum: The Clarkston Heritage Museum, located at the address above, is open 10 a.m. to 9 p.m. Mondays through Thursdays, 10 a.m. to 6 p.m. Fridays, 10 a.m. to 5 p.m. Saturdays, and 1 p.m. to 5 p.m. Sundays. Holdings include photographs, documents, and settler artifacts.
Publications: Books include *Heritage,* $15; *The Way We Remember,* $20; *Our Children's Heritage,* $25. See the society's Web site <www.clarkstonhistorical.org/merchandise.htm> for more information.
Research service: "Nothing official, but we will help when we can."

Farmington Genealogical Society
c/o Farmington Community Library
23500 Liberty St.
Farmington, MI 48335-3570
Web site: <www.rootsweb.com/~mifarmgs/>

Franklin Historical Society
P.O. Box 25007
Franklin, Mich. 48025
Date founded: 1969
Membership dues: $25 and up
Number of members: 300
Purpose: "To preserve the history of Franklin."

Museum: The Franklin Historical Museum has various exhibits about the history of Franklin. It is open from 1 p.m. to 3 p.m. Wednesdays and Saturdays.

Magazine/newsletter: *Kit and Key,* a quarterly.

Publications: *All About Franklin,* $15.

Research service: "We're not really organized yet, but we do offer what we have."

French-Canadian Heritage Society of Michigan
c/o Gail F. Moreau
9513 Whipple Shores Dr.
Clarkston, Mich. 48348
Telephone: (248) 625-4988
E-mail: <gfmoreau1@aol.com>
Web site: <fchsm.habitant.org/index.htm>
Date founded: 1980
Membership dues: $20
Number of members: About 600

Purpose: "Promote the study of French Canadian history and heritage."

Library/archives: The society's collection is housed at the Mount Clemens Library (see page 326-327) and may be viewed by appointment. Contact members Mary Freer (810) 791-4126 or Al Trudeau (810) 751-4284.

Magazine/newsletter: *Michigan's Habitant Heritage* is published quarterly in January, April, July, and October.

Research service: "We do not do research. To put a query in our journal, *Michigan's Habitant Heritage,* one has to be a member."

Other: "On May 18, 2002, a plaque honoring the first 51 French-Canadian voyaguers who accompanied Antoine de Lamothe Cadillac to Detroit on July 24, 1701, was dedicated at Hart Plaza in Detroit. It's the only historical plaque in the state of Michigan erected by a genealogical society."

Highland Township Historical Society
P.O. Box 351
Highland, Mich. 48357
Telephone: (248) 887-5976
E-mail: <deneedham@peoplepc.com>
Date founded: 1991
Membership dues: $5
Number of members: 15
Publications: *Our Highland Heritage.*

Holly Historical Society
306 S. Saginaw St.
Holly, Mich. 48442
Telephone: (248) 634-9233
Date founded: 1972

Membership dues: $10
Number of members: 12
Museum: The Victorian Home Museum is open 1 p.m. to 4 p.m. Sundays and a.m. to 2 p.m. Tuesdays through Thursdays.
Research service: Donation required.

Jewish Genealogical Society of Michigan
P.O. Box 251693
West Bloomfield, Mich. 48325-1693
Web site: <www.jgsmi.org/>
Date founded: 1985
Membership dues: $36, individuals; $50, families
Library: The society's library, located at the Temple Beth El Library, 7400 'elegraph Rd., Bloomfield Hills, is open to members only.
Magazine/newsletter: Members receive *Generations,* a quarterly.

Jewish Historical Society of Michigan
6600 W. Maple Rd.
West Bloomfield, Mich. 48322-3003
Web site: <www.michjewishhistory.net/>
Date founded: 1959
Membership dues: $36, individuals and families
Purpose: "To preserve and commemorate our past for future generations."
Magazine/newsletter: "*Michigan Jewish History* is the longest continuously ublished journal of local Jewish history in North America and is carried in ibraries and universities throughout the world." It is sent to members.

Lyon Township Genealogical Society
c/o Lyon Township Public Library
27025 Milford Rd.
New Hudson, Mich. 48165
Telephone: (248) 437-8800
Fax: (248) 437-4621
E-mail: <lyon.library@yahoo.com>
Number of members: 24
Purpose: "Love of genealogy."
Library: Collection located at Lyon Township Pubic Library. Includes crapbooks, local newspaper, CDs, and census records on microfilm.
Research service: "We have local scrapbooks. Will copy the pages for 10 cents copy. We accept donations."

Michigan Society
Order of Founders and Patriots of America
2961 Woodcreek Way
Bloomfield Hills, Mich. 48304-1974

Telephone: (248) 644-3654

Web site: <www.founderspatriots.org/mi.htm>

Date founded: 1954

Membership dues: $25 per year

Number of members: 40

Purpose: "Discover, collect and preserve records, documents, manuscripts monuments and history relating to first colonists; recognize patriots of th Revolutionary War."

Magazine/newsletter: *Bulletin* is published semi-annually. Subscription rat is $2.

Milford Historical Society
124 E. Commerce St.
Milford, Mich. 48381

Telephone: (248) 685-7308

Date founded: 1973

Museum: Located at the address above, holdings include the *Milford Times* o microfilm from 1871 and Oak Grove Cemetery records.

Publications: *Ten Minutes Ahead of the Rest of the World,* a Milford histor book, $35 (includes shipping and handling).

Research service: $10 per hour, plus 10 cents per regular copy and 20 cent per microfilm copy.

Northeast Oakland Historical Society
1 N. Washington St.
Oxford, Mich. 48371

Telephone: (248) 628-8413

Date founded: 1971

Membership dues: $10

Number of members: 50

Purpose: "Alive and active to preserve the past."

Library/archives: "The Museum Library contains many family histories Oakland County histories, and atlases. There is an extensive file of clippings an pictures. Researchers are welcome."

Museum: The Northeast Oakland Historical Museum, located at the addres above, is open 1 p.m. to 4 p.m. Saturday year round, and 1 p.m. to 4 p.m Wednesdays during June, July, and August.

Publications: "Oxford cemetery books, *Michigan Cyclone of 1896,* books b local authors, and a video of Oxford history."

Research service: "Limited to materials in our files. Accepts donations. Pleas call for appointment for researching."

Oakland County Genealogical Society
P.O. Box 1094
Birmingham, Mich. 48012-1094

Telephone: (248) 643-0019

Web site: <www.metronet.lib.mi.us/ROCH/OCGS/>

Date founded: 1977

Membership dues: $15

Number of members: About 400

Purpose: "To promote and encourage an interest in genealogy and related fields among its members and the general public."

Library/archives: The society's holdings are located at the Troy Public Library (see page 336).

Magazine/newsletter: Members receive *Acorns to Oaks,* published quarterly.

Publications: Several books are available, including cemetery transcriptions, census records, first landowners, vital records, and funeral home records. For more information, see the society's Web site <www.metronet.lib.mi.us/ROCH/OCGS/Publications.html>.

Research service: "We maintain a non-circulating library. Society volunteers will answer brief research requests related to Oakland County and check society and other Oakland County publications in the library collection. Society has some vital records and probate index microfilms. Local newspapers can be checked for obituaries if a death date is provided. Donation appreciated. Cost of photocopies and postage."

Other: "The society is active in locating, transcribing/extracting primary records for Oakland County and publishing those in book form, on fiche, or in the society quarterly. The Society has the 'Ruth S. Kennedy Oakland County Records Preservation Fund,' which is used to microfilm original records and/or preserve Oakland County genealogical and historical materials."

Oakland County Pioneer and Historical Society

405 Oakland Ave.

Pontiac, Mich. 48342

Telephone: (248) 338-6732

Fax: (248) 338-6731

E-mail: <ocphs@wwnet.net>

Web site: <wwnet.net/~ocphs/index.html>

Date founded: 1874

Membership dues: Individuals, $20

Number of members: More than 300

Purpose: "To identify, record, correct, preserve, and make available objects and materials reflecting the history of the people, places, and events of Oakland County. To restore and maintain the Gov. Moses Wisner estate, known as Pine Grove, as a recognized national and state historic site."

Library/archives: Located at the address above, the research library is open 9 a.m. to 4 p.m. Tuesdays through Saturdays. Resources include Brace Funeral Home Records from 1887 to 1951; obituaries and death notices; bound volumes of newspapers; gazetteers and directories; maps and atlases; periodicals; and manuscript collections. Cost for use is $5 per day for non-members or free to members.

Museum: The Pine Grove Historical Museum is located at the address above and includes the Gov. Moses Wisner Mansion and the Pioneer Museum. **Magazine/newsletter:** Members receive *The Oakland Gazette,* a quarterly newsletter.

Research service: Requests can be sent by e-mail, phone, or mail. Cost is $15 per hour for non-members (one hour minimum), with additional research at $10 per hour or $7.50 per hour for members (one hour minimum), with additional research at $5 per hour.

Oakland Township Historical Society
4393 Collins Rd.
Rochester, Mich. 48307
Telephone: (248) 651-8715
Fax: (248) 651-7340
E-mail: <claygro@juno.com>
Date founded: 1974
Membership dues: $10 and up
Number of members: 100

Purpose: "Gather, interpret, and preserve the history of the Oakland Township community for the purpose of offering opportunities for education and entertainment to the community and all other interested persons."

Publications: *Heritage In Oakland Township,* $7; and *A Footpath Through Goodison History,* $1.

Oceana County

Oceana County Historical and Genealogical Society
114 Dryden St.
Hart, Mich. 49420
Telephone: (231) 873-2600
E-mail: <info@oceanahistory.org>
Web site: <www.oceanahistory.org/>
Date founded: 1967
Membership dues: $15
Number of members: 225

Purpose: "Collect and preserve the history of Oceana County for future generations."

Archives: An archives, located at the Chadwick Munger House, 114 Dryden St., Hart, is open 10 a.m. to 5 p.m. Wednesdays and other times by appointment. Holdings include census records, newspapers on microfilm, county history books, an extensive obituary file, cemetery files, surname file, and family genealogies.

Museum: The Oceana County Historical Park Museum Complex is located on Fox Rd. in Mears and is open on 1 p.m. to 4 p.m. weekends from Memorial Day through Labor Day and from 1 p.m. to 4 p.m. Wednesdays during July and August. It has artifacts and exhibits and special events.

Publications: Books include the two-volume set, *Oceana County History; Oceana County Pioneers and Businessmen of Today;* and cemetery records.

Research service: "$7 per research hour plus copying costs. Minimum one-hour research charge."

Ogemaw County

Family Research Institute

P.O. Box 653
West Branch, Mich. 48661-9695
Telephone: (989) 345-1061
Fax: (989) 345-4645
E-mail: <donnieb@i-star.com>
Date founded: 1988
Membership dues: $12
Number of members: 8

Purpose: "To encourage and teach family history by supporting and using the LDS Family History Centers."

Magazine/newsletter: *Family Legacy Newsletter,* a quarterly, $12.

Research service: $10 per hour, plus expenses.

Other: The Family History Center, located at 315 Fairview Rd., West Branch, has a research collection geared for Michigan, Canada, and Native Americans.

Ogemaw Genealogy and Historical Society

123 S. 5th St.
West Branch, Mich. 48661-0734
Web site: <www.rootsweb.com/~mioghs/_sgt/f10000.htm>

Osceola County

Marion Area Historical Society

P.O. Box 276
Marion, Mich. 49665
Telephone: (231) 743-6632
Date founded: 1991
Membership dues: $5
Number of members: 90

Purpose: "Preservation of historical information and artifacts relating to Marion, Michigan."

Library/archives: The archive, located at the museum, has obituaries, genealogies, family narratives, and clippings.

Museum: The museum is located at 223 W. Main St., Marion, and is open June through September from 1 p.m. to 4 p.m. on Wednesdays, Fridays, and Saturdays. There are three buildings: the main building contains household, school, and military artifacts as well as the archives research desk; the cabin contains early 20th century furnishings; and a shed contains farming, logging, and trapping artifacts.

Publications: *Marion – 100 Years – Moving Ahead,* $12, plus shipping; *Heritage Recipes,* $6, plus shipping; and *Upon Becoming a Young Lady,* $7, plus shipping.

Osceola County Genealogical Society
Old Rugged Cross Historical Museum
4918 Park St.
P.O. Box 27
Reed City, Mich. 49677
Telephone: (231) 832-5431
Membership dues: $8, individuals; $10, families

Purpose: "To encourage and promote the study of genealogy; to assist others in collecting personal genealogical information; to preserve and publish local and historical and genealogical material."

Library/archives: Holdings in the archives include Reed City newspapers on microfilm through 1999; Lake, Mecosta, and Osceola county census records; atlases and platbooks; family histories; and miscellaneous records and periodicals.

Museum: The museum is open daily from 1 p.m. to 4 p.m. May 1 to September 30 and other times by appointment.

Magazine/newsletter: Members receive *The Osceolean,* published twice a year.

Publications: Books include *Osceola County Tombstone Inscriptions,* $26, plus postage and *McDowell Funeral Home Records 1910-1950,* $25, plus postage.

Research service: $7 per hour for members and $10 per hour for non-members.

Otsego County

Gaylord Fact-Finders Genealogical Society
P.O. Box 1524
Gaylord, Mich. 49734
Telephone: (231) 584-2625
E-mail: <dmarz@avci.net>
Web site: <www.otsego.org/factfinders>
Date founded: 1986
Membership dues: Individuals, $10; families, $12
Number of members: 18

Purpose: "Promotion of genealogy."

Library/archives: Society's material are available at the Otsego County Library, 700 S. Otsego Ave., Gaylord <www.otsego.org/factfinders/materials.htm>.

Publications: The society has several books for sale, including *Otsego County Cemetery Headstones,* $20. For more information, see the society's Web site <www.otsego.org/factfinders/publications.htm>.

Research service: $10 per hour, plus mileage and cost of copies.

Ottawa County

Grand Haven Genealogical Society

c/o Loutit District Library
407 Columbus Ave.
Grand Haven, Mich. 49417
Telephone: (616) 842-5560
Fax: (616) 847-0570
E-mail: <ghgs_2000@yahoo.com>
Web site: <www.geocities.com/ghgs_2000>
Membership dues: $15
Number of members: 30

Purpose: "To preserve genealogical and local history materials and make them available for use in genealogical research."

Library/archives: Holdings are located at the Loutit District Library (see pages 337-338).

Research service: Yes

Roscommon County

Roscommon Area Historical Society

P.O. Box 627
Roscommon, Mich. 48653
Telephone: (989) 275-5042
Date founded: 1984
Membership dues: $10
Number of members: About 100

Purpose: "To preserve the history of the area and the collection of artifacts on display."

Museum: The Gallimore Boarding House and Richardson Schoolhouse, a home and school furnished with local artifacts, are located at 404 Lake St., Roscommon. They are open from noon to 4 p.m. Fridays and Saturdays from Memorial Day weekend through September. Holdings include reference materials on cemeteries, oral history tapes, school pictures and records, and old photographs.

Publications: *A Memoir of Roscommon,* $10; *Memories of Higgins Lake,* $6; and *Historical Highlights of the Village of Roscommon,* $8.

Roscommon County Genealogical Society

2597 S. Gladwin Rd.
P.O. Box 983
Prudenville, Mich. 48651

Telephone: (989) 366-1774
Date founded: 1999
Membership dues: $20, individuals; $30, families
Number of members: 56
Purpose: "Non-profit genealogy research and education."

Library/archives: The Roscommon County Genealogy Society Research and Education Center, located at the address above, is open noon to 4 p.m. Mondays, Wednesdays, and Saturdays and Wednesday evenings by appointment. Holdings include Roscommon County census records 1860 to 1920 and more than 2,000 books, periodicals, and newsletters.

Research service: "For Roscommon County only. $5 per hour with a two-hour minimum, plus document costs."

Saginaw County

Cass River Genealogy Society
c/o Wickson Memorial Library
359 S. Franklin St.
Frankenmuth, Mich. 48734
Telephone: (989) 652-8323
Fax: (989) 652-3450
E-mail: <wickson@frankenmuthcity.com>
Web site: <www.frankenmuthcity.com/library/genealogy.htm>
Date founded: 1996
Membership dues: $10
Number of members: 15

Purpose: "Support people who have an interest in genealogy; preserve, compile, and index genealogy records; present genealogy programs."

Library/archives: A local history and genealogy collection for Saginaw County is located at the address above.

Magazine/newsletter: Members receive a monthly newsletter, issued September through May.

Publications: "Volumes of scanned articles from the *Frankenmuth News* concerning births, birthdays, deaths, baptisms, marriages, and military service. Indexed. CD-roms for each year also have been produced. 1930s to 1970s."

Research service: $10 per hour.

Frankenmuth Historical Association
613 S. Main St.
Frankenmuth, Mich. 48415
Telephone: (989) 652-9701
Fax: (989) 652-9390
Web site: <frankenmuth.michigan.museum>
Date founded: 1963
Membership dues: $40, families; $15, seniors

Number of members: 325

Purpose: "Document the history of the Frankenmuth area including local families, sister colonies, and emigration from Germany in the late 19th century."

Museum: The library/archives of the Frankenmuth Historical Museum, located at the address above, is open by appointment. "The collection focuses on Frankenmuth's history as a German Lutheran missionary settlement (1845), socialization in a German-American community, and the subsequent development of the community as a tourist destination. We maintain genealogy files on local residents of four German communities; *Frankenmuth News* (1905-1927) on microfilm; indexed translations of church records; and a translation of 'Emigrants from Central Franconia to North America in the 19th Century' (Nuremberg State Archives)."

Magazine/newsletter: Members receive a newsletter.

Publications: *Teach My People the Truth,* a community history, and *A Valuable Work Ethic: A Pictorial History of Frankenmuth Business.* For more information, see the society's Web site <frankenmuth.michigan.museum/selling.html>.

Research service: $15 per hour, plus 25 cents for copies or $3 per scanned photograph or document.

Historical Society of Bridgeport
6190 Dixie Highway
P.O. Box 337
Bridgeport, Mich. 48722
Telephone: (989) 777-5230
Date founded: 1969
Membership dues: $10, families; $8, individuals; $5, senior
Number of members: About 100

Purpose: "Preserve and collect historical materials and artifacts."

Museum: Organization has an archives/library. Collection includes various books and tax records.

Publications: *History of Bridgeport,* $5; *Historical Cookbook,* $5; and *History of Schoolhouse,* free.

Saginaw Genealogical Society
c/o Saginaw Public Library
505 Janes Ave.
Saginaw, Mich. 48507

Web site: <www.saginawlibrary.org/Genealogy_History/Genealogy_Society/genealogy_society.html>

Date founded: 1971
Membership dues: $15, individuals; $17, families
Number of members: More than 200

Library/archives: The society's holdings are at the Saginaw Public Library (see page 339).

Magazine/newsletter: Members receive *Timbertown Log,* a quarterly, and a monthly newsletter.

Publications: Several books are available, including cemetery transcriptions; *First Land Purchasers of Saginaw County,* $7, plus $1.25 postage; *History of Bridgeport,* $5.75, plus $1.25 postage; and *History of Frankenmuth,* $7.75, plus $1.25 postage.

Research service: "The corresponding secretary will answer simple requests. Some members will do research for a fee. Donations are always welcome."

Saginaw Valley Chapter, AHSGR
c/o Carol L. Niederquell
6910 Trowbridge Circle
Saginaw, Mich. 48603
Telephone: (989) 799-4266
E-mail: <clniederusa@netscape.net>
Web site: <www.ahsgr.org/saginaw_valley_chapter.htm>
Date founded: 1972
Membership dues: $5
Number of members: About 75

Purpose: "Discover, collect, preserve, and disseminate information related to history, cultural heritage, and genealogy of the Germans from Russia and their descendants. To bring together people interested in our history and promote a better appreciation of the culture through the descendants."

Library/archives: "Local library for members available by phone or at meetings."

Publications: Ethnic cookbooks.

Research service: "The international group charges (for research service). Limited research available locally."

Tittabawassee Township Historical Society
P.O. Box 294
Freeland, Mich. 48623
Telephone: (989) 695-9439
Date founded: 1990
Membership dues: $5, individuals; $4, seniors
Number of members: 20

Purpose: "To be a source of historical information for the community as well as genealogical purposes."

Publications: "We are working on a book of all the cemeteries in Freeland."

Written queries: Will answer. "We have files on people of Freeland."

Saint Clair County

Capac Community Historical Society
401 E. Kempf Ct.
Capac, Mich. 48014

Telephone: (810) 395-2859
Date founded: 1977
Membership dues: $10, individuals; $15, couples
Number of members: About 80
Purpose: "To preserve and promote the history of the Capac community."
Library/archives: Located in the museum, the archives is open by request.
Museum: Located at the address above, the museum is open from 1 p.m. to 4 p.m. Saturdays and Sundays June through September or by appointment. Holdings include a postcard and picture collection and a display of school graduates from 1910 to present.
Publications: *Books include 125 years of the Capac Community, 1857-1982* and *A Pictorial History of Capac.*
Research service: There is no research service, but "... we do [research] and have looked up information for people at no cost."

Marysville Historical Museum
887 Huron Blvd. East
Marysville, Mich. 48040
Telephone: (810) 364-5198
Web site: <www.marysvillemuseum.org>
Date founded: 1977
Number of members: "The Marysville Recreation Department operates the museum."
Library/archives: Marysville Historical Museum Archives is located at the museum at the address above. The facilities may be used year round by appointment. It is open from 1:30 p.m. to 4 p.m. Sundays Memorial Day through Labor Day. Holdings include photos, maps, documents, and books about schools, community organizations, city records, local industries, and early founding families.

Saint Joseph County

Community Historical Society
P.O. Box 136
Colon, Mich. 49040-0136
Date founded: 1974
Membership dues: $5, annual; $100, lifetime
Number of members: About 75
Purpose: "To gather and preserve our local history."
Museum: The society's museum is located on Blackstone Ave. in Colon.
Research service: Offers a "limited" service for donations.

Saint Joseph County Genealogical Society
P. O. Box 486
White Pigeon, Mich. 49099-9734
Web site: <www.famgen.net/sjcgs/>

Saint Joseph County Historical Society
P.O. Box 492
Centreville, Mich. 49093
Telephone: (269) 467-7723
Date founded: 1840; reorganized 1930
Membership dues: $10
Number of members: About 90
Purpose: "Preservation of county history."
Museum: The museum in Centreville was purchased in 1998 but isn't open yet. An office in White Pigeon is open upon request.
Publications: *1827-1877 County History Book,* $50 postpaid and *1858 Atlas,* $10, plus $5 postage.
Research service: $20 per hour.

Three Rivers Genealogy Club
13724 Spence Rd.
Three Rivers, Mich. 49093

Shiawassee County

Shiawassee County Genealogical Society
P.O. Box 841
Owosso, Mich. 48867
Telephone: (989) 725-8549
Date founded: 1968
Membership dues: $15, individuals; $20, families
Number of members: 125
Purpose: "To help those researching their lines and to preserve our history."
Library/archives: The society's holdings are at the Shiawassee District Library (see page 342).
Magazine/newsletter: Members receive *Steppin' Stones,* published three times a year.
Publications: Several books are available, including cemetery transcriptions; *Early Land Owners of Shiawassee County,* $12, plus $1.50 shipping; and *Rush Township Death Records,* $7, plus $1.50 shipping.
Research service: $5 per hour, plus copies and postage.

Shiawassee County Historical Society
Shiawassee County Archives
P.O. Box 526
Owosso, Mich. 48867
Telephone: (989) 723-2371
E-mail: <arch@shianet.org>
Date founded: 1963
Membership dues: $12, individuals

Number of members: 350

Purpose: "To preserve historical artifacts and paper work."

Library/archives: "We are in the process of getting a museum and archives, so our material is unavailable at this time."

Magazine/newsletter: A newsletter is published three times a year.

Publications: Several publications are available and listed on the Web site <www.usgennet.org/usa/mi/county/shiawassee/geneasoc.html>.

Research service: $5 per hour, plus copies and postage.

Tuscola County

Mayville Area Museum of History and Genealogy
2124 Ohmer Rd.
P.O. Box 2423
Mayville, Mich. 48744

Telephone: (989) 843-7185

Date founded: 1972

Membership dues: $5, individuals; $100, lifetime

Number of members: 103

Purpose: "Gathering and displaying historical artifacts, compiling genealogical information and family histories."

Museum: The Mayville Area Museum is open 10 a.m. to 4 p.m. Fridays and Saturdays during the summer. The facility includes a former depot, log cabin, and one-room rural schoolhouse.

Newsletter: Members receive a yearly newsletter.

Van Buren County

Van Buren County Historical Society
6215 East Red Arrow Hwy.
P.O. Box 452
Hartford, Mich. 49057

Telephone: (269) 621-2188

Date founded: 1970

Number of members: 300 to 400

Purpose: "Preservation, education."

Library/archives: Located at the address above.

Publications: Some pamphlets and books.

Research service: $5 per search, copies 10 cents each.

Other: A "demonstration day" of old crafts takes place in August. Society offers tours of historical buildings from 1920s and 1930s.

Van Buren Regional Genealogical Society
P.O. Box 143
Decatur, Mich. 49045

Telephone: (269) 423-4771
Fax: (269) 423-8373
E-mail: <tbenson@vbdl.org>
Web site: <www.rootsweb.com/~mivbrgs/vbrgs.htm>
Date founded: 1987
Membership dues: $14, individuals; $17, families
Number of members: 150

Purpose: "Promote and preserve local/family history for the Michigan counties of Allegan, Berrien, Cass, Kalamazoo, and Van Buren."

Library/archives: A regional collection is co-owned with the Van Buren District Library (see pages 343-344). Special collections include the Southwest Michigan Military Registry, the Southwest Michigan Pioneer Certificate Program, photographs, and yearbooks.

Magazine/newsletter: Members receive *Van Buren Echoes,* a quarterly.

Publications: See the society's Web site <www.rootsweb.com/~mivbrgs/vbrgs.htm#pub> for a list of publications.

Written queries: "Brief lookups" may be addressed to the Van Buren District Library, 200 N. Phelps St., Decatur, Mich. 49045.

Washtenaw County

Dexter Area Historical Society
3443 Inverness St.
Dexter, Mich. 48130
Telephone: (734) 426-2519
E-mail: <DexMuseum@aol.com>
Date founded: 1972
Membership dues: $3
Number of members: 100

Purpose: "To preserve the history of the Dexter area."

Museum: The Dexter Area Museum, located at the address above, is open 1 p.m. to 3 p.m. Fridays and Saturdays May to mid-June. "Museum contains donated items that demonstrate the history of Dexter, from furniture to toys to tools and much more. We also have a genealogical department and have many local records of churches and cemeteries, also township records. The *Dexter Leader* is available on microfilm from 1869 to 1969."

Research service: "Donation to cover costs of copies and materials, plus postage if necessary."

Genealogical Society of Washtenaw County
P.O. Box 7155
Ann Arbor, Mich. 48107-7155
Telephone: (734) 483-2799
Web site: <www.hvcn.org/info/gswc>
Date founded: 1974

Membership dues: $14, individuals; $15, families; $12, seniors

Number of members: 300

Purpose: "Collect, assist, and research the genealogical history of Washtenaw County and surrounding areas."

Library/archives: The society's holdings are housed at the LDS Family History Center, 914 Hill St., Ann Arbor, Mich. 48104. Call (734) 995-0211 for hours.

Magazine/newsletter: Members receive *Family History Capers,* a quarterly magazine, and a quarterly newsletter.

Publications: Several books are available, including *Washtenaw County, Michigan, Plat Maps 1856 and 1864,* $35, plus $4 postage, and *Directory of Cemeteries of Washtenaw County, Michigan,* $8, plus $3 postage. For more information, see the society's Web site <www.hvcn.org/info/gswc/publications.htm>.

Research service: "Limited research is available on request. Send all pertinent information, including a statement of information being sought and resources previously consulted, and a self-addressed, stamped envelope. We request a $10 donation for our book fund."

Other: The society's Web site includes an index of life events (obituaries, deaths, marriages, birthdays, and other notices) from Washtenaw County newspapers.

Washtenaw County Historical Society
P.O. Box 3336
Ann Arbor, Mich. 48106-3336
Telephone: (734) 662-9092
Web site: <www.washtenawhistory.org>
Date founded: 1857
Membership dues: $25
Number of members: 450

Purpose: "To preserve and educate regarding Washtenaw County."

Newsletter: Members receive a newsletter seven times per year.

Ypsilanti Historical Society Museum
220 N. Huron St.
Ypsilanti, Mich. 48197
Telephone: (734) 482-4990
Date founded: 1967
Membership dues: $10
Number of members: 275

Purpose: "To preserve the story of this city, its families, schools, churches, and businesses – past and present."

Archives: The museum archives is open from 9 a.m. to noon Mondays, Wednesdays, and Fridays.

Museum: The museum is open from 2 p.m. to 4 p.m. Thursdays, Saturdays, and Sundays. Special visits and tours may be arranged at any time by calling the number above or (734) 482-2929.

Publications: Many books are available, including *The Story of Ypsilanti, Mayors of Ypsilanti 1858-1976,* and *African-American Settlers in Ypsilanti.*

Research service: "No charge, but donations are gratefully received." Copies are 10 cents each.

Other: "We are located within walking distance of Depot Town, the oldest part of town, and two other museums, the Firefighters Museum and the Auto Heritage Museum."

Wayne County

Canton Historical Society
P.O. Box 87362
Canton, Mich. 48187
Telephone: (734) 397-0088
E-mail: <ronnikay@comcast.net>
Date founded: 1975
Membership dues: $10, individuals; $13, families; $100, lifetime
Number of members: 135

Purpose: "Preservation of Canton Township history and to maintain a museum."

Library/archives: The archives of the Canton Historical Museum, located at the corner of Canton Center Rd. and Heritage Dr., is open from 1 p.m. to 4 p.m. Tuesdays and Saturdays and by appointment. Holdings include family histories, Civil War pension papers, photographs, and scrapbooks.

Magazine/newsletter: Members receive the *Canton Historical Society News.*

Publications: *Cornerstones,* a history of Canton's families, $39, plus $4 postage; *Canton Cemetery Records,* $5, plus $2 postage; and *Canton's Country School Book,* $30, plus $5 postage.

Other: "We have identified more than 60 Civil War soldiers from Canton. We are getting the pension papers, if available, for each one and are attempting to find where each is buried to take pictures of their tombstones."

Dearborn Genealogical Society
P.O. Box 1112
Dearborn, Mich. 48121-1112
Web site: <www.rootsweb.com/~midgs/index.htm>

Detroit Society for Genealogical Research
c/o Detroit Public Library
Burton Historical Collection
5201 Woodward Ave.
Detroit, Mich. 48202
Web site: <www.dsgr.org>
Date founded: 1936
Membership dues: $20

Number of members: 850

Purpose: "The preservation and perpetuation of the records of ancestors and families."

Magazine/newsletter: "Our magazine is published four times a year, with an all-name index in the summer issue."

Publications: The society's Web site has a publications list.

Downriver Genealogical Society

P.O. Box 476
Lincoln Park, Mich. 48146
Telephone: (313) 382-3229
E-mail: <sherry@localonline.net>
Web site: <www.rootsweb.com/~midrgs/drgs.htm>
Date founded: 1980
Membership dues: $10
Number of members: 270

Purpose: "To preserve and perpetuate the records of our ancestors; to encourage and assist members in genealogical research."

Library/archives: The society's collection is housed in the Lincoln Park Historical Museum, 1335 Southfield Rd. and Fort Park Blvd., Lincoln Park. It is open to the public at no charge from 1 p.m. to 5 p.m. Tuesdays through Thursdays. Numbering more than 1,200 volumes, the collection includes "extensive Michigan and Canadian books and sources, census microfilm for many Michigan counties, and books for other states and foreign countries."

Magazine/newsletter: Members receive *The Downriver Seeker,* published four times per year.

Publications: "There are many publications for sale. Some cover Wayne County, others are for the downriver area and include cemetery transcriptions, funeral home records, an 1876 atlas for Wayne County, and 1904 landowners." For more information, see the society's Web site <www.rootsweb.com/~midrgs/drgspubs.htm>.

Flat Rock Historical Society

P.O. Box 337
Flat Rock, Mich. 48134
Telephone: (734) 782-5220
Date founded: 1976
Membership dues: $7, individual; $100, lifetime
Number of members: 150

Purpose: "To preserve Flat Rock history."

Library/archives: Located behind the City Hall and Library at the corner of Gibralter Rd. and Aspen Blvd., the facility is open from 1 p.m. to 4 p.m. the second Sunday of each month or by appointment. The facility has "school class pictures, old newspaper articles, maps, obituary files, and death records."

Publications: *Fields of Honor: The Battle of Fort Freeland, July 28, 1779,* the story of Flat Rock founder Michael Vreeland's capture in Pennsylvania, $10.

Research service: Volunteers will assist researchers.

Ford Genealogy Club
P.O. Box 1652
Dearborn, Mich. 48126-1652
E-mail: <miprofgenie@wwnet.net> or <diane@dianesgenealogy.com>
Web site: <wwnet.net/~krugman1/fgc/>
Date founded: 1994-95
Membership dues: $12
Number of members: 35

Purpose: "To encourage others to pursue and enjoy the hobby of genealogy; to provide assistance and encouragement to our membership in their pursuit of family history."

Magazine/newsletter: Members receive a newsletter, published four times per year.

Research service: "We don't offer a research service, but we do have members who answer inquiries and do minor lookups for people in local resources. We also have three professional genealogists in our club who offer to help but do charge."

Other: "Our club is made up primarily of Ford/Visteon employees. We do accept membership from other persons on a limited basis. We also accept Ford/Visteon retirees and spouses."

Fred Hart Williams Genealogical Society
c/o Detroit Public Library
Burton Historical Collection
5210 Woodward Ave.
Detroit, Mich. 48202
Telephone: (313) 438-3233
Fax: (313) 340-0587
E-mail: <fredhartwilliams@yahoo.com>
Web site: <www.fhwgs.org>
Date founded: 1979
Number of members: 200

Purpose: "Researching and preserving African American family history."

Library/archives: The society's collection is housed at the Burton Historical Collection (see pages 346-347).

Publications: *Our Untold Stories: A Collection of Family History Narratives,* $35, plus $3.50 shipping.

Grosse Ile Historical Society
P.O. Box 131
Groose Ile, Mich. 48138
Telephone: (734) 675-1250

Date founded: 1959

Membership dues: $10, individuals; $20, families; $300, lifetime

Number of members: 300

Purpose: "To collect, preserve, and interpret historical information and materials relative to Grosse Ile, Michigan, and to teach, to promote study and research, and to generate interest in Grosse Ile history."

Library/archives: "The archives are housed in the museum. An appointment is necessary to study our archives."

Museum: "We maintain a museum, which was a Michigan Central Railroad Depot (1904) and an old U.S. customs house (ca. 1873). The museum is open 1 p.m. to 4 p.m. Sundays and 10 a.m. to noon Thursdays or by appointment. We are closed in January and February and on major holidays. It is located at the corner of East River Rd. and Grosse Ile Parkway."

Publications: "We have a few books for sale which are centered on Grosse Ile history. We are not set up for mail order, though occasionally we will fill an order and charge shipping and handling."

Written queries: "If people request information in writing we recommend enclosing a stamped, self-addressed envelope. We do not encourage people to call and ask for a return call unless they are located in this area."

Research service: "We offer assistance with research when requested. Any costs would be negotiated on a case-by-case basis, depending on what is wanted. There is a charge for reproducing photos and for photocopies. Our service is limited by the fact that we are all volunteers and have no paid curator or staff."

Irish Genealogical Society of Michigan

c/o Irish American Club
2068 Michigan Ave.
Detroit, Mich. 48216

Telephone: (248) 540-7294

Fax: (248) 540-7297

E-mail: <igsm@topicsinc.com>

Web site: <www.rootsweb.com/~miigsm>

Date founded: 1996

Membership dues: $10, individuals; $12, families. Membership is required to use the society's services/resources.

Number of members: 200

Purpose: "To create interest and aid members of the society and the general public in the compilation of their genealogies."

Library/archives: "The library is available to members only, before and after monthly meetings. The collection consists of books, periodicals, magazines, computer software, and CD indexes. Also, the library contains computers and microfiche/microfilm readers."

Publications: *Our Roots Began in Ireland,* Irish families that settled in Detroit and Michigan, pre-Revolutionary War to present, $13, plus $4 postage.

Other: "We have monthly lectures on topics of genealogical interest, especially Irish-related. They are free and open to the public."

Northville Genealogical Society
P.O. Box 932
Northville, Mich. 48167
E-mail: <richpats@hotmail.com>
Web site: <www.rootsweb.com/~mings/>
Date founded: 1987
Membership dues: $15, individuals; $20, couples
Number of members: 67
Purpose: "Share knowledge, learn from speakers."

Archives: The Archive Collection of the Northville Historical Society <www.northville.lib.mi.us/community/groups/history/> is located on the second floor of the Cady Inn, part of the society's Mill Race Historical Village, located off Griswold St., Northville. It is open to the public from 9 a.m. to 1 p.m. Thursdays or by appointment. Staffed by a professional librarian, holdings include original documents, newspaper clippings, photographs, scrapbooks, family histories, city directories, microfilmed newspapers (*Northville Record,* 1869 to present), Northville census records (1810-1920), and Sanborn Fire Insurance Maps.

Museum: Mill Race Historical Village, a living museum, "consists of a church, gazebo, school, blacksmith shop and general store, Interurban station, and several homes reminiscent of a bygone era." It is open to the public from 1 p.m. to 4 p.m. Sundays June through October and is located off Griswold St., Northville.

Magazine/newsletter: Members receive a quarterly newsletter.

Publications: The society has several books for sale, including cemetery inscriptions, *Early Northville,* and *Northville – Ideal Suburban Village*. For more information, see the society's Web site <www.rootsweb.com/~mings/publications.html>.

Research service: $7.50 per hour, plus 10 cents per copy.

Polish Genealogical Society of Michigan
c/o Burton Historical Collection
Detroit Public Library
5201 Woodward Ave.
Detroit, Mich. 48202
Telephone: (586) 247-3583
E-mail: <jan@zaleski.net>
Web site: <www.pgsm.org>
Date founded: 1978

Membership dues: $20 annually. Membership is required to use the society's services/resources.

Number of members: 566

Purpose: "Dedicated to promoting interest and encouraging research in Polish genealogy as well as preserving historical materials, which would aid in researching Polish family history."

Magazine/newsletter: Members receive *The Polish Eaglet,* the Journal of the Polish Genealogical Society of Michigan, three times per years. Past issues are available for sale.

Western Wayne County Genealogical Society
P.O. Box 530063
Livonia, Mich. 48153-0063
Web site: <www.rootsweb.com/~miwwcgs>
Date founded: 1876
Membership dues: $15, individuals; $18, families
Number of members: 125

Library/archives: "Our holdings are in the Livonia Civic Center Library, 32777 Five Mile Rd., Livonia, 48154. They consist of more than 200 books and a genealogical computer with more than 200 CDs from Family Tree Maker and other sources."

Magazine/newsletter: Members receive a bi-monthly newsletter and a quarterly.

Publications: Several books are available, including *Union Church and Livonia Cemetery,* $10; *Maple Grove Cemetery,* $15; and *1870 Livonia Census,* $1.00. Add $3 per book for shipping and handling.

Research service: Will research for "donation, if desired." Limited to materials in the local area.

Westland Historical Commission
36601 Ford Rd.
Westland, Mich. 48185
Telephone: (734) 326-1110 (leave message)
Date founded: 1972
Membership dues: None
Number of members: 9

Purpose: "To gather and preserve the history of Nankin Township and Westland."

Museum: The Westland Historical Museum is located at 857 N. Wayne Rd., Westland, 48185. It is open 1 p.m. to 4 p.m. Saturdays and by appointment. Holdings include early Nankin Township birth records, Eloise death records (incomplete 1867-1957), cemetery records of Nankin Township and neighboring communities, and census records 1850 to 1880 for Nankin Township.

Publications: Maps of Nankin Township, 1876, 1905, 1915, or 1924; $1 each.

Research service: "Limited to Nankin Township, Wayne County. Fee depends on research."

Wyandotte Historical Society
2610 Biddle Ave.
Wyandotte, Mich. 48192

Telephone: (734) 324-7297
Fax: (734) 324-7283
E-mail: <wymuseum@ili.net>
Date founded: 1958
Number of members: 500
Purpose: "To educate, preserve, and present Wyandotte history."
Library/archives: Yes.
Museum: Yes.
Publications: Books include *Proudly We Record,* a history of Wyandotte, and *Pictorial History of Wyandotte.*

Wexford County

Wexford Genealogy Organization

P.O. Box 226
Cadillac, Mich. 49601
Telephone: (231) 779-7331
Date founded: 2002
Membership dues: $9, individuals; $12, couples
Purpose: "To preserve records and genealogical resources and to promote ethical genealogical research."
Library/archives: The society's holdings are located in the Genealogy Room of the Cadillac-Wexford Public Library (see page 349).
Publications: Several books are available, including cemetery transcriptions, death records, and marriage records.
Research service: "$1 per page, plus 50 cents postage for look-ups in our resources; $5 for courthouse records in Wexford County; $10 for courthouse records in Missaukee, Osceola, or Manistee counties. Contact us for census search prices and prices for more in-depth research."
Other: "We offer a location for records the townships don't have room to store and so have available information from several townships. We have every obituary published in the *Cadillac Evening News/Cadillac News* since 1988 and a large number dating before that."

Notes

Chapter 1

[1] In a 25 September 1702 letter to French authorities, Cadillac gave a glowing description of the present-day Detroit area. "This river or strait of the seas is scattered over, from one lake to the other, both on the mainland and on the islands there, in its plains and on its banks, with large clusters of trees surrounded by charming meadows … Game is very common there, as wild geese and all kinds of wild ducks. There are swans everywhere; there are quails, woodcocks, pheasants, rabbits – it is the only place on the continent of America where any have been seen. There are so many turkeys that 20 or 30 could be killed at one shot every met with. There are partridges, hazel-hens, and a stupendous number of turtle-doves. … This country, so temperate, so fertile, and so beautiful that it may justly be called the earthly paradise of North America …" The entire letter can be found in Cadillac's "Account of Detroit," published in *Michigan Pioneer and Historical Collections*, volume 33, or online through the Clarke Historical Library Web site <clarke.cmich.edu/detroit/cadillac1702.htm>, accessed 7 September 2004.

[2] Willis Frederick Dunbar, *Michigan: A History of the Wolverine State* (Grand Rapids: William B. Eerdmans Publishing Co., 1965), 47.

[3] Harry Stapler with Berenice Lowe and Amy South, *Pioneers of Forest and City: A History of Michigan for Young People* (Lansing: Michigan Historical Commission, 1985), 25.

[4] John Kern, *A Short History of Michigan* (Lansing: Michigan Department of State, 1977), 5.

[5] Frank Angelo, *Yesterday's Michigan* (Miami: E.A. Seemann Publishing Inc., 1975), 26.

[6] Eric Freedman, *Pioneering Michigan* (Franklin, Michigan: Altwerger and Mandel Publishing Co., 1992), 47.

[7] *Detroit in Its World Setting: A Three Hundred Year Chronology, 1701-2001,* ed. David Lee Poremba (Detroit: Wayne State University Press, 2001), 112.

[8] Dunbar, 39.

[9] George P. Graff, *The People of Michigan* (Lansing: Michigan Department of Education, 1974), 20.

[10] Stapler, 95.

[11] Kern, 66.

[12] *Detroit in Its World Setting,* 149, 183.

[13] *Atlas of Michigan,* ed. Lawrence M. Sommers (East Lansing: Michigan State University Press, 1977), 64

[14] Kern, 2.

[15] *Detroit in Its World Setting,* 330.

[16] Sources for this section include Stapler; *Detroit in Its World Setting; Chronology and Documentary Handbook of the State of Michigan,* ed. Robert I. Vexler (Dobbs Ferry, New York: Oceana Publications, 1978); and *Michigan Manual 2001-2002* <www.michiganlegislature.org/documents/publications/manual/2001-2002/2001-mm-0030-0046-Chron.pdf >, accessed 9 May 2004.

Chapter 2

[1] Willis F. Dunbar, and George S. May, *Michigan: A History of the Wolverine State,* 3rd ed. (Grand Rapids: William B. Eerdmans Publishing Co., 1995), 21.

[2] Dunbar and May, 45.

[3] Alec R. Gilpin, *The Territory of Michigan* (East Lansing: Michigan State University Press, 1970), 47.

[4] Frank Angelo, *Yesterday's Michigan* (Miami: E.A. Seemann Publishing Inc., 1975), 21.

[5] Angelo, 21.

[6] Dunbar and May, 75.

[7] John Kern, *A Short History of Michigan* (Lansing: Michigan Department of State, 1977), 8.

[8] Angelo, 25.

[9] Kern, 12-13.

[10] Dunbar and May, 131.

[11] Le Roy Barnett and Roger Rosentreter, *Michigan's Early Military Forces* (Detroit: Wayne State University Press, 2003), 72; Angelo, 29; and Kern, 14.

[12] Theodore J. Karamanski, *Deep Woods Frontier: A History of Logging in Northern Michigan* (Detroit: Wayne State University Press, 1989), 16.

[13] Gilpin, 11.

[14] Annette Newcomb, *Awesome Almanac: Michigan* (Fontana, Wisconsin: B and B Publishing, 1993), 6, and *Facts About the States,* 2nd ed. ed. Joseph Nathan Kane, Janet Podell, and Steven Anzovin (New York: H.W. Wilson, 1993), 248.

[15] *Atlas of Michigan,* ed. Lawrence M. Sommers (East Lansing: Michigan State University Press, 1977), 2, and *Michigan: A Guide to the Wolverine State* (New York: Oxford University Press, 1941), 60.

[16] Larry Wakefield, *Ghost Towns of Michigan* (Holt, Michigan: Thunder Bay Press, 2002), III, 43.

[17] Kenneth E. Lewis, *West to Far Michigan: Settling the Lower Peninsula, 1815-1860* (East Lansing: Michigan State University Press, 2002), 57.

[18] Richard A. Santer, "Great Lakes Island Guru," *Michigan History,* 87-6 (November-December 2003), 46.

[19] Lewis, 22.

[20] Dunbar and May, 156.

[21] Dunbar and May, 156-157.

[22] Dunbar and May, 157.

[23] LeRoy Barnett, "Milestones in Michigan Mapping: Part I," *Michigan History,* 63-5 (September-October 1979), 38.

[24] Lewis, 170, 219.

[25] Lewis, 197.

[26] Dunbar and May, 161.

[27] Dunbar and May, 161.

[28] Harry Stapler with Berenice Lowe and Amy South, *Pioneers of Forest and City: A History of Michigan for Young People* (Lansing: Michigan Historical Commission, 1985), 89.

[29] Dunbar and May, 271.

[30] David G. Chardavoyne, *A Hanging in Detroit: Stephen Gifford Simmons and the Last Execution Under Michigan Law* (Detroit: Wayne State University Press, 2003), 32.

[31] Lewis, 222.

[32] Dunbar and May, 159.

[33] Fred C. Hamil, "Michigan in the War of 1812," *Michigan History,* 44-3 (September 1960), 260.

[34] Stapler, 68.

[35] Kern, 17.

[36] Kern, 18.

[37] Chardavoyne, 33.

[38] Jeremy W. Kilar, *Michigan's Lumbertowns: Lumbermen and Laborers in Saginaw, Bay City, and Muskegon, 1870-1905* (Detroit: Wayne State University Press, 1990), 86.

[39] Dunbar and May, 165.

[40] Lewis, 224.

[41] Frank N. Elliott, *When the Railroad Was King* (Lansing: Bureau of History, 1988), 66, and George S. May, *Pictorial History of Michigan: The Later Years* (Grand Rapids: William B. Eerdmans Publishing Co., 1969), 40.

[42] Lewis, 198.

[43] Elliott, 43.

[44] Elliott, 44.

[45] Stapler, 71.

[46] Elliott, 17-18.

[47] Roy L. Dodge, *Michigan Ghost Towns of the Lower Peninsula* (Las Vegas: Glendon Publishing, 1990), II, 2-3.

[48] Dodge, *Michigan Ghost Towns of the Lower Peninsula*, I, 7.

[49] Dunbar and May, 244.

[50] Dunbar and May, 374.

[51] Stapler, 150.

[52] Lewis, 128.

[53] Dunbar and May, 163-164.

[54] Dunbar and May, 164.

[55] Daniel E. Sutherland, "Michigan Emigrant Agent: Edward H. Thomson," *Michigan History*, 59-1-2 (Spring-Summer 1975), 6.

[56] John Cumming, "Michigan for Sale," *Michigan History*, 70-6 (November-December 1986), 16; Angelo, 31; and Susan E. Gray, *The Yankee West: Community Life on the Michigan Frontier* (Chapel Hill: The University of North Carolina Press, 1996), 44.

[57] Lewis, 100.

[58] Lewis, 1.

[59] George S. May, *Pictorial History of Michigan: The Early Years* (Grand Rapids: William B. Eerdmans Publishing Co., 1967), 156-158.

[60] Lewis, 249.

[61] Sutherland, 3, 5.

[62] C. Warren VanderHill, *Settling the Great Lakes Frontier: Immigration to Michigan, 1837-1924* (Lansing: Michigan Historical Commission, 1970), 18.

[63] Sutherland, 15, 21.

[64] VanderHill, 18.

[65] VanderHill, 22.

[66] Carlton C. Qualey, *Norwegian Settlement in the United States* (New York: Arno Press, 1970), 183.

[67] Kilar, 176.

[68] George P. Graff, *The People of Michigan* (Lansing: Michigan Department of Education, 1974), 65.

[69] Lewis Walker, Benjamin C. Wilson, and Linwood H. Cousins, *African Americans in Michigan* (East Lansing: Michigan State University Press, 2001), 18.

[70] Elliott, 26-27.

[71] Graff, 60.

[72] Carlton C. Qualey, "Pioneer Scandinavian Settlement in Michigan," *Michigan History*, 24 (Autumn 1940), 438.

[73] Lewis, 131.

[74] Lewis, 132.

[75] Lewis, 133.

[76] Stapler, 128.

[77] Kilar, 21.

[78] Dunbar and May, 340.

[79] Dunbar and May, 339.

[80] Burton W. Folsom Jr., *Empire Builders: How Michigan Entrepreneurs Helped Make America Great* (Traverse City, Michigan: Rhodes and Easton, 1998), 55.

[81] Karamanski, 186.

[82] Dunbar and May, 340.

[83] Lawrence M. Sommers with Joe T. Darden, Jay R. Harman, Laurie K. Sommers, *Michigan: A Geography* (Boulder: Westview Press, 1984), 109.

[84] Kilar, 63.

[85] Stapler, 128.

[86] Rolland H. Maybee, *Michigan's White Pine Era* (Lansing: Michigan Department of State, 1988), 44.

[87] George B. Engberg, "Who Were the Lumberjacks?" *Michigan History,* 32-3 (September 1948), 241.

[88] Karamanski, 105.

[89] Dunbar and May, 344.

[90] Kilar, 216.

[91] Karamanski, 206.

[92] Stapler, 130.

[93] Karamanski, 224.

[94] George S. May, *Pictorial History of Michigan: The Later Years,* 80.

[95] Larry Lankton, *Cradle to Grave: Life, Work, and Death at the Lake Superior Copper Mines* (New York: Oxford University Press, 1991), 8.

[96] Angus Murdoch, *Boom Copper: The Story of the First U.S. Mining Boom* (New York: MacMillan Co., 1943), 27.

[97] Virginia Jonas Dersch, "Copper Mining in Northern Michigan: A Social History," *Michigan History,* 61-4 (Winter 1977), 300-301.

[98] Lankton, 5.

[99] Arthur W. Thurner, *Strangers and Sojourners: A History of Michigan's Keweenaw Peninsula* (Detroit: Wayne State University Press, 1994), 13, and Dunbar and May, 357-358.

[100] Thurner, 64.

[101] Stapler, 146.

[102] William B. Gates Jr., *Michigan Copper and Boston Dollars: An Economic History of the Michigan Copper Mining Industry* (Cambridge, Massachusetts: Harvard University Press, 1951), 95.

[103] Dunbar and May, 365-366.

[104] Dunbar and May, 359.

[105] Dunbar and May, 365.

[106] Michigan History Magazine, *Introducing Michigan's Past: An Overview for Teachers* (Lansing: Michigan Department of State, 2001), 18.

[107] Sommers, 113.

[108] *Introducing Michigan's Past,* 18.

[109] Sommers, 114.

[110] May, 162.

[111] Dunbar and May, 396.

[112] Dunbar and May, 401.

[113] Dunbar and May, 401.

[114] Mike Smith, and Thomas Featherstone, *Labor in Detroit: Working in the Motor City* (Chicago: Arcadia Publishing, 2001), 11.

[115] Kern, 40.

[116] Kern, 41.

[117] *Detroit in Its World Setting: A Three Hundred Year Chronology, 1701-2001,* ed. David Lee Poremba (Detroit: Wayne State University Press, 2001), 160.

[118] *Detroit in Its World Setting,* 184, and Lewis, 438.

[119] Stapler, 170.

[120] Kern, 45-46.

[121] Smith and Featherstone, 32.

[122] *Michigan Voices,* ed. Joe Grimm (Detroit: Wayne State University Press, 1987), 121.

[123] Smith and Featherstone, 27.

[124] *Michigan Remembered: Photographs From the Farm Security Administration and the Office of War Information, 1936-1943,* ed. Constance B. Schulz (Detroit: Wayne State University Press, 2001), 17.

[125] *Michigan Remembered,* 18, 20.

[126] Smith and Featherstone, 8, and Kern, 59.

[127] Dunbar and May, 533.

[128] Dunbar and May, 534, and Larry Lankton, "Autos to Armaments: Detroit Becomes the Arsenal of Democracy," *Michigan History,* 75-6 (November-December 1991), 48.

[129] Dunbar and May, 394.

[130] *Michigan Remembered,* 15-16.

[131] Ray Allen Billington, *Westward Expansion: A History of the American Frontier,* 4th ed. (New York: MacMillan Publishing Co. Inc., 1974), 291.

[132] Billington, 292.

[133] Dunbar and May, 483.

[134] Eric Freedman, *Pioneering Michigan* (Franklin, Michigan: Altwerger and Mandel Publishing Co., 1992), 61.

[135] Amos Henry Hawley, *The Population of Michigan, 1840 to 1960: An Analysis of Growth, Distribution and Composition* (Ann Arbor: The University of Michigan Press, 1949), 35.

[136] Dunbar and May, 484.

[137] Dunbar and May, 484.

[138] Sommers, 108.

[139] Dunbar and May, 483.

[140] Angelo, 151.

[141] *Michigan Remembered,* 16.

[142] Kern, 41.

[143] Angelo, 151.

[144] *Michigan Remembered,* 16.

[145] Sommers, 108.

[146] Lewis, 134.

[147] Lewis, 134-135.

[148] Lewis, 142.

[149] Dunbar and May, 303.

[150] Roger L. Rosentreter, "Michigan's 83 Counties: Benzie County." *Michigan History,* 63-6 (November/December 1979), 8-9.

[151] Roger Rosentreter, "Brother Benjamin: The Author of the Newest Book on the House of David Talks with Michigan History Magazine," *Michigan History,* 75-4 (July-August 1991), 15.

[152] Dunbar and May, 600.

[153] Gray, 18.

[154] Gray, 19.

[155] Roger L. Rosentreter, "Michigan's 83 Counties: Charlevoix County," *Michigan History,* 64-5 (September-October 1980), 8, and Bradley A. Rodgers, *Guardian of the Great Lakes: The U.S. Paddle Frigate Michigan* (Ann Arbor: The University of Michigan Press, 1996), 62-63.

[156] Rosentreter, "Michigan's 83 Counties: Charlevoix County," 8.

[157] Dunbar and May, 302.

[158] Lewis, 144.

[159] Lewis, 144.

[160] Jeremy W. Kilar, *Germans in Michigan* (East Lansing: Michigan State University Press, 2002), 15; and Lewis, 150.

[161] Lewis, 151.

[162] A. James Rudin, "Bad Axe, Michigan: An Experiment In Jewish Agricultural Settlement," *Michigan History,* 56-2 (September 1972), 126.

[163] Roger L. Rosentreter, "Michigan's 83 Counties: Clinton County," *Michigan History,* 65-3 (May-June 1981), 10.

[164] Lewis, 142.

[165] Lewis, 145.

[166] Kilar, *Germans in Michigan,* 16.

[167] Lewis, 145.

[168] Ralph Crandall, "From New England to Michigan: Patterns of Migration and Settlement," presentation given at the State Library of Michigan, 12 October 2002.

[169] Gilpin, 135.

[170] Jean Lamarre, *The French Canadians of Michigan: Their Contribution to the Development of the Saginaw Valley and the Keweenaw Peninsula, 1840-1914* (Detroit: Wayne State University Press, 2003), 105, 150.

[171] Gray, 102.

[172] A. L. Rowse, *The Cousin Jacks: The Cornish in America* (New York: Charles Scribner's Sons, 1969), 177.

[173] Rowse, 178.

[174] Eleanor Myers, *A Migration Study of the Thirty-two States and Four Organized Territories Comprising the United States in 1850 Based Upon the Federal Census of 1850* (Syracuse, New York: Central New York Genealogical Society, 1977), 17.

[175] Andrew D. Perejda, "Sources and Dispersal of Michigan's Population," *Michigan History,* 32-4 (December 1948), 365.

[176] Mary Lou Straith Duncan, *Passage to America, 1851-1869: The Records of Richard Elliott, Passenger Agent, Detroit, Michigan* (Detroit: Detroit Society for Genealogical Research, 1999), vii.

[177] Duncan, xi.

[178] U.S. Citizenship and Immigration Services: U.S. Ports of Entry in Canada – Saint Albans Ship Lists <uscis.gov/graphics/aboutus/history/POELIST/CAN2.htm>, accessed 3 February 2004.

[179] Loretto Dennis Szucs, *They Became Americans: Finding Naturalization Records and Ethnic Origins* (Salt Lake City, Utah: Ancestry Inc., 1998), 81.

[180] Szucs, 22.

[181] Szucs, 25.

[182] Szucs, 155.

[183] Szucs, 39.

[184] Marian L. Smith, "Any Woman Who Is Now or May Hereafter Be Married: Women and Naturalization, ca. 1802-1940," *Prologue,* 30-2 (Summer 1998), <www.archives.gov/publications/prologue/summer_1998_women_and_naturalization_1.html>, accessed 17 September 2002.

[185] Szucs, 161.

[186] Szucs, 162.

[187] Smith.

[188] U.S. National Archives and Records Administration: Naturalization Records <www.archives.gov/research_room/genealogy/research_topics/naturalization_records.html>, accessed 17 September 2002.

[189] Szucs, 42-43.

[190] Christina K. Schaefer, *The Great War: A Guide to the Service Records of All the World's Fighting Men and Volunteers* (Baltimore: Genealogical Publishing Co. Inc., 1998), 141.

[191] U.S. National Archives and Records Administration: Naturalization Records <www.archives.gov/research_room/genealogy/research_topics/naturalization_records.html>, accessed 17 September 2002.

[192] U.S. National Archives and Records Administration: Naturalization Records <www.archives.gov/research_room/genealogy/research_topics/naturalization_records.html>, accessed 17 September 2002.

[193] Neagles, 39.

[194] Szucs, 3.

[195] U.S. National Archives and Records Administration: Naturalization Records <www.archives.gov/research_room/genealogy/research_topics/naturalization_records.html>, accessed 17 September 2002.

[196] Szucs, 92.

[197] Joseph Oldenburg, *A Genealogical Guide to The Burton Historical Collection: Detroit Public Library* (Salt Lake City, Utah: Ancestry Inc., 1988), 33.

[198] James C. Neagles and Lila Lee Neagles, *Locating Your Immigrant Ancestor* (Logan, Utah: Everton Publishers Inc., 1975), 48.

Chapter 3

[1] *The Source: A Guidebook of American Genealogy,* ed. Arlene Eakle and Johni Cerny (Salt Lake City, Utah: Ancestry Publishing Co., 1984), 49. An earlier version of the Michigan Department of Community Health Web site said there were more than 30 million vital records at the state level.

[2] *Laws of the Territory of Michigan* (Lansing: W.S. George and Co. 1871), 1, 30-32.

[3] *Laws of the Territory of Michigan,* 1, 646-649.

[4] *Laws of the Territory of Michigan* (Lansing: W.S. George and Co. 1874), 2, 312-414.

[5] *The Revised Statutes of the State of Michigan* (Detroit: John S. Bagg, 1838), 333-335.

[6] Public Act 23 of 1883

[7] *The Revised Statutes of the State of Michigan,* 330-332.

[8] *Michigan Compiled Laws,* 2001, 551.201-551.204.

[9] *Laws of the Territory of Michigan,* 1, 183.

[10] *Laws of the Territory of Michigan,* 1, 494-499.

[11] *Laws of the Territory of Michigan* (Lansing: W.S. George and Co. 1874), 3, 931-932.

[12] *Laws of the Territory of Michigan,* 3, 1005-1007.

[13] David G. Chardavoyne, *A Hanging in Detroit: Stephen Gifford Simmons and the Last Execution Under Michigan Law* (Detroit: Wayne State University Press, 2003), 52.

[14] Chardavoyne, 52.

[15] *The Revised Statutes of the State of Michigan,* 336-341.

[16] *The Revised Statutes of the State of Michigan* (Detroit: Bagg & Harmon, 1846), 332-337.

[17] Larry Lankton, *Beyond the Boundaries: Life and Landscape at the Lake Superior Copper Mines, 1840-1875* (New York: Oxford University Press, 1997), 149-150.

[18] *Michigan Compiled Laws,* 2001, 333.2827 and 333.2828.

[19] Marilyn Ferris Motz, *True Sisterhood: Michigan Women and Their Kin 1820-1920* (Albany: State University of New York Press, 1983), 89.

[20] See *Vital Statistics Holdings by Government Agencies in Michigan. Birth Records* (Detroit: The Michigan Historical Records Survey Project, 1941); *Vital Statistics Holdings by Government Agencies in Michigan. Death Records* (Detroit: The Michigan Historical Records Survey Project, 1942); *Vital Statistics Holdings by Government Agencies in Michigan. Divorce Records* (Detroit: The Michigan Historical Records Survey Project, 1942); and *Vital Statistics Holdings by Government Agencies in Michigan. Marriage Records* (Detroit: The Michigan Historical Records Survey Project, 1941).

[21] During the 1996 Michigan Genealogical Council Seminar, Glen Copeland presented a session on "Michigan's 29,000,000 Vital Records." He said 23 Michigan cities in Macomb, Oakland, and Wayne counties still record vital statistics and forward these to the state.

[22] Copeland.

Chapter 4

[1] Laura Arksey, Nancy Pries, and Marcia Reed, *American Diaries: An Annotated Bibliography of Published American Diaries and Journals* (Detroit: Gale Research Co., 1983), I, ix.

[2] Joseph Oldenburg, *A Genealogical Guide to the Burton Historical Collection Detroit Public Library* (Salt Lake City: Ancestry Publishing, 1988), 15.

[3] *Michigan Family Register,* Volume 1.

[4] Eric Freedman, *Pioneering Michigan.* (Franklin, Michigan: Altwerger and Mandel Publishing Co., 1992), 15.

[5] *Michigan Surname Index.* (Lansing: Michigan Genealogical Council, 1989), II, vii.

[6] Edward F. Rines, "Some Historic Churches in Michigan," *Michigan Heritage,* 4-2 (Winter 1962), 71.

[7] Saralee R. Howard-Filler, "'A Jubilee Shall That Fiftieth Year Be Unto You': Michigan Churches in 1884," *Michigan History,* 67-4 (July-August 1983), 22.

[8] Willis F. Dunbar, and George S. May, *Michigan: A History of the Wolverine State,* 3rd ed. (Grand Rapids, Mich.: William B. Eerdmans Publishing Co., 1995), 192.

[9] Howard-Filler, 23.

[10] Howard-Filler, 23.

[11] Alec R. Gilpin, *The Territory of Michigan* (East Lansing: Michigan State University Press, 1970), 73.

[12] Howard-Filler, 19.

[13] Marilyn P. Watkins, "Civilizers of the West: Clergy and Laity in Michigan Frontier Churches, 1820-1840," *Michigan: Explorations in its Social History,* ed. Francis X. Blouin Jr. and Maris A. Vinovskis (Ann Arbor: Historical Society of Michigan, 1987), 166.

[14] Howard-Filler, 19.

[15] C.M. Burton, *Cadillac's Village, or Detroit Under Cadillac, with List of Property Owners and a History of the Settlement 1701 to 1710* (Detroit: Detroit Society for Genealogical Research, 1999), 30.

[16] Kenneth E. Lewis, *West to Far Michigan: Settling the Lower Peninsula, 1815-1860* (East Lansing: Michigan State University Press, 2002), 138.

[17] Howard-Filler, 17.

[18] Howard-Filler, 19.

[19] Howard-Filler, 20.

[20] Howard-Filler, 21.

[21] Howard-Filler, 25.

[22] Dunbar and May, 196.

[23] Dunbar and May, 196.

[24] "Quaker Monthly Meetings in Michigan Established Prior to 1900," *Family Trails,* 3 (1983), 35; Lewis Walker, Benjamin C. Wilson, and Linwood H. Cousins, *African Americans in Michigan* (East Lansing: Michigan State University Press, 2001), 6.

[25] Robert A. Rockaway, *The Jews of Detroit: From the Beginning, 1762-1914* (Detroit: Wayne State University Press, 1986), 31.

[26] Judith Levin Cantor, *Jews in Michigan* (East Lansing: Michigan State University Press, 2001), 11.

[27] Robert A. Rockaway, "The Detroit Jewish Ghetto Before World War I," *Michigan History,* 52-1 (Spring 1968), 33.

[28] Irving I. Katz, "Jews in Michigan," *Family Trails,* 3 (1983), 43; "Oldest Synagogue," *Michigan History,* 65-2 (March-April 1981), 5.

[29] Dunbar and May, 599.

[30] Dunbar and May, 397.

[31] Gertrude Enders Huntington, *Amish in Michigan* (East Lansing: Michigan State University Press, 2001), 2.

[32] Dunbar and May, 602.

[33] Michigan Historical Records Survey, *Vital Statistics Holdings of Church Archives in Michigan, Wayne County* (Detroit: The Michigan Historical Records Survey Project, 1942), ix.

[34] The Rabbi Leo M. Franklin Archives <www.tbeonline.org/leofranklinarchives.htm>, accessed 8 September 2003.

[35] Society of American Archivists. Detailed List of Counties, Municipalities, and Denominations/ Sample HRS Forms. 1980, a microfiche distributed with Loretta L. Hefner, *The WPA Historical Records Survey: A Guide to the Unpublished Inventories, Indexes, and Transcripts,* (Chicago: The Society of American Archivists, 1980).

[36] *Marriage Records, Ste. Anne Church, Detroit, 1701-1850,* ed. Sharon A. Kelley (Detroit: Detroit Society for Genealogical Research, 2001), vi.

[37] Roy L. Dodge, *Michigan Ghost Towns of the Lower Peninsula* (Las Vegas, Nevada: Glendon Publishing, 1990), xii.

[38] *Cemeteries of the U.S.: A Guide to Contact Information for U.S. Cemeteries and Their Records* (Detroit: Gale Research, 1994), 501.

[39] Public Act 217 of 1897.

[40] Gilpin, 72.

[41] George S. May, *Pictorial History of Michigan: The Early Years* (Grand Rapids: William B. Eerdmans Publishing Co., 1967), 125.

[42] Willis Frederick Dunbar, *Michigan: A History of the Wolverine State* (Grand Rapids: William B. Eerdmans Publishing Co., 1965), 390.

[43] Dunbar, 720.

[44] Georges J. Joyaux, "French Press in Michigan," *Michigan History,* 37-2 (June 1953), 156.

[45] *Atlas of Michigan,* ed. Lawrence M. Sommers (East Lansing: Michigan State University Press, 1977), 205.

[46] Dunbar and May, 274.

[47] Michigan Newspaper Project Web site <www.michigan.gov/hal/0,1607,7-160-17449_18643-50500--,00.html>, accessed 2 September 2003, and Kendel Darragh, Michigan Newspaper Resources, presentation made 9 August 2003 at the Library of Michigan, Lansing, Michigan.

[48] A 1973 fire at the National Personnel Records Center destroyed about 18 million military personnel records, including 80 percent of those for army personnel who were discharged from 1 November 1912 to 1 January 1960 and 75 percent of those for air force personnel who were discharged 25 September 1947 to 1 January 1964 and with the last names of Hubbard through Z.

[49] Gilpin, 47.

[50] Valerie Gerrard Browne, and David Jerome Johnson, *A Guide to the State Archives of Michigan: State Records* (Lansing: Michigan Department of State, 1977), 123.

[51] Le Roy Barnett and Roger Rosentreter, *Michigan's Early Military Forces* (Detroit: Wayne State University Press, 2003), 27.

[52] Barnett and Rosentreter, 12.

[53] Gilpin, 168.

[54] *Michigan Voices,* ed. Joe Grimm (Detroit: Wayne State University Press, 1987), 47.

[55] Roger L. Rosentreter, "Brigands or Paragons: Michigan Officials During the Patriot War," *Michigan History,* 73-5 (September/October 1989), 25.

[56] Barnett and Rosentreter, 341.

[57] Barnett and Rosentreter, 20.

[58] Dunbar and May, 321.

[59] Frederick D. Williams, *Michigan Soldiers in the Civil War* (Lansing: Bureau of Michigan History, 1994), 12.

[60] Dunbar and May, 323.

[61] DeAnne Blanton, and Lauren M. Cook, *They Fought Like Demons: Women Soldiers in the Civil War* (New York: Vintage Books, 2002), 17.

[62] Dunbar and May, 324.

[63] John Kern, *A Short History of Michigan* (Lansing: Michigan History Division, Michigan Department of State, 1977), 36.

[64] Dunbar and May, 323, and John Robertson, *Michigan in the War* (Lansing: W.S. George and Co., 1882), 740-746.

[65] Williams, 48.

[66] Public Act 147 of 1903.

[67] *The Roster of Union Soldiers, 1861 to 1865,* ed Janet B. Hewett. (Wilmington, North Carolina: Broadfoot Publishing Co., 1997), XVII, 30.

[68] Paul D. Mehney, "The War With Spain," *Michigan History,* 86-3 (May-June 2002), 30.

[69] *The Almanac of American History,* ed. Arthur M. Schlesinger Jr. and John S. Bowman (New York: G.P. Putnam's Sons, 1983), 389.

[70] Dunbar and May, 389.

[71] George S. May, *Pictorial History of Michigan: The Later Years* (Grand Rapids: William B. Eerdmans Publishing Co., 1969), 52.

[72] Mehney, 40.

[73] *The Almanac of American History,* 432.

[74] Christina K. Schaefer, *The Great War: A Guide to the Service Records of All the World's Fighting Men and Volunteers* (Baltimore: Genealogical Publishing Co. Inc., 1998), 123.

[75] Dunbar and May, 460.

[76] Douglas Galuszka, "Michigan in the Great War," *Michigan History,* 77-4 (July-August 1993), 31.

[77] John J. Newman, *Uncle, We Are Ready! Registering America's Men, 1917-1918: A Guide to Researching World War I Draft Registration Cards* (North Salt Lake, Utah: Heritage Quest, 2001), 163.

[78] Bentley Historical Library, Polar Bear Expedition <www.umich.edu/~bhl/bhl/mhchome/polarb.htm>, accessed 13 September 2003.

[79] Faye Clark, *As You Were: Fort Custer* (Galesburg, Michigan: Kal-Gale Printing, 1985), 44.

[80] Debra Johnson Knox, *World War II Military Records: A Family Historian's Guide* (Spartanburg, South Carolina: MIE Publishing, 2003), 50-54.

[81] Knox, 53.

[82] Knox, 18.

[83] Knox, 91.

[84] Information from the cover jacket of the book.

[85] Barnett and Rosentreter, 342.

[86] Gregory Hayes, "The Grand Army of the Republic," *Michigan History,* 84-1 (January-February 2000), 42.

[87] Dunbar and May, 604.

[88] Reinder Van Til, "Fulfilling a Sacred Trust: The Michigan Veterans' Facility," *Michigan History,* 70-3 (May-June 1986), 48.

[89] Veterans History Project <www.loc.gov/folklife/vets/vets-registry.html>, accessed 14 September 2003.

[90] May, *Pictorial History of Michigan: The Early Years,* 159.

[91] James N. Jackson, *Guide to the First Fifty Years of The Detroit Society for Genealogical Research Magazine* (Detroit: Detroit Society for Genealogical Research, 1990), i.

[92] Harmison, Eva Murrell, and Donna Valley Russell, "Michigan," *Genealogical Research: Methods and Sources,* ed. Kenn Stryker-Rodda (Washington, D.C.: American Society of Genealogists, 1983), II, 98.

[93] Harmison and Russell, II, 99.

[94] *Family Trails* (Lansing: Michigan Genealogical Council, 1983), I, iii.

Chapter 5

[1] Donna Valley Russell, *Michigan Censuses 1710-1830 Under the French, British, and Americans* (Detroit: Detroit Society for Genealogical Research Inc., 1982), 1.

[2] LeRoy Barnett, "State Censuses of Michigan: A Tragedy of Lost Treasures," *Family Trails,* 6-1 (Summer-Fall 1978), 3.

[3] Barnett, 1.

[4] Barnett, 2.

[5] Barnett, 6, 8.

[6] "Early Michigan Census Records," *Family Trails,* 6-1 (Summer-Fall 1978), 28, and Russell, 1.

[7] Peggy Tuck Sinko, *Michigan Atlas of Historical County Boundaries,* ed. John H. Long. (New York: Charles Scribner's Sons, 1997), xix.

[8] Kathleen W. Hinckley, *Your Guide to the Federal Census for Genealogists, Researchers, and Family Historians* (Cincinnati: Betterway Books, 2002), 6, 12.

[9] Hinckley, 18.

[10] Hinckley, 59, 64.

[11] Hinckley, 66.

[12] Hinckley, 70.

[13] Hinckley, 101.

[14] Hinckley, 76, 78.

[15] Barnett, 12.

[16] *The Source: A Guidebook of American Genealogy,* ed. Arlene Eakle and Johni Cerny (Salt Lake City, Utah: Ancestry Publishing Co., 1984), 103.

[17] Hinckley, 134.

[18] Val D. Greenwood, *The Researcher's Guide to American Genealogy,* 3rd ed. (Baltimore: Genealogical Publishing Co, 2000), 273.

[19] Hinckley, 142.

[20] Hinckley, 137.

[21] Hinckley, 137.

[22] Hinckley, 143.

[23] Richard J. Hathaway, "Michigan Directories," *Family Trails,* 5-4 (Summer 1975), 4.

[24] George S. May, *Pictorial History of Michigan: The Later Years* (Grand Rapids: William B. Eerdmans Publishing Co., 1969), 39.

[25] Alec R. Gilpin, *The Territory of Michigan* (East Lansing: Michigan State University Press, 1970), 25.

[26] Gilpin, 75.

[27] Willis F. Dunbar, and George S. May, *Michigan: A History of the Wolverine State,* 3rd ed. (Grand Rapids, Mich.: William B. Eerdmans Publishing Co., 1995), 207.

[28] *Detroit in Its World Setting: A Three Hundred Year Chronology, 1701-2001,* ed. David Lee Poremba (Detroit: Wayne State University Press, 2001), 149; Ronald P. Formisano, "The Edge of Caste: Colored Suffrage In Michigan, 1827-1861," *Michigan History,* 56-1 (Spring 1972), 27; Benjamin C. Wilson, "Kentucky Kidnappers, Fugitives, and Abolitionists In Antebellum Cass County, Michigan," *Michigan History,* 60-4 (Winter 1976), 341; and Dunbar and May, 313.

[29] Dunbar and May, 473.

Chapter 6

[1] Alan S. Brown, "Mr. Tiffin's Surveyors Come to Michigan," *Michigan History,* 74-5 (September-October 1990), 33.

[2] Charles E. Cleland, *A Brief History of Michigan Indians* (Lansing: Michigan History Division, 1975), 25.

[3] Kenneth E. Lewis, *West to Far Michigan: Settling the Lower Peninsula, 1815-1860* (East Lansing: Michigan State University Press, 2002), 84.

[4] Alpheus Felch, "The Indians of Michigan and the Cession of Their Lands to the United States by Treaties," *Michigan Historical Collections,* 26 (1896), 283.

[5] Lewis, 88.

[6] LeRoy Barnett, "Land for Family and Friends: The Saginaw Treaty of 1819," *Michigan History,* 87-5 (September-October 2003), 29.

[7] Felch, 282.

[8] Willis F. Dunbar, and George S. May, *Michigan: A History of the Wolverine State,* 3rd ed. (Grand Rapids, Mich.: William B. Eerdmans Publishing Co., 1995), 146.

[9] Felch, 284.

[10] Charles E. Cleland, *Rites of Conquest: The History and Culture of Michigan's Native Americans* (Ann Arbor: The University of Michigan Press, 1992), 222.

[11] Felch, 283.

[12] Felch, 284.

[13] LeRoy Barnett, "Mapping Michigan's First Land Sales," *Michigan Out-of-Doors,* 53-2 (February 1999), 44.

[14] Willis Frederick Dunbar, *Michigan: A History of the Wolverine State* (Grand Rapids: William B. Eerdmans Publishing Co., 1965), 240-241.

[15] Dunbar, 162.

[16] Lewis, 105.

[17] Lewis, 105.

[18] Lewis, 124-125.

[19] Robert K. Clarke, "Homesteading in Michigan," *Family Trails,* 3-3 (Spring-Summer 1971), 10, and George S. May, *Pictorial History of Michigan: The Early Years* (Grand Rapids: William B. Eerdmans Publishing Co., 1967), 154.

[20] Val D. Greenwood, *The Researcher's Guide to American Genealogy,* 3rd ed. (Baltimore: Genealogical Publishing Co, 2000), 385.

[21] Susan E. Gray, *The Yankee West: Community Life on the Michigan Frontier* (Chapel Hill: The University of North Carolina Press, 1996), 39.

[22] Information in a Family History Month Exhibit, State Archives of Michigan, October 2003.

[23] E. Wade Hone, *Land and Property Research in the United States* (Salt Lake City: Ancestry, 1997), 111.

[24] Brown, 34.

[25] *The Source: A Guidebook of American Genealogy,* ed. Arlene Eakle and Johni Cerny (Salt Lake City, Utah: Ancestry Publishing Co., 1984), 226.

[26] Hone, 113.

[27] Alec R. Gilpin, *The Territory of Michigan* (East Lansing: Michigan State University Press, 1970), 133.

[28] *Grassroots of America: A Computerized Index to the American State Papers – Land Grants and Claims (1789-1837),* ed. Phillip W. McMullin (Greenville, South Carolina: Southern Historical Press, 1944), i.

[29] Greenwood, 397.

[30] *Governor and Judges Journal; Proceedings of the Land Board of Detroit,* ed. by M. Agnes Burton (Detroit: 1915), 6.

[31] Gilpin, 34.

[32] Michigan's Centennial Farm Program <www.michigan.gov/mda/0,1607,7-125-1566_1733_22582_22586-67115--,00.html>, accessed 4 October 2003.

[33] Letter to the author dated 13 August 1986.

[34] E-mail to the author from Squire Jaros, Centennial Farm Coordinator, dated 27 June 2003.

[35] W.O. Hedrick, "The Financial and Tax History of Michigan," *Michigan History,* 22-1 (Winter 1938), 97.

[36] Hedrick, 97-98.

[37] Hedrick, 98.

[38] Richard J. Hathaway, "Michigan Landownership Maps and Atlases," *Family Trails,* 3 (1983), 55.

[39] LeRoy Barnett, "Milestones in Michigan Mapping: Early Settlement," *Michigan History,* 63-5 (September-October 1979), 42.

[40] Hathaway, "Michigan Landownership Maps and Atlases," 5.

[41] Kathleen W. Hinckley, *Your Guide to the Federal Census for Genealogists, Researchers, and Family Historians* (Cincinnati: Betterway Books, 2002), 130.

[42] John R. Hébert, and Patrick E. Dempsey, *Panoramic Maps of Cities in the United States and Canada: A Checklist of Maps in the Collections of the Library of Congress, Geography and Map Division,* 2nd ed. (Washington D.C.: Library of Congress, 1984), 3.

[43] *The Source,* 521.

[44] Diane L. Oswald, *Fire Insurance Maps: Their History and Applications* (College Station, Texas: Lacewing Press, 1997), 93.

[45] Roy L. Dodge, *Michigan Ghost Towns of the Lower Peninsula* (Las Vegas: Glendon Publishing, 1990), I, 1.

[46] Richard J. Hathaway, "Michigan Directories," *Family Trails,* 5-4 (Summer 1975), 4.

[47] Graydon M. Meints, *Along the Tracks: A Directory of Named Places on Michigan Railroads* (Mount Pleasant, Michigan: Clarke Historical Library, 1987), ix.

[48] Dodge, *Michigan Ghost Towns of the Lower Peninsula,* I, 13; and Lewis, 185.

[49] Dodge, *Michigan Ghost Towns of the Lower Peninsula,* vii.

[50] Dodge, *Michigan Ghost Towns of the Lower Peninsula,* vii.

[51] Dodge, *Michigan Ghost Towns of the Lower Peninsula,* I, 13.

[52] Roger L. Rosentreter, "Michigan's 83 Counties: Ingham County," *Michigan History,* 67-5 (September-October 1883), 8.

[53] Greenwood, 452.

[54] *Michigan Manual, 1937,* 189.

[55] Gilpin, 66.

[56] *Michigan Manual, 1937,* 189.

[57] *Michigan Manual, 1937,* 192.

[58] *Michigan Manual, 1937,* 193.

[59] *Michigan Manual, 1999-2000,* 606.

[60] *Michigan Manual, 1937,* 195.

[61] *Michigan Manual, 1959-60,* 151.

[62] Gray, 69.

[63] *Michigan Manual, 1937,* 195.

[64] *Michigan Manual, 1937,* 195.

[65] *Michigan Manual, 1937,* 194.

[66] *Michigan Manual, 1937,* 193.

[67] *Michigan Manual, 1937,* 193.

[68] *Michigan Manual, 1999-2000,* 615.

[69] Charles E. Harmon, "Cases at the Court of Appeals," *Michigan History,* 87-5 (September-October 2003), 43.

[70] *Michigan Manual, 1999-2000,* 578.

[71] *Michigan Manual,* 1999-2000, 597.

[72] Marilyn Ferris Motz, *True Sisterhood: Michigan Women and Their Kin, 1820-1920* (Albany: State University of New York Press, 1983), 23.

[73] Motz, 23.

[74] Section 1, Public Act 168 of 1855.

[75] Motz, 121.

[76] Motz, 121.

[77] Motz, 121.

[78] Motz, 85.

[79] *The Source,* 192.

[80] Public Act 77 of 1891.

[81] The Adoption History Project: Timeline of Adoption History <www.uoregon.edu/~adoption/timeline.html>, accessed 18 November 2003.

[82] Public Act 105 of 1933.

Chapter 7

[1] NUCMC Frequently Asked Questions <lcweb.loc.gov/coll/nucmc/newfaqs.html>, accessed on 25 August 2003.

[2] Barbara Speas Havira, "A Treasure and a Challenge: Michigan Bureau of Labor Reports," *Michigan History,* 72-5 (September-October 1988), 37.

[3] John P. DuLong, "Engagements: Guide to Fur Trade Employment Contracts, 1670-1821," *Michigan Habitant Heritage,* 10-3 (July 1989), 48.

[4] DuLong, 55.

[5] Donna Valley Russell, *Michigan Voyageurs* (Detroit: Detroit Society for Genealogical Research, 1982), 1.

[6] John Cumming, "Michigan Lumber and Lumbermen," *Family Trails,* 2-1 (Winter 1968-69), 5.

[7] Beacons in the Night: A Light House Keeper's Life <www.lib.cmich.edu/clarke/lighthouses/lhkeep1.htm>, accessed 25 August 2003.

[8] The list is found on page 27.

[9] Morris C. Taber, "New England Influence in South Central Michigan," *Michigan History,* 45-4 (December 1961), 309.

[10] Willis F. Dunbar, and George S. May, *Michigan: A History of the Wolverine State,* 3rd ed. (Grand Rapids: William B. Eerdmans Publishing Co., 1995), 190.

[11] Valerie Gerrard Browne, and David Jerome Johnson, *A Guide to the State Archives of Michigan: State Records* (Lansing: Michigan Department of State, 1977), 61.

[12] Dunbar and May, 286.

[13] Dunbar and May, 296.

[14] Charles E. Cleland, *A Brief History of Michigan Indians* (Lansing: Michigan History Division, 1975), 26.

[15] Bruce Rubenstein, "To Destroy a Culture: Indian Education in Michigan, 1855-1900," *Michigan History,* 60-2 (Summer 1976) 137.

[16] Rubenstein, 146.

[17] Rubenstein, 155.

[18] Rubenstein, 155.

[19] Charles E. Cleland, *Rites of Conquest: The History and Culture of Michigan's Native Americans* (Ann Arbor: The University of Michigan Press, 1992), 246; Emerson F. Greenman, *The Indians of Michigan* (Lansing: Michigan Historical Commission, 1961), 42.

[20] *Laws of the Territory of Michigan* (Lansing: W.S. George and Co. 1871), 1, 90-91.

[21] *Laws of the Territory of Michigan* (Lansing: W.S. George and Co. 1874), 2, 40-42.

[22] *Laws of the Territory of Michigan,* 2, 115-116.

[23] Dunbar and May, 517, 523.

[24] Toni I. Benson, *Van Buren County Poorhouse/Infirmary Records: An Abstract of the Births, Deaths, Burials and General Register* (Decatur, Michigan: F-AMI-LEE Publishing Co., 1996), 1, iii.

[25] Poorhouse Holdings of the Michigan State Archives <www.poorhousestory.com/MICH_Archives_holdings.htm>, accessed 28 August 2003.

[26] Henry M. Hurd, "A History of the Asylums for the Insane in Michigan," *Michigan Pioneer Collections,* 13 (1888), 293.

[27] Browne and Johnson, 109.

[28] Patricia Ibbotson, *Eloise: Poorhouse, Farm, Asylum, and Hospital 1839-1984* (Chicago: Arcadia Publishing, 2002), 7.

[29] Ibbotson, 7.

[30] Ibbotson, 8, and Tales of Eloise <www.talesofeloise.com/>, accessed 28 August 2003.

[31] Tales of Eloise <www.talesofeloise.com/>, accessed 28 August 2003.

[32] Dunbar and May, 455.

[33] Dunbar and May, 455.

[34] Browne and Johnson, 330.

[35] Browne and Johnson, 272.

[36] Browne and Johnson, 272-273.

[37] State Archives of Michigan Circular No. 3 <www.michigan.gov/documents/mhc_sa_circular03_49682_7.pdf>, accessed 28 August 2003.

[38] Tom Powers, *Michigan Rogues, Desperados, Cut-throats* (Davison, Michigan: Friede Publications, 2002), vi.

[39] Grant Parker, "Disaster in Bath," *Michigan History,* 65-3 (May-June 1981), 12.

[40] David G. Chardavoyne, *A Hanging in Detroit: Stephen Gifford Simmons and the Last Execution Under Michigan Law* (Detroit: Wayne State University Press, 2003), 157.

[41] Chardavoyne, xii.

[42] *Laws of the Territory of Michigan* (Lansing: W.S. George and Co. 1871), 1, 70-71.

[43] Joseph Oldenburg, *A Genealogical Guide to the Burton Historical Collection Detroit Public Library* (Salt Lake City: Ancestry Publishing, 1988), 13.

[44] Thomas H. Roderick, V. Elving Anderson, Robert Charles Anderson, Roger D. Joslyn, and Wayne T. Morris, "Files of the Eugenics Record Office: A Resource for Genealogists," *National Genealogical Society Quarterly,* 82-2 (June 1994), 101.

[45] Information from the Family History Library card catalog <www.familysearch.org>, accessed 2 December 2002.

[46] Dunbar and May, 458.

[47] Charles Loring Brace, *The Dangerous Classes of New York and Twenty Years' Work Among Them* (Montclair, New Jersey: Patterson Smith, 1967), 246. An account of the first trip to Dowagiac is on pages 246-254.

[48] Section 10, Public Act 33 of 1895.

[49] E-mail message from Al Eicher to the author, dated 6 June 2003.

[50] Alan T. Forrester, *Scots in Michigan* (East Lansing: Michigan State University Press, 2003), 47.

[51] Alvin J. Schmidt, *Fraternal Organizations* (Westport, Connecticut: Greenwood Press, 1980), 3.

[52] Ronald A. Bremer, *Compendium of Historical Sources* (Salt Lake City, Utah: Butterfly Publishing Inc., 1983), 355.

[53] *Michigan: A Centennial History of the State and Its People,* ed. George N. Fuller (Chicago: The Lewis Publishing Co., 1939), 2, 618.

[54] *Michigan: A Centennial History of the State and Its People,* 2, 618.

[55] Frank N. Elliott, *When the Railroad Was King* (Lansing: Bureau of History, 1988), 48.

[56] Fred Trump, *The Grange in Michigan* (Grand Rapids: Dean-Hicks Co., 1963), v.

[57] Calvin Enders, "White Sheets in Mecosta: The Anatomy of a Michigan Clan," *The Michigan Historical Review,* 14-2 (Fall 1988), 61.

[58] Michael Newton, and Judy Ann Newton, *The Ku Klux Klan: An Encyclopedia* (New York: Garland Publishing Inc., 1991), 388.

[59] Clarke Historical Library online catalog entry for the Ku Klux Klan Collection, 1916-1974 <catalog.lib.cmich.edu/>, accessed 25 August 2003.

[60] Clarke Historical Library online catalog entry for the Ku Klux Klan Membership cards, 1923, 1926 <catalog.lib.cmich.edu/>, accessed 25 August 2003.

[61] Ethel W. Williams, *Know Your Ancestors: A Guide to Genealogical Research* (Rutland, Vermont: Charles E. Tuttle Co., 1976), 98.

[62] Charles A. Symon, *We Can Do It! A History of the Civilian Conservation Corps in Michigan: 1933-1942* (Escanaba, Michigan: Richard Printing, 1983), 1.

[63] State Archives of Michigan Circular No. 16 <www.michigan.gov/documents/mhc_sa_circular16_49706_7.pdf>, accessed 25 August 2003.

[64] John W. Heisey, *The W.P.A. Historical Records Survey Sources for Genealogists* (Indianapolis: Heritage House, 1988), 1.

[65] Heisey, 19.

[66] Helen Taylor, "Primarily Archives," *Michigan History,* 77-4 (July-August 1993), 6.

[67] *The Almanac of American History,* ed. Arthur M. Schlesinger Jr. and John S. Bowman (New York: G.P. Putnam's Sons, 1983), 319-320.

[68] Betty Sodders, *Michigan on Fire* (Holt, Michigan: Thunder Bay Press, 1997), 7.

[69] Sodders, 3, 5.

[70] Dunbar and May, 348.

[71] Sodders, 150.

[72] Dunbar and May, 349.

[73] *Michigan Voices,* ed. Joe Grimm (Detroit: Wayne State University Press, 1987), 76.

[74] Sodders, 298.

[75] Sodders, 320, and Gerald Micketti, "The Day Metz Burned," *Michigan History,* 65-5 (September-October 1981), 16.

[76] Sodders, 318.

[77] Larry Lankton, *Cradle to Grave: Life, Work, and Death at the Lake Superior Copper Mines* (New York: Oxford University Press, 1991), 111.

[78] Virginia Jonas Dersch, "Copper Mining in Northern Michigan: A Social History," *Michigan History,* 61 (Winter 1977), 308.

[79] Lankton, 131.

[80] Lankton, 122-124.

[81] Larry Wakefield, *Ghost Towns of Michigan* (West Bloomfield, Michigan: Northmont Publishing Inc., 1994), I, 100.

[82] Roy L. Dodge, *Michigan Ghost Towns of the Upper Peninsula* (Las Vegas: Glendon Publishing, 1990), 109.

[83] Arthur W. Thurner, *Strangers and Sojourners: A History of Michigan's Keweenaw Peninsula* (Detroit: Wayne State University Press, 1994), 153-154.

[84] Public Act 123 of 1897.

[85] Lankton, 134.

[86] Thurner, 213.

[87] Lankton, 237.

[88] Eva Koskimaki, "Finns," *Ethnic Groups in Michigan.* ed. James M. Anderson and Iva A. Smith (Detroit: Ethnos Press, 1983), 114.

[89] C.M. Burton, *Cadillac's Village, or Detroit Under Cadillac, with List of Property Owners and a History of the Settlement 1701 to 1710* (Detroit: Detroit Society for Genealogical Research, 1999), 37.

[90] Dunbar and May, 157.

[91] Earl E. Kleinschmidt, "Prevailing Diseases and Hygienic Conditions in Early Michigan," *Michigan History,* XXV (Winter 1941), 59.

[92] Kleinschmidt, 62. Unless otherwise indicated, all statistics in this section are from the Kleinschmidt article.

[93] Larry Wakefield, *Ghost Towns of Michigan* (Holt, Michigan: Thunder Bay Press, 1995), II, 203.

[94] Kleinschmidt, 78.

[95] *Atlas of Great Lakes Indian History,* ed. Helen Hornbeck Tanner (Norman: University of Oklahoma Press, 1987), 172.

[96] *Atlas of Great Lakes Indian History,* 173-174.

[97] *Michigan Voices: Our State's History in the Words of the People Who Lived It,* ed. Joe Grimm (Detroit: Detroit Free Press and Wayne State University Press, 1987), 39.

[98] *Michigan Voices,* 39.

[99] David G. Chardavoyne, *A Hanging in Detroit: Stephen Gifford Simmons and the Last Execution Under Michigan Law* (Detroit: Wayne State University Press, 2003), 166.

[100] George Newman Fuller, *Economic and Social Beginnings of Michigan: A Study of the Settlement of the Lower Peninsula During the Territorial Period, 1805-1837* (Lansing: Wynkoop Hallenbeck Crawford Co., 1916), 61.

[101] Dunbar and May, 179, and Chardavoyne, 166.

[102] Kleinschmidt, 71-72.

[103] Bradley A. Rodgers, *Guardian of the Great Lakes: The U.S. Paddle Frigate Michigan* (Ann Arbor: The University of Michigan Press, 1996), 65.

[104] Kleinschmidt, 68.

[105] James R. Acocks, *History of Tuberculosis in the Upper Peninsula of Michigan* (Marquette: Privately Printed, 1990), 1.

[106] Dunbar and May, 457.

[107] Tiffany Dziurman, "Tragedy on the Tracks," *Michigan History,* 77-6 (November-December 1993), 37.

[108] Elliott, 42.

[109] The Great Lakes Shipwreck File <greatlakeshistory.homestead.com/temp.html>, accessed 25 August 2003.

[110] E-mail message from David Swayze to the author, dated 25 February 2003.

[111] Katherine Scott Sturdevant, *Bringing Your Family History to Life Through Social History* (Cincinnati: Betterway Books, 2000), 6, 8.

[112] Robert R. Hubach, *Early Midwestern Travel Narratives: An Annotated Bibliography, 1634-1850* (Detroit: Wayne State University Press, 1998), 1.

[113] George S. May, *Pictorial History of Michigan: The Early Years* (Grand Rapids: William B. Eerdmans Publishing Co., 1967), 86.

[114] *Michigan Quilts: 150 Years of Textile Tradition,* ed. Marsha MacDowell and Ruth D. Fitzgerald (East Lansing: Michigan State University, 1987), ix.

[115] Michigan Quilt Project <www.museum.msu.edu/s-program/MQuilt/mqp.html>, accessed 25 August 2003.

[116] Michigan Quilt Project: It's Beginnings <www.museum.msu.edu/s-program/MQuilt/mqp.html>, accessed 25 August 2003.

[117] *African American Quiltmaking in Michigan,* ed. Marsha MacDowell (East Lansing: Michigan State University Press, 1997), 1.

[118] Kenneth E. Lewis, *West to Far Michigan: Settling the Lower Peninsula, 1815-1860* (East Lansing: Michigan State University Press, 2002), 65.

[119] *Detroit in Its World Setting: A Three Hundred Year Chronology,1701-2001,* ed. David Lee Poremba (Detroit: Wayne State University Press, 2001), 264.

[120] Richard A. Keen, *Michigan Weather* (Helena, Montana: American and World Geographic Publishing, 1993), 32.

[121] Larry Massie, *From Frontier Folk to Factory Smoke: Michigan's First Century of Historical Fiction* (AuTrain, Michigan: Avery Color Studios, 1987), 7.

[122] Dunbar and May, 88.

[123] Chardavoyne, 67.

Chapter 8

[1] John P. DuLong, *French Canadians in Michigan* (East Lansing: Michigan State University Press, 2001), ix.

[2] Willis F. Dunbar, and George S. May, *Michigan: A History of the Wolverine State,* 3rd ed. (Grand Rapids, Mich.: William B. Eerdmans Publishing Co., 1995), x.

[3] Dunbar and May, 63; and DuLong, 13.

[4] Dunbar and May, 170.

[5] Barbara Bilge, "Yankees," *Ethnic Groups in Michigan,* ed. James M. Anderson and Iva A. Smith (Detroit: Ethnos Press, 1983), 279.

[6] Dunbar and May, 163.

[7] George P. Graff, *The People of Michigan* (Lansing: Michigan Department of Education, 1974), 23.

[8] John Kern, *A Short History of Michigan* (Lansing: Michigan History Division, Michigan Department of State, 1977), 18.

[9] Gregory S. Rose, "South Central Michigan Yankees," *Michigan History,* 70-2 (March-April 1986), 32.

[10] Graff, 22; and Bilge, 279.

[11] Susan E. Gray, *The Yankee West: Community Life on the Michigan Frontier* (Chapel Hill: The University of North Carolina Press, 1996), 12.

[12] Dunbar and May, 170.

[13] Kenneth E. Lewis, *West to Far Michigan: Settling the Lower Peninsula, 1815-1860* (East Lansing: Michigan State University Press, 2002), 134.

[14] Eleanor Myers, *A Migration Study of the Thirty-Two States and Four Organized Territories Comprising the United States in 1850 Based Upon the Federal Census of 1850* (Syracuse: Central New York Genealogical Society, 1977), 17.

[15] Kern, 18; Rose, 34.

[16] Dunbar and May, 170.

[17] George Newman Fuller, *Economic and Social Beginnings of Michigan: A Study of the Settlement of the Lower Peninsula During the Territorial Period, 1805-1837* (Lansing: Wynkoop Hallenbeck Crawford Co., 1916), 482.

[18] Lewis, 134.

[19] Kern, 32.

[20] Kern, 42; and Geostat Center: Historical Census Browser <fisher.lib.virginia.edu/collections/stats/histcensus/>, accessed 15 April 2004.

[21] Kern, 43-44; and *Detroit in Its World Setting: A Three Hundred Year Chronology, 1701-2001*, ed. David Lee Poremba (Detroit: Wayne State University Press, 2001), 183.

[22] Theodore J. Karamanski, *Deep Woods Frontier: A History of Logging in Northern Michigan* (Detroit: Wayne State University Press, 1989), 205.

[23] *Atlas of Michigan.* ed. Lawrence M. Sommers (East Lansing: Michigan State University Press, 1977), 2, and *Michigan: A Guide to the Wolverine State* (New York: Oxford University Press, 1941), 67.

[24] The Immigration Restriction Act of 1921 gave to each European nation a quota of 3 percent of the total number of its residents living in the United States in 1910 for its amount of annual immigration. Total immigration to the United States was limited to about 350,000 each year. In 1924, the National Origins Act changed the quota to 2 percent of those living in the United States in 1890. Since more northwestern Europeans were living in the United States in 1890, fewer southern and eastern Europeans were able to immigrate after 1924. In 1929, quotas were allocated based on the national origins of the total U.S. population, and in 1965 the national origins quota system was abolished.

[25] Dunbar and May, 511.

[26] Jack Glazier and Arthur W. Helweg, *Ethnicity in Michigan: Issues and People* (East Lansing: Michigan State University Press, 2001), 30.

[27] *Michigan Voices,* ed. Joe Grimm (Detroit: Wayne State University Press, 1987), 140.

[28] Glazier and Helweg, 30.

[29] Glazier and Helweb, 34.

[30] Charles E. Cleland, *Rites of Conquest: The History and Culture of Michigan's Native Americans* (Ann Arbor: The University of Michigan Press, 1992), 39.

[31] James A. Clifton, George L. Cornell, and James M. McClurken, *People of the Three Fires: The Ottawa, Potawatomi, and Ojibway of Michigan* (Grand Rapids: The Grand Rapids Inter-Tribal Council, 1986), 2.

[32] Dunbar and May, 14.

[33] Charles E. Cleland, *A Brief History of Michigan Indians* (Lansing: Michigan History Division, 1975), 14.

[34] Cleland, *A Brief History of Michigan Indians,* 14.

[35] Edwin McClendon, "Native Americans," *Ethnic Groups in Michigan,* ed. James M. Anderson and Iva A. Smith (Detroit: Ethnos Press, 1983), 212-213.

[36] Cleland, *A Brief History of Michigan Indians,* 14.

[37] Cleland, *A Brief History of Michigan Indians,* 14.

[38] Lewis, 87.

[39] Cleland, *A Brief History of Michigan Indians,* 13.

[40] *Atlas of Great Lakes Indian History,* ed. Helen Hornbeck Tanner (Norman: University of Oklahoma Press, 1987), 35.

[41] Dunbar and May, 151.

[42] Dunbar and May, 151.

[43] Dunbar and May, 151; and William J. Kubiak, *Great Lakes Indians: A Pictorial Guide,* 2nd ed. (Grand Rapids: Baker Books, 1999), 147.

[44] Dunbar and May, 14.

[45] Kubiak, 89.

[46] Kubiak, 92.

[47] Cleland, *A Brief History of Michigan Indians,* 14.

[48] Dunbar and May, 13.

[49] Kubiak, 108-109.

[50] Clifton, Cornell, and McClurken, 27.

[51] Dunbar and May, 152.

[52] Lewis, 90.

[53] Clifton, Cornell, and McClurken, 31.

[54] Cleland, *A Brief History of Michigan Indians,* 14.

[55] Cleland, *A Brief History of Michigan Indians,* 14.

[56] Cleland, *A Brief History of Michigan Indians,* 15.

[57] Cleland, *A Brief History of Michigan Indians,* 15.

[58] Cleland, *A Brief History of Michigan Indians,* 15.

[59] Dunbar and May, 47.

[60] Beatrice A. Bigony, "A Brief History of Native Americans in the Detroit Area," *Michigan History,* 61-2 (Summer 1977), 138.

[61] Cleland, *Rites of Conquest,* 129.

[62] Charles E. Cleland, *The Place of the Pike: A History of the Bay Mills Indian Community* (Ann Arbor: The University of Michigan Press, 2001), 12.

[63] Cleland, *A Brief History of Michigan Indians,* 30.

[64] Cleland, *A Brief History of Michigan Indians,* 23.

[65] Elizabeth Neumeyer, "Michigan Indians Battle Against Removal," *Michigan History,* 55-4 (Winter 1971), 278.

[66] Dunbar and May, 151.

[67] Neumeyer, 285, 287.

[68] Dunbar and May, 151.

[69] Neumeyer, 280-281.

[70] Daniel Cetinich, *South Slavs in Michigan* (East Lansing: Michigan State University Press, 2003), 36.

[71] Cleland, *Rites of Conquest,* 234.

[72] Kathleen W. Hinckley, *Your Guide to the Federal Census for Genealogists, Researchers, and Family Historians* (Cincinnati: Betterway Books, 2002), 195, 198.

[73] Native American Research in Michigan. Lesson One: U.S. Census Records, <members.aol.com/RoundSky/lesson1.html>, accessed 3 May 2004.

[74] Hinckley, 199.

[75] Cleland, *The Place of the Pike,* 49.

[76] Durant Index of the Grand Traverse Band <members.aol.com/VWilson577/durant-gtb.html>, accessed 2 May 2004.

[77] Ottawa Native Americans <www.us-census.org/native/other_tribal/ottawa.html>, accessed 2 May 2004.

[78] Ottawa Native Americans <www.us-census.org/native/other_tribal/ottawa.html>, accessed 2 May 2004.

[79] Cleland, *The Place of the Pike,* 39.

[80] Native American Material in the Clarke Historical Library <clarke.cmich.edu/nativeamericans/index.htm>, accessed 3 May 2004.

[81] Cleland, *The Place of the Pike,* vii.

[82] Donat Gauthier and George Graff, "French," *Ethnic Groups in Michigan,* ed. James M. Anderson and Iva A. Smith (Detroit: Ethnos Press, 1983), 120.

[83] DuLong, 7.

[84] Irvin Rabideau, "French Canadians," *Ethnic Groups in Michigan,* ed. James M. Anderson and Iva A. Smith (Detroit: Ethnos Press, 1983), 124.

[85] Frank Angelo, *Yesterday's Michigan* (Miami: E.A. Seemann Publishing Inc., 1975), 21.

[86] DuLong, 7.

[87] Rabideau, 124.

[88] DuLong, 8.

[89] DuLong, 12.

[90] DuLong, 3, 12-13.

[91] DuLong, 3, 15.

[92] Rabideau, 126.

[93] DuLong, 22.

[94] Jean Lamarre, *The French Canadians of Michigan: Their Contribution to the Development of the Saginaw Valley and the Keweenaw Peninsula, 1840-1914* (Detroit: Wayne State University Press, 2003), 27; and DuLong, 31.

[95] DuLong, 18.

[96] Lamarre, 25; and DuLong, 21.

[97] Rabideau, 125.

[98] DuLong, 21, 23.

[99] DuLong, 21.

[100] C. Warren VanderHill, *Settling the Great Lakes Frontier: Immigration to Michigan, 1837-1924* (Lansing: Michigan Historical Commission, 1970), 13.

[101] The French in America <www.euroamericans.net/french.htm>, accessed 13 May 2004.

[102] David A. Badillo, *Latinos in Michigan* (East Lansing: Michigan State University Press, 2003), 15.

[103] John P. DuLong, *French Canadians in Michigan* (East Lansing: Michigan State University Press, 2001), 14.

[104] Grace Lee Nute, *The Voyageur* (Saint Paul: Minnesota Historical Society, 1955), 88.

[105] C.M. Burton, *Cadillac's Village, or Detroit Under Cadillac, with List of Property Owners and a History of the Settlement 1701 to 1710* (Detroit: Detroit Society for Genealogical Research, 1999), 22.

[106] DuLong, 14.

[107] Richard J. Hathaway, "From Ontario to the Great Lake State: Canadians in Michigan," *Michigan History,* 67-2 (March-April 1983), 42.

[108] Lewis, 370.

[109] VanderHill, 6.

[110] VanderHill, 6.

[111] Hathaway, 44.

[112] Hathaway, 42.

[113] Alan T. Forrester, *Scots in Michigan* (East Lansing: Michigan State University Press, 2003), 7.

[114] Hathaway, 43.

[115] Geostat Center: Historical Census Browser <fisher.lib.virginia.edu/collections/stats/histcensus/>, accessed 15 April 2004; VanderHill, 7-8; and Hathaway, 43.

[116] VanderHill, 6.

[117] Forrester, 6, 31.

[118] Geostat Center: Historical Census Browser <fisher.lib.virginia.edu/collections/stats/histcensus/>, accessed 15 April 2004.

[119] "English," *Ethnic Groups in Michigan,* ed. James M. Anderson and Iva A. Smith (Detroit: Ethnos Press, 1983), 103.

[120] Graff, 111-112.

[121] Forrester, 9-10.

[122] Forrester, 13.

[123] Forrester, 39.

[124] Forrester, 17, 44; Graff, 111.

[125] Forrester, 15.

[126] Forrester, 31-33.

[127] Scots in America <www.euroamericans.net/scottish.htm>, accessed 13 May 2004.

[128] Forrester, 44.

[129] Forrester, 19.

[130] Richard A. Rajner, "Nineteenth Century Irish Settlement in the State of Michigan" (M.A. thesis, University of Toledo, 1994), 52.

[131] Rajner, 52-53.

[132] Kathleen Lavey, "Influx from Ireland Has Had Profound Effect on Michigan," *Lansing State Journal,* 14 March 2004, accessed online <www.lsj.com/things/etc_in/040314_irish_1d.html> 20 April 2004; Geostat Center: Historical Census Browser <fisher.lib.virginia.edu/collections/stats/histcensus/>, accessed 5 April 2004; VanderHill, 37; Rajner, 52.

[133] Graff, 114.

[134] VanderHill, 36.

[135] Lavey.

[136] Lavey.

[137] VanderHill, 36.

[138] Lavey.

[139] Graff, 114.

[140] VanderHill, 37.

[141] Mary Clare Carolan Duran, "Irish," *Ethnic Groups in Michigan,* ed. James M. Anderson and Iva A. Smith (Detroit: Ethnos Press, 1983), 163.

[142] Lavey.

[143] Roy L. Dodge, *Michigan Ghost Towns of the Upper Peninsula* (Las Vegas: Glendon Publishing, 1990), 9.

[144] VanderHill, 27.

[145] Margaret Rabideau and Todd Earl Rhodes, "Cornish," *Ethnic Groups in Michigan,* ed. James M. Anderson and Iva A. Smith (Detroit: Ethnos Press, 1983), 86; Graff, 35.

[146] Graff, 35.

[147] Rabideau and Rhodes, 87.

[148] A. L. Rowse, *The Cousin Jacks: The Cornish in America* (New York: Charles Scribner's Sons, 1969), 427; Rabideau and Rhodes, 85; Graff, 36.

[149] Graff, 113.

[150] Graff, 112.

[151] Graff, 113.

[152] Graff, 112.

[153] Graff, 115.

[154] Graff, 116.

[155] Reginald Larrie, *Black Experiences in Michigan History* (Lansing: Michigan Department of State, 1975), 1.

[156] *African American Quiltmaking in Michigan,* ed. Marsha MacDowell (East Lansing: Michigan State University Press, 1997), 19.

[157] Dunbar and May, 103.

[158] Graff, 27.

[159] Norman McRae, "Crossing the Detroit River to Find Freedom," *Michigan History,* 67-2 (March-April 1983), 35.

[160] McRae, 35.

[161] Alec R. Gilpin, *The Territory of Michigan* (East Lansing: Michigan State University Press, 1970), 29.

[162] Darlene Clark Hine, *Black Women in the Middle West: The Michigan Experience* (Ann Arbor: Historical Society of Michigan, 1990), 3.

[163] Lewis Walker, Benjamin C. Wilson, and Linwood H. Cousins, *African Americans in Michigan* (East Lansing: Michigan State University Press, 2001), 6; and Gilpin, 98.

[164] Walker, Wilson, and Cousins, 7.

[165] Walker, Wilson, and Cousins, 8-9.

[166] Dunbar and May, 303.

[167] Larrie, 12.

[168] Walker, Wilson, and Cousins, 10.

[169] Benjamin C. Wilson, "Kentucky Kidnappers, Fugitives, and Abolitionists In Antebellum Cass County, Michigan," *Michigan History,* 60-4 (Winter 1976), 348.

[170] Charles Lindquist, *The Antislavery-Underground Railroad Movement in Lenawee County, Michigan, 1830-1860* (Adrian: Lenawee County Historical Society, 1999), 54.

[171] Public Acts 162 and 163 of 1855.

[172] Graff, 27.

[173] Geostat Center: Historical Census Browser <fisher.lib.virginia.edu/collections/stats/histcensus/>, accessed 20 May 2004.

[174] Walker, Wilson, and Cousins, 11.

[175] Harold B. Fields, "Free Negroes in Cass County Before the Civil War," *Michigan History,* 44-4 (December 1960), 381-382.

[176] Benjamin C. Wilson, "Kentucky Kidnappers, Fugitives, and Abolitionists In Antebellum Cass County, Michigan," *Michigan History,* 60-4 (Winter 1976), 340, 346.

[177] Reginald R. Larrie and DeWitt S. Dykes Jr., "Black Americans," *Ethnic Groups in Michigan,* ed. James M. Anderson and Iva A. Smith (Detroit: Ethnos Press, 1983), 40.

[178] Larrie and Dykes, 40.

[179] Betty DeRamus, "Native Americans Forge Bonds With Former Slaves," *Detroit News,* 22 February 2000, 6C.

[180] Geostat Center: Historical Census Browser <fisher.lib.virginia.edu/collections/stats/histcensus/>, accessed 20 May 2004.

[181] Hondon Hargrove, "Their Greatest Battle Was Getting Into The Fight: The 1st Michigan Colored Infantry Goes to War." *Michigan History,* 75-1 (January-February 1991), 26.

[182] Larrie and Dykes, 41.

[183] Willis F. Dunbar, "Frontiersmanship in Michigan," *Michigan History,* 50-2 (June 1966), 106.

[184] Ronald J. Stephens, *Idlewild: The Black Eden of Michigan* (Chicago: Arcadia Publishing, 2001), 13.

[185] Benjamin C. Wilson, "Idlewild: A Black Eden in Michigan," *Michigan History,* 65-5 (September-October 1981), 33, 36.

[186] Larry Wakefield, *Ghost Towns of Michigan* (West Bloomfield, Michigan: Northmont Publishing Inc., 1994), I, 43.

[187] Geostat Center: Historical Census Browser <fisher.lib.virginia.edu/collections/stats/histcensus/>, accessed 20 May 2004.

[188] Charles Lindquist, "Afro-American Journal and Directory, 1895." *Michigan History,* 64-2 (March April 1980), 42.

[189] Ursula Dibner and Peter J. Tappert, "Germans," *Ethnic Groups in Michigan,* ed. James M. Anderson and Iva A. Smith (Detroit: Ethnos Press, 1983), 129.

[190] John Andrew Russell, *Germanic Influence in the Making of Michigan* (Detroit: University of Detroit, 1927), 50-51.

[191] Jeremy W. Kilar, *Germans in Michigan* (East Lansing: Michigan State University Press, 2002), 10.

[192] VanderHill, 15.

[193] Kilar, 10.

[194] VanderHill, 15.

[195] Graff, 41.

[196] Kilar, 13.

[197] Dibner and Tappert, 129-130.
[198] Kilnar, 25; VanderHill, 16, 22.
[199] Graff, 40.
[200] Kilnar, 2.
[201] VanderHill, 23.
[202] Kilnar, 25.
[203] Graff, 43-44.
[204] Kilnar, 32.
[205] Graff, 43.
[206] Dibner and Tappert, 131.
[207] VanderHill, 45.
[208] Hero Bratt and Paul Trap, "Van Raalte's Settlement at 150," *Michigan History,* 81-2 (March-April 1997), 22.
[209] VanderHill, 47.
[210] Larry ten Harmsel, *Dutch in Michigan* (East Lansing: Michigan State University Press, 2002), 8.
[211] Robert P. Swierenga, *The Dutch Transplanting in Michigan and the Midwest* (Ann Arbor: Historical Society of Michigan, 1986), 6.
[212] Bratt and Trap, 23; Graff, 64.
[213] Ten Harmsel, 8.
[214] Elton J. Bruins, "Holocaust in Holland: 1871," *Michigan History,* 55-4 (Winter 1971), 295.
[215] VanderHill, 52.
[216] Cornelius Steketee, "Hollanders in Muskegon: 1850-97." *Michigan History,* 31-4 (December 1947), 382.
[217] VanderHill, 53.
[218] Swierenga, 6.
[219] VanderHill, 55.
[220] Swierenga, 9.
[221] Josias Meulendyke, "Dutch Settlement North of Muskegon: 1867-1897," *Michigan History,* 31-4 (December 1947), 392-398.
[222] Graff, 67.
[223] Graff, 66.
[224] Ten Harmsel, 18.
[225] Swierenga, 4.
[226] Riet Haas, "Dutch," *Ethnic Groups in Michigan,* ed. James M. Anderson and Iva A. Smith (Detroit: Ethnos Press, 1983), 99; Swierenga, 8.
[227] Swierenga, 8.
[228] Myers, 17; Dunbar and May, 243.
[229] Swierenga, 9.
[230] Haas, 100.
[231] The Dutch in America <www.euroamericans.net/dutch.htm>, accessed 13 May 2004.
[232] ten Harmsel, 26.
[233] Belgians in America <www.euroamericans.net/belgian.htm>, accessed 5 April 2004.
[234] Graff, 95.
[235] James DeWorken, "Belgians," *Ethnic Groups in Michigan,* ed. James M. Anderson and Iva A. Smith (Detroit: Ethnos Press, 1983), 23; Graff, 95.
[236] DeWorken, 23.
[237] Graff, 97.
[238] Geostat Center: Historical Census Browser <fisher.lib.virginia.edu/collections/stats/histcensus/>, accessed 5 April 2004.
[239] Geostat Center: Historical Census Browser <fisher.lib.virginia.edu/collections/stats/histcensus/>, accessed 5 April 2004.

[240] Dunbar and May, 511.

[241] Graff, 52.

[242] Carlton C. Qualey, "Pioneer Scandinavian Settlement in Michigan," *Michigan History,* 24 (Autumn 1940), 435; and VanderHill, 60.

[243] Armand Gebert, "Swedes," *Ethnic Groups in Michigan,* ed. James M. Anderson and Iva A. Smith (Detroit: Ethnos Press, 1983), 266.

[244] Graff, 58.

[245] Graff, 60.

[246] VanderHill, 60.

[247] Qualey, "Pioneer Scandinavian Settlement in Michigan," 444.

[248] Graff, 59; Gebert, 266.

[249] Gebert, 266; VanderHill, 60-61.

[250] The Swedish in America <www.euroamericans.net/swedish.htm>, accessed 13 May 2004.

[251] Eva Koskimaki, "Finns," *Ethnic Groups in Michigan,* ed. James M. Anderson and Iva A. Smith (Detroit: Ethnos Press, 1983), 110.

[252] John Wargelin, "The Finns in Michigan," *Michigan History,* 24 (Spring 1940), 180.

[253] Matti Enn Kaups, "Finnish Place-Names in Michigan," *Michigan History,* 51-4 (Winter 1967), 338.

[254] VanderHill, 58-59.

[255] Karamanski, 105.

[256] VanderHill, 66.

[257] Finnish/American Heritage Center <www.finlandia.edu/fahc.html>, accessed 4 April 2004.

[258] Koskimaki, 111; and Kaups, 338.

[259] Kaups, 338.

[260] Graff, 55; and Koskimaki, 112.

[261] Koskimaki, 112.

[262] Graff, 54.

[263] The Finnish in America <www.euroamericans.net/finnish.htm>, accessed 13 May 2004.

[264] Theodore C. Blegen, *Norwegian Migration to America: 1825-1860* (New York: Arno Press, 1969), 199.

[265] These statistics are from Carlton C. Qualey, *Norwegian Settlement in the United States* (New York: Arno Press, 1970), 176, 247. However, other sources report as few as 52 Norwegians and as many as 110 listed in the 1850 census.

[266] Qualey, 176.

[267] Qualey, 178.

[268] Qualey, 173.

[269] Qualey, 248; and VanderHill, 60.

[270] Carlton C. Qualey, "Pioneer Scandinavian Settlement in Michigan," *Michigan History,* 24 (Autumn 1940), 435.

[271] Qualey, "Pioneer Scandinavian Settlement in Michigan," 441.

[272] Graff, 49.

[273] Graff, 49.

[274] Qualey, "Pioneer Scandinavian Settlement in Michigan," 441.

[275] Eva Koskimaki and Rigmor Coulahan, "Scandinavians," *Ethnic Groups in Michigan,* ed. James M. Anderson and Iva A. Smith (Detroit: Ethnos Press, 1983), 241.

[276] Lois Rankin, "Detroit Nationality Groups," *Michigan History,* 23 (Spring 1939), 134. Rankin places the date of arrival of the first Finn in Detroit as 1832, other sources, including *Ethnic Groups in Michigan,* set the date at 1852.

[277] Koskimaki and Coulahan, 239.

[278] Rankin, 135; Qualey, 182.

[279] Gary Durkin, "Czechs," *Ethnic Groups in Michigan,* ed. James M. Anderson and Iva A. Smith (Detroit: Ethnos Press, 1983), 92.

[280] Durkin, 92.

[281] Durkin, 92.

[282] Geostat Center: Historical Census Browser <fisher.lib.virginia.edu/collections/stats/histcensus/>, accessed 15 May 2004

[283] Graff, 126.

[284] Graff, 127.

[285] Gary Durkin, "Slovaks," *Ethnic Groups in Michigan,* ed. James M. Anderson and Iva A. Smith (Detroit: Ethnos Press, 1983), 251.

[286] Judith Levin Cantor, *Jews in Michigan* (East Lansing: Michigan State University Press, 2001), 1.

[287] Cantor, 3.

[288] Lisa L. Rush, "Jews," *Ethnic Groups in Michigan,* ed. James M. Anderson and Iva A. Smith (Detroit: Ethnos Press, 1983), 181.

[289] Cantor, 12.

[290] Cantor, 31.

[291] Cantor, 20.

[292] Robert A. Rockaway, *The Jews of Detroit: From the Beginning, 1762-1914* (Detroit: Wayne State University Press, 1986), 52.

[293] Rush, 181.

[294] Robert A. Rockaway, "The Detroit Jewish Ghetto Before World War I," *Michigan History,* 52-1 (Spring 1968), 32.

[295] Russell M. Magnaghi, *Italians in Michigan* (East Lansing: Michigan State University Press, 2001), 2.

[296] Magnaghi, 3.

[297] Magnaghi, 22.

[298] Magnaghi, 1.

[299] Russell M. Magnaghi and Vittorio Re, "Italians," *Ethnic Groups in Michigan,* ed. James M. Anderson and Iva A. Smith (Detroit: Ethnos Press, 1983), 169.

[300] Magnaghi, 22.

[301] Magnaghi and Re, 173.

[302] Rev. John C. Vismara, "Coming of the Italians to Detroit," *Michigan History,* 2-1 (January 1918), 120.

[303] Magnaghi and Re, 170.

[304] Magnaghi, 2.

[305] Magnaghi, 7.

[306] VanderHill, 79-80.

[307] VanderHill, 80.

[308] Cetinich, 39.

[309] Cetinich, 39-40.

[310] Barbara McCann, "Women of Traunik: A Story of Slovenian Immigration," *Michigan History,* 68-1 (January-February 1984), 41.

[311] Cetinich, 40.

[312] Cetinich, 41.

[313] Cetinich, 44; Daniel Obed, "Slovenes," *Ethnic Groups in Michigan,* ed. James M. Anderson and Iva A. Smith (Detroit: Ethnos Press, 1983), 252.

[314] Cetinich, 7.

[315] Steven F. Talan, "Croatians," *Ethnic Groups in Michigan,* ed. James M. Anderson and Iva A. Smith (Detroit: Ethnos Press, 1983), 89.

[316] Cetinich, 12-13; Graff, 125.

[317] Cetinich, 27.

[318] Cetinich, 50.

[319] Cetinich, 54; and Macedonians in America <www.euroamericans.net/macedonian.htm>, accessed 13 May 2004.

[320] Cetinich, 61.

[321] Willis F. Dunbar, "Frontiersmanship in Michigan," *Michigan History,* 50-2 (June 1966), 106.

[322] The Polish in America <www.euroamericans.net/polish.htm>, accessed on 25 May 2004.

[323] Dennis Badaczewski, *Poles in Michigan* (East Lansing: Michigan State University Press, 2002), 2.

[324] Badaczewski, 2.

[325] Graff, 88.

[326] Badaczewski, 8.

[327] Grafff, 87.

[328] Badaczewski, 7.

[329] Badaczewski, 8.

[330] Badaczewski, 10.

[331] Badaczewski, 25.

[332] Badaczewski, 23.

[333] Rankin, 177.

[334] Badaczewski, 4, 13.

[335] Leonard S. Chrobot, "Poles," *Ethnic Groups in Michigan,* ed. James M. Anderson and Iva A. Smith (Detroit: Ethnos Press, 1983), 221.

[336] Badaczewski, 4.

[337] Badaczewski, 15.

[338] Rankin, 178.

[339] Badaczewski, 4.

[340] Frances Trix, *The Albanians in Michigan* (East Lansing: Michigan State University Press, 2001), 4.

[341] Trix, 10.

[342] Dennis Papazian and Carolyn Sirian, "Armenians," *Ethnic Groups in Michigan,* ed. James M. Anderson and Iva A. Smith (Detroit: Ethnos Press, 1983), 16.

[343] Graff, 76-77.

[344] Geostat Center: Historical Census Browser <fisher.lib.virginia.edu/collections/stats/histcensus/>, accessed 5 April 2004.

[345] Armenians in America <www.euroamericans.net/armenian.htm>, accessed on 5 May 2004.

[346] Mary Jo Clarken and Mable F. Lim, "Chinese," *Ethnic Groups in Michigan,* ed. James M. Anderson and Iva A. Smith (Detroit: Ethnos Press, 1983), 82.

[347] Dunbar and May, 591.

[348] Laura Zarrugh, "Arabic-speaking Peoples," *Ethnic Groups in Michigan,* ed. James M. Anderson and Iva A. Smith (Detroit: Ethnos Press, 1983), 10.

[349] Dunbar and May, 512.

[350] Anan Ameri and Yvonne Lockwood, *Arab Americans in Metro Detroit: A Pictorial History* (Chicago: Arcadia Publishing, 2001), 9.

[351] Dunbar and May, 512.

[352] Graff, 82.

[353] Graff, 130; Atanas Doxcheff, "Bulgarians," *Ethnic Groups in Michigan,* ed. James M. Anderson and Iva A. Smith (Detroit: Ethnos Press, 1983), 53.

[354] Geostat Center: Historical Census Browser <fisher.lib.virginia.edu/collections/stats/histcensus/>, accessed 5 April 2004.

[355] Rankin, 130.

[356] Basil P. Kardaras, "Greeks," *Ethnic Groups in Michigan,* ed. James M. Anderson and Iva A. Smith (Detroit: Ethnos Press, 1983), 133.

[357] Geostat Center: Historical Census Browser <fisher.lib.virginia.edu/collections/stats/histcensus/>, accessed 5 April 2004.

[358] Rankin, 141.

[359] Marios Stephanides, "Greeks and Cypriots of Detroit," *Michigan History,* 56-2 (Summer 1972), 135; Graff, 91.

[360] Rankin, 142.

[361] Geostat Center: Historical Census Browser <fisher.lib.virginia.edu/collections/stats/histcensus/>, accessed 5 April 2004.

[362] The Greeks of Berrien County, Michigan, <www.pahh.com/bcha>, accessed online 5 May 2004.

[363] Rankin, 147; and Eva W. Huseby-Darvas, *Hungarians in Michigan* (East Lansing: Michigan State University Press, 2003), 18.

[364] Geostat Center: Historical Census Browser <fisher.lib.virginia.edu/collections/stats/histcensus/>, accessed 5 April 2004.

[365] Huseby-Darvas, 20.

[366] Graff, 130; Jonas Urbonas, "Lithuanians," *Ethnic Groups in Michigan,* ed. James M. Anderson and Iva A. Smith (Detroit: Ethnos Press, 1983), 193-194.

[367] Rankin, 173.

[368] Geostat Center: Historical Census Browser <fisher.lib.virginia.edu/collections/stats/histcensus/>, accessed 5 April 2004.

[369] Rudolph Valier Alvarado and Sonya Yvette Alvarado, *Mexicans and Mexican Americans in Michigan* (East Lansing: Michigan State University Press, 2003), 13.

[370] Alvarado and Alvarado, 14.

[371] Badillo, 8.

[372] Alvarado and Alvarado, 29.

[373] Badillo, 13.

[374] Rankin, 184; Geostat Center: Historical Census Browser <fisher.lib.virginia.edu/collections/stats/histcensus/>, accessed 5 April 2004.

[375] Paul Edson, "Romanians," *Ethnic Groups in Michigan,* ed. James M. Anderson and Iva A. Smith (Detroit: Ethnos Press, 1983), 229.

[376] Geostat Center: Historical Census Browser <fisher.lib.virginia.edu/collections/stats/histcensus/>, accessed 5 April 2004.

[377] Romanians in America <www.euroamericans.net/rumanian.htm>, accessed 13 May 2004.

[378] Rankin, 189.

[379] Geostat Center: Historical Census Browser <fisher.lib.virginia.edu/collections/stats/histcensus/>, accessed 5 April 2004.

[380] Graff, 131.

[381] Rankin, 200.

Chapter 9

[1] Making of America <moa.umdl.umich.edu>, accessed 22 June 2004.

Chapter 10

[1] Alec R. Gilpin, *The Territory of Michigan* (East Lansing: Michigan State University Press, 1970), 22.

[2] Peggy Tuck Sinko, *Michigan Atlas of Historical County Boundaries,* ed. John H. Long (New York: Charles Scribner's Sons, 1997), xviii.

[3] Gilpin, 22.

[4] Sinko, xviii.

[5] Gilpin, 104.

[6] Sinko, xviii.

[7] Sinko, xviii.

[8] Sinko, xix.

[9] Sinko, xix.

[10] Sinko, 280.

[11] Sinko, 282.

[12] Roy L. Dodge, *Michigan Ghost Towns of the Upper Peninsula* (Las Vegas: Glendon Publishing, 1990), 25.

[13] Dates for the creation and organization of counties and information about attachments and boundaries are taken from Sinko's *Michigan Atlas of Historical County Boundaries* (1997).

[14] Information about townships in this chapter is taken from Andriot's *Township Atlas of the United States* (1991).

[15] Information about records, in-person research, and written queries is taken from surveys mailed to all of Michigan's county clerks in 2002. Seventy-two of Michigan's 83 county clerks responded. If survey questions were unanswered or if dates reported conflicted with the results of the author's 1985 survey, the author consulted other standard sources, including Bentley's *County Courthouse Book* (1995) and *The Handybook for Genealogists* (2002).

[16] Dodge, *Michigan Ghost Towns of the Upper Peninsula*, 26.

[17] Sinko, 37.

[18] Sinko, 57.

[19] Roger L. Rosentreter, "Michigan's 83 Counties: Charlevoix County," *Michigan History*, 64-5 (September-October 1980), 9.

[20] Roger L. Rosentreter, "Michigan's 83 Counties: Clare County," *Michigan History*, 65-2 (March-April 1981), 8.

[21] Sinko, 81.

[22] Sinko, 106.

[23] Sinko, 138.

[24] Wakefield, Larry, *Ghost Towns of Michigan* (West Bloomfield, Michigan: Northmont Publishing Inc., 1994), I, 121.

[25] Sinko, 154.

[26] Sinko, 165.

[27] Sinko, 204.

[28] Larry Wakefield, *Ghost Towns of Michigan* (Holt, Michigan: Thunder Bay Press, 1995), II, 50

[29] Sinko, 282.

[30] Roy L. Dodge, *Michigan Ghost Towns of the Lower Peninsula* (Las Vegas: Glendon Publishing, 1990), II, 178.

Chapter 11

[1] Library of Michigan brochure, printed May 2002.

[2] State Archives of Michigan brochure, printed June 2002.

[3] In fall 2002 the author mailed surveys to 201 libraries, archives, and museums with Michigan genealogical or historical collections. One-hundred-twenty libraries (about 58 percent) responded to the survey, and the results are listed in this chapter. Unless otherwise indicated, all material quoted in this chapter is from the surveys or brochures and other promotional materials returned with the surveys.

Chapter 12

[1] In fall 2002 the author mailed surveys to 278 historical or genealogical societies in Michigan. One-hundred-forty-three societies (51 percent) responded to the survey, and the results are listed in this chapter. A few societies with Web sites also are listed. Unless otherwise indicated, all material quoted in this chapter is from the surveys or brochures and other promotional materials returned with the surveys.

Sources

The following bibliography is not a comprehensive list of published sources for Michigan genealogy and history. It is a listing of sources used in the preparation of this book. For information about other published sources, family history researchers should consult online card catalogs of the Library of Michigan <www.michigan.gov/hal>, the Family History Library <www.familysearch.org>, the Allen County (Indiana) Public Library <www.acpl.lib.in.us/genealogy/index.html>, or other libraries with large genealogy collections.

Articles and Books

1870 Michigan Census Index. 10 vols. Lansing: Library of Michigan, 1991. Also available online <envoy.libraryofmichigan.org/1870_census/>.

1877 Tax Assessment Roll, Odessa Township, Ionia County, Michigan. Lake Odessa, Michigan: Ionia County Genealogical Society, 2000.

1890 Residents of Livingston County, Michigan. Ed. Kernie L. King. Howell, Michigan: Livingston County Genealogical Society, 2000.

Acocks, James R. *History of Tuberculosis in the Upper Peninsula of Michigan.* Marquette: Privately Printed, 1990.

African American Quiltmaking in Michigan. Ed. Marsha MacDowell. East Lansing: Michigan State University Press, 1997.

Alphabetical General Index to Public Library Sets of 85,271 Names of Michigan Soldiers and Sailors Individual Records. Lansing: Wynkoop Hallenbeck Crawford Co., 1915.

Alvarado, Rudolph Valier, and Sonya Yvette Alvarado. *Mexicans and Mexican Americans in Michigan.* East Lansing: Michigan State University Press, 2003.

Ameri, Anan, and Yvonne Lockwood. *Arab Americans in Metro Detroit: A Pictorial History.* Chicago: Arcadia Publishing, 2001.

American Biographical History of Eminent and Self-made Men: Michigan. Cincinnati: Western Biographical Publishing Co., 1878.

"American Revolutionary Soldiers in Michigan." *Family Trails,* 5-2 (Summer 1976), 4-30.

American State Papers: Documents, Legislative and Executive, of the Congress of the United States. 9 vols. Greenville, South Carolina: Southern Historical Press, 1994.

Ancestral Charts. 2 vols. Charlotte, Michigan: Eaton County Genealogical Society, 1998.

Anderson, Alloa, and Polly Bender. *Genealogy in Michigan: Its What, When, Where.* Ann Arbor: Washtenaw County Genealogical Society, 1978.

Anderson, William M. *They Died to Make Men Free: A History of the 19th Michigan Infantry in the Civil War.* Dayton, Ohio: Morningside, 1994.

Andrews, Clarence. *Michigan in Literature.* Detroit: Wayne State University Press, 1992.

Andriot, Jay. *Township Atlas of the United States.* McLean, Virginia: Documents Index, 1991, 431-463.

Angelo, Frank. *Yesterday's Michigan.* Miami: E.A. Seemann Publishing Inc., 1975.

Annual Report of the Adjutant General of the State of Michigan. 6 vols. 1862-1866.

Applegate, T.S. "A History of the Press in Michigan." *Michigan Pioneer and Historical Collections,* 6 (1883), 62-98.

Arksey, Laura, Nancy Pries, and Marcia Reed. *American Diaries: An Annotated Bibliography of Published American Diaries and Journals.* 2 vols. Detroit, Michigan: Gale Research, 1983-1987.

Atlas of Great Lakes Indian History, Ed. Helen Hornbeck Tanner. Norman: University of Oklahoma Press, 1987.

Atlas of Michigan. Ed. Lawrence M. Sommers. East Lansing: Michigan State University Press, 1977.

Atlases of Saginaw County, Michigan: 1877, 1896, 1916. Mount Vernon, Indiana: Windmill Publications, 1992.

Badaczewski, Dennis. *Poles in Michigan*. East Lansing: Michigan State University Press, 2002.

Badillo, David. *Latinos in Michigan*. East Lansing: Michigan State University Press, 2003.

Banner, Melvin E. *The Black Pioneer in Michigan*. Midland, Michigan: Pendell Publishing Co., 1973.

Barber, Edward W. *The Vermontville Colony: Its Genesis and History*. Lansing: R. Smith Print Co., 1897.

Barfknecht, Gary W. *Murder, Michigan*. Davison, Michigan: Friede Publications, 1983.

Barnett, LeRoy. *Checklist of Printed Maps of the Middle West to 1900*. Vol. 5. Ed. Robert W. Karrow, Jr. Boston: G.K. Hall, 1981.

__________. "Land for Family and Friends: The Saginaw Treaty of 1819."*Michigan History*, 87-5 (September-October 2003), 28-34.

__________. "Mapping Michigan's First Land Sales." *Michigan Out-of-Doors*, 53-2 (February 1999), 44-49.

__________. "Milestones in Michigan Mapping: Early Settlement." *Michigan History*, 63-5 (September-October 1979), 34-43.

__________. "Milestones in Michigan Mapping: Modern Waymarks." *Michigan History*, 63-6 (November-December 1979), 29-38.

__________. "State Censuses of Michigan: A Tragedy of Lost Treasures," *Family Trails*, 6-1 (Summer-Fall 1978), 1-25.

__________, and Roger Rosentreter. *Michigan's Early Military Forces: A Roster and History of Troops Activated Prior to the American Civil War*. Detroit: Wayne State University Press, 2003.

Baxter, Angus. *In Search of Your Canadian Roots*. 3rd ed. Baltimore: Genealogical Publishing Co., 2000.

Beasecker, Robert. *Michigan in the Novel 1816-1996: An Annotated Bibliography*. Detroit: Wayne State University Press, 1998.

Beets, Henry. "Dutch Journalism in Michigan." *Michigan History*, 6-2 (1922), 435-441.

Bell, Mary McCampbell, Clifford Dwyer, and William Abbot Henderson. "Finding Manuscript Collections: NUCMC, NIDS, and RLIN." *National Genealogical Society Quarterly*, 77-3 (September 1989), 208-218.

Bench and Bar of Michigan: A Volume of History and Biography. Ed. George Irving Reed. Chicago: The Century Publishing and Engraving Co., 1897.

Bench and Bar of Michigan: Nineteen Hundred Eighteen. Detroit: Bench and Bar Publishing Co., 1918.

Bench and Bar of Michigan, 1938. San Francisco: C.W. Taylor, Jr., 1938.

Benson, Toni I. *Van Buren County Poorhouse/Infirmary Records: An Abstract of the Births, Deaths, Burials, and General Register*. 2 vols. Decatur, Michigan: F-AMI-LEE Publishing Co., 1995.

Bentley, Elizabeth Perry. *County Courthouse Book*. 2nd ed. Baltimore: Genealogical Publishing Co., 1995.

__________. *The Genealogist's Address Book*. 4th ed. Baltimore: Genealogical Publishing Co., 1998.

Bentley, Jeanie Huntley, Cynthia Newman Helms, and Mary Chris Rospond. *Artists in Michigan, 1900-1976: A Biographical Dictionary*. Detroit: Wayne State University Press, 1989.

Biennial Report of the Board of Managers of the Michigan Soldiers' Home. 17 vols. Lansing: Wynkoop Hallenbeck Crawford Co., 1887-1918.

Bigony, Beatrice A. "A Brief History of Native Americans in the Detroit Area." *Michigan History*, 61-2 (Summer 1977), 135-163.

Billington, Ray Allen. *Westward Expansion: A History of the American Frontier*. 4th ed. New York: MacMillan Publishing Co. Inc., 1974.

Bingham, Stephen D. *Early History of Michigan, With Biographies of State Officers*. Lansing: Thorp and Godfrey, 1888.

Birchbark Belles: Women on the Michigan Frontier. Ed. Larry B. Massie. Allegan Forest, Michigan: Priscilla Press, 1993.

Blanton, DeAnne, and Lauren M. Cook. *They Fought Like Demons: Women Soldiers in the Civil War.* New York: Vintage Books, 2002.

Blegen, Theodore C. *Norwegian Migration to America: 1825-1860.* New York: Arno Press, 1969.

Blois, John T. *Gazetteer of the State of Michigan, in Three Parts.* Detroit: S.L. Rood and Co., 1838.

Bozich, Stanley J. *Michigan's Own: The Medal of Honor, Civil War to Vietnam War.* Frankenmuth, Michigan: Polar Bear Publising Co., 1987.

Brace, Charles Loring. *The Dangerous Classes of New York, and 20 Years' Work Among Them.* Montclair, New Jersey: Patterson Smith, 1967, 246-254.

Bratt, Hero, and Paul Trap. "Van Raalte's Settlement at 150." *Michigan History,* 81-2 (March-April 1997), 18-26.

Bremer, Ronald A. *Compendium of Historical Sources: the How and Where of American Genealogy.* Bountiful, Utah: AGLL Inc., 1997.

Brown, Alan S. "Mr. Tiffin's Surveyors Come to Michigan." *Michigan History,* 74-5 (September-October 1990), 33-36.

Browne, Valerie Gerrard, and Johnson, David Jerome. *A Guide to the State Archives of Michigan: State Records.* Lansing: Michigan History Division, Michigan Department of State, 1977.

Bruins, Elton J. "Holocaust in Holland: 1871." *Michigan History,* 55-4 (Winter 1971), 289-304.

Burton, Ann, and Conrad Burton. *Michigan Quakers: Abstracts of 15 Meetings of The Society of Friends, 1831-1960.* Decatur, Michigan: Glyndwr Resources, 1989.

Burton, C.M. *Cadillac's Village, or Detroit Under Cadillac, with List of Property Owners and a History of the Settlement 1701 to 1710.* Detroit: Detroit Society for Genealogical Research, 1999.

Bush, Karen Elizabeth. *First Lady of Detroit: The Story of Marie-Thérese Guyon, Mme. Cadillac.* Detroit: Wayne State University Press, 2001.

Cantor, Judith Levin. *Jews in Michigan.* East Lansing: Michigan State University Press, 2001.

Castle, Amelia B. *1888 Assessment Roll for Cass County, Michigan.* Dowagiac, Michigan: The Author, 1997.

Ceasar, Ford Stevens. *Forgotten Communities of Central Michigan.* Lansing: Wellman Press, 1978.

Cemeteries of the U.S.: A Guide to Contact Information for U.S. Cemeteries and Their Records. Detroit: Gale Research, 1994.

A Census for Pensioners of Revolutionary or Military Services. Baltimore: Genealogical Publishing Co., 1965.

Census of the State of Michigan 1894: Soldiers, Sailors, and Marines Volume 3. Lansing: Washington Gardner, 1896.

Cetinich, Daniel. *South Slavs in Michigan.* East Lansing: Michigan State University Press, 2003.

Chardavoyne, David G. *A Hanging in Detroit: Stephen Gifford Simmons and the Last Execution Under Michigan Law.* Detroit: Wayne State University Press, 2003.

Chronology and Documentary Handbook of the State of Michigan. Ed. Robert I. Vexler. Dobbs Ferry, New York: Oceana Publications, 1978.

The City of Detroit, Michigan, 1701-1922. Ed. Clarence M. Burton. 5 vols. Detroit: The S.J. Clarke Publishing Co., 1922.

City Directories of the United States 1860-1901: Guide to the Microfilm Collection. Woodbridge, Connecticutt: Research Publications, 1984.

Clark, Faye. *As You Were: Fort Custer.* 1985.

Clark, Murtie June. *Index to U.S. Invalid Pension Records, 1801-1815.* Baltimore: Genealogical Publishing Co., 1991.

__________. *The Pension List of 1820.* Baltimore: Genealogical Publishing Co., 1991.

Clarke, Robert K. "Homesteading in Michigan." *Family Trails,* 3-3 (Spring-Summer 1971), 8-11.

Cleland, Charles E. *A Brief History of Michigan Indians.* Lansing: Michigan History Division, 1975.

__________. *The Place of the Pike: A History of the Bay Mills Indian Community.* Ann Arbor: The University of Michigan Press, 2001.

__________. *Rites of Conquest: the History and Culture of Michigan's Native Americans.* Ann Arbor: The University of Michigan Press, 1992.

Classified Finding List of the Collections of the Michigan Pioneer and Historical Society. Detroit: Wayne University Press, 1952.

Clifford, Mary Louise, and J. Candace Clifford. *Women Who Kept the Lights: An Illustrated History of Female Lighthouse Keepers.* 2nd ed. Alexandria, Virginia: Cypress Communications, 2001.

Clifton, James A., George L. Cornell, and James M. McClurken. *People of the Three Fires: The Ottawa, Potawatomi, and Ojibway of Michigan.* Grand Rapids: The Grand Rapids Inter-Tribal Council, 1986.

Colletta, John Philip. *They Came in Ships: A Guide to Finding Your Immigrant Ancestor's Arrival Record.* 3rd ed. Provo, Utah: Ancestry, 2002.

Combined 1829-1929 Land Ownership Atlas of Branch County, Michigan. Coldwater, Michigan: Branch County Genealogical Society, 1996.

Combined 1859 Wall Map, 1875 Atlas, 1895 Plat Book Atlas, and 1915 Atlas of Shiawassee County, Michigan, Indexed. Owosso: Shiawassee County Historical Society, 2003.

Combined 1874, 1893, 1916 Atlases of Lenawee County, Michigan. Adrian, Michigan: Lenawee County Historical Society, 1997.

Combined Ingham County, Michigan 1874 and 1895 Atlases. Lansing: Mid-Michigan Genealogical Society, 1988.

Conover, Jefferson S. *Freemasonry in Michigan: A Comprehensive History of Michigan Masonry from Its Earliest Introduction in 1764.* 2 vols. Coldwater, Michigan: The Conover Engraving and Printing Co., 1897-1898.

Coombs, Leonard A. *American Intervention in Northern Russia, 1918-1919, The Polar Bear Expedition: A Guide to the Resources in the Michigan Historical Collections.* Ann Arbor: Michigan Historical Collections, 1988.

Corliss, Lois Streeter. *First Land Owners of Van Buren County, Michigan.* Lansing: Michigan State Library, 1965.

Corwin, Nancy. *Declaration of Intent, 1859-1890, Muskegon County, Michigan.* Dowagiac, Michigan: N. Corwin, 1998.

Crawford, Kim. *The 16th Michigan Infantry.* Dayton, Ohio: Morningside, 2002.

Cumming, John. "Michigan Lumber and Lumbermen." *Family Trails,* 2-1 (Winter 1968-69), 3-5.

__________. "Michigan for Sale." *Michigan History,* 70-6 (November-December 1986), 12-16.

__________. *A Preliminary Checklist of 19th Century Lithographs of Michigan Cities and Towns.* Mount Pleasant, Michigan: Clarke Historical Library, 1969.

Curry, John Carlyle. "Michigan Revolutionary War Pension Payments." *Michigan Heritage,* 1-3 (Spring 1960), 95-100; 1-4 (Summer 1960), 149-152; 2-1 (Autumn 1960), 50-54; and 2-2 (Winter 1960), 105-113.

Denissen, Christian. *Genealogy of the French Families of the Detroit River Region, 1701-1911.* 2 vols. Detroit: Detroit Society for Genealogical Research, 1976.

DeRamus, Betty. "Native Americans Forge Bonds With Former Slaves." *Detroit News,* 22 February 2000, 6C.

Dersch, Virginia Jonas. "Copper Mining in Northern Michigan: A Social History." *Michigan History,* 61-4 (Winter 1977), 291-321.

Detroit in Its World Setting: A Three Hundred Year Chronology, 1701-2001. Ed. David Lee Poremba. Detroit: Wayne State University Press, 2001.

Devlin, Dennis S. *Muskegon's Jewish Community: A Centennial History, 1888-1988.* Muskegon: Congregation B'nai Israel, 1988.

Dilts, Bryan Lee. *1890 Michigan Census Index of Civil War Veterans or Their Widows.* Salt Lake City: Index Publishing, 1985.

Directory of Historical Organizations in the United States and Canada. Nashville: American Association for State and Local History, 2002.

Dodge, Roy L. *Michigan Ghost Towns of the Lower Peninsula.* Las Vegas: Glendon Publishing, 1990.

__________. *Michigan Ghost Towns of the Upper Peninsula.* Las Vegas: Glendon Publishing, 1990.

__________. *Ticket to Hell: A Saga of Michigan's Bad Men.* Tawas City, Michigan: Northeastern Printers, 1975.

Douglass, Samuel T. *Reports of Cases Argued and Determined in the Supreme Court of the State of Michigan.* Detroit: C. Willcox, 1846-1849.

Draeger, Carey L. "They Never Forgot: Michigan Survivors of the Titanic." *Michigan History,* 81-2 (March-April 1997), 28-43.

Druse, Joseph L., and Eleanor Bachmann LeDuc. *Abstracts of the Early Probate Records of Ingham County, Michigan, 1838-1869.* Lansing: Mid-Michigan Genealogical Society, 1980.

Dubester, Henry J. *State Censuses: An Annotated Bibliography of Censuses of Population Taken After the Year 1790 by States and Territories of the United States.* Washington, D.C., 1948.

DuLong, John P. "Engagements: Guide to Fur Trade Employment Contracts, 1670-1821." *Michigan's Habitant Heritage,* 10-3 (July 1989), 47-58.

__________. *French-Canadian Genealogical Research.* Palm Harbor, Florida: Lisi Press, 1995.

__________. *French Canadians in Michigan.* East Lansing: Michigan State University Press, 2001.

Dunbar, Willis Frederick. "Frontiersmanship in Michigan." *Michigan History,* 50-2 (June 1966), 97-110.

__________. *Michigan Through the Centuries.* 4 vols. New York: Lewis Historical Publishing Co., 1955.

__________. *Michigan: A History of the Wolverine State.* Grand Rapids: William B. Eerdmans Publishing Co., 1965.

__________, and George S. May. *Michigan: A History of the Wolverine State.* 3rd ed. Grand Rapids: William B. Eerdmans Publishing Co., 1995.

Duncan, Mary Lou Straith. *Passage to America, 1851-1869: The Records of Richard Elliott, Passenger Agent, Detroit, Michigan.* Detroit: Detroit Society for Genealogical Research, 1999.

Dziurman, Tiffany. "Tragedy on the Tracks." *Michigan History,* 77-6 (November-December 1993), 37-41.

"Early Michigan Census Records." *Family Trails,* 6-1 (Summer-Fall 1978), 26-29.

Early Western Travels. Ed. Reuben Gold Thwaites. New York: AMS Press, 1966.

Edgar, Irving I. *A History of Early Jewish Physicians in the State of Michigan.* New York: Philosophical Library, 1982.

Elliott, Frank N. *When the Railroad Was King.* Lansing: Bureau of History, 1988.

Ellis, David M. *Michigan Postal History: The Post Offices, 1805-1986.* Lake Grove, Oregon: The Depot, 1993.

Enders, Calvin. "White Sheets in Mecosta County: The Anatomy of a Michigan Clan." *The Michigan Historical Review,* 14-2 (Fall 1988), 59-84.

Engberg, George B. "Who Were the Lumberjacks?" *Michigan History,* 32-3 (September 1948), 238-246.

Ethnic Groups in Michigan. Ed. James M. Anderson and Iva A. Smith. Detroit: Ethnos Press, 1983.

Ethnic Newspapers and Periodicals in Michigan: A Checklist. Ed. Richard Hathaway. Ann Arbor: Michigan Archival Association, 1978.

Evolution of Michigan Townships. Lansing: Mid-Michigan Genealogical Society, 1972.

Fairbairn, J., and Charles Fey. *History of Freemasonry in Michigan.* Michigan: Most Worshipful Grand Lodge Free and Accepted Mason of Michigan, 1963.

Farmer, Silas. *History of Detroit and Wayne County and Early Michigan: A Chronological Cyclopedia of the Past and Present.* 2 vols. Detroit: Silas Farmer and Co., 1890.

Feddersen, Christian T. *Scandinavians in Michigan With Special Reference to Detroit and Environs.* Romeo, Michigan: Christian T. Fedddersen, 1968.

Federal Land Patents Kent County, Michigan. Grand Rapids: Western Michigan Genealogical Society, 1984.

Felch, Alpheus. "The Indians of Michigan and the Cession of Their Lands to the United States by Treaties." *Michigan Historical Collections,* 26 (1896), 274-297.

Fields, Harold B. "Free Negroes in Cass County Before the Civil War." *Michigan History,* 44-4 (December 1960), 375-383.

Finding Aid No. 15: Records of the Michigan Department of the Grand Army of the Republic 1861-1957 (Record Group 63-19). Lansing: Michigan Department of State, 1966.

Fire Insurance Maps in the Library of Congress. Washington D.C.: Library of Congress, 1981.

First Land Owners of Oakland County, Michigan. Birmingham: Oakland County Genealogical Society, 1981.

Fitzmaurice, John W. *The Shanty Boy, or, Life in a Lumber Camp.* Upper Saddle River, New Jersey: Literature House, 1970.

Flagg, Charles A. *An Index of Pioneers From Massachusetts to the West, Especially the State of Michigan.* Baltimore: Genealogical Publishing Co., 1975.

Folsom, Burton W. Jr. *Empire Builders: How Michigan Entrepreneurs Helped Make America Great.* Traverse City, Michigan: Rhodes and Easton, 1998.

Formisano, Ronald P. "The Edge of Caste: Colored Suffrage In Michigan, 1827-1861." *Michigan History,* 56-1 (Spring 1972), 19-41.

Forrester, Alan T. *Scots in Michigan.* East Lansing: Michigan State University Press, 2003.

Fountain, Daniel R. *Michigan Gold: Mining in the Upper Peninsula.* Duluth, Minnesota: Lake Superior Port Cities Inc., 1992.

Freedman, Eric. *Pioneering Michigan.* Franklin, Michigan: Altwerger and Mandel Publishing Co., 1992.

French Canadian Sources: A Guide for Genealogists. Ed. Patricia Keeney Geyh, Joyce Soltis Banachowski, Linda K. Boyea, Patricia Sarasin Ustine, Marilyn Holt Bourbonais, Beverly Ploenske Labelle, Francele Sherburn, Karen Vincent Humiston. Orem, Utah: Ancestry Publishing, 2002.

Friggens, Thomas G. *No Tears in Heaven: The 1926 Barnes-Hecker Mine Disaster.* Lansing: Michigan Historical Center, 2002.

Fuller, George Newman. *Economic and Social Beginnings of Michigan.* Lansing: State Printers, 1916.

Galuszka, Douglas. "Michigan in the Great War." *Michigan History,* 77-4 (July-August 1993), 31.

Gates, William B. Jr. *Michigan Copper and Boston Dollars: An Economic History of the Michigan Copper Mining Industry.* Cambridge, Massachusetts: Harvard University Press, 1951.

Genealogical Periodical Annual Index. 40 vols. Bowie, Maryland: Heritage Books, 1962-2001.

Genealogical Resources in Michigan. Ed. V.C. Clohset, E.C. Erwin and H.F. Powell. Detroit: Detroit Society for Genealogical Research, 1973.

A General Index to a Census of Pensioners for Revolutionary or Military Service, 1840. Baltimore: Genealogical Publishing Co., 1965.

George Croghan's Journal of his Trip to Detroit in 1767. Ed. Howard H. Peckham. Ann Arbor: The University of Michigan Press, 1939.

George, Sister Mary Karl. *The Rise and Fall of Toledo, Michigan: The Toledo War.* Lansing: Michigan Historical Commission, 1971.

Gibson, Arthur Hopkin. *Artists of Early Michigan: A Biographical Dictionary of Artists Native to or Active in Michigan, 1701-1900.* Detroit: Wayne State University Press, 1975.

Gilpin, Alec R. *The Territory of Michigan.* East Lansing: Michigan State University Press, 1970.

Glazier, Jack, and Arthur W. Helweg, *Ethnicity in Michigan: Issues and People.* East Lansing: Michigan State University Press, 2001.

Goodfriend, Joyce D. *The Published Diaries and Letters of American Women: An Annotated Bibliography.* Boston: G.K. Hall, 1987.

Governor and Judges Journal; Proceedings of the Land board of Detroit. Ed. M. Agnes Burton. Detroit: 1915.

Grabowski, John, and Billie Jo Grabowski. *List of County Sheriffs of Michigan, 1869-1986.* Cheboygan, Michigan: The Authors, 1987.

Graff, George P. *The People of Michigan.* 2nd ed. Lansing: Michigan Department of Education State Library Services, 1974.

Grassroots of America: A Computerized Index to the American State Papers – Land Grants and Claims (1789-1837). Ed. Phillip W. McMullin. Greenville, South Carolina: Southern Historical Press, 1994.

Gray, Susan E. *The Yankee West: Community Life on the Michigan Frontier.* Chapel Hill: The University of North Carolina Press, 1996.

Greenman, Emerson F. *The Indians of Michigan.* Lansing: Michigan Historical Commission, 1961.

Greenwood, Val D. *The Researcher's Guide to American Genealogy.* 3rd ed. Baltimore: Genealogical Publishing Co., 2000.

Groene, Bertram Hawthorne. *Tracing Your Civil War Ancestor.* 4th ed. Winston-Salem, North Carolina: John F. Blair, 1995.

Guide to the Michigan Genealogical and Historical Collections at the Library of Michigan and the State Archives of Michigan. Lansing: Michigan Genealogical Council, 1996.

Guide to the Western Michigan University Regional History Collections. Ed. Phyllis Burnham. Kalamazoo: New Issues Press, 1998.

Gutsche, Andrea, and Cindy Bisaillon. *Mysterious Islands: Forgotten Tales of the Great Lakes.* Toronoto: Lynx Images, 1999.

Hamil, Fred C. *Michigan in the War of 1812.* Lansing: Michigan History Division, Michigan Department of State, 1977.

The Handy Book for Genealogists. 10th ed. Draper, Utah: Everton Publishers, 2002.

Hargrove, Hondon. "Their Greatest Battle Was Getting Into The Fight: The 1st Michigan Colored Infantry Goes to War." *Michigan History,* 75-1 (January-February 1991), 24-30.

Harley, Rachel Brett, and Betty MacDowell. *Michigan Women: Firsts and Founders.* 2 vols. Lansing: Michigan Women's Studies Association, 1992-1995.

Harmison, Eva Murrell, and Donna Valley Russell. "Michigan." *Genealogical Research: Methods and Sources.* Ed. Kenn Stryker-Rodda. Washington D.C.: American Society of Genealogists, 1983. II, 79-99.

Harmon, Charles E. "Cases at the Court of Appeals." *Michigan History,* 87-5 (September-October 2003), 43.

Harrington, E. Burke. Reports of Cases Determined in the Court of Chancery of the State of Michigan. Detroit: Bagg and Harmon, 1845.

Hatcher, Patricia Law. *Locating Your Roots: Discover Your Ancestors Using Land Records.* Cincinnati: Betterway Books, 2003.

Hathaway, Richard J. "From Ontario to the Great Lake State: Canadians in Michigan." *Michigan History,* 67-2 (March-April 1983), 42-45.

__________. "Michigan Directories." *Family Trails,* 5-4 (Summer 1975), 1-8.

__________. "Michigan Landownership Maps and Atlases." *Family Trails,* 3-3 (Spring-Summer 1971), 1-7.

Hatten, Ruth Land. "The 'Forgotten' Census of 1880: Defective, Dependent, and Delinquent Classes." *National Genealogical Society Quarterly,* 80-1 (March 1992), 57-70.

Haulsee, William M. *Soldiers of the Great War.* Vol. 2. Washington, D.C.: Soldiers Record Publishing Association, 1920.

Hauptman, Laurence M. *Between Two Fires: American Indians in the Civil War.* New York: The Free Press, 1995.

Havira, Barbara. "A Treasure and a Challenge: Michigan Bureau of Labor Reports." *Michigan History,* 72-5 (September-October 1988), 36-43.

Hawley, Amos Henry. *The Population of Michigan, 1840 to 1960: An Analysis of Growth, Distribution and Composition.* Ann Arbor: The University of Michigan Press, 1949.

Hayes, Gregory. "The Grand Army of the Republic." *Michigan History,* 84-1 (January-February 2000), 42.

Hébert, John R., and Dempsey, Patrick E. *Panoramic Maps of Cities in the United States and Canada: A Checklist of Maps in the Collections of the Library of Congress, Geography and Map Division.* 2nd ed. Washington, D.C.: Library of Congress, 1984, 63-68.

Hedrick, W.O. "The Financial and Tax History of Michigan." *Michigan History,* 22-1 (Winter 1938), 34-106.

Hefner, Loretta L. *The WPA Historical Records Survey: A Guide to the Unpublished Inventories, Indexes, and Transcripts.* Chicago: The Society of American Archivists, 1980.

Heisey, John W. *The W.P.A. Historical Records Survey Sources for Genealogists.* Indianapolis: Heritage House, 1988.

Heiss, Willard C. "Early Quaker Meetings in Michigan." *Michigan Heritage,* 12 (1971), 13-14.

Helweg, Arthur. *Asian Indians in Michigan.* East Lansing: Michigan State University, 2002.

Herek, Raymond J. *These Men Have Seen Hard Service: The First Michigan Sharpshooters in the Civil War.* Detroit: Wayne State University Press, 1998.

Hinckley, Kathleen W. *Your Guide to the Federal Census for Genealogists, Researchers, and Family Historians.* Cincinnati: Betterway Books, 2002.

Hine, Darlene Clark. *Black Women in the Middle West: The Michigan Experience.* Ann Arbor: Historical Society of Michigan, 1990.

Historic Women of Michigan: A Sesquicentennial Celebration. Ed. Rosalie Riegle Troester. Lansing: Michigan Women's Studies Association, 1987.

Historical and Genealogical Record of the Michigan Daughters of the American Revolution. DAR, 1940-.

Historical Record of the Michigan Daughters of the American Revolution, 1893-1930. 2 vols. The Michigan Daughters, 1930.

Hixson, James W. "A May Day to Remember." *Michigan History,* 83-3 (May-June 1999), 34-38.

Holmio, Armas K. E. *History of the Finns in Michigan.* Trans. Ellen M. Ryynanen. Detroit: Wayne State University Press, 2001.

Hone, E. Wade. *Land and Property Research in the United States.* Salt Lake City: Ancestry, 1997.

Howard-Filler, Saralee R. "'A Jubilee Shall That Fiftieth Year Be Unto You': Michigan Churches in 1884." *Michigan History,* 67-4 (July-August 1983), 16-25.

Hubach, Robert R. *Early Midwestern Travel Narratives: An Annotated Bibliography, 1634-1850.* Detroit: Wayne State University Press, 1998.

Huntington, Gertrude Enders. *Amish in Michigan.* East Lansing: Michigan State University Press, 2001.

Hurd, Henry M. "A History of the Asylums for the Insane in Michigan." *Michigan Pioneer Collections,* 13 (1888), 292-307.

Huseby-Darvas, Eva V. *Hungarians in Michigan.* East Lansing: Michigan State University Press, 2003.

Hydrick, Blair D. *A Guide to the Microfiche Edition of Civil War Unit Histories: Regimental Histories and Personal Narratives.* Part 4. Bethesda, Maryland: University Publications of America, 1994, 75-96.

Ibbotson, Patricia. *Eloise: Poorhouse, Farm, Asylum, and Hospital, 1839-1984.* Chicago: Arcadia, 2002.

Index to the First 37 Volumes of Michigan D.A.R. Bible and Pioneer Records. 1967.

Index of Naturalization Records at Alpena County Courthouse for the 26th Judicial Circuit 1878-1978. Alpena: Northeastern Michigan Genealogical and Historical Society, 1980.

Index to Personal Names in the National Union Catalog o Manuscript Collections, 1959-1984. 2 vols. Alexandria, Virginia: Chadwyck-Healey, 1988.

Index to Subjects and Corporate Names in the National Union Catalog of Manuscript Collections, 1959-1984. 3 vols. Alexandria, Virginia: Chadwyck-Healey, 1994.

Index to the Great Lakes Lighthouse Keepers Association Oral History Tape Collection. Southfield, Michigan: Great Lakes Lighthouse Keepers Association, 1986.

Index, First Land Owners of Shiawassee County, Michigan. Owosso: Shiawassee County Genealogical Society, 1984.

Irish Genealogical Society of Michigan. *Our Roots Began in Ireland.* Detroit: Irish Genealogical Society of Michigan, 2001.

Isham, Asa B. *Historical Sketch of the Seventh Regiment Michigan Volunteer Cavalry.* Huntington, West Virginia: Blue Acorn Press, 2000.

Jackson, James N. *Guide to the First Fifty Years of The Detroit Society for Genealogical Research Magazine.* Detroit: Detroit Society for Genealogical Research, 1990.

__________. *Index to the List of Pensioners on the Roll, January 1, 1883.* Troy, Michigan: Words on Disk, 1989.

Jarboe, Betty M. *Obituaries: A Guide to Sources.* Boston: G.K. Hall & Co., 1982, 125-130.

The Jesuit Relations and Allied Documents; Travels and Explorations of the Jesuit Missionaries in New France, 1610-1791. Ed. Reuben Gold Thwaites. 73 vols. New York: Pageant Book Co., 1959.

Johnson, Georgia A. Lewis. *Black Medical Graduates of the University of Michigan (1872-1960 inclusive) and Selected Black Michigan Physicians.* East Lansing: Georgia A. Johnson Publishing Co., 1994.

The Joint Archives of Holland: Guide to the Collections Holland Historical Trust, Hope College, Western Theological Seminary. Ed. Larry J. Wagenaar. Holland: The Joint Archives of Holland, 1989.

Joint Documents of the Senate and House of Representatives at the Annual Session of 1848. Detroit: Bagg and Harmon, 1848, 31-43.

Journal of the Annual Encampment. Grand Army of the Republic. Department of Michigan. Lansing: Grand Army of the Republic, 1882-1948.

Joyaux, Georges J. "French Press in Michigan: A Bibliography." *Michigan History,* 36-3 (September 1952), 260-278.

__________. "French Press in Michigan." *Michigan History,* 37-2 (June 1953), 155-165.

Karamanski, Theodore J. *Deep Woods Frontier: A History of Logging in Northern Michigan.* Detroit: Wayne State University Press, 1989.

Karpinski, Louis C. *Bibliography of the Printed Maps of Michigan 1804-1880.* Lansing: Michigan Historical Commission, 1931.

Katz, Irving I. "Jews in Michigan." *Family Trails,* 4-3 (Spring 1974), 5-7.

__________. *The Jewish Soldier from Michigan in the Civil War.* Detroit: Wayne State University Press, 1962.

Kaups, Matti Enn. "Finnish Place-Names in Michigan." *Michigan History,* 51-4 (Winter 1967), 335-347.

Kavieff, Paul R. *The Purple Gang: Organized Crime in Detroit, 1910-1945.* Fort Lee, New Jersey: Barricade Books, 2000.

__________. *The Violent Years: Prohibition and the Detroit Mobs.* Fort Lee, New Jersey: Barricade Books, 2001.

Kebler, Geneva. *Finding Aid for the Records of the Michigan Military Establishment 1838-1941.* Lansing: Michigan Department of State, 1966.

Kedzie, Robert C. *The Cholera in Kalamazoo.* Kalamazoo: Kalamazoo Public Museum, 1961.

Keen, Richard A. *Michigan Weather.* Helena, Montana: American and World Geographic Publishing, 1993.

Keenan, Stanislas M. *History of Eloise.* Detroit: Thomas Smith Press, 1913.

Keesee, Dennis M. *Too Young to Die: Boy Soldiers of the Union Army, 1861-1865.* Huntington, West Virginia: Blue Acron Press, 2001.

Kemp, Thomas Jay. *The American Census Handbook.* Wilmington, Delaware: Scholarly Resources, 2001.

Kent, Timothy J. *Fort Pontchartrain at Detroit: a Guide to the Daily Lives of Fur Trade and Military Personnel, Settlers, and Missionaries at French Posts.* Ossineke, Michigan: Silver Fox Enterprises, 2001.

Kern, John Kern. *A Short History of Michigan.* Lansing: Michigan Department of State, 1977.

Kerstens, Elizabeth Kelly. "Ship Wrecks of the Great Lakes." *Ancestry,* 21-1 (January-February 2003), 34-39.

Kilar, Jeremy W. *Germans in Michigan.* East Lansing: Michigan State University Press, 2002.

__________. *Michigan's Lumbertowns: Lumbermen and Laborers in Saginaw, Bay City, and Muskegon, 1870-1905.* Detroit: Wayne State University Press, 1990.

Kistler, Mark O. "The German Language Press in Michigan: A Survey and Bibliography." *Michigan History,* 44-3 (September 1960), 303-323.

Kleinschmidt, Earl E. "Prevailing Diseases and Hygienic Conditions in Early Michigan." *Michigan History,* 25 (Winter 1941), 57-99.

Knapp, Michael. "World War I Service Records." *Prologue,* 22-3 (Fall 1990), 300-302.

Knox, Debra Johnson. *World War II Military Records: A Family Historian's Guide.* Spartanburg, South Carolina: MIE Publishing, 2003.

Kohl, Cris. *Titanic, The Great Lakes Connections.* West Chicago: Seawolf Communications Inc., 2000.

Kolchmainen, John Ilmari. "Finnish Newspapers and Periodicals in Michigan." *Michigan History.* 24 (Winter 1940), 119-127.

Kristiansen, Soren. *Diary of Captain Soren Kristiansen, Lake Michigan Schooner Captain, 1891-1893.* Iron Mountain, Michigan: Mid-Peninsula Library Cooperative, 1981.

Kubiak, William. *Great Lakes Indians: A Pictorial Guide.* Grand Rapids: Baker Book House, 1970.

Lajeunesse, Ernest J. *The Windsor Border Region, Canada's Southernmost Frontier: A Collection of Documents.* Toronto: Champlain Society, 1960.

Lamarre, Jean. *The French Canadians of Michigan: Their Contribution to the Development of the Saginaw Valley and the Keweenaw Peninsula, 1840-1914.* Detroit: Wayne State University Press, 2003.

Lamport, Warren Wayne. *Michigan Poets and Poetry, with Portraits and Biographies.* Leslie: Michigan Publishing Co., 1904.

Landrum, Charles Hanford. *Michigan in the World War: Military and Naval Honors of Michigan Men and Women.* Lansing: Michigan Historical Commission, 1924.

Lankton, Larry. "Autos to Armaments: Detroit Becomes the Arsenal of Democracy." *Michigan History,* 75-6 (November-December 1991), 42-49.

__________. *Beyond the Boundaries: Life and Landscape at the Lake Superior Copper Mines, 1840-1875.* New York: Oxford University Press, 1997.

__________. *Cradle to Grave: Life, Work, and Death at the Lake Superior Copper Mines.* New York: Oxford University Press, 1991.

Lantz, Raymond C. *Ottawa and Chippewa Indians of Michigan, 1855-1868.* Bowie, Maryland: Heritage Books, 1993.

__________. *Ottawa and Chippewa Indians of Michigan, 1870-1909.* Bowie, Maryland: Heritage Books, 1991.

__________. *The Potawatomi Indians of Michigan, 1843-1904.* Bowie, Maryland: Heritage Books, 1992.

Larrie, Reginald. *Black Experiences in Michigan History.* Lansing: Michigan Department of State, 1976.

Lavey, Kathleen. "Influx from Ireland Has Had Profound Effect on Michigan." *Lansing State Journal,* 14 March 2004. Accessed online <www.lsj.com/things/etc_in/040314_irish_1d.html> 20 April 2004.

Laws of the Territory of Michigan. 4 vols. Lansing: W.S. George and Co., 1871-1884.

Lewis, Kenneth E. *West to Far Michigan: Settling the Lower Peninsula, 1815-1860.* East Lansing: Michigan State University Press, 2002.

Lincoln, James H., and James L. Donahue. *Fiery Trial.* Ann Arbor: Historical Society of Michigan, 1984.

Lindquist, Charles. "Afro-American Journal and Directory, 1895." *Michigan History,* 64-2 (March April 1980), 42-43.

__________. *The Antislavery-Underground Railroad Movement in Lenawee County, Michigan, 1830-1860.* Adrian: Lenawee County Historical Society, 1999.

List of Pensioners on the Roll January 1, 1883. Washington, D.C.: Government Printing Office, 1883.

"List of Real Estate Owners and Values at the Time of the Detroit Fire in 1805." *Michigan Pioneer and Historical Collections,* 36 (1908), 114-115.

Living at a Lighthouse: Oral Histories from the Great Lakes. Ed. LuAnne Gaykowski Kozma. Allen Park, Michigan: Great Lakes Lighthouse Keepers Association, 1987.

Lockwood, Charles. *Indian Patents Issued in Leelanau County from Allotment List in the National Archives.* Lansing, 1978.

Loomis, Francis. *Michigan Biography Index.* Detroit: Detroit Public Library, 1946-1958.

Lucas, Richard E. *First Landowners of Ingham County, Michigan.* Lansing: Michigan Genealogical Council, 1982.

"Mackinac Register of Baptisms and Interments, 1695-1821." *Wisconsin State Historical Society Collections,* 19 (1910), 1-192.

"The Mackinac Register of Marriages, 1725-1821." *Wisconsin State Historical Society Collections,* 18 (1908), 469-513.

Magnaghi, Russell M. *Italians in Michigan.* East Lansing: Michigan State University Press, 2001.

__________. *Miners, Merchants, and Midwives: Michigan's Upper Peninsula Italians.* Marquette: Belle Fontaine Press, 1987.

__________. *The Way It Happened: Settling Michigan's Upper Peninsula.* Iron Mountain, Michigan: Mid-Peninsula Library Cooperative, 1982.

The Making of Michigan: 1820-1860. Ed. Justin L. Kestenbaum. Detroit: Wayne State University Press, 1990.

Mansfield, John Brandt. *History of the Great Lakes.* 2 vols. Chicago: J.H. Beers and Co., 1899.

Marriage Records, Ste. Anne Church, Detroit, 1701-1850. Ed. Sharon A. Kelley. Detroit: Detroit Society for Genealogical Research, 2001.

Martin, John Bartlow. *Call It North Country: The Story of Upper Michigan.* Detroit: Wayne State University Press, 1986.

Mary Austin Wallace: Her Diary, 1862; A Michigan Soldier's Wife Runs Their Farm. Ed. Julia McCune. Lansing: Michigan Civil War Centennial Observance Commission, 1963.

Massie, Larry. *From Frontier Folk to Factory Smoke: Michigan's First Century of Historical Fiction.* AuTrain, Michigan: Avery Color Studios, 1987.

May, George S. *Pictorial History of Michigan: The Early Years.* Grand Rapids: William B. Eerdmans Publishing Co., 1967.

__________. *Pictorial History of Michigan: The Later Years.* Grand Rapids: William B. Eerdmans Publishing Co., 1969.

Maybee, Rolland H. *Michigan's White Pine Era.* Lansing: Michigan Department of State, 1988.

McCann, Barbara. "Women of Traunik: A Story of Slovenian Immigration." *Michigan History,* 68-1 (January-February 1984), 41-45.

McGee, John W. *The Passing of the Gael.* Grand Rapids: Wolverine Print Co., 1975.

McRae, Norman. "Crossing the Detroit River to Find Freedom." *Michigan History,* 67-2 (March-April 1983), 35-39.

__________. *Negroes in Michigan During the Civil War.* Lansing: Michigan Civil War Centennial Observance Commission, 1966.

Meints, Graydon M. *Along the Tracks: A Directory of Named Places on Michigan Railroads.* Mount Pleasant, Michigan: Clarke Historical Library, 1987.

Men of Progress: Embracing Biographical Sketches of Representative Michigan Men with An Outline History of the State. Detroit: Evening New Association, 1900.

Merriman, Brenda Dougall. *Genealogy in Ontario: Searching the Records.* Toronto: Ontario Genealogical Society, 1996.

Mehney, Paul D. "The War With Spain." *Michigan History,* 86-3 (May-June 2002), 28-41.

Meulendyke, Josias. "Dutch Settlements North of Muskegon: 1867-1897." *Michigan History,* 31-4 (December 1947), 392-398.

Mevis, Daniel S. *Pioneer Recollections: Semi-historic Sidelights on the Early Days of Lansing.* Lansing: Robert Smith Printing Co., 1911.

Michigan: A Centennial History of the State and Its People. Ed. George N. Fuller. 5 vols. Chicago: The Lewis Publishing Co., 1939.

Michigan: A Guide to the Wolverine State. New York: Oxford University Press, 1941.

Michigan Appeals Reports: Cases Decided in the Michigan Court of Appeals. Rochester, New York: Lawyers Cooperative Publishing Co., 1967-.

Michigan Biographies, Including Members of Congress, Elective State Officers, Justices of the Supreme Court, Members of the Michigan Legislature, Board of Regents of the University of Michigan, State Board of Agriculture and State Board of Education. Lansing: The Michigan Historical Commission, 1924.

Michigan Cemetery Atlas. Lansing: Library of Michigan, 1991.

Michigan Cemetery Compendium. Spring Arbor, Michigan: HAR-AL Inc., 1979.

Michigan Cemetery Source Book. Lansing: Library of Michigan, 1994.

Michigan County Histories: A Bibliography. Lansing: State Library Services, 1970 and 1978.

Michigan Family Register. 9 vols. 1969-1971.

Michigan Historical Collections: Collections and Researches made by the Michigan Pioneer and Historical Society. 28 vols. Lansing: Michigan Pioneer and Historical Society, 1888-1916.

Michigan Historical Records Survey. *African Methodist Episcopal Church, Michigan Conference.* Detroit: Michigan Historical Records Survey Project, 1940.

__________. *Alger County.* Detroit: Michigan Historical Records Survey Project, 1940.

__________. *Alpena County.* Detroit: Michigan Historical Records Survey Project, 1942.

__________. *Baraga County.* Detroit: Michigan Historical Records Survey Project, 1937.

__________. *Bay County.* Detroit: Michigan Historical Records Survey Project, 1940.

__________. *Calendar of the Baptist Collection of Kalamazoo College, Kalamazoo Michigan.* Detroit: Michigan Historical Records Survey Project, 1940.

__________. *Calhoun County.* Detroit: Michigan Historical Records Survey Project, 1941.

__________. *Cheboygan County.* Detroit: Michigan Historical Records Survey Project, 1938.

__________. *Churches of God, Michigan Assemblies.* Detroit: Michigan Historical Records Survey Project, 1941.

__________. *Church of the Nazarene, Michigan District Assembly.* Detroit: Michigan Historical Records Survey Project, 1942.

__________. *Dearborn Churches.* Detroit: Michigan Historical Records Survey Project, 1940.

__________. *Directory of Churches and Religious Organizations, Greater Detroit 1941.* Detroit: Michigan Historical Records Survey Project, 1941.

__________. *Evangelical, Michigan Conference.* Detroit: Michigan Historical Records Survey Project, 1941.

__________. *Evangelical and Reformed Churches.* Detroit: Michigan Historical Records Survey Project, 1941.

__________. *Genesee County.* Detroit: Michigan Historical Records Survey Project, 1940.

__________. *Iosco County.* Detroit: Michigan Historical Records Survey Project, 1938.

__________. *Iron County.* Detroit: Michigan Historical Records Survey Project, 1938.

__________. *Jackson County.* Detroit: Michigan Historical Records Survey Project, 1941.

__________. *Jewish Bodies.* Detroit: Michigan Historical Records Survey Project, 1940.

__________. *Marquette County.* Detroit: Michigan Historical Records Survey Project, 1940.

__________. *Muskegon County.* Detroit: Michigan Historical Records Survey Project, 1941.

__________. *Pilgrim Holiness, Michigan District.* Detroit: Michigan Historical Records Survey Project, 1942.

__________. *Presbyterian Churches in U.S.A., Presbytery of Detroit.* Detroit: Michigan Historical Records Survey Project, 1940.

__________. *Presbyterian Church in U.S.A., Presbytery of Flint.* Detroit: Michigan Historical Records Survey Project, 1941.

__________. *Protestant Episcopal Bodies, Diocese of Michigan.* Detroit: Michigan Historical Records Survey Project, 1940.

__________. *Protestant Episcopal Church, Diocese of Northern Michigan.* Detroit: Michigan Historical Records Survey Project, 1940.

__________. *Protestant Episcopal Church, Diocese of Western Michigan.* Detroit: Michigan Historical Records Survey Project, 1940.

__________. *Roman Catholic, Archdiocese of Detroit.* Detroit: Michigan Historical Records Survey Project, 1941.

__________. *Salvation Army in Michigan.* Detroit: Michigan Historical Records Survey Project, 1942.

__________. *Vital Statistics Holdings of Church Archives, Michigan: Wayne County.* Detroit: Michigan Historical Records Survey Project, 1942.

__________. *Vital Statistics Holdings by Government Agencies in Michigan. Birth Records.* Detroit: The Michigan Historical Records Survey Project, 1941.

__________. *Vital Statistics Holdings by Government Agencies in Michigan. Death Records.* Detroit: The Michigan Historical Records Survey Project, 1942.

__________. *Vital Statistics Holdings by Government Agencies in Michigan. Divorce Records.* Detroit: The Michigan Historical Records Survey Project, 1942.

__________. *Vital Statistics Holdings by Government Agencies in Michigan. Marriage Records.* Detroit: The Michigan Historical Records Survey Project, 1941.

Michigan History Magazine. *Introducing Michigan's Past: An Overview for Teachers.* Lansing: Michigan Department of State, 2001.

Michigan Manual. Lansing: State of Michigan, 1836-.

"The Michigan Newspapers on Microfilm Project." *Family Trails,* 3-4 (Fall-Winter 1971-72), 6-8.

Michigan Quilts: 150 Years of Textile Tradition. Ed. Marsha MacDowell and Ruth D. Fitzgerald. East Lansing: Michigan State University, 1987.

A Michigan Reader: 11,000 B.C. to A.D. 1865. Ed. George May and Herbert Brinks. Grand Rapids: William B. Eerdmans Publishing Co., 1974.

A Michigan Reader: 1865 to the Present. Ed. Robert M. Warner and C. Warren VanderHill. Grand Rapids: William B. Eerdmans Publishing Co., 1974.

Michigan Remembered: Photographs From the Farm Security Administration and the Office of War Information, 1936-1943. Ed. Constance B. Schulz. Detroit: Wayne State University Press, 2001.

Michigan Reports: Reports of Cases Determined in the Supreme Court of Michigan. Chicago: Callaghan, 1878-.

The Michigan Supreme Court Historical Reference Guide. Ed. Ellen Campbell. Lansing: The Michigan Supreme Court Historical Society, 1998.

Michigan Surname Index. 2 vols. Lansing: Michigan Genealogical Council, 1984-1989.

Michigan Voices, Ed. Joe Grimm. Detroit: Wayne State University Press, 1987.

Michigan Volunteers of '98: A Complete Photographic Record of Michigan's Part in the Spanish-American War of 1898. Detroit: G.F. Sterling and Co., 1898.

Michigan Women in the Civil War. Lansing: Michigan Civil War Centennial Observance Commission, 1963.

Micketti, Gerald. "The Day Metz Burned." *Michigan History,* 65-5 (September-October 1981), 12-16.

Miles, William. *Michigan Atlases and Plat Books: A Checklist, 1872-1973.* Lansing: Michigan Department of Education State Library Services, 1975.

Miller, Alice Turner. "Soldiers of the War of 1812 Who Died in Michigan." *Michigan Heritage,* 4-1 (Autumn 1962), 9-60; 4-4 (Summer 1963), 201-212; 5-4 (Summer 1964), 164-167; 6-4 (Summer 1965), 184-185; 7-4 (Summer 1966), 206-208; 8-4 (Summer 1967), 199.

__________. Soldiers and Widows of the War of 1812 Who Died in Michigan. Ithaca, Michigan: Miller, 1962.

__________. "War of 1812 Soldier's Widows Who Died in Michigan." *Michigan Heritage,* 4-1 (Autumn 1962), 60-66.

Miller, Sharon L. *1860 United States Census, Muskegon County, Michigan.* Muskegon: Miller, 1985.

Milner, Anita Cheek. *Newspaper Indexes: A Location and Subject Guide for Researchers.* 3 vols. Metuchen, New Jersey: Scarecrow Press Inc., 1977-1982.

Moon, Elaine Latzman. *Untold Tales, Unsung Heroes: An Oral History of Detroit's African American Community, 1918-1967.* Detroit: Wayne State University Press, 1994.

Moore, Charles. *History of Michigan.* 4 vols. Chicago: The Lewis Publishing Co., 1915.

Motz, Marilyn Ferris. *True Sisterhood: Michigan Women and Their Kin, 1820-1920.* Albany: State University of New York Press, 1983.

Murdoch, Angus. *Boom Copper: The Story of the First U.S. Mining Boom.* New York: MacMillan Co., 1943.

Myers, Eleanor Myers. *A Migration Study of the Thirty-two States and Four Organized Territories Comprising the United States in 1850 Based Upon the Federal Census of 1850.* Syracuse, New York: Central New York Genealogical Society, 1977.

Nagel, Herbert. *The Metz Fire of 1908.* Rogers City, Michigan: Presque Isle County Historical Society, 1979.

Neagles, James C. U.S. Military Records: A Guide to Federal and State Sources, Colonial America to the Present. Salt Lake City: Ancestry, 1994.

__________, and Lila Lee Neagles. *Locating Your Immigrant Ancestor.* Logan, Utah: Everton Publishers Inc., 1975.

Neumeyer, Elizabeth. "Michigan Indians Battle Against Removal." *Michigan History,* 55-4 (Winter 1971), 275-288.

Newberry, Phelps, and George C. Waldo. *History of Michigan Camps.* Military Training Camps Association, 1929.

Newcomb, Annette. *Awesome Almanac: Michigan.* Fontana, Wisconsin: B and B Publishing, 1993.

Newman, John J. Uncle, We are Ready! Registering America's Men, 1917-1918: A Guide to Researching World War I Draft Registration Cards. North Salt Lake, Utah: Heritage Quest, 2001.

Nowlin, William. *The Bark Covered House.* Detroit: Nowlin, 1876.

Nute, Grace Lee. *The Voyageur.* Saint Paul: Minnesota Historical Society, 1955.

Oakland County, Michigan, Genealogical Society Surname Directory. 7 vols. Birmingham, Michigan: Oakland County Genealogical Society, 1983-1999.

Oldenburg, Joseph. *A Genealogical Guide to the Burton Historical Collection Detroit Public Library.* Salt Lake City: Ancestry Publishing, 1988.

"Oldest Synagogue." *Michigan History,* 65-2 (March-April 1981), 5.

Oswald, Diane L. *Fire Insurance Maps: Their History and Applications.* College Station, Texas: Lacewing Press, 1997.

Parisville Poles: First Polish Settlers in U.S.A.? Ed. Harry Milostan. Mount Clemens, Michigan: Masspac Publishing Co., 1977.

Parker, Grant. "Disaster in Bath." *Michigan History,* 65-3 (May-June 1981), 12-15.

__________. *Mayday: The History of a Village Holocaust.* Perry, Michigan: Parker Press, 1980.

The Pension Roll of 1835. 4 vols. Baltimore: Genealogical Publishing Co., 1992.

Perejda, Andrew D. Perejda. "Sources and Dispersal of Michigan's Population." *Michigan History,* 32-4 (December 1948), 355-366.

Phillips, Althea Cascadden, and Donald J. deZeeuw. *First Landowners of Ogemaw County, Michigan.* Lansing: Michigan Genealogical Council, 1980.

Physicians', Dentists' and Druggists' Directory of Michigan. Chicago: Galen Gonsier, 1893.

Powers, Thomas E., and William H. McNitt. *Guide to Manuscripts in the Bentley Historical Library.* Ann Arbor: University of Michigan, 1976.

Powers, Tom. *Michigan Rogues, Desperados, and Cut-Throats: A Gallery of 19th Century Miscreants.* Davison, Michigan: Friede Publications, 2002.

Preparedness. Sixth Corps Area, Camp Custer, Michigan. Prepared by the Men of the Citizens Military Training Camp. Chicago: Military Training Camps Association of the U.S., 1922-1926.

Priestley, Kenneth H. *Michigan Territorial Post Offices.* Vassar, Michigan: Peninsular Philatelist, 1961.

Proceedings of the Grand Chapter of the Order of Eastern Star of the State of Michigan. Coldwater, Michigan: The Order, 1879-1900.

Proceedings of the Annual Session of the Michigan State Grange of Patrons of Husbandry. Michigan: The Grange, 1875-2002.

Quaife, Milo M. *The Kingdom of Saint James.* New Haven: Yale University Press, 1930.

"Quaker Monthly Meetings in Michigan Established Prior to 1900." *Family Trails,* 4-2 (Summer 1972), 7-9.

Qualey, Carlton C. *Norwegian Settlement in the United States.* New York: Arno Press, 1970.

_________. "Pioneer Scandinavian Settlement in Michigan." *Michigan History,* 24 (Autumn 1940), 435-450.

Quigley, Maud. *Index to Michigan Research Found in Genealogical Periodicals.* Grand Rapids: Western Michigan Genealogical Society, 1979.

Rajner, Richard A. "Nineteenth Century Irish Settlement in the State of Michigan." M.A. Thesis, University of Toledo, 1994.

Rankin, Lois. "Detroit Nationality Groups." *Michigan History,* 23 (Spring 1939), 129-205.

Ranney, George E. *List of Regular Physicians Registered in Michigan.* 1885.

Record of Service of Michigan Volunteers in the Civil War 1861-1865. 46 vols. Kalamazoo: Ihling Brothers and Everard.

Reed, Ruth M., and Sister Marciana Hennig. *Post Offices of Michigan.* 1976.

Reel Index to the Microform Collection of County and Regional Histories of the "Old Northwest," Series V, Michigan. Woodbridge, Connecticut: Research Publications, 1975.

The Revised Statutes of the State of Michigan. Detroit: John S. Bagg, 1838.

The Revised Statutes of the State of Michigan. Detroit: Bagg & Harmon, 1846.

Reynolds, D.B. *Early Land Claims in Michigan.* Lansing: Michigan Department of Conservation, Lands Division, 1940.

Riddell, William Renwick. *Michigan Under British Rule: Law and Law Courts 1760-1796.* Lansing: Michigan Historical Commission, 1926.

Rines, Edward F., "Some Historic Churches in Michigan." *Michigan Heritage,* 4-2 (Winter 1962), 70-81.

Robertson, John. *Michigan in the War.* Lansing: W.S. George and Co., 1882.

Rockaway, Robert A. "The Detroit Jewish Ghetto Before World War I." *Michigan History,* 52-1 (Spring 1968), 28-36.

_________. *The Jews of Detroit: From the Beginning, 1762-1914.* Detroit: Wayne State University Press, 1986.

Roderick, Thomas, Elving Anderson, Robert Charles Anderson, Roger D. Joslyn, and Wayne T. Morris. "Files of the Eugenics Record Office: A Resource for Genealogists." *National Genealogical Society Quarterly,* 82-2 (June 1994), 97-113.

Rodgers, Bradley A. *Guardian of the Great Lakes: The U.S. Paddle Frigate Michigan.* Ann Arbor: The University of Michigan Press, 1996.

Romig, Walter. *Michigan Place Names: The History of the Founding and the Naming of More Than Five Thousand Past and Present Michigan Communities.* Detroit: Wayne State University Press, 1986.

Rose, Gregory S. "South Central Michigan Yankees." *Michigan History,* 70-2 (March-April 1986), 32-39.

Rosemond, Irene. *Reflections: An Oral History of Detroit.* Detroit: Broadside Press, 1992.

Rosentreter, Roger L. "Brigands or Paragons: Michigan Officials During the Patriot War." *Michigan History,* 73-5 (September/October 1989), 24-31.

_________. "Michigan's 83 Counties: Benzie County." *Michigan History,* 63-6 (November/December 1979), 8-9.

_________. "Michigan's 83 Counties: Charlevoix County," *Michigan History,* 64-5 (September-October 1980), 8-11.

_________. "Michigan's 83 Counties: Clare County." *Michigan History,* 65-2 (March-April 1981), 7-9.

__________. "Michigan's 83 Counties: Clinton County." *Michigan History*, 65-3 (May-June 1981), 9-11.

__________. "Michigan's 83 Counties: Ingham County." *Michigan History,* 67-5 (September-October 1883), 8-12.

__________. "Brother Benjamin: The Author of the Newest Book on the House of David Talks with Michigan History Magazine." *Michigan History,* 75-4 (July-August 1991), 12-19.

Roster of Union Soldiers, 1861-1865: Michigan. Ed. Janet B. Hewett. Wilmington, North Carolina: Broadfoot Publishing Co., 1998.

Rowse, Alfred L. *The Cousin Jacks: The Cornish in America.* New York: Charles Scribner's Sons, 1969.

Royce, Charles C. *Indian Land Cessions in the United States.* New York: Arno Press, 1971.

Rubenstein, Bruce. "To Destroy a Culture: Indian Education in Michigan, 1855-1900." *Michigan History,* 60-2 (Summer 1976), 137-160.

Rudin, A. James. "Bad Axe, Michigan: An Experiment In Jewish Agricultural Settlement." *Michigan History,* 56-2 (September 1972), 119-130.

Russell, Donna Valley. *Michigan Censuses 1710-1830 Under the French, British, and Americans* Detroit: Detroit Society for Genealogical Research Inc., 1982.

__________. *Michigan Voyageurs.* Detroit: Detroit Society for Genealogical Research Inc., 1982.

Russell, John Andrew. *The Germanic Influence in the Making of Michigan.* Detroit: University of Detroit Press, 1927.

Sabbe, Philemon D., and Leon Buyse. *Belgians in America.* Tielt: Lanno, 1960.

"The Saint Joseph Baptismal Register." Ed. Rev. George Pare and M.M. Quaife. *Mississippi Valley Historical Review,* 13-2 (September 1926), 201-239.

Saginaw Valley and Lake Shore Business Gazetteer and Directory. East Saginaw: R.A. Sprague, 1873.

Sanders, Rhonda. *Bronze Pillars: An Oral History of African-Americans in Flint.* Flint: Flint Journal and Alfred P. Sloan Museum, 1995.

Schaefer, Christina K. *The Great War: A Guide to the Service Records of All the World's Fighting Men and Volunteers.* Baltimore: Genealogical Publishing. Co., 1998.

__________. *Guide to Naturalization Records of the United States.* Baltimore: Genealogical Publishing Co., 1997.

Schmidt, Alvin J. *Fraternal Organizations.* Westport, Connecticut: Greenwood Press, 1980.

Schultz, Gerard. *Walls of Flames.* Elkton, Michigan, 1968.

Sherman, Alonzo J. *Index to Poor Farm Inmates, Iosco County, Michigan, 1874-1893.* Oscoda, Michigan: Huron Shores Genealogical Society, 1993.

__________. *List of the Grand Army of the Republic Posts in Michigan, 1872-1948.* Oscoda: Huron Shores Genealogical Society, 1994.

Silliman, Sue Imogene. *Michigan Military Records.* Lansing: Michigan Historical Commission, 1920.

Sinko, Peggy Tuck. *Michigan Atlas of Historical County Boundaries.* Ed. John H. Long. New York: Charles Scribner's Sons, 1997.

Smith, Juliana Szucs. *The Ancestry Family Historian's Address Book.* Orem, Utah: Ancestry, 2003.

Smith, Marian L. "Any Woman Who Is Now or May Hereafter Be Married: Women and Naturalization, ca. 1802-1940." *Prologue,* 30-2 (Summer 1998), 146-153.

Smith, Mike, and Thomas Featherstone. *Labor in Detroit: Working in the Motor City.* Chicago: Arcadia Publishing, 2001.

Sodders, Betty. *Michigan On Fire.* Holt, Michigan: Thunder Bay Press, 1997.

__________. *Michigan On Fire 2.* Holt, Michigan: Thunder Bay Press, 1999.

Sommers, Lawrence, with Joe T. Darden, Jay R. Harman, Laurie K. Sommers. *Michigan: A Geography.* Boulder: Westview Press, 1984.

The Source: A Guidebook of American Genealogy. Ed. Loretto Dennis Szucs and Sandra Hargreaves Luebking. Rev. ed. Salt Lake City: Ancestry, 1997.

Sourcebook of Michigan Census, County Histories and Vital Records. Lansing, Michigan: Library of Michigan, 1986.

The Speaking Telephone! Detroit, 1941.

Spear, Dorothea E. *Bibliography of American Directories Through 1860.* Worcester, Massachusetts: American Antiquarian Society, 1961.

Spooner, Harry L. *Postoffices and Postmasters of Muskegon County.* Spooner, 1962.

__________. *Postoffices and Postmasters of Newaygo County.* Spooner, 1961.

__________. *Postoffices and Postmasters of Oceana County.* Spooner, 1961.

__________. *Postoffices and Postmasters of Ottawa County.* Spooner, 1962.

Sprenger, Bernice. *Guide to the Manuscripts in the Burton Historical Collection Detroit Public Library.* Detroit: Burton Historical Collection, 1985.

Stapler, Harry Stapler with Berenice Lowe and Amy South. *Pioneers of Forest and City: A History of Michigan for Young People* Lansing: Michigan Historical Commission, 1985.

State Land Patents, Kent County, Michigan. Grand Rapids: Western Michigan Genealogical Society, 1984.

State Summary of War Casualties: Michigan. Washington, D.C.: U.S. Navy, 1946.

Stefaniuk, Myroslava, and Fred E. Dohrs. *Ukrainians of Detroit.* Detroit: Wayne State University, 1979.

Steketee, Cornelius. "Hollanders in Muskegon: 1850-97." *Michigan History,* 31-4 (December 1947), 382-387.

Stephanides, Marios. "Greeks and Cypriots of Detroit." *Michigan History,* 56-2 (Summer 1972), 131-150.

Stephens, Ronald J. *Idlewild: The Black Eden of Michigan.* Chicago: Arcadia Publishing, 2001.

Stephenson, Richard W. *Land Ownership Maps: A Checklist of 19th Century United States County Maps in the Library of Congress.* Washington, D.C.: Library of Congress, 1967, 18-20.

Steuart, Raeone Christensen. *Michigan 1890 Veterans Census Index.* Bountiful, Utah: Heritage Quest, 1999.

Stevens, J. Harold. "The Influence of New England in Michigan." *Michigan History,* XIX (Autumn 1935), 321-353.

Streeter, Floyd Benjamin. *Michigan Bibliography.* Lansing: Michigan Historical Commission, 1921.

A Study in Valor: Michigan Medal of Honor Winners in the Civil War. Lansing: Michigan Civil War Centennial Observance Commission, 1966.

Sturdevant, Katherine Scott. *Bringing Your Family History to Life Through Social History.* Cincinnati:Betterway Books, 2000.

A Subject Guide to Michigan History Magazine, 1978-1994. Lansing: Michigan Historical Center, 1995.

Sutherland, Daniel E. "Michigan Emigrant Agent: Edward H. Thomson." *Michigan History,* 59-1-2 (Spring-Summer 1975), 3-37.

Swan, L. B. *Journal of a Trip to Michigan in 1841.* Rochester, 1904.

Swayze, David D. *Shipwreck! A Comprehensive Directory of Over 3,700 Shipwrecks on the Great Lakes.* Boyne City, Michigan: Harbor House, 1992.

Swierenga, Robert P. *Dutch Households in U.S. Population Censuses, 1850, 1860, 1870: An Alphabetical Listing by Family Heads.* 3 vols. Wilmington, Delaware: Scholarly Resources, 1987.

__________. *The Dutch Transplanting in Michigan and the Midwest.* Ann Arbor: Historical Society of Michigan, 1986.

Symon, Charles. *We Can Do It! A History of the Civilian Conservation Corps in Michigan: 1933-1942.* Escanaba, Michigan: Richard Printing, 1983.

Szucs, Loretto Dennis. *Naturalizations: Declarations of Intent and Final Oaths, Circuit Court, Eastern District of Michigan, Detroit.* 1977.

__________. *Naturalizations, Declarations of Intent and Final Oaths: District Court, Eastern District of Michigan, Detroit.* 1977.

__________. *They Became Americans: Finding Naturalization Records and Ethnic Origins.* Salt Lake City: Ancestry, 1998.

Taber, Morris C. Taber. "New England Influence in South Central Michigan." *Michigan History,* 45-4 (December 1961), 305-336.

Taylor, Hilda A. *First Land Owners of Saint Clair County, Michigan.* Lansing: Michigan Genealogical Council, 1978.

Ten Harmsel, Larry. *Dutch in Michigan.* East Lansing: Michigan State University Press, 2002.

Territorial Papers of the United States. Ed. Clarence Edwin Carter. Vols. 2-3, 7-8, 10-12. Washington, D.C.: Government Printing Office, 1934, 1939, 1942-1945.

Thavenet, Dennis. "The Michigan Reform School and the Civil War: Officers and Inmates Mobilized for the Union Cause." *The Michigan Historical Review,* 13-1 (Spring 1987), 21-46.

They Made a Difference: Highlights of the Swedish Influence on Detroit and Michigan. Royal Oak: Detroit-Swedish Council, 1976.

Thomas, N. Gordon. "The Alphadelphia Experiment." *Michigan History,* 55-3 (Fall 1971), 205-216.

Thorndale, William, and William Dollarhide. *Map Guide to the U.S. Federal Censuses, 1790-1920.* Baltimore: Genealogical Publishing Co., 1987.

Thurner, Arthur W. *Strangers and Sojourners: A History of Michigan's Keweenaw Peninsula.* Detroit: Wayne State University Press, 1994.

Transactions of the Grand Lodge of Free and Accepted Masons of the State of Michigan at Its Annual Communication. Detroit: The Grand Lodge, 1841-1936.

Transactions of the Supreme Court of the Territory of Michigan. Ed. William Wirt Blume. Ann Arbor: University of Michigan Press, 1935-1940.

The Tree That Never Dies: Oral History of the Michigan Indians. Ed. Pamela J. Dobson. Grand Rapids: Grand Rapids Public Library, 1978.

Treppa, Allan R. *An Index to Detroit's Polonia in the Michigan Catholic, 1872-1900.* Livonia: A. R. Treppa, 1981.

Trix, Frances. *The Albanians in Michigan.* East Lansing: Michigan State University, 2001.

Trump, Fred. *The Grange in Michigan.* Grand Rapids: Dean-Hicks Co., 1963.

Unreported Opinions of the Supreme Court of Michigan, 1836-1843. Ed. William Wirt Blume. Ann Arbor: University of Michigan Press, 1945.

Van Buren County Gazetteer and Business Directory. Decatur, Michigan: Hill and Leavens, 1869.

Van Til, Reinder. "Fulfilling a Sacred Trust: The Michigan Veterans' Facility." *Michigan History,* 70-3 (May-June 1986), 45-48.

__________. *Michigan's Veteran's Facility Centennial: A Century of Caring.* Grand Rapids, 1986.

VanderHill, C. Warren. *Settling the Great Lakes Frontier: Immigration to Michigan 1837-1924.* Lansing: Michigan Historical Commission, 1970.

Vismara, John C. Rev. "Coming of the Italians to Detroit." *Michigan History,* 2-1 (January 1918), 110-124.

Wakefield, Larry. *Butcher's Dozen: 13 Famous Michigan Murders.* West Bloomfield, Michigan: Altwerger and Mandel, 1991.

__________. *Ghost Towns of Michigan.* 3 vols. Holt, Michigan: Thunder Bay Press, 1994-2002.

Walker, Henry N. *Reports of Cases Argued and Determined in the Court of Chancery of the State of Michigan.* Detroit: Harsha and Willcox, 1845.

Walker, Lewis, and Ben C. Wilson. *Black Eden: The Idlewild Community.* East Lansing: Michigan State University Press, 2002.

__________, Benjamin C. Wilson, and Linwood H. Cousins. *African Americans in Michigan.* East Lansing: Michigan State University Press, 2001.

Wantz, Terry E. *Post Offices of Newaygo County.* White Cloud, Michigan: Newaygo County Society of History and Genealogy, 1992.

Wargelin, John. "The Finns in Michigan." *Michigan History,* XXIV (Spring 1940), 179-203.

Warren, Francis H. *Michigan Manual of Freedmen's Progress.* Detroit: The Commission, 1915. (Reprinted in 1968 and 1985 under the title of *Negroes in Michigan History.*)

Waterstreet, Darlene E. *Biography Index to the Michigan Manuals, 1923-1973.* Milwaukee: Badger Infosearch, 1975.

Watkins, Marilyn P. "Civilizers of the West: Clergy and Laity in Michigan Frontier Churches, 1820-1840." *Michigan: Explorations in its Social History,* Ed. Francis X. Blouin Jr. and Maris A. Vinovskis. Ann Arbor: Historical Society of Michigan, 1987, 161-190.

Weddon, Willah. *First Ladies of Michigan.* Lansing: NOG Press, 1994.

__________. *Michigan Governors: Their Life Stories.* Lansing: NOG Press, 1994.

__________. *Michigan Press Women: Today and Yesterday.* Stockbridge, Michigan: Weddon Press, 1996.

Weeks, George. *Stewards of the State: The Governors of Michigan.* 2nd ed. Detroit and Ann Arbor: Detroit News and Historical Society of Michigan, 1991.

Welch, Richard W. *County Evolution in Michigan 1790-1897.* Lansing: Michigan Department of Education State Library Services, 1972.

__________. *Michigan in the Mexican War.* Durand, Michigan, 1967.

Wermuth, Mary L., and the Michigan Centennial Farm Association. *Michigan's Centennial Family Farm Heritage, 1986: A Michigan Sesquicentennial History.* Hillsdale, Michigan: Ferguson Communications, 1986.

Wilkins, Gene H. *My Scrapbook on the Bath School Bombing of May 18th, 1927.* TimberWolf Ltd., 2002.

Williams, E. Gray, and Ethel W. Williams. *First Land Owners of Barry County, Michigan.* Kalamazoo: Michigan Heritage, 1965.

__________, and __________. *First Land Owners of Eaton County, Michigan.* Kalamazoo: Michigan Heritage, 1967.

__________, and __________. *First Land Owners of Hillsdale County, Michigan.* Kalamazoo: Michigan Heritage, 1968.

__________, and __________. *First Land Owners of Mason County, Michigan.* Kalamazoo: Michigan Heritage, 1967.

__________, and __________. *First Land Owners of Monroe County, Michigan.* Kalamazoo: Michigan Heritage, 1968.

__________, and __________. *First Land Owners of Wayne County, Michigan.* Kalamazoo: Michigan Heritage, 1964.

Williams, Elizabeth Whitney. *A Child of the Sea and Life Among the Mormons.* Harbor Springs, Michigan: E. W. Williams, 1905.

Williams, Ethel W. *Tracing Your Ancestors in Michigan.* Salt Lake City: Genealogical Society of the Church of Jesus Christ of Latter-day Saints, 1969.

Williams, Frederick D. *Michigan's Soldiers in the Civil War.* 3rd ed. Lansing: Bureau of Michigan History, 1994.

Wilson, Benjamin C. "Idlewild: A Black Eden in Michigan." *Michigan History,* 65-5 (September-October 1981), 33-37.

__________. "Kentucky Kidnappers, Fugitives, and Abolitionists In Antebellum Cass County, Michigan." *Michigan History,* 60-4 (Winter 1976), 339-358.

Wilson, Victoria. *Native American Research in Michigan: A Genealogical Guide.* Grawn, Michigan: Kinseekers Publications, 1997.

Woodford, Arthur M. *This Is Detroit 1701-2001.* Detroit: Wayne State University Press, 2001.

World War, 1939: Michigan Casualties. Detroit: Detroit Public Library, 1946.

World War II Honor List of Dead and Missing: Michigan. Washington D.C.: War Department, 1946.

Wytrwal, Joseph Anthony. *The Polish Experience in Detroit.* Detroit: Endurance Press, 1992.

Yates, John S. *Researching Masonic Records: A Guide for Genealogists.* 4th ed. Yates, 1998.

Yockelson, Mitchell. "They Answered the Call: Military Service in the United States Army During World War I, 1917-1919." *Prologue,* 30-3 (Fall 1998), 228-234.

__________. "The United States Armed Forces and the Mexican Punitive Expedition: Part 1." *Prologue,* 29-3 (Fall 1997), 256-261.

__________. "The United States Armed Forces and the Mexican Punitive Expedition: Part 2." *Prologue,* 29-4 (Winter 1997), 334-343.

Young, Frank J. *Strangite Mormons: A Finding Aid.* Vancouver, Washington: F.J. Young, 1996.

Zehnder, Herman F. *Teach My People the Truth! The Story of Frankenmuth, Michigan.* Frankenmuth: Zehnder, 1970.

Microform

Civil War Unit Histories: Regimental Histories and Personal Narratives. Ed. Robert E. Lester and Gary Hoag. Bethesda, Maryland: University Publications of America, 1990-1993.

County Histories of the Old Northwest. Series V: Michigan. New Haven, Connecticut: Research Publications, 1973.

Land Ownership Maps: Michigan. Washington, D.C.: Library of Congress Geography and Map Division, 1983.

Videos

Keweenaw Copper: A Michigan Story. Lansing: Michigan Department of State, 2000.

The Orphan Train in Michigan, 1854 to 1927. Program Source International, Broomfield Hills, Michigan 2002.

Web Sites

American Memory's Pioneering the Upper Midwest: Books from Michigan, Minnesota, and Wisconsin, ca. 1820-1910 <memory.loc.gov/ammem/umhtml/umhome.html>

Ancestry.com <www.ancestry.com>

FamilySearch <www.familysearch.org>

Michigan Family History Network <www.mifamilyhistory.org>

Michigan Genealogy on the Web <www.rootsweb.com/~migenweb>

Michigan Manual <www.michiganlegislature.org/> Select "Publications."

Michigan.gov's History, Arts, and Libraries <www.michigan.gov/hal>

National Archives and Records Administration <www.archives.gov/>

RootsWeb.com <www.rootsweb.com>

Index